George Henry Thomas

George Henry Thomas

As True As Steel

Brian Steel Wills

 University Press of Kansas

Published by the University Press of Kansas (Lawrence, Kansas 66045), which was
organized by the Kansas Board of Regents and is operated and funded by Emporia State
University, Fort Hays State University, Kansas State University, Pittsburg State University,
the University of Kansas, and Wichita State University

Library of Congress Cataloging-in-Publication Data

Wills, Brian Steel, 1959–

George Henry Thomas : as true as steel / Brian Steel Wills.

p. cm.

Includes bibliographical references.

ISBN 978-0-7006-1841-5 (cloth : alk. paper)

1. Thomas, George Henry, 1816–1870. 2. Generals—United States--Biography. 3. United
States. Army—Biography. 4. Unionists (United States Civil War)—Virginia—Biography.
5. United States—History—Civil War, 1861–1865—Campaigns. 6. Thomas, George Henry,
1816–1870—Military leadership. I. Title.

E467.1.T4W55 2012

973.7'41092—dc23

[B]   2011046016

British Library Cataloguing-in-Publication Data is available.

Printed in the United States of America

10 9 8 7 6 5 4 3 2 1

To Nick and Elliot

Contents

A photograph section appears following page 171.

Illustrations

Maps

Photographs

Acknowledgments

Growing up as I did in old Nansemond County, Virginia, adjacent to Southampton County to the west, I found the existence of a Union general from that region of a state that was so vital to the fate of the Confederacy intriguing. My interest in George Henry Thomas has grown through these years and developed in sophistication from mere curiosity to an increasing understanding of who this man was and the important role he played in sustaining the Union cause during the American Civil War.

Unlike some figures from the conflict, Thomas left no voluminous correspondence to reveal his thinking on the critical issues of his day. Yet, the materials that give access to aspects of his life and perspectives are more numerous than expected, and his long career of military service to the United States provides ample opportunity to understand the issues that Thomas confronted and the manner in which he responded to them, as well as the personality features and foibles he exhibited.

Such a study of the life of an individual requires assistance from many sources. The members of the Department of History and Philosophy at the University of Virginia's College at Wise were helpful, and the institution supported this project by providing the means required for research and writing, including a semester leave. The Kenneth Asbury Chair of History made time available in the summer and funding for travel that supported numerous research trips to libraries and archives. Special appreciation goes to Provost and Senior Vice Chancellors David Smith and Gil Blackburn, as well as to Darlene Moore. Robin Benke and his excellent staff at the John Cook Wyllie Library contributed with timely arrivals of interlibrary loans. Rhonda Bentley helped in many ways, but especially with regard to the production of drafts of the manuscript.

Since my arrival at Kennesaw State University in Georgia to assume the directorship of the Center for the Study of the Civil War Era there, the same has been true. Assistance with sources through the Horace W. Sturgis Library has been superb, as has the support from Dean Richard Vengroff, the Dean's Office personnel, and Megan MacDonald and Gayle Wheeler in the Department of History and Philosophy. Thanks especially to my colleagues Randy Patton and David Parker in the History Department and my assistant at the Center, Mike Shaffer, for their unswerving support and unbounded good cheer while I put the finishing touches to revisions of the manuscript.

Various persons at the libraries and archives found in the endnotes were extraordinarily generous with their time and assistance. Archivists and students at major university repositories, the National Archives, and the Library of Congress were particularly helpful. I was fortunate to have the support of fellowships at the Filson in Louisville, Kentucky, and the Virginia Historical Society in Richmond. The personnel at both institutions were unfailingly kind and generous regarding this project. The Huntington in San Marino, California, provided microfilm copies of materials related to Thomas that I could then access locally. Likewise, the University of Colorado at Boulder Library's Archives unit was extremely helpful in making available their important source material from one of the general's closest aides in his final years. The Virginia Military Institute and Yale University Library also provided important assistance.

Special thanks go to my friend Wiley Sword, who provided me with a copy and a transcript of a letter George Thomas wrote to his brother John from West Point. I appreciate his friendship and support. Thanks also to Jim Ogden for his aid and advice. I am grateful to Mark Johnson, who made many of the maps in the volume available with a sense of comradeship that would have made George Thomas proud. Heather Harvey produced the other maps with fortitude and good cheer, while maintaining her own family and career. I am also grateful for the careful editing and thoughtful queries of Carol Kennedy and Larisa Martin. Finally, Fred Woodward has proven to be stalwart in his shepherding of the manuscript through various incarnations and over more time than either of us would have calculated as necessary to see the project to completion.

For each of the primary documents included in this study of George Thomas, it should be noted that where emphasis occurs in this volume, that emphasis originated in the letter itself. The attempt to indicate this in each instance proved cumbersome.

To my wife and our family in Wise, Virginia, in Peachtree City, Georgia, and for a time, in Lakeland, Florida, I owe the greatest appreciation. I have chosen to dedicate this volume to grandsons Nick and Elliot. Both of these vivacious young men have brought joy into our lives and shared, in their own ways, their Paw Paw's love of history, the Georgia Bulldogs, and the Green Bay Packers. George and Frances Thomas had no children of their own, but when he wrote about young people his characterizations were among his most enthusiastic. I hope in due time as they get older they will enjoy reading about an important figure from history just as I did from my youth and come to appreciate his many contributions, perhaps as a spur to their own.

George Henry Thomas

Introduction: Embattled Virginian

"George Thomas, you know, is slow, but as true as steel."
—William T. Sherman on George Henry Thomas
 before the battle of Atlanta, Georgia, 1864

*"[To] not prepare is the greatest of crimes; to be prepared
beforehand for any contingency is the greatest of virtues."*
—Chinese theorist, Sun Tzu

Everything about Union general George Henry Thomas exuded stability and dependability. As an adult, the rock-jawed Virginian was massive and strong, standing five feet ten inches tall. A contemporary writer might as well have chiseled his description in rock for the readers who sought to know something of the general: "Well, if you will just think what manner of man he must be that should be hewn out of a large square block of the best-tempered material that men are made of, not scrimped anywhere, and square everywhere . . . and the whole giving the idea of massive solidity, of the right kind of man to 'tie to,' you will have a little preparation for seeing him as he is."[1]

Steadiness and coolness marked his outward appearances, even in the most stressful situations. Yet, beneath the solid exterior seethed a powerful force of character exemplified by an insatiable curiosity, a surprising sense of humor, an intense sensitivity, a painful tendency toward privacy, a stubborn adherence to right as he understood it, and an unquenchable quest for personal honor and integrity without insistence upon overblown recognition for himself, or in any sense that it might be thought to have come to him at the expense of another.

Thomas's military accomplishments mirrored his physical stature. Ezra Warner, the compiler of two volumes of biographical sketches of Union and Confederate generals, described Thomas as the "third of the triumvirate who won the war for the Union."[2] A former soldier who had served in the Western Theater declared him "one of the four master spirits of the war."[3] In the circular that announced the death "of one of our most exalted generals," William T. Sherman placed Thomas "in the very front rank of our war generals."[4] Nor has George Thomas's reputation diminished with the years. Popular modern-era Civil War historian Bruce Catton labeled him "certainly one of the four or five best soldiers on either side in the whole war."[5]

On another occasion, in his assessment of the Union side of the Civil War, Catton conceded that the notion of Thomas being better suited to the defense could be termed "correct." But the record also demonstrated an unmistakably effective tendency toward the offensive as well. "It may also be worth making note that just twice in all the war was a major Confederate army driven away from a prepared position in complete rout—at Chattanooga and at Nashville," he explained. "Each time the blow that routed it was launched by Thomas."[6] Of even more interest was the fact that the man who bore this distinction hailed from the South's Commonwealth of Virginia, not from a state in the North or Midwest that remained in the Union during the sectional crisis of the 1860s. His geographical lineage was well known at the time of the war and since and has generated speculation as to the origin and legitimacy of his decision to remain loyal to the Union at its greatest moment of national strife.

George Henry Thomas was a man of complexities, reflected in the names by which contemporaries, historians, and students of the war and the man have known him. Yet, even these badges of recognition and familiarity have lent themselves more to questions than to answers concerning the sturdy Virginian. Was he the "Rock of Chickamauga," as he became known in the wake of his stand on Snodgrass Hill and Horseshoe Ridge in September 1863, or "Old Pap" as some of the soldiers named him? He became the "Sledge of Nashville" after driving John Bell Hood's Confederate command from the doorsteps of the Tennessee capital in December 1864, despite almost being relieved of his responsibilities when Ulysses Grant determined he had been too reticent in his actions. "Old Tom" and "Old Slow Trot," names that were supposed to have emanated from his days at West Point, offered additional insights into his martial character, as did the affectionate titles "Old Reliable" and "Uncle George."[7] One soldier applied the familiar term "Pappy" to his wartime superior.[8] In each of these cases, a historian's assertion certainly applied to George Thomas: "The commanding general's persona was deemed an important indication of his capabilities."[9]

Many of his contemporaries held Thomas in high esteem. While especially true of those who served with him in some capacity, this was also the case with other observers as well. George W. Cullum, whose compilation of service records of West Pointers has offered scholars an outstanding resource on so many of these military figures, noted in his response to an invitation to attend the unveiling of the statue of General Thomas located in Washington, "Beside my warm personal regard for Thomas, I had an enthusiastic admiration of him as the unsurpassed soldier of our great civil contest—the general who had never been defeated, and the leader of armies whose victories had placed him among the greatest heroes of the republic." Cullum saw in Thomas admirable qualities that appeared most conspicuously in the white heat of combat, a characteristic frequently associated with the general and often illustrated with allusions to battles ranging from Mill Springs and Stones River to Chickamauga and Nashville.[10]

A newspaper correspondent from Philadelphia remarked, "General

Thomas is one of the most even-tempered men in the army without a doubt." He recognized the regard that officers had for their commander, but added firmly, "the men would die for him—do die for him." The writer was particularly struck with the manner in which the command performed its tasks. "Everything goes on like clock[work] in his army. No irregularities, no procrastination." His final analysis would have brought a smile to the "grim old warrior's" face, as he had described an earlier version of George Thomas: "Every man is at his post at the proper time."[11]

Scholars have generally agreed that the Virginian was an exceptional contributor to Union victory in the American Civil War, while also maintaining that he was methodical in his approach. If there was "no procrastination" in his ranks, Thomas himself has remained opened to this criticism regarding his generalship. Yet, George Thomas hardly preferred to avoid tasks or responsibilities by shifting them to another time or by substituting matters of less significance for those that should enjoy the highest priority. No criticism has suggested that he did not want to act, but rather that his preparations beforehand were too extensive. Historian T. Harry Williams observed, "Thomas was a good general, a hard-hitting attacker, but he always took a long time to get ready to attack. He moved like a sledgehammer when he moved, but he never advanced until his army was prepared down to the last knapsack."[12] Prolific author Stephen Ambrose concurred with the latter sentiment in observing of Thomas, "Old Pap would not advance until every button on every private had been secured and every Springfield loaded."[13] The delicate balance of being sufficiently ready to move so as to offer a greater assurance of success and the timeliness of acting in concert with larger strategic imperatives has remained an area of contention for Thomas. Yet, his subsequent record in these instances has seemed to bear out his wisdom in following the general course he chose.

More than a keenness for preparation accounted for Thomas's successes. Although close observers consistently labeled him as intellectual, they did not consider the Virginian to be brilliant. Nevertheless, he demonstrated himself to be an exceptional student of the military arts and an astute observer of human nature. During a discussion that Thomas had with staff members and subordinates in the course of the 1863 Tullahoma Campaign on the merits of particular commanders, the general chose to focus on a broader level of analysis. "Put a plank six inches wide five feet above the ground and a thousand men will walk it easily," he explained. "Raise it five hundred feet and [only] one man out of a thousand will walk it safely." As he saw it, the experiment indicated the primacy of the mental challenge over a physical one. "It is a question of nerve we have to solve," he concluded, "not one of dexterity." Thomas then turned the lesson in theory to one of practical application. "It is not [enough] to touch elbows and fire a gun, but how to do them under fire," he argued in a way that justified his views on the need for adequate training. "We are all cowards in the presence of immediate death. We can overcome that fear in war through familiarity." He felt his opponents had an advantage in this regard. "Southerners are more accustomed to violence and therefore more familiar with death," he observed. "What we have to do is to make veterans." Thus, when Thomas looked at the performances of high-profile comrades, he thought he understood the difference between their successes and failures as commanders. "[George B.] McClellan's great error was in his avoidance of fighting. His congratulatory report was, 'All Quiet along the Potomac.' The result was a loss in morale. His troops came to have a mysterious fear of the enemy."[14]

Similarly, the Virginian passed along his views of martial mastery to James Garfield following the war. "The success of an army depends more on the drill and discipline of the men than on the ability of their officers. Recognizing this, I applied myself to that [idea] from the start."[15] Clearly, George Thomas, the scientific soldier and West Point–trained professional officer, wanted to eliminate any element of "mysterious fear" on the part of either himself or his men. He had already achieved this mastery through a long, and often distinguished, career that included service on the frontiers of Florida, California, and Texas, as well as participation in portions of the War with Mexico under Zachary Taylor, and in the American Civil War. He knew the artillery and cavalry branches of the service well and had time amidst the swirl of black powder smoke and in the saddle to prove it. In every phase of the conflict to which he would devote himself for four years, Thomas also demonstrated growth and capacity.

The discipline that George Thomas applied to the battlefield, he also applied to himself. As he had once pointedly observed to a colleague, he "had educated himself not to feel."[16] One can but marvel at such self-control, but this was a tendency in him that he had nurtured from his earliest years. As a middle child he grew up in circumstances that developed tendencies toward mediation and peaceful resolution of difficulties. Thomas held passionate views about justice and justness, championed those causes in behalf of others, believed in the proprieties of discipline and duty, and allowed expressions of emotions to reach the surface only after what he deemed to be severe and unnecessary provocations.

Thomas's sense of detachment and self-control provided him with a level of protection from the slings and arrows of others and allowed him to take greater positions of moral authority without pretension. He was too much the scientist and the careful observer of the human condition not to understand that such a defensive mechanism was important for him to continue in whatever course lay before him. As one contemporary and biographer noted, "He served honestly and faithfully under any and all circumstances, and at all times bore true allegiance to his country and to his commander."[17]

Writer Carl Sandburg, in his work on Abraham Lincoln, touched upon this sense of development in one of the president's most able lieutenants. "At Mill Springs Thomas had shown a flash, at Murfreesboro fire and flint, at Chickamauga granite steadiness and volcanic resistance."[18] Sandburg's assessment ended with the engagement that won the Virginian undying fame, but it could have been easily extended to the fortitude and determination Thomas showed in the Atlanta Campaign and the "volcanic" element he displayed in a different sense against John Bell Hood at Nashville.

In the aftermath of the frustration of wresting Atlanta from the grips of Joseph E. Johnston and Hood, William T. Sherman paused to offer his colleague, Henry Halleck, some personal thoughts. Within the communication the Ohioan delivered a short, but generally blistering, critique of some of his generals in the recent campaigning. Although he would be critical of George Thomas as well in many ways, Sherman gave his old West Point classmate the most positive evaluation and captured the essence of both popular perceptions and personal characteristics of the man he knew so well. "George Thomas, you know, is slow, but as true as steel."[19] Sherman would be as responsible as anyone for solidifying the impression that his colleague was "slow." He seldom referred to the Virginian in the context of a critique that he did not apply that description, and usually in a way so as to emphasize that quality over all others. An evaluation Sherman offered in mid-1862 was typical: "Thomas [is] slow, cool & methodic."[20]

In some ways, George Thomas proved to be his own worst enemy in his associations with others. There was nothing quite so perplexing for those who had to deal with him as the complications of the Virginian's personality. He often came across to the casual viewer as diffident and distant. War correspondent William Shanks especially honed in on this aspect of his character. "His undemonstrative manner has given to many the idea that he was incapable of strong affections, firm friendships, or noble emotions." For this individual at least, the general sometimes appeared to be "selfishly cold."[21] Yet, the newspaperman softened his critique slightly when he added, "His countenance is at all times severe and grave, but not necessarily stern. He seldom smiles; but the constant seriousness of his countenance is not repulsive."[22]

A subordinate remembered the general's demeanor differently. "There was nothing more fascinating than the face of General Thomas when it broke into a smile," friend and biographer Donn Piatt observed. "His laugh was of the same sort, not loud but musical in its brief, hearty enjoyment. The rarity of the expression made them in their surprise all the pleasanter."[23] Thomas would hardly be termed effusive, even by close associates, but in working on a biography of the general, Piatt heard from a wartime associate who recalled a more gregarious side of the austere commander. "Those [who] often heard him tell the story of a soldier who applied for leave of absence, and as he told it, it was a little poorer [in grammar and expression] than you have printed it."[24]

Another person asserted, "I should have enjoyed hugely hearing Thomas laugh aloud," and thought that in three years of relatively close contact he had seldom seen him smile. In this instance, the writer recalled, it was not so much the hilarity of the subject matter that affected Thomas as the involvement of a very sober and serious subordinate in an incongruous situation that caused his merriment.[25] The Virginian could be struck by irony and enjoyed a subtle insight that could be lost on others. His expressions of humor occasionally failed to resonate with others because of their sophistication.

Thomas was aware of the image that any public expression of emotion on his part projected. He could be practiced and cultivated, but most often seemed natural and instinctive. Biographer Francis McKinney was quick to point out that Thomas himself "regretted that his own solemn, undemonstrative temperament kept him from getting closer to the men of his command." When the Virginian let down his guard, he displayed a dry wit and an impulsive sense of humor. Even so, the characterization of "his rare laugh, soft and musical," was less a comment on its nature than its uncommon occurrence.[26] William Shanks observed, "He never laughs and jokes with soldiers or officers, but his mild voice and quiet manner win him more of the love of his men than any momentary familiarity could do."[27]

That Shanks did not see instances of Thomas's familiarity with the men in the ranks did not mean they did not occur. One of the common soldiers under the Virginian's command convinced an especially talented colleague to display for the general some items he had carved from wood found on the ground at Chickamauga over which they had fought. Nicholas Phieffer's skill with a pocketknife and James Haynie's audacity combined when the men slipped from camp to venture to Thomas's headquarters. The napkin rings Phieffer had carved found favor with the general, who praised the artist's craftsmanship "as he turned the rings over and over in his hands," summoning others from his staff over to admire the workmanship as well. Then, true to a nature that mixed a deft common touch with practicality, Thomas insisted that he "would hardly dare to use such beautiful and valuable articles for his mess service" and asked the soldier instead if he might be allowed to forward the items for inclusion in a Sanitary Fair auction. Pheiffer explained that while he had made the rings for the general's personal use, Thomas could do with them as he wished, "if he did the sending." Haynie recalled that General Thomas "laughed heartily at this" and promised to "attend to that part of the affair." The men returned to their camp without censure for either their absence or their defiance of military protocol, and the napkin rings fetched a total of 600 dollars in the sale that occurred subsequently.[28]

Such lighter moments aside, the general's associates were just as likely to notice an anger that could burst forth with the power of a Southern summer thunderstorm and as quickly dissipate and allow him to return to the calm that usually marked his demeanor. A New York newspaperman noted this aspect of the general's personality. "He grows really enthusiastic over nothing, though occasionally his anger may be aroused. When it is, his rage is terrible."[29] Comrade and early biographer Chaplain Thomas Van Horne observed, "His chief fault was violence of temper, but the recurrence of outbursts of passion only after long intervals, proved that he overcame a strong natural tendency in maintaining habitual self-control."[30] Mistreatment of anyone he deemed less than capable of providing a defense and demonstrations of infidelity were liable to loosen his wrath more quickly than anything else, although Thomas could seethe internally when he felt himself to be the victim of disrespect for his office and service or disregard for the strictures of military tradition. "He was positive in his opinions but free from intolerance," Van Horne recalled. "To him wrong and revenge were equally abhorrent, right and mercy equally attractive."[31]

A contemporary explained, "His calm, dignified bearing under circumstances that deeply wounded his nature, so intensely sensitive, has led to the belief that he was indifferent to rank and corresponding command. But in this, as in other matters affecting chiefly his inner life, he was utterly misapprehended by those who supposed that they knew him well." Thomas's personality kept him somewhat insulated from others, and this seemed to be a strategy that developed from his earliest years and that he chose to cultivate deliberately. Thomas Van Horne concluded, "He was really known only by the few who called forth confiding friendship."[32]

Thomas made strong personal connections, yet he surely challenged them, too, as he exposed layers of his thinking and aspects of his personality and character over time and through various circumstances. He appeared to express himself most openly in his younger years to his older brother, John, and later in life to his wife, Frances. A handful of trusted staff members saw or heard the most unvarnished side of their general's personality and viewpoints. Complexities nevertheless remained. William T. "Cump" Sherman was among those who claimed a close association, and the evolving relationship between them featured affection and volatility that remained in equal measure throughout their lives. Sherman was as critical of his friend as anyone, yet argued that he maintained a high regard and personal affection for him, too.

Thomas's relationships with other comrades in blue were just as complex as the one he had with Sherman. Much of the earliest work on the Virginian reflected a powerful bias against Ulysses Grant, often fed by the personal views of the writers themselves, but also reflective of the sense of alienation and frustration Thomas felt in the latter stages of his life. It became standard fare to dismiss Grant because he had seemingly dismissed Thomas. Yet, the two men, who were not so very far apart from each other in their mutual devotion to the Union and their bulldog determination to defeat those arrayed against it, could not prevent their differences in approach and strategic thinking from frequently overriding all other considerations between them. Often Thomas and Grant simply did not mesh well together, and just as often the incongruity was not based on past slights or current wrongs as much as it reflected two strong-willed and stubborn warriors intent on holding the ground they had determined to defend. Thomas's solution to dealing with discomfort was to draw in upon himself, and diffidence was not the means by which one could best reach Grant. Even so, Ulysses Grant insisted as he reflected on the life of his comrade, "I yield to no man in my admiration of Thomas."[33] One indication of the closeness of the men in one sense was the insistence of a contemporary that only William T. Sherman and George H. Thomas referred to their comrade as "Grant," while "no other subordinate ever addressed him except by his title."[34]

This was not to say that the Virginian did not have detractors. In his postwar memoirs, wartime subordinate John M. Schofield coldly asserted, "I believe it must now be fully known to all who are qualified to judge . . . that General Thomas did not possess in a high degree the activity of mind necessary to foresee and provide for all the exigencies of military operations, nor the mathematical talent required to estimate 'the relations of time, space, motion and force' involved in great problems of war."[35] Schofield's unbounded ambition and antagonism plagued Thomas, especially in the latter portion of his life, but such a criticism prompted one of Thomas's foremost biographers to note, in one specific refutation of the general's supposed deficiencies, that under the Virginian's command, the Army of the Cumberland "harnessed" the railroads to such an extent as to give "to the science of transport and supply a division of time and a multiplication of tonnage never seen before."[36]

Likewise, many Southerners diminished Thomas's military contributions or dismissed him altogether by labeling him as a traitor to his state and region. They simply could not square the circumstances of the Virginian's birth with the dictates of duty and conscience as he saw them. Proud Southerner Catherine Edmonston remained so disturbed with the course that Thomas had taken that when she learned erroneously that he had perished during the assault on the Crater at Petersburg in 1864 she rejoiced. "Amongst the Yankee dead within our lines was found the renegade and traitor Gen. Thomas a base son of Virginia," whose "blood," she declared, it was most fitting that her violated soil now lapped up.[37]

Character and circumstance provided challenges for the Virginian to overcome in life and in memory. His reticence to promote himself combined with a personality that tended toward a less spectacular persona that often found itself engulfed in the shadows of those who preferred the limelight. The era produced many more charismatic figures that limited Thomas's exposure in the tapestry of the great national struggle. Others were simply better equipped to assert themselves and advance their own interests and those of their subordinates and close compatriots. The general assumed that his record would speak for itself and was content to let what official or public praise might come his way be cast on his commands and thus less directly upon himself. His was a worthy purpose, but the choice left him perplexed and not infrequently angry at the lack of recognition to which he felt his contributions in the service had entitled him without his having to demand it in some overt, and therefore unseemly, fashion.

George Thomas turned his training and knowledge to account in the American Civil War. His sense of duty and obligation joined with the quiet force of his personality to affect the outcome of the conflict and secure the values he cherished most. He embodied the spirit that President Abraham Lincoln reflected when he admonished a grousing general, "'Act well your part, there all honor lies.'" It was better, Lincoln argued, to "do *something*" on whatever level one operated than to have greater responsibility and do nothing.[38]

General Thomas needed no such exhortation. This sort of devotion to duty was what his character demanded of him without additional prodding. The irony was that it took some time for Lincoln and others to understand the application of the principle in the Virginian's case, not only because he was a Virginian, but because of the nature of his personality. George Thomas's ultimate triumph was not in what he was able to achieve for himself, but in the fulfillment of his duty in the service to his country. In this sense, he frequently "did something" at whatever point the opportunity presented itself to him, and in the process he tempered his "steel" to the purest substance of which he was capable.

1   Young George (1816–1840)

"Well, George Thomas, when a boy, never did what the other boys wanted, unless he thought it was right."
—Southampton County neighbor

"He never allowed anything to escape a thorough examination, and left nothing behind that he did not fully comprehend."
—Mathematics professor Albert Church at West Point on Thomas

Although George Henry Thomas won fame as a Federal general in the American Civil War, he hailed from a state that seceded from the Union. His parents, John and Elizabeth Rochelle Thomas, were residents of an area near the small community of Newsoms, in Southampton County, Virginia. The farm was located just a few miles from the North Carolina border, well away from any significant commercial centers, the nearest hamlet of any size being Jerusalem, now modern-day Courtland, Virginia.[1]

John and Elizabeth Thomas had been married for eight years, since February 9, 1808, when George Henry was born into that union on July 31, 1816. George was a middle child, bracketed by two brothers and six sisters. The eldest was John William. Judith Elvira was next in age, followed by Benjamin. George was the fourth child and last of the males, although the lack of specific dates for some of his sisters make exact birth order difficult to know with precision. Two of the siblings did not seem to survive infancy.[2]

John Thomas established himself as a successful planter on land that had passed down from the earliest settlement of the Thomas descendents in Colonial America. In 1816, the estate encompassed 438 acres of land and nine slaves.[3] By 1850, the family holdings had increased slightly to 500 acres, but the slave property now reached twenty-one.[4] This level of property ownership placed the family in the upper echelons of Southampton citizenry.

Growing up on the family's extended acreage in rural Virginia, George had the world as his playground and siblings with whom he could share experiences and from whom he would learn life's lessons. In reply years after Thomas's death to an inquiry by General Oliver O. Howard for information on the general's life as a youth, his sister Judith, still obviously sensitive to her brother's choice of service in the Civil War, managed to scribble briefly on the envelope before returning it, "I can only inform you that he was as all boys are who are well born and well reared."[5]

A eulogy including a description of George Thomas in this period termed him as "obedient, frank, respectful, and for his years singularly sedate and sensible." It would be hard to say the extent to which these qualities prevailed over other childhood characteristics, for the same source indicated that he also possessed his share of youthful energy. "Fond of out-door sports, an admirable horseman and a good shot, he was a favorite with the sons of the neighboring planters." Even so, there were signs of an independence of thought and deed in these early years, too.

George's subsequent life offered additional hints of the development his personality and character underwent in those formative childhood years. A contemporary noted "his grave demeanor, his quiet good sense and reliable nerve, even as a lad, commended him to the liking and respect of his elders." Yet, young Thomas was not afraid to carve his own path. At least one neighbor recalled this tendency in him. "Well, George Thomas, when a boy, never did what the other boys wanted, unless he thought it was right."[6]

Tragedy struck early to jolt the security of that world when his father John died of an apparent farm accident on February 19, 1829.[7] George would just be entering his teenaged years, and would have to do so now without this parent's influence, beyond the impact already made upon him. Perhaps this death, so early in his life caused the young man to withdraw somewhat. George never seemed to have completely divested himself of at least a latent sense of insecurity about himself, although he rarely offered glimpses in either his public actions or his private expressions. Throughout his life that same uncertainty provided a springboard for the ambition that propelled him forward.

Family meant a great deal to George Thomas. He developed important relationships with his siblings. John William was not significantly older than George, but enough so that he represented something of an authority figure for the younger man, especially in the absence of their father. The older brother's focus on his livelihood created a void that continued through their lives. The bittersweet relationship the brothers shared was also marked by genuine affection.

Thomas's relationships with others remained as complex as it was difficult to label. He had a tendency to keep to himself, and remain in control of a smoldering temper that seldom found public release. One contemporary explained, "Thomas possessed an even temperament, and was never violently demonstrative," but Thomas did not suffer individuals he considered foolish lightly and would usually make that stance clear to the offender. Regular army comrade and fellow Union general Erasmus Keyes explained simply that the Virginian's "deportment was dignified" and in the company of "strangers and casual acquaintances he was reserved."[8] Thomas displayed these qualities too commonly in subsequent years to make it likely that they were not present in his formative ones.

Above all, Thomas learned early to embody the virtue of duty as he saw it, regardless of the stage of his development or the benefits or detriments that might accrue accordingly. Frugal when it came to personal finance and conservative in his approach to the issues of his day, Thomas reflected the characteristics that would serve him well on the battlefield, but often tended to work against him through his refusal to curry favor or seek personal or career advancement at any costs. In the sense that any excess is a flaw, his greatest one was a tendency to rely so often upon himself.

The record has been exceptionally limited in some respects for young George Thomas. This was true of his connections to the institution of slavery. Much of what he did concerning African Americans, especially in his early years, appeared to be without particular reference to race. Such evidence as existed was anecdotal and would have been supplied years later in the context of a Southerner who had chosen to side with the Union in the Civil War. Thus, when colleague and friend Oliver Howard sought information on Thomas's background and received only a curt reply to his inquiries from the general's immediate family, he searched elsewhere and located an elderly individual of African descent who offered an additional— and despite its distance and the patina of memory, credible—account. The gentleman, named Artise, recalled Thomas as being "as playful as a kitten when he was a boy," and suggested the observation that the planter's son "seemed to love the Negro quarters more than he did the great house." Perhaps he was drawn by the life and energy he saw expressed there, but it is almost certain that he wanted to be in that area because that was where his friends were located. "Many times he would obtain things out of the great house for the Negro boys," the now eighty-year-old man remembered, noting that Thomas himself seemed to refer to the contemporaries as his "playmates." The gesture would not have been out of place for the good-hearted young man, who recognized that he had something the others did not and wanted to share what he had with them. The boys traded items and seemed to enjoy each other's company immensely. Artise added that when he started attending school, Thomas offered some of those lessons to his black friends, as well.[9]

There were no indications of public expressions during his youth where Thomas divulged a position on the "peculiar institution," or exposed his views concerning race. He did not outwardly question the validity of the slave system in which he had grown from childhood, except as Artise intimated, through a desire to pass along what he was learning in school to those friends, too. Essentially reared in a paternalistic world, Thomas neither embraced the harsher elements of mastery over others nor exhibited notions of race and equality that were out of line with his contemporaries or his age. Even as his personal views developed over time, his position as a paternalist, with regard to helping those he deemed to be weak or in need of assistance, prevailed until his death.

The complacent world in which young Thomas lived would be especially shaken when a number of slaves in the area followed the dynamic leadership of Nat Turner into one of the nation's greatest slave uprisings. Turner had labored under a searing sense of hostility and religious fatalism that reached a violent denouement in 1831. He stoked those fires of rebellion not only in himself but in a small band of compatriots for whom their "general," as he was called, gave guidance. The charismatic figure unleashed his vision of rebellion on the unsuspecting white community and instantly began to wreak havoc as his group hacked and bludgeoned their way from farm to farm.

The number of participants grew as the violence spread. Additional weapons came from ransacked homes, barns, and sheds. The Thomas household was in the path of the bloodshed and destruction. A timely warning allowed the widow and the children to dash for the safety of the county seat, Jerusalem. Even with the alarm, the fear of pursuit and the likelihood of not being able to avoid any insurrectionists who would be traveling along the farm lanes prompted the family to abandon their conveyance and take their chances on foot. The trek across the low-lying countryside was grueling, but the decision allowed the distraught family to reach the town safely. Given the coolness with which he faced every emergency later in life, it would be difficult to imagine the fifteen-year-old boy exhibiting much emotion beyond a steadied determination, but the event surely presented him with a starkly drawn firsthand picture of the volatility and dangers inherent in a system of forced servitude.

Turner's Insurrection instilled terror in many white community members and an intense desire for retribution against those slaves or free blacks who happened to be in the wrong place at the wrong time, as well as the participants who fell into the hands of authorities. White patrols eventually captured Turner himself, although he managed to elude pursuit for a time, to the considerable chagrin of local residents. If Thomas expressed himself on such matters those views have been lost to history, but he remained an adherent to order and control for his entire life and thus would have found such proceedings troublesome to say the least.

Naturally reluctant to reveal matters he considered private to even his closest colleagues, Thomas nevertheless exposed something of his character in its earliest development, undoubtedly from his teenaged years. One such story focused on the inquisitive nature that seemed to have imbued the Southampton Countian. By his admission he enjoyed learning the way things operated. Such puzzles challenged him and brought out in him a desire to master any situation through the sheer force of his mind. In this instance the curiosity involved the creation of saddles. The young man regularly visited the local shop that specialized in the making of that product and observed carefully as the work was being undertaken. The busy saddler must have noticed the boy's continuing presence and interest, but seemed neither to have minded it enough to send him away nor embraced it sufficiently to make him a formal apprentice. Still, George watched and learned. At length, he had gathered enough information to make an attempt himself, and as Thomas later related with pride, "succeeded in his first effort in making a good saddle," simply from having observed how it was done by a master craftsperson. The general related that he had done similarly with other handiwork as well, including making "boots and furniture."[10]

When not teaching himself, Thomas engaged in the schooling that then was available to a few of the established white families of the region. Although early biographer Thomas Van Horne observed that at twenty Thomas "completed with honor the prescribed course of study of the Southampton Academy located near his home," he probably received little more than what another writer termed "the rudiments of his education."[11]

Upon his graduation from the local school, Thomas contemplated his future and apparently gave some thought to legal training. One source noted only, "His father wished him to study law, and he turned to it for a while."[12] That young Thomas had an aptitude for such endeavors could be confirmed in later years by his knowledge and experience with courts-martial and military law. In any case, the time for such study could not have been an extended one, for the young man was destined to follow a different path.

Thomas's uncle, James Rochelle, appeared to have discerned such a desire in his nephew and broached the possibility of an appointment to the United States Military Academy with a family friend, Congressman John Young Mason. "Let us call the boy [in] and ascertain what he thinks of the proposition," the uncle was supposed to have suggested, although there is no record of how any discussions they had at that time might have gone.[13] It is also not known how long after this initial query before the August 17, 1835, death of his uncle, but Thomas at least temporarily followed in the relative's footsteps when he was sworn in as deputy clerk on November 18 of the same year.

Benefiting in this way from family and political connections, Thomas also had an aptitude for organization and administration that must have been appealing for such a position. Yet, George did not seem to view the clerical position as either a sinecure or a permanent avocation and clearly, given his subsequent actions after only a few months on that job, demonstrated that he was not content to remain where he had found himself at this early stage of his life.[14]

Congressman Mason's experience with the young man prompted the politician to author a short letter of recommendation to Secretary of War Lewis Cass for George Thomas. "He is seventeen or eighteen years of age, of fine size and of excellent talents with a good preparatory education," the representative observed in his March 1 note.[15] Thomas had obviously accepted the nomination for the cadetship at the United States Military Academy, and the appointment came through as expected. Elizabeth Thomas extended her permission as well as her blessing. But when the young man approached the legislator on his way to West Point to express his gratitude he received a surprisingly cold reception. Mason proved quite direct to his Southampton County constituent. His track record with such appointments had not been stellar in the past, and he did not want another disappointing performance to add to this unflattering record. "No cadet appointed from our district has ever graduated from the Military Academy," the politician explained pointedly. If Thomas could not perform satisfactorily, he added bluntly, "I never want to see you again."[16]

It is difficult to know whether the challenge was meant to inspire the young man or was more of a jestful gibe at the serious fellow who stood before him, but the congressman need not have worried. Still, Mason, in his third term of office and already having achieved what one historian has called "far greater prominence than any other antebellum Southamptonite," undoubtedly wanted to be able to point to one successful appointment and thought that the prod of motivation would not be lost on the earnest young man.[17]

Indeed, the rather unorthodox method worked; Thomas took the charge literally. As it was, he had all of the proper authorization to take his chance, having formalized his acceptance of the appointment in a letter to Secretary of War Cass, dated April 25, 1836, and sent from West Point, where he had already arrived to embark on this phase of his life and prospective career. His paperwork included his mother's written consent for her son to "sign any articles by which he will bind himself to serve five years as a cadet in the United States Military Academy at West Point," unless, of course, he should be discharged or found deficient at an earlier point.[18]

The West Point experience represented an opportunity to obtain an education that would carry George Thomas beyond whatever he might have attained by remaining in southeastern Virginia. Thus, the quiet lad found himself thrust into a new world. Yet, he had the advantage of relative maturity. A contemporary observed that when he "entered the Military Academy he was twenty years of age, or four years beyond the average of cadets at the time of his admission."[19]

Upon his arrival at West Point on July 1, 1836, he would have registered with the adjutant, as entrants were required to do, and then taken his place as a "plebe." Thomas found himself assigned for this initial year to billet with Ohioan William Tecumseh Sherman and Vermonter Stewart Van Vliet.[20] The Virginian was only a year younger than Vliet, with both men bent toward more serious study, and both appreciably older than Sherman at sixteen and a half.[21] Despite their age difference, "Cump" Sherman would claim the Virginian as his "best friend," and one of Sherman's biographers later asserted, "Although in the succeeding three years Thomas would room with Van Vliet, it was Sherman who became his closest friend."[22]

In 1893, Stewart Van Vliet still recalled the heady days of the academy. "Sherman, George H. Thomas, and I arrived at West Point on the same day," he explained to Henry Coppée, "and all three were assigned to the same room, on the south side of the old south barracks." The men, whom he remembered as "all three sturdy fellows," hit if off quickly and established a "warm friendship [that] commenced in that room, which continued, without a single break, during our lives."[23]

One would have had to venture long to find more taciturn individuals than Thomas and Vliet. On the occasion of the Virginian's death, his old comrade offered comments on their relationship at the academy that were concise and straightforward, although obviously genuine and heartfelt. "We entered West Point together; we studied together; we roomed together; we graduated together." Vliet capped off his brief tribute to Thomas by noting, "in all that time I never knew him to be guilty of an unkind word or act."[24] However, it was also Vliet who recalled at least one "unkind word or act" on his roommate's part when a hazing effort brought forth Thomas's impressive wrath.[25]

Among Thomas's other classmates were fellow Virginians Richard S. Ewell and Richard B. Garnett, and Northern-born George Washington Getty, Bushrod R. Johnson, and William H. C. Whiting.[26] Students who arrived in subsequent years after Thomas had established himself seemed to have formed attachments to the Virginian as well. A future adversary, James Longstreet, entered West Point in 1838, and according to one of that general's biographers, "became a valued companion for two years," of the upperclassman.[27]

George Thomas possessed sufficient educational preparation and political connections to get him into the military institution. But like everyone else, he would have to demonstrate stamina and determination as well as academic prowess to remain until graduation. "Thoroughness rather than alertness was the chief virtue of this young man," one writer explained.[28] This quality, as well as a consistent determination, served Thomas well then and throughout his career.

Even so, the plebe found himself tested early. Part of the informal indoctrination process frequently involved hazing. The older cadets often enjoyed harassing the new arrivals. Although one historian of the institution observed, "Most of the hazing resulted in nothing more painful than the loss of a plebe's dignity,"[29] Thomas made sure that any indignity would be visited on the oppressor rather than upon himself or his companions. Thus, when an upperclassman entered the room, the Virginian turned on him and abruptly demanded, "Get out of this room or I will throw you out that window." The fellow hastily departed, and word must have spread of Thomas's intent, for no further attempts were aimed in his direction.[30]

One West Pointer recalled the academy as "a great place to wean one from home," and declared it to be "a great place in every respect, great for the facilities for education as a finished school for manners and refinements, for studying human nature learning the ways of the world for straightening the form."[31] All of these elements fit into the process of indoctrination whereby the youthful civilian would be transformed into his new military persona. Author Stephen Ambrose concurred with this assessment in his observation that "West Point made life hard for the cadets in order to turn out finished soldiers."[32]

Aside from hazing, another form of indoctrination, perhaps even a rite of passage for many, was the application of a nickname for the new arrivals. Such colorful terms usually projected messages about the individual's physical character or personality, especially if some feature stood out to observers. Sometimes these socializing methods offered unflattering assessments, although Thomas did not generate a title with negative connotations. Oliver O. Howard observed that in his cadet days, Thomas took the name "Washington."[33] For this Virginian, the appellation implied a measure of respect, perhaps in recognition of his comparative age and maturity. But, these practices also served a double purpose, by establishing the superiority of the veteran cadets over the newcomers and binding them to the institution and each other. Breaking down the individuality that characterized each person as he came to the academy served to progress the development of the class as a whole in addition to making soldiers of the civilians.

Despite an impassive disposition, Thomas made an impression on some of the individuals with whom he came into contact at West Point. The chaplain at the military academy remembered "Young Thomas" sufficiently to observe, "His deliberate care in the preparation of his lessons, and his punctiliousness in the performance of every duty, won for him the sobriquet of 'Old Pap Thomas' while at the Point."[34] Another description of him during this time reflected the traits for which he would become known later in life. "Always faithful in study, and conscientious in the exact performance of every assigned duty, he was regarded as reliable, rather than brilliant, and was esteemed to be a cadet of great common sense rather than of rare promise of genius." One ought not to read too much into the emphasis on common sense as opposed to an exceptional academic prowess. Thomas was as capable in the classroom as he was on the parade ground or would be later on the battlefield, but his knowledge came principally from hard work and application rather than reliance on natural gifts. The same contemporary recalled, "If he gained entrance to the Academy because of the influence of an aristocratic family, he won his sure way upward by sterling merit and the most unremitting devotion to duty." Perhaps for this reason, at West Point, Thomas "deserved and received the sincere respect and regard alike of his instructors and comrades."[35]

Thomas embraced his new life enthusiastically. He traded the civilian garb he had worn in Southampton for the spit-and-polish uniform of West Point. The double-breasted gray coat presented three rows of buttons below a stiff collar, with white canvas belts at the waist and shoulders, and the uniform also featured a brass breastplate and white trousers. A tall felt hat adorned with a visor, leather bands, a pompon, and a brass plate in the shape of a castle represented the headgear the cadet wore while on duty, as opposed to the infinitely more comfortable small blue cloth cap that served as his covering otherwise. A musket and cartridge box completed the uniform.[36]

Thomas had his first experiences with the other incoming "plebes" in the general encampment established for all cadets on the Plain at West Point. There he learned the rigors of drill and the regulations of army life, designed to assist the civilian in making the transition to military life. This first summer exercise also introduced the young men to the order and discipline of the military, with its prescribed times for rising, policing the grounds, drilling, facing inspection, going on parade, eating meals, and going to bed.[37] The activities were meant to be impressive visually, with vast rows of tents and well-ordered company streets that stretched across the broad plain. The ceremonies that occurred when the cadets struck the tents and returned to the barracks for the colder seasons were particularly memorable to those who witnessed or participated in them.

Celebrations made the whole experience more palatable. The Fourth of July prompted an entire day of activities, while a ball marked the close of the summer season at the end of August. Despite the nearly constant drilling and instruction, there was time for other activities as well, and there were always the visitors who stopped to watch the pageantry.[38]

A second form of honorific ceremony occurred soon after the cadets entered the fall term. Richard Ewell, Thomas's classmate, explained to his brother on November 6, "Major Alden died last Saturday, the 6th, and was buried on Sunday with the honors of war."[39] Alden had been a Revolutionary War figure and the storekeeper of the academy for better than a decade.[40] The solemn occasion would have been one of the earliest opportunities Thomas and his comrades had to see displayed before them the panoply of the profession they were seeking to enter. "I admired the procession very much," Cadet Ewell noted blithely, before illustrating the lack of connection the young men had for their venerated elder by adding, "but there appeared to be none who cared the least for the deceased."[41]

The students soon settled into the academic routine so important to their development as soldiers. The educational regimen at the military academy was quite rigorous. Daily recitations were meant to guarantee that the participant engaged properly in his preparation and studies. Class ranking ultimately depended upon examinations in January and June, but the demands were quite heavy from day to day. As one historian explained, "All told, the boys spent between nine and ten hours daily in class or studying, approximately three hours in military exercises, two hours in recreation, and two hours at meals."[42]

By the end of his first year at the academy, termed the Fourth Class there, Thomas stood twenty-sixth out of a class of seventy-six and had only twenty demerits to blemish his record.[43] Thomas's first two years would be taken up in the most part by mathematics and French. As such, one of the Virginian's instructors, mathematics professor Albert Ensign Church, had an extended introduction to the young Virginian. Church had just arrived at West Point when Thomas sat before him with slate in hand, prepared to take his lessons. Already balding atop a head that seemed constantly tilted to one side, the forty-year-old instructor was considered "dry as dust," but receptive to those who demonstrated a willingness to prepare for class.[44] Professor Church recalled the strengths in Thomas's academic personality that reflected his character throughout his life. "He never allowed anything to escape a thorough examination," he explained, "and left nothing behind that he did not fully comprehend."[45]

Church may not have been present on one occasion when the ordinarily reliable young student failed in his preparation. During one of the ubiquitous blackboard recitations, the Virginian found himself in the unenviable position of not knowing the material well enough. Thomas might be, as one scholar assessed, "the most imperturbable cadet of his generation," but William Sherman later recalled that the moment flustered his friend so much that the color faded from his face as he stood at the blackboard dumbfounded. Sherman did not record any immediate reaction other than Thomas's physical manifestations, but as the Ohioan later observed, there was no subsequent occasion in which his colleague "didn't know his lesson."[46]

In the Third Class year, Thomas moved up to fifteenth out of fifty-eight overall and secured a position as corporal at the academy.[47] His improvement slipped back slightly the following year where he held the seventeenth slot out of a total of forty-six, but advanced to the position of sergeant among his peers.[48] Thomas achieved his highest level in his final stanza, a pattern that also might have proven symbolic for the soldier who often saved his best for the end.

Thomas was clearly preparing for a profession at arms at West Point, but he also developed an interest in science that would remain with him for the rest of his life. As a boy playing in the rural countryside of Southampton County, he undoubtedly came to appreciate nature in his own, youthful way, but now he had a chance to expand that interest. One person who certainly played a role in this aspect of his academic and intellectual life was a new professor, Jacob W. Bailey. Termed a "walking science department," by a later historian, Bailey was apparently proficient at all of the natural sciences.[49]

For the military academy, Bailey's presence was novel and, in the sense of the culture of the institution, revolutionary. Although a product of West Point himself, in the class of 1832, Bailey seemed to have defied the mold when it came to instruction and enthusiasm for his subject. A later scholar deemed the science professor "a kindly figure, a cadet favorite because of his willingness to try to stimulate the cadets to learn rather than forcing them to memorize massive amounts of material." What particularly must have appealed to a student like George Thomas was that the scientist "applied the principles of science to practical situations that cadets might encounter while on active duty." Not far removed from their position as cadets, having graduated himself less than ten years before, Bailey also struck a chord with the Virginian through their common interest in science. Indeed, Thomas sat at the feet of this influential teacher in chemistry in his Second Class or junior year and in mineralogy and geology in his First Class or senior year.[50] One of Thomas's modern biographers argued that it was in this period that the Virginian "replaced his curiosity about human-made objects with an interest in the scientific study of minerals, animals and plants."[51] Of course, such a position suggested that these studies were mutually exclusive, a point that Thomas himself seemed to dispel.

Not all was smooth at the military academy during Thomas's tenure. Rene E. DeRussy, the superintendent who had been there when the Virginian arrived in 1836, left the institution in September 1838 under a cloud of dissatisfaction, particularly with regard to laxness in discipline, the cardinal sin of the profession. Upon his death, a description of DeRussy lent itself to such an interpretation, describing him as possessing "great kindness of heart," and serving as "the kindest of fathers."[52] One of Thomas's classmates described the situation that had formerly prevailed in a letter home. "It is better for the institution that the Superintendent should have a character for strictness," Dick Ewell explained, for "under DeRussy's administration, it was going down hill with increasing velocity."[53]

DeRussy's replacement by Major Richard Delafield, first in the Class of 1818, brought almost instantaneous and thoroughgoing change. Delafield wanted to place his imprimatur on the academy from the outset.[54] Thomas's fellow cadet Richard Ewell no doubt expressed the feelings that most, if not all, of his colleagues held concerning the new man. "Major Delafield seems to pride himself upon having everything different from what it used to be." Considering some of the changes to be good ones, Ewell concluded, "A new broom sweeps clean." Still, he predicted that inertia would be difficult to overcome: "I expect after a while things will go on in the old way."[55]

Life at West Point became increasingly disciplined in ways that exceeded the ordinary course of life there in prior years. Thomas expressed himself rather vigorously to his brother concerning this new state of affairs in a letter in mid-February 1839. He described "a court of Enquery [that] had been ordered here for the purpose of enquiring into a riot (our *worthy* Superintendent was pleased to call it) of Cadets which took place last Christmas night." Obviously, holiday celebrations had gotten out of hand and the superintendent wanted to discourage such unmilitary behavior in his charges when the matter came to his attention. "It appears that one of the officers got his hand and head pretty severely bruised that night and complained to Maj. Delafields who wrote to Washington for this court."

The case made its way to the attention of the nation's highest authority, where the Virginian thought that the matter went astray. Chiding President Martin Van Buren for "considering the matter with his usual *wisdom*," Thomas revealed an underlying disdain for politics that he would cultivate through the years. In particular he condemned the action taken against one of his fellow cadets on the basis of "circumstantial" evidence "which would be rejected in any Court Martial," and took a perverse pleasure in noting that the other individual summarily dismissed had actually already "*graduated last January* and left the military service long before his sentence came over." Such inattention to detail and uninformed decision making on the part of the president left an indelible mark on the impressionable young soldier and helped to color his assessment of the relationship between the worlds of martial discipline and political capriciousness.

Thomas was having little better fortune with regard to Richard Delafield personally. "I tried to get a leave to visit Ben while he was in New York but *Old Dick the democrat* (our Superintendent) would not consent to let me go." Then he rather irreverently observed of both DeRussy and Delafield, "I use[d] to think that old *Red* poor fellow was rather close with money, but Dick rather overreached him, for I believe that he would not only *skin* a *flie* his hide and tallow, but would eat the meat."[56]

Thomas was not the only one finding his new superior difficult to work with, despite the positive changes that he had wrought in a relatively short time. An assessment offered as part of Delafield's biographical entry for the academy's members noted that he improved the grounds and facilities, enlarged the library holdings, and enhanced the educational experiences of the students, particularly with regard to the sciences and artillery and cavalry instruction. Such "salutary reforms" raised the level of discipline and the reputation of the institution, but not without a cost. "Major Delafield, however, was not a popular superintendent. The young are ever restive under restraint, and even the elder members of his command, while freely admitting his superior administrative abilities, did not take kindly to the iron rule of his arbitrary will."[57]

Like all of those who were fortunate to survive their first two years at West Point, Cadet Thomas looked forward to the rare experience of a furlough in the third summer. In late April 1839, Thomas informed his brother that a friend studying medicine in Philadelphia could talk only about his upcoming furlough. Then he confessed that "he is not worse in that respect than everyone else, for I believe I can say from experience that a furlough is the last thing thought of at night, and the first thing in the morning that a *third classman* thinks of."[58]

When he returned to the barracks and the routine of the academy, Cadet Thomas prepared for the final phases of his West Point career. In his last year, Thomas placed at or near the top ten in rankings in all of his classes. His highest rating was in artillery, where he placed seventh, edging out classmates William T. Sherman and Richard Ewell. His score of eleventh was also slightly above Sherman, who rated twelfth, but the Ohioan took the honors in every other class. Still, Thomas's eleventh in engineering and tenth in ethics were quite respectable, and he placed ninth in "Mineralogy and Geology." Overall, George Thomas stood at twelfth in the class, one ahead of Ewell and six behind Sherman.[59]

The sparse circulation records for Cadet Thomas revealed an interest in science that may have helped to account for his success in "Mineralogy and Geology."[60] Correspondence with his family indicated that he engaged in other reading as well. In a short postscript to a February 16, 1839, letter to his brother, Thomas inquired about farming, then noted, "By the way I see that [Edmund] Ruffin has published Davy's Agricultural Chemistry which is a very valuable thing as it gives the nature of all soils properties etc. of clays, muds, etc."[61] In March 1839 he read volumes on botany and shades and shadows. Earlier in the year, Thomas had checked out a book on Florida.[62]

The Virginian was as aware as anyone that completing his education at West Point meant service in the field, and given the likelihood that such an assignment might take him to Florida, he wanted to familiarize himself as much as possible with information on that destination. Thus, he selected *The Territory of Florida*, by John Lee Williams.[63] A colleague who served with him there remarked on the tendency Thomas had still to indulge in reading as circumstances allowed. "He was an accomplished officer," Erasmus

Keyes recalled, "and although his turn of mind inclined him more to science than to literature, his reading was extensive and varied."[64]

Perhaps with Congressman Mason's challenge in the back of his mind, and determined to make something of himself in any account, Thomas remained dedicated to completing the work he had set before him. Dogged determination served him well at the academy. Even so, the rigors of the classroom were having a somewhat debilitating impact, as he admitted in a letter to his brother John. Explaining that "if anything" he was "a little more tired of studying, and just as sleepy head[ed] as usual at this time of the year," George knew that he had only to redouble his efforts to finish his education successfully. As always practical and observant, he assured his elder sibling, and perhaps himself, "I think there is no reason to apprehend being found deficient."[65]

Lack of sleep might have been a factor plaguing cadets, but lack of scrutiny was never an issue for them. Although Thomas would not achieve an unblemished record as did another Virginian, Robert E. Lee, who had preceded him, his "delinquencies" were hardly an indication of his ability to adapt to a martial world. Among his earliest infractions were a single mark for being "Late to Reveille" on April 22 and five for "Introducing Citizens in qrs." between the hours of "5 & 6 PM." Thomas had additional demerits for "Visiting" and "Loitering" and was gigged for not having swept his floor and failing to keep his bedroom "policed."[66] But his overall nineteen delinquent strikes were hardly sufficient to worry him about his ranking among his peers.

Through the next year, Cadet Thomas had difficulty being "Out of bed after Taps" on more than one occasion and was found "Visiting" again during "Study Hours." Those five demerits collected on May 24 were the largest individual blemish on a record that ended with one less negative mark than the previous year. Perhaps most troubling to the disciplinarian that he would become were the three demerits each he accrued for being "Absent from drill roll call" on October 4 and for "Neglect[ing] duty as file closer not reporting men Looking to the rear at insp." on April 7.[67] He never amassed large numbers and received his lowest total of fourteen in his last year (again being tagged for being late to roll call, reveille, or class and for "Visiting," on two occasions). He may well have been running late another time in September when he received a demerit for his "Coat not buttoned."[68]

Despite the focus on academics, class rankings, and discipline, the cadets remained at least nominally familiar with issues arising outside of the confines of the academy. In the spring of 1839, Thomas recorded the arrival of General Winfield Scott at West Point. Scott raised the possibility of hostilities with the British, but discounted the likelihood of a war, especially if cooler heads prevailed. Thomas seemed to have considered preparation reasonable under the circumstances. "I suppose the object is to have the troops prepared in case there should be any necessity for calling [them] out to fight."[69]

The subordination of the individual to the good order and discipline of the service helped to limit troublesome political expressions. Melding persons of varying backgrounds and viewpoints into a larger whole was an essential part of the process of turning citizens into soldiers.[70] The description that historian John Marszalek has used for Henry Halleck, one of Thomas's contemporaries at the academy, fit the Virginian as well: "He had become a military man and, as such, had to stay clear of politics."[71] Early biographer Thomas Van Horne noted, "He was originally a Whig in political faith, but in deference to army traditions and personal taste, never was a partisan."[72] The political controversies that would characterize the next decade had not broiled to the point of intensity they would reach subsequently, but George Thomas was certainly aware of the world around him. Little has been recorded concerning his views on the subjects of the day by his academy contemporaries, but Thomas tended toward moderation, even when controversial matters entered his world.

Nor did Thomas seem to allow distractions of a more social nature to complicate his life as much they did for others, including his roommate Sherman. He did not have the type of personality to indulge in the temptations that lay just outside the regimented world of the academy. Despite the demerits he received, his penchant for personal discipline kept the most unsavory elements at a safe distance and assisted him mightily in instances where many of his comrades would go astray.[73] Of the stellar career of Robert E. Lee at West Point, historian and biographer Emory Thomas observed, "But in one sense life at West Point was easy. Cadets simply obeyed orders."[74] Like the focus on studying that did not permit him to proceed without fully comprehending the material, this assessment of academy life suited Thomas, too. He had learned the chain of command, the rudiments of military leadership with the positions of authority he had assumed, and he understood, perhaps better than most, the value and importance of following orders.

Arriving at West Point at a more mature age and prone to a more serious bent than many of his fellows, George Thomas certainly learned a great deal from his experiences at the military academy. His training there enhanced his sense of order and discipline. He excelled at cavalry tactics, the importance of which would also be driven home to him in his future service on the frontier. But as one student of the old army asserted, West Point was not the best place to obtain preparation for confronting the Indians or their specialized tactics. The academy, Robert Utley observed of its graduates, "sent them forth to learn Indian fighting by hard experience."[75] Nor, as a student of West Point noted, was the focus intended to be as much on the practical as on the theoretical side of military matters. "The men who controlled the institution," historian James Morrison asserted, "viewed its mission as being the production of engineers who could also function as soldiers rather than the reverse."[76]

Upon leaving West Point, Thomas had the benefit of continuing his association with Stewart Van Vliet, who was assigned to the same regiment and ordered to Florida as well. But, in many ways, the world that the two men were about to enter was as unfamiliar as a young man from Southampton County, Virginia, even by way of West Point, New York, could ever have imagined. If the roommates remained "together," as Vliet later recalled, each nevertheless had to determine his own path, starting in an unglamorous war against the Seminoles in the exotic environment of the Everglades.[77]

2   First Duties (1840–1845)

*"I shall have to depend upon my sword for a living for some time
at least if not always."*
—Thomas to his brother John

*"This will be the only opportunity I shall have of distinguishing
myself, and not to be able to avail myself of it is too bad."*
—Thomas on his service in Florida

George Thomas may have left the confines of West Point
when he graduated, but he did not venture far, at least initially. His first
posting was as a second lieutenant in Company D of the Third Artillery at
Fort Columbus, New York, with orders to report there from leave by
September 30, 1840.[1] Fort Columbus dated to 1806 as a part of the defenses
of New York Harbor, and its proximity to the city offered the young officer
access to that metropolitan center as well, although there is no evidence that
Thomas indulged in activities that cast a disparaging aspect on his budding
career.[2]

Anxious to start his career appropriately, Lieutenant Thomas reported to
his post a few days early. The young officer was already developing the
habits that would remain with him throughout his career. A colleague who
had the opportunity to analyze him at about this same period concluded,
"He was seldom much in advance of the appointed time in his arrival at the
post of duty, and I never knew him to be late, or appear impatient or in a
hurry." Thomas exuded confidence, but not to the degree that others became
offended or put off by the trait. "All his movements were deliberate," the
same friend recalled, "and his self-possession was supreme, without being
arrogant."[3]

On September 27, he wrote his brother John in Norfolk, "I arrived here
last Wednesday and made the necessary preparations for living as
comfortably as we can that is I reported took a room and bought a few
articles of bed clothing a chair etc. to make it inhabitable for as to living
comfortably it is out of the question." In the cool chill of approaching
autumn, he expressed himself satisfied that he had managed to keep warm,
"and that is all that we can do towards living comfortable."

Thomas informed his brother that he had found that he should be
expecting to be ordered to proceed to Florida "about the end of next month."
He was already becoming sensitive to the demands of a career in the
military and heard complaints from officers who threatened resignation.
Perhaps not yet able to sympathize with those who had been in the service
longer, or simply attempting to project positively on the career path he had

chosen, Thomas observed, "if that should be the case I shall not be so much displeased as I shall be a little higher in the army list, and as I shall have to depend upon my sword for a living for some time at least if not always I shall not grumble a great deal."

Thomas did not anticipate many extravagances if he were to be deployed to the distant territory, but in as practical a mind-set as ever, regarded that likelihood as more beneficial than detrimental. "If I should remain in Florida for any length of time I could soon raise money enough to pay all of your debts as I have been told that in the part of the territory I am going to an officer cannot spend more than ten dollars a month let him live as extravagantly as he pleases." Aside from being in a position to husband his resources, Thomas wanted to do his part in sustaining his family. "If this be the case I am in hopes there will be no necessity of your moving to any other part of the state for now," he explained. He was now "able" to help, and asked only to be allowed "to assist you."

George Thomas would often be depicted through much of his life as reserved. Yet, the letter also revealed a more creative and expressive side of his personality that focused on an appreciation of the fine arts. He expressed the desire to examine personally the work of one stage performer in particular. "I want to see the celebrated . . . Power act, some of his Irish characters," he told his brother. "He is decidedly the best actor I have ever seen." Even when he was a tourist, practicality and curiosity remained mainstays, and Thomas's interests lent themselves to wide varieties of topics. "I have enclosed you a Baltimore shinplaster which you may be able to pass of[f] in Norfolk," he observed before admitting, "it is of no earthly use to me, and I am afraid it will be of little to you."[4]

Thomas was already on the books of his new duty station at Fort Lauderdale, Florida, in October; he just was not present at the post.[5] Some of the troops were set to sail for Florida over a period of the next couple of weeks, Thomas explained to his brother. He anticipated leaving "at the end of October, but he was still in New York at mid-month."[6] From Fort Wood, he wrote brother John another letter in which he confessed, "I can not learn when we sail for Florida, not before the 1st of next month."[7] Finally, on November 23, he and the regiment received orders to travel to Florida. The post report confirmed his presence there in December.[8] Second Lieutenant George H. Thomas, Third Artillery, was now in the field. The assignment took the young officer to the country's distant and troubled southern frontier, where hostilities had broken out once more with the Seminoles. Among the passengers who traveled with the Virginian as he made his way from New York to Florida, via Savannah, Georgia, was Braxton Bragg, whom Thomas would confront on battlefields in the future.[9]

By December 9, 1840, Thomas had reached Fort Lauderdale, Florida, and found that the post was nothing like he had previously experienced, even in the Spartan world of the military academy. The officers and men lived in cane huts, and the amenities were not sparse, they were nonexistent.[10] Arriving as he did in the winter, Thomas was fortunate not to experience any of the difficulties of heat and humidity associated with warmer periods. Indeed, he wrote his brother John in Norfolk in early January a glowing letter. "I am very much pleased with the situation of this post and should like to live here very much if we could get the mails regularly." He predicted that despite its current isolation, people would be drawn to the area. "After the war is ended if it ever should be, I would not be at all surprised if this became a very populous country. The soil is very good and well adapted to the cultivation of cotton."

Thomas apparently had already had the opportunity to indulge his interest in science in the new locale, and enjoyed sharing his initial impressions with his kinsman. "By the way the Everglades is one of the greatest natural curiosities in existence, it covers nearly the whole of the southern portion of the territory. It is overflowed with water coming from no known source, and what is more singular, this water though apparently stagnant is perfectly sweet and palatable, indeed I think it is as good water as is generally met with any where in the U.S." The beauty and the isolation were both appealing to the young officer. "There are also several large and fertile islands, about 15 miles west of this place which would make a beautiful abode for a man disgusted with the world."[11]

While at Lauderdale, Thomas served as acting assistant commissary of subsistence and acting assistant quartermaster. The routine kept him occupied sufficiently to prevent him from replying to the letter of a friend stationed at Watervliet Arsenal in New York, dated May 22, until near the end of July. He was at Fort Lauderdale when he finally put his thoughts on paper to his friend and fellow West Pointer Lieutenant C. P. Kingsbury. "My duties at this post are so many that my whole time is taken up," he explained. "I have to do the duty of commissary, quartermaster, ordnance officer, and adjutant; and if I find time to eat my meals, I think myself most infernal fortunate." Thomas did not address his sleeping habits, but later experience suggested that he required his full measure, and thus his days and weeks passed in his exotic posting.

Like other young officers in such circumstances, Thomas wanted to demonstrate his proficiency at something other than generating paperwork. He noted that an officer had arrived with a detail heading to Fort Dallas "below this place, with sixty men from his post and sixty from here, for the purpose of making an expedition into the Everglades to oust Sam Jones from his cornfields." This last reference to the Native American leader suggested that an engagement was probable, and Thomas was convinced that the troops "may do something if they will go to work properly, for the Indians are there, I know, as we have frequently seen their fires at night, and they do not expect to see any of our men there at this season of the year." Thomas felt disappointment at missing the potential for action and the prospect for "laurels" to be won as a result. He offered his emotions on the matter with a force he seldom allowed others to see. "I have been left behind to take care of this infernal place in consequence of being commissary, etc." It was one time where the responsibility he craved came at a price he wished he did not have to pay. "This will be the only opportunity I shall have of distinguishing myself," he complained, "and not to be able to avail myself of it is too bad."[12]

It is difficult for those who have not had experience in the military service to understand such expressions of disappointment for going into danger. For Thomas the fact that the realities of combat remained in his future may have fed his desire to participate in an operation where fighting might occur. He recognized that he and his comrades had chosen a profession, trained for it, and he understood that advancement seldom came from working strictly behind the scenes. Another contemporary agreed with the concern of being left out of any action: "We who were then at West Point as cadets were also very fearful that the Florida War would end without giving us a chance."[13]

Thomas also had reason to understand further the frailties of life, regardless of whether one sought deliberately to go into harm's way or not. In the same letter in which he lamented the lack of opportunity for active service in the field, he addressed the fates of other friends. "I have just heard that poor Job Lancaster has been killed by lightning. I have heard no news lately which has distressed me more, for he was one of the very best of men." Then there was another friend, who had died of "the fever which had been prevailing in the western part of the territory."[14] Thomas must have considered those outcomes, occurring as they did far from the battlefield, in his preference to take his chances where one had the expectation of defending oneself against a dangerous foe and winning accolades in the process.

In the late spring and summer of 1841, Lieutenant Thomas finally escaped the confines of the post for a "short leave of absence" and "detached Service, [per] Verbal permission."[15] By July he was not only back at his station but given the opportunity to exercise greater authority than he had done in his short professional career. As of July 24, 1841, he was in command at Fort Lauderdale in the absence of the others on a scouting expedition into the Everglades.[16] While at Fort Lauderdale, Thomas had occasion to find means of recreation and study that reflected his interests in science and nature. William T. Sherman recalled seeing him during this period on the beach, "spearing the sharks in the surf, or hauling in red fish." Sherman saw him in other pursuits as well, "paddling his canoe, and steering it in the intricate waves of the Everglades, hunting for our then wily foe; marching for days and weeks in the swamps, carrying his five day's rations, to last ten; piling up brush to make his bed above water; sitting by the camp-fire, testing the comparative merits of the alligator and coon as human food."[17]

A month later, Thomas was back in the field himself, "Temporarily absent on Detached Service Verbal Orders."[18] The next two months saw him back at his post, but for all of the adventure that Sherman's account suggested of his friend's service in Florida, the Virginian had not seen significant combat action.[19] That situation was about to change, as another scouting expedition formed to march into the Everglades under the command of Captain Richard D. A. Wade in search of the usually elusive Seminoles. Wade's report noted in November 1841, in "pursuance of the instructions . . . I set out on the 5th instant, accompanied by Lt. Thomas, 3d artillery." The next day, the expeditionary force "surprised and captured twenty Indians, men, women and children, took six rifles, destroyed fourteen canoes, and much provision of the usual variety." The troops proceeded to surround another settlement a couple days afterward and secured twenty-seven more captives, along with "six rifles and one shot-gun, and destroyed a large quantity of provisions and four canoes."[20] By November 11, the force was back at Fort Lauderdale, and Wade filed his after-action report. The total number of prisoners seized throughout the operation varied, but the figures included more women and children than warriors.[21] One Thomas biographer captured the essence of the conflict as well as the outcome from the army's perspective: "As Indian raids went in this feckless war, this one was successful."[22]

These excursions were clearly destructive to the Seminoles, but they were not without cost to the forces that executed them; the price to be paid through disease, however, was consistently far greater than that produced by combat. By the time the Third Artillery departed from the region it would have been understandable if the survivors considered Florida pestilential, as eight of the command's officers fell to disease, compared to the three who died in combat. Another 125 enlisted men likewise succumbed to those effects, while 33 perished from battle.[23]

His brief exposure to combat in the field may not have been enough to prevent Thomas from experiencing the frustrations of sedentary postings, but the freedom of the region offered its own relief from what one historian has labeled "the tedious monotony of garrison life."[24] Thomas also found diversion and built on his scientific interests by analyzing the rich local flora and fauna. Biographer Thomas Van Horne noted, "In Florida, he studied botany, geology and mineralogy in regions fruitful in specimens."[25]

Among the individuals with whom Thomas made contact in Florida was

Erasmus Keyes. The latter had been at Fort Lauderdale for only a short time when word arrived that a scouting party had returned from the interior. Keyes reached the landing in time to see "stepping on shore from a boat a young lieutenant whose name was George H. Thomas." Keyes set the officer's age as "twenty-six years old" and described him in some detail at this phase of his life. "His height was exactly six feet, his form perfectly symmetrical, inclining to plumpness; his complexion was blonde, eyes deep blue and large." He recalled thinking that the fellow reminded him of an ancient Roman patrician and was clearly struck on first impression. "From the first we were companions," he explained, "and my confidence in him was at once complete." Keyes would have occasion to examine his comrade even more closely as they served on the isolated frontier together.[26]

Certainly the conflict itself would not prove spectacular. One historian described the struggle as simply having "dragged itself out," as the "few Seminoles remaining in Florida withdrew into the Everglades."[27] Yet, for action that involved relatively few combatants, the Second Seminole War not only left a significant casualty list, but made a lasting impression on its survivors. "These men and others necessarily learned something from the Florida War which they employed later," historian John Mahon maintained. "Surely, too, they caught a glimpse of how grim the practice of their profession could be."[28]

Thomas's Florida experiences not only brought him exposure to combat, but won him distinction and recognition as well. On November 6, 1841, President John Tyler and Secretary of War John G. Spencer signed the commission that elevated Second Lieutenant George H. Thomas to "the rank of First Lieutenant BY BREVET," for "gallantry and good conduct in the war against the Florida Indians."[29]

By the summer Thomas was out of Florida altogether, but remained in the South, briefly assigned to the New Orleans Barracks in Louisiana. In July 1842, he left the Crescent City for a posting at Fort Moultrie, a historic fort at Charleston, South Carolina.[30] Post reports from Fort Moultrie listed Thomas as joining the garrison there on July 27, and carried him as present for duty until December, when he enjoyed a thirty-day furlough that dated from the thirteenth.[31]

Many years later, the Virginian recalled his experiences in both places with great fondness. Toward the end of the Civil War, he reminisced with feeling to Unionist A. A. Draper of New Orleans. "I often think of the pleasant time we had at New Orleans Bks where I was always cordially welcomed at your house, also of Fort Moultrie where the who[le] garrison lived on as cordial and friendly terms as the members of a family, and where we also had so many sincere friends as I thought among the inhabitants of Charleston and neighboring country." In the aftermath of the turmoil of civil war he remained inquisitive and solicitous of those connections: "I often wonder what has become of them."[32]

William T. Sherman shared a posting at the installation and remembered the time as filled with a mixture of mundane duties and more appealing diversions. "Our life there was of strict garrison duty," he recalled, "with plenty of leisure for hunting and social entertainments." He echoed the sentiments of his more sober Virginia comrade when he noted that the men in the post "formed many and most pleasant acquaintances in the city of Charleston."[33]

Sherman also noted the desire among the officers to improve themselves as soldiers. He explained that while stationed at the fort, "we were studying and practicing the new tactics." The numerous diversions included "Reading history, discussing the relative merits of the old flint lock, and the new percussion musket, experimenting with round shot, shrapnel and canister; lamenting that our fate had been cast in an era of eternal peace, and grumbling at the slowness of promotion."[34]

Thomas's service had warranted him a leave of absence, and he availed himself of it, with plans to visit family in Virginia among other business. As a traveling companion on this excursion he had a young lieutenant and future Union general, John Pope, since the latter could take the same transportation on his way to Baltimore. A boat ride to Wilmington, North Carolina, proved uneventful, but once the two soldiers were on land, their adventures took a more exciting turn. Arriving at Goldsboro, another pilgrim and future Confederate general joined their little band. Samuel G. French recorded that the three decided to continue their opportunity for companionship by proceeding to Norfolk, where they could catch a steamer to their final destinations. However, rather than their enjoying a leisurely trip, brutal winter weather began to play havoc with the travelers, and on several occasions they had to descend to help push the train along the ice-slicked rails. "There was not much comfort on the trains in those days," French later concluded.[35] Thomas would certainly have concurred, especially later when an accident while traveling nearly derailed his military career.

Thomas returned from his leave of absence in mid-January and had his brevet to first lieutenant recorded on the post registry in March, dated by general orders from March 6, 1843.[36] In September, greater responsibilities again fell to the Virginian with the designation of "Acting Staff Officer of the Dept." for a brief time, but his work must have proven satisfactory enough to place him in the same position under "Extra Duty" the following month.[37] He remained at the post only until December 1843, when he received orders transferring him to Company C of the Third Artillery. He accepted reassignment to famous Fort McHenry in Baltimore, Maryland, the site that had inspired the "Star Spangled Banner" during the War of 1812, reaching that post by the end of the month.[38]

A contemporary pronounced this location "one of the most desirable posts to be stationed at in the whole country."[39] Thomas biographer Francis McKinney noted that in addition to the assignment being welcomed for its social possibilities, it was "even more desirable from a professional point of view." Fort McHenry presented the young officer with his "first assignment to a fully equipped battery."[40]

In March, Thomas and the troops of Company C also received an important honor, although it was one associated with a terrible national tragedy. Near the end of a Potomac cruise aboard the USS *Princeton* that had taken place in late February, a number of visitors on the vessel for the occasion, including Secretary of State Abel P. Upshur and Secretary of the Navy Thomas Gilmer, had perished in an explosion. The incident occurred when one of the pieces of ordnance burst during a firing demonstration. Although aboard the vessel, President John Tyler was unharmed. He opened the East Room of the White House for the bodies of the victims to lie in state on March 1. Funeral services occurred the following day.[41] Thomas's company served as part of the escort for the cortege through the streets of Washington, returning from their special detached service at the beginning of April.[42] The July report for Fort McHenry acknowledged Thomas's promotion to first lieutenant, and the newly advanced junior officer had a short twenty-day leave in September.[43] Things seemed to be going well for the soldier, who was enjoying a comfortable posting and the sense of accomplishment that had come with advancement in rank.

On October 17, Thomas told his brother that he expected to leave Maryland momentarily. "As nothing has been said about joining my post immediately, I have some idea of [visiting], if Norfolk is more agreeable than usual I shall remain with you two days. I wish you could arrange it so that you could go to So.hampton with me and we would take a [trip] together. However I shall not be able to stop at home more than three or four days and perhaps it would hardly be worth the time and expense of traveling on the road." Later circumstances would appear to make his connections to his Southampton relatives seem tenuous, but Thomas remained attached to family in a way that was clearly close and comfortable, including sharing the fact that he had taken notice of "one of the prettiest Ladies I have ever seen."[44]

The Virginian had barely returned from his time away from the post when orders came down taking him back to Fort Moultrie, in South Carolina.[45] Although he would undoubtedly miss the amenities in Baltimore, and the proximity to New York City, being stationed through the late fall and winter months back on the southern coast must have been pleasant in its own regard. He also remained in contact with his brother from Fort Moultrie, complaining in November, "I shall annoy you with a very dry and uninteresting communication." Matters continued at the post much as he had left them earlier. "I found every thing and every body about the Garrison nearly or quite the same as when I left." But some of the changes were noticeable and affected his circle of personal companions. "Some of my favorites have been ordered away which I regret as one dislikes to be parted from friends; but our life is such an unstable one that we all have to learn to live with those we do not much admire." Yet, he did not want his relative to read too much in his remark. "You must not suppose from what I say about that I do not admire my present companions, on the contrary I like them all very much, and only regret that some of my more intimate friends are away."

Thomas informed his brother that he had not ventured into the nearby port city, and therefore, "I have not seen any of the Charlestonians yet but I know that they are all in 'status quo.'" He hoped to do so, although he despaired that one of the reasons was waning. "My desire for female society is fast leaving me so much so I have not paid a single visit except in the families of my military friends, although several of my old acquaintances among the Charlestonians are residing on the island yet." There was a nagging sense that one part of his life was slipping away from him while he focused so heavily on his martial obligations. "I begin to have all the whims and notions of an old Bachelor and if I do not alter my condition soon, I shall never do so."

Thomas was ever practical in his approach to his life and career. A tendency to stress preparation, for which he became famous later, was already present in his mind-set as he now considered interactions of a more social nature. "I am not in a condition to marry now and shall not be in five years to come, therefore I may as well cease thinking of the charms of matrimony at once, for the sooner I do so, so much sooner shall I be contented with the state of single blessedness." His self-consciousness returned as he apologized "for writing all this nonsense about matrimony for really I have nothing else to write about, and although I never expect to be a married man, still I am fond of talking about it, and always bring up matrimony when all other subjects are wanting in interest." He concluded that at any rate, "It is the most animatory topic of all others."[46]

Another letter to John on January 11, 1845, revealed some of the ennui that George was feeling. "I fear you will think you have thrown away a quarter when you have perused this letter, for I know no more what I am going to write than one who had never written a line. I have already waited so long that I feel as if I had to commence our correspondence anew." Perhaps the opportunity to chide his brother on matters of the heart prevailed. "You are certainly one of the most cautious lovers I have ever known; whilst you are reflecting upon the consequences of matrimony one half of the present generation would be married and in a fair way to increase their families. Indeed I have many acquaintances who have given you the start by two years and who are at this time more than two years ahead of you." Then, he began to recognize the way he would have reacted had the position been different. "But don't let my remarks alter your determination pro or con for in a matter of that sort," he explained. Perhaps as a way of heading off any criticism that might be returned, he concluded, "I think every man is his best adviser. I know if I were in that way of thinking I should have my own way notwithstanding the advice of others." The relationship between the brothers was clearly a deep and meaningful one. Although some six years separated them, the younger sibling had developed an attachment to his elder that allowed for trust and introspection.

After requesting that his brother present his respects "to the young lady," George openly revealed the doubts that had crept in as he admitted, "I fear my prospects in this quarter are rather gloomy." The younger Thomas then immediately tried to deflect such concerns by employing humor and history to bolster his position. "The South Carolina girls flirt very charmingly, but when matters become serious they give a very decided practical illustration of the domestic policy of their state, by nulefying instantly." Of course, in this case, Thomas's interest rested not as much in an assertion of state's rights as in allaying the underlying fear that he would never succeed in locating suitable companionship.

The soldier next shifted the subject to a topic with which he was more comfortable. By recalling the productive qualities of Southampton soil, he exhibited his interest in science and agriculture, but also tied his discussion to the financial possibilities that supported his thinking. "That branch below the house if cleared up would pay for itself in two years, besides being of immense advantage to the machine field." He contemplated the possibility of purchasing land and wanted his brother to make inquiries. "I am out of debt at this time and I have a notion that we could do something with that place if we had it besides it would be such a magnificent range for hogs and cattle, and might with but little expense be converted into a grazing farm."

Thomas found that even in a short time changes had occurred in his native Virginia that he found unsettling. "It shocked my feelings when I was home in the fall to see such fine places . . . going to ruins," he observed. He asked his brother to "inquire" about a part of these properties and speculated, "I think under good management that portion of the tract would pay for itself at the present price of land in about three years, and if I had it unencumbered I should regard myself as worth not less than thirty thousand dollars." Breaking down the elements into their constituent parts, Thomas displayed his methodical approach in observing, "The orchard alone will yield $1000 a year if it is attended to . . . and then, besides the mill which I suppose will yield nearly, if not quite, another thousand. The crop and stock would yield more than $500 more, which would be quite sufficient with economical management to pay all the expenses of the place." The soldier's whirring mind was never far from determining the most advantageous course to follow. "I heard that the whole tract could be purchased for $12000 so I suppose that part about the house including the mill might be bought for 6 or 8 thousand."

Thomas's correspondence revealed aspects of his character and personal motivations. His "hope" that a person might "gain satisfaction" from "a fine situation" that would "be of enormous advantage to him" reflected as much on the soldier's assessment of his own life and career. Happily, circumstances seemed to be turning to advantage for him, too.[47] He remained concerned about both his social and economic well-being, and approached both more with calculation than romantic notions or emotions.

Lieutenant George Thomas had reached a point in his still developing career when he could project himself more accurately into a lifetime of service to his nation. His first assignments produced experiences in a variety of settings and exposed him to a range of responsibilities that enabled him to critique his capabilities and gain valuable confidence in himself and them. The Virginian could be proud that he found himself up to the requirements that seemed necessary for advancement, although his mastery of affairs of the heart must have appeared as remote and uncertain as ever. Still, the realities of his obligations had replaced the imaginings of a cadet. Perhaps fittingly, when he rejoined the garrison from leave on April 4, Thomas spent a portion of his time in recruitment.[48] But this service would last only until June 26, 1845, when new duties required him to embark on the most significant test he had faced since beginning his military career.

3   "Under Fire" in Mexico and Virginia (1845–1848)

"I saved my section of Bragg's battery at Buena Vista by being a little slow."
—Thomas to Colonel Thomas Anderson

"I was under fire from 6 o.c. A.M. to 4 P.M."
—Thomas on his service at Buena Vista

"If I could get off with a dinner only I should have great cause to congratulate myself."
—Thomas expressing concern about public recognition for his service in Mexico

Years after the Civil War had ended, Colonel Thomas Anderson recalled a conversation with General George Thomas that related to the Virginian's service in Mexico. The topic suggested both an element of criticism that nagged at the Virginian and an innate sense of pride that overrode it. Anderson remembered, "General Thomas once told me himself that he had always been called slow, but he added with a grim smile: I saved my section of Bragg's battery at Buena Vista by being a little slow."[1]

The statement reflected the future general's personality and the importance that Thomas's service had during the Mexican-American conflict that raged during the mid-1840s and provided the Virginian and many of his colleagues with combat experience. Of the many officers participating in a wide range of capacities in this earlier conflict, historian James McPherson noted that "the competence of these men foreshadowed the ultimate irony of the Mexican War, for many of the best of them would fight against each other in the next war."[2]

The situation had been volatile between the neighboring countries, including the Texas War for Independence, which had involved figures such as Davy Crockett and Jim Bowie. When the United States annexed Texas in 1845, Mexico refused to accept the claim. Further, the two countries disputed the area of the Rio Grande River. Then an American patrol clashed with their Mexican counterparts in April 1846, and the United States had its pretext for war. The U.S. Congress issued its declaration in May and prepared to back its demands with force. The mobilization of that force followed.

There seemed to be little trepidation from the regulars who would be headed for active service. William Sherman later recalled that when Thomas and the rest of the men who were going to Texas departed from the beach at Fort Moultrie to board the brig *Hayne*, he could not help but give them "three hearty cheers." The gesture garnered the Ohioan a reprimand from his more sedate commander, Robert Anderson, "for making such unmilitary noise on the beach." But Sherman's action reflected the general feeling of being left behind, and as he put it, "how we all envied them the opportunity for glory and renown!"[3]

George Thomas was soon on his way to Texas. The command reached New Orleans in mid-July and proceeded to Corpus Christi, arriving at that destination on August 2, 1845.[4] Since the unit had traveled without horses to encumber them, one of the first responsibilities for the young officer was to procure sufficient animals for the battery. In addition to purchasing horses, Thomas and the command had to obtain the resources necessary for them to perform their operational duties.[5] There could be no better practical example of the challenges of adequate preparation for a person who came to see such activity as paramount to the chances for success on the battlefield.

During this period Thomas spent much of his time in close association with three future Civil War generals, including his battery commander, Braxton Bragg. Carolinian Daniel Harvey Hill recalled that in addition to himself, the other lieutenants of the unit were Thomas and John F. Reynolds. "We four had been in the same mess there," he explained referring specifically to Corpus Christi."[6] Under the command of Zachary Taylor, Thomas and his comrades remained stationed in Corpus Christi until March 11, 1846, when their unit joined other troops already moving on to the Rio Grande River.[7]

In the meantime, tensions in the border region continued to mount. Mexican movements threatened Taylor's base of supplies, and he moved to respond to them, leaving a small contingent of infantry and artillery in a post called Fort Texas. George Thomas was among the defenders, commanding a six-pounder attached to a battery under Bragg. By May 3, the Mexicans had begun to target the relatively weak position, not the least because its construction remained incomplete. Much of this initial contact was confined to the trading of artillery fire, for which Thomas's smaller-caliber piece was largely ineffective.

Perhaps for this reason, circumstances reduced the young artillerist primarily to the role of observer. On one occasion, he sat placidly on a portion of the works watching the exchange of long-range fire when someone asked for his critique of the effectiveness of the American weapons. "Excellent," he immediately replied; then in a manner reflective of his priorities as an officer he added, "but I'm thinking that we'll need, after a while, the ammunition you're throwing away."[8] A commonsense approach to his duties and the husbanding of resources were already priorities for him, but the assessment could hardly have appealed to the vanity of those who sought only praise for their endeavors.

As the bombardment continued, the Mexicans substituted weapons that could lob projectiles into the position. While this type of firing was little more than a nuisance, it succeeding in wearing on nerves and caused a few casualties among the already small band of defenders, which could count only about 500 against an opposing force estimated at 8,000. The most chilling of these blows came with the ultimately fatal wounding of Major Jacob Brown, in command of the post at the time. Sharp firing prevented the Mexican infantry from closing in, but their commander felt sufficiently satisfied at his position to call upon the Americans to surrender. Although the effects of the engagement were starting to show, the defenders refused the demand, and the indirect fire continued.[9]

For the next two days, the defenders alternately endured the firing and found small ways to strike back at their numerically superior foe. During lulls in the firing at Fort Texas, the men could hear the distant rumbling of other fighting and deemed correctly that Taylor must be encountering opposition. Taylor's command had come into contact with their adversaries at Palo Alto on May 8 and at Resaca de la Palma the following day. Despite being significantly outnumbered, his forces used their artillery in the first engagement, and infantry and dragoons in the second, to secure victories.

During this trying period, the garrison at Fort Texas continued to sustain fire, and morale further received a test when Major Brown succumbed to his wounds in mid-afternoon on May 9. Still, sounds of the fighting at Resaca de la Palma grew, and by late afternoon there were unmistakable indications that the Mexicans, despite their advantages, were retiring from the field and back across the Rio Grande River.[10]

Taylor's return to the area and the Mexican withdrawal from it meant that the way was now open for the Americans to move into Mexico proper. Taylor decided to push toward the Sierra Madre Mountains along a road that ran through the town of Camargo and on to Monterrey. Because of its access by road and water, Camargo became Taylor's forward supply base for the operation. On June 6, a small, mixed expedition of infantry, cavalry, and two pieces of artillery under the command of George Thomas moved forward to secure the town. Because they had been among the lead elements of troops into Camargo, Thomas's men found relatively satisfactory accommodations. Except for the oppressive heat that bore down on them, the movement was relatively uncomplicated.

Whatever Thomas may have learned from his experiences in Mexico, the difficulty of supplying troops over considerable distances must have been one of these lessons. General Taylor did what he could to prepare for further operations, while enduring the scolding that came from impatient newspaper editors and political figures. He also watched as disease decimated the ranks and morale sank to dangerous lows. It had taken a third of a year to set up the next move to the commander's satisfaction, but finally the Americans drove forward in early September.

Thomas was among the troops to set out on the second day of the march from the base camp, leaving Camargo on September 6. He was one of three lieutenants who led Company E, including John F. Reynolds and Samuel G. French, future Union and Confederate generals respectively. The lead elements of this force arrived before the city of Monterrey on September 19. Reconnoitering the position and waiting for the remainder of the command to come up filled the greater portion of this period. A council in the evening set the stage for an audacious assault the next day to be carried out by the regulars and volunteers comprising the American army. The Battle of Monterrey that followed demonstrated many of the problems that plagued American forces during this portion of the conflict. Based upon investigation by his engineer officers Taylor had designed an elaborate movement against the defenses that would require timing and coordination. The city had a citadel to its front and left, facing the direction from which Taylor's command had generally approached it. On the front and right was a smaller work, called La Teneria, which derived its name from a nearby tanyard. Essentially a redoubt with an open rear, it boasted four artillery pieces and covered the roads that led directly to Taylor's camp. A third work covered the area to the left of the Teneria and earthworks, and makeshift barricades completed the defenses. To the rear, the town had the natural defenses of the San Juan River and the mountains.[11]

Mexican general Pedro de Ampudia had assembled 7,303 soldiers and at least forty artillery pieces to hold the town against a smaller American force of about 6,000. Taylor had no heavy ordnance to batter down walls or subdue fortifications, but instead had to rely on pluck and maneuver to win the day. In accordance with the latter, he planned to let William J. Worth smash into the town to the rear of the Citadel, while David Emmanuel Twiggs kept the Mexican forces focused on his feint against the Teneria that could be turned into a more serious movement as the battle unfolded.[12]

On the morning in which this cooperative effort was to take place, Twiggs became preoccupied by other matters. Although a subordinate took the men in and grandiosely advised that they "take any of them little forts down there with the bayonet," the attack lost the focus for which it had been intended. What was supposed to have been a mere diversionary action now became a full-blown engagement. As one historian termed the effort, "It was an ill-starred movement."[13]

Opposing artillery quickly lashed at the troops as they surged forward, as much to get to the cover of houses as to capture any position of value. American artillery support raced the same gauntlet, only to find movement through the narrow streets difficult, if not impossible. Even the initial entry of the pieces into the town met with significant obstacles that had to be overcome. Taylor had assigned John Pope the task of assisting the "advanced troops [in] entering, or trying to enter, the place." To that end, Pope moved toward the defenses with the mission of "tearing away with a small body of pioneers, the rough abatis which lined the face of the town, so as to admit more easy passage of troops, especially of artillery." One of the momentary spectators of this effort was George Thomas, whom Pope described, "as always, tall and stalwart" with an "impassive, unmoved countenance." The officer noted that in answer to his request, Thomas dispatched "a man of the battery with a lighted port-fire to set fire to the dry branches and brush of the abatis," which Pope accomplished, and then watched as Thomas disappeared back into the smoke of battle.[14]

The artillery pieces quickly created a logjam that prevented further movement and exposed the gunners to a terrific enemy fire. Only by old-fashioned manhandling were the pieces cleared and brought into service, and even then few shots poured forth from the American tubes. When those shots came they had the unhappy side effect of creating huge plumes of dust from the adobe buildings to add to the smoke created from firing black powder charges. The effect was frequently a blinding cloud that made sight adjustments impossible. Enemy fire compounded the situation, with artillery rounds from the defenders decimating the horse teams and adding to the carnage and confusion of the battle.[15] Other troops came to the rescue of those pinned down in the streets by attacking and taking the Teneria directly. The respite allowed the Americans to consolidate their gains and rest their battered units.

In one sense there was little to show for the first day of heavy fighting. The defenders remained largely in place, and the hopes of a coordinated assault that would carry the town had thus far been dashed. But the Americans had gained an important foothold, and the artillery unit of which Thomas was a part was in a position to help maintain those gains. In the meantime, fighting continued on the other end of the town around a heavily defended eminence that the Americans captured in dramatic fashion.

By nightfall, it was the defenders who chose to consolidate themselves by abandoning some of the positions they had been holding. The Mexican troops had pulled back to a more defensible line around the plaza, where they remained in hopes of preventing the capture of the town with a stout resistance. One participant recalled that the configuration of most of the structures in the city offered them distinct advantages. "The dwelling houses all had flat roofs, surrounded by walls three feet high forming so many small fortresses."[16] Jefferson Davis reported similarly on the effectiveness of these defenses, which could also be turned to the benefit of the attackers. "We continued to advance and drive the enemy by passing through courts, gardens and houses, taking every favorable position to fire from the house tops; which from their style of architecture furnishes a good defense against musketry."[17] The army commander explained, "The streets were at different and well chosen points, barricaded by heavy masonry walls, with embrasures for one or more guns." These barriers would have to be blasted through if the Americans were going to be able to proceed, and even the pugilistic Taylor recognized the difficulty his troops faced in making that attempt. "These arrangements of defences gave to our operations at this moment a complicated character, demanding much care and precaution."[18] At the plaza itself, the Americans confronted makeshift barricades of debris and stone ringed with the weapons of defenders determined to hold this last stronghold.[19] Davis was similarly impressed, noting that "near the Plaza . . . we found all the streets barricaded and swept by a fire so severe that to advance from our last position it became necessary to construct a defence across the street."[20]

Taylor wisely decided that frontal assaults would prove bloody, if not futile. Such a fruitless strategy would cost the Americans dearly while offering little promise of success. A gathering of commanders to consider their options produced a more viable solution. Thomas was to be part of that solution, as was the same Samuel French whom the Virginian had traveled with and helped push train cars over icy tracks while on leave. Thomas and French were now responsible for the placement of an artillery piece at a strategic location from which the Mexican barricades could be tested and potentially breached. The nature of the road system was such that all of the work would have to be done in the open, although French recalled employing a technique he had learned from an incident of street fighting in Philadelphia where the gun crew used ropes and the gun's recoil to reload while remaining relatively unexposed.[21]

Generals Taylor and John A. Quitman had worked their way into the town and over to the point of contact. Quitman wanted to use the artillery to clear the area and thought that one piece might move while the other fired to provide it cover. Since French's tube was already located on the main road, he ordered Thomas to use the smoke as a screen for shifting his piece.[22]

Thus French provided cover for Thomas while the latter put his tube into position, but with only relatively light ordnance, the Virginian found that he could make no headway against the defenses themselves. Unperturbed, Thomas filled the gun with canister rounds that proved effective in covering an advance by the foot soldiers and provided them with a precious few seconds of covering fire of their own. Even so, the position of the defenders held the American infantry at bay and prevented the line from being breached. Increasingly frustrated, and without proper communication with the other forces under Worth that were making headway, Taylor ordered the effort in this quarter discontinued. Thomas disengaged and brought his weapon safely from its exposed position.[23]

Other developments quickly negated whatever joy the Mexican defenders may have derived from repulsing the threat on their front and right. Worth's command pushed its way into the city and reached a point from which it could bring the plaza defenders under fire. On the morning of September 24, the Mexican commander, General Pedro de Ampudia, broke off the fighting and opened negotiations. The Americans understandably rejected his request for permission to march out of the city without restrictions, but the combatants reached an accommodation that was satisfactory enough for the Mexicans to surrender. The formal turnover of Monterrey took place three days later. The Americans had won the prize, but at a cost of 120 killed, 368 wounded, and 43 missing. Ampudia's casualties stood at 367 killed and wounded.[24]

George Thomas emerged from the engagement with recognition, when he received a brevet to captain on September 23, "for gallant conduct in the several conflicts at Monterrey, Mex."[25] Thomas had come under severe fire and by all accounts measured himself well in the test. As Bragg received a promotion and transfer elsewhere, command of the battery devolved upon Thomas, and he soon had the more mundane, but necessary, duties of restoring the unit to fighting trim.

From November 21, 1846, Lieutenant George Thomas commanded the company and was the responsible officer during that period when the men and horses suffered so terribly from the exposure of marching through the difficult country. It was likely in this period that Thomas had a confrontation with a superior officer that would haunt him for years to come. David Twiggs had been engaged in the fighting around Monterrey, but his next run-in was with the willful subordinate from Virginia who refused to allow rank to intimidate him from claiming what he perceived to be his just prerogatives.

The situation developed when Twiggs sought to obtain a mule team from his young artillerist. Twiggs wanted the animals for the benefit of his headquarters, while the junior officer preferred to use them in the field as originally intended. Consequently, Thomas demurred, then appealed up the line for relief, and obtained it, much to the chagrin of his superior.[26] Twiggs undoubtedly thought the subaltern's refusal to adhere to his demands, exacerbated by the disgruntled officer's willingness to carry the issue further along the chain of command, constituted an unacceptable insubordination. One Thomas biographer concluded of the strained relationship, "Twiggs was one of Thomas's very few personal enemies during his lifetime."[27]

But the Twiggs-Thomas tiff was only a side drama. Zachary Taylor's army remained in the region anticipating further action. A lieutenant in the Fourth Infantry, Cadmus Wilcox, recalled seeing Thomas while they were in the staging process for the next campaign after Monterrey. "Near the Third Infantry was Bragg's battery, and with it were George H. Thomas and John F. Reynolds. The tall spare form of the first, his large black eyes and heavy brows, nervous, tremulous voice, attracted notice; and his industry, attention to duty, and strict regard for discipline, ensured the efficiency and gallantry subsequently exhibited with such splendor and success on the field of Buena Vista."[28] In the meantime, on February 14, 1847, a returning Thomas W. Sherman replaced Thomas, relegating the officer once again to a subordinate position. Reynolds and French, his comrades from the engagement at Monterrey, served as junior officers as well.[29]

Taylor knew that one engagement would not mean that the war was over. Consequently, he planned for further operations. Unfortunately, political infighting among the Americans and the difficulty of moving troops over great distances while maintaining their sharpness for combat proved problematic.[30] Trouble also came from the capture of a duplicate copy of a message sent from Winfield Scott meant for Taylor. Scott's charge from President Polk was to lead a force to Vera Cruz on the coast and march inland directly to Mexico City. To accomplish this, Scott directed the transfer of substantial numbers of Taylor's troops to his command. In order to assure that Taylor received his instructions, two copies went out, but the one in the possession of Lieutenant John A. Richey never made it to its intended destination. The young officer was waylaid and the dispatch recovered and forwarded to Antonio Lopez de Santa Anna. With this intelligence coup to bolster him, the Mexican leader decided upon a bold course by moving against Taylor's depleted force and inflicting a devastating blow against it before turning back on Scott.

In January 1847, Santa Anna set out to accomplish his daring mission. At the same time, Taylor's command had passed through Monterrey and moved on to Saltillo. Just beyond that town was a house called Buena Vista, or "Beautiful View," that stood just outside a point at which the road proceeded through a narrow passage flanked by steep ravines and gullies.[31]

The Americans had fanned out, but with indications that Santa Anna was approaching with a substantial force, including the capture of some of the outlying U.S. patrols, Taylor opted to pull back and take up what he hoped would be a naturally strong defensive position. The Americans would have to contend with the geographical challenges presented by the numerous depressions, but the terrain offered some distinct advantages as well as obstructions that would disrupt any concerted movements being made against them by a larger force. Taylor dispersed his artillery so as to support the infantry, placing French's and Thomas's pieces on the left and right, respectively, of the Second Illinois.

Against an array of some 20,000 troops the United States forces could

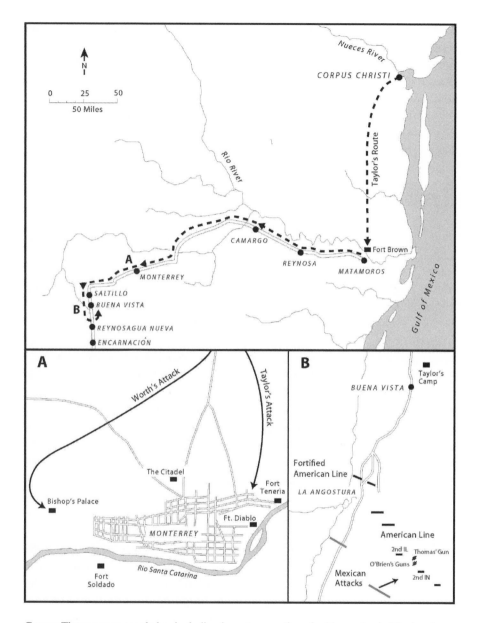

George Thomas won accolades, including brevet promotions for his service in Mexico, in action that occurred at Monterrey (A) and Buena Vista (B). Map created by Heather Harvey.

muster only about one-quarter of that strength, with few regulars to bolster them in any combat that developed. By mid-morning on February 22, 1847, the likelihood of a collision between the opposing forces reached a crescendo of hooves and stamping feet as Mexican lancers rode into view, followed by what appeared to be an endless stream of infantry. It took the rest of the morning and into early afternoon for the Mexican troops to establish their battle formations. Once he was satisfied with his dispositions, Santa Anna sent a demand for surrender to his counterpart. Overcoming the language barrier between the antagonists mellowed the reply somewhat as the translator softened Taylor's response, but the message was unmistakable. The Americans had declined the offer.

Presumably, Taylor's terse reply took less time for the Mexican leader to interpret, but by mid-afternoon he was ready to send his troops into battle. The disposition of the American forces called for Thomas and the other artillery positions to be supported by infantry. Wilcox noted that "six companies of the Second Illinois," under Colonel William H. Bissell, "were posted on the plateau opposite the head of the ravine; in their left and a little retired was a 12-pound howitzer, under Lieut. S.G. French, Third Artillery, and in like position a 6-pounder, under Lieut. George H. Thomas, Third Artillery." Wilcox completed his description of the American dispositions by noting, "To the right and rear of Thomas were two companies of the First Dragoons, under Capt. Enoch Steen, and to their right and near the head of the ravine was [Ben] McCulloch's company of mounted Texans."[32]

A single artillery round opened the action. Miscommunication and pressure from their opponents exposed the left flank of Taylor's position, which had been the weakest portion of the line from the outset, but the Americans held. Evening brought a brief serenade from Santa Anna's personal band, but the weather was hardly hospitable for the combatants themselves. One participant asserted, "I cannot recall a night when I came so near perishing from cold."[33]

As morning broke, it became clear that Santa Anna would test American resolve on this field on this day. Three heavy columns surged forward. The artillery pieces of Thomas and French worked determinedly to stem the tide. The latter recalled that they "used canister as rapidly as men (so well trained as ours were) could serve the guns." Thomas W. Sherman later observed in his report, "Early on the morning of the 23rd Lieut. Thomas' section took a position on the plateau on our left: a 6 pdr. under Lieut. Thomas in support of the right of a brigade of infantry and a 12 pdr. howitzer under Lieut. French in support of the left." Sherman watched as the fight unfolded. "Soon after this section had taken its position the action became general upon this flank and indeed throughout the line, and my reserve section was ordered up and took position on the right of Lieut. Thomas' pieces."

The combined "sharp fire of cannister and shells from my battery, supported by that of Capt Bragg on the left and some pieces under Lieuts. [John Paul Jones] O'Brien and Thomas upon the plateau on our right," held the enemy at bay for a time. Sherman recalled, "I joined Lt. Thomas who had been constantly engaged during the forenoon in the preservation of that important position and whom I found closely engaged with the enemy and that time in a very advanced position."[34]

Cadmus Wilcox noted that "Bissell's regiment, Steen's squadron of Dragoons, and Thomas and French, each with a gun, had remained in position, the last two firing an occasional shot at [General Francisco] Pacheco's troops while engaged with [Joseph] Lane. This force (Pacheco's) was ordered to advance, whilst the Second Indiana and O'Brien were engaged, and had barely reached a point from which to fire with effect, when Lane's men gave way, as previously described, and [General Francisco] Perez's command then advanced against them." In conjunction with the Second Illinois, Thomas and French fired at close range and, according to Wilcox, "literally strewed the ground with the enemy's killed and wounded." As the American horsemen retired for their own protection, Wilcox recalled, "The Mexicans continued their advance, passed beyond the left of Bissell and his men, and those with Thomas' and French's guns, received a fire on their left flank, as well as in front."[35]

Abject fear compounded the chaos and confusion as some of the panic-stricken Americans streamed into a deep ravine, hoping for cover or an avenue of escape, only to find that they were trapped under heavy Mexican fire and threatened by lancers from virtually all sides. A participant noted with unvarnished honesty that he was surprised to have survived the ordeal. "They are most miserable shots," the soldier concluded of his adversaries, "or they would have killed every one of us huddled as we were in the utter confusion."[36] William H. L. Wallace eventually made it to safety, but many of his comrades were not so fortunate, including a number who found no mercy from the Mexican lancers.[37]

Unfortunately for the defenders, the rate of fire proved insufficient as the tired and bedraggled volunteers from the American Midwest gave way under the growing pressure. In the ensuing chaos, a round struck French in the leg while he was attempting to mount his horse, and he consequently had to be helped into the saddle. Cannoneers were suddenly running in short supply. Sherman and Reynolds had to be ordered up from the reserve. Repositioning prevented the tubes themselves from falling into enemy hands, but the threats continued from every corner.[38]

General John E. Wool struggled to hold his position, improvising a defensive line that could sustain itself, but bending perilously toward a final breaking point. The Mexican assault threatened to unhinge it at its most vulnerable spot. Thomas once more moved into the critical position with artillery. His six-pounder and French's twelve-pounder would somehow have to stem that opposing tide before it overwhelmed the tottering American defenses. Even with infantry support, the odds were stacked against them fearfully, and they must have realized that it was only a matter of time before the strength of enemy numbers proved telling. The difficulty of the ground compounded matters by not allowing much opportunity for adjustment.

An early historian of the battle related the hectic nature of the contest at this critical juncture. "As our left was now the most seriously menaced, not only by the forces which had turned it in the beginning of the battle, but likewise by more than half of the enemy's centre column, General Taylor ordered Captain Sherman and Captain Bragg, each with a section of his battery, to proceed there and strengthen it." This movement of forces, as necessary as it might be to secure the endangered American left, diminished the forces available to maintain the center. "This left on the plateau Lieutenant O'Brien with his two pieces, and Lieutenants Thomas and Garnett, each with one."[39] Robert S. Garnett, a cousin of Thomas's West Point classmate Richard, had taken French's place when the latter left the field with his wound and served his gun valiantly. But the mere weight of numbers was likely to prove overwhelming for the limited firepower that remained.

Wilcox noted the difficulty presented to the Americans when the Mexican right received infantry reinforcements and Taylor responded to the deployment by sending a portion of his artillery to bolster the threatened sector. Now, the four pieces left with O'Brien, Thomas, and Garnett "fired successively upon the enemy in front, on the heavy guns near the foot of the mountains, then on the masses threatening the left and rear."[40] Other demands required additional shifts of personnel as Santa Anna probed for what he hoped would be a fatal weakness in the American position. Taylor had committed everything he had, and if that weakness materialized it would mean more than a lost battle. Yet, as so often happens on battlefields, fate shifted the balance from one side to the other, and certain victory turned into sure defeat. Thus it was for Santa Anna, who had appeared so close to a decisive win, only to watch the opportunity slip away. Now Thomas and O'Brien fed as much canister as they could bring to bear on the troops opposite them. One account suggested that the effect of the fire was so terrific that the opposing forces gave way, encouraging an impromptu American counterattack. Santa Anna quickly sent in his reserves, and the fortunes of war threatened to shift once more. Even with a concerted and concentrated fire, the Mexican forces seemed poised to overwhelm the guns and their infantry supports.[41]

Cadmus Wilcox noted that Mexican troops advanced in the face of a withering fire. "O'Brien's and Thomas' guns opened upon it with grape, directed first upon the head of the column, and when this changed to the left upon both its head and right flank." The advance continued, forcing some of the defenders to fall back into the ravine, and soon positioned itself so as to rake the occupants with a heavy fire of their own. "There was no obstacle at this time to the advance of this 1st column but the three guns under O'Brien, Thomas, Fourth and Third Artillery." Wilcox identified this as "the crisis, the issue to be decided in a few minutes, and the chances were strongly in favor of the Mexicans." Taylor's presence and influence remained, despite the fact that for this moment, "there was nothing" between the general and the enemy "but O'Brien and Thomas, the one with two, the other with one gun."[42]

Employing a tactic that allowed them to fire and pull back with the recoil of the tubes from each shot, the artillerists gave ground grudgingly. Thomas held on grimly. John Paul Jones O'Brien was not so fortunate. Mexican troops swarmed his pieces and captured them. One contemporary concluded, "It never occurred to O'Brien to save his pieces; there was too much at stake. To delay the enemy, to hold him in check, was his determination, even if he lost his guns and life, for the plateau held, the battle was won."[43]

Under such conditions the fire continued unremittingly. Wilcox noted that even with "no time being lost in aiming, that the enemy could not fail to receive the full effects of each discharge, the distance being so short and their columns covering so much of the plateau." He wrote admiringly of the advance over ground that "was strewn with their dead and wounded." But the effect of the Mexican fire was devastating to the Americans as well. "O'Brien's little squad was also falling; two horses had been killed under him and this third bleeding, he himself wounded, and nearly every horse of his two pieces killed or wounded; the horses of Thomas had been equally unfortunate."[44]

Assistance was finally able to reach the beleaguered defenders in time to avert complete disaster. Bragg's much-traveled tubes appeared. Taylor continued to provide moral support himself, thrusting his sword in the direction of the opposing line and instructing the new arrivals, "Double shot your guns and give 'em hell, Bragg."[45] Braxton Bragg would forever be associated with a different, but inaccurate, popular version of these fighting words.[46]

General Wool later noted simply, "Without our artillery we could not have maintained our position for a single hour."[47] A contemporary account of the fighting underscored the important role Thomas and his compatriots on the plateau played in helping to secure an American victory. "As occasion seemed to render it necessary, the fire of these four guns was directed, now toward the front, now toward the battery at the head of the plateau, and now toward the heavy masses threatening our left and rear, and always with marked effect."[48]

Even with the stout efforts of the artillerists, the position was uncertain until other troops could reach them. Finally, the Americans were able to stabilize the situation and at length turn the attacking forces back. Santa Anna had put everything he had into the effort to catch Taylor while he was vulnerable and win a decisive victory before responding to other American threats. Instead, his withdrawal concluded a desperate fight that had depleted his ranks without producing the desired result.

An American officer and future Union general, Abner Doubleday, rode to the scene of the fighting. "As I entered the little village or rancho I came upon the Artillery Batteries," he recalled. "There were Bragg, Thomas, and Reynolds leaning upon their guns surrounded on all sides by the dead. It was a picture I shall never forget." Doubleday rode on across the landscape of ridges and ravines to find "corpses doubled up in every attitude of death and pain." The impact of the desperate struggle remained powerfully evident as he worked his way through the dead and wounded. "The field of battle was very large in extent and it took a long time to ride over the whole of it," he explained. "I had seen similar scenes before, and the force of habit prevented the suffering from making a very deep impression upon me," even when he located the body of "a tall handsome" Mexican officer whose "leg had been completely severed from his body by a cannon ball."[49]

Casualties on both sides were significant. A Mexican newspaper correspondent who had attached himself to that army subsequently observed, "The nation has cause to lament the serious losses in this battle. There the blood of her bravest sons flowed copiously." Ramon Alcaraz also declared the Mexican forces victorious in the engagement, although he praised the efforts and the sacrifices of the soldiers of both sides.[50]

Taylor had succeeded with approximately 4,600 troops, but at a cost of 272 killed, 387 wounded, and 6 missing. By contrast, Santa Anna set his own losses at 591 killed, 1,048 wounded, and 1,894 missing.[51] Some twenty officers and men from the Third Artillery were among these U.S. casualties.[52] One of the American wounded, Lieutenant Samuel French, was struck by the sight of the struggling men in a makeshift field hospital in Saltillo. "The whole floor was covered with wounded," he recalled. Then, in the understatement that came from the years of experience in combat he had seen since, he added, "The scene almost beggars description."[53]

General Taylor's official report, sent from Agua Nueva, and dated March 6, 1847, offered considerable praise for the forces that had struggled along the hills and valleys in the difficult engagement. The commander's observations were especially positive toward the artillery. "The services of the light artillery, always conspicuous, were more than usually distinguished. Moving rapidly over the roughest ground, it was always in action at the right place and the right time, and its well-directed fire dealt destruction in the masses of the enemy." Taylor had depended upon that arm of the service and was careful to single out not only the commanding officers, but also their subordinates. "I deem it no more than just to mention all the subaltern officers," he wrote. "They were nearly all detached at different times, and in every situation exhibited conspicuous skill and gallantry." Lieutenants Thomas, Reynolds, and French all found their names in the report, the latter identified as having been "severely wounded."[54]

Thomas Sherman ladled the praise thickly and appropriately for his subordinates. "Lieuts. Thomas and Reynolds behaved nobly throughout the action and their coolness and firmness contributed not a little to the success of the day." He then singled out the Virginian for particular attention and distinction. "Lieut. Thomas more than sustained the reputation he has long enjoyed in his regiment as an accurate and scientific artillerist."[55]

One of the participants in the fight who had been fortunate just to survive wrote exuberantly using a phrase that would become popular among recruits in the Civil War to symbolize an initial exposure to combat. "I've seen the elephant," William H. L. Wallace observed, "in every attitude, walking, running, at bay and fighting!" But, as he continued his descriptive letter, Wallace concluded, "It is a terrible thing, this fighting!"[56]

A little over a decade later, the Virginian offered a much more concise assessment of his service in the engagement to George Cullum, who was compiling information for West Point graduates in biographical sketches that highlighted their military careers. Thomas communicated with his colleague from Camp Cooper in Texas, and declared, "my military history as given in your Register of Graduates of the Military Academy for 1850 is correct up to that date." He supplied additional updated material, but returned to the earlier service already covered by the volume that related to actions in the war with Mexico. Of his participation in the fighting around Monterrey Thomas offered nothing but confirmation of his presence. Then, with regard to his subsequent actions at Buena Vista, the Virginian compressed the action into a single day, labeling it February 22, when he was actually referring to the following one. In any case, he still recalled the extent of the action a decade after. "I was under fire from 6 o.c. A.M. until 4 P.M."[57]

Thomas's participation in the battle of Buena Vista, February 22–23, once again secured recognition for his service. This time the brevet, for his "gallant and meritorious conduct in the battle of Buena Vista, Mex.,"[58] was to the rank of major. As one biographer succinctly concluded, "Three brevets in seven years marked Thomas as one of the outstanding junior officers in the army."[59] Thomas would shortly learn that this was not the only form of recognition he would receive.

Yet, the soldier George Thomas was sufficiently realistic to understand that in the aftermath of the fighting at Buena Vista, the war would have to move to other, more distant locales, if American arms were going to prevail. In a letter to one of the officers associated with the operation being undertaken by General Winfield Scott in the direction of Mexico City after a successful landing at Vera Cruz, Thomas shared his strategic assessment. "We are all anxiously awaiting news from your column for upon its success depends the duration of the war." As for the victory at Buena Vista, "Although they have been whipped at this place at least four to one the disaster will produce little effect upon the nation because we have not been able to follow up our victory." The lesson thus learned would remain with Thomas in the future. Victories had to be "followed up" to be complete.

Another lesson that he had learned, and expressed in his letter to his colleague serving under Scott, related to the attitudes of Mexican civilians to the occupying forces. In this case, the concern was not so much in bushwhacking as earlier in the conflict, but in the veracity of information being provided, almost too willingly. Thomas found that as people returned to their homes after the fighting at Buena Vista, they indulged in "making all manner of protestations of their inocence in the affair." Despite these public appearances, the Virginian was both savvy and skeptical enough not to place too much credence on them or the information the local populace was supplying.[60]

Back in Southampton County, public manifestations were afoot of a different nature, which would nevertheless also prove distressing to the distant warrior. Thomas had served with distinction, and the citizenry sought to recognize and honor him in a fitting and significant manner. Local farmer and diarist Daniel William Cobb noted in an entry on July 19, 1847, "Lutenant Thomas was presented with a sourd price $2 or 300." The occasion must have impressed him to the point that he was still considering it several days later and took time to elaborate. "On Munday our last Cort day the people noticed our neighbour Loutenant Thomas who has been so suckscessfull in the Flordia war and also Texas war was in several engagements and won the prise[.]" The farmer was especially impressed that Thomas "never has been defeated in no battle what ever he has been engaged in[.]"

Swelling with community pride, "the people of Southampton his oald friends and neighbours . . . want him to now we feel much regoiced at his keen and suond management of the gun he had in command and the successful manner [in which] he managed his men[.] That we have purched a soward of the amt of value of $3 or 400 and seluted him with it or may be said presented to him in be half of his sucksess and Bravery."[61]

The citizen's meeting produced a resolution, noting "our attention has been especially drawn to the military skill, bravery and noble deportment of our fellow countryman George H. Thomas as exhibited in the campaign of Florida at Fort Brown Monterey and Buena Vista in which he has given ample proof of the best requisition of a soldier, patience fortitude firmness and daring intrepidity." The grateful community affirmed Thomas's "character as a citizen and a soldier" in a tangible form that would be an ever-present reminder of their esteem. The resulting proposal called for "a sword with suitable emblems and devices" to be commissioned. For that purpose a special committee would be tapped with responsibility "to collect by subscription a sum sufficient for the purpose and cause to be fabricated a sword to be presented to the said George H. Thomas through the hands of his noble and heroic commander Maj. Genl. Zachary Taylor."

The proud neighbors planned to disseminate the proceedings broadly, as well as making them available to Thomas family members and the recipient himself. In correspondence with Judith Thomas, dated July 20, 1847, James Maget informed her of the unanimous resolution of thanks and the "token of their regard be tendered to Lieut. George H. Thomas (Capt. by Brevet) of the Artilery, and now with the army in Mexico, for galantry, skill and noble daring displayed by him, in the various battles in which he has been engaged." Maget's next duty, "as chairman of [the] meeting," was to request her assistance in assuring that the weapon being designed for the honored son of Southampton be accurate concerning "in what particular battles, your distinguished brother participated and their dates, as well in Florida as Texas & Mexico[.]"[62]

It was not until early in the following month that the Southampton official communicated with Elizabeth Thomas about the recognition being planned. "I herewith present you with the subjoined proceedings at a meeting of the Citizens of our county," Maget explained on February 4, "held more particularly in compliment to our distinguished fellow citizen your gallant son Capt. George H. Thomas 3d. Artilery he in whose heroic fame we all glory and which redounds to his mother & sisters." In a flowing expression of esteem for the mother who had brought such a champion in their midst, Maget observed, "Inestimably honoured is she who add[s] a jewell to the briliant escutheon of old Virginia."[63]

In the meantime, the recipient of the honors was still in the field in Mexico when he responded to the honor bestowed on him by his Southampton County neighbors. Thomas explained modestly, "Your letter of the 8th February transmitting the Resolution of the citizens of Southampton at a meeting in their Court House on the 19th July 1847 was received by the last mail." The need for some form of acknowledgment of such recognition was less painful in this manner for Thomas than it would have been in person, but for an acutely reserved soldier who considered himself as only doing his duty the task was difficult enough. "In accepting the Sword presented me by my fellow countrymen, and in acknowledging the very high compliment paid me in those resolutions, I beg you will present to the committee, and through them, to my old friends of Southampton my sincere and heartfelt thanks," he explained. "Aware that the little service that I have been able to render my country, although performed with cheerfulness, and to the utmost of my ability does not in the least entitle me to this very high compliment from my old friends and fellow citizens, I shall always regard it as the result of kindness of heart and a friendliness of feeling on their part, which renders the obligation doubly grateful, and as such will ever be a proud recollection to the last hour of my life. 'Next to the consciousness of having done his duty the Sympathy of friends is the highest reward of the Soldier.'" Thomas closed with sincere gratitude for the communication itself. "I beg you will accept my hearty acknowledgements for the very flattering and friendly manner in which you have communicated to me, these resolutions."[64]

A student of Southampton County's politics and culture has described the Captain James Maget to whom Thomas corresponded and with whom the family had indisputably cordial relations as "an active Democrat and prosperous lower-county member of the county court."[65] Thomas's West Point patron, Congressman John Young Mason, was also a wealthy Democrat with substantial property holdings. Ironically, Mason's personal history mirrored Thomas's in an intriguing way, in that as he proceeded with his career his connections with Southampton County became more tenuous.[66] Thus, whatever disdain Thomas might have held for politics, the figures that exerted the most political impact and had the strongest links to him were associated with the Democratic Party.

Thomas also had a prominent friend in Braxton Bragg. With regard to the Virginian's temporary assignment to his battery, Bragg expressed a strong sentiment for the appointment to become permanent. "It has been the wish of Captain Thomas and myself, to effect this arrangement ever since my promotion to the [command of] the company." Bragg laid the argument that Thomas's "distinguished services as an officer of Light Artillery will be considered as entitling him to a choice."[67] To Colonel William Gates of the Third Artillery, he wrote on the same day from his camp near Monterrey, Mexico: "I enclose an application to the Adjutant General for the permanent transfer to my Company of Brevet Capt. Thomas who is now serving temporarily with me."[68]

Bragg's endorsement and Thomas's record did not suitably impress the War Department, as the Virginian remained where he was for the time being.

He undertook detached duty with Captain Braxton Bragg and Company C of the Third Artillery later that year and then rejoined Company E in February 1848 at Buena Vista. By June, Thomas was on his way back through Monterrey and Camargo to Fort Brown, Texas. Arriving at that point, the men learned that the conflict had ended. The regiment departed, but Thomas stayed behind to supervise a supply depot at Brazos Santiago, Texas, from August 9, 1848 to February 1, 1849.

While there, Thomas had the opportunity to display not only his administrative skills, but his human relations abilities, too. When a young and admittedly naïve recent graduate from West Point arrived on his way into duty in the region, Thomas had a beneficial influence on the newly minted officer. "At the Brazos, I met Lieutenant Thomas, then a brevet major for gallantry in the battles of the war just ended," and now "on detached duty at the Brazos depot," Lieutenant John Tidball noted. The Virginian took a "fatherly interest" in his junior officer's transition, which won the young man's affection and appreciation. Tidball gratefully acknowledged that he "got from him many hints that I found most sound and practical in my subsequent career as an officer."

The colloquial nature of some of this advice revealed an ease and "kindness which he possessed to such a high degree" that made the suggestions more likely to be followed. In one primary instance, Tidball wanted to know more about the personality of the commander with whom he would be working shortly. George Thomas explained that Captain Thomas Sherman frequently displayed an eccentricity that some found unfavorable, but suggested that this did not make him a "bad man." The Virginian warned his new protégé not to "buck against him," regarding the temperamental captain. "And he went on to remark that if a lieutenant did his duty properly . . . he would get along well enough; but on the other hand, if he did not toe the mark, according to his notions, he, Sherman, would make it hot for him."[69]

From "Brazos Island" Thomas wrote his brother John on October 25 concerning his anticipated trip home. The company itself was departing shortly for Fort Adams in Rhode Island after making a stopover in New Orleans. His obligations as commissary officer prevented him from accompanying them, but he expected to "wait only long enough to turn over the stores and arrange my papers for settlement at Washington." Most importantly, George was looking forward to visiting with family. Brother Ben was in Vicksburg, John in Norfolk, and there were the others in Southampton. He was also contemplating other steps to secure a future for the Thomas clan.

"Whilst in Washington I shall apply for a leave of absence and should I obtain one I shall pass the most of it in Southampton and Norfolk so we shall have ample time to look about and decide what will be the best plan to addopt, purchase a farm on the Nansemond river or a house in Norfolk." When he reached Vicksburg, he planned to "speak to Ben on the subject and try to get him to contribute something, for if all three of us contribute we can get quite a nice place and perhaps one [that] will provide with all the conveniences for a valuable farm."

Thomas was pleased to have kept in contact with his sisters, but they had sent him word of activities in his home county that caused the soldier no little distress. "I have heard from the girls two or three times since my arrival here, and they have mentioned that it appears to be the determination of the Southamptonians to do something when I go home." Such public displays were unsettling for him. "This will be a great source of annoyance to me and will take away a great deal of the pleasure I anticipated on having in visiting the County again." Thomas's concern almost caused him to vary his plans. "I have thought of it a great deal, at first I was determined not to go to the County for one or two years, but upon reflection I had concluded to go as soon as I could get a leave and have the thing off my mind, before I received your letter. I hope they will not enact the absurd ceremony of presenting me with the sword for in truth it has already been presented and accepted by letter some months since."

George Thomas would never be comfortable receiving such public accolades. Future circumstances suggested that it was not so much the demonstration of appreciation he abhorred, but the likelihood that in the process he would have to offer remarks to the gathering. "If I could get off with a dinner only I should have great cause to congratulate myself," he noted wistfully.

George maneuvered to another delicate subject. "I am sorry you are not successful in your selection of a fair lady to share her fortunes with me, as I should prefer one from the old state to any other," he observed of his brother's matchmaking efforts on his behalf. The reference revealed the degree to which the state of his birth retained a connection with him, but his subsequent note suggested the beginning of the fraying of that link. "I am now so much of a stranger there I am afraid I should not know where to look for one." The bond of soldier to native state would have significant ramifications in the future, but George Thomas was not yet a complete "stranger" to Virginia.

Even with regard to national political developments, Thomas had a sense of estrangement. "We are so much removed from the world here that we have not been able to keep [up with] the run of politics atall," he explained. "I have had a sort of presentiment that Genl. Taylor will be elected and I am more confirmed now than ever." Thomas noted that he had a reason for believing that his old army commander in Mexico would be a successful presidential candidate. "Our last mail brings us the news that in the . . . elections of Ohio and Pennsylvania the Democrats were successful. Therefore I have put those states down for Taylor for I believe it has never failed that when a state or town has been [taken] by any vote immediately preceding the voting for President that they go differently from what they do in voting for President." Thomas's assessment demonstrated that he paid attention to such trends, although he professed to disdain politics himself. "I am no politician and don't care which is the successful candidate for I believe the world will wagg as usual in either case."

At this stage in his life, Thomas's relationships with family members were certainly cordial. Even when discussing potentially divisive topics the tone was hardly hostile or antagonistic. Indeed, the soldier closed this piece of correspondence warmly. "Present my regards to any friends of mine you may meet with and expect me about Christmas."[70]

In the meantime, Thomas's old battery mate, Braxton Bragg, continued to work diligently to advance his friend's interests. In November 1848, he corresponded with Congressman John Y. Mason, the same man who had secured the West Point appointment for Thomas: "Information has just reached me that a vacancy is about to occur in the chief of the department of artillery at West Point. The position I think would suit your young friend Brevet Maj. George H. Thomas, 3d artillery, and it is one for which he is eminently qualified." Bragg had not broached the subject with the Virginian, either with regard to his desire for such a post or his approval of such personal intervention, but he was sure, "No officer of the army has been as long in the field without relief, and to my personal knowledge no one has rendered more arduous, faithful and brilliant service. He is yet on duty at Burgar Island, tho' his company is at home, and he is certainly entitled to some consideration from his government."[71]

Although the assignment to the supply station offered a respite from campaigning and played to his strengths as an organizer, it could not have been an easy duty to perform following active service in the field. Thomas had experienced combat in Mexico with all of its attendant dangers and subsequently sampled the benefits and rewards that could be obtained from it. The opportunity to test his mettle and improve the skills that would continue to serve him well as his career progressed was certainly gratifying. One student of Civil War leadership asserted that the primary lessons Thomas took from his Mexican War service related to "secure lines of supply," "a dogged persistence," and the importance of "well-placed artillery" to any defensive stand on a battlefield.[72]

In the meantime, George Thomas headed off to the quieter world he had left after five months of duty to enjoy a leave of six months and a chance to visit family in Virginia. Major Thomas could expect to be welcomed and feted by proud friends and family members, although he remained perplexed as to why they thought the service he considered part of his duties and obligations required such fuss. The Virginian also knew that public expressions of acknowledgment would be required of him in order for him to demonstrate appropriately his appreciation for such esteem, and Thomas deemed this type of activity a fate worse than facing all the deadly missiles a hostile foe could fling in his direction.

4   New Frontiers (1848–1854)

"It would be by far the best policy to make this treaty with them and get rid of this business."
—Thomas to his brother John on the situation in Florida

"Having done what you conscientiously believe to be right, you may expect, but should never be annoyed, by a want of approbation on the part of others."
—Thomas recalling advice he had received from his brother

Following his brush with martial glory in the War with Mexico, George Thomas returned to more mundane duties. For the moment there was the opportunity to visit with friends and family, prompting Thomas to travel the great distance to Virginia and his home in Southampton County. The end of a furlough brought him to Fort Adams, Rhode Island, where he joined Company B of the Third Artillery in August and remained until September. The command left the post on September 12, 1849, making its way southward to the remote regions Thomas had first experienced after he left West Point.[1]

One of the duties Thomas had to perform while in Florida brought him into association with another future Union colleague, George Gordon Meade, who was surveying the area for a new series of posts as part of General Twiggs's plan to create a cordon system to protect settlers. In the course of this assignment, Thomas moved from Tampa to Fort Myers. The post returns indicated that he reached the fort on July 14, 1850, where he assumed command of Company B, as well as the post itself, and that he remained in those capacities until relieved later in the year.[2]

George Thomas was located in eastern Florida at Fort Vinton at the end of August 1850 when he wrote his brother John, in Norfolk, Virginia. Contrary to any sense of isolation that he might be expected to have felt regarding his family in Virginia, the letters reflected a poignant connection. Thomas began by noting that his last letter "from home" was from sister Judy, "who informed me that you have become disgusted with farming and had or was about to return to Norfolk. She affected to be considerably annoyed at having to take the farm in hand again, but I expect really she will be more contented after a little, and no doubt after leading so active a life she found it rather irksome." George had a strong sense of compassion for his sibling. "Since receiving her letter I have had their situation in my thoughts very often. They lead a most lonely life; it is time they appear to be contented but they really have no associations which are more than barely tolerable, and it could give me the utmost satisfaction to see them settled in Norfolk where they might form some desirable acquaintances at all events." Locating her in Norfolk might ease matters considerably, and as the eldest, John ought to know how to help. While finances were never far from the young officer's mind, Thomas seemed not to be absorbed with them strictly on his own account. If he could find the means to assist with family matters, any personal investment would be well spent. "With my Bank Stock and what I can save from my pay I will guarantee to pay $3,000 in three years towards defraying any expenses you may incur," he offered John as inducement.

His brother seemed also to be acting as his agent for some investments for which Thomas forwarded some of his army pay. For the time being Thomas felt himself a prisoner to the military bureaucracy, with no funds immediately available to him and the paymaster temporarily absent. "I shall endeavor to send you $800 before the end of the year but can't say yet whether I can do or not." A sense of security could come with a new posting. "Should I be successful in obtaining the appointment of Commissary I should not hesitate a moment, but should urge the family to move to Norfolk as soon as they could conveniently do so. I received a letter from Genl. Jackson saying he would take great pleasure in assisting me to get the appointment."

Militarily, the lieutenant seemed to think that the situation in Florida was also becoming more stable. "We are comparatively settled now and I hope to remain at this place until we are ordered north again." The primary culprit, from the army's perspective at least, was a prominent Seminole leader who remained troublesome. "[Billy] Bowlegs has refused to move west but has agreed to have the limits of their territory defined so as to give them no pretext for wandering around the whole country and has agreed to abide by any treaty which he and his people may make with Genl. Twiggs." Thomas and Twiggs would have a number of connections in the years to come, most of which would be terribly strained and particularly frustrating for the Virginian, but Thomas thought his superior's efforts in this instance might lead to a satisfactory conclusion. "I suppose the result of it will be that a treaty will be made with the Indians [part scratched out] and the troops withdrawn with the exception of those stationed in the Country before the difficulties commenced." For their part, Thomas believed that the "Indians have thus far acted in good faith, and although it has been expected that they have agreed to move west, they have never done so, on the Contrary Bowlegs has always said that he did not believe his people would consent to move." At any rate, he could see no harm in accommodating, rather than continuing to fight, the Seminoles. "As they have also agreed to take their territory out of lands which would never be settled by the whites. It would be by far the best policy to make this treaty with them and get rid of this business. Genl. Twiggs expects to hear from the Sec. [of] War by the middle of May."[3]

George Thomas soon left Florida himself. The orders sending him back to West Point had actually been cut in September, but they were contingent upon his being replaced in command of Company B and the post at Fort Myers. Consequently, he remained in place longer than he had expected, through the month of October and into November. Finally, the official relief of his duties came on November 17, and Thomas traveled northward toward his new assignment.[4] The transfer was expected to send him back to the site at which he had learned his profession and graduated ten years before. But this time he would return to the United States Military Academy as a respected war veteran and instructor.

The journey for the already much traveled soldier to his assigned destination took longer than he had planned and was more harrowing than he had hoped. He and his comrades boarded the steamer *Thomas Leopard* for transport to New England, but off the often-troubled coast of North Carolina dire circumstances arose. Wrecks of all types littered the sandbars and seabeds of the region, vessels victimized by sudden storms and squalls, but in this case, the actions of the captain were as dangerous as the conditions themselves. The drunken skipper's behavior concerned the first officer to the extent that he approached Thomas to plead that despite the threat to all hands, he was powerless to depose the captain on the grounds of mutiny. Having no such restrictions to constrain him, Thomas located the captain and demanded that he remain confined to the stateroom during the crisis, while the vessel came under the control of the officer who had raised the alarm. The *Thomas Leopard* maneuvered safely out of that danger, although the major had to report that another threat, an outbreak of cholera aboard, had cost the lives of nine of his men and two of the crew.[5] The harrowing voyage brought Thomas once more to Fort Independence in Boston Harbor, Massachusetts, where he joined the garrison by transfer from the New Orleans Barracks in Louisiana on January 4, 1851. He assumed command of the company and the post as a first lieutenant and brevet major on the same day.[6]

Thomas had been in the area for only a month when he wrote his brother John, back in Southampton County, from his new posting, where he was "anxiously awaiting some news of Capt. [E. O. C.] Ord, that I might inform you which time they would probably relieve me from my duties here, and permit me to go to West Point. Ord has not been heard from yet, but the Superintendent of the Academy has written to know if my duties are absolutely required here, and if not he intends making application to Hd. Qrs. of the Army that I may be ordered to West Point immediately, as my services are very much required at the Academy." Thomas knew that even as an instructor, time was of the essence. "When they will act upon his application I do not know but hope it may be soon, for it will be pretty hard work for me to be fully prepared for the June examination even should I be able to get there in the course of this month. It will require close application on my part at least for one or two months after which time I shall endeavor to pay you a flying visit of a fortnight or three weeks." Thomas knew that once he undertook his responsibilities, the chance for interruption, even for family business, would be extremely limited. "My duties at the Academy will be such that I can not well leave there for more than a month at a time."

Thomas was pleased that aside from the professional experience and the occasional indulgence in his scientific interests, there was another tangible benefit from his service in the Seminole War. To his brother, he explained, "Whilst in Florida I have been saving up my pay and expected at the end of the last year to be able to send you something like seven or eight hundred dollars to add to my small gains, but this move to West Point has knocked it all into [pieces] for the present, as I shall require considerable [expenses] to make myself comfortable there, but I am in hopes of being able to send at least that amount perhaps a thousand before the end of this year to invest in the same manner as my other investments."

There was also better news from home. "I am pleased to hear you say that you are getting better satisfied with farming. I take it from that some of the gloom has disappeared from our sister's brow." This latter point particularly bothered him and foreshadowed the family difficulties he would face from his own decisions in the future. "God grant it may have done so," he observed solemnly, "for domestic differences are to me the most horrible of which I can conceive. I sincerely hope that time will gradually deaden all feeling of irritation, and our home will once again become as happy as it had previously been." Benjamin Thomas was apparently a source of irritation for some of the family members because of his stinginess. George noted that Ben "made" his money himself, felt he "has a right to enjoy in his own fashion," and thus, "we have no right to quarrel with him because we consider him more unfortunate or willful than we could wish." As a middle child, George Thomas continued to see himself as the mediator in delicate family matters, with a desire to limit family quarrels and maintain peace and harmony through his efforts. "He is his own master," George concluded, "and I am sure will never do anything unbecoming." His advice dispensed, the soldier closed affectionately, "Give my best love to all the family."[7]

Toward the end of March, Thomas was at last able to report some positive developments to his brother in Virginia. "I have been waiting some time before answering yours of the 1st . . . hoping to be able to announce my approaching departure from this inhospitable climate." That welcome occurrence came with the appearance of his replacement. "Capt. O. C. Ord has at last arrived and nothing is to be done now but to turn over my public property to him and be off. So I hope to be able to start for West Point about the end of this week."

Ord had brought troubling word from his last posting. "The Capt. gives rather an unfavorable account of affairs in California," Thomas explained. "He says the state is in terrible embarrassment overwhelmed with debt, and possessing no means of raising money to pay off. It has already borrowed as much money as its Constitution will allow, and now has no means of raising funds to pay its state officers except by means of taxation. The taxes are so enormous that all wealthy persons will be ruined, in as much as they can not without the greatest difficulty pay their taxes when they become due." The allure of California had lost much of its luster for Thomas. "Such is the conditions of things in the 'el dorado' and any [one] may consider himself fortunate, who succeeds is saving one fourth of what the world gives him credit for possessing." It now seemed as if his life and career were not nearly so objectionable. "I therefore begin to think that we are fortunate who have not had the opportunity of trying our fortunes in that part of the world and not so unfortunate after all."

Apparently, George's brother was suffering from difficulties that the soldier sibling was powerless to alleviate regarding friction in the family. Thomas lamented that he had been "unable to think of any advice other than general that I can give." He felt the distance between them acutely. "It is a difficult matter to deal with and unless I could be with you for a sufficient time to make myself more intimately acquainted with the Circumstances, advice from me might do more harm than good." For this reason, he observed, "I shall endeavor to get a short leave and spend it with you, when it shall be my particular aim to try and unwind the mystery of this unnatural estrangement."

While embracing this pensive mood, Thomas reflected back nostalgically on his initial arrival at the military academy as a young lad fresh from the countryside of Southampton County. "I still recollect a piece of advice you gave me when on my way to West Point, and which is applicable in your case. 'Having done what you conscientiously believe to be right, you may expect, but should never be annoyed, by a want of approbation on the part of others.'" George took such advice to heart and offered it back with sincerity. Whatever family troubles might bring, he had reached a state of contentment, maintaining that he thought he was "getting things arranged at West Point," and in a position "to add to my investments." But Thomas was especially proud of a purchase he had recently made. "I have nearly forgotten to tell you of a perfect jewel of a Gun, which I have just received made to order: it has been the admiration of all beholders."[8]

As he had expected, the Virginian relinquished command of his post and duties in Boston on March 27 to Captain Ord, at last freeing him to assume his new role.[9] Thomas's departure from the post illustrated one of the difficulties that all post commanders faced in the Army of the United States before the Civil War. He continued to be listed on the rolls at Fort Independence, albeit on detached duty, for more than a year. His successors scrambled to find sufficient levels of replacement officers to run the post efficiently. Finally, Captain Francis O. Wyse complained in February 1852 that his senior lieutenant was essentially "permanently absent as though he did not belong to the Co. for he cannot live in this climate, & the other 1st Lt. [Thomas] is on duty at West Point. Therefore I would respectfully request an available 1st Lt. may be assigned to my company."[10] Wyse anticipated the creaking bureaucracy by naming another officer to temporary assignment on the staff until he finally received the new first lieutenant he had requested in September. Thomas remained on the rolls throughout, until June 1853, when he transferred to Fort Adams, Rhode Island, for the purposes of reporting, while, of course, continuing to be located actually at West Point.[11]

On April 1, 1851, he returned to the United States Military Academy in a very different capacity from which he had left the institution. It had been just over a decade since he had trod the grounds as a cadet; he was coming back as a distinguished veteran and as an instructor of artillery and cavalry. Of George Thomas during this period, Henry Coppée wrote, "Those, who like the writer of this sketch, served with him during his tour of duty at West Point, will readily recall his serious, practical, almost stern face; his stately form his firm, martial tread; his cool and equable temper; his impartial justice; and withal his courteous bearing and kindly spirit toward the cadets, which they fully recognized and appreciated. He certainly taught them by example as well as by precept; with entire recognition of military law and regulations, he treated them as gentlemen of honor as well as soldiers."[12]

Perhaps the most enduring legacy of this period was the name frustrated cadets bestowed on him when he reined them in during their riding demonstrations. A fellow West Pointer recorded, "When, he was instructor of cavalry and artillery at West Point, the cadets, who were hard riders, and the horses, which understood the drill just as well as the cadets, wanted to gallop and charge; so when the command to trot was given they expected it to be followed by that to gallop." With the exuberance of youth, the tendency was to give in to the anticipation of the next phase of the standard procedure. Instead, Thomas used the opportunity to instill discipline and good order into their minds. Just as some were preparing to lurch forward, "the deep and sonorous voice of Thomas would check their ardor with the order 'Slow trot!' Thus was born the name that would remain with him for the rest of his life."[13]

Military historian Joseph Mitchell pointed out in his examination of the principal military leaders of the Civil War that George Thomas would hardly have been the only one to insist that his charges maintain control of their animals. "Every riding instructor at the academy followed the same general practice when first teaching new cadets to ride." Thus, he contended, "There is no more reason why Thomas should have been given the name 'Slow Trot' than any other officer who taught equitation." Instead, he explained, it was more likely that the young men were addressing the character traits they had noticed in their instructor rather than to comment on the relative speed of the exercises he was putting them through. "From the very beginning," Mitchell insisted, "they were aware of the fact that their commander was a deliberate, slow-speaking, careful person who was not to be hurried, no matter how great the crisis."[14]

In any case, the Virginian was apparently popular among his peers. Dabney Maury recalled a gala Christmas meal with his messmates. "Old George Thomas was then the president of the mess, and a more genial and kindly president we never had." Among his colleagues, some of Thomas's traditional reticence seemed to have faded, but the future Confederate general who hailed from the same state as the native of Southampton County had no doubts as to his loyalties at this stage. "Everybody loved him," Maury remembered, "and he was at that time a Virginian before everything else."[15]

September 1852 proved to be a significant time in the life of George Henry Thomas. At the first of the month fellow Virginian Robert E. Lee became superintendent, succeeding Captain Henry Brewerton and remaining in that position through Thomas's tenure as an instructor.[16] Then, on September 9, an unusual court-martial convened that would have a powerful impact upon Thomas, although the effects would take a number of years to be felt in full.

The court met to consider the case of a cadet who had held good standing at the academy until incidents relating to hazing occurred. For Cadet Lieutenant John M. Schofield the most disturbing aspect was that the accusations ran counter to Superintendent Henry Brewerton's desire to curtail such unsavory activity. Schofield sought a formal court-martial, by which he undoubtedly hoped to vindicate himself, but the secretary of war, Charles Conrad, took the much more drastic step of dismissing the cadet. Schofield had to travel to the nation's capital and engage actively in reversing the decision, even appealing to the powerful senator from Illinois, Stephen Douglas, in doing so. Ultimately, the struggling cadet succeeded in his appeal.

But the crisis was hardly over. Successful appeal had only meant the opportunity to appear before a court-martial to have the matter heard and adjudicated. George Thomas was among those tapped to serve. Schofield's was not the only case considered, and three other cadets received negative outcomes that called for suspension until July 1, 1853. In addition to the allegations of disorderly conduct and disobedience of orders that doomed his comrades, Schofield faced neglect of duty, and the result was a finding of dismissal from the service.

On the positive side was Schofield's record of good conduct preceding the point from which these charges emanated. Apparently, the mitigating circumstances were sufficient to obtain some leniency from the majority of those sitting on the panel. Schofield claimed not to know until many years later that Thomas and Fitz John Porter had not been swayed to vote to reduce or reverse the original outcome of the court-martial.[17]

The great irony for Thomas was that he tended to take such matters personally much harder than the individuals who had committed the infractions in the first place. Richard Johnson noted that the Virginian had proven to be "very popular with the cadets, not because he was lax in discipline, for he was quite the opposite, but for the reason that he was eminently just." Whenever he felt compelled to impose a disciplinary response the toll was as certain to fall on him. "It gave him great pain to be compelled to punish a cadet," Johnson explained, "and he never did so unless duty imperatively demanded it." There were to be no frivolous expressions of power simply because he had the cloak of authority, and the gnawing sense of acting appropriately remained with him. Even after many years had passed from the time he had left the academy as an instructor, when he saw a former cadet he had felt the necessity for reporting he offered an apology for having had to do so and hoped that there were no lingering hard feelings on the matter.[18]

Thomas had spent a considerable portion of his professional life serving his country in isolated stations or occupied with the demands of conflict. West Point offered him a welcome respite and the opportunity to engage in pursuits of a more social nature. Among these were the chances to meet visitors who came to the academy, often during the summer months, and resided at the hotel there. The relatives of cadets were frequent visitors and one of these, the widowed Abigail Kellogg, from Troy, New York, brought her daughters Frances and Julia as companions.[19] Frances was the elder daughter, born on January 25, 1821, and was thus five years younger than Thomas.[20] It is uncertain when and under what exact conditions the bachelor major and Frances first became acquainted, but the soldier was smitten. Richard Johnson described her as "pleasing in her manner, handsome in her appearance, with a fluency in conversation rarely equaled," and concluded, "it was not strange that they should be mutually fascinated with each other."[21]

The next important personal step came for George Henry Thomas when he married Frances Lucretia Kellogg on November 17, 1852. The Reverend Dr. Van Kleeck performed the ceremony at St. Paul's Episcopal Church in the bride's hometown of Troy, New York. Frances's immediate family, a brother and an uncle, recorded their names in the registry as witnesses to the occasion.[22] The groom proudly wore the presentation sword he had received from the citizens of his home county.[23]

Everyone who met the couple subsequently considered them to be well matched. Often the observations came with regard to physical characteristics such as height, but those who knew Frances well recorded an intelligence and self-possession that was similar to her husband's. A contemporary and friend recalled, "Seldom is such a congenial union to be recorded. She was, like him, large and of stately presence; she made for him a charming home, when he could be at home; she entered into all his interests and made them her own."[24] Thomas offered a rare personal glimpse, when in 1865 he observed that he and Frances had been "very happy in one another," having developed a relationship in which "our mutual love and confidence has sustained us from desponding," despite the long periods of separation his service had required of them.[25]

Yet the conditions in which the couple now lived were hardly ideal to close-knit relations between them. Biographer Donn Piatt noted that the absence Frances Thomas almost immediately experienced became exacerbated "by her husband's absorbing devotion to military duty."[26] Even with long separations, the nature of the relationship between them was strong and caring. George referred to her in personal correspondence with family as Fanny, a name he had grown to adulthood with in reference to one of his siblings. He became quite solicitous regarding his mother-in-law. Family would always be important to him, and Frances's now by extension became his, too.[27] Unfortunately, the Thomases had little opportunity to enjoy a honeymoon in New York City before he had to return to his duties at West Point.[28]

In the Spring of 1853, the duties required of Thomas as an instructor at the academy were rather wide-ranging. Superintendent Lee offered a glimpse of this activity in official correspondence that occasionally referenced Thomas. When such mentions occurred, they illustrated the structure of the world of West Point outside of the classroom. In one instance, the superintendent's personal inspection of the saddles the cadets used for their mounted instruction demonstrated the equipment to be woefully inadequate. Lee included a letter from "Major Thomas, Inst. of Arty. & Cavy. Tactics" to buttress his assessment that only six saddles would pass muster, while the "remainder cannot be used without extensive repairs." Then, after detailing the effort that would be required, he concluded rather abruptly, "But if thoroughly repaired they would still be unsuited to the use of the Cadets." In a meticulous manner, Lee offered his reasoning and, perhaps recalling his own days in the field, observed that even for the "heavy dragoon" for whom the saddle was intended it proved to be a terrible physical ordeal. If absolutely required the students could forgo the equipment, Lee explained, "But I think it poor economy to be at the expense of the Instructors, horses & Cadets & without the means of using [the lessons] to the greatest advantage." Simply, the saddles were so poor in quality that they "have not been used for more than three years & probably never will be again" at the academy and could be replaced efficiently with more appropriate equipment in greater quantity "that could be bought for the price of repairing these."[29] In Lee's assessment of this situation, Thomas could see enacted before him requests that reflected practicality and frugality, while adhering to army protocol. Lee's model approach meshed well with his subordinate's notions of propriety and practicality.

In addition to the quality of equipment, the artillery and cavalry instructor soon had other matters to add to his concerns. After determining that a number of the mounts available were unfit for the duty required of them, Thomas brought the matter to the attention of the superintendent for his disposition. The maladies and afflictions ranged from lameness and blindness to conditions that "forbid all expectation of their recovery," that also indicated "no sign of improvement" and "baffled all efforts to cure." Lee was convinced that the conditions of such animals rendered them "unfit for Cavalry service" and provided concerns they would not "be able to perform during the winter sufficient service to pay for their forage." The most cost-effective solution would be to sell the horses rather than continue to try to maintain them under the circumstances.[30]

In August 1853, official references from the superintendent's office also dealt with Thomas's role as "Police officer of the Post." He had experienced the frustration of finding that some individuals were working at circumventing restrictions and repeatedly violating "police regulations and orders." The Virginian was not content simply to report such matters; he preferred to enforce the law, particularly in the case of those who seemed to flout it or want to thwart it. He must have also felt that his inability to secure the grounds properly against "persons" of "notoriously bad character" was a blemish on his capacity to fulfill his duty and reflected poorly on his office.

Thomas was fortunate to have strong support. George Cullum, who held the office for a portion of the summer, wrote that the transgressions had "become so frequent and daring, that measures more summary and stringent than mere expulsion must be resorted to, to prevent existing orders from being utterly disregarded and the discipline of the post destroyed." Thomas would hardly have condoned such threats to the integrity of the institution and undoubtedly welcomed the call for stronger measures. Without censure to his comrade, Captain Cullum observed, "At a large post like this, it is impossible to guard every avenue of approach," and the inability to do more than remove the culprits if apprehended hampered enforcement and limited options, especially when it came to determined resistance. "They must be made to feel the weight of military authority by confinement of their persons, or suffer pecuniarily by the imposition of fines, or the award of Courts."[31] Thus, Thomas learned a valuable lesson concerning relations with individuals who had no intention of adhering to rules, which enhanced his sense of indignation at those who challenged so arbitrarily good order and discipline or violated accepted regulations.

The instructor also experienced a reinforcement of the camaraderie of his profession when news arrived of a tragic accident that shook the West Point community. Just before Christmas, while transporting members of the Third Artillery and some of their families to California, the *San Francisco* foundered in the treacherous waters off the Outer Banks of North Carolina. Some one-third of the six hundred men aboard perished in the wreck, and the effects of the tragedy reached George Thomas at West Point in the most intensely personal manner possible.[32] Were it not for his service at the military academy, he might have been among those who had perished in the disaster.

Thomas was apparently instrumental in organizing an effort to honor the rescuers of the survivors. At a meeting held at West Point, on January 19, "Bt. Major G. H. Thomas, 3rd Art., called the meeting to order and stated its object." The gathering then designated Thomas, Superintendent Robert E. Lee, and mathematics professor A. E. Church as a drafting committee to convey to the captains of the vessels who had assisted the victims "the grateful appreciation entertained by the Professors and officers at the U.S. Military Academy of the humanity and daring acts of heroism displayed in rescuing the passengers and crew from the ill-fated Steamer San Francisco in her recent disaster."[33]

With regard to his educational duties, Thomas would have been pleased to know that his instruction was exerting a positive influence on his charges. The biographer of future Confederate general Stephen Dill Lee termed Thomas "the professor who had the greatest impact upon Lee." Historian Herman Hattaway noted that critics felt the instructor was too generous with his grading, "but if a teacher's success is measured by the future performance of his students, Thomas was remarkable." If Stephen Lee "received superior grades from Thomas, particularly in cavalry," as Herman Hattaway noted, "the ratings stood second in importance to the real knowledge gained."[34] This was especially noteworthy given that the Virginian would not have the long-standing service at the military academy that many of his colleagues did.

Edward L. Hartz, in his second or next to last year in 1854, made an important personal transition that related directly to Thomas's instruction, which he shared in a letter to his father. "Thus far I have done well in artillery, and in cavalry I have entirely exceeded my anticipations," he proudly related to his father. "I came here one of the most ignorant men of my class as regards horses and horsemanship," and although illness limited his time in the saddle, he managed to become "one of the best riders in the class and for several weeks had the *highest* mark."[35]

Students who would be called upon to perform well on more trying future stages could be found among the upper echelons of Thomas's classes. S. D. Lee stood at four in cavalry tactics, six places ahead of Virginian Jeb Stuart and immediately prior to North Carolinian William Dorsey Pender, while his position of nineteen in artillery was six places behind Stuart and two ahead of his good friend Pender.[36] Another Lee performed extraordinarily well under Thomas, too, in both cavalry and artillery instruction, as he did for every other class in which he was a member in 1854. George Washington Custis Lee's class ranking of one in both courses was unanimous among all of the subjects he took for that year (his only blemish being thirteen demerits for the six-month period).[37]

Thomas was at West Point at an important period in its institutional development and as such was part of an evolving curriculum at the military academy. Change was a novel experience, but in this instance brought the cadets significant improvements in their instructional opportunities. Cadet Hartz left extensive written impressions of these changes as he saw them. The young man noted that "from the 15th of March to the commencement of the June Examinations will be taken by the Plebes to learn pyrotechnics or rather as much of it as relates to making cartridges, sewing bags for powder, making grape & canister, filling shells, etc., by the second and third classes of the study and practice of artillery." The second class undertook the "*study* [of] artillery and [its] use," serving as officers in command of the "Field Light Battery," while the third class "acted as canonneers." Others were "taught the management and fighting of the siege and harbour Batteries."

Although the alteration in the educational program meant imposing "additional duties upon us," Hartz nevertheless considered it "very desirable" for the break it represented from an otherwise monotonous routine. "A better reason is this, however, we will not now be obliged to cram nearly the whole of our practical instruction into one year, as has been the case heretofore, but having more time for each, we can gain a more general and satisfactory knowledge of those things upon which our usefulness as officers depends, and without which all the dry abstract mathematics, visionary philosophy and endless chemistry would be but a poor compensation for the miserable life of cadets."[38]

One of Thomas's students wrote a family member in February 1854, "Unlike other Colleges, where the studies and duties become a mere trifle

[in] the last year, at West Point they are multiplied ten fold; we have a great deal to do and little time to do it in."[39]

The records of the Board of Visitors indicate that on Monday, June 14, Thomas and his successor, Fitz John Porter, spent the better part of the day supervising the examination of the first class in artillery tactics. They finished the process later in the afternoon with "experiments in target firing" for the benefit of the board members.[40] Thomas and Porter completed their duties with the cadets the following morning with assessments of their knowledge of "artillery tactics."[41]

But Thomas's time to enjoy the satisfactions of teaching and working with the young persons in this stint at West Point was drawing short. In April, Superintendent Lee received orders to relieve Thomas and two other officers from their duties at the academy. He immediately attempted to forestall the reassignment, arguing, "The withdrawal of these officer[s], just as the classes they instruct are preparing for the review of their course, previous to the Examination, is a serious injury to the Acady., the Cadets, & the Army." Lee singled out his fellow Virginian's presence particularly as indispensable. "Major Thomas is in the midst of his instruction of the 1st Class in Theoretical & Practical Arty. No one is acquainted with their proficiency or progress but himself, nor could manage their standing in that branch with equal justice." In addition to expressing the desire to retain Thomas until the June examinations had been completed, Lee added, "He is besides in command of the Arty. & Dragoon detachments, is charged with the instruction in Fencing of the 1st & 4th classes & is responsible for much property." The list of the subordinate's duties was indeed impressive and the argument that Lee had "no one to place in charge of his Dept." was compelling, but Lee would have difficulty retaining Thomas at West Point, even for a short while.[42]

Within a week, Colonel Lee learned that the secretary of war had denied his request. Major Thomas would have to submit to his instructions regarding a new assignment. Lee could not help but express his disappointment once more at losing so valuable an officer "before [the completion of] the present course of instruction of the classes under his care." Before dutifully proceeding to outline the steps he planned to take to implement a replacement, the colonel observed, "I had hoped the necessities of service, could not have required the withdrawal at such a time, of the head of a Dept. which I fear will be as injurious to the Army as to the Academy." Lee designated Brevet Major Fitz John Porter to succeed Thomas as the best individual to carry the academic term to completion with the least interruption.[43] On May 1, 1854, Thomas was officially relieved from duty at West Point and replaced by Porter as Lee had projected.[44] It was now time for the Virginian to answer a new call.

5   The West Beckons (1854–1860)

"I shall begin to feel as if I had something besides my pay to live on."
—Thomas on his economic prospects

"I am anxious to get through with the move as soon as possible to be able to go for my wife."
—Thomas in Texas

Leaving the comfortable environment of West Point to travel to more remote regions was part and parcel of the life Thomas had chosen for himself. He had already seen assignment to numerous posts throughout much of the eastern United States, and his involvement in the war with Mexico took him to that border and brought him combat experience and recognition for his bravery. Frances Thomas had known much less transience, but her husband's new posting would be the first of many new experiences for her as well. For the moment, she returned to the embrace of her own family as Thomas headed out, not to see him again for two years.[1]

As he was captain of the Third Artillery, dating from December 24, 1853, the chief reason for Thomas's call from West Point was the departure of his unit for the West Coast. The command traveled across Panama to California, where it reached San Francisco at the end of May 1854. Colonel Joseph K. F. Mansfield was in the area, having just completed a tour of the department, and recorded the strength of Thomas's command when it arrived. Setting the total in the four companies of D, G, I, and K at 220 enlisted personnel and 10 commissioned officers, he added that "Major Thomas's field and staff number 2 assistant surgeons, one lieutenant, and 9 enlisted men." The companies themselves scattered to various locations.[2]

While in San Francisco, Thomas had occasion to become reacquainted with an old friend and comrade who was no longer in the service himself. The relationship was cordial, as indicated by William T. Sherman's later recollection: "In 1854, as Captain of artillery, he came to California, where I was a citizen, and we there interchanged the memories and experiences of that interval of our lives."[3] Sherman was now engaged in banking, and Thomas turned to him for investment advice, among other shared interests. They would stay in touch as the Virginian set out for his official posting.

In early summer Thomas led a battalion composed of the First and Third Artillery to Fort Yuma, reaching that post on July 1, 1854. The Virginian assumed command of the post in relief of Brevet Major Samuel P. Heintzelman of the Second Infantry on the fifteenth.[4] Yuma constituted another of the small outposts being formed in that decade in Southern

California. Dating from 1850, it was situated so as to control the region at an important crossing point of the Colorado River via the Gila Trail that connected posts in Arizona to those in California.[5]

Just before Thomas arrived, Colonel Mansfield inspected the site as part of his larger tour of the Pacific region. He was not impressed with the quarters for officers or men, but complimented Heintzelman for making improvements in the roads and for establishing ample supplies for the garrison. Mansfield's observations might have given Thomas and the new arrivals pause had they been able to read the report of the location in which they were about to reside. Demonstrating a keen observation of weather and terrain as well as military matters throughout his journey, Mansfield recorded of Yuma, "It seldom rains here, and the sand storms from the desert, at times, fill the whole atmosphere and shut out the rays of the sun."[6] The state of the weather at Fort Yuma would impress George Thomas, too, with searing heat that achieved legendary status among the regulars who billeted there.

On September 11, 1854, Thomas wrote to his brother John in Norfolk, concerning his new duty station. Conditions at Fort Yuma were certainly enough to test a person's endurance, and Thomas shared that aspect of life in the service with his brother. "The weather has become quite cool for this place the thermometer standing . . . for the last two weeks at 84 in the shade during the day, and frequently at night falling below summer heat." Even so, he was making the best of the situation in his usual temperate fashion. "It really begins to look quite like living, & I could enjoy life here very well with this weather if we had decent quarters, fit for my wife to live in," he concluded.

The other element that made the assignment almost palatable was Thomas's continuing ability to engage his interests in his surroundings. He had an almost instinctive tendency toward the study of the sciences that he had embraced at the academy and in Florida. This new world gave him fresh fields to explore, and the inquisitive Virginian seemed to make the most of the opportunity. The soldier's studies of the region and its habitat also appealed to another connected interest. "I wish you could be here this fall for the hunting," he wrote his brother John. "There are any quantities of quail now coming in and the old residents tell me that in winter there is an abundance of Geese and ducks. I should think also that the snipe would resort to this river bottom to winter, for I have never seen finer feeding ground for them than this is."

Farming, health, and family also remained on his mind. He explained that sister Judith was "much pleased with the success of her experiments with guano. She writes me her Crop for this year is better than her last years Crop." Sickness was always a concern. "My wife writes me that there is a great deal of Colera throughout the country, but that there have been no cases at West Point yet. I hope it will not get there. She was very well. She intends paying Mother and the girls a visit next winter, when I hope you will be able to see her often. Do you ever hear from Ben now. How is he getting on in the world?"

He focused on his long-term plans for financial security and the assistance he had received from various quarters in achieving it. John had apparently advanced his brother money to be invested by the soldier. Thomas had also turned to an old friend for monitoring the fund. "Capt. Sherman has promised me to invest the $2000 for me and the end of every year invest the interest also. If the rates continue as they are now I am in hopes of doubling this amount in four years." Aside from the capital that investment ought to accrue, there was an equally important sense of security this effort should provide. "By that time I shall begin to feel as if I had something besides my pay to live on. I shall leave the whole in his hands as long as he continues the Banking business or until it reaches such an amount as will give me a respectable interest at the usual rates, before I begin to draw upon it at all."[7]

Thomas's diversity of discussion with his brother on interests that ranged from finances and the wildlife of California to the use of fertilizer on a farm in Virginia once again illustrated the eclectic nature of his mind. This broad interest found expression for his energies in many levels and fields. One contemporary noted that it was while at Fort Yuma that Thomas "gave attention to the language and traditions of the neighboring Indians." In the process, "He learned to speak the language of the Yumas, and made [an] effort to reduce it to a written form."[8] The soldier continued to pursue the interests he had generated many years later, after the Civil War, when he consulted his notes and shared his efforts with George Gibbs of the Smithsonian Institution in Washington, D.C.[9]

This pursuit of elements outside of a narrow field of martial studies and responsibilities was part of his nature, but it was also framed by his official duties. His superiors were among many agencies and interest groups that sought to gain additional information about the regions beyond the Mississippi River. As historian William Goetzmann has explained, "Virtually every expedition conducted by the Corps of Topographical Engineers operated under orders to make a general examination of the plants, animals, Indians, and a geological examination of the country traversed." Reinforcing this exploratory spirit was the sense that the West represented, according to Goetzmann, "a vast laboratory—a bonanza of exotic specimens and wonders of nature whose meaning and interconnectedness it had been the job of science to describe since the eighteenth century."[10]

Thomas was happy to oblige in adding to this cache of knowledge, melding his personal interests with his professional duties extraordinarily well in this instance. The annual report of the board of regents of the Smithsonian Institution in 1856 credited Major G. H. Thomas with supplying information about the species he found inhabiting the region in which he was stationed. Thomas's name appeared under the listing of "specimens received" for the categories of "mammals" and "reptiles." His work at Fort Yuma, in conjunction with a subordinate officer from the post, resulted in an expansion of "our knowledge of the zoology of the Mexican boundary line" that included "several new species, the most important of which was a *Phyllostome* bat, the first member of that family ever found within the limits of the United States."[11] Another report recognized Thomas's efforts in collecting and submitting samples of "small flowers" in the vicinity of Fort Yuma.[12] Altogether, the soldier scientist forwarded at least a dozen jars of specimens and "one bat" for the benefit of the Smithsonian's collections.[13]

Thomas also wrote fairly extensively while at Fort Yuma. One of his regular correspondents was his former West Point classmate and current financial advisor William T. Sherman. During this period the two men were unusually close, especially as reflected in the terms of familiarity with which Thomas exchanged his views. His letters to Cump were frank and personal, touching on a wide range of subjects. Indeed, in some ways, the Thomas-Sherman relationship mirrored that of Cump and his brother John. As one biographer explained, "Sherman's younger brother John, the future senator, turned out to be a deeply reserved, carefully controlled, cold and conventional adult," while William T. exhibited quite different and often volatile characteristics.[14]

In a November 30, 1854, letter to Cump Sherman, Thomas opened on the subject of the dangers of transportation, based upon what he had read in the newspapers that had reached him from the East. Both men had experienced their share of close calls and dangerous situations, and the Virginian was especially sympathetic to the plight of those who had suffered similarly. "My papers from N. York contain some accounts of the wreck of the Arctic. It is a most distressing affair, worse than the disaster to the San Francisco."[15] Thomas had been at West Point as an instructor when the latter maritime tragedy occurred, costing the lives of numerous members of the Third Artillery.[16] Now, repeated headlines from the *New York Times* trumpeted the "frightful loss of life" that attended the collision of the *Arctic* with another vessel in fog-shrouded waters, and waged an ongoing investigation that revealed flaws in the number and size of lifeboats, desertion by members of the crew, and questions about the behavior of the captain.[17] Being in a profession that required many of its members to be transported for often impressive distances by water, Thomas must have felt the vulnerability deeply.

But Thomas took a different tack regarding such tragedies. He expressed the wish that this latest incident would cause people to "look with more charity" on the individuals involved in these situations. Clearly having had the matter weigh on his mind, he told Sherman that he hoped "that people should not criticize too severely the behaviour of people placed in such a position." Thomas may well have been thinking of his own extensive travels by water when he expressed the question of "how we would act when suddenly called upon to sacrifice our lives for the safety of others." The Virginian appeared to be particularly troubled that so many dependent passengers had not "escaped according to the accounts."[18]

Sherman shared a concern about traveling by water that biographer John Marszalek called a "fear of shipwreck."[19] But unlike Thomas, who met the worry with introspection and sympathy, Cump chose hyperbole and bravado. "All travelers should experience a wreck once," he had once observed facetiously, "to know how it feels to experience that delightful sensation of timbers grinding and crashing," and more graphically "copper cracking and splitting under the ocean's powerful grasp, like dry leaves in the hands of a strong man."[20]

Having shared his views on this "distressing" matter, Thomas turned to recent events on the world stage. He had obviously been watching developments, albeit through news reports, of the conflict that had erupted in Europe primarily between England, France, and Turkey against Russia, centered on the Crimean Peninsula. Already, the antagonists had clashed in several important land battles along the Alma River (September 20), at Balaclava (October 25), and at Inkerman (November 5). Although the charge of the Light Brigade, made famous for its noble sacrifice in the teeth of Russian artillery, had occurred at Balaclava, the more recent engagement, a one-sided victory for the Allied forces, had been most recently prominent.[21]

As a professional soldier, Thomas was acutely interested in the developments that he watched from afar. His sense was that the British and French forces had appropriately demonstrated their resolve and "certainly commanded their operations in a brilliant and Skillfull manner." The Virginian predicted that the victorious Allies would present the Russian leader, Czar Nicholas I, with little option but to sue for peace. "It appears to me that Nicholas must if he has any regard for the sacrifice of life or the future welfare of his own government, yield to the suggestions of the Western Powers."[22] Thomas's assessment that Nicholas would only be demonstrating that "he must therefore be a weak man to continue the contest any longer" revealed an interesting mind-set for a soldier who would prove his own determination to prevail against all odds and a stubborn unwillingness to accept defeat.[23] In any case, his prognostifications proved inaccurate. The Crimean War continued for two more years, encompassing a long siege of Sevastopol, and Nicholas's death in March 1855, before peace finally came through treaty in the spring of 1856.

On a more personal level, Thomas told his friend that he had recently heard from Braxton Bragg. "He writes that having become thorough[ly] disgusted with the service he thinks it more than likely that he will resign his commission soon." Bragg was giving his former subordinate the chance to position himself favorably as a replacement, and Thomas was certainly anxious to consider the proposal. But Bragg should have reckoned with the Virginian's sense of honor. Thomas had already made an application for a transfer to a position as pay master. He could follow Bragg's suggestion only if that request did not receive approval. In the meantime, he admonished Sherman to "say nothing of this to any one as yet you and B[ragg] are the only persons to whom I have communicated."[24] Thomas may well have meant for the last statement to reflect persons outside of his family circle, but if taken at face value, it suggests that he may well not have discussed such sensitive matters with his wife or brother John, with whom he had corresponded so regularly.

The wide range of discussions with his friend Sherman continued in March 1855, with a letter that contained information and opinions on everything from investments and recent discoveries of gold in the region to lessons in the human condition and the circumstances of old comrades in the service. Thomas remained consumed with the fate of the $2,000 investment he had made with the banker. He also kept an eye on the prospects and prospectors in gold. In one case, he had heard that the wealth being extracted amounted to about five dollars per day and concluded, "These discoveries have created quite an excitement in this community." Thomas did not say if he shared in the "excitement," but one factor that might have dulled any gold fever that he experienced was the nature of the individual who flocked to the region to take advantage of the chance for quick wealth. He expressed concern about "these speculators" and was so perturbed with the characters that had emerged that he noted harshly of one of the gold settlements, "I sincerely wish the first flood of the river will wash [it] away with the inhabitants."[25] At any rate, the Virginian seemed untroubled by any contradiction between his own capitalistic endeavors and those of others.[26]

Thomas was more likely to be governed by his tendency to see his wealth as a means, not only of providing security for himself, but of helping others. Still, the same George Thomas who had spent a good portion of his time at this post in his scientific studies of plants, animals, and geology, as well as taking the trouble to learn and appreciate local Native American culture and language, allowed himself to indulge in a harsh and racially tinged critique of the region and some of its recent inhabitants. "I cannot comprehend," he noted coldly, "how a decent white man could desire to live in this terrible country."[27]

Thomas had sought the means of removing himself from the area through a transfer of one form or another. His old battery commander had offered one possibility, but nothing had as yet transpired along that line. "Have you heard from Bragg recently?" he asked Sherman. "How is he satisfied now?" There was not much more to do than to wait for the rest of the company to arrive, which he expected sometime in midsummer. "As you said the day I left San Francisco," he reminded Sherman, "Genl. Wool has ordered it here. Such conduct is enough to make one play old fogy."[28]

In addition to the time he spent corresponding with friends and family, as well as attending to official duties, the Virginian seemed to enjoy sitting with the other officers and listening to the stories they told to wile away the hours. One featured an ill-begotten soldier who had died, but after the burial returned to complain that he was returning to get blankets because he was "near freezing to death" in Hades, which also happened to only be "about a half-mile from Fort Yuma." Richard Johnson later recalled that Thomas "could enjoy a good story and laugh as heartily as any one," and would "sit for hours" listening to the exchanges unless the humor became too ribald.[29]

Another spring brought that notorious heat back to Fort Yuma, causing Thomas to complain to his friend Sherman, "Our nights still continue to be cool but the days are becoming exceedingly hot and uncomfortable." He put a temperature reading at 105 degrees "in the shade in the middle of the day.[30] But sweltering heat or not, he continued to maintain the kind of control over his command that reflected his character and training. In February, he reported dutifully to the Adjutant General's Office that although the company had been relieved of duty at Fort Yuma, he left six men too ill to travel and one man in confinement "under going sentence of a Genl. Court Martial" at the post.[31] Thomas remained at Fort Yuma himself until July 21, 1855, when he received new orders relieving him of duty with the Third Artillery and transferring him formally to the Second Cavalry. The new cavalryman left the post two days later.[32]

Major Thomas joined the Second Cavalry on September 25, 1855, reporting to his posting at Jefferson Barracks in Missouri. From there he wrote his brother a letter that opined on matters of health and personal economics. The former subject reminded him of the unpredictability of life. "It is distressing to learn of the death of so many one knows in so short a time," Thomas observed, "but at the same time we feel thankful that many have escaped." The latter underscored his anxiety for financial security as he contemplated his debts and investments.

In the meantime, Thomas was "busy getting the Regt. in marching order for Texas, and I suppose we shall start sometime next week, probably about the 20th, which will be none too soon, for we have already had one snow storm and no doubt in such a fickle climate as this, there is more or less danger of them all the time." Although he might be detained by circumstances, the soldier announced himself "anxious to get through with the move as soon as possible to be able to go for my wife." Thomas wanted his brother to know that he still planned to obtain a leave, using the time for "paying you all a short visit, and squaring up my affairs with the audators, [then] take my wife with me to Texas." If not, the Virginian thought he could still benefit. "Perhaps after all it will be better for me to go to Texas first as I can then see for myself what things will be necessary & what others can be dispensed with."[33]

At the end of the year, the 750-man Second United States Cavalry set out from Jefferson Barracks, Missouri, to head southwestward for Texas. Thomas biographer and contemporary Richard Johnson noted that the command had the advantage of purchasing better mounts than usually were made available to the cavalry due to financial constraints. Because the "best horses" could be bought "without regard to price," the regiment benefited tremendously by having sturdier animals that had a superior record of standing the strains of service.[34] Consequently, the command became, in the words of a later historian, "a crack outfit."[35]

The appearance of these troops in Texas and their emphasis on taking the offensive meant less untrammeled activity on the part of those Kiowas and Comanches who had chosen to challenge white settlement of the region. The command prepared to employ aggressive measures to assert greater control over their area of responsibility. Historian Robert Utley calculated that some portion of the Second Cavalry clashed with hostile forces in forty engagements through a four-year period, and this would not have taken into account the seemingly endless scouting expeditions that produced no contact or casualties.[36]

Thomas was not at Fort Mason long before he received orders to participate in general court-martial proceedings at Fort Washita.[37] From November 11 he was absent from the post on this detached duty for the remainder of the year. At the close of that assignment, Thomas garnered an unusual one. He was detached once more to travel to New York with the specific task of "Enlisting a band for the 2nd Regt. Cavalry." His term for this special assignment stretched from January 17 to May 29, 1856, when he was once more listed as present with the command at Fort Mason in Texas.[38]

It was about this time that George Meade and his wife had occasion to meet Frances Thomas and visit briefly with her. In a letter written just after Thomas's great success at Nashville against John Bell Hood, Meade reminded his spouse of their earlier acquaintance with Mrs. Thomas. "Don't you remember, when we were at West Point, meeting his wife, who was at the hotel?" he asked. "He was then in Texas, and she was expecting him home." The general concluded with a description to help assist with her memory. "She was a tall good-natured woman, and was quite civil to us."[39]

Thomas needed the support of his wife when he experienced the sudden death of his mother, Elizabeth Rochelle Thomas, on January 27, 1856. In the midst of his loss, the opportunity to fulfill his duty in New York City also had the tangible benefit of putting him in closer proximity to the Kellogg family. The ties to Southampton were becoming more tenuous and distant at a time when they seemed to be cementing with regard to Frances's family. Future developments would suggest that the connection he was creating with them would have an increasingly strong influence upon him as well.

Still, by the end of May Thomas was back in Texas. Although listed on the returns for Fort Mason, he actually was at the site of his first encounter with the Mexican forces during that conflict at what was then called Fort Texas. The site had subsequently taken the name Brown in honor of the commander who received a mortal wound while defending it. But this time there was to be no exposure to combat or hostile enemy fire; instead the danger was likely to be more from tedium than anything else. Thomas was at the fort as part of a court-martial proceeding.

Robert E. Lee was also involved in the series of courts-martial that seemed to flourish in the Texas dust. In early September Lee noted in his diary that he had reached Fort Mason. His next entry recorded: "Accompanied Major Thomas in his wagon, taking his baggage in mine." They were headed for San Antonio en route to a court-martial there. On the first day of October Lee duly noted the opening of the "Court for the trial of Major Giles Porter 4th Arty." at 10 AM and indicated "All the members present." The court, "having been in continuous session from day to day," adjourned to reconvene at Fort Brown on the Texas coast.[40]

On November 8, 1856, Lee observed, "On the following day I embarked aboard the Steamer with the other members of the Court." He had been compelled to leave his "waggon tent" and a sick servant and was only able to secure a single empty room. "Major Thomas & I encamped in it," he explained, but the accommodations were hardly deluxe, since neither man came prepared. "We each brought along no bedding," although they were able to locate "a very good restaurant in Brownsville."

The setting for the officers' stay might initially have seemed primitive, but Lee pronounced Fort Brown "the most Comfortable Post that I have yet seen in Texas." He was not overly impressed with the surrounding landscape, "but within the limits of the Post there is an air of Comfort & life of which the others I have visited are destitute." He found the complex to be pleasant and nearby Brownsville "a quiet little village," many of whose small residences "have very pretty gardens around them."[41] Thomas left no such record of his impressions, but with a practiced eye and an interest in science he must have made similar observations.

As the proceedings at Fort Brown unfolded, officers who could do so made arrangements for their wives to join them. The new arrivals necessitated some creative accommodations in living quarters. Thomas and Lee graciously sacrificed their room to one of the wives and took up residence elsewhere. "Major Thomas and I are gone into a room with Lt. Howard who being recently married, his wife living with her friends in Brownsville he only occupies his room in the day, & at night the Major & I will have it to ourselves." The unconventional arrangement was almost comical. "He has moved his things in one Corner, the Major occupies another, & I the third." But the prospect existed for still more cooperation among the new roommates. "I think it probable that we will soon have an applicant for the fourth [corner]." Lee and Thomas would have to put the best face on the situation, but both Virginians probably felt what Lee expressed to his wife when he noted, "You know I am not fond of this Community living. I would definitely prefer my tent to myself in all occa[sions] than to a room in Common, but [I] must accommodate myself to Circumstances."[42]

When Lee wrote Mary two days after Christmas, the colonel had more on his mind than accommodations or courts-martial. He had attended a church service and prepared to celebrate the holiday with his comrade in arms and on the bench. "By previous invitation," he told Mary, "Major Thomas & I dined with him [the minister] at 9 P.M." The festive repast included "quail turkey, & plumb pudding."[43]

The time must have seemed to pass interminably for the members of the Court. Not until February 18 was the matter closed. Many of those who had sat through the frustrating four and a half months of sessions, including Lee and Thomas, boarded a steamer for the return trip to Ringgold Barracks. Despite experiencing difficulties with a broken wagon and poor weather, Lee "Sent wagons & men to Fort Mason with Major Thomas with instructions to continue on to Camp Cooper if opportunity offered, otherwise to await there [for] my arrival."[44]

In June, command of the post devolved upon Thomas for the remainder of the summer months. Then, in September, court-martial duty summoned Thomas again, this time at Ringgold Barracks. He left Fort Mason on September 7 and continued in the onerous assignment into the spring of the following year. When not at Ringgold Barracks, he served on the same type of panel at Indianola, Texas.[45]

From San Antonio Colonel Lee explained on March 7, "I am ordered to Indianola on another Court [Martial] . . . Major Thomas Came with me & went on to day to [Fort] Mason to bring down Mrs. Thomas."[46] In his diary, Lee noted the opening of these proceedings and the presence of George Thomas as one of the adjudicators, although the timetable proved shorter than expected for the procedures, and this alteration challenged the participants' calculations.[47] Lee noted the presence of "Mrs. T," on March 20, but subsequently observed, "Major Thomas anticipating a longer sojourn brought down Mrs. T & not knowing what to do with his Servants brought them too, Cook, dining room Servant, etc."[48]

The situation offered additional insight into the relationship the couple enjoyed and the willingness of Frances Thomas to discuss matters freely with others, or at least with Colonel Lee. "Mrs. Thomas was telling me last evg of her troubles in relation to her womenkind," he wrote. Bringing a woman from New Orleans who was supposed to be "under obligations to remain in her Service two years" proved problematic when the woman became "enamored of a Soldier at Fort Mason, & has engaged herself to marry him."[49]

The situation created a dilemma for the Thomases. They felt the need for domestic assistance, but none could be had on a for-hire basis. The alternative, and one that Thomas was not unfamiliar with from his days of youth, was the purchase of a slave as a domestic servant. His contemporary and early biographer, Thomas Van Horne, explained of the Virginian, "He had been accustomed to the service of slaves all his life, and felt no scruples in purchasing one, when in need of a servant."[50] In any case, the soldier managed to overcome whatever squeamishness he might have felt about engaging in this business, although it put him in what he would later regard as an untenable position if he should wish to divest himself of such property.

A brief return to Fort Mason on April 6 provided little respite for Thomas from his court-martial duty. He was quickly off on the twentieth of the same month to Camp Cooper, Texas, to sit once more for a proceeding there.[51] On April 26, 1857, Colonel Lee wrote his wife from Camp Cooper informing her that a general court-martial was being convened at the post. Lee explained that he had "pitched a couple of tents by the side of mine for Major & Mrs. Thomas, for she has accompanied him again & they are to take their meals with me." The circumstances concerned the colonel, but less for the purposes of sociability than the conditions they would be sharing. "The Major can fare as I do," he explained in soldierly fashion, "but I fear she will fare badly." Lee was concerned about his cook, who he deemed "both awkward & unskilled," but he was satisfied that she could be supplied with "plenty of bread & beef, but with the exception of the preserved vegetables & fruits, I fear I can give her little else." Even so, the officer and gentleman from Virginia would do what he could, and had already sent "to the Settlements below & got a few eggs some butter and 1 old hen." Of this last he had thought better upon examination, before determining "I shall not inflict [it] on her." Still, with wild game "out of season" even a scrawny chicken might have seemed most delectable.[52]

In all other respects, Lee need not have worried about Frances Thomas and her contentedness with her husband's posting in a land a world apart from her home of Troy, New York. Almost twenty years after the Civil War and long after the specifics of life in Texas would have been lost to memory, she still held affection for the region, as evidenced in a warm closing in a letter to a family friend. "Hoping your health is good in the climate of northern Texas, which I found so splendid."[53]

For all of the dullness of the proceedings Thomas, Lee, and others had to endure, the former seemed to have made the most of his duties. A later subordinate attested glowingly to Thomas's capabilities in the varied elements of his chosen profession. "When I became a member of his staff, as judge advocate," Gates Thruston remarked, "it was a matter of surprise to me to find how remarkably familiar and accomplished he was with all matters of military law and precedent; and other officers of his staff in the various departments often remarked to me that he seemed to know the usage, details and system of each department of service as thoroughly as though he had passed his entire military service in it." Thruston attributed the legal expertise to service in the field rather than any formalized training. "During his earlier days he had made a careful study of military and court-martial law, and had prepared notes of decisions from various works on the subject, showing how painstaking and systematic he was." Of course, Thomas was making sure that he understood the responsibilities he was now regularly undertaking in Texas as fully as possible. But the officer concluded admiringly that the Virginian demonstrated himself to be "master of them all."[54]

In the meantime, Albert Sidney Johnston left for other duties in the spring of 1857. His replacement in the department by the grizzled veteran of the War of 1812 and the Mexican War, David E. Twiggs, represented a change in authority for Thomas that threatened to dredge up old difficulties. A perceived slight in Mexico over the proper disposition of animals might have seemed insignificant at the time, but the junior officer's insistence did not sit well with a superior who apparently did not forget the affront and was now in a position to retaliate if he chose.[55]

Action was also beginning to heat up with the approach of summer. On May 11, 1857, Thomas dispatched Captain Richard W. Johnson on a scouting expedition that took the detail to the headwaters of the Concho River. Thomas always submitted meticulous reports that included orders read before the command, and in this case, as well as for several months to come, there was a reference to the services of "One Indian Guide at $40 for month, 1 ration and 1 ration of forage."[56]

Thomas typically felt bound by the protocols and procedures of his profession, but when he thought the circumstances warranted he was not above going outside normal channels. The Virginian demonstrated this degree of flexibility, as well as his disposition for gathering and assessing intelligence wherever he might gain it, in a letter to Adjutant General Samuel Cooper in July. He deemed it important to pass along information he had obtained concerning the likelihood that the Colorado River could be used as "not only the most direct but the most convenient and safest route to convey supplies to the troops stationed in Utah Territory."[57] Thomas was as aware as anyone of the importance of establishing viable lines of communication and supply for troops in the field. His attention to this type of detail would be a hallmark in the planning he insisted upon making throughout his career.

The most significant subsequent operation came in August when Thomas dispatched a lieutenant and a detachment of 24 troopers after a band of hostile Native Americans. Thomas duly recorded the outcome, noting that the squad "while on Scout in the month of July had an engagement with a large party of Comanche Indians near the head of Devil's River Texas on the 20th of the same month." Unfortunately for the command, the confrontation had resulted in casualties, with one private killed and a second "missing, supposed to be killed." The lieutenant and four of his men suffered wounds as well, but were able to return to the post with the rest of the detachment on August 8, 1857.[58]

Within a few days after the return of the battered expedition, Major Thomas forwarded a letter to Adjutant General Samuel Cooper in Washington, D.C. Apparently, Cooper had reprimanded Thomas as commander of the post for not properly documenting the death of one of the noncommissioned officers in an earlier report. Thomas's response was instructive of the officer he was at the time and the personality traits and characteristics that defined him throughout his career. "I presume that the reason that the special mention of the death of Sgt. Gardner was not made on the post return of the month of April was from the fact that the then commanding officer, Capt. R.W. Johnson was not familiar with the manner of making out the Post Returns." Furthermore, the deficiency had occurred, he explained, while "I was absent from the post at the end of that month."[59] He has been careful not to place blame on a subordinate, but he was equally concerned not to accept it for himself under the circumstances, preferring to acquaint his superior with plausible explanations.

Thomas was listed as on detached service on a scout on August 8, 1857. His future Civil War opponent John Bell Hood was on the same expedition. During the period, he painstakingly listed on the monthly reports every variation from "joined" to "transferred" to "present." In October the headquarters of Second Cavalry transferred from San Antonio Barracks to Fort Mason. The following month, he was again absent on detached service as a member of a court of inquiry at San Antonio, Texas. This service concluded on December 13, when he returned and relieved Captain Johnson of command of the post, remaining there through April 1858. On June 26, 1858,

Companies C and K and the headquarters of the Second Cavalry left Fort Mason for Fort Belknap, where Thomas assumed command in July.[60]

Throughout his tenure in Texas, General Twiggs clashed with his junior officer from Virginia. The department commander seemed to enjoy finding the means of creating conditions that Thomas would find intolerable. Thomas exacerbated matters by communicating directly to the attention of Secretary of War John B. Floyd, who uniformly backed the junior officer. But such victories proved small and short-lived. The assignment to Belknap with a fraction of the command was meant in part to send a message to the troublesome officer, but Twiggs surely came to realize that he had met his match in stubbornness and determination.[61]

Thomas made the best of his time at the post and seemed not to have lost his sense of humor in the bargain. Undoubtedly for the two imperatives of discipline and diversion, he ordered officers to identify men with musical talent for the purpose of organizing a band. Richard Johnson recalled that the standards were pretty lax, and individuals might be eligible "if they could not play on an instrument, but could whistle a tune." One of the men, "a soldier by the name of Hannah," tapped for the duty proved unable to do even that, and the frustrated bandmaster finally had to report as much to the major. Thomas was unperturbed, noting simply that the "poor fellow" would be returned to his company since he had "possibly" been "mistaken" for "a sister by that name that could play on some instrument."[62]

While the Second Cavalry was at Fort Belknap, Texas, awaiting orders that would likely take the command to Utah, General Twiggs took the opportunity to designate a commander for the expedition. The department commander might understandably have turned to George Thomas, the second in command, and present for duty at the post, but the old soldier gave the nod to Earl Van Dorn instead, a protégé he touted as having the "capacity and energy to conduct such an expedition."[63] Twiggs explained that it was his "confidence" in that officer that led to this selection.[64] A Van Dorn biographer concluded more tellingly, "This choice assignment of leading an expedition against the Indians was just one of many favors that Twiggs offered Van Dorn in their years of service together."[65]

From Fort Belknap in Texas, Thomas dashed off a letter in late December 1858 to his sister Fanny in Southampton County. He was still waiting for Robert E. Lee or another field officer to arrive so that he could take his own leave; Lee's had been extended into the spring. But Thomas's anxiety seemed to be allayed somewhat as the health crisis for his mother-in-law that had in part sparked the desire for some time off from his official responsibilities, passed. "Fanny is no longer anxious about her," he told his sister about his wife. "However I must manage somehow to get out next May as She is almost out of clothes but I promised her mother to take her north this last Spring and should not like to delay it any longer than the next." He observed, "This place continues as wretchedly dull as ever, and we have had one or two as cold spells, as I ever experienced in New York." Thomas particularly noted the "high winds during the whole winter here," calling them "as bleak and disagreeable as the March winds in VA." The extremes were particularly taxing, for "it frequently and very unexpectedly turns exceptionally cold, so we are constantly uneasy about the weather all winter." But even in the cold climate, the letter ended in warm fashion. "Fanny joins me in wishing you all, a happy Christmas, & sends much love."[66]

As things turned out, the Virginian did not have to wait until spring to leave Fort Belknap. Orders arrived on February 23, 1859, to close the post for active duty.[67] Thomas supervised the movement of the regimental head-quarters and two companies to Camp Cooper, reaching the new post the next day. Three days later, he reported to Adjutant General Cooper in Washington from the site. "After carefully examining the country in the vicinity of this place, including the site of New Camp Cooper, and other points heretofore designated by officers as suitable for military positions, I have selected this place for the Cavalry Camp, as the buildings are in a tolerable state of preservation, and the grass and water as abundant and of as good quality as at any other point." The basic elements were always essential, and the com-mander was conscientious to meet the needs of both men and animals in the name of efficiency. "For the infantry camp I have selected [a] position on the Clear Fork about one fourth of a mile at and above the Comanche Agency, and between one and two miles below and S.E. from this place. The position is sufficiently near the present Indian Village, S. one mile to exer-cise a controlling influence over them, and in other respects contains all the requisites for a large Infantry camp."[68] If trouble arose, the cavalry was in close enough proximity to support the foot soldiers if required. As usual, Thomas seemed to have thought of everything and duly reported his actions to his superiors for their approval.

Thomas leveled his powers of observation on the terrain for the purposes of meeting the requirements of his troops, but he also took great pleasure in examining the geological features for their own sake. He had spent time in the swamps of Florida, sampling the flora and fauna of each environment with the scientist's curiosity, and applying the same interests in California. Now he did the same regarding a totally different world of vegetation and animal life. In each case, his inquisitive nature and the practical desire to procure information that would be useful to the army again joined together, in what one contemporary described as the gathering "of much valuable geological and geographical knowledge." Thomas Van Horne concluded, "He was especially fitted for this service by habits of close observation, through scientific attainments, and unbounded enthusiasm."[69] Another colleague noted simply, "His mind was disciplined to study, and even on the frontier posts he had devoted it to the analyization of flowers and rocks."[70]

Thomas also continued to battle with Twiggs in what was rapidly becoming a full-blown rhetorical war. The department commander had violated one of the sacred tenets of the military chain of command by elevating Van Dorn to lead the expedition against the Comanche when Thomas was the one who held seniority. But when Twiggs rejected Thomas's complaint, the irate junior officer refused to let the matter go. Winfield Scott now threw his considerable weight behind Twiggs, and the stunned subordinate demanded a court of inquiry. Secretary of War Floyd closed the matter by continuing his pattern of supporting Thomas. Floyd had to do so again later in the summer when Twiggs decided that outbreaks of violence between Texans and Native Americans confined to reservations were civil matters in which the army could not intervene and Thomas disagreed.[71]

Despite these difficulties, Thomas presided over a relatively quiet station through the first half of 1859. The first indications that this phase might be drawing to a close came with the appearance of reinforcements on June 20 that included two additional companies each of the Second Cavalry and First Infantry. This enabled Thomas to execute orders more securely, and in July those included escorting "Texas Indians to their new location in the Indian Territory."[72] The Virginia-born superintendent for Indian affairs for Texas, Robert S. Neighbors, had requested army assistance in effecting the move, and Thomas obliged with two companies of the Second Cavalry and one of the First Infantry. The transfer expedition set out in the early morning hours of August and required Thomas's absence from the post through most of the month.[73]

Thomas also now had his hands full with Texas civilians who were incensed toward the Indians and prone to express their frustrations and antagonism through vigilantism. Hostilities among whites reached the point at which Superintendent Neighbors fell victim to assassination in September 1859. Thomas had been concerned enough about the potential for violence in the volatile atmosphere that he had offered a military escort, which the official had turned down.[74]

On October 1 Thomas again carried a detachment from the post on scouting operations that lasted until near the end of the following month. At least two efforts seem to have been made to determine the status of Native Americans in the region, but neither of these proved successful. Consequently, there was little on that score to report beyond a disappointing "No recent signs of Indians were discovered by either portion of the Command."[75]

Robert E. Lee's return to command of the Department of Texas was now a significant development for George Thomas. In addition to welcoming the fact that Twiggs no longer represented an impediment, Thomas appreciated the opportunity to revisit a relationship that had worked so well in their previous interactions. The arrival of another spring also suggested the likelihood of renewed operations that the wintry weather had largely precluded. On May 2, Thomas was once more out in the field on detached service, engaged in a scout, and the same designation appeared in subsequent post returns for the early summer months. On July 23, 1860, Thomas led four companies consisting of just over a hundred men "on an expedition to the head waters of the Concho and Colorado rivers for the month of July 1860."[76]

As the summer dragged on, Thomas decided to return to Camp Cooper in what a formal report termed an "extensive scout of thirty-nine days." When signs of a fresh Indian trail appeared, the major decided to streamline his command by sending most of the troops back to the post, while engaging in pursuit with the remainder. His command now consisted of "himself, Lieutenant William W. Lowe, two non-commissioned officers, [and] twenty-two privates of the Band and company D." The unit put another 60 miles into the effort when the troopers detected eleven Indians moving rapidly with a remuda of stolen horses early on August 26, 1860. The cavalry force "hotly pursued" their adversaries "for a few miles" until it became clear that the only chance for escape for the Indian party would be to abandon their prizes.[77]

The soldiers, with Thomas in the lead, allowed exuberance to overcome prudence and followed as rapidly as possible. Suddenly, one of the warriors broke off from the others for the purpose of holding the troopers at bay while the rest made good their escape. The Indian dismounted and began to unleash a torrent of arrows with remarkable accuracy against the cavalrymen as they approached. Four of the army personnel, including George Thomas, sustained wounds from the barrage. An arrow glanced off Thomas's chin as he leaned forward and lodged in his chest, making the only instance in which he suffered a battle wound in his long career.[78]

The Indian succeeded in wounding five more of his attackers, although no other as severely as the major, but numbers quickly began to tell against him. Despite calls for him to surrender, the courageous warrior refused, finally falling himself with a number of wounds. In perishing as he did, he managed to accomplish the goal of allowing the others to put sufficient distance between themselves and the patrol so that further pursuit did not occur. The soldiers gathered up twenty-eight horses and started out for the post.[79]

Rain and the pain from their wounds made the return journey less pleasant, but Thomas was back at Camp Cooper at the end of August, assuming command once more while he recovered from his wound. He remained in this position until November, when the Second Cavalry transferred back to Fort Mason on the fifth.[80]

About the same time Thomas led the expedition out that resulted in his wound in battle, he put in his paperwork for a twelve-month leave of absence. Given the state of bureaucracy and the distance over which word had to travel, it was not surprising that it was August 28 before the request received approval and November 12 when it went into effect. The move prompted one consideration of a domestic nature. Thomas still had the slave woman he had purchased, and his efforts to determine the best disposition of her met with frustration on several levels. She was unwilling simply to go free, and he could not bring himself to sell her to anyone else. The only recourse he could determine was to bring her back to Virginia.[81] Those who knew him best understood that his own stubbornness limited his options.

The moment indeed represented something of a crossroads for Thomas with regard to the institution of slavery and his attitudes toward it. Biographer Van Horne observed that "when the question of the sale of a slave became a practical one, the nature of the transaction" became objectionable, even if it simultaneously went "against his pecuniary interest."[82] Thomas was always weighing matters as to their likely costs and benefits. He was practical as well as paternalistic and had been largely insulated from the more unsavory aspects of slavery by his choice of career. He had not overtly questioned the status of individuals who occupied what were supposed to be their traditional deferential roles in society. Similarly, the George Thomas who had experienced the terrors of slave insurrection firsthand and for whom order and ranking were affirming notions would not have had much reason to find his sensibilities on the subject challenged until this moment.

The incident also revealed the approach George Thomas took on most issues. One of the Virginian's associates, Donn Piatt, described him as being opposed to slavery, but without taking an extreme stance in the matter. Thomas certainly was no abolitionist. Piatt caught the essence of the man in the observation, "He had little patience with the man who, not content with walking himself in the direction of the sunlight, sought, as a special agent of God, to drag others into the same path." As Thomas himself had told his friend, "he could not sell a human being," and thus the matter would have to be resolved in another manner.[83]

Even with such troubling issues to address, Thomas must have been delighted with the opportunity to travel to the East. According to one report of the period, he made "no reference to the arrow wound, from which he speedily recovered and never felt any effects afterward." But he was not to be as fortunate as he crossed Virginia by train and took the opportunity during a watering stop at Lynchburg to stretch his legs. He stepped off the car, searching in the dim moonlight of night for solid ground, but failing to detect a steep embankment when the darkness and shadows implied otherwise. The contemporary account placed the consequent fall at "twenty feet or more." The unexpected tumble jarred him, seriously wrenching his back and causing him considerable pain.[84] Thomas later confirmed the effects and the location of the accident as he reported on his ability to perform active duty. "I am still quite lame from an injury which I received last November in Lynchburg, Va."[85]

The hobbled warrior continued the journey rather than immobilize himself immediately in order that he could complete a rendezvous with his wife in Norfolk, Virginia. A contemporary of the general's noted that afterward he remained "confined in his bed in Norfolk" for six weeks, under Frances's care. He explained that although the injured soldier recovered from the impact of the fall, Thomas "always felt the effects of that accident."[86] Another associate of the general's maintained that the Virginian "never entirely recovered" from the accident. "This continued spinal lameness was one cause, at least, of his slow riding and deliberate personal movements so noticeable during the war."[87] He certainly had a period of forced prostration ahead of him, even as national events were spiraling out of control in a way that would impact his life and career with a force he could not have foreseen.

Up to this point in his life and career, George Thomas had enjoyed as much variety and opportunity as anyone in his situation would have a right to expect. His postings had carried him to every corner of the country, presenting him with myriad challenges that helped him hone his personal talents and professional skills. Thomas had also seen combat and knew how he would react to situations as they developed in places as diverse as Florida, Mexico, and parts of the American West. Each of these old army experiences had a long-standing impact on Thomas's career and development as a soldier. The numerous courts-martial introduced or reinforced lessons on military jurisprudence. Command of the small posts and the necessary paperwork associated with them did the same for his knowledge of quartermaster, commissary, and ordnance demands, as well as for the routines of garrison life. All seemed to be preparing him for the challenges to come, whatever they might turn out to be. For now, as Thomas contemplated an indefinite period of recuperation, he planned, in the words of one contemporary, to "be able to take care of his health and cultivate the art of war by [the] studious perusal of the campaigns of great generals."[88] Any other decisions hardly seemed pressing, even if some of them were bound to be the most contentious and significant of his career.

6   Duty Calls (1860–1861)

*"There was never a word passed between General Thomas and
myself, or any one of the family, upon the subject of his
remaining loyal to the United States Government."*
—Frances Thomas on influencing her husband

"I would like to hang hang him as a traitor to his native state."
—Jeb Stuart on George Thomas, 1861

Incapacitation from his injury left George Thomas with
plenty of time to mull over matters of all types. National developments in
the latter part of 1860 were occurring with a rapidity that could not have
escaped his notice. The election of Republican presidential candidate
Abraham Lincoln in November and the subsequent secession of South
Carolina in December were only the most dramatic. Speculation naturally
followed as to the course other Southern states might follow and the choices
that their native sons would have to make for themselves if they did. By the
end of the year, Federal troops were out of Thomas's old stomping grounds
at Fort Moultrie, occupying instead an incomplete facility in the heart of
Charleston Harbor called Fort Sumter. Conflicting rumors of impending
violence and the possibilities for compromise and reconciliation abounded
in a charged atmosphere that was rife with uncertainty. Such larger issues
were bound to affect George Thomas in ways he could not fully comprehend
or adequately anticipate.

On at least one important issue, Thomas was clear. Evidence suggested
that he viewed the question of secession with deep skepticism. Even if the
"fire-eaters," as the most radical proponents of state's rights were called,
embraced such views, he did not believe that as a general rule all white
Southerners, including many of those in his native state, would join them.[1]
Hotheads were leading others astray, and it remained for cooler heads like
his to persist and prevail.

It benefited George Thomas enormously that he was naturally disposed
toward calm when others seemed more likely to succumb to the emotions of
the moment. Even so, recollections of Thomas's positions on sectional
issues generated varying views of intensity. On the one hand, Erasmus
Keyes asserted, "Of all the hundreds of Southern men with whom I have
been intimate, he and Robert E. Lee were the fairest in their judgment of
Northern men." As if to underscore his sincerity, Keyes added, "In this
conclusion I make no exception."[2] On the other, Daniel Harvey Hill recalled
that during the time of their service together in Mexico, the Virginian was

"the strongest and most pronounced Southerner of the four" of the men who shared a mess together.[3]

Thomas did not make a habit of expressing himself extensively in any public forum on current political events, but he grappled with the inner turmoil of fulfilling the obligations of his military duty and remaining true to Virginia and the South. Again, his comrade Erasmus Keyes may have summarized the situation best for his friend. "He was strictly conscientious, he loved Virginia, which was his birthplace, and the bias of his affections was towards the South." But, Thomas also felt "warmly attached to the Union," and this competing affection would prove to be a powerful countervailing force if and when circumstances thrust a decision upon him.[4]

Another individual remembered that when they discussed these matters the general took a strong stance. Thomas explained that "he could not believe officers of the army were so ignorant of their own form of government as to suppose such proceedings [as secession] could occur." At the very least, he was convinced that the "government cannot dissolve itself; it is the creature of the people, and until they had agreed by their votes to dissolve it, and it was accomplished in accordance therewith, the government to which they had sworn allegiance remained."[5]

Of course, this sort of process was exactly what the secessionists in the South were arguing was occurring. The voters of the states, or at least their representatives in assembled conventions, were making choices about their continued adherence to the union that had bound them since the ratification of the United States Constitution. This expression of alienation, sanctified by the tenets of "states rights," was causing not a few white Southerners to embrace increasingly radical solutions to the questions that had plagued the nation since its inception.[6]

Clarity on such issues may have come less easily for George Thomas prior to the Civil War as he, and the rest of the nation, watched developments unfold. He also was still "suffering severely" from his fall when he made his way for a short visit with family in Southampton County, Virginia. The time that had elapsed since the accident was already reaching "several weeks."[7] But a time to test his resolve, not only to remain in the service, but to decide what the exact nature of that service would entail, was also rapidly approaching. Even so, practical concerns continued to occupy the soldier's attentions. From all appearances it looked to him that he might not recover sufficiently in the short term, at least, for active service, and he would have to make an adjustment under the circumstances regardless of his future career path. The George Thomas who would spend his entire life preparing for contingencies did so again here. He wanted to have a reserve in place and remained open to the possibility of one that would enable him to remain in the service in a capacity that would be less demanding of him physically.

Ultimately, the recovering husband and his wife returned to New York, after a brief stopover in Washington, but it became increasingly clear that the effects of the injury he had sustained were lingering and that he might be worse off than he had initially realized. It was at that point, in the midst of the occasionally excruciating pain that he was enduring, that Thomas had to face the fact that physically he might not be able to return to active service, and the couple began to contemplate what alternatives might exist for him to undertake realistically. One of these choices, and what would have been the easiest one for him to select under the circumstances, seemed not to have merited much consideration. A contemporary explained that Thomas "was in New York when his regiment arrived from Texas and could easily have obtained a surgeon's certificate for inability to do any duty, but preferred to make the effort suffering and disabled as he was."[8] Certainly, a medical exemption could have freed him from the requirement of choosing any side in a civil conflict. But Thomas was not one to select a path solely for its apparent ease and personal comfort. As long as the government existed, he later maintained, "I should have adhered to it."[9]

In this critical phase of their lives, Frances scanned the newspapers and happened upon an advertisement that offered another intriguing possibility. The Virginia Military Institute in Lexington was searching for a suitable candidate to assume the role of commandant and instructor of cadets. According to a personal source, she "read it aloud to him, and asked if he could do that duty." His initial response to her inquiry was that "he thought he could," and then after contemplating the matter Thomas determined to write a letter to the superintendent to seek additional information concerning the position. She concluded, "He never supposed from the great injury he had sustained in his back that he could ever do any duty with his regiment a cavalry regiment; and we were talking over the future prospects when *I* saw in the National Intelligencer the advertisement."[10]

Frances Thomas later recalled that during that period considerations for the future lay in practical terms rather than philosophical or political ones. "I was with him from early December when I joined him in Norfolk, Va., after he had met with his very severe accident on his return from Texas—so severe that it was four or five weeks before he was able to travel to reach New York." As he convalesced Thomas had ample opportunity to contemplate his next course. "At the time he made the inquiries concerning a position at the Virginia Military Institute no person (at the North at least) *thought*, or had *any idea* of War, and *I know* it was *solely* as a means of support that he thought of the position."[11]

The soldier referenced the circumstances generally in his letter to VMI superintendent Francis Smith on January 18, 1861. "In looking over the files of the 'National Intelligencer' this morning," Thomas began, "I met with your advertisement for a commandant of cadets and instructor of tactics at the Institute." His teaching at West Point had been a pleasant experience for him, and Thomas must have considered that an opportunity to return to that aspect of the profession would allow him to continue associating with this form of service even if his physical limitations altered the level and extent of that participation. "If not already filled," he continued, "I will be under obligation if you will inform me what salary and allowances pertain to the situation, as from present appearances I feel it will soon be necessary for me to be looking for some means of support."[12]

Ironically then, it was Frances who saw the advertisement in the newspaper for a vacancy at the Virginia Military Institute in 1861. It was she who encouraged her husband to inquire concerning it out of their mutual worry that his recent fall and resulting injury would require a less strenuous line of work. The operative phrase appeared to be that the job would be meant to provide "some means of support." The situation was revealing in several ways. First, Thomas shared such matters with his wife, sought her counsel, and seemed to act in response accordingly. Second, although Virginia remained in the Union currently, the national crisis looked to be close to a breaking point of some type, and it would have been unlikely that she would have encouraged him to consider employment at a Southern institution if his opposition to it on principle were clear in her mind. Third, while he made the inquiry with a view to providing for their mutual welfare, he did so on his terms. George Thomas was his own man, if also a happily married one.

The inquiry met with a rebuff, there then being "no vacancy in the Va. Mil. Institute," as Smith recalled later. But the superintendent interpreted the tone of the letter unmistakably. "From the terms of his letter to me," he explained to Frances Thomas in February 1876, well after the general's death, "I had no doubt at the time that his sympathies were with the South, and these, not any physical disability, prompted his purpose to resign." Smith explained that he then proposed that Thomas look into a possible appointment as chief of ordnance for Virginia, through the offices of Colonel William Gilham. In turn, that officer showed Smith the letter to Gilham in which Thomas asserted, "*I have not determined what I will do, but I have made up my mind never to draw my sword against a state struggling for its constitutional rights.*"[13] Clearly, Thomas's reference to "present appearances" in the Smith letter and to states that were "struggling for constitutional rights" in the Gilham correspondence left the matter in enough doubt to allow the VMI official to interpret Thomas's motivation for seeking employment outside of the regular army as he did.

At the beginning of March, Thomas also drafted a letter for the adjutant general that indicated he was prepared to make adjustments within the service in response to whatever action his home state might take with regard to secession. "I have the honor respectfully to ask to be detailed as Superintendent of the mounted recruiting service for the next two years." The former cavalry instructor at West Point felt comfortable about his ability to relate to young men and perhaps induce them to join the cavalry. But he remained less certain of his ability to perform the duties he normally would be required to undertake in that capacity. As one of the reasons he offered for the application, Thomas explained that despite the severe injury he had sustained on the journey home from Texas at Lynchburg, he believed that he "could attend to all my ordinary duties," but added, "I fear that I shall not have sufficient strength to perform every duty which might be required of me if with my regiment."[14]

From his temporary New York Hotel residence, Thomas sent a letter out on March 12 to Virginia governor John Letcher. The correspondence occurred in response to one sent him three days earlier by William Gilham. That letter had presented the possibility for the veteran army officer to become the chief of ordnance for the Commonwealth of Virginia. Gilham had asked his old West Point colleague to respond directly to the governor, and Thomas was happy to oblige.[15] Letcher had been trying for some time to fill the slot with an appropriate candidate, and Thomas seemed made to order. The governor's biographer, F. N. Boney, observed, "Letcher's court-ship of Major George H. Thomas was typical of his efforts to recruit army talent."[16] The third-party invitation was a way of saving face for all parties if the targeted individual declined.

Thomas offered neither an outright rejection nor an acceptance to the governor. "I have the honor to state, after expressing my most sincere thanks for your very kind offer," he began, "that it is not my wish to leave the service of the United States as long as it is honorable for me to remain in it, and therefore, as long as my native State remains in the Union, it is my purpose to remain in the army, unless requested to perform duties alike repulsive to honor and humanity."[17] His opening had suggested a refusal, but the latter elements left several escape clauses in the eventuality that Virginia left the Union or he felt compelled to engage in functions he found repug-nant. He wanted his options left open to him so that no appearance of deception or impropriety might interfere.

Of course, Thomas could have believed that the crisis would pass without a sword leaving its scabbard in anger. Although he could do so from hindsight, Thomas wrote a family friend on March 22, 1865, to thank her for supporting Frances and her sister at the time of their mother's death. He explained that reminders of their "long and friendly acquaintance" had the effect of "carrying me back to days of joy and happiness, the remembrance of which now fill my heart with gladness." Indeed, that opportunity for reflection reminded him of his earlier moment of decision. "How little in those happy days did I think we should have to go through such a terrible trial as is now upon us." Then, in typical Thomas fashion, he expressed no remorse for his course in the conflict, but regretted that he had not prepared himself better for it. "Could I possibly have conceived of such a calamity, I should have devoted my entire life to preparations to meet the emergency instead but possibly all had happened for the best."[18]

A state of uncertainty for soldiers and civilians alike was understandable under the constantly changing circumstances. While lamenting the difficulty he was having in finding a suitable officer for the position of which Thomas had inquired, Virginia governor John Letcher advised Francis Smith in mid-February that he had word from Washington "the controversy will be settled." Then he hastened to add, "Such was my own decided conviction when I left the city, last Sunday."[19]

Even in the midst of the swirl of events, Frances Thomas remained as sure of her husband's intentions as anyone else possibly could be. "*He* went with his troops, and *I* was to follow in two or three days," she explained the sequence to a family friend, "*then* was the time *I* wanted to *dissuade* him from going on duty, knowing as I did, how *very far* from well he was, but he would go, and said 'he could attend to the remounting of the regiment, although he could not ride on horseback.'" She insisted that there was no ambivalence in her husband's actions despite his fragile physical state. "Not one in a dozen injured as he was would have reported for duty." As he took his leave of her, Thomas stopped to wire her "to remain in NY" and "wrote me at length of his course, which as he said, 'turn it every way he would the one thing was uppermost, his duty to the government of the United States.'"[20] On another occasion, Frances Thomas reiterated her belief that her husband's attitude on the subject was firm. "In Gen. Thomas' own words from a letter he wrote me at the time of the attack on Fort Sumpter, every time he thought of the matter his duty to his country was uppermost."[21]

Frances Thomas may have felt certainty about her husband's course, but he sent messages to his family in Southampton, Virginia, that left them perplexed as events unfolded. After the war, one of his sisters insisted that her brother had given every indication of his remaining loyal to Virginia and the South. He had taken steps to secure his personal property with them, including his servants and the sword Southampton Countians had bestowed upon him, so that he might retrieve them at the appropriate moment. Since he had been in the Virginia household during this critical period from December 15, 1860, to January 8, 1861, there was no reason to disregard her reminiscence or question her understanding of the circumstances she would have been in a reasonable position to witness. Yet, Fanny Thomas, a favorite sibling of the general's, was writing many years later in 1900 and with her sister peering figuratively, if not literally, over her shoulder. Fanny explained,

"While here he said he should side with the South and my sister says to tell you the last word he said to her was he should be back in March."[22]

Although his decision to remain under the old flag would trouble all of them greatly, Thomas's brother Benjamin, residing in Vicksburg, later insisted to the general's widow that he was not surprised by the course George had chosen to follow. "[O]f course he would remain in the U.S. Army," she quoted the general's elder sibling observing, "as he did not see *how* he could *do otherwise* with the oath he had taken on his entering the Army to serve the United States."[23] To underscore this perception on her part, Frances Thomas simply asserted a few years later, "Genl Thomas would never have gone to Carlisle to remount his regiment if he had not intended to remain in the Army."[24]

In a postwar letter to the general's widow, Francis Smith provided numerous examples of individuals whom he argued confirmed Thomas's pro-Southern sentiments at the time. "Other corroborating statements left no doubt on my mind that the views entertained by Gn. T. in the spring of 1861, coincided with the ultra secession party of Va., and were more pronounced in this respect," he argued, than the positions taken by men who subsequently became prominent Confederate generals. Frances Thomas was not going to agree, especially when Smith concluded, "If correct, as I believe them to be, it may be remarked that such sentiments as were understood to be held by him were the common sentiments of Virginians."[25] Any sensitivity that she felt toward such statements was not entirely ill-placed, if judged by the assessment of a later scholar that "No man vilified Thomas with more gusto" than Smith.[26]

Ulysses Grant later recalled that during this period Thomas suffered from the effects of a tendency toward thorough deliberation. "It was his slowness that led to the stories that he meant to go with the South," the wartime commander of the Union armies insisted. "When the war was coming Thomas felt like a Virginian, and talked like one, and had all the sentiment then so prevalent about the rights of slavery and sovereign States and so on. But the more Thomas thought it over, the more he saw the crime of treason behind it all." Grant cast no doubt on the ultimate decision and thought that Thomas had arrived at it honestly. "So, by the time Thomas thought it all out, he was as passionate and angry in his love for the Union as any one. So he continued through the war."[27]

Grant's early assertion of Thomas's mind-set gibed with Francis Smith's recollection. But if George Thomas's connection to Virginia was tenuous, perhaps biographer Francis McKinney best explained why. "In the quarter century preceding the outbreak of the Civil War, the aggregate of the time Thomas spent at home was less than eighteen months."[28] It was true that some of the old army postings were in the South, too, as fond memories of life in the vicinity of Charleston, South Carolina, and New Orleans, Louisiana, or service in Texas and Florida attested, but Thomas had also spent considerable months outside of his native region. His reach was distinctly national, rather than sectional or regional.

That George Thomas was ambivalent in the face of such a crucial decision would not be as out of the question for his personality as it might seem. He would have wanted to weigh all options before plunging in to any course, regardless of how right philosophically he believed either one or the other to be. Gamaliel Bradford, an early analyst of the principal Union figures in the conflict, argued, "In view of all this evidence, I do not see how any unprejudiced person can doubt that up to the middle of March, at any rate, Thomas was divided between his loyalty to the Union and his loyalty to Virginia."[29] Bradford might have added wife to the first and family to the second half of the equation, for they were also contributors to Thomas's unsettled mind-set. External forces pulled at him from either direction, and the risk of familial "estrangement" that he had lamented in his brother's case a few years earlier now threatened him as well.

Frances Thomas was adamant that she never exerted any undue influence upon George to make a decision as to what course he would take in the national crisis. After the war, when she read that Erasmus Keyes had suggested that her influence was crucial to Thomas's decision for the Union, she explained, "His *private opinion* that I was the cause of Genl Thomas' remaining in the Union is *decidedly* a *mistake*." She further insisted, "There was never a word passed between General Thomas and myself, or *any one* of our family, upon the subject of his remaining loyal to the United States Government." In obviously the best position to know how her husband was liable to treat such an intensely emotional matter, Frances insisted, "We felt that whatever his course, it would be from a conscientious sense of duty; that no one could persuade him to do what he felt was right."[30]

As Keyes suggested, the strongest intimation from the outset, regardless of side in the conflict, concerned the influence upon Thomas by his New York–born wife and her family. Frances Thomas bristled at each source, questioning the motivation, if not the veracity, that provided the foundation for it. In a series of letters to a former close associate of the general's she repeatedly deflected any notion that she exerted herself in any direct sense on her husband's decision making in this crucial period. "As long as Southern papers published these wilful misrepresentations I did not care to have any notice taken of them as that was nothing more than I could expect after the terms they applied to *me* during the War," she explained to Alfred Hough as an expression of the resignation she felt toward the statements of her husband's opponents. But for her the notion that "a Northern paper with such a circulation as the N.Y. Herald's published it, and embellished by their correspondent at Richmond in so totally false an article," required a response, and she "did not hesitate to tell them as plainly as possible that Genl. Thomas' object and motives had been wilfully misrepresented, whatever others may say to the contrary."

The general's wife explained that she had been with him "from early in December for he was in the house most of the time; only walking out a short time each day," but that she "never had a doubt what his course would be." Of course, she could not know what he contemplated on his strolls, but Frances Thomas insisted, "I never tried to influence him, (although I have been denounced by his Southern friends) for I knew what he did would be from a conscientious sense of duty."[31] She understood her husband best and may have reckoned the cost of appearing to apply pressure on him, although her later willingness to engage in an often vehement defense of her late husband's reputation offered proof that Frances Thomas was not afraid of asserting herself. Indeed, in her later correspondence, she offered at least two references where she noted seeing messages her husband planned to send "*before* they were sent" and learning "the reason" for them from him directly or discussing "matters" that were current at the time with him.[32] Clearly, the couple had established lines of communication and a willingness to employ them on sensitive issues.

Even if George Thomas remained uncertain during these whirlwind months, events were quickly rendering the time short for the Virginian to consider whatever course he might choose to pursue. Confederate general Pierre Gustave Toutant Beauregard sent his counterpart at Fort Sumter and Thomas's old commander, Major Robert Anderson, an ultimatum to surrender the installation. When that Union officer could not comply, the Confederate shore batteries blazed forth in the early morning hours of April 12, 1861, and a state of war existed between the United and Confederate States of America.

The firing on Fort Sumter spurred United States president Abraham Lincoln to call for 75,000 volunteers to suppress a rebellion too great for ordinary forces to handle. He expected a quota of troops from each of the remaining "loyal" states. But Sumter had also created the conditions, exacerbated now by the actions of the president, that would force additional Southern states out of the Union. One of these was bound to be Virginia. An individual who studied the general closely felt that it was Fort Sumter that proved the final determinant in Thomas's decision for the Union. "Whatever may have been Thomas's doubts when the dispute was in the theoretical stage," Gamaliel Bradford astutely concluded, "the guns at Sumter settled the question for him."[33]

Thus, George Henry Thomas, the man who had grown up in Southampton County, Virginia, and who had received his education at West Point and his professional experience in the service of the United States, was confronted with the final choice. In many ways he had already indicated the path that he would follow in his acceptance of the honorary sword bestowed on him by Southampton Countians less than a decade before. He indicated afresh that if circumstances required it, as they now did, he would choose one allegiance and loyalty over the other.

Much has been written to compare the choices made by Thomas and by another famous Virginian and old army comrade, Robert E. Lee. Although he agonized in the process, Thomas's former colleague indicated that his choice was really no choice. Thomas did not have to pace the floors of Arlington (or his hotel room in New York) as his conflicted fellow Virginian felt compelled to do. Yet, like Lee, the future Union general did not make his decision mindlessly. As Thomas indicated to his wife, he had considered the matter from every angle, almost as an intricate geometrical problem that had to be solved. One biographer has even labeled his decision "supreme unemotional objectivity."[34] As true as this might be, and he was almost clinical in his approach to the question of his loyalty, it was not done without thought or careful consideration.

Lee also seemed to have been affected in his decision by his wife, who espoused the cause of the South vehemently. One biographer noted that the Virginian might have reached his decision in part because it would provide him with a measure of domestic tranquility. "In a real sense," that historian observed of the marriage, "Lee went to war in order to avoid conflict."[35] Although such a conclusion is open to other interpretations and suggested motives less noble than those many would ascribe to the future Confederate general, Lee's motivations were nonetheless human. So were those of George Thomas.

The same comparisons might have been done with profit regarding the choices of Thomas Jonathan Jackson and James Ewell Brown Stuart. Unlike "Stonewall" Jackson, George Thomas was not an overwhelmingly religious person. He believed in a higher power and ascribed to that entity the ultimate position of authority over humanity, but he did not feel himself to be only an instrument of that being, subject to his understanding of God's will above all else. Furthermore, what we know about him suggested that he had that most earthly of reactions to things divine. "Above all painful doubts," he once observed, "we feel that there is an overwhelming Power ever wise and just." The extent of that "Power" was unclear, but the nature of it was "ever wise and just." Still, George Thomas did not find the existence of this "Power" sufficient to use it to determine his personal decisions for him.

For Jackson, every choice was simple: "God will decide." As his biographer, James I. Robertson Jr., has noted, "Faith, tinged by the ambition to do God's will, were his impulses."[36] Jackson would listen to the rhetoric, he would watch the actions of anxious Virginia Military Institute students and hotheaded politicians, but he would "listen and remain silent," preparing for the day that a Christian soldier might be called to war under the banner of the Commonwealth of Virginia.

For Thomas, a choice made upon such a basis was not so obvious. His religion was of a more practical bent, the will of God less inflexibly certain. "I fail to comprehend what is meant by natural religion, it is so vague and uncertain," he once observed, "but revealed religion, that is given us in the teachings and character of Christ, is clear in all things." He saw in this view of things spiritual the "goodness of Christ" and the "purity or divinity of his teachings." Upon that premise, he revealed much of himself in assessing, "Whether they will get us into heaven or not after death, there is one thing certain, and that is to obey them is to make us better and happier on earth. Accepting that I will chance the rest."[37]

Unlike the pious Jackson, George Thomas seemed not to have felt it necessary to depend upon the Deity to guide his course. He accepted the responsibility that an individual given free will would exert over his own actions. Even so, his beliefs were not for public consumption, but for his private and personal edification. A military associate later observed that Thomas "was a man of deep religious convictions," but practiced this faith "without parading it."[38]

Clarity for fellow West Pointer and former Thomas student Jeb Stuart came in another form. "I go with Virginia," he remarked repeatedly and, his biographer Emory Thomas added, almost "liturgically" to anyone who inquired of his position. Labeling the plumed cavalier a "Virginiaphile," the scholar asserted that Stuart "did not have to decide whether he was more Southern than American or vice versa, Virginia would decide for him."[39]

Such a passing of the decision for George Thomas was not so easy, nor in the least bit desirable. He loved Virginia as well as any man. He cherished family connections and lifetime friends, but he loved duty more and treasured loyalty to the military oath he had taken most. A modern cultural allusion may offer the clearest insight into the position that Thomas took with regard to such matters. In the John Huston film *The Searchers,* John Wayne, as Ethan Edwards, a disgruntled Confederate veteran facing life after the war, observed when asked to take an oath as a Texas Ranger, "I am only good for one oath at the time."[40] His had been to the Confederate States of America. Thomas's was to the Union.

George Thomas took such an oath as a sacred trust. He was especially critical of those brethren in the old blue who claimed some justification for violating theirs. In his eyes there could be none. In this regard, as he told another officer, these former comrades "had sworn allegiance to the government [and] they were bound to adhere to it, and would have done so [if] they had been so inclined." He dismissed constitutional explanations particularly as poor "excuses," noting that the "government to which they had sworn allegiance remained, and as long as it did exist, I should have adhered to it."[41]

Interestingly, Thomas appeared to have held these men less responsible for their actions than the government that allowed them to take those actions. To at least one individual he remarked that he believed the United States should not have accepted the resignations of these officers in the first place, even if they had provided them in good faith. Such a course certainly would have placed the onus back on the individual hoping to resign his commission with his honor intact, but it would surely not have altered the course of those who, as Thomas put it, were "so inclined" to follow that course anyway.

A few years after the war, the general received an invitation to share his political views publicly. He declined, citing the need for professional officers to avoid such partisan expressions. He also admonished those officers who sought to influence the votes of soldiers during the war, arguing that the men in the ranks cared more about the outcome of elections than the officers themselves. Then, in assessing what he felt may have motivated those who volunteered to serve, he unwittingly revealed something of his own motivations. "My experience during the late war was that the Volunteers laid aside for the time being *politics* and joined the Army to sustain the Constitution & Government."[42]

One of the men who served with Thomas and later wrote about him observed, "A democrat by birth and breeding, he had an old fashioned belief that a soldier, like a clergyman or a judge, was precluded from taking an active part in the partisan contentions of the country."[43] Thomas would have been mortified by the thought that his actions could be construed as politically charged or unprofessionally motivated. Indeed, he ever insisted that service to the nation overrode all else. "We must remember that this is a civil war," he said later in a discussion on the treatment of Southern civilians that also revealed his personal motivations concerning the conflict, "fought to preserve the Union that is based on brotherly love and patriotic belief in the one nation."[44]

Nevertheless, allegations persisted that Thomas chose his course in part because it offered him the swiftest and surest means of advancement in his career. Promotion in the old army was notoriously slow by any standard, but at the outbreak of hostilities, as others left the service to follow their states out of the Union, the path opened for those who remained. Yet, a staff officer who formed a close attachment to Thomas found the suggestion of the Virginian's motivation based in this way as preposterous. In a statement he wrote in 1876, indicating that it was meant for private purposes only, Alfred Hough took on a spate of recent public statements to elaborate on Thomas's position, as he understood it, in the early part of 1861. Hough thought that Fitzhugh Lee, one of the most outspoken persons on the subject, labored under a "misapprehension." In the course of his discussion of the matter, Hough even offered an additional factor, when he asserted, "General Thomas had also become tired of frontier life, and in addition saw very little in store for the prospects of the army," as men who now "were in possession of the government had always been considered unfriendly to the army." Contrary to a calculation for professional advancement based on the resignation of fellow Southerners, and apparently influenced by the often tedious service in California and Texas he experienced, Thomas seemed intent upon considering a different career path. "Under all these circumstances," the aide insisted, "he was anxious for employment out of the army," as indeed his friend Sherman and others had done at some point in their own careers.[45]

Perhaps one interesting observation remained concerning the Virginian's determination to "stand by the Union" beyond the influence of a wife or other family ties, adherence to duty or the Constitution, the personal ambitions to rise in rank, or the will of God. He had that injured back. His wife referred to him at this stage as "very much crippled from the accident he had met with a few months before."[46] Suffering acutely from that spinal injury, he could have used that very real issue as an excuse to vacillate. Subsequently criticized as slow in some circles, he had every reason to slow the process here to his benefit, had he been sufficiently ambivalent about his intentions. He could have postponed any decision to see how matters would develop. If we were talking about another time and profession, we could say simply that he could have "held out" like a modern professional athlete. That Thomas did no such thing, even in the face of criticism he was bound to face whatever path he chose, redounded to his credit and reaffirmed the notion that once he set his mind on a course he stayed with it. In one sense, going with Virginia would have been a simpler choice for him to make as it would have constituted the path of least resistance concerning the welcome he would have received from his would-be comrades in that cause, but his character clearly would not make it so for him. That was the essence of the man—the core of the rock—and remaining with the Union was the course he had set.

An old nemesis, General David E. Twiggs, may actually have caused the decision to be an even easier one for the Virginian to embrace. When that officer not only refused to turn over his command, but surrendered the troops and their equipage to Southern control in Texas, Thomas felt a deep sense of betrayal. Had he remained in the region, he was certain the outcome would have been different. "I would have taken command of the men, marched them north until they reached the loyal states, and the rebels should not have taken a prisoner or captured a cannon or a flag."[47] That he now had a small role to play in the reconstitution of the same command compensated in a limited way for his absence from the scene at such a crucial time.

Thomas was soon confident enough that he had recovered sufficiently to take some role in the events that were unfolding. Under orders to report for duty, he left New York for Carlisle to see about the remounting of the regiment with a portion of the command that had reported to him there before his departure. The party had reached the Pennsylvania capital of Harrisburg when commotion erupted in their midst. Newsboys dashed into the cars holding copies of hastily produced news "extras" that announced the firing by Southern forces on Fort Sumter in Charleston, South Carolina. Frances Thomas recalled years later that her husband wired her promptly with the news and his reaction. "Immediately he telegraphed me from Carlisle to wait," rather than join him at his new duty post as he had anticipated. She was to remain with family until events crystallized, but Frances was convinced that now George "clearly saw what was coming, [and] wrote me his course."[48] The post reports for Carlisle Barracks indicated Thomas's presence there in April 1861.[49]

For the next several extremely hectic days, George Thomas remained focused on his duties. A flood of messages inundated Carlisle and Harrisburg, passed between the Virginian and his former West Point and old army colleague Fitz John Porter. Both officers scrambled to obtain the equipment needed to return the depleted Second Cavalry to field-grade service as quickly as possible. "Send here by train at 7 a.m. to-morrow four companies armed, equipped with ammunition, and four days provisions in haversacks, if you have them—[with] as little baggage as possible," Porter instructed on April 20. "I will go with my entire force, as efficiently equipped as the means we have will admit, by train this afternoon," Thomas replied the same day.[50]

A sense of urgency pervaded as Porter scoured every corner for supplies that could be forwarded quickly to Carlisle. To Colonel H. L. Scott in New York City, he wrote, "Major Thomas' command, ordered to Washington, requires immediately 400 Sharp's carbines, 300 Colt's revolvers, 300 cavalry sabers, 32,000 rounds of ammunition and caps for carbines."[51] The scramble for supplies and equipment underscored the degree to which events had overtaken the command structure. These myriad challenges added a level of intensity to an already highly charged atmosphere.

Even so, Thomas faced the crisis with his accustomed calm and deliberation. His communications were dispassionate and professional. For instance, he listed as having at his disposal Companies B, D, G, and I, with himself and four other commissioned officers, along with 216 enlisted personnel. Apparently other new recruits were due to arrive, but in a time of crisis, any schedule was bound to be difficult to maintain. The next day, Thomas and his men were still at Carlisle. "Have not yet got recruits," he wired. "Will move as soon after as possible."[52]

Just when it must have seemed that the sense of urgency could not be greater, Major Thomas received orders on April 22 to bring his four companies of cavalry to Washington "as fast as they are mounted (which must be done with all possible dispatch), and by the route which will insure their arrival at the earliest moment practicable." The troopers were to be prepared for all contingencies, including the possibility that they would be called on to "encounter opposition and to overcome it."[53]

In accordance with these instructions, Thomas proceeded to Harrisburg, where he was supposed to rendezvous with Major Porter and any recruits coming with him at that point. From Carlisle came the hardly unexpected communication that the men being sent to "report to Major Thomas at Harrisburg . . . are by no means well instructed. They have been too short a time at the depot for them to be well drilled."[54]

In the meantime, Porter sought to provide as much assistance as possible. "Send as fast as can be procured 2,500 shoes and 100 pounds of horse-shoe nails and 6 sets of shoeing tools to Major George Thomas, Carlisle Barracks," he instructed the commander in Philadelphia. "Send by express train to Major George H. Thomas, 2d Cavalry, at Carlisle Barracks Pa., 500 complete sets of cavalry equipments, saddles, bridles, saddle-bags, blankets, etc.," he wired the head of the arsenal in Pittsburgh. From Harrisburg, Porter communicated directly with the Virginian, "I will give you and collect where you may say, everything you wish. Horses are being purchased here."[55]

The chaotic nature of these early days of the war could not have appealed to Thomas's sense of order and discipline, but such were the conditions with which he had to contend. From York on the twenty-fourth, he explained that he preferred to return to Carlisle, "as horses etc can be collected there much easier than here." He had ordered a train to transport the command and expected to leave early the following morning.[56]

Thomas quickly sent another somewhat plaintive communication racing along the wires. "Can [an] officer be sent here from Harrisburg to muster in the volunteers?" he inquired of Major Porter. "I have been so busy that I could not attend to it."[57] The dismounted cavalry arrived from their service in Texas on board the steamer *Empire City* and proceeded to Carlisle Barracks.[58] R. W. Johnson recalled the atmosphere as the recruits and dismounted veterans attempted to mesh in short order into a cohesive and efficient potentially combat-ready unit. "When our companies reached Carlisle Barracks great confusion existed, as is the case when cavalrymen have no horses."[59]

Porter observed in a full report that at the beginning of May, "Major

Thomas, with 400 cavalry (dismounted) tolerably equipped arrived at Harrisburg." But he noted that another element of concern arose. "The officers accompanying Major Thomas were, without exception, southern men." Porter felt that these circumstances would create an explosive situation. "They were all anxious, excited, in doubt as to what should be their immediate action and gloomy as to the future." These officers were also conversing among themselves. "I knew Major Thomas' views. I had no doubt of his course," Porter explained. "But I did fear that some, if not all his subordinates would tender their resignations and ask to be left behind."

Already one officer had taken that action, returning to his home in Maryland. In an initial moment of uncertainty, another approached the Virginian and deliberately and publicly posed the question, "What shall we do?" In one sense, Thomas's answer was unequivocal. "We are ordered to Washington, and there we go." But he quickly followed that definitive statement with recognition of the doubts that persisted. "There will be time enough after getting there for you to decide what to do." Porter took the message to mean that Thomas would see that the entire command adhered to its duty. Accordingly, he observed, "This incident and other events satisfied me that whatever the obstacle we should meet with, these officers would do their full duty so long as in the service, and until officially relieved at Washington."[60]

As an additional surety of loyalty, those who had already taken oaths of allegiance received notice that they would be required to undergo a renewal of that pledge. Richard W. Johnson, who had seen his share of service in numerous spheres, still felt a sense of bitterness years later when he recalled that the U.S. Government required the step of its officers, even in the light of the national crisis. "This was thought to be an uncalled-for insult to every officer in the army, and I spoke to Major Thomas in relation to it," he explained. "His reply was, 'I do not care a snap of my finger about it. If they want me to take the oath before each meal I am ready to comply.'"[61]

In the heated atmosphere, matters continued to escalate as tempers flared and emotions soared. Thomas once again demonstrated a steady and decisive hand concerning the news of an early defeat suffered by Federal forces at Big Bethel, in eastern Virginia. This issue came to a head when one of Thomas's officers expressed a strong and obviously undiplomatic opinion about the setback, by exclaiming, "I'm glad the damned old abolitionist was whipped." A colleague took exception, arguing, "It seems to me, sir, that you are fighting on the wrong side." The verbal sparring threatened to turn into something more than words.

At the evening meal, the air was thick with tension, but decorum demanded that the erstwhile comrades remain civil in the presence of their fellow officers and commander. Thomas's entrance required the usual response of stiffening to attention while the Virginian moved to his seat. He had heard the rumors and before he sat to partake of the meal, he wanted matters clearly understood. As he saw it, the offensive statement suggested that the initial response was an honest assessment, but no conflict among brother officers was to be tolerated. "Let there be no more talk about this being a damned Abolition war," he observed, closing the matter as he took his seat to begin the meal he had unceremoniously but effectively delayed.[62]

Referring to the conflict in this manner was about as far as George Thomas was prepared to go, and certainly he had no intention of assigning blame or articulating his political views concerning it with his subordinates. He held extremists of both sides responsible for the nation's misery, but increasingly came to see the Southerners who insisted upon taking up arms against the Union to be worthy of his greatest opprobrium. These feelings remained with him to the end of his life and served as the heart of a pointed comment to a comrade after he had returned from a postwar trip to Alaska. He insisted that "Alaska would have been an excellent purchase in 1861, as a kind of water and cold air cure for the hot-headed Southerners who fell into our hands as prisoners of war." He imagined that a few months in such a climate back in those days might have had a palliative effect on any desires for rebellion and war.[63]

However opponents might try to impugn Thomas's motives, the fact was that the departure of comrades for the Confederacy cleared a path for the Virginian to experience rapid promotion. The resignation of Robert E. Lee from the service of the United States opened the way for Thomas to become a lieutenant colonel in the Second Cavalry on April 25, 1861. Likewise, he rose quickly to colonel of the regiment on May 3, when Albert Sidney Johnston also stepped aside to join the Southern cause.[64]

Because of the choice he had made as to which flag he would follow, the Virginian alienated himself from those of his former comrades from the old army who sided with the South. Edmund Kirby Smith had studied under Thomas at West Point and served as a subordinate in the Second Cavalry. Now, having chosen the Confederate banner, he dismissed his onetime teacher and colleague in a homebound letter as "a Virginia renegade."[65] Such views were not uncommon in these circles, but Thomas refused to be goaded into public displays or disputes over the merits of his service.

Fellow Virginian and old army compatriot General Winfield Scott was not among that number. Like Thomas, he followed the banner under which he had served with such distinction for decades, including army command in the war with Mexico. As he contemplated a commander for an expeditionary force, Scott felt comfortable in turning to Robert Patterson. "I have flanked him with two good army officers," the old veteran remarked, one of whom was George H. Thomas.[66] Accordingly, that soldier received his marching orders on May 27 and reported at Chambersburg, Pennsylvania, in compliance with them on June 1, at the head of "four companies of the second cavalry and the Philadelphia City troops."[67]

An old comrade certainly concurred with General Scott's assessment of Thomas's capabilities. "There are two A no. 1 men there," William T. Sherman wrote his brother John in June concerning Patterson's command. One was Thomas, "a Virginian from near Norfolk, and Say what we may he must feel unpleasant at leading an invading army." Although professing that "if in the varying chances of war" he had the opportunity to name Thomas for a "high" place, and deeming his Southern-born friend above suspicion or doubt, Cump Sherman could not resist a playful jab. "But if he says he will do it I think he will do well—He was never brilliant but always Cool, reliable, & steady—maybe a little slow."[68] It was about this time that Thomas and a group of Union officers spent what their host termed "a pleasant May evening" dining in the home of Republican lawmaker and inveterate observer Alexander McClure. While they were "enjoying their cigars on the porch" after their meal the conversation inevitably turned to national events. The group engaged in a wide-ranging discussion that included speculation about the section of the nation they might shortly be called to enter to quell the rebellion. McClure recalled that most of the participants expressed enthusiasm for the sentiment that any conflict would be short-lived. "The only silent guest of the occasion was Colonel Thomas," he explained. The attitude represented the Virginian's character, but also reflected a sobering assessment of any conflict between North and South. Consequently, McClure added, "only very few questions were asked of him at any time during the conversation, to which he always answered very courteously and without expressing any decided opinion."[69] In another recollection of the events, the attorney observed that Thomas exhibited on the occasion "that modesty that always characterized him." The Virginian had additional distinctions from his comrades on this occasion. While the others indulged in their bombastic predictions amidst clouds of cigar smoke, Thomas not only remained largely silent, if respectful, he also did not participate in the consumption of tobacco.[70] "He never smoked," a contemporary recalled.[71] Another officer who later had opportunities to be in Thomas's company indicated that this inclination persisted through the war, claiming the Virginian "never used tobacco, at least I never saw him indulge in the habit in any form."[72]

McClure had desired to discern Thomas's views on the subjects of Southerners and secession, only to be disappointed at how little he divulged for the benefit of others. The dinnertime host recalled, "I saw him several times during that campaign, and much enjoyed visits to his camp; but even in the privacy of personal conversation he was most reluctant to discuss the situation." McClure speculated that despite a tendency to keep his own counsel Thomas recognized "the determined purpose of the Southern people to win independence."[73]

Another individual, who would become a close associate and biographer of the Virginian, remembered that about this time period the two men "messed together, and frequently conversed freely together in regard to the war." As in so much that had dictated his approach thus far to his duty as he saw it, Thomas declared himself prepared to "help whip" Virginia, and ostensibly the rest of the seceded South, "back again" into the Union.[74] There was no rancor in such a view. Given what his wife would one day write about her husband's attitude in these fateful days, the strongest emotion in him must have been incredulity. As Frances Thomas observed in an 1876 letter, "Genl Thomas was very unwilling to believe there would be War, that the South would be so crazy, and unjust to herself."[75]

The proximity of his troops to civilians added further concerns and required close and almost constant attention, particularly if he hoped to practice a conciliatory policy toward any who harbored Southern sympathies. One local, A. T. Caperton, seemed to have had personal difficulties with the officer who requisitioned the use of his property to house and drill his men. In early May and again later in the month, Caperton broached the matter directly with Thomas. In the initial contact, the citizen sought the soldier's help in reining in a subordinate by asking Thomas to take "such steps . . . as will at least protect me from further insults & outrages."[76] His second letter suggested that the Federal commander had indeed acted, but that the subordinate had failed to abide by the spirit of his orders. "While the instructions to Capt. Conrad made special reference to the erection of buildings on my grounds they were no doubt intended to signify to him that he was not to occupy my premises for any purpose without my written consent. He has not so interpreted them as without any such consent he still occupies them for drilling purposes." The two principals had reached an impasse. "I am satisfied that I can have no sort of relations with Captain Conrad, without hazard of unpleasant collisions & must therefore respectfully ask that you will cause him to be instructed to find some other place for the accommodations of his command."[77]

This incident was just one of the early indicators of the fine line George Thomas would be called upon to make in distinguishing civilian concerns from military ones. Thomas was not one to allow subordinates, particularly commissioned officers, to flout orders, and justified his position for the good of the discipline of the service as well as for the results he hoped to achieve by issuing his orders. The fact remained that in this conflict he was going to find his priorities and policies challenged, and the nature and necessities of the war expanded, from the beginning of the war.

Thomas had the chance to test his theories concerning Southern determination on June 12 when a circular emanating from Chambersburg, Pennsylvania, instructed him to march his command to Williamsport and encamp there. "He will hold Williamsport and protect the ford by artillery."[78] He used the time to prepare his men in every facet to assume their responsibilities. Thomas understood the importance of topography and had maps created that indicated meticulously features of all types for reference. For instance, one of his maps for the Martinsburg, Virginia, area identified not only roads and farmhouses, but "high ground" and "cleared" fields. Should an advance occur, it was best to know the circumstances that one would face in the best sense that was possible. As historian Thomas Buell explained, it was this kind of "attention to detail" that made George Thomas successful as a field commander.[79]

By the end of June, the command of General Robert Patterson was ready to shake itself into motion and cross the Potomac River. William T. Sherman remembered visiting his brother, then acting as a volunteer staffer, and watching as the first troops moved through the "waist-deep" water into Virginia. "My friend and classmate, George H. Thomas, was there, in command of a brigade in the leading division."[80] On July 2, Colonel Thomas proceeded with his brigade on the road from Williamsport, Maryland, toward Martinsburg, Virginia (later West Virginia). The column was pushing ahead when Confederate resistance emerged from a timbered area alongside the road. Artillery aided the Southern effort and forced the Federals to deploy in response.

Thomas's brigade occupied a position behind that of J. J. Abercrombie's, which veered to the right-hand side of the road. Thomas shifted his command to the left and brought his own battery into action against their Confederate counterparts. The advantage turned to the men in blue as the Federal forces managed to reach the Southern right flank, compelling the Confederates to retreat. Thomas's men, along with Abercrombie's, took up the pursuit, which carried over a distance of several miles.[81]

During the action, the old artillerist could not resist making his way over to the point where Lieutenant D. D. Perkins was working his pieces. The tubes had swerved "through several fields" looking for a vantage point against their opponents, but changing circumstances required new positioning. Thomas rode over in part to order the unit back into the road in pursuit of the broken foe. Not much farther, Perkins nearly captured a couple of Confederate officers who had ridden forward without realizing that the approaching forces were Union. A timely discovery and the lack of small arms for the artillerists saved these Southerners from the ignominy of becoming prisoners, but the lieutenant soon had his command hurling rounds of canister and spherical case after them for good measure.[82]

In textbook fashion, Thomas retained a force of cavalry to facilitate the pursuit, but he learned that on this field, as he had experienced in Florida and in the West against Native American opponents, and in Mexico against his adversaries there, not everything would go according to the book. "I hoped that I might have an opportunity of charging the enemy after the retreat commenced," he noted in his after-action report, "but no such opportunity was offered, on account of the broken and wooded nature of the country over which we had to operate." Thomas knew as well as anyone the foolishness of breaking down horses over such terrain and risking the success he had enjoyed thus far to unforeseen difficulties that should prudently be avoided. Never one to indulge himself in wasteful enterprises, Thomas recalled the men and reorganized them for more effective service when the next opportunity presented itself.

Even so, the fruits of victory included a substantial amount of camp equipage captured and destroyed, although an insufficient amount of transportation prevented the victorious troops from hauling off much of the forage the Confederates had abandoned during their hasty retreat. The commander noted the most favorable news from the operation. "There were no casualties in my brigade." But also of immense satisfaction was the knowledge that his men had performed handsomely under fire. The veteran of many prewar campaigns felt justified in exulting in the only fashion he knew. "It gives me much pleasure to say that the troops behaved with the utmost coolness and precision during the engagement."[83]

The overall commander of the Confederate forces opposing the Federals at Falling Waters or Hoke's Run was Colonel Thomas Jonathan Jackson. His report reflected his orders to determine the strength of the Federals, not to hold the ground at all hazards. Consequently, Jackson became satisfied that he had accomplished his mission, and as the Union forces began to flank his position he ordered the withdrawal. The immediate commander on the field, Colonel Harper, noted the loss of 11 men wounded and 9 missing out of the 380 men engaged. He reported the Union casualties as being "much greater" and cited "eight dead bodies of the enemy" as evidence.[84] Generally the numbers stood at 75 for the Federals and 25 for the Confederates.[85]

Thomas may not have known that another former West Point associate also was across the way. Writing his wife on June 11 from under "The Old Oak Tree," Jeb Stuart observed, "I have been so constantly in the saddle . . . for several days," although he deemed his health to be "excellent." Then, of the war news, he explained, "We turned suddenly across from that route to meet Gen. Patterson's Division crossing at Williamsport. After a long & fatiguing march my advanced scouts met those of the enemy, the latter being in much larger force 80 men to 10, nevertheless retired first & spread consternation and alarm in the enemy's camp by the news of the Va forces advancing." For this combatant at least, the action was not of as much interest as the opponent the Confederates had faced. "Old Geo H. Thomas is in command of the Cavalry of the enemy," he wrote, then offered passionately, "I would like to hang *hang* him as a traitor to his native state."[86]

In the aftermath of the success at Falling Waters, Patterson continued to determine what the best course would be for his forces to follow. At Martinsburg a council of war took place on July 9 for that purpose, in which Thomas offered a brief suggestion, attested to by the notes generated from the meeting. "Colonel Thomas: approves of a flank movement to Charlestown."[87] The Virginian wanted to maintain the initiative and thereby keep his opponents off-balance and on the defensive, but thought that Union purposes could be served best by maneuver rather than pushing ahead on a more direct line solely for the sake of the appearance of aggression.

Thomas was still in Maryland on August 25 when he responded to queries about the recent campaign from one of Patterson's staff officers. The commander had taken criticism for allowing Confederate troops under Joseph Johnston to slip out of the Shenandoah Valley and reinforce other Southerners in the vicinity of the little rail town of Manassas. The Confederates had won the great battle that resulted on July 21 and established the fame and provided the nickname "Stonewall" for the Thomas J. Jackson that George Thomas had so recently and successfully confronted at Falling Waters. For his inability to contain or react appropriately to Johnston's movements, Patterson subsequently gave way in command to Nathaniel Banks. Thomas's suggestion on the matter was that his chief should state the facts, supporting them with documentation, "and demand justice" from the government. He advised that if no such justice was forthcoming, he would, if in Patterson's place, insist on a court of inquiry into the matter. Interestingly, the Virginian also recognized that the appetite for placing blame had diminished somewhat over the time that had elapsed since the campaign and concluded in a revealing postscript, "I think, however, that time will set the general all right, as I see the papers are much more favorable to him than at first."[88] As things turned out, there was no inquiry and Patterson faded from the scene, while the Virginian soon transferred to another location to win laurels of his own.

In August 1864, while situated near Atlanta, Georgia, Thomas had occasion to revisit the earliest of his campaigns with his old chief. "In the council of war, at Martinsburg, I in substance advised an advance toward Winchester, at least as far as Bunker Hill," he recalled. Patterson then would have been in a position to react accordingly to whatever move Joseph Johnston chose to make. The only factor that had given him pause, as he reflected on those days, was the nature of the Union command itself. "They were all, with the exception of the Second U.S. Cavalry and two batteries of the regular artillery, three months men," with a term of service that was due to expire "in a few days." Thomas had seen volunteers in action in Mexico and watched them carefully in this opening campaign. "Judging of them as of other volunteer troops, had I been their commander, I should not have been willing to risk them in a heavy battle."

Thomas considered his superior's management of the campaign "able and judicious," especially given the difficult circumstances under which he had operated.[89] By the point he was writing in retrospect the soldiers were combat veterans, but Patterson had not enjoyed that luxury at the time. Thomas, in the words of one comrade, "saw no material in the peace parade contingent" of the ninety-day wonders of the summer of 1861.[90]

In the whirlwind of those months, George Thomas had watched the unraveling of the union he had committed to protect with the studied emotion that characterized him. His precise point of determining finally to remain with the United States service was not likely tied to a specific moment, but was made certain by the outbreak of hostilities between the contending parties. In the volatile days of early 1861, Thomas demonstrated important traits as he became engaged in the largest conflict in which he had ever participated. A display of his logistical and administrative skills became evident immediately as he undertook the challenge of preparing his command for the potential of hostilities. His diplomatic abilities proved useful in diffusing tension and distrust among his officers. Similarly, his steadiness and unflappability in the emerging crisis reminded subordinates and superiors alike that duty came foremost for him. Thomas had experienced combat previously in places as varied as Florida and Mexico, but this time the fighting was against fellow countrymen, some of whom had formerly served alongside him in those earlier conflicts. Whatever doubts some might have harbored about his loyalty, the Virginian demonstrated that he would lead troops onto his native soil and play his part in opposing rebellion against the Union. In the great national turmoil, George Henry Thomas was now more committed than ever to the flag under which he had served for his entire professional career and the government he had obligated himself faithfully to support and defend.

7   Keeping the Blue in the Bluegrass (August 1861–January 1862)

"Damn this speech making. I won't speak."
—George Thomas at Camp Dick Robinson

"Hang it Fry, I never once thought of it."
—Thomas to Speed Fry at Mill Springs, January 1862

George Thomas was not always blessed with the finest sense of timing. As he made his way westward, he was not able to reach Louisville before a powerful group of Union generals, Bluegrass officials, and Tennessee refugees convened to assess the state of affairs in Kentucky. Among the attendees at the session were Generals Robert Anderson and William T. Sherman, as well as the U.S. senator from Tennessee, Andrew Johnson. Thomas's presence may not have offered assurances of his loyalty and devotion to everyone who was there, but it might have allowed him to assuage any concerns and interject his positions on the subjects under discussion.[1]

Thomas's Southern roots provided some basis for skepticism among those who did not know him well. But he did not let any doubts cloud his determination to do his duty as he saw it. Historian Larry Daniel has concluded of Thomas at this time, "The loyal Virginian took the criticism stoically, but the fact remained that, despite his competency, Thomas remained largely unproven and highly unpopular in some influential political circles."[2]

Thomas had friends who could prove helpful to him, even if he did not actively cultivate their assistance. One of these was the man who would be tapped to command the Department of the Cumberland, General Robert Anderson. The "Hero of Fort Sumter" had already identified William T. Sherman, a former subordinate at Fort Moultrie, as critical to his success in the field. To his wife, Anderson noted confidently, "The Prest. has consented to let me have Brig. Genl. Sherman as my right hand man. He will relieve me of a great deal of the care of arranging & organizing my Dept."[3] In his *Memoirs* Sherman indicated that about the middle of the month of August Anderson asked to see him. The men met in the famous Willard's Hotel in Washington, D.C., and exchanged views about the new command. Anderson wanted individuals with him who were familiar and whom he could trust. His other preferences, in addition to Sherman, included George H. Thomas.

The next day the men took their case to President Lincoln for his approval. Apparently, Thomas was one of the sticking points in the conversation, with the chief executive concerned about the trustworthiness of the Virginian,

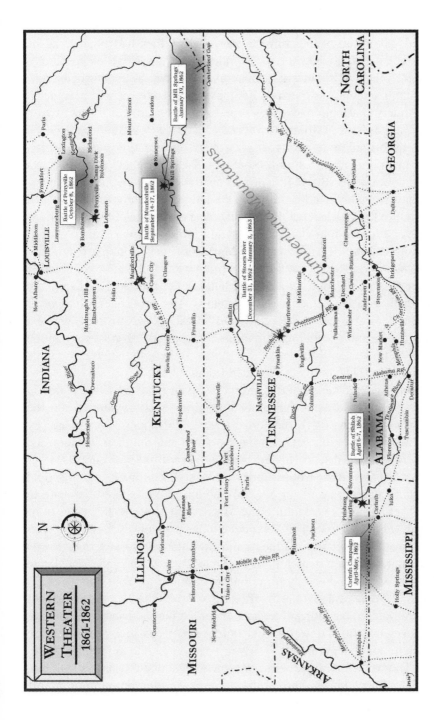

The Western Theater of the Civil War provided the platform for Thomas and his commands in the military operations of 1861–1862. © Mark W. Johnson.

knowing that so many other native-born Southerners had not chosen to remain faithful to the Union. Sherman was convinced—in part, he explained, as a result of the conversation in which they had engaged at the time of Patterson's movement into Virginia—and the assurance appeared to assuage the president's concerns.[4] General Orders No. 57 established a new department to encompass much of Kentucky and Tennessee and designated Robert Anderson as commander.[5] A series of announcements followed with the appointments of William T. Sherman, Don Carlos Buell, and G. H. Thomas as brigadier generals under Anderson.[6] In this new capacity, Thomas quickly confronted issues that would have strained even the most composed personality. But before he was done with the Bluegrass Commonwealth he had established a military reputation for effective service and helped to turn the Confederate flank in its most crucial theater of operations by virtue of a resounding victory against an aggressive opponent.

From his "Camp near Hyattstown, Maryland," the Virginian paused on August 26, 1861, to write a short but heartfelt reply to his new commander to express his appreciation for his "kind letter of the 19th inst. enclosing my appointment as a Brig. Genl. of volunteers." The subsequent display of emotion was as effusive as Thomas could be. "It will give me the greatest pleasure to be under your command," he asserted. "I was very much gratified to find from your letter that I was to be associated with Genls Sherman & Burnside, both old & valued friends."[7]

Kentucky was indicative of the amorphous state of affairs in the nation in the late summer and early fall of 1861. Following Fort Sumter and the second wave of secession by the border states of the upper South, Kentucky held a "neutral" position between the Northern and Southern antagonists. Martial activities had to be muted, although recruitment occurred within Kentucky borders, until troops under the overall command of Episcopal bishop and Confederate major general Leonidas Polk entered the state to occupy high ground overlooking the Mississippi River in the vicinity of Columbus. Polk's incursion on September 3 opened the way for corresponding Union movement into Paducah and Smithland, two key river towns situated on the northern border along the Ohio River. Union and Confederate leaders now scrambled openly for optimum positions for their commands.

General Thomas's departure for Kentucky represented a commitment of duty to the soldier, but entailed a sacrifice for the husband and wife. George and Frances had little time together before the necessities of the service thrust them apart geographically. Even years after her husband's death, Frances Thomas recalled the sense of separation she felt as orders sent him to Carlisle Barracks in April 1861 to oversee the remounting of his command. For the next three and a half years the couple largely remained apart from each other. The lone exception came at New Haven, Connecticut, as Thomas made ready to "report to Genl. Anderson at Louisville."[8] Despite the lengthy separation, both focused on honoring the demands that marriage and warfare imposed upon them with a commendable sense of fortitude and self-denial.

Anderson had selected Thomas partially upon the recommendation of those who vouched for him. Now the Kentucky-born defender of Fort Sumter turned to Thomas to accomplish a vital task. From the newly established headquarters at Louisville, he released Special Orders No. 3 on September 10, dispatching Thomas to take command of a brigade organizing at a camp located on land owned by a proud Unionist farmer named Richard Robinson, in Central Kentucky.[9]

Camp Dick Robinson had been under the supervision of a barrel-chested and contentious naval officer named William Nelson. As of September 15, 1861, it became Thomas's responsibility, and he quickly assessed that there was much work to be done with regard to his new assignment. The initial mission was to raise recruits and prepare those newly minted soldiers to take the war to the enemy.

General Thomas found that upon his arrival at Camp Dick Robinson on September 15 he would be under no shortage of advice from seemingly every corner. From Frankfort, the speakers of the House and Senate of Kentucky dashed off a communication that the Virginian must have found at once annoying and amusing. The politicians suggested the manner in which he should operate with regard to security and called upon him to meet with a delegation from the legislature before he did anything else.[10]

Another similar communication came out of Berry, Kentucky, with Thomas the recipient of extensive views on the dispositions of his forces.[11] Then, two days later, a third party explained, "Not being possessed of the future military plans of the United States Government, I am not prepared to offer you any views that even I myself would consider to be entitled to any reflection," and the writer proceeded to provide his viewpoint anyway.[12] The implication was that in the chaotic state of affairs that prevailed for the moment in Kentucky, the professionally trained Thomas would need all of the assistance these civilian leaders could provide, and they were only too happy to oblige. The difficulty for him was the need to balance their imperatives with his, or at least appear to do so. George Thomas was not one to do very much for appearance's sake alone.

An account from a contemporary noted the difficulties the Virginian faced in his new responsibility with a command "not half equipped" and a scarcity of staff officers to implement any changes, but concluded that Thomas was a better one than Nelson to get the work done. His boisterous predecessor had alienated many, including key political constituencies, a situation that the more soft-spoken Thomas might be able to avoid. "More patient than Nelson," the writer explained, "he was yet greatly tried by the importunities of the East Tennessee troops, and of the prominent politicians from that region, who made his camp their rendezvous, as well as by military suggestions from civilians more zealous than was wise in such matters."[13]

The requirements that demanded Thomas's attentions indeed had to be prioritized, but the Virginian was going to do so in his own manner. A staff officer who had worked with Nelson on recruiting recalled that when Thomas first appeared at the camp, he was confronted with a "crowd of half-clad, undisciplined men and boys gathered from every walk of life" that would have to be molded "into an army of fighting men." These would-be soldiers came from across the spectrum of society, but many of them "had been reared in the mountains of Kentucky and Tennessee, [and were] ignorant, uncouth, and independent of control." Even so, as the writer went on to recount, they were also the stuff from which an army could be made. "To us came Thomas," he explained, "to mould, to guide, to instruct, to form from this unpromising material a body of disciplined soldiers of which the nation may well be proud."[14]

Thomas ever afterward attributed his renown to his men. "I made my army and my army made my success," he explained succinctly to an inquisitive comrade. "I learned at an early day that a good army with a poor commander was better than a good general with poor men." Consequently, he noted, "I took my commission as an order to find an army, and I began from the first to organize, drill and discipline the men upon whom after all falls the real work of the war." Fortunately, the Virginian felt confident from the outset, considering even these rawest of volunteers, "splendid material, quick to learn and ready to obey."[15] On another occasion he used the same descriptor for the troops, before adding that "the rawest recruit becomes an efficient soldier in thirty days."[16]

Thomas's greatest task would be to win the men's confidence, and he knew that high expectations and rigorous demands, without seeming to be arbitrary or pettifogging, were the answer. He was convinced he could create such a force, given the time to do so, and set out at once to prepare the command for the supreme test of combat. A later scholar maintained, "He was inclined to distrust volunteers and he was very stiff about matters of training."[17] Shortcuts would not do.

The challenge of shaping an army would indeed prove to be a formidable one. Virtually every conceivable obstacle seemed to confront Thomas as he took stock. The general knew that he could not wait while all of the paperwork got sorted out, so he took immediate steps to provide his men with desperately needed supplies. A lack of officers to train the citizens and turn them into soldiers beset the command and complicated Thomas's efforts.

When the Virginian communicated with his superior in Louisville concerning the shortages he faced, Anderson understood the circumstances well himself. "I regret that you have not been able to get staff officers," Anderson offered sympathetically, assuring his subordinate that he was "in the same condition." Indeed, the situation might become worse before it could get better as the Confederate incursion into Kentucky held out the tantalizing possibility that the Union cause might be inundated with anxious recruits. "I hope that the Kentuckians will rally now rapidly and in strength," Anderson observed optimistically.[18]

Thomas was certainly not working to create an entourage of sycophants for himself in his search for staff officers. He simply wanted sufficient administrative support for bringing Camp Dick Robinson under some semblance of order and control. As he witnessed the earliest recruits fumble with their attempts to perform the most basic functions, his inquiries toward them took on a similar simplicity. To those who planned to join the mounted service, he asked, "Can you ride?"

In his interactions with his young staff members there was also to be no favoritism or special treatment. Lieutenant Thomas Anderson, the nephew of Thomas's superior, became so flustered by the threat of one disgruntled recruit to shoot up the camp that he hastened to his commander for instructions. A laconic Thomas maintained his gaze out of the window as the officer blurted out his story, before replying, "In the last resort death." The perplexed lieutenant received no further guidance, as Thomas intended him to handle the matter using his own wits. When later confronted with a different situation, Anderson benefited from the difficult lesson he had received and demonstrated enough self-confidence to act without troubling his commander a second time. Thomas must have gotten word of the incident, which related to the presence of unauthorized whiskey, and sent for the subordinate. The officer recounted the incident, and his superior validated his personal initiative. "Well, I am glad you did not come to ask this time what you should do."[19] One of the individuals who watched such developments unfold complained in a letter home, "It would astonish you to see the Volunteer officers," and concluded that they did little more than "bother the life out of the general."[20]

Later critics would suggest that Thomas came to enjoy the comforts and amenities of camp life often available to general officers. If that were to be the case someday, there was no evidence of such lavish behavior in Kentucky. Thomas biographer Francis McKinney observed, "There are no records of grand reviews at Dick Robinson, no requisitions for white gloves or paper collars." McKinney concluded that the lack of extravagances indicated that Thomas "did not believe that his commission gave him an army or invested him with any more than the symbols of command," but the general undoubtedly realized that with funds so tight wasteful expenditures would not constitute a furtherance of his duty to prepare the command.[21] Thomas experienced at least one uncomfortable moment when he had to back some of his requisitions with a bank draft to cover costs of items already procured.[22]

Of course, Thomas was not making any purchases for himself. Indeed, when he had first arrived at Camp Dick Robinson, his coat continued to bear the insignia of a lesser rank. A contemporary recalled, "He still wore his colonel's uniform with the buff shoulder-straps of a colonel of cavalry."[23] Apparently, this tendency followed him throughout his career, fed by a sense of frugality as well as general humility. One student of the general insisted that Thomas "hated new clothes, and when his promotions began to come faster than he could wear out his uniforms, he was always one uniform behind."[24]

Undoubtedly unconcerned with appearance for its own sake, the Virginian remained focused on the work at hand. He called upon his past experience for more than a choice of wardrobe. As cavalry instructor at West Point, and with active mounted service to bolster his resume, Thomas set out to create a force of such troops by selecting men with equestrian aptitude. He gathered these horsemen together, formed a cavalry regiment, and kept a close watch on their progress.[25]

During the period General Thomas did not overlook details that might easily have been left to others. His was hardly a desire to micromanage or a symbol of distrust in those below him, but an example of his consummate attention to the preparations with which he had been charged. Consistent drill and constant inspection would bring the command into an acceptable state. Besides, with a shortage of staff officers many of the duties others might have performed fell his way by default.

Even as he scraped together a staff, he spent a great deal of his time teaching them how to perform their tasks efficiently. One of the Virginian's lieutenants in this period remembered, "He was as respectful, and in all regards as attentive, to a remark made by a subordinate as to General Anderson or General Sherman, both of whom visited our camp." Thomas exhibited a patience that was astounding to this young man, who also noted that the commanding officer "wasted no time in complaints nor useless upbraidings." For this forbearance, the junior officers gave him genuine affection. "All his staff officers were young men, whose hearts were easily won by kindness and appreciation of the difficulties surrounding them, and step by step the process went on."[26] One writer later praised General Thomas's power "to attract and retain the devoted loyalty of [his] men."[27] A future staff officer, Gates Thruston, also thought that Thomas's penchant for attentiveness paid off for him in his relationships with his subordinates. "He also always gave a willing and patient consideration to every case or question brought before him."[28]

Thoroughness and versatility were tremendous assets to add to patience and professionalism in these early days. Thomas would need all of these qualities as Camp Dick Robinson evolved rapidly. According to one contemporary, he soon "covered the fields for miles around with squads of men engaged in company drill." For a time the Virginian must have imagined summer encampment again at West Point and then blended that thought with his role as instructor; he could now be found seemingly everywhere. "He attended [the] dress parade of each regiment, inspected clothing, arms, and accoutrements." Then, Thomas's methodical approach began paying dividends. "On every side the signs of improvement were visible. It began to be apparent that military life meant something more than for men to come together and be fed and clothed, waiting for an opportunity to shoot at a crowd of rebels in battle." Indeed, Thomas was ensuring that if they had to confront an enemy in combat they might have a greater chance for personal survival and collective success.[29] One of the first orders he gave one of his field commanders mirrored this focus on adequate preparation. Among the items Thomas set for Colonel Theophilus T. Garrard to accomplish was to "commence drilling" his command, "which must be continued until the men are perfect in drill as much as possible."[30]

On September 21, Thomas expressed a sense of satisfaction with the progress he had already begun to make in the mass of humanity that confronted him. "I am beginning to work some order out of the confusion which I found existed in every part of the camp when I arrived."[31] But Thomas was also genuinely concerned about security, as well as preparation. He instructed Colonel Garrard to "take up a strong position [in] the Rockcastle Hills on the road from this place to London & fortify so as to enable you to defend yourself against any force that may come to attack you." Such defenses were to have priority over the building of winter quarters. "I also wish you to get all the information you can of the enemies movements and report to me from time to time, sending at once, however, when anything of importance occurs." Finally, to decrease the likelihood that intelligence would pass to the Southerners, Thomas suggested that Garrard exercise diligence in guarding the roads. "Be careful to stop all persons who wish to go to London unless you know who they are—perhaps it would be best to station a party at the ford so as to keep all strangers out of your camp. It is important that you conceal your exact condition as much as possible."[32]

Security would be a difficult, if not impossible, task, since Camp Dick Robinson also attracted more than its share of observers. Part of the usual process for stirring a sense of patriotism among civilians resided with long-winded politicians and oratorically gifted generals. Such rhetoric rendered the atmosphere less martial than a professional like Thomas could tolerate easily. Yet, the thought of imposing himself upon the festivities, particularly in the presence of civilian visitors who expected to see and be able to participate in such pageantry, caused the Virginian no small amount of angst. The general also understood that he had no obligation to engage in such activities himself, much less subject himself to the circus. So Thomas quietly excused himself and returned impatiently to his office, where he waited for the procession of speakers to conclude the unhappy business.

An unseen staff officer working quietly in a corner watched as his commander paced "up and down the floor in growing irritation." Thomas was particularly chagrined to hear the cry suddenly lifted for him to come forward and offer his comments to the anxious crowd. He would have none of it. "Damn this speech making," Thomas growled. "I won't speak." Then, as if to emphasize the sentiment to himself, he inquired rhetorically, "What does a man want to make a speech for?" The reaction was vintage George Thomas. He would submit to virtually anything in the name of service to his country, but frivolous speeches were another matter. As one contemporary put it in an understated fashion, "The speech-making of distinguished visitors became a burden to him."[33]

Historian Larry Daniel has speculated that Thomas's strong reaction came as a result of his contempt for the East Tennessee politicians who arrived in his camp to offer the men these stirring speeches. He argued that Thomas "now hated the East Tennessee politicians, a fact that he made no pretense of hiding," as the reason for the vehement response he had toward them. Certainly the Virginian could seethe beneath a stolid exterior, but his uncharacteristic outburst would not have been different had the visitors been more acceptable to their host. He had work to do, and the distraction was not only unnecessary but personally unsettling to a man who had no craving for the limelight.[34]

There was an unmistakable sense of urgency in these early days of the war in Kentucky as well as among the Unionists of East Tennessee. Perhaps none felt it as clearly as President Abraham Lincoln, who insisted to a friend in a "private & confidential" communication, "I think to lose Kentucky is nearly the same as to lose the whole game." Citing the potential of failing to retain Missouri and possibly Maryland if Kentucky slipped from the national grasp, Lincoln pondered the worst. "These all against us," he concluded, "and the job on our hands is too large for us."[35] Of course, the job on George Thomas's hands was the requirement of converting raw volunteers into soldiers capable of holding Kentucky in the Union.

Much of the work Thomas was doing was meant to be instructive to the men he was trying to turn into soldiers. But, as one of the staff officers who worked with him at this stage observed, the lessons could prove beneficial to the commander as well. "The schooling that we were receiving at the hands of the master was not without its effect upon himself. If he was the first trained soldier we had seen, so was ours the first volunteer camp of instruction which he had been assigned to command." To this officer, Thomas "was studying human nature from a new standpoint, and mastering the subject."[36] Of course, the Virginian had been exposed to volunteers while serving under Zachary Taylor in Mexico, but these men were now his responsibility.

At the same time, the Virginian had a number of other changes to consider as well. On October 8, 1861, General Orders No. 7 related the news that Robert Anderson had stepped aside and would be replaced by William Tecumseh Sherman, Thomas's old roommate from West Point.[37] Historian Larry Daniel assessed the replacement of Anderson with Sherman as offering little hope for improvement since it meant elevating "an officer as psychologically unprepared for the post as his predecessor."[38] Furthermore, the fog of war was descending upon Central Kentucky in a manner that almost derailed a Federal advance into East Tennessee before it had a chance to start.

On October 11, Andrew Johnson brought Thomas a communication from Ormsby Mitchel to the effect that the War Department had ordered that officer to proceed to Camp Dick Robinson to supervise an "onward movement" into East Tennessee, effectively replacing Thomas. The Virginian considered resignation, but in the meantime contented himself with a letter to General Mitchel in which he revealed a complex set of emotions. "I have been doing all in my power to prepare the troops for a move on Cumberland Ford and to seize the Tennessee and Virginia Railroad," Thomas explained dutifully, "and shall continue to do all I can to assist you until your arrival here; but justice to myself requires that I ask to be relieved from duty with these troops, since the Secretary has thought it necessary to supersede me in the command, without, as I conceive, any just cause for doing so." There were ample reasons for the pace of operations and planning, not the least of which was lack of financial support. "I have also been very much embarrassed in my operations from the want of funds, not having received any since my arrival here, nearly a month ago," he observed by way of explaining the situation that his successor would find himself entering shortly.[39] Clearly, the "embarrassment" that Thomas mentioned was the government's responsibility, but its ramifications would fall, as they always did, on the commander and the troops in the field. A later historian's assessment projected, "In truth, the Virginian had been the one bright spot in an otherwise gloomy picture."[40]

George Thomas's willingness to lay his positions bare, even in well-crafted communications such as this one, could leave him vulnerable to unscrupulous individuals who sought to embarrass him in a different sense of that word. In any event, he could not help himself. He felt aggrieved, yet without any personal animosity toward any individual who would benefit from the injustice done him, or enough against the system of which he was a part to separate himself from it. His actions were based not upon his loyalty or disloyalty to the North or South, but on his single-minded adherence to duty above all else. If one suffered, one persevered to the best of one's ability. One did one's duty.

Favorable biographers and friends of the general have sought to elevate Thomas to the level of "American patriot" for his actions in the face of such expressions.[41] Even so, his old commander Robert Patterson captured Thomas's personality well when he observed that whereas "most men in the army have two reputations,—one which exists among their brother-officers, the other that by which they are known to the public at large," the Virginian was the rare figure in which "the two coincide."[42] One of his men in Kentucky forwarded a similar view of the ways in which the Virginian differed from other officers at this stage in the war. "General Thomas is—in contrast to so many, so stiff, dandified higher officers—very ordinary and conducts himself very nicely towards everyone."[43] Thomas would likely have been amused that some wished to see so much in him and read so much into his words. He was a soldier, and that fact dictated above all other considerations, even when he was sorely tempted to remain angry at the illogical positions others frequently took with regard to him.

Closer to the mark was the assessment biographer Wilbur Thomas offered that the incident and George Thomas's response to it illustrated a tendency in the general to behave according to his character. "His objection is proof positive that he had a keen sense of justice, that he had the courage to stand up to anyone in protest when he deemed his rights were violated, and that he had the utmost confidence in his ability to exercise command independently, despite the arguments of some that he shrank from responsibility."[44]

In the volatile and chaotic setting of Kentucky, Thomas had every reason to believe that he was being superseded at Camp Dick Robinson for reasons beyond his control. The incident seemed to have remained with him, adding to the general disdain for political machination that already existed within him. Nevertheless, duty precluded rash personal defense in the matter. He would absorb the blow and press on until a suitable moment arrived to address the issue. Even so, Thomas was sensitive to the situation and clearly did not either ignore what he saw happening or sacrifice his feelings entirely regarding it. The Mitchel reassignment failed to materialize and Thomas remained in command, but the lessons of the incident were significant. Political interference could occur at any moment and alter the ability of the commander to exercise his duties and implement directives, regardless of his intentions and abilities.

Thomas's counterpart in the region, fiery newspaper editor and now Confederate brigadier general Felix Zollicoffer, labored under many of the same constraints. His arrival in the department came with explicit directives from Adjutant and Inspector General Samuel Cooper to "Preserve peace, protect the railroad, and repel invasion."[45] Zollicoffer had reason to worry, not only about the Federal forces to his front under Thomas, but also about threats by Unionists to his rear. In August, Reverend William Blount Carter had made his way out of East Tennessee into Union territory. He approached everyone who would listen with an extraordinary idea: why not cripple the Confederate infrastructure in the region he had just left by damaging or destroying nine bridges on the East Tennessee and Virginia Railroad? With the diversion thus created, a force of Union troops could march into and occupy the area, liberating the Unionist citizens and impairing the major rail line that connected Virginia with the Deep South states of the Confederacy. Even with the administration's blessing and an undetermined amount of money, it was the possibility of an accompanying invasion by Federal troops that held out the greatest promise for success in the bold enterprise.

George Thomas was enthused. On September 30, 1861, from his headquarters in a commandeered tavern at Camp Dick Robinson, he wrote George B. McClellan in Virginia to broach the subject with him of an invasion of East Tennessee and obtain his support for it. "I have just had a conversation with Mr. W. B. Carter, of Tennessee," he explained, "on the object of the destruction of the Grand Trunk Railroad through that State." For a man usually devoid of hyperbole, General Thomas concluded enthusiastically, "It would be one of the most important services that could be done for the country."[46]

In the meantime, the Confederates were unwilling to concede the initiative in Kentucky to their opponents in blue. Hoping to establish a presence and challenge the Union foothold in the region, Felix Zollicoffer advanced through southeastern Kentucky. On October 16, after having pushed his way tentatively through the area of Barbourville, where he defeated and dispersed a small Unionist force gathered there at an aptly named Camp Andy Johnson, Zollicoffer contemplated a bolder move. Using the Wilderness Road as the main avenue of advance, he planned to strike Union forces located at Camp Wildcat in the vicinity of Rockcastle Hills, between London and the Rockcastle River.

The opposing forces converged on Camp Wildcat, with Zollicoffer brushing aside Union cavalry at a crossing on the Little Rockcastle River before advancing against the main Union position. In the subsequent battle of Wild Cat Mountain, fought on October 21, 1861, the Federals under Albin Schoepf ably defended their ground against the Confederates and then hurled them back with a successful counterattack.[47] The whole affair cost the Confederates 11 killed and 42 wounded by their account. The Federals recorded having lost 4 men killed and 18 wounded while retaining the field and barring further Southern threats to the Kentucky Bluegrass.[48] Zollicoffer slipped back, but remained ensconced on the border area. The Federals followed him to London, settling there where they could guard the Wilderness Road approaches or support their own long-awaited advance into East Tennessee should it come. "Many say we lost a great victory by not pursuing the enemy," one of the officers in the engagement explained to Thomas. "It is true, if we had have known as much then as now we might have done wonders." Still, realities being what they were, the moment had slipped past. "But we expected an attack the next morning and every one was sleeping on their arms, and we never knew the enemy had left camp until near 8 o'clock."[49]

Thomas prepared to move to the scene of the fighting himself and wanted to take advantage of the momentum achieved to relocate a forward depot at Crab Orchard.[50] He probably did not hear any grumbling personally, but likely would have agreed with one assessment of the second guessing. "We have a great many here who know precisely how to manage affairs when the enemy is out of hearing," one officer recalled, "but would be as much at a loss to do so in a fight as I would be."[51] The Federals could bask in the afterglow of their firefight with the Southerners, but Zollicoffer remained as a viable opponent, and Sherman was once again developing second thoughts. By the end of the month he sent word for Thomas to keep his forces from advancing too far, and the Virginian dutifully instructed Schoepf accordingly.[52]

Active operations could not entirely demand the Virginian's attentions. In late October, Thomas complained to the new department commander that two business firms assigned responsibility for producing overcoats for the men had failed to do so. "I fear from what I can learn that they were led away from the path of common honesty by the tempting offer of the governor of Ohio."[53] Thomas would not have seen any more justification for war profiteering than he did for political meddling, especially in the face of the enemy. He planned to keep his focus as much as possible on the front. In the meantime, there was a forward movement into East Tennessee to consider. Circumstances remained dire for the Unionists and were bound only to get worse. Indeed, following another session with Thomas, William Blount Carter returned to East Tennessee, where he reported on the desperate state of affairs he had found in the region.[54]

Thomas remained anxious to go, Sherman much less so. The Ohioan had already warned his subordinate, "Don't push too far. Your line is already long and weak."[55] He was undoubtedly still concerned about an array of possibilities for disaster. Thus, Thomas only probed forward cautiously, looking to secure his supply lines while seeking instructions. "I will be glad to know whether we are to make preparations for a winter campaign or go into winter quarters," he inquired of Sherman from Crab Orchard on November 3.[56]

Sherman responded with a convoluted communication. "In the present aspect of affairs it is impossible to say how or where we shall winter," he explained somewhat nervously. "This will depend on our enemies," he added hastily before declaring, "They will not allow us to choose."[57] An overwhelming sense of impending crisis was rising to the surface and pouring itself out into the message, and it would be up to Thomas to decipher his commander's real intent. Either way, there would be no Union invasion of East Tennessee for the time being, whatever the East Tennesseans might do to encourage or pave the way for one. Unfortunately, the people behind the scenes there could have no knowledge of the alteration in Union thinking and strategy.

Historian Noel Fisher has speculated that while Carter may not have known what had transpired of the supposed invasion, he might also have proceeded with the bridge-burning operation as a means of putting pressure on Sherman, Thomas, and others to act. As it was, on November 8, the Unionists took matters into their own hands and succeeded in knocking out five of nine bridges in the region. In the aftermath of the monumental undertaking, they seemed to come out of the woodwork. Hundreds gathered in groups that frightened local Confederates. The largest assemblage brought some 1,000 Unionists out to organize themselves.[58]

Even with the developments unfolding in East Tennessee that had been meant to help open the path for the triumphant arrival of a Union force from Kentucky, the tone there was completely opposite in its effect. "If you can hold in check the enemy in that direction, is all that can be attempted," Sherman offered as one suggestion to Thomas. Of course, Thomas could "fall back," in the direction of Lexington, Kentucky. If in any event he found himself outnumbered, he must understand, "you are not bound to sacrifice the lives of your command." There was no talk of advance in any of the scenarios Sherman presented.[59]

As the commanders of the Federal forces vacillated, the initially panicked Southerners loyal to the Confederacy quickly regained their equilibrium, even in the face of numbers expanded through rumor and exaggeration. As a result, no further damage was able to be accomplished against the remaining bridges. No invasion by Federal troops meant that there was little hope of sustaining resistance against organized Confederate efforts, and those who were not killed or captured sought refuge elsewhere.

Confederate troops also began to converge on East Tennessee to confront a situation that seemed to have exploded out of control. Brigadier General

William Carroll proclaimed martial law in Knoxville, and troops spread across the region to locate and apprehend or eliminate any individuals affiliated with the uprising.[60] The situation could not help but to devolve into Unionist-hunting expeditions whose members sought to root out anyone whose politics inclined in the wrong direction.

The actions of the bridge-burners hastened Felix Zollicoffer to a conclusion that many of the opposing commanders would eventually reach concerning a "hard war" approach to the conflict. He had once been convinced that Unionists could be reached with a kinder and gentler approach, including authorizing the release of a statement in August promising, "The general in command gratified at the preservation of peace and the rapidly increasing evidences of confidence and good-will among the people of East Tennessee strictly enjoins upon those under his command the most scrupulous regard for the personal and property rights of all the inhabitants."

Now in the wake of the activities behind his lines, Zollicoffer adopted a different tactic. Unionist leaders and their followers were to be "seized," if not "pursued to extermination if possible." The most severe measures were the only appropriate ones to convince these people of their "folly." Zollicoffer concluded coldly, "They should be made to feel in their persons and their property that their hostile attitude [toward the Confederacy] promises to them nothing but destruction."[61] Two days afterward, the former newspaperman was still steaming with anger. "They should now be pursued to extermination, if possible," he declared unequivocally.[62]

Confederate secretary of war Judah Benjamin concurred. Captured bridge-burners were to be "tried summarily by drum-head court-martial, and, if found guilty, executed on the spot by hanging." Then, in a demonstration as old as the Ancient World, "their bodies [might well be left] hanging in the vicinity of the burned bridges" as moot testimony of the fate of such individuals. The secretary thought that an object lesson of this type could not fail to have a powerful deterrent effect.[63]

Such military tribunals would have their day. Courts stood in Greeneville, no doubt with the connection of Unionist Andrew Johnson in mind as well as the proximity to a burned bridge, and in Knoxville. From the proceedings, seven bridge-burners received convictions and four suffered the supreme penalty called for by Secretary Benjamin.[64] One student of the period concluded: "East Tennessee Unionists suffered greatly from Confederate repression, and they would attempt no more massive uprisings. But, Confederate oppression did not destroy the Unionist resistance." That flame had flickered briefly before being extinguished; yet it remained ready to be rekindled when the opportunity again presented itself. The Confederates would not be able to postpone the moment indefinitely, especially if the Federals under George Thomas moved into the region in force.

All the while, Thomas remained diligent in his efforts to progress the state of his forces, while maintaining his vigilance against further Confederate incursions. The Southern forces seemed less a threat than ever, with intelligence reports suggesting that they had retreated and were experiencing difficulties retaining strength.[65] He worked to solidify his positions by inspecting and improving the roads, and calling for permission to relocate supply depots to forward positions that would support his troops more efficiently and effectively. At such a point, Thomas maintained, he could be less concerned with the bridge over the Kentucky River over which supplies currently flowed, and he could move his own headquarters forward to either London or Somerset. The move would have additional benefits as well. "With my headquarters at Somerset," he observed, "I can easily seize the most favorable time for invading East Tennessee, which ought to be done this winter." All that remained were a few additional "well organized and drilled" regiments that were "prepared to take the field on their arrival."[66]

The next day, Albin Schoepf reported not only that Thomas's directives regarding road improvements "have been complied with," but that badly needed clothing had arrived for the troops, "much to their relief." Consequently, the men were "in good spirits."[67] Of course, even in relatively good spirits, patience and deliberation were not virtues in the eyes of the rank and file. Hard work and preparation could seem to pay off only if allowed to be tried on the battlefield. Soldiers were anxious to test their mettle. Recruits from East Tennessee were particularly desirous to push forward, with broad opinion supporting an advance in the direction of a home region roiling under the occupation of Southern forces.

Samuel Carter maintained a steady stream of correspondence and corresponding pressure on General Thomas to do something sooner rather than later to provide relief for the people of that area. In mid-November he had tried a positive approach, informing the Virginian, "We thank you, general, for your assurance that as soon as you can you will move towards East Tennessee. Our men and officers have entire confidence in you and shall be most happy to see you in our midst."[68] Without allowing much opportunity for that appeal to take hold, he stepped up the rhetoric. Simultaneously reporting the successes sympathetic individuals had achieved in the region by disrupting Confederate rail transportation and communications through their bridge-burning efforts, Carter declared, "The Union men are waiting with longing and anxiety for the appearance of Federal forces on the Cumberland Mountains, and all are ready to rise up in defense of the Federal Government."[69]

For the moment, even such urgent calls for relief for the East Tennessee Unionists had to be shelved as the higher echelons of departmental command once more changed hands. On November 16, Sherman sent

Thomas a brief note announcing that Don Carlos Buell had just arrived in Louisville and assumed authority.[70] The next day, the Virginian passed along the news to Carter. Although usually a stickler for military procedures, Thomas may have thought he could enhance the chances for success by offering his anxious subordinate permission to communicate directly with Buell "for instructions" if he wished.[71]

Within a matter of days, the situation reached a crisis point. Far from sharing the desire of the East Tennesseans to march into and liberate their land from the Confederate grip, General Buell preferred more conventional methods of advance at a much more deliberate pace. Hasty actions could well result in costly setbacks, to careers if not the cause itself, and consequently, Buell stressed caution above all else. Thomas, who well knew the condition of his men, was not averse to such a pace, even if he supported a move into East Tennessee personally. To Carter and his men, the difference amounted to little in the way of distinction.

Carter insisted that his men exhibited "a great dread of the Blue-grass country," at least in terms of pulling back toward the heart of it as Thomas and Buell seemed to be advocating. Indeed, they remained "most desirous of driving the rebels from East Tennessee in the quickest possible time."[72] Carter continued to work the military channels for the outcome he preferred, but he did not neglect the political ones and found a willing assistant in Congressman Horace Maynard from Tennessee.[73]

Maynard had offered considerable pressure of his own, along with Andrew Johnson, whose home lay in East Tennessee. Johnson had written directly to Thomas earlier in the month and must have been disappointed by the response, which was characteristically straightforward. "I have done all in my power to get troops and transportation and means to advance into Tennessee," Thomas explained at the beginning of November. Sherman had done likewise, but neither had been successful in pressing the case. He promised not to move any troops farther back into Kentucky, "unless ordered."

The Virginian understood the pressure. "I am inclined to think that the rumor (of a pull-back) has grown out of the feverish excitement which seems to exist in the minds of some of the regiments that if we stop for a day that no further advance is contemplated." Thomas may have been intending for Johnson to read himself in this as well, but he more likely meant exactly what he said, since his focus tended to be on things military rather than things political. In any case, he explained, "I can only say that I am doing the best that I can. Our commanding general is doing the same, and using all his influence to equip a force for the rescue of Tennessee." In the meantime, everyone was going to have to exercise patience, as trying as that might be. "In conclusion," Thomas closed methodically, "I will add that I am ready to obey orders, and earnestly hope that the troops at London will see the necessity of doing the same."[74] Historian Larry Daniel has asserted that these exchanges illustrated that "Thomas and Johnson by now hated each other."[75] But most of this intensity of feeling and expression appeared to be attributable to the extraordinary pressures both of these strongly willed men faced at the time.

Practical and reasonable as any advice might be, it would hardly assuage individuals who felt the fate of their region hanging in the balance while potential liberating forces dawdled. Supporters of a forward movement called upon Secretary of War Simon Cameron to remove officers who seemed to be recalcitrant in supporting an offensive into the region and viewed George Thomas as one of the culprits. One individual noted rather pointedly to Johnson that when it came to the Virginian, "the troops have no confidence with him." The disgruntled attorney added to his friend concerning Thomas, "I am not alone in the belief he is not in the right place."[76]

General Buell also sought to provide assurances that he understood the message being conveyed to him. In a joint communiqué with Congressman Maynard and Senator Johnson, he explained almost plaintively, "I assure you I recognize no more imperative duty and crave no higher honor than that of rescuing our loyal friends in Tennessee, whose sufferings and heroism, I think I can appreciate." As if to confirm the nature of his awareness of their concerns, Buell pointed out that he had recently "seen Colonel Carter, and hope he is satisfied of this."[77]

Thomas disdained political maneuvering in the ranks, and not just because he was not very effective at using it as a tactic in advancing himself. He felt that it undercut the army's effectiveness and undermined the war effort. On the same day he communicated with Andrew Johnson from his headquarters at Crab Orchard, Thomas dashed off a message to his subordinate, Albin Schoepf. "It is time that discontented persons should be silenced both in and out of the service," he complained. Lest there be any doubt as to the source of his references, he added hastily that he sympathized "most deeply with the Tennesseans on account of their natural anxiety to relieve their friends and families from the terrible oppression which they are now suffering; but to make the attempt to rescue them when we are not half prepared is culpable." Thomas had never been one for half measures and would certainly not advocate them in this instance. Prudence demanded adequate preparation; preparation required time. "I hope you will therefore see the necessity of dealing decidedly with such people," he concluded, "and you have my authority and orders for doing so."[78] This type of pace was a George Thomas hallmark and would remain so for the duration of the war.

Schoepf felt so strongly in conjunction with Thomas on the matter that he replied immediately, "This outside pressure has become intolerable and must be met with firmness, or the Army may as well be disbanded." Schoepf particularly complained about the newspaper reporters who lingered around camp, scrapping for every piece of information that could be obtained and frequently embellishing what they found as "expressed opinions," to the chagrin of the officers who supposedly made the remarks in the first place. Sickness plagued the troops as well, rendering any movement "imprudent" in any case for the time being.[79]

The tug-of-war represented by the various constituencies and blocs of interest continued. While in command, Sherman had to admit reluctantly that he did not have the trained troops Thomas requested available to send to him, but added that he understood the need to placate influential voices. "Mr. Maynard still presses the East Tennessee expedition," he observed, but the troops were simply not present in sufficient strength to make the operation possible. In any case, Sherman felt consolidating Federal troops would be better than dispersing them to various points. "In the mean time," he offered, "do the best you can."[80]

President Abraham Lincoln and General in Chief George B. McClellan were more susceptible to the demands made known in Washington, while Don Carlos Buell concerned himself more with the dictates of the department and localized pressure groups. Buell preferred more conventional approaches along rail lines that existed and offered better chances to support any advance with supplies and reinforcements. Central Kentucky had such an infrastructure; Eastern Kentucky did not. Thus, it seemed not only appropriate but necessary, in Buell's eyes at least, that any forward movement occur there, with a target of the Tennessee capital of Nashville.

Buell confessed as much to President Lincoln and immediately received a blistering response meant to reorder the field commander's priorities. McClellan dutifully followed suit, and Buell had no choice but to comply if he wished to retain his position. Thomas would be sent ahead, and the East Tennessee advocates' sense of relief must finally have been palpable.

Captain S. M. Mott of the Thirty-first Ohio may have represented the frustration men on the ground at Somerset were feeling about the lack of advancement when he wrote to Senator Andrew Johnson comparing Thomas to George McClellan and concluded that the Virginian seemed "never in a hurry." It particularly irked him that his commander appeared perfectly content to leave the Confederates free to roam the region scouring supplies while men who were "very willing to attack if we were permitted" remained idle.[81]

As the Union officer had understood, the Confederates had not been quiet in the region. Zollicoffer moved westward of his last foray into eastern

Kentucky, crossing the Cumberland River and establishing a strong camp in the area of Beech Grove, not far from the Union position at Somerset. This allowed the Southerners to remain a viable threat, but also left them susceptible to disaster in a defensive posture with a substantial river to their rear. Defeat could easily mean the loss of the entire force if it became trapped.

Thomas also had new responsibilities. Special Orders No. 39 designated him as commander of the First Division in the Department of the Ohio.[82] But like all subordinate commanders, he found that his hands remained tied by superiors who saw challenges on a broader scale. It was almost the end of January when Buell finally determined that Zollicoffer posed enough of a presence on the north side of the Cumberland River to require his attention. Historian Larry Daniel noted the limited aspect of Buell's intentions for the Confederates. "His plan, often misunderstood by historians, was simply to maneuver Zollicoffer back across the Cumberland River," with the implication that any means of doing so would be acceptable.[83]

Buell was now convinced that time was of the essence and that an attack must be carried out. He admonished Thomas to march accordingly, with the operation "conducted with secrecy and without any tarrying on the road."[84] In a subsequent communication Buell reiterated for effect, "the movement should be made rapidly and secretly and the blow should be vigorous and decided. There should be no delay after your arrival."[85]

Thomas started two of his brigades down the Columbia Pike on the last day of December. The indications were that the new year would see fighting, despite the typically difficult wintry conditions that often prevented active operations of any size. Volunteer aide James Scully, who would later secure a commission and assignment to Thomas's staff, explained to his wife, "I am in the same Mess with *General Thomas*. Our Mess consists of the General, the Adjutant General, two aids, Gillem & myself." As a matter of course, Thomas put the seating arrangements in order at the initial meal. "On the first day of our camping out, the General gave us our positions at table." Appropriately, the Virginian placed himself at the head and his adjutant at his right, but quickly called out, 'Come Scully, you're the oldest soldier you take my left ahead of the *Vol.* aids.'" Scully recognized that Thomas had made his choice for a reason. "I think he done it to show them that he placed me on a footing with any of them. One of his aids is 1st cousin to John C. Breckenridge."[86] Clearly, there was going to be no respecting of persons outside of that required for the efficiency of good order and military protocol. On Thomas's staff each individual would be called upon to function with their comrades regardless of former status or position.

Order would prove hard enough to maintain as all struggled through conditions that taxed men and animals alike. The column endured harassing rains that caused rivers to rise and even the better roads to deteriorate under the weight of troops and animals as they churned through the mud to rendezvous with Albin Schoepf and take on the Confederates. Thomas indicated something of the conditions while still well out along the route of march toward Somerset: "The road, which has been represented as good, is the worst I ever saw, and the recent rains have made it one continuous quagmire." What was even more troubling, indications suggested that conditions would not be improving, as the shortest route to the vicinity of the Southern forces "is represented by my scouts as much worse than the roads the command has already passed over."[87]

At the same time, the aide who had benefited from his seating arrangement at the general's table complained bitterly about the situation presented by the wintry weather. "We are in an awful predicament," James Scully observed; "it took us 3 days to come ten miles. The mud on the road is about two feet deep and nearly impassable for such a large train as we have got." The circumstances reminded him of other locations in which he had served. "I thought the Arkansas roads bad enough but this gets ahead of any I have ever seen." Even so, the men were anxious to slog through whatever might bring them closer to contact with the Confederates, and the only concern was that Zollicoffer might slip away before they could reach him and his command. "We are only 19 or 20 miles from the enemy and are afraid he will get away before we reach him as the road is so bad. The men are very cheerful notwithstanding the hardships they have gone through and are anxious to meet old Zolly so as to pay him back for all the depredations he has committed upon their homes."[88]

But if conditions made the Virginian and any of his subordinates take pause, Buell had made up his mind and insisted that the operation proceed regardless. With Thomas's communication in hand, the department commander ordered unequivocally, "It is not sufficient to hold Zollicoffer in check; he must be captured or dispersed." With the swollen Cumberland River at the Southerners' backs, Buell was quite certain that "his situation offers the opportunity of effecting the former." In any case, Thomas was to take the route to Somerset. "I am aware that the roads are in a horrible condition," Buell expressed sympathetically, but he considered corduroying the worst portions as offering the only hope for improvement in the near term. Thomas was to see that the effort "was pushed forward energetically."[89] A participant recalled the grueling nature of the work. "All along our route we had to cut down trees and saplings and make what we called 'corduroy' roads, over which the wagons, when lifted out of the [hub-deep] mud, would be placed by the soldiers."[90] It was clear from such strenuous efforts that obstacles would simply have to be surmounted or overcome.

On January 17, Scully informed his wife that the command had reached a point "5 miles from the Enemy." He explained, "We arrived at this place to day and will remain around here until the General sees fit to attack 'Zolly.' Our pickets are in sight of his. We are confident of Whipping him, as we have more men, and better equipped than he." Certainly, the staffer antici- pated a battle to occur shortly. "I suppose this will be the last letter I can send you until after the Battle. I hope to be able to send you the account of a glorious victory." Offering a succinct assessment of the limited options the Confederates faced, he observed, "Old Zolly would retreat now if he had any way of doing so, but with Thomas on one side, Shoepf on the other, and the Cumberland River in his rear he has no alternative but fight or surren- der." Scully concluded of Zollicoffer's predicament, "I think he will fight."[91]

Thomas pushed on through the mire and reached the vicinity of Logan's Cross Roads on January 18. He had an array of forces available and others on the road approaching as fast as conditions would allow. Thomas deployed the troops of the Ninth Ohio, Second Minnesota, and Tenth Indiana, supported by the First Kentucky cavalry under Frank Wolford and artillery. Schoepf rode in to confer with his commander, and the officers made further decisions concerning the disposition of Schoepf's men.

Zollicoffer's superior, Major General George B. Crittenden, had now reached the area as well. Both of the Confederate commanders were aware of the drama unfolding before them and equally cognizant of the ways that weather constrained their choices in dealing with the approaching Union forces. Crittenden dashed off a hurried message to Albert Sidney Johnston requesting a diversion if possible, but his tone was hardly encouraging. "I am threatened by a superior force of the enemy in front, and finding it impossible to cross the river, I will have to make the fight on ground I now occupy."[92]

Understandably, Crittenden may have felt that the options at his disposal were limited, but a council of war that included the belligerent Zollicoffer quickly convinced him that the best defense was attack. If Thomas were expecting more troops, as Crittenden believed, he would only grow stronger with delay. Better to take the risk and trust in boldness to cover weakness. Seizing the initiative was a time-honored method of offsetting other disadvantages.

Having resolved his course of action, Crittenden turned to Zollicoffer to lead a mixed force of men into the darkness of a dreary night. Brigadier General William H. Carroll, the other attendee at the session, would follow with a second wave of Confederates, while a reserve held the fortified camp at Beech Grove pending the outcome of the expected engagement. Rain set in to make conditions more difficult for the Southerners as they groped toward the Union positions. Crittenden would later report that the rain had a dampening effect on the Southerners in another crucial manner than simply adding to their physical discomfort. "Many of the men were armed with flint-lock muskets," the Confederate general wrote, "and they became soon unserviceable."[93]

Such were the conditions that prevailed in the early morning hours of January 19, 1862, when the battle of Mill Springs or Logan's Cross Roads began as the lead elements of the Confederate advance stumbled onto Union pickets.[94] "About 7 oclock this morning we were roused from our beds by the beating of the 'long roll,'" a participant noted. "Our pickets together with the Camp of the 10th Indiana regiment were attacked by the enemy in *full force*. He came out of his fortification with Eight Regiments and surprised us."[95]

Colonel Mahlon Manson, commanding the Second Brigade of Thomas's force, found that the storm of battle might not be as difficult as the ire of his superior. The officer, whom one contemporary described as "a rough, excitable, but gallant old Indianian," was doing his best to determine the nature of the enemy force he faced and the proper disposition for his troops when he rode to find Thomas and get instructions from him personally. In the turmoil of the moment, Manson lost his hat and consequently presented a disheveled appearance to his normally composed commander. Thomas barely listened to the opening statement of his subordinate when he burst out, "Damn you, sir, go back to your command and fight it." In a real sense, these were all the instructions the officer needed, and he raced back to his men to lead them into the battle.[96]

Despite the dressing down, Manson responded to the appearance of the Confederates by thrusting troops forward to oppose them. Waterlogged Mississippians and Tennesseans confronted Hoosiers, soon supported by troops from the Fourth Kentucky under Colonel Speed Fry, as the fight developed. The combatants began trading volleys as the men fanned out on either side of the road and sought to take advantage of such terrain features as they could identify. Fry's men held a central position along a fence line and overlooking a ravine through which the Confederates sought to gain their flank.

Zollicoffer had accompanied the lead elements and during the confusion of the fighting rode forward to give himself a better vantage point. He believed that the troops that he was approaching were his own, mistakenly firing into their own ranks. Unfortunately, it was he who was mistaken. The troops were members of the Fourth Kentucky. It was Union colonel Speed Fry whom he admonished to cease firing. Dressed as he was in a garment that covered his uniform and insignia, Zollicoffer gave the impression that he was a Federal. The situation might have gone undetected had one of the general's well-meaning subordinates not panicked and hastened to his side,

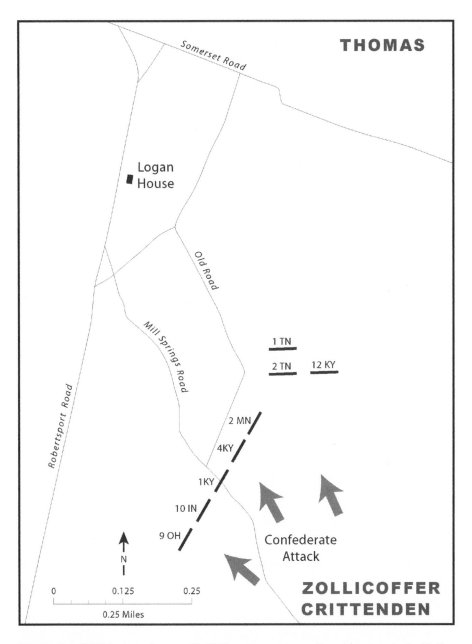

The Battle of Mill Springs, January 19, 1862, represented one of two occasions in the Civil War when Thomas decimated an opposing force, and in this instance, provided the first significant Union victory in the Western Theater. Map created by Heather Harvey.

firing at the Federal officer in front of him, while calling out, "It is the enemy, General!" Zollicoffer turned his horse, but could not pull himself clear before shots brought him down. The volley cost the messenger and another aide their lives as well.

Union staffer James Scully recalled, "The rebels fought like tigers for about an hour, during which there was an incessant roar of musketry." The nature of the fight made predicting its outcome difficult. "The 4th Kentucky, 10th Indiana & 2nd Minnesota regiments were the first in the fight, as their camps were convenient to the Battle ground, and for 20 minutes it was very doubtfull which side was gaining ground, until at length Col. [Robert L.] McCook at the head of his regiment (German) charged them with the *Bayonette*, and at the same time Col. Fry of the 4th Kentucky shot Zollicoffer through the heart killing him instantly."[97]

Yet, even with the death of their commander, the Confederates continued to fight. Indeed, the outcome of the contest remained in doubt as Thomas reached the field himself. One contemporary credited the Virginian's instinctive understanding of his men and the situation they faced for his ultimate success on this battlefield. "At Mill Spring, Thomas knew that his or any green troops were incapable of maneuvering under fire, and he determined that no attempt to make a single useless movement should mar the grand result." This was one reason for chiding Colonel Manson and ordering him to return to his command. The men would need his steady hand as an example. "Thomas told the writer that he placed himself, so to speak, like a marker on the line of battle, and saw or felt each regiment file into its proper or assigned position. Then he faced them, indicated the enemy, and bade them go in and do their duty."[98]

Thomas found the Tenth Indiana formed in front of their encampment, but unsure of their role until someone instructed them. He obliged by ordering them forward to support their comrades. He also quickly assessed that the Union left flank was in danger of being reached and scrambled to find troops to meet that crisis. The Second Minnesota advanced to the fence line from which the earlier Union defenders had withdrawn and stubbornly clung to it. Men from both sides grappled with each other without achieving advantage for either of them.

As the stalemate continued, Thomas fed other troops into the fight and brought the Union artillery into a more effective position from which to add to the amount of metal being thrown at the Southerners. Historian Thomas Buell particularly lauded the Virginian's use of his artillery arm. "Thomas knew how to use it, how to place it where it was most needed, and when and how to reposition it as situations unfolded."[99] These were the lessons of the drill range at West Point and the battlegrounds of Monterrey and Buena Vista coming back to benefit him once more.

Boldness and determination could sustain troops for just so long, as the Federals seemed to find new men to thrust into the fight at every critical juncture. Finally, the Confederates began to give way, and while a remnant sought to gain time, most broke and fled for the camp from which they had marched the previous evening. "We run them clear into their intrenchments," one of the participants recorded in a letter he would send shortly to his wife, "and kept shelling them there until it got too dark to see them, but will commence bright and early tommorrow morning." James Scully thought that Zollicoffer's death had tipped the balance, but reported happily, "the 'Secesh' mad[e] a *precipitate retreat throwing away every thing* that would impede their progress until the road was literally covered with knapsacks, Haversacks, Blankets, Arms, & every thing else that would impede their flight."[100]

A highly stylized account noted the reaction of a demoralized Southerner who insisted colloquially to his captors, "Well, we were doing pretty good fighting till old man Thomas rose up in his stirrups, and we heard him holler out: 'Attention, Creation!' 'By kingdoms right wheel!' and then we knew you had us." The colorful description concluded with a comment that surely reflected the state of mind for many of the Confederates when the retreat began, when he explained, "it was no time to carry weight."[101]

Although the field was indisputably theirs, disorder and chaos in the ranks of the victorious bluecoats prevented a more concerted pursuit. The central portion of the fighting had concluded by 10 AM, but the bulk of Thomas's men lost momentum while engaged in re-forming and receiving a fresh supply of cartridges to replace those expended in the short, but fearful, engagement. In addition to the time spent in reorganizing the units and re-plenishing ammunition, 207 wounded Federal troops had to be recovered. The loss of 14 dead and wounded officers impacted the command as well in the form of lost or diminished leadership.[102] The Union combatants spent most of the remaining daylight hours moving toward Beech Grove and the Cumberland River.

Buell's instructions had been to capture or disperse Zollicoffer's forces. In one sense the latter had already been accomplished, while the former still remained a very real possibility. By late in the afternoon, the first Union troops reached the Confederate defenses at Beech Grove. Southerners manned the works they had erected painstakingly before the attack, and the effort seemed now to be ready to pay off. Thomas moved his men to the high ground overlooking the Southern position and worked to deploy his forces for a bombardment and final assault until darkness prevented further efforts in that regard. With the benefit of a commanding position and a demoralized and defeated opponent at his fingertips, it surely appeared as if it would only be a matter of waiting until morning to accept a Confederate surrender.

But Crittenden was in no mood to capitulate, whatever the odds might be that he faced. More fortuitously, from his perspective, the Confederates had an unlikely source of salvation. The stern-wheel paddleboat *Noble Ellis* remained in the Cumberland, having reached Beech Grove earlier on January 7. The vessel had been of little meaningful assistance by itself, but now its efficacy could not be disputed. Crittenden jammed as many men as he could aboard the craft and ferried them across through the night. Although the Southerners lost some casualties to the panic that ensued in the difficult operation, most escaped the trap that Thomas believed he had laid for them. Living up to its first name in its final role, the steamer suffered the ignoble fate of being burned by the Confederates following the last debarkation of soldier refugees, to prevent it from falling into Union hands.[103]

In the midst of a heavy downpour and illuminated by lightning, the Federals awoke to complete their work with the Southern forces. Several rounds of artillery screamed toward the formidable defenses, but when these missiles prompted no response, the bluecoats moved forward gingerly, as one participant explained, "looking every moment for the rebels to open fire upon us."[104] Instead, they found that the Confederates were gone. The haste of the abandonment was so great that in some cases horses remained saddled and wagons hitched, but the soldiers themselves had scurried to the far side of the raging Cumberland River.[105]

Of course, not all of the Union troops were elated at the departure of their adversaries. Speed Fry was beside himself and wanted to know why his commander had not demanded a Confederate surrender the previous evening. Thomas had focused so thoroughly on the pursuit and establishment of a dominant position in the waning daylight that he apparently had not considered such an alternative. Rather than dodge the responsibility or assign the blame to someone else, the weather conditions that had hampered operations all day long, or the rapidly approaching nightfall on a gray and dismal afternoon, he replied simply and honestly, "Hang it Fry, I never once thought of it."[106] Such missed opportunities were the bane of any commander's existence, although Thomas did not appear to dwell on such matters.[107]

In any case, the substantial spoils of the battle and the abandoned camp remained in the hands of the Federals. Twelve pieces of Confederate artillery and their complement of limbers and caissons, 150 wagons, and over 1,000 horses and mules were now property of the United States government, along with the many other forms of camp equipage and military stores that had been left behind.[108] Among the spoils of victory was a copy of "all of General Zollicoffer's orders from the organization of his brigade until a few days before the battle."[109] Federal losses amounted to 39 killed, 207 wounded, and 15 captured or missing, for a total of 261. By contrast, the battle produced 533 casualties for the Southern forces, broken down into 125 killed, 309 wounded, and the relatively small number of 99 persons captured or missing, given the nature and scope of the defeat.[110]

Thomas broke the elements of the engagement down in his after-action report. He considered Union victory attributable to Zollicoffer's demise, observing that the Confederate leader's death "contributed materially to the discomfiture of the enemy." But stubborn fighting that included bayonet charges and artillery exchanges wore the Confederate resistance down as well. Timely reinforcements sealed the victory for the Federals, although the inability of the victorious bluecoats to decimate their opponents rankled. Despite his honesty toward Speed Fry on the field, Thomas must have been disappointed that he had failed to capture the Confederate force essentially intact. He carefully conceded that "steam and ferry boats having been burned by the enemy in their retreat, it was found impossible to cross the river and pursue them; besides their command was completely demoralized and retreated with great haste and in all directions, making their capture in any number quite doubtful if pursued." The fact was that Thomas's troops had pursued the broken Southerners, driving them not only from the field but to the original base camp from which they had set off in hopes of victory. The Virginian left unaddressed in any official capacity the opportunity that had slipped away to apply the coup de grâce. Yet, he was absolutely convinced that the success he had enjoyed had an even larger impact than the mere crushing of an enemy force. "There is no doubt but what the moral effect produced by their complete dispersion will have a more decided effect in re-establishing Union sentiments than though they had been captured," he argued.[111]

Therein lay another crucial, and debatable, factor involving George Thomas in the days following Mill Springs. Terming the Virginian "an enterprising commander," historian Steven Woodworth asserted that Thomas was effectively hamstrung. "He would have been glad to exploit his success at Mill Springs for all it was worth, but he was not allowed to." Between the difficulty of supplying troops, Buell's focus elsewhere, and subsequent Union successes in Tennessee, Thomas's moment of opportunity passed.[112] General Buell later described the battle as "at the time one of the most important that had occurred during the war . . . but the lack of transportation and the conditions of the roads rendered it impossible to follow up."[113]

Another modern historian attributed stronger emotions to the Virginian at this period, by suggesting, "Thomas would always remember the campaign with a smoldering rage."[114] This may have been true. Circumstances had certainly thwarted him, and were doing so again, but these were as much of Thomas's making as they were of anyone or anything else's. Even so, he was not one to engage in second-guessing what might have been, or lingering on missed opportunities. His focus turned to the tasks that lay ahead and the work that would have to be done to prepare his battle-weary men for it.

For Thomas, then, any additional assessment would have to wait, but for one participant the effect was immediate. "General Thomas will be highly applauded for the splendid way in which he managed this Battle," James Scully explained enthusiastically. "For the seven or eight miles that we pursued and advanced on the enemy, the line was kept up as uniform as I ever saw a drill. There was the right and left flank & centre all through without a waver, and every regiment and battery in its proper place, that one would imagine he was at a grand review instead of a Terrific battle." As for the commander's personal demeanor throughout the engagement, the witness observed that "the General was as 'Cool as a cucumber.'"[115]

Local reaction remained mixed in the immediate aftermath of the battle. One Unionist recorded testily in her diary, on Wednesday, January 22, 1862, "The secessionists will not believe a word of the late battle, but put it off by saying that Zollicoffer has whipped Thomas."[116] The next day Frances Peter noted definitively, "Our victory is more complete than we thought. Thomas is still in pursuit." Even so, her neighbors continued to persist "in saying there is no battle."[117] Finally, she concluded, "The secesh always boasted that Zollicoffer would come here and he will, but not by any means in the way they expected."[118]

General Buell was grateful for the success, coming as it did on his watch as departmental commander, but he was hardly effusive at the time. This had not been his idea until later in the process, and there had been enough anxiety with the torn-up road systems and supply shortages to dull any satisfaction success might have offered. He brought himself to report to George McClellan that Thomas had "repulsed the enemy handsomely" and had done so despite having been "on half rations for some days."[119] Several days later, General Orders No. 4b did a better job of reflecting glory on the engagement and its participants. Terming the battle "an important victory" and a "brilliant" one, the words of the announcement nevertheless took a more qualified stance when it came to assessing the outcome. "Night alone, under cover of which his [the enemy's] troops crossed the river from their intrenched camp and dispersed, prevented the capture of his entire force."[120]

The tone of the congratulatory order released by Secretary of War Edwin Stanton on behalf of President Lincoln was also unusually stilted. Once again, "brilliant victory" proved the operative phrase for describing the battle, but there was little beyond the perfunctory about the statement and nothing that could be attached personally to George Henry Thomas.[121] General Thomas had done his duty, despite questions about his loyalty, but official Washington seemed little intent upon lavishing with plaudits an individual about whom so many of its principal actors had initially harbored doubts and uncertainties.

Interestingly, the person who praised Thomas in the most unqualified fashion was the individual with whom he had previously experienced some heated communications. Congressman Horace Maynard opened with a message that must have made the general smile. "You have undoubtedly fought the great battle of the war," the politician began. "The country is still reverberating [with] the shout of victory." Maynard remained vitally concerned about liberating East Tennessee from the Confederate grip, but he was wise enough, perhaps politic enough, to offer a hand to the man who might yet be called upon to do it. As further evidence of his goodwill, the Tennessean informed the Virginian, "Yesterday the Senate confirmed your promotion as brigadier general."[122]

A contemporary who served a good portion of the war with Thomas offered the most substantial assessment of the engagement. Calling the battle "most disastrous to the enemy," Henry Cist added that it had "inflicted the most severe blow they had up to that time experienced." For Cist, an officer in and postwar historian of the Army of the Cumberland, "The victory for the Federal forces was the first complete success of the war, and was hailed everywhere with joy and hope."[123] One historian has described the victory as singularly important given its scope. "Few Civil War battles had results so disproportionate to the numbers involved," Gerald Prokopowicz explained.[124]

Thomas's response to one letter of commendation also revealed some of the sentiments and motivations that lay beneath his steady persona. When Ohio governor David Tod forwarded the state legislature's resolution on the battle, the Virginian expressed his gratitude also "for the complimentary manner in which they have approved our endeavors to reinstate the Constitution and laws over our distressed country."[125] There was no spirit of vindictiveness or triumphant preening. Duty had dictated the task at hand and moderation characterized the tone.

Still, the success he had enjoyed against Zollicoffer did not mean that Thomas was free from all setbacks at the hands of other opponents. One of these occurred when the Virginian attempted to establish more effective communications by ordering the installation of telegraph lines in the region the victory had supposedly secured. The exposure of some of the personnel tasked with carrying out the assignment proved too tempting a target for an inveterate gambler and raider named John Hunt Morgan. The Confederate horseman dashed into the region at the head of a small handpicked team of daredevils, plucking prisoners and supplies from an outpost before slipping away wearing the Union overcoats they had just procured.[126]

In the larger scheme, such efforts were little more than embarrassing nuisances. Northern victories, including Thomas's at Mill Springs or Logan's Cross Roads in Kentucky, and Ulysses Grant's at Fort Donelson in Tennessee, following the navy's capture of nearby Fort Henry, had a much greater strategic impact. When coupled with successes of Union arms on the Atlantic coast characterized by Ambrose Burnside's defeat of the defenders of Roanoke Island in North Carolina, this string of Federal victories created a compelling synergy that deeply challenged Confederate morale. The defeats were the fledgling Southern nation's stiffest tests to date, causing an early crisis of confidence and threatening to lay the foundations for further deterioration in the integrity of the Confederacy.[127] The Virginian could be pleased that he had done more than his share to cause such discomfort for the rebellion, and he was determined to continue until he had helped to bring about its final collapse.

8 A Difficult Interlude (February 1862–January 1863)

"We were classmates, intimately acquainted, had served together before in the old army, and in Kentucky, and it made to us little difference who commanded the other, provided the good cause prevailed."
—William T. Sherman on Thomas

"This army can't retreat."
"Gentlemen, I know of no place better to die than right here."
—Quotations attributed to George Thomas at Stones River at the close of the first day's fighting

George Thomas's victory at Mill Springs shattered the right end of the Confederate flank that had been meant to secure portions of Kentucky and all of Tennessee from Union incursion. It also rendered Albert Sidney Johnston's position at Bowling Green, Kentucky, untenable, causing the Southern commander to withdraw from the exposed position into Tennessee and beyond. Thomas had shifted in that direction when Johnston's decision rendered the effort moot, and the Virginian continued on to Louisville to await further orders.

The Federal cause in the Western Theater continued to flourish in the campaigns that occurred over the next several months. The Union navy subdued a token force of Confederate artillerists at Fort Henry, while Ulysses Grant won a reputation for himself when he secured the surrender of the indifferently led defenders of Fort Donelson. Johnston was now in Corinth, Mississippi, and the victorious Federals took up advanced positions near Pittsburg Landing in southern Tennessee, with additional troops posted at nearby Crump's Landing and Grant headquartered at the little village of Savannah. Thomas proceeded to Nashville by water and arrived there on March 2.[1] In the meantime, the Confederate general chose the moment to plan an audacious offensive that he hoped would surprise his opponents and recoup the ground that had been lost in western Tennessee from the earlier defeats.[2]

The troops around Nashville were planning to move toward a rendezvous with their comrades near Pittsburg Landing in mid-March. But the move became imperative when, despite almost every conceivable warning sign, the Confederates managed essentially to achieve the advantage they had sought with an early morning April 6 assault in that vicinity. Broken terrain, the confusion of battle, and increasingly stubborn Union resistance prevented the Southerners from completing the victory. Johnston's mortal wounding by his own men compounded the difficulties for the attackers and left the command to P. G. T. Beauregard. But the Federals were battered and teetering, reduced to hunkering along a line that stretched from the river at the landing.[3]

Frantic messages reached Thomas through the day on April 6, calling upon him to "Hurry forward your troops." The additional demand for him to "Bring your ammunition and three days' rations" was the signal phrase for active operations. As if the suggestion for speed were not clear enough, the staff officer who passed the orders along directed the Virginian, "Leave your baggage."[4] Thomas prepared to comply, but apparently the frenetic pace being asked for initially was not as important as the potential need for supplies once the men reached the scene of action around Pittsburg Landing. In a subsequent dispatch sent from Savannah, Tennessee, the staffer directed, "Instead of leaving your train, push forward your troops and train as rapidly as the roads will permit."[5]

During the night the vanguard of Don Carlos Buell's forces under General William "Bull" Nelson began to filter into the vicinity and, with the troops that had been at Crump's Landing under General Lew Wallace and the battered commands Grant cobbled together, managed to stabilize a defensive line. The Confederates who attempted to assault it late in the day found the position formidable and settled onto the ground they had won for the night.

The next day it was the Confederates' turn to pull back, offering such resistance as they could to buy time. In some ways the battle had been a near thing for the Federals, who suffered some 13,000 killed, wounded, and captured or missing. But it was the Southerners who staggered back to their staging ground at Corinth, having experienced almost 11,000 casualties of their own.[6] General Beauregard prepared for a defense of the rail town, knowing that the effort to drive Union forces from West Tennessee had failed.

George Thomas was still enroute when the tide turned at Shiloh. Perhaps as much to reflect the differences in style between the officers that would help to explain the subsequent estrangement between them as to illuminate the situation the Federals faced on the battlefield, one of Grant's early biographers noted an exchange between the men that was supposed to have occurred at some point on the second day of the fighting. "General, those fellows are completely demoralized," Grant presumably observed to Thomas. "Take your division and another and pursue. We can cut them to pieces and capture a great many." Thomas was reported then to have responded, "My men are completely used up. They marched all Saturday and Sunday, and have been fighting all day. If you say so, of course, they shall march, but they are hardly able to move."[7]

Any pursuit of the retreating Confederates could use all the fresh troops that could be brought to bear, but Thomas's men, regardless of their condition, were not yet on the battlefield to be directed against the beaten foe. His troops marked the rear of Buell's extended line of march. On Monday, April 7, Thomas received orders to "move your command with the utmost dispatch to the landing at Savannah, where steamboats will be waiting to transport you to this place."[8] Although the Virginian had pushed the command relentlessly to reach their embattled comrades as quickly as circumstances would allow, the troops did not arrive until after the fighting had subsided.[9]

In the aftermath of Shiloh, Henry Halleck arrived to assume command. He reconfigured his forces and shuffled personnel to suit his purposes. In the process, the overall command divided into wings, with George Thomas given responsibility for one of them. Placed under his command would be his own division and those of William T. Sherman, Thomas W. Sherman, Stephen A. Hurlbut, and Thomas A. Davies.[10] Halleck prepared to send a three-pronged thrust toward Corinth, with the Army of the Ohio under Don Carlos Buell acting as the center portion, the Army of the Mississippi under John Pope on the left, and Thomas's Army of the Tennessee on the right.[11]

Cump Sherman later observed in his *Memoirs*, "General Thomas at once assumed command of the right wing, and, until we reached Corinth, I served immediately under his command." Sherman professed not to be concerned with the assignment. "We were classmates," he observed, "intimately acquainted, had served together before in the old army, and in Kentucky, and it made to us little difference who commanded the other, provided the good cause prevailed."[12]

James Scully, the volunteer aide who had witnessed Thomas's performance at Mill Springs, was no less animated by the prospects of a new campaign, even in the aftermath of the bloodletting of Shiloh. "Genl. Halleck is now in command here," he explained to his wife on April 14, "and will move 'upon the enemy's works' at Corinth in a very few days. I believe that the next battle will be even greater than the last one."[13]

In addition to being the location of the Confederates who had so brazenly attacked at Shiloh, now under the command of General Beauregard, Corinth was an important rail junction in North Mississippi. Taking it would deprive the Southerners of the full use of the east–west running Memphis and Charleston and the north–south oriented Mobile and Ohio railroads. A victory could also open the way for operations deeper into Mississippi.

The effort consumed Halleck's energies as he sought methodically and cautiously to move his heavily augmented force of three armies toward the Confederate stronghold. Halleck hoped to capture the city through maneuver rather than combat while securing the advance in such a way as to avoid inviting an attack, and these became the overriding principles in his first, and what turned out to be only, field command. To avoid any untoward developments as the Federals drew closer to Corinth, Halleck instructed Thomas to entrench at every interval, and spadework became the order of the day for most of the men in blue.

One of the officers with Halleck wrote favorably of the strategy of "[Winfield] Scott: [George] McClellan the little-loss-as-possible method of warfare," particularly in preference to the "slaughter-pen style of conquering" exhibited earlier at Shiloh and elsewhere. Historian Stephen Ambrose noted that Halleck was drawn to the slower-paced process, as indicated by his operations against Corinth. "Careful advances, meticulous planning, and no thought of attacking the enemy," were the imperatives that drove the campaign, according to Ambrose.[14]

Years after the war, John Pope, who commanded the Army of the Mississippi, recalled that the operations around Corinth had included the names of some of the most successful generals the war would produce, including George Thomas. But his next observation was as telling. In his noting the presence of "nearly every one of the generals who attained the highest rank and won the greatest honors in the war" there was also the comment that they had been "active" participants, "if any such word as active can be applied to any of the operations around Corinth." He explained that there was "little opportunity for distinction in such military work as we then executed, except, indeed, in the amount and massiveness of the fieldworks we built at every step of our advance upon that ill-fortified village."[15]

Interestingly, the charges that would be laid at Thomas's feet in future campaigns such as Atlanta and Nashville would sound eerily similar, from Sherman's criticism that Thomas dug in whenever possible to the pressure Henry Halleck placed on the Virginian for faster-paced movement in Tennessee. Thomas had seen Halleck's version of speed at first hand and clearly did not find it repugnant to his ideas for waging war. Corinth was one of the first major campaigns in which Thomas had been a member after his success at Mill Springs. The Virginian experienced a slower, more methodical approach that must have appealed to the engineering-oriented education he had received at West Point and exacerbated his personal tendencies toward rhythmic routine and deliberate pace.

In his post-campaign report Thomas referenced the requirement on several occasions to entrench. On May 4, as the command went into motion, "Major-General Sherman's right flank being much exposed, was intrenched immediately." Twelve days later, as the troops encountered Confederate resistance, the same focus on security prevailed. "The ground [we had] taken up was strongly intrenched the same day by all the troops." On May 21, Thomas anticipated an attack that prompted his men to fortify "a strong position" with which to "receive" an assault. Although none proved forthcoming on that occasion, the soldiers had once again employed their entrenching implements fully.[16] Indeed, the proliferation of spadework led the Virginian to include a final word of praise that the men would nevertheless have found amusing, as he singled out the "cheerfulness with which labor in the trenches was performed by the officers and men."[17]

By May 30, the Federals seemed poised to battle with their foes over the fate of the Mississippi rail town. Sherman drew his forces into position and was pleased with what he saw from them in the face of the enemy. He was also satisfied that a strong performance came under the gaze of his superiors. "Generals Grant and Thomas were present during the affair, and witnessed the movement," he recorded in his post-campaign report, "which was admirably executed, all the officers and men keeping their places like real soldiers."[18]

The end came swiftly and unexpectedly. Thomas recalled, "About 5 a.m." on the thirtieth of May, he and his men picked up the sound of "several explosions being heard in the direction of Corinth." This prompted an investigation that revealed that far from moving up reinforcements, as earlier reports had indicated, the Confederates were actually pulling out of their defenses. Corinth fell anticlimactically, almost as an afterthought to the rest of the campaign.[19]

At the time, Thomas dashed off a hasty message to Halleck that announced the successful culmination of the seemingly endless Union descent upon Corinth. "The enemy commenced evacuating Tuesday night," he explained. "Their main body retreated last night." Henry Halleck, or "Old Brains," as many liked to refer to him, had worked to create the conditions for capturing the important rail junction, and it had occurred not due to a dramatic engagement, but with a whimper.

Halleck's first inclination was to secure the prize without exposing himself to some unexpected turn of events by the enemy until he was absolutely certain that no threat from the vicinity of Corinth continued to exist. "I do not wish Corinth occupied in force," he told Buell, Pope, and Thomas. Instead, each was to focus on a safe position. "General Thomas' forces, except his cavalry, will fall back to the enemy intrenchments, and hold the Corinth and Purdy road to Russellville." There was no talk in this instance of giving the retreating army no rest or pursuing with vigor, or even, apparently, of holding "in force" the town that they had worked so diligently to obtain.[20]

In the aftermath of the siege of Corinth and the conquest of the town the Virginian issued his report of the recent campaign, concluding that his men had demonstrated "their steady, energetic, and soldierly bearing on every advance [which] evinces a state of discipline, highly commendable."[21]

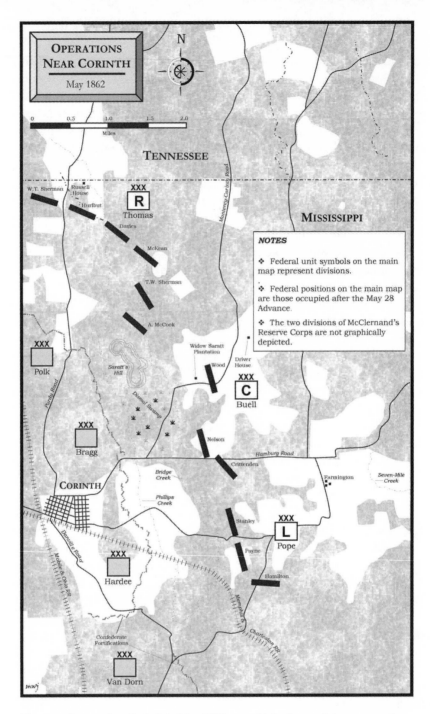

The operations against Corinth in May 1862 proved laborious and time-consuming, but ultimately successful, as Henry Halleck's forces captured the critical northern Mississippi rail junction. © Mark W. Johnson.

Thomas also held temporary command in Corinth, but this duty was not destined to be a prelude to larger levels of responsibility for him.[22] In fact, within a short period, he received very different orders. "General Thomas will resume the immediate command of his division on its arrival at Corinth."[23] The assignment had lasted but a few days before Thomas returned to his position with the Army of the Ohio's First Division, at his own request on June 22.[24]

Later, Thomas offered a brief assessment of his participation in the Corinth campaign. "Before Corinth I was intrusted with the command of the right wing of the Army of the Tennessee. I feel confident that I performed my duty patriotically and faithfully and with a reasonable amount of credit to myself. As soon as the emergency was over I was relieved and returned to the command of my old division. I went to my duties without a murmur, as I am neither ambitious nor have any political aspirations."[25]

Well after the war, as she assessed the nature of her husband's sometimes rocky relationship with Ulysses Grant, Frances Thomas offered her views on the origins of their personal difficulties. She explained that in the aftermath of the fighting at Pittsburg Landing and the subsequent advance on Corinth "Genl Thomas was placed in command of a column in Genl Grant's place [and] he wrote me that Genl Grant did not like it." Noting her husband's desire to ameliorate any bitterness on his colleague's part, "after the fall of Corinth he (Genl T) went to Genl Halleck and asked to be put back in Genl Buell's army, as he did not wish to stand in Grant's way." Even so, as far as she was concerned the damage had been done. "Genl Thomas always felt that Genl Grant *never* forgave him."[26] Of course, aside from the distance in time from these events, such an appraisal also came from an individual whose opinions were colored by circumstances in the interim as well as her relationship with one of the principal protagonists.

Be that as it may, other duties remained paramount for the Virginian at the time. His next responsibility entailed setting the men at work repairing the Memphis and Charleston Railroad and deploying them so as to protect the line from enemy raids. Thomas established his base at Tuscumbia, Alabama, but he had elements scattered from Decatur in Alabama to Iuka in Mississippi. Part of his troop dispositions included cavalry pickets at advanced locations.[27]

Early in the morning on July 3, 1862, Confederate cavalry struck suddenly at members of the First Ohio Cavalry near Russellville, Alabama. The sharp fight produced significant casualties for so small an engagement and lasted for approximately an hour and a half. In addition to the serious wounding of the Union captain, A. B. Emery, the Federals lost four others wounded and two killed. Confederate losses were difficult to ascertain, although as the Union horsemen pulled back from the ground over which the fighting had occurred they carried away at least one prisoner.[28]

The lesson was a clear one for Thomas. The distances he had to cover with limited cavalry made some of these detached parties vulnerable to such attacks. "The force of cavalry I have is too small for so extended a line as that from Iuka to Decatur," he explained.[29] Buell recognized the demands being placed on his subordinate. Indeed, the additional responsibilities regarding the railroad "detained General Thomas's division a month longer in guarding it," Buell explained, "so that division did not reach Athens and Huntsville [in Alabama] until the last of July."[30]

On the fourth of July, Thomas took time from his duties to host a celebration of the nation's declaration of independence from Great Britain. At the gathering, Brigadier General Robert McCook, of the "Fighting McCooks" from Ohio, availed himself of the opportunity to express his sentiments unabashedly toward his wayward Southern brethren. "If they will not submit reasonably," he blurted regarding the Confederates, "they must be exterminated." McCook declared that his men were ready to follow this course, "even if it means the South must be laid waste."[31] There was no record of Thomas's response. But even with the commander's scornful attitude toward such public displays of emotion, in many ways these sentiments represented the steady alteration in the outlook of many Northern soldiers toward the war and their opponents. General Thomas himself would have to confront the changing nature of war as the fighting and killing continued.

The Virginian had heard fiery rhetoric before and kept any sensitivity he might have experienced from it to himself, although he shared the opinion that his wayward Southern brethren had to be brought out of a state of rebellion. His own background and heritage had been an occasional hindrance with his Union superiors, but he was finally enjoying a heightened status in important circles. About this time, secretary of the treasury Salmon P. Chase recorded a visit with Henry Halleck, observing that he "talked a good while with him." Chase kept the conversation from becoming contentious, but took mental note of the soldier's assessments. "Judged it prudent not to say much of the war," the secretary recalled, before adding, "He spoke of Buell as slow but safe; of Grant, as a good general and brave in battle, but careless of his command. Of Thomas, he spoke very highly."[32]

Thomas had a distasteful report to make in August, when the same boisterous Brigadier General Robert L. McCook became the victim of an ambush. Thomas noted that McCook was being transported in an ambulance and had stopped at a local residence when the shooting occurred. "His regiment were very much enraged, and before they could be stopped burned and destroyed some four or five farmhouses; but Colonel [Ferdinand] Van Derveer, by great exertions, succeeded in subjecting them to discipline before night, and they are now quiet."[33] Thomas heard conflicting reports concerning the nature of the force that had been responsible for McCook's death. "I am inclined to the belief that citizens were giving assistance, but do not know who."[34] Colonel Van Derveer elaborated on the attack and the reaction of the Union troops in a report several days later.[35]

Thomas looked at such incidents and the reactions to them through the prism of his concepts of civilization and professionalism. If the famed military theorist Carl von Clausewitz could argue, "War is an act of force . . . which theoretically can have no limits." Thomas was not one to adhere to that pronouncement strictly. Civilized people imposed limits. Professionals had standards. "Reciprocal action" might lend a sense of satisfaction and send what some would deem an appropriate message to an opponent who was acting in an unacceptable fashion, but it smacked of a continuous state of escalation that represented a loss of control that was equally unacceptable to the Virginian. The case for each person would be different, even if by degrees, as the writer Michael Walzer observed. "As soon as we focus on some concrete case of military and moral decision-making, we enter a world that is governed not by abstract tendencies but by human choice."[36] At this point, and even with the provocation of what he deemed to be an act of murder, Thomas would have no truck with those who sought only to exhibit an unbridled vengeance or wanton retaliation on whoever crossed their paths.[37]

By the fall of 1862, Braxton Bragg and Edmund Kirby Smith were making provision for an invasion of Kentucky that they hoped would be met with waves of Southern sympathizers who might be induced to join the ranks. Buell was trying to anticipate and if possible counter the Confederate movements. But Thomas was fending off more than Buell's uncertainty or Bragg's likely next course of action. Andrew Johnson had once more been angling for a movement into East Tennessee and wanted Thomas to be at the head of it. The Virginian responded carefully, but definitively. He was always disdainful of appearing as if he supported machinations that would promote him at another's expense, but he was also concerned that any command he might receive had to offer him sufficient autonomy, too. "I most earnestly hope I may not be placed in that position for several reasons," he told Johnson. "One particular reason is that we have never yet had a commander of any expedition who has been allowed to work out his own policy, and it is utterly impossible for the most able General in the world to conduct a campaign with success when his hands are tied."[38] Thomas did not stipulate as to whether he considered himself "the most able General in the World," but he was convinced that he should not be in command of any army for which he did not have primary control and authority.

Thomas had an interesting, if misplaced, confidence in Buell. In the same communication with Johnson, he asserted, "I am sure that I can confidently assure you that General Buell's dispositions will eventually free all Tennessee and go very far to crush the rebellion entirely." Indeed, the Virginian believed that Union success in the war was bound to occur quite soon. "If our Army will not permit itself to degenerate with idleness," he speculated, "the rebels will be crushed in 60 days, for the Confederacy cannot possibly subsist its troops a great while longer." Thomas had already explained that he thought the Confederates to be in desperate straits, and that without reclaiming Kentucky and Tennessee, they must recognize "their cause is lost," but the current campaign should have done more to temper his optimism.[39]

In the meantime, Buell sent Thomas to the area of Altamont to assess the situation there for moving the army through that region. The Virginian did not like what he saw and was straightforward in his report. "Water is very scarce here, only one spring; not forage enough in the neighborhood to last but one day." Even if that situation were to improve, the transportation system was still abysmal. "The road up the mountain is almost impassable," he explained, offering the example of the difficulty of getting his artillery to keep up with the infantry. "I deem it next to impossible to march a large army across the mountains by Altamont," he concluded. Thomas had already proposed a better location for gathering the army, and he decided to offer it one more time. "As I mentioned in one of my dispatches, I regard McMinnville as the most important point for occupation of any."[40] By the end of the month, Thomas was located there, expressing the "wish to fortify this place" and suggesting that Buell travel to McMinnville to see the advantages of the position for himself.[41]

Even so, Buell remained uncertain of what to expect from Bragg, still believing that the Confederate chieftain planned to target Nashville. Thomas responded as instructed, including moving to the Tennessee capital to oversee its defense, but Bragg saw the opportunity to steal a march into Kentucky and took it. The prospect of Southern banners waving over the region received a further boost when elements of Kirby Smith's column confronted Federals under the immediate command of Mahlon D. Manson, who had served under Thomas at Mill Springs. The sharp fighting near Richmond, Kentucky, on August 29–30, ended in a rout of the Union forces, with the overall commander, William Nelson, barely escaping the fate of some 4,500 bluecoats. Kirby Smith did not press his advantage, but the specter of victorious Confederates in the bluegrass greatly concerned Union leadership in Washington.

If Kirby Smith's path seemed disturbingly clear, Bragg's remained perplexingly uncertain. The argument over McMinnville or Altamont as the point from which to be able to block Bragg from either approaching Nashville or entering into Kentucky quickly became trumped by Murfreesboro. Buell sought to keep an eye on all approaches by using that town as his base.

Thomas appeared to concur, signaling his approval on September from McMinnville: "By concentrating at Murfreesborough we shall be within striking distance of this place." If Bragg moved as everything indicated, that point would provide the Federals with the chance to "drive him toward Sparta, his longest line of retreat."[42] Thomas later became obsessed with what he remembered were the possibilities for Sparta as a point of concentration of Union forces and confrontation with Bragg, but this was due more to hindsight than to anything he expressed on the record at the time. That Thomas was aware of the benefits of Sparta could be seen from his reference to it as the "longest line of retreat" for Bragg, but there was no overt recommendation to move the army there at the time.[43]

Matters seemed to be compounded when Bragg's course suddenly became clearer. His troops besieged the approximately 4,000-man Federal garrison defending Munfordville on September 14–17, compelling its surrender. Buell had hastily, if belatedly, dispatched Thomas to Bowling Green just before the fall of Munfordville, and then slowly dragged the army toward a possible engagement with Bragg, while waiting for the Virginian to arrive. The pressure mounted for Buell to defeat the Confederates and drive them from the region, although Louisville's fate became secure when a few days later the Southerners sidled away from its path and opened the way for Federal troops to reach the city. The symbolic importance of inaugurating Richard Hawes as a friendly governor in Frankfort and the opportunity to draw closer to Kirby Smith's troops had pulled Bragg in that direction. Thomas was able to join his comrades in Louisville by September 27, where his appearance drew attention from at least one witness, who contrasted the general's calm demeanor and reassuring presence with the "excited and fearful" state of the local citizenry.[44]

In the midst of these active operations, General in Chief Henry Halleck determined that a change in leadership had to be made. On September 29, he instructed General Buell to turn over his command to Thomas. The subordinate hastened over to his superior's headquarters in the Galt House to discuss the matter with him and found Buell prepared to comply. Thomas insisted that he would reject the assignment, but Buell instructed that he not do so on personal grounds. Thomas read the message that he planned to send Halleck. "I could make no personal objection to his reasons," Buell recalled, "but I encouraged him to accept the duty assigned to him, saying that nothing remained to be done but to put the army in motion, and that I would cheerfully explain my plans to him and give him all the information I possessed."[45]

Whatever Buell thought about his motivation, Thomas's chief argument proceeded on specific grounds. "General Buell's preparations have been completed to move against the enemy," he explained to Halleck, "and I therefore respectfully ask that he may be retained in command."[46] The army commander had been most generous in offering his assistance, but the Virginian clearly preferred to avoid assuming command under the circumstances unless compelled to do so. Buell biographer Stephen Engle observed that Thomas likely recognized that despite the suggestion that the army had only to be put into motion, the situation actually would take time for him to assess adequately and that the army he inherited might have been "in no condition to fight."[47]

Thomas biographer Christopher Einholf has postulated that the Virginian's explanation for turning the slot down was "unconvincing, however, because the army was not on the eve of battle at the time of Halleck's orders but was safe in its base at Louisville. There was time for Thomas to take over the army and learn its dispositions before taking the field against Bragg."[48] Of course, with Bragg still lurking in Kentucky and pressure from Washington clearly mounting, it is difficult to imagine that Thomas had the luxury of time that the historian considered was available to him. What was more, the Virginian's own notions of adequate preparation worked against this idea that he could simply order the army into motion and expect success. A newspaper correspondent from Chicago used the same argument to suggest that the exchange of commanders would bring no relief, representing as it did a case of "out of the frying pan into the fire, for Gen. Geo. H. Thomas is a slower man than Buell. It takes Thomas half an hour to say no."[49]

The reticence Thomas had shown for displacing Buell was misunderstood by virtually everyone. Buell attributed the gesture to personal friendship, an idea that subsequent testimony before a court of inquiry dispelled. Others were sure that the failure to step forward represented a flaw in the Virginian's makeup. In any case, his reaction was certainly commendable. Rather than advance his own interests, he preferred to let the commander who had inaugurated a campaign see it to its conclusion. But in doing so, Thomas also revealed the vulnerability he felt at assuming authority over a situation he had not developed for himself. He would have to take on someone else's plans, with the efforts that individual had set into motion to carry them out. Just as he preferred not to be subjected to undue political interference as an army commander, he was not keen on accepting a situation over which he had not previously exercised the kind of planning and control he expected a commander to be able to utilize. In his halting way, Thomas tried to explain this reluctance. "My position is very embarrassing," he asserted, "not being as well informed as I should be as the commander of this army and on the assumption of such a responsibility."[50] To do anything else was tantamount, in military parlance, of going into a pending engagement half-cocked, which was not the preferred choice for George Thomas in any case.

General Thomas later asserted his position in the Buell saga. "I am not as modest as I have been represented to be. I did not request the retention of General Buell in command through modesty, but because his removal and my assignment were alike, unjust to him and me." Then he elaborated for clarity's sake, "It was unjust to him to relieve him on the eve of battle, and unjust to myself, to impose upon me the command of the army at such a time."[51]

Now aware of Thomas's feelings in the matter, Halleck took the step of informing him that the change had been meant to be made earlier. Still, he assured the general, "You may consider the order as suspended till I can lay your dispatch before the Government and get instructions."[52] Subsequently, Halleck informed both parties that the removal of Buell and his replacement with Thomas was indeed "by the authority of the President, suspended."[53]

Spurred by his near dismissal, the army commander reorganized his command, placing Alexander M. McCook in charge of the First Corps, Thomas L. Crittenden the Second, and Charles C. Gilbert the Third.[54] William Nelson would have commanded the Third Corps, except that on the same day that the Buell drama unfolded, a disgruntled colleague, Brigadier General Jefferson C. Davis, shot and mortally wounded Nelson on the steps of the Galt House following a heated exchange of bitter denunciations.[55]

Thomas accepted the post of second in command, but as Grant might have told him from his experience in the same role under Halleck at Corinth, the largely honorific position carried no real authority. Even so, he managed to perform an important function almost immediately when he prevented the newly named corps commander, General Gilbert, from firing on some of his own troops when they resisted orders after not being paid.[56] Despite all of the confusion, the message from Washington had nevertheless been received, and the Army of the Ohio moved out from Louisville on October 1 in search of Bragg.[57]

The Kentucky Campaign that had caused Washington and Buell such angst culminated in the battle of Perryville on October 8, 1862, which began as the opposing forces groped for each other and for water to slake the thirst of an unusually hot and dry period. The engagement moved across the rolling hill terrain and proved desperate and bloody for those who engaged in it. Thomas could not count himself among that number, largely remaining on the fringe of the fighting with a substantial portion of Buell's command under Thomas L. Crittenden. As their comrades slogged against the Confederates over trampled cornfields, dry creek beds, and grassy slopes, Thomas held firm where he was, insisting, "I know nothing of General Buell's plan, and I must wait here where he knows I am for orders."[58]

Historian Larry Daniel assessed the lapse harshly. "At the very moment when Buell, both physically and emotionally, needed Thomas the most, the

Virginian sulked." Daniel attributed the subordinate's failure to report to Buell as a "passive-aggressive gesture." The historian concluded speculatively that with Thomas being "as methodical as Buell," Thomas's advice would not likely have changed anything.[59] Concerning such points, Thomas himself later offered a reasonable explanation in his testimony before a commission formed to assess the campaign. "I did not know a battle had been fought on the left until after night-fall, when, as I was riding to my tent, Lieutenant Fitzhugh, of Buell's staff, over took me and told me." He estimated the time to be "about 7 o'clock."[60] Lieutenant C. L. Fitzhugh corroborated the timing and nature of their conversation, although he remained adamant that he thought Buell's verbal orders were not open to interpretation. "It was about an hour after sundown," the staffer explained. "I gave him the orders. He asked me then if it was intended to advance at night after dark, and I repeated the order and left him to draw his own inference for the order, which was to advance at once."[61] When queried as to the length of time it had taken him to leave Buell's headquarters and pass the instructions to Thomas, the aide explained, "I was all that time hunting up the general, and discovered him accidentally. He was not at his own headquarters; he was out in front, and I lighted on him accidentally." Fitzhugh attended to his horse and took supper with the general, but remained incredulous that Thomas had not acted immediately. "There was a bright moon," he recalled, "and it was almost as light as day."[62] Thomas finally rode over to Buell's headquarters, apparently thinking that he would personally coordinate his plans for the next day's actions with his superior. They talked until well into the morning, but there was no indication that Buell was displeased with his subordinate's decisions.[63]

Watching the testimony, Buell provided the most substantial support for his subordinate's decision to await any movement until the next day. "I wish, Mr. President, in justice to General Thomas, to explain what interpretation I put upon this order myself," Buell asserted. "I never interpreted when I gave the order that it would be executed after night." Twice, he pointed out that for Thomas to do otherwise, under the conditions and in violation of his own discretion and experience, would have brought him censure.[64] Given the timing of the situation, Thomas had acted most reasonably and acceptably in the estimation of the commander who had sent him the order in the first place.

Only occasionally did the faint thump of artillery reach Thomas and his compatriots, prompting his none-too-urgent inquiries. That general would later refer to a high wind blowing, which created conditions that made firm identification of the nature of any fighting problematic.[65] A phenomenon known as "acoustic shadow" seemed largely to have prevented any knowledge of the vicious combat that raged only a short distance away.[66] On this occasion and under these circumstances, Thomas fell back on the conservative course of awaiting orders. There was no question that the initiative he had shown, and would demonstrate again, on other fields was missing at Perryville.[67] But it is by no means certain that Thomas's behavior came as a result of petulance.

The circumstances after Perryville were similar in some respects to those that had prevailed following Mill Springs. It was not sufficient to hold a hard-won battleground. But destruction of the defeated forces required active pursuit, and the victorious Federals were unable to follow effectively as Bragg slipped away. On the morning of October 12, Thomas forwarded local reports that the Confederates were "scared and scattered like pigeons through the country." He translated the vernacular as "in other words, demoralized," but saw in the chaotic state of their opponents less an opportunity to complete the victory than an indication that further pursuit of the remnants would not be productive.[68] In any case, overextension, even for the sake of finishing a foe, might produce more harm than good and negate all that had been accomplished thus far.

Thomas's lackluster role in the campaign prompted justifiable criticism, but he demonstrated stronger elements of his character during the period as well. The Virginian took a particular interest in the protection of the rights of citizens, in part because he seemed to have an innate sense of justice and because such a policy made sense when dealing with a foe that shared so much common history and heritage. During the course of the Kentucky Campaign, the actions of some of the more rowdy and rambunctious recruits toward civilians drew his attention and ire. One incident occurred when a farmer approached the general to complain that a Union officer had made off with his horse. Since the animal was the only one he had on his small establishment, the requisition had hit him hard. Thomas reacted in such a way as to astound those who did not think him capable of emotion. He wanted to know the identity of the culprit, and in glancing around the farmer happened to see the fellow with the horse with which he had absconded.

Although the procurer was not a member of his staff, Thomas took the matter seriously as reflecting upon the uniform regardless. He hurried over to the officer, insisting that he explain on what authority he had acquired the animal. Perhaps not appreciative of the tone of accusation, the gentleman offered the flippant response that he had "impressed" the horse. But he had failed to reckon with the Virginian's sense of justice and propriety, both of which had been violated. Thomas suddenly drew his sword and snatched the shoulder straps indicating rank from the uniform, all the while berating the officer for his behavior and insisting that he would not only return the animal, but pay for its use.[69]

A similar illustration appeared in the general's obituary, with the prefatory remark, "He never tolerated the slightest evasion of duty from his Brigadiers down to his Orderlies." As part of his routine, Thomas made unannounced visits to hospitals for the purpose of inspecting the treatment of the sick and wounded. But on one such occasion, Thomas surprised an officer who had neglected his duty, and with his own face "hardened into a white heat of passion," taking "out his penknife, he ripped off the fellow's shoulder-straps," while instructing him, "Go home, Sir, by the next train. You may do to feed cattle: you shall not feed my soldiers."[70]

One of the individuals who had a chance to view Thomas closely and recorded his impressions noted that the Virginian was "absolutely honest," and that when pushed "could show considerable acerbity at incompetence or dissembling." Officers, such as the miscreant in Kentucky or the negligent hospital attendant, would have understood the assessment that George Thomas "had little patience with what we term general worthlessness." Actions reflected on the uniform, and Thomas could not sanction poor ones, especially from those who purported to lead. "He utterly detested any habit or custom that detracted from the character of either the army as a whole, or of an officer individually."[71]

Of course, the discipline that he insisted upon was meant to make the command ready for the tests of combat when they came. But any future fighting was going to have to be undertaken by a new commander. On October 24, Don Carlos Buell learned that he was to turn over the reins of the army to William S. Rosecrans.[72] It took several days for official word to filter through the system that Buell was out as army commander. Secretary of War Edwin Stanton insisted to Governor David Tod of Ohio that if it had been left to him the move would have been made earlier. "I had been urging his removal for two months," the official explained, "had it done once, when it was revoked by the President."[73] There was now to be no revocation or reprieve. Buell was out.

"I am ordered to Indianapolis to report for further orders," the general informed his second in command on October 30 of his departure. As a gesture of appreciation, Buell inquired, "Can I do anything for you privately?" Then, resignedly he closed, "I can hardly flatter myself that I can do anything officially, though I would be glad to try."[74] The next official duty Thomas was called upon to perform with regard to his former superior would strain that friendly tone as he provided testimony at an inquiry into the Kentucky campaign. But for the moment, the Virginian had a bigger and more personal battle to wage on matters of seniority and military protocol.

Thomas's previous self-deprecating refusal to accede to the command over Buell had worked against him here. What may have appeared to him to be high-minded and reasonable suggested to others a reluctance that might bode ill on the battlefield. Even with Mill Springs on his record as an example of what he could accomplish against a foe, Thomas could not overcome the appearance that his refusal had generated. "Let the Virginian wait," Abraham Lincoln observed, with a reference to the home state that undoubtedly played a factor in the decision as well, "we will try Rosecrans."[75]

Buell's replacement with William Rosecrans infuriated Thomas. He could not imagine a manner in which someone inferior to him in rank could be elevated beyond him, especially when he had turned down the command only due to the fact that Buell's campaign had already gotten under way and Thomas did not see the wisdom of changing commanders in the midst of active operations. A later historian noted in connection with the incident, "Seniority was sacred in the army, and generals knew their place precisely in the pecking order."[76] Thomas certainly thought he knew his.

For once George Thomas did not mince words or attempt to conceal his feelings in a cloak of duty. For the man who would claim that he had taught himself "not to feel," there was plenty on his mind now, and he was determined to air it out. It is certainly possible that he figured that he had nothing to lose from expressing himself fully and the freedom to do so was too great a temptation for him to resist. "On the 29th of last September I received an order through your aide, Colonel McKibbin, placing me in command of the Department of the Ohio and directing General Buell to turn over his troops to me," Thomas began with a brief history lesson that he knew Henry Halleck already understood. But like the general he was, he recognized that for battle to be joined successfully, one had to prepare the ground appropriately. "This order reached me just as General Buell had by most extraordinary exertions prepared his army to pursue and drive the rebels from Kentucky. Feeling convinced that great injustice would be done him if not permitted to carry out his plans, I requested that he might be retained in command." Thus, Buell had been allowed to continue when "the order relieving him was suspended," and he went on to engage Bragg in the battle of Perryville.

With the campaigning ended, the proper time for a change in leadership seemed to have arrived, except that the person tapped for the position was not to be him. Instead, "today I am officially informed that he is relieved by General Rosecrans, my junior. Although I do not claim for myself any superior ability, yet feeling conscious that no just cause exists for overslaughing me by placing me under my junior, I feel deeply mortified and aggrieved at the action taken in this matter."[77]

Halleck responded to the discontented general by offering assurances of his personal esteem. "I cannot better state my appreciation of you as a general than by referring you to the fact that at Pittsburg Landing I urged upon the Secretary of War to secure your appointment as major-general, in order that I might place you in command of the right wing of the army over your then superiors. It was through my urgent solicitations that you were commissioned."

Halleck believed that his support of Thomas was beyond question. To reiterate the point, he asserted, "When it was determined to relieve General Buell another person was spoken of as his successor and it was through my repeated solicitations that you were appointed." Instead, Thomas had, perhaps with good reason, spurned the promotion. "You having virtually declined the command at that time it was necessary to appoint another, and General Rosecrans was selected."

Then Halleck took the matter in a different direction. He understood the importance of seniority to the army as well as to this subordinate in particular. "You are mistaken about General Rosecrans being your junior," he explained to Thomas. "His commission dates prior to yours." Regardless, the Virginian also had to understand and accept the prerogatives of the commander in chief, "for the law gives the President the power to assign with regard to dates, and he has seen fit to exercise it in this and many other cases."

Perhaps "Old Brains" recognized the harshness of the verdict, for he repeated his own level of regard for Thomas. "Rest assured, general, that I fully appreciate your military capacity, and will do everything in my power to give you an independent command when an opportunity offers." In any case, as he had already pointed out, "It was not possible to give you the command in Tennessee after you had once declined it."[78]

Thomas replied to Halleck on November 21, 1862, expressing his appreciation for "the kindness of its tone." He also accepted at face value the assertion that his biggest concern had been properly addressed. "I should not have addressed you in the first place if I had known that General Rosecrans's commission dated prior to mine. The letter was written not because I desired a command but for being superseded as I supposed, by a junior in rank when I felt there was no cause for so treating me."

Thomas's complaint had not focused on the individual choice of successor. His chief distress was predicated on their relative seniority. "I have no objection whatever to serving under General Rosecrans now that I know his commission dates prior to mine, but I must confess that I should feel deeply mortified should the President place a junior over me without just cause, although the law authorizes him to do so should he see fit."[79]

The new commander wisely sought to do what he could not to alienate his subordinate through any actions of his own. Rosecrans appealed to the Virginian in an effective manner as a sage colleague rather than a subordinate. He observed that they had been "friends for many years and I shall especially need your support and advice." Rosecrans seemed genuinely to appreciate Thomas in a way that made the situation more palatable. He reminded his staff that in their days at West Point, he had been prone to refer to his classmate as "General Washington" out of respect for "points of strong resemblance between his character and that of Washington."[80]

Thomas biographer and contemporary Thomas Van Horne felt the need to assert that "while General Thomas desired an independent command it was not pleasant to him to supersede another general. His idea of enlarged command was to have his forces multiplied in his own hands, and thus be promoted without the displacement and mortification of another commander."[81] The Buell business in Middle Tennessee in 1863 had illustrated Thomas's wariness at appearing to undermine a commander or creating undue disruptions and distractions during active operations. The dilemma for him now that he had been passed over for the command that could already have been his was that he should appear to operate out of that same sense of self-interest, while also protesting the treatment of which he felt victimized.

The combination of appearing to have turned down a command that he now wanted, the desire to have independence in any command he assumed, the unwillingness to appear conniving, and the preference that President Lincoln expressed to "try Rosecrans" all worked against Thomas in this instance. He would have to have overcome each of these elements to prevent Rosecrans from "overslaughing" him and he could not do it. Yet, Thomas was as responsible for the position he found himself in as was anyone else. Mill Springs had been a long time ago in the memory of a nation and its leaders who had watched engagements unfold on subsequent fields, and the difficult period that had followed for the Virginian offered little indication of the service that was to come.

To be sure, Thomas's prized equilibrium had undergone a severe test when Rosecrans assumed command. It was about to undergo another one, but this time at the behest of the Confederate cavalry raider John Hunt Morgan. The troops affected were two regiments of infantry and three of cavalry assigned to protect the area of Hartsville, Tennessee. Thomas duly reported the matter to Rosecrans, insisting that he had sent out an officer to investigate "and report to me the actual state of affairs."[82] The army commander grasped the inference and understandably took the news with a sense of incredulity. "Do I understand that they have captured an entire brigade of our troops without our knowing it, or a good fight? P.S.—Answer quick."[83]

Apparently, even with additional information now available, the Virginian could only reply that the "fight lasted about an hour and a quarter" and that those who did not break and run had indeed been captured. He held out the possibility that the attacking force could be "intercepted" before it slipped away, but this could not have inspired confidence in Rosecrans.[84] The whole business hardly cast glory on Thomas or the army commander. A disappointed Rosecrans reported glumly to Henry Halleck, the general in chief,

"General Thomas dispatches me that one of his brigades, Dumont's, posted at Hartsville, was probably surprised by two regiments of infantry and three of cavalry, and captured."[85]

Confederate cavalry raids would continue to harass Rosecrans and Thomas. General Morgan seemed to take special delight in wreaking havoc. In addition to trying to protect the lines of communication and supply, and prevent as much damage as possible from being done before it happened, Thomas also adapted himself to the effective restoration of broken rail lines. As one historian explained, "The key was to fix the damage fast." Combining the "brute force" of work crews with the establishment of repair shops and standardized pieces for downed trestles, the Virginian perfected a system that stood well for him long after he had left the region to engage in other campaigns.[86]

Raids reminded the men and their commanders that threats could emerge at any time. Thomas tried to keep the command vigilant by putting them through their paces in drills and reviews. He also used these opportunities to instill pride and confidence in the troops. One soldier described "our grand *Review* which we had by major Gen. Thomas on the 5th [of December]," to a sister a few days later. "[T]he Gen. complimented us very highly Said the 31st was as good a Regiment [as] he had in his whole command."[87]

Unfortunately for him, unpleasant developments of a more personal nature continued for Thomas in the near term. As one of the principals in the Kentucky Campaign, he journeyed to Nashville in December to appear before a panel investigating the campaign and Buell's leadership in it. The commission had already been meeting, asking questions of various witnesses and sifting through the testimony, when Thomas appeared on the morning of December 18. Properly sworn in by the judge advocate, the general settled into his chair to submit to questions. Buell would be among those listening, and subsequently pose inquiries of his own. Thomas's examination continued through the next day.[88]

The Virginian's testimony contained one interesting feature. During his cross-examination by his former superior officer Thomas consistently referred to Buell formally in the third person.[89] Clearly a relationship that had been amicable was now purely to be treated as professional. As it was, the commission heard from a number of individuals and accepted a substantial statement from Buell himself. The ultimate finding went against Buell, but hardly on any grounds to which most commanders who had experienced setbacks in their careers would not also be susceptible. The general's biographer concluded of the proceedings, "In some ways Buell had won his only true victory of the war."[90] It would be a hollow one.

By the end of the year, William S. Rosecrans was ready to place his own stamp on the army he had inherited from Buell. He divided his command into three wings. Thomas would take command of the center wing. As Peter Cozzens has explained, "It was no accident that the Center was the largest command in the army, or that it went to Thomas. In fact, it was the price of his continued service in the department."[91] There is no evidence of a quid pro quo on the parts of Rosecrans or Thomas, but it was true that the center wing had more divisions and artillery than either of the other elements, and in raw numbers almost doubled them both with 29,337. Alexander McCook and Thomas Crittenden led the 15,832-man right and 14,308-man left wings of the army, respectively.

As the command approached Murfreesboro, the plan was for the wings to move in concert in such a way as to be able to support each other. Thomas had marched more due south of Nashville than either McCook or Crittenden, who angled in a southeastwardly direction, the latter moving along the Murfreesboro Pike, close to the Nashville and Chattanooga Railroad.

Both Rosecrans and Bragg formulated a plan that would allow their commands to outflank the other, and each of the opposing commanders planned to seize the initiative for himself. Enveloping the right flank would mean turning a position that would make it easier to expose an opponent to brutal punishment. Bragg particularly hoped to drive Rosecrans away from his line of supply and communication back to Nashville.

On the eve of battle, Rosecrans sought the input of his subordinates. Thomas later recalled, "On the evening of the 30th of December you came with a portion of your staff to where I had made my headquarters during that day, and after inquiry as to the position of my troops and my dispositions for the night." Having dispensed with the routine business, Thomas and the army commander "then mounted our horses and rode in the direction of your headquarters tents, during which time you explained to me in substance that McCook's corps was to engage the enemy's attention and hold him in his front the next day (the 31st), whilst our left, supported by the center, was to attack and crush the enemy's right."[92] Other commanders joined Rosecrans at his headquarters, where his conversation with Thomas may have blended in his mind, but the Virginian insisted that he spoke to Rosecrans about the expected battle only as the two men rode together between their respective headquarters camps.

Whatever Rosecrans, Thomas, and the other Union commanders may have anticipated, the probability of a collision was certainly a strong one. Through a statement delivered by his chief of staff, J. P. Garesché, General Rosecrans implored the troops to remember that "the eyes of the whole nation are upon you, the very fate of the nation may be said to hang on the issue of this day's battle." But the energizing exhortation moved swiftly from high-toned rhetoric to the advice of a sergeant on the drill field that called for the men to make their shots count and aim and fire low.[93]

Rosecrans and his officers were not the only ones anticipating imminent action. A junior officer with responsibility for supplying ammunition for Thomas's command was vitally concerned that he place his wagons where the general wanted them to be. Alfred Pirtle rode out to where Thomas was supposed to be encamped and found the chief of staff, to whom he reported. "While I did so I noticed General Thomas sitting astride a chair, on the opposite side of the fire, apparently asleep, resting his arms on the back of the chair." Pirtle supposed that the general was too tired to sleep tradition-ally, and too worn out to remain awake. Thomas suddenly "roused up, ask-ing who I was." The subordinate repeated his report, to which the superior "gave polite and interested attention." Never one to avoid taking lessons, especially from difficult situations that had occurred earlier, the Virginian explained that at Perryville, "there had been much valuable time lost at a critical time in the battle by the ammunition wagons being too far in the rear, and he would like to have my train within a short distance of the rear line in case of a battle the next day." They subsequently agreed that the reserve line would be placed 600 yards back from the front and the wagons loaded with ordnance would be located another 600 yards beyond that.[94]

Whatever the Federals had hoped, it was the Confederates who got in the first of those shots on that fateful last day of 1862. Thomas recorded in his after-action report that on "December 31, between 6 and 7 a.m., the enemy having massed a heavy force on McCook's right during the night of the 30th, attacked and drove it back, pushing his division in pursuit *en echelon*." The force of the Confederate blow shoved the Federals back upon the Union center. Thomas made dispositions to hold such ground as he could while supporting the exposed units as they readjusted. "About 11 o'clock," he recorded, "General Sheridan reported to me that his ammunition was entirely out, and he would be compelled to fall back to get more." The resulting developments forced Thomas to realign his position. Having to "fall back out of the cedar woods" he had been defending, Thomas established "a line along a depression in the open ground, within good musket-range of the edge of the woods, while the artillery was retired to the high ground to the right of the turnpike."[95]

Artillery would be one of the keys to Union success at Stones River, and, just as he had succeeded in doing on a much smaller scale at Buena Vista those many years ago, the Virginian used his cannon to secure this vital position. Even so, the combat was brutal for the men who fought alongside the batteries, too. Thomas recalled that the effect of the fighting was particularly costly for the Eighteenth U.S. Infantry, under Lieutenant Colonel Oliver Shepherd. The regulars endured "a most murderous fire, losing 22 officers and 508 men in killed and wounded, but with the cooperation of [Benjamin F.] Scribner's and [John] Beatty's brigades and [Francis L.] Guenther's and [Cyrus O.] Loomis' batteries, held its ground against overwhelming odds."[96]

In most respects, Thomas remained cool in the midst of the turmoil that swirled around him, reputedly instructing his embattled subordinate, "Shephard, take your brigade there and stop the Rebels."[97] A participant in the heavy fighting at the Round Forest recalled that when an anxious General Alexander McCook advised that the commanders who had gathered at one spot "thin out" a little so as not to be as likely to draw enemy fire on them, Thomas responded nonchalantly that either side of the road would be about the same.[98]

But the Virginian's demeanor under fire left differing impressions on witnesses, depending on when they took notice of him. One remembered a distinctive change in the general's attitude, observing "General Thomas had plenty on his mind; this was the first occasion I had ever observed him trotting his horse. Walking was his pace, his quiet, grand presence always inspiring confidence."[99] Another considered Thomas's presence "ubiquitous," but maintained that "his charger never broke out of the slow pace that had given its master the nickname Old Slow Trot." In any case, he remained active, "now directing the firing to repulse a charge, now placing a regiment in line, and again marking a point to which his troops must retire and take up the fight anew."[100]

Thomas was particularly proud of the manner in which, although initially driven from and then giving some of the ground his men were charged with defending, the line had stabilized and solidified in the face of mounting pressure. "The center having succeeded in driving back the enemy from its front, and our artillery concentrating its fire on the cedar thicket on our right, drove him back under cover" he explained without any sense of hyperbole, "from which, though repeatedly attempting it, he could not make any advance."[101] In a subsequent report, the Virginian highlighted the efforts of his men to defend this last position against a foe who "was straining every nerve to gain possession of the same point."[102]

A specific incident remained with Thomas long after the battle. In the midst of the carnage, he rode up to a noncommissioned officer supervising two artillery pieces. "I said to a sergeant, the only man left in command of two guns at Stone[s] river, who, of course, was [anxious] about getting away, 'I want you to save those pieces, my good fellow.'" When Thomas next saw the man that evening, the soldier "reported to me . . . that the guns were right where I saw them, only he [had] 'shoved 'em round.'" Thomas was impressed by more than the bravery this effort had exhibited. "The good fellow did not seem to think he had accomplished any thing extraordinary, for when I made him a lieutenant he hesitated about accepting as he preferred remaining with the boys, but took it on the ground that it would enable him to run home and see the old woman."[103]

Of course, the time to "run home" had not arrived yet. Rosecrans mulled over his options after a hard day of fighting, but was anxious to hear and willing to consider the positions and advice of his subordinates. Exhausted from his part in the engagement, Thomas took the opportunity to doze as the discussions flashed back and forth. Apparently even as he rested the Virginian had the capability of keeping up with the gist of what was going on around him. An inquiry concerning retreat brought him to attention to indicate that his sharp mind was never sleeping. There is some debate as to the exact response that he uttered. O. O. Howard recorded it simply as, "This army can't retreat!"[104] But, a more colorful phrase was attributed to Thomas in this instance as well. One witness recalled the night council, with Thomas looking, "as he always did, calm, stern, determined, silent and perfectly self-possessed, his hat squarely on his head." John Yaryan did not notice the Virginian dozing. "I watched him closely to see if I could discern any proposition to be stated, already showing in his face, but he never changed a muscle; his eye never left the bed of red coals that were now aglow on the old hearth; he did not appear to hear any of the replies; the same set, determined look I saw when I came in, was there." The staffer vividly recalled Thomas rising, adjusting his uniform and buttoning "his great coat from bottom to top," before turning to his comrades and declaring succinctly, "Gentlemen, I know of no place better to die than right here." Then he walked out into the night.[105]

So much is often made of such events as if they were immutable affairs that must be corroborated fully by all present in order to be appropriately authenticated. Instead, gatherings like the council of war that Rosecrans had convened were transmutable moments, witnessed by individuals with varying degrees of receptivity and understanding to what was occurring around them. The positioning or proximity of one individual to another, the degree of distraction or absentmindedness, the extent to which memory then served or failed the participant in rendering the account after the fact, all played a part, as they do in any of these cases. The frailties of human beings and their perceptions and interpretations may provide accounts that appear on the surface to be contradictory when they merely reflect different individuals capturing varying elements of the same occasion.

Thomas may very well have stirred himself to insist that the army ought not to retreat before subsequently rising and preparing to leave the assembly with the dramatic declaration that there would be no better place to die than the one the army was now holding and from which he believed it ought not to withdraw. Scholars can occasionally become so fixated on details as to miss the larger point: regardless of the expression Thomas used to illustrate his position, he wanted to stand his ground. The determination suited his personality and fit the staunchness for which he had already made, and would later add to, his military reputation.

Whatever the Virginian actually said, he was as determined as ever not to give the ground that he and his men had ultimately defended and so stubbornly refused to abandon in the thick of the fighting after the fact. If the Confederates wished to deprive him of it they would have to find the means to do so themselves after already having tried valiantly and failing. He also understood the perils of attempting to withdraw an army in the face of an undefeated foe. In many ways it would be preferable to stay and die than attempt to undergo a retreat. Stubbornness, in this instance, was a decided virtue, and George Thomas could exhibit a rare brand of the commodity when he wished. It was up to the rest of the army whether or not a stand would be made with him. The sense of steadiness and determination that Thomas exhibited in the face of extreme difficulties had already proven significant for him on the battlefield and would do so again. At Stones River, it provided a tonic to those who might waiver or find their devotion wanting.

On January 1, one of the Federal general officers recalled seeing both Rosecrans and Thomas "riding over the field, now halting to speak words of encouragement to the troops, then going to inspect portions of the line."[106] If Thomas had strengthened his superior's resolve through his positions at the night council, he was actively demonstrating the same trait to the men in the field, too.

Dissension within the Confederate ranks, Rosecrans's inspirational leadership, and Thomas's solid performance contributed mightily to Union victory at Stones River. A contemporary historian concluded, "At Stone's River, Thomas was a tower of strength. His crucial section of the line held firm and became the key to stopping the Confederate assault. His sturdy influence steadied Rosecrans through the ordeal."[107]

An assault by John C. Breckinridge's division against an isolated Union division represented the anticlimactic conclusion to the battle on January 2. Union artillery tore the Southern ranks to shreds, and both sides settled into a mode of engagement marked mostly by exhaustion and desultory skirmish fire. The Confederates opted to retreat on the night of January 3, and Rosecrans largely acquiesced. Thomas's men spent the next day recovering the dead and counting their costs. Scuffling with Confederate cavalry represented the final contact with Bragg's departed forces.[108]

The costs for Thomas had indeed been significant. Of the 5,786 officers and men Lovell Rousseau had taken into the engagement, 179 were killed, 946 wounded, and 325 were captured or missing. James Negley's division of 4,869 suffered 178 dead, 748 wounded, and 311 missing. Over half of

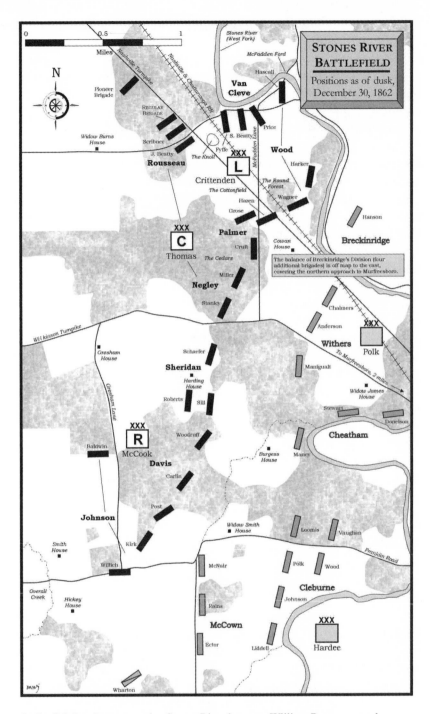

In the fighting that occurred at Stones River between William Rosecrans and Braxton Bragg, Thomas proved instrumental in holding the threatened Union center. Positions at dusk, December 30, 1862. © Mark W. Johnson.

that division's artillery pieces had been lost or disabled in the bitter combat, and a substantial number of the teams used to pull them were killed or otherwise out of commission, too.[109] Even members of Thomas's staff had not been immune. Acting chief of commissary Captain O. A. Mack took a severe wound to the hip and abdomen in the course of delivering important orders, while a member of the general's escort fell to an artillery round on the relatively quiet second day of fighting.[110] Such exposure was proof that Thomas expected his staff to be more than supernumeraries, contributing to whatever demands arose. It would take some time to reconcile these losses and restore the survivors to fighting trim, but George Thomas was certainly the man to do the job, and he embraced the challenge with his usual gusto. It remained to be seen if 1863 would prove to be as eventful a year as 1862 had been, but for the moment the army needed to rest and recuperate.

Photographic images abound for the man who ordinarily disdained public expressions. This one portrays George H. Thomas as a major general of volunteers. Photograph courtesy of the National Archives.

The urban warfare style of street fighting in Monterrey, Mexico, proved especially troublesome for the Americans, including Thomas, who struggled to subdue the stubborn resistance of citizens and soldiers firing from rooftops and barricades. Photograph by Terry Shortt.

George Thomas recalled that Buena Vista was one instance where his reputed "slowness" worked to his advantage against repeated and determined Mexican assaults. Photograph by Terry Shortt.

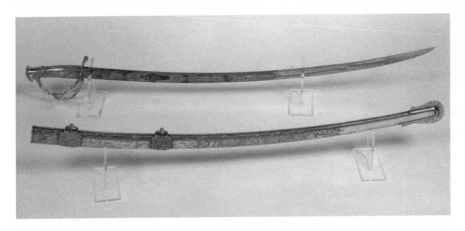

Specially designed by citizens from Southampton County, Virginia, to honor their native son for his regular army heroics and presented in 1847, this ceremonial sword and scabbard became symbolic of the emotions associated with Thomas after his decision to adhere to the Union rather than to Virginia and the Confederacy in the Civil War. Photograph courtesy of the Virginia Historical Society.

Thomas's penchant for good order and discipline in camp is reflected in this sketch. Photograph by Terry Shortt.

Eyeing the camera with the resolve that he brought to the battlefield, George Thomas proved "as true" as the steely look he displayed for the studio photographer. Photograph courtesy of the Library of Congress.

Felix Zollicoffer's brush with Thomas at Mill Springs cost the near-sighted former newspaper editor and Confederate general his life in fighting that also critically compromised the defense line of the Western Theater for the South. Photograph courtesy of the Library of Congress.

Thomas served under Don Carlos Buell in the early part of the war and refused to replace him as army commander in Kentucky in 1862. Photograph courtesy of the Library of Congress.

Braxton Bragg had been a prewar comrade but became a key Confederate adversary for Thomas during the Civil War. Photograph courtesy of the Library of Congress.

William S. Rosecrans commanded Thomas throughout 1863 before giving way to him at Chattanooga in the wake of the disastrous defeat at Chickamauga. Photograph courtesy of the National Archives.

A reflection of the scale of fighting at Snodgrass Hill and Horseshoe Ridge, at Chickamauga, this illustration features a mounted Thomas and staff in the foreground observing the progress of the action as it unfolds. Photograph courtesy of the Library of Congress.

The tandem that took Atlanta in 1864 included Ulysses S. Grant (top left), William T. Sherman (top right), George H. Thomas (bottom left), and James B. McPherson (bottom right), with the latter's death coming before the city fell. As also reflected in this period, Thomas's relationships with Grant and Sherman were at best complicated throughout their professional careers. Photograph courtesy of the Library of Congress.

Famous for his meticulous preparations, George Thomas sits with staff officers at Ringgold, Georgia, during planning sessions in the early phases of the Atlanta Campaign. Photograph courtesy of the National Archives.

The rugged landscape of Kennesaw Mountain in Georgia proved to be only a brief, if bloody, obstacle to the Union advance against Atlanta that included Thomas's command engaged in heavy fighting there. Photograph courtesy of the National Archives.

John Bell Hood had the duty of trying to wrest Nashville, Tennessee, from Thomas's grasp in a late 1864 campaign that ended in a crushing defeat for the Confederate Army of Tennessee. Photograph courtesy of the National Archives.

The Capitol Building in Nashville took on the aspect of a fortification as Thomas successfully defended the city against Hood's Confederates in December 1864. Photograph courtesy of the National Archives.

Popularly known as "Old Brains," Henry W. Halleck served as Thomas's commander at Corinth in 1862, as the army's chief of staff in 1864–1865, and as the Virginian's predecessor in the Division of the Pacific after the war. Photograph courtesy of the Library of Congress.

This image of the equestrian statue of George Thomas in Washington, D.C., captured the majesty of the work meant to honor the service and cement the legacy of the Virginian who had helped to save the Union in the Civil War. Photograph courtesy of Terry Shortt.

Worn by the years of hard campaigning and facing the uncertain prospects of
Reconstruction, George Thomas nevertheless struck a stalwart pose as the Union emerged
victorious in the Civil War. Photograph courtesy of the Library of Congress.

9 "The Rock of Chickamauga" (February–October 1863)

"Why, my good man, I haven't seen my wife for three years."
—Thomas in response to a request for a furlough

"That's right. Stand by that and we will stand by you to the last."
—Thomas to Rosecrans

"It will ruin the army to withdraw it now. This position must be held until night."
—Thomas to James Garfield at Snodgrass Hill

While the forces of the Union struggled to turn back Confederate invading columns from Kentucky and Maryland, General George Thomas remained focused on his duties in the field. Consequently, the actions of President Abraham Lincoln with regard to the Preliminary Emancipation Proclamation announced on September 22, 1862, and the final Emancipation Proclamation, which went into effect on January 1, 1863, drew no public comment from the Virginian. In any case, for the career soldier, manuvering on the hills and fields of Kentucky and Tennessee must have seemed considerably distant from the political maneuvers in the halls of Washington. Once the fighting on the Western Front subsided, attention shifted again to the necessary recuperation and reconfiguration that followed active campaigning. Thomas's lackluster performance at Perryville had not tarnished his reputation as seriously as had his refusal to replace Don Carlos Buell in command of the army, but his solid performance at Stones River reinvigorated his image. In early 1863, he stood poised to take a significant role in a new season of campaigning.

On February 2, 1863, George Thomas received notice that he was now in command of the newly designated Fourteenth Corps.[1] But Thomas's endorsement of the report, dated February 11, also raised an important point of discussion. "The question is what policy to adopt—the conciliatory or the rigid." The Virginian had grappled with the notion that Southern civilians might be won over, but he was becoming more exasperated with each passing day. "The conciliatory [policy] has failed," he observed, "and however much we may regret the necessity, we shall be compelled to send disloyal people of all ages and sexes to the south, or beyond our lines." With logistics being stretched to the limits, the notion of adding to that strain by supporting those with wavering loyalties no longer seemed to be a useful option. "Secessionism has so degraded their sense of honor that it is next to impossible to find one tinctured with it who can be trusted."[2]

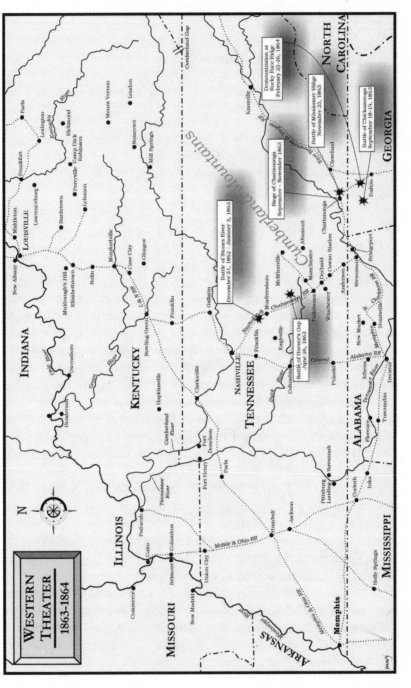

Thomas continued to play a pivotal role in the Western Theater in 1863–1864, as Union troops penetrated deeper into the Confederate heartland. © Mark W. Johnson.

From Washington, General in Chief Henry Halleck considered the advice that had come his way from Middle Tennessee. He observed that Thomas's suggestions "in regard to a more rigid treatment of all disloyal persons within the lines of your army are approved."[3] It remained to be seen how the commander in the field would implement the new approach. In any case, he had clearly determined that Southern civilians could not be treated with kid gloves if the Union effort were going to be effective. Quashing rebellion—a course to which Thomas had committed himself from the beginning—would require stringent methods.

George Thomas was not prepared to abandon good order and discipline in the ranks for the sake of implementing a hard-war policy against their opponents. From the headquarters of the Fourteenth Army Corps, the general's aide sent an unequivocal message: "On account of the depredations committed by the different divisions of this command, the general commanding directs that the most energetic measures be adopted to put a stop to them at once, and that hereafter, whenever this so-called impressments is resorted to, no means [should] be spared to trace the guilty party to the division, regiment, and company, and that the amount for the property so taken be paid out of the company savings, by withholding the commutation of rations until the amount is fully paid." Thomas had reached the point where he would use extraordinary measures to curb excesses. "The general commanding is determined that pillaging shall be put down in his command, and hopes this circular will have the desired effect." Thomas was also ready to make examples of anyone who transgressed and thereby brought dishonor to the uniform. "If not," he explained simply in that regard, "more strenuous measures will be adopted to arrest the guilty, and to make such examples of them as shall effectually put it down throughout the entire command."[4]

In addition to determining a policy for troublesome Southerners and an unruly soldiery, Thomas also dealt with a commander who was obsessed with the battle they had just experienced at the turn of the year. Rosecrans pestered several subordinates, including the Virginian, to determine their recollections of a night meeting that was supposed to have preceded the battle of Stones River and included the issuance of verbal instructions for the coming engagement. Rosecrans wanted affirmation against charges that he had no plan, but Thomas was not one to provide cover for a commander, just for convenience's or loyalty's sake. Thus, when Thomas responded on March 12, he explained that while he and Rosecrans rode together and "you explained to me in substance" the scheme of attack designed for the next day's actions, he did not remember proceeding to Rosecrans's headquarters itself for a nighttime council. "I did not ride up to your tent that evening, but called there the next morning (the 31st) before the battle commenced."[5] Neither man disagreed that a plan had been laid out, just over the location of their discussions. But the incident illustrated that Thomas could be a stickler for such details, to the point of negating the larger point that needed to be made.

Unlike the great battle that Rosecrans was continuing to try to dissect, there was not much action during this period. An expedition from Murfreesboro to McMinnville produced a report from the leader, Major General J. J. Reynolds, to Thomas, in which he assessed the state of loyalty among local residents. Reynolds not only argued that these citizens could be divided by class and loyalty, but that the wealthier ones had tended, especially in initial contacts with Union forces, to be "quite defiant" in their attitudes. Nevertheless, time and circumstances had worked wonders. As he assessed the situation with the passage of several months, Reynolds detected a change in the posture of the citizens in the area that indicated they "have discovered their mistake. They had been misled." Should he give such people an oath and trust them to uphold it? He thought not, but wanted Thomas's advice.[6]

The commander responded to the inquiry in a manner totally consistent with what he had said only a short time before. Confederate sympathizers existed, whatever they might say to the contrary when confronted with the presence of Union troops. The safest course for "those who have heretofore been active rebels" was to remove them and "put [them] beyond our lines." This action would free the troops to "penetrate and occupy the insurgent territory, with much more certainty, as we would not then be under the necessity of keeping up with such strong guards in our rear to secure our lines of communication."[7] Thomas would struggle with the delicate balancing act of treating potentially hostile civilians humanely, while also protecting and advancing his own military interests.

At the same time, duty required that he remain fully committed to the welfare of his command. As such, a contemporary noted that the general spent the months after Stones River productively by taking "the supply departments in his own hands" in order for the "rank and file" to be satisfied that "their wants were being considered." Thomas was not about to neglect the discipline of his men, but he wanted the training to be meaningful and practical. "Most of these tactics were gotten up for show and are something worse than useless," he explained to the aide, "for we waste time on what are as unnecessary in actual war as a dancing-school would be." He wanted his methods to produce efficient soldiers, not parade-ground automatons. "By simplifying the movements to the actual demand of the service we have full time to make veterans." Thomas also wanted the training to reflect his personal values. "It is too common," he observed of most officers, "to believe that they can maintain and enhance their own dignity by degrading the men." He had been consistent on that score whether the setting was West Point or the Western Theater of the Civil War. Arbitrary mistreatment was not going to be the case in his command if he could help it. "I am naturally reserved and have found it difficult to be on familiar, easy terms with my men," he admitted. But because they considered his treatment to be fair and evenly implemented, his men had responded well to his demands of them.[8]

As one element of this process, Thomas monitored the progress of his troops through reviews and drills. One Indiana volunteer noted the general's presence repeatedly in his diary and used the occasion of one of the visits to describe his commander. "Genl Thomas is a very large man [who] will weigh about two hundred and twenty five pounds," William Miller wrote. "About fifty years old and [he] makes a fine appearance and our Boys think there is no body like him. I always hear men speak of him with praise," the Indianan continued, "and we are proud to be led by him." Miller speculated that the popular general they all referred to as "Pap Thomas," and a general he termed "one of the main Stays of our department," was destined to accomplish great things. He thought Thomas would "lead his men to glory and make his mark before the summer is gone."[9]

An additional part of Thomas's approach to the preparation of his men for the work that lay ahead was to keep them exposed to contact with the enemy as often as possible. He considered the exercise a curative for the new recruits especially in facing down their own fears of the dangers of the battlefield. However, keeping the men sharp in this manner also brought exasperating deficiencies to the forefront. "It is a great error in the government not to supply us with enough horses to enable us to feel daily the enemy at our front," he lamented one day. "It is the best training to give our men, while it gives us information and the enemy a healthy regard for us." He saw as a critical mistake the refusal of some commanders to avoid such activity and concluded with a homespun observation: "It was like the poor woman who consented to have her daughter learn to swim, but warned her not to go near the water."[10] Left unsaid was the notion of whether or not soldiers who were allowed to become idle or who avoided exposure to the dangers of duty might prove less prepared for the campaigning that lay ahead of them.

Thomas seemed to have his hand in every phase of his command, although he delegated authority regularly as part of his official routine. Perhaps as a tribute to his intellectual instincts, he also appeared to take notice of wide-ranging matters, including the presence in his command of a youth who displayed uncommon musical acumen. The young bugler thought his father should know that he had adapted well to army life. "[T]he fact is I have learned how to soldier," John Dow explained. "[I] take things easy as possible. I do no guard or fatigue duty [and] have about 9 or ten Bugle calls to make each day." Mostly, he was proud that his commanders had taken notice of his skills, telling his father that "there is no bugler but Dow as they call me." The recognition had come from one source in particular. "Gen. Thomas told Col. [Moses B.] Walker that I was the best Bugler in the Division."[11] Despite his quiet demeanor, Thomas connected with the men themselves and was unafraid to lavish praise on them when the situation warranted.

Thomas's monitoring of leaves and furloughs was also exasperating to some of the subordinate commanders during this largely inert period. One complained that Thomas's actions illustrated that he "is an officer of the regular army; the field is his home, the tent his house, and war his business." John Beatty noted that his commander "regards matters coolly, therefore, to applications of volunteer officers for leaves of absence. Why should they not be as contented as himself?" Then, as Beatty considered the matter further, he relented in his adamancy toward his superior's seeming insensitivity to the plight of his men. "But, then on second thought, I incline to the opinion that the old man is right. Half the army would be at home if leaves and furloughs could be had for the asking."[12]

Even during these momentary lapses when personal demands conflicted with professional ones for the officers who served under him, Thomas remained a galvanizing force. At the end of a long summer of maneuvering, a staff officer informed his wife, "I am not displeased at being with Genl. Thomas for awhile, who I consider the 'model soldier' so far as I have yet seen in this war."[13]

General Beatty needed only to have looked in the ranks for concurring sentiment. Some of the enlisted personnel were equally desirous of obtaining extended leave to visit home. One of these men even broached the matter with Thomas himself. "Mister, I want to get a furlough," the soldier insisted. When the general inquired as to the reason, he replied, "I want to go home and see my wife." Thomas asked how long it had been since he had last done so and the fellow allowed, "Ever since I enlisted—nigh on to three months." Unimpressed, Thomas quickly retorted, "Why, my good man, I haven't seen my wife for three years."[14] But the foot soldier was uninspired by the example his commander had set and with a mischievous glance explained, "well general, me & my old woman ain't them kind."[15] Reportedly, Thomas "rocked with laughter" at the answer he had received, before riding off, leaving the soldier to ponder whether his encounter with his commander had been successful or not.[16] Of course, Thomas knew that morale was a critical matter for all of the components that comprised his command, not the least the men who shouldered the muskets.

Frances Thomas later corroborated the point her husband had tried to make to the despairing soldier. In correspondence with one of Thomas's wartime lieutenants, she explained candidly that after his recall to service at the beginning of the war, "I never saw General Thomas but once from the day he left me to go to Carlisle April 14th 1861, until after the fall of Atlanta at Nashville Oct. 1864, 3½ years."[17]

There was soon to be business serious enough to make such pleasantries seem idyllic. In March, John Beatty noted that the conditions of the roads were improving and the army was showing signs of movement. Indeed, he perceived, "The Army . . . looks better than it ever did before."[18] But prodding remained necessary to turn expectations into reality, while most eyes turned elsewhere to see the fate of the Mississippi River settled in an audacious operation.

In the spring, Ulysses Grant managed initially to put 22,000 men in position at Bruinsburg, with others set to follow, to threaten the last grip of the Confederacy on the Mississippi River at Vicksburg from the south. Methodically approaching the state capital at Jackson with numbers that increased to over 40,000 by mid-May, Grant worked to cut off the defenders under John Pemberton from potential reinforcements under Joseph Johnston and force the Southerners to make a crucial choice whether to abandon or defend the river city. Critical engagements at Port Gibson and Raymond, in Mississippi, on May 1 and 12 respectively, set the stage for the capture of the state capital a couple of days later. The subsequent push westward against the increasingly isolated river town led to heavy fighting at Champion Hill, on May 16 and the Big Black River on the following day. Grant closed on Vicksburg, but early assaults on the Confederate positions revealed that Pemberton and his men were not too demoralized to resist effectively. By May 25, it was clear that a more systematic approach would be necessary, and Grant called for the beginning of siege operations.[19]

The larger strategic picture called for Rosecrans to do something actively in Middle Tennessee that could divert Confederate attention and resources, or at least prevent them from being utilized against Grant's efforts before Vicksburg. Henry Halleck laid the matter squarely before his general. "If you can do nothing yourself, a portion of your troops must be sent to Grant's relief."[20] The long delay for refitting his command after the Battle of Stones River had, in the words of a couple of modern historians, "exhausted" Rosecrans's "credit" with the general in chief, but he remained firm in resisting any precipitate action.[21]

Thomas understood Rosecrans's dilemma. If the army moved prematurely there were bound to be complications, but the real adverse effect might well be the opposite of what was intended. The Confederates could simply choose to "fall back" while "keeping up a sufficient force to hold us in check, draw us away from our base, attack and destroy our communications, or threaten them so strongly as to greatly weaken our main force, and then send reinforcements of artillery and infantry to Johnston."[22] In this type of scenario, the situation would work against Union interests. Better to stand pat and compel the Confederates to deal with a force that could move at any time against them than press an issue through aggressiveness that could produce more problematic results. Even the normally aggressive Philip Sheridan counseled caution under the circumstances.[23] The problem was not identifying strategic imperatives, but determining what action to take that would benefit them the most.

Some voices in the South remained skeptical of George Thomas's ability to contribute to his cause in any meaningful way. In the June 13, 1863, edition of *Southern Illustrated News*, a query regarding the Second Cavalry of prewar days led to a harsh assessment of the man who had been its major. "Major Thomas was a Virginian," the writer noted, employing the past tense to the identification, "and belongs to the 'Black List' of old army men native-born in the South who adhered to the Lincoln Government." Then, perhaps conveniently forgetting the Mill Springs campaign and its decisive results, he added sarcastically, "He is a General now in the Yankee army, if we are not mistaken, but he has achieved nothing which causes his name to be much known in the war."[24]

George Thomas had the opportunity to prove himself to such critics as the summer finally brought military operations into full swing in Middle Tennessee. Up to this time, as one modern historian put it, Rosecrans "refused to budge until he was sure the army was ready, and the general had a very exacting idea of what constituted readiness."[25] But by June 23, he felt sufficiently prepared to move against the Confederates, who had taken up a line of defense at the Duck River, stretching from Shelbyville to McMinnville, for the purpose of protecting Chattanooga, Tennessee. Rosecrans also advanced with a deftness that his opponents found overwhelming as he deployed troops to hold the Southerners in place with a feint toward Shelbyville while he sent Thomas on a flanking movement that threatened them if they remained in place. In the nick of time, the Confederates realized their dilemma and pulled back. Within relatively short order, the retrograde movement did what no battle had yet accomplished. "After just eleven days," a later student of the operation explained, "and at a cost of only 560 men, the Army of the Cumberland had swept its old foes nearly out of the state in one of the most brilliant campaigns of the war."[26]

Thomas continued to push his command forward, cautiously securing ground that enabled him to keep his advance moving while minimizing the possibility of surprises by the enemy. In one of the initial encounters, his men performed better than he had anticipated in reaching and securing Hoover's Gap, and this prompted an unusual public expression of emotion from the Virginian. One participant wrote his wife, "In a few minutes up came General Thomas, our corps commander, his grave face beaming with delight as he grasped our brigade commander by the hand and said, 'You have saved the lives of a thousand men by your gallant conduct today. I didn't expect to get this Gap for three days.'"[27] The general had obviously

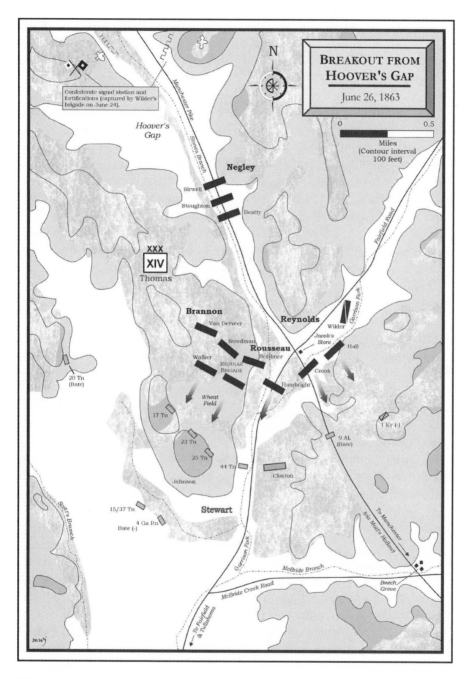

The breakout of Thomas's forces from Hoover's Gap, June 26, 1863, represented a significant point in the Tullahoma Campaign that cleared Confederate defenders under Braxton Bragg from Middle Tennessee. © Mark W. Johnson.

anticipated the outcome he got, just not the rapidity with which his men obtained it or the relatively light cost expended to do so. A Union soldier observed simply to a friend on June 25th on the subject, "Gen. Thomas Commanding 14th Army Corps occupied Hoover's Gap last night. *no* resistance whatever very strong position."[28]

For Thomas, such incidents were also less about accumulating accolades than building up necessary experience for the combat that was sure to come. "My men are being taught the art of war in the only school of practical instruction, and that is in the field," he explained to a gathering of staffers. "All the training, however necessary, is as nothing to that training which is done in the face of death." Even then, there was the danger of complacency that came with repeated successes. He planned to press the enemy rather than avoid contact with them, but wanted to assure the officers that a formidable opponent remained before them that ought not to be underestimated. "Well, gentlemen," he concluded, "we will defer bragging until we capture Bragg."[29]

This attempt to "capture Bragg" was certainly not aided by nature. Heavy rains plagued the advance almost from the start and doused the troops, rendering movements tedious and cumbersome. While most of the men understandably groused at the misfortune, Thomas reacted in his normally even-keeled and practical manner. "We have time to accomplish all that is necessary for my boys to do," he explained to a complaining subordinate, "and the storms that embarrass us keep the enemy from annoying us or discovering our intent."[30] Thomas understood that rain created havoc for both sides, aiding his movements by masking them, and that with persistence even nature could be overcome.

Another young officer's frustration offered the general the unusual chance to illustrate the spiritual faith he practiced. Thomas had apparently been standing at the flap of his tent when he offhandedly remarked, "We are getting more cold water thrown on our campaign than we deserve." Overhearing him, a soldier stepped forward to ask if his commander believed in the Divinity. "Most assuredly," Thomas quickly responded. The individual then followed with a query about the Almighty's intent. The Virginian quietly reflected. "I am not prepared, my young friend, to throw any light upon that matter. I have never made religion a study, and I am not equipped for its discussion." But he could attest to his faith and no more questioned that, he explained, "than I would doubt and question the love of my mother," or, he might have added, his country.[31]

The weather did not much improve, but by the end of June the Union troops reached Manchester, Tennessee. Then, at the same time that fighting was occurring on the distant ridges near the little Pennsylvania crossroads town of Gettysburg and the final stages of a siege against the defenders of the Mississippi River town of Vicksburg unfolded, they marched into Tullahoma. Thomas's men pursued the retreating Southerners to the Elk River, where the heavy rains, downed bridges, and some of Bragg's horsemen impeded their progress. The bluecoats were trading shots with Confederates across the river when the Virginian rode up to inquire as to the nature of the resistance they had encountered. The situation threw Thomas into his first meeting with a staff officer with whom he would be closely associated for much of the remainder of his life.

Alfred Lacey Hough recalled that when the general approached he made numerous inquiries and, most importantly for the future staff officer, "listened attentively" before deciding that nothing further could be accomplished. His sent the aide to locate General James Negley and instruct him to "cease firing as it was no use wasting ammunition across the river."[32] Such an order was vintage George Thomas. Waste accomplished nothing. There was no need for artificial display for the sake of an impression of aggressiveness. Once a reasonable expectation of any military benefit no longer existed, further efforts would only be detrimental. Unfortunately, despite his careful husbanding of supplies, the subsequent crossing resulted in "damaging much of their ammunition by the water getting into their cartridge boxes." Thomas was proud of his men and commended them for their "manly endurance and soldierly conduct" in "marching day and night, through a most relentless rain, and over almost impassable roads."[33]

A short time after this encounter, Thomas's name became one of those featured at the highest levels for recognition. In mid-July, Henry Halleck expressed his preference to Ulysses Grant as to which generals he thought deserved promotion to the rank of brigadier in the regular army. As he saw it the short list included William T. Sherman, James B. McPherson, George H. Thomas, John Sedgwick, and Winfield Scott Hancock. He did not indicate that the list reflected a particular priority in the order of the individuals, other than expressing his belief that Sherman and McPherson "have rendered the best service and should come in first." To facilitate this process, he suggested that Grant indicate his own preferences and justifications for them as well. "The feeling is very strong here [in favor] of your generals," Halleck concluded.[34]

Just over a week later, Grant found time to dictate a lengthy communication with President Abraham Lincoln that offered his assessment on Sherman and McPherson as the best qualified to receive regular army promotions. He did not mention the others, including Thomas, either by way of suggesting one or more of them in addition to his choices or to offer any criticism or disqualification of them. The Virginian and his other comrades simply got no advocacy on their parts by Grant for such recognition.[35] His brigadiership in the regular army would not occur until the following October.[36]

Despite the positive developments in the field, affairs remained troubling for William Rosecrans. Thomas had witnessed interference at first hand with Sherman and Buell in Kentucky, and the lesson remained an indelible one for him. The success of General Rosecrans in driving Braxton Bragg from the heart of Tennessee had given way to a period of consolidation. Halleck and the War Department pressured Rosecrans to mount an offensive, and while the desire for maintaining momentum was understandable, the intervention of such officials in the operations of field commands was not. Rosecrans was livid. Historian W. J. Wood catalogued the issues. "Here was an army commander up to his ears in restoring a vital railroad line, clearing mountain roads, pushing to establish essential supply dumps, assembling and training a pontoon bridge train in secrecy, accumulating ammunition for two major battles, preparing thousands of wagons and draft animals for the vital supply trains that would enable the army to operate far from its supply bases beyond the Tennessee—all the preparations required to move an army over three mountain ranges, cross an unfordable river, and move to outmaneuver and defeat a wily enemy on his own ground."[37] The list of concerns was formidable and the obstacles to success significant.

Rosecrans brought the matter to his principal commanders for their reactions and input. Thomas's strong response might have caught him unprepared, but the tenor of it likely did not. "That's right," the Virginian asserted with uncommon public passion. "Stand by that and we will stand by you to the last."[38] This was not mere posturing. Thomas was as incensed as his superior at the interference, seeing it as ample confirmation of his demand for independence for any commander, but especially one engaged in ongoing and complex operations in the field against an opponent. This was why he had refused to supersede Buell in the 1862 Kentucky campaign that nevertheless had ended triumphantly for the Union.

Thomas deployed the Fourteenth Corps for crossing the Tennessee River in the vicinity of Bridgeport with the intention of moving through Trenton toward Steven's Gap, then on through Dug Gap and toward the Georgia town of LaFayette. The problem was that Rosecrans did not realize that while he had maneuvered Bragg out of Tennessee with deftness and precision, the terrain and the Confederate commander's determination to reverse that trend threatened all that he had accomplished thus far. Proceeding through mountain passes to different destinations might leave the Southerners with greater ground to cover, but it enhanced Rosecrans's vulnerability by keeping all of his columns separated in such a fashion as to make it difficult for them to be able to support each other in time of need. Thus, while Thomas L. Crittenden worked his way around Lookout Mountain to descend on Chattanooga, Thomas pushed through Steven's Gap and Alexander McCook approached Winston Gap. Each was easily a day's march from the other, which made them open to attack and destruction in detail. Rosecrans had sacrificed security in the belief that Bragg's army was too demoralized to turn on him.[39]

Until now, there had been no indication that the Confederate commander intended to do anything but continue to withdraw. Thomas's moment of reckoning came on September 9 and 10 when the Confederates turned to confront their tormenters with the Federals seemingly vulnerable in a long valley known as McLemore's Cove. Bragg fashioned a plan to launch a blow, but then failed to execute it, largely because of disgruntled subordinates who refused to follow his orders. Other chances slipped through Southern fingers by virtue of the general incompetence of Leonidas Polk, the bishop-turned-general who had shed his vestments for a different sort of armor. Suddenly and finally alerted to the precarious nature of his divided advance, Rosecrans closed up his formation, and this chance for a Southern reversal passed.

Rosecrans was indeed fortunate that Bragg could not muster the coordinated assault that would have severely damaged, perhaps even destroyed, his command, but the Southerner had demonstrated a return to aggressiveness that once more made him a potent adversary. The opposing forces soon settled along Chickamauga Creek. Bragg hoped to redeem the situation with a bold and unexpected strike that could flank the Union position and threaten their supply and communication routes back to Chattanooga. Rosecrans hoped to consolidate his command in time to prevent disaster, and perhaps to strike a blow of his own if the opportunity presented itself.

In the early morning hours of September 17, George Thomas roused to meet another day in the field. It was approximately 3:30 AM, and the general followed his routine of allowing ten minutes to prepare himself for his daily activities. Chief of staff George E. Flynt appeared to generate the orders for the day. On this occasion, these instructions related not just to the order of march, but to the requirements necessary to ready the men for battle. The troops were to be provided with twenty rounds of ammunition in addition to full cartridge boxes. If there was fighting to be done on this day, it would be well for them to have sufficient resources at hand.[40]

Thomas then settled into a breakfast prepared by the servant he kept in his employ. A contemporary described his "style of living in camp" as "comfortable and even elegant." The sense of elegance came from the general's use of silver "mess ware" rather than the surroundings, since on the occasion that William Shanks ate with Thomas the "breakfast table was spread under the fly of the tent, which served as a kitchen." Of the "smoked fresh beef, ham, and strong black coffee" that constituted the fare, the visitor concluded, "Better beef and better coffee could not have been found in the country in which the army was campaigning, while the hot rolls and potatoes, baked in the hot ashes of a neighboring fire, would have made many a

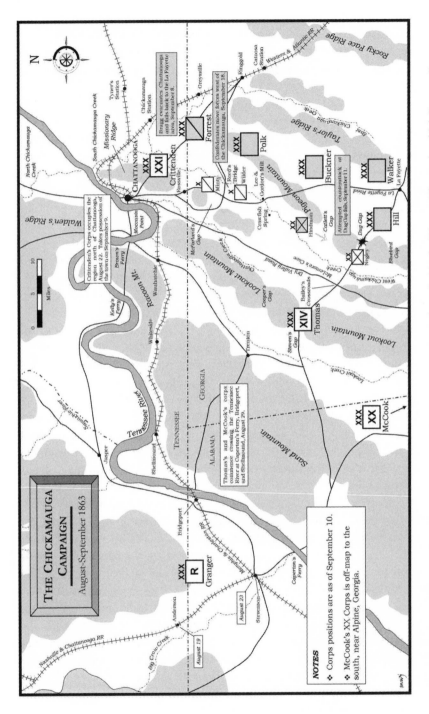

The Chickamauga Campaign in August–September 1863 represented a dramatic period in the Western Theater in which Braxton Bragg attempted to reverse the successes William Rosecrans had experienced for Union arms after Stones River. © Mark W. Johnson.

French cook blush." Shanks had been equally impressed with the presentation, which he termed could have rivaled that found in many fine hotels.[41]

The general might take his rest on a regular army cot in preference to other forms of bedding, but he seemed to have preferred to allow himself and those who dined with him a measure of civilization despite being in the midst of an active campaign. Even so, the affectation must not have been offensive, for the same breakfast guest who marveled at the silver plates, water goblets, and tableware, garnished by folded napkins and china cups, recalled of Thomas, "He is perhaps as free from display and pretension as any man in the army."[42] Apparently, his chief of staff, George Flynt, added a special element to the morning repast. Shanks recalled that the servant "brought me an excellent punch, with 'Colonel Flynt's compliments,' as an appetizer."[43]

Slogging through mountain passes and along the winding roads meant that Thomas's wearied warriors would not have a chance to enjoy much rest themselves. This was especially true when Rosecrans determined to shift his command further to the north, requiring these men to take a circuitous route from near the middle of the line to the left end of it in the direction of Chattanooga. In effect, the move inverted the army's previous position in order to prevent Bragg from being able to flank it himself. Furthermore, the effort had to be undertaken immediately and largely in darkness if the troops were going to be in the appropriate position by daylight. By approximately 4:00 PM on the afternoon of September 18, the men were under way, passing behind Crittenden's lines in the vicinity of Lee and Gordon's Mill. In the jerky motion of columns groping through the night, the troops worked their way to the new positions with only minimal delays for rest.[44] The grueling effort paid off. Historian Steven Woodworth noted the significance of the maneuver: "Without fully realizing it, they had been marching across the front and beyond the flank of the Army of Tennessee."[45]

One observer recalled the evening. "On this night ride through the woods, Generals Thomas and [Absalom] Baird rode side by side, and the two staffs mingled together behind, like the long tail of a kite." The ride afforded an opportunity to record his thoughts about the Virginian. "General Thomas was a very sedate man, who said but little. There was about him at all times, the very atmosphere of solid merit and reserve strength. There was nothing that suggested that he was conscious of his high position, or that he could anticipate any of the glory that afterwards came to him. So we rode along in the gloom and foreboding stillness of that autumn night."[46]

Once the riders had settled into their makeshift camp, Thomas took a place near a campfire. "On the ground near him lay [Captain J. P.] Willard and several others, members of his staff, who, worn with the fatigues of a hard day's battle, had fallen asleep. The General sat with his face to the fire, bending forward, studying a map held at an angle to allow the light to fall upon it." Although he would be oblivious to the fact, men began to gather at a short distance to attempt to discern what they could from their commander's expression as he remained lost in thought while pondering over his map. All the while, Thomas "sat there studying the topography of the ground over which his army must fight, and the lines that must be held at all hazards."[47]

Another visitor found the general out in the open, "no house, no tent, no pomp, no show, no anything, nothing but a man . . . standing erect by the side of a few smoldering embers." He recognized the divergence of the scene when it came to the men and their commander. "All about him lay his sleeping men, stretched upon the ground, completely worn out and exhausted with their long and continued hardships. With great powers of endurance, the general held up when all others were worn out."[48]

One of the participants recalled that it was not until "four o'clock, on the morning of the 19th, about daylight," when the Federal column reached the area of Kelly's Farm. "There was an inferior looking log house on the opposite side of the road, and here General Thomas halted under a spreading tree." The troops deployed, and the general now took the opportunity to "lay down on some blankets, saying to his aide not to let him sleep more than an hour." Thomas had not been resting long when the arrival of Colonel Daniel McCook caused a stir. "He was immediately awakened," the witness recalled, "and McCook reported that he had burnt a bridge after a brigade of rebels had crossed this side of it." The sense was that the isolated Confederate brigade might be cut off and captured if the Union forces acted expeditiously. "Just then [John M.] Brannan's division was passing to our rear to take position on our left," and Thomas sent them "in the direction of this burnt bridge." Unfortunately, the bluecoats quickly learned that their opponents would not be so easily overwhelmed.[49]

Confederates under the renowned cavalry commander Nathan Bedford Forrest had probed the Reed's Bridge Road and prompted the Union response, spearheaded by Ferdinand Van Derveer of Brannan's division. Forrest's gray-clad horsemen, who preferred to fight dismounted as mobile foot soldiers, could call on their infantry colleagues for support if any fight became a general one. Both sides were doing their best to determine the scope and dispositions of their opponents, and a bloody, multiday affair was about to commence with what was in effect initially heavy skirmishing.

Thomas's night was already demanding, even before the first shots rang out. He had anticipated battle and spent considerable energy working to ensure that the pieces would be in place for whatever might transpire with daylight. He made dispositions for supporting troops that could be sent in if and where needed as the renewed contest unfolded. A sure reserve was more than prudent; it could be essential to exploit success or stave off disaster. Historian Glenn Tucker explained, "Thomas, who left nothing more to chance than circumstances compelled, was making doubly sure that he could rely on [General James] Steedman."[50]

Now the moment of combat, with an admittedly undeveloped foe, was at hand. Despite his reputation for seriousness and the appearance of being dour in the presence of others, Thomas's sense of humor remained intact and his tolerance of it in others was not lessened. When he sent John Croxton on a mission into a wooded area that both thought contained only a handful of disorganized Confederates, for the purpose of capturing or dispersing them, the investigation did not last long. Croxton found considerably more rebels than he had bargained for and hastily returned to Thomas to report. "General, I would have brought them in if I had known which ones you wanted."[51]

The combat thus far seemed more piecemeal than concerted on either side. Local advantages allowed one unit to succeed and another to break and run, without much distinction. The Virginian pushed Absalom Baird's division forward to support Brannan's right, and Bragg responded by shoving St. John R. Liddell into the fight as well. The cacophony of shot and shell, interspersed by peels of volleys from small arms and the effects of these projectiles on flesh and bone, filled the air. Now Daniel Govan urged his Arkansas troops forward against Benjamin Scribner's boys from Wisconsin. The Union line faltered and then folded under the weight of pressure added by the Mississippians of Edward Walthall's brigade as the Confederates extended their reach to find the flanks of individual units.

Yet, it is not here that George Thomas secured his famous title as the "Rock of Chickamauga." That recognition was destined for his actions on the next day. Thomas knew only that the struggle would continue and that it had been a near enough thing for him as it was to hold his portion of the line and resist the progression of blows the Confederates had sent against his men. Repeatedly witnesses reported the calmness and coolness he displayed under fire. Thomas seemed imperturbable, and officers and enlisted personnel frequently noted that they drew strength from him in those instances. "I have seen him on many battle-fields," one veteran recalled. "Calm, cool, and brave, his countenance bore no trace of excitement." His presence reassured the men and allowed him to respond to circumstances as they arose. "Watchful of every move of his antagonist, he covered every point." Consequently, there was a sense of security knowing that he was in command, and on the evening of that hard day of fighting at Chickamauga men strained to see signs of assurance in his face and found only studied thought.

Interestingly, this sense of coolness and confidence was part of Thomas's quiet practice of religious faith. "I can not see how a man can be an infidel and remain a brave man," he once observed. "Belief in God is like confidence in one's general, it holds us to the front." In his own fashion, the Virginian was prepared to accept the grace of God on the battlefield. "We feel that the power above has a wise design in making us face the deadly peril." But while he expressed doubt that "any sane mind ever does positively disbelieve," Thomas was aware that his sense of imperfection remained a part of his fabric, too. "One may have painful doubts," he explained, "for we are brought continually face to face with mysterious and apparent contradictions, but back and above all these, we feel that there is an overruling power ever wise and ever just."[52]

Intermittent and interrupted sleep interspersed by marching and fighting over a forty-eight-hour period had left Thomas exhausted. Thus, when General Rosecrans summoned his officers to assess with them the situation and determine their next course of action, the Virginian lapsed into sleep. Occasionally he awakened to inquiries, replying groggily that the army commander should "strengthen the left." A perplexed Rosecrans wanted more detail and plaintively asked, "Where are we going to get the men from?" Thomas had no answer, and finally, after the session had dissolved, most of the officers scattered into the night to complete their duties while James Garfield, Rosecrans's chief of staff, drafted orders to comport with the discussions.[53]

Braxton Bragg had been doing some alterations of his own in anticipation of another day's fighting. In the midst of an ongoing battle and in the face of the enemy, he reorganized his entire command into two wings. Leonidas Polk assumed command of the Confederate right wing, opposite Thomas's position, while the recently arrived James Longstreet commanded the left wing. The Southerners still planned to turn the Union left if possible, but the blue-coated Virginian's realignment had at least temporarily thwarted that possibility. A delay in the morning attacks due to fog, poor communication, and even poorer execution prevented the full cascading effect that Bragg had hoped for against the Union defenders. Driving the Federals from their positions would have to take old-fashioned slugging and perhaps a little bit of luck.

Finally, at approximately 9:30 AM on September 20, well after the hour Braxton Bragg had appointed for a concerted advance, the Confederates tested the part of the Union line for which George Thomas and his troops had responsibility. John Beatty was in the path of the oncoming wave of Confederates, but he had insufficient numbers available to stem the tide. Southerners under the command of former United States vice president John C. Breckinridge had little difficulty finding the flank, and the Federal line shattered under the weight of the assault. Beatty's lack of numbers made the decision to send the command to hold that ground a dangerous move, and the gambit had failed. One historian termed the positioning of this command in an isolated position by Thomas as "one of his rare mistakes," and the Federals soon paid a dear price for the miscalculation.[54] The Confederates were now in a position on the extreme Union left to turn the entire flank and, more ominously, cut the Federals off from their line of retreat to Chattanooga.

It certainly must have seemed as if the Southerners would roll through the Northern defenders with ease. But appearances proved deceiving. Into the difficult situation strode the men of Colonel Timothy R. Stanley, who sought also to rally as many of Beatty's broken men as possible. They confronted one of the regiments Breckinridge had faced south to sweep the Union line. In the hail of shot and shell, the Confederate commander, Daniel Adams, fell wounded, and the Southerners shrank back. To Adams's left was Marcellus Stovall's regiment, bringing pressure to bear directly on Thomas's right flank. A brief attempt by a brigade to shift to react to the threat disintegrated, but other Federals, under Van Derveer, moved into the maelstrom. With almost parade-ground precision, the troops maneuvered through the fire and battle smoke, and it was Stovall's turn to fall back in disorder. Thomas's ability to draw on reserves at critical junctures was decisive in the contest for Kelly's Field.

Among the other Southerners who surged forward against the blazing Union line of breastworks was the redoubtable Irish expatriate Patrick R. Cleburne. Cleburne had tried a hectic night assault at the end of the first day that produced as much friendly fire in the confused darkness as anything else. A few captures of men and cannon offered what little satisfaction that could be had, and in the morning light it became brutally clear that the Federals were in ideal positions to exact a substantial measure of revenge. Cleburne's people pressed against a crucial salient held by John Starkweather and crowned with artillery pieces. Closer to the Kelly house, August Willich and Charles Cruft were also dug in with plenty of artillery support. William B. Hazen performed stoutly, too, as he had done to such advantage at Stones River; only the breastworks prevented heavy casualties from being inflicted as they had been previously on that earlier field. It was the Confederates under James Deshler whose advance suffered devastating repulse as he lost his life directing them in the futile assaults.

Disjointed even in success, the Confederates lost momentum at the very point at which they stood poised to turn Rosecrans's defensive line. The failure to provide additional supporting troops doomed the best opportunity for the Confederates to crush the Union left and essentially finish the battle and Rosecrans's army in one fell swoop. Thomas's relatively compact position and the availability of reinforcements proved decisive. Thanks to

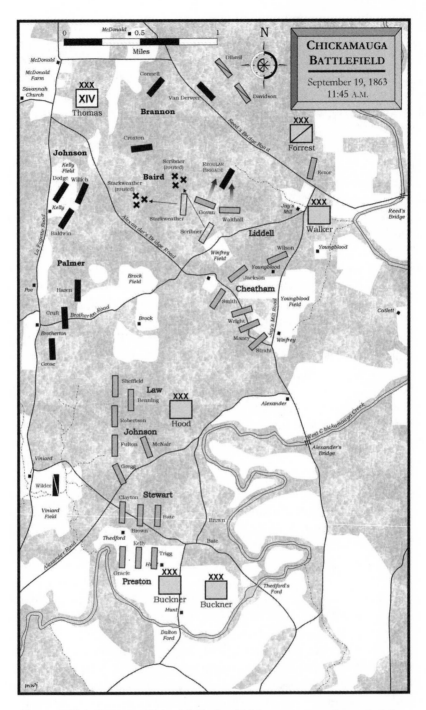

Thomas held the important Union left flank at Chickamauga as combat exploded there. Situation on September 19, 1863, 11:45 A.M. © Mark W. Johnson.

the efforts of these stalwart veterans, it was possible to keep the Union left flank intact, if other pressures did not overwhelm it or cause some other portion of the line to fail in the meantime.[55]

Thomas may not have been of much help to William Rosecrans in the council the night before, but the army commander was among those who sought his counsel the next morning. As the fighting resumed he rode to Thomas's section of the lines and found the Virginian in an unusual mood. Their discussion tended to focus on the issues of the previous day, when both sides had suffered from sudden reverses of fortune. Suddenly and rather uncharacteristically, Thomas burst from the reflection of what he had seen, "Whenever I touched their flanks they broke, general, they broke." A witness of the exchange noted the animation in his face as he spoke, but when Thomas noticed that he was being watched, he returned to a more somber cast. The momentary dropping of his carefully constructed guard actually caused him to blush in embarrassment. "His eyes were bent immediately to the ground," William Shanks remembered, "and the rest of his remarks were confined to a few brief replies to the questions addressed to him."[56] There was no record as to whether Rosecrans noticed the change or was so absorbed as to miss it entirely, but exposure of the inner core of feelings was rare for his studied subordinate.

Thomas also liked to reconnoiter personally, and the desire to do so occasionally led him into danger from enemy fire. Even when he did not expose himself recklessly, the general's proximity to the front could lead to difficulties. On the morning of September 20, as he and a staff officer sat just behind the Union lines, Confederate artillery began to open on the position. "While thus exposed," a participant remembered, "a shell passed between the general and his aid, causing them to look at each other with a quiet smile." Apparently, the men had little chance to contemplate the close call they had just experienced before a second projectile followed a similar path. "Major, I think we had better retire a little," the general explained calmly, perhaps considering the notion that the third time might not be the charm for them.[57]

Calmness in the face of danger did not prevent George Thomas from being concerned with the fate of the army. As commander of the force occupying the left of the Union line, he had responsibility for maintaining the flank that, if turned, might be fatal to Northern chances for success. Some historians have criticized him for repeated calls for assistance and William Rosecrans for responding so uncritically to them, with Larry Daniel asserting that Thomas's subsequent performance on that day "barely made up for his mistakes in the morning."[58] In fairness, Thomas recognized the critical nature of his position and understood, even with his penchant for preparation, that no battle was free of risk. Allowing this flank to be turned would mean that the Federals lost their most direct connection to Chattanooga, and thus the potentially negative results would accelerate greatly.

As the fighting developed through the morning, the gray-clad soldiers experienced both hard fighting on their right and good fortune elsewhere. At just after 11 AM, General James Longstreet launched an assault against the Union center; his men found and poured through an inadvertent gap created when defenders shifted out of the position unnecessarily. Rosecrans had chided General Thomas Wood openly for not following orders expeditiously, and when that officer received instructions to relocate his command and align with another he did not hesitate a second time. No gap had existed to cover until now, and Longstreet's Confederates picked this most opportune moment to press their attack in that sector. Eight Southern brigades smashed into the area Wood had vacated. The penetration shattered the Union forces to their front, detaching the right and left flanks and creating widespread pandemonium among the terrified defenders. The Rebel tide engulfed the few units that made any attempt to halt or delay them. As both center and right gave way to the forces arrayed against them, Thomas's men prepared for a crucial fight on wooded high ground that took its name from the nearby Snodgrass house and the oddly shaped ridge adjacent to it.

Thomas had assessed the breakdown of positions around Dyer Field and correctly understood that a stand would have to be taken elsewhere if greater portions of the Union army were to be able to retreat. He rode over to the area of Snodgrass Hill where he could have a reasonably good vantage point. How serious his presence was for the success of Union arms in the desperate action to come may be best attested to by the reaction he received from the men who would defend the ground around him. The survivors of the carnage remembered seeing the general calmly bestriding his horse, surveying the scene, and for them, at least, it had a profound affect. Historian Peter Cozzens termed the general's example on this field as "electrifying" and attested to "the uplifting effect this had on morale."[59] Establishing a field headquarters at the site, Thomas spent his time in the saddle and, according to a modern account, "rode back and forth between this point and his Kelly Field positions issuing orders and inspiring confidence by his presence."[60]

Personal example was important for the Virginian. At one point in the thickest of the fighting, men from one of the units broke ranks and hastened toward the rear. Two of the officers ran headlong into the general, who admonished them to regain their composure and go back to the front. "Gentlemen," he noted simply, "your regiment is there, or ought to be there, and you will join your commands instantly." According to the account, Thomas watched impassively amidst the storm raging around them, but "saw the order obeyed to the letter."[61]

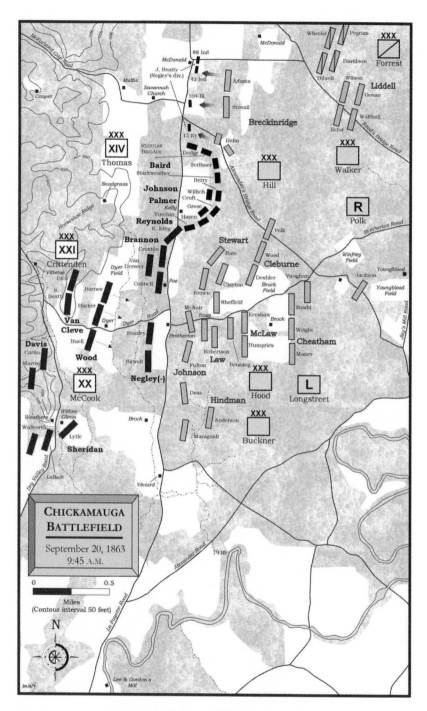

On the second day of sustained fighting at Chickamauga, Thomas remained
ensconced in positions on the Union left in the vicinity of the Kelly Farm. Situation
on September 20, 1863, 9:45 A.M. © Mark W. Johnson.

Another of the participants caught glimpses of the general while helping to distribute ammunition to the men on the embattled Union line. "Every soldier knew that Thomas was there," William Calkins recalled, "and turned instinctively as he rode from one point to another in the lull that was only a prelude to another and fiercer attack." Thomas inspired the Illinois volunteer in terms the witness could not describe in other than superlatives as Calkins remembered the engagement in which he also suffered the fate of falling into Confederate hands as a wounded prisoner.[62]

Thomas knew men and he understood morale. A stern example in the face of uncertainty or adversity could be a key to success. Exhibiting trust, or at least appearing to do so, was equally important. A commander simply could not be everywhere at once and had to rely on those who were where he was not to perform as he would have done in their stead. Thus, to Colonel Charles G. Harker he stated, "This hill must be held and I trust you to do it." The confidence exuded from "Little Charlie," who assured his commander, "We will hold it or die here." Under the circumstances, such words were not histrionics, they were statements of fact, and alternate versions of them spread as Thomas presented the same challenge to other subordinates.[63]

The Confederates were finally making headway at Kelly's Field, largely because the defenders had received word to withdraw. Others took up positions before Thomas's Snodgrass/Horseshoe Ridge line and deployed for the purpose of driving the bluecoats from that ground. Unfortunately, decisions had to be made on the spur of the moment and with partial information and poor intelligence. Thomas had sent word for James Negley to assume responsibility for artillery in the new position, and that officer managed to accumulate an impressive array of tubes and supporting troops. As conditions deteriorated around him, the officer, who had battled illness and limited rest, determined that the best course would be to withdraw the guns in order to assure their safety from capture. The act created difficulties for Negley in the aftermath of the battle, but more significantly deprived the Federals of substantial firepower for their defense of the critical point.[64]

Such concerns gathered on Thomas's broad shoulders as the Southerners pushed forward their attacks. At various points in the difficult day, he allowed his features to betray the doubt that he was attempting to suppress as the Confederates tore at his position. Those careful observers might have noticed, like someone sitting across from another at a gambling table, the general's "tells" or physical manifestations of what was in his mind. One officer watched the ways in which Thomas fidgeted with his whiskers as a sign of his thought processes, recalling "when satisfied he smoothes them down; when troubled he works them all out of shape."[65] A newspaper correspondent noted the same tendencies, explaining "if everything progresses satisfactorily he caresses his whiskers, moving his right hand down upon them from the chin." Under more adverse conditions, the writer observed, the general reversed the process, "the strokes upward being more numerous."[66] In these circumstances especially, the Virginian's mustache and beard must have been disheveled indeed.

Gordon Granger, commanding the reserve, had spent a good portion of the morning anxiously attempting to determine what was going on and what he might do to lend a hand. It was almost midday, following a reconnaissance that had yielded little except more lost time, when he and his subordinate, James Steedman, rode into their camp. "Thomas is having a hell of a fight over there," one of the officers remarked, and the words were the spur Granger had needed to spring into action, all the while hoping that it was not already too late. He went to see Rosecrans, who was so out of sorts by what he had experienced that he resorted to overcompensation in drafting an order for Thomas to withdraw. As Rosecrans laid out the instructions in painful detail, Granger's subordination departed from him. "Oh, that's all nonsense, general," he blurted. "Send Thomas an order to retire. He knows what he's about as well as you do." Either too worn or beaten down by events, Rosecrans tore up the message and drafted another. He understood that George Thomas would indeed know what to do.[67]

By late in the day, it was becoming more difficult to obscure concern as casualties mounted and exhaustion and depletion of available supplies set in for the troops themselves. The strain of the combat was starting to show. Thomas was soon directing commanders to have their men take ammunition from the dead and wounded if necessary to continue the fight. It would be vital to hold until dark, when a withdrawal might be undertaken with less Confederate harassment.

When Thomas detected a rising cloud of dust coming from the distance and located at such a point in the rear of his position that if it were a sign of enemy movement the day might indeed be lost, his normally controlled demeanor underwent its severest test of that difficult day. The cloud bore no identifying mark to ease his mind. "The anxiety of General Thomas increased with every moment of delay in the development of the character of the advancing column," a participant recalled. "At one time he said nervously to his staff, 'Take my glass, some of you whose horse stands steady—tell me what you see.'" The spectacle of the normally sedate general passing his field glasses from one set of eyes to another as the knot of officers collectively tried to figure out the nature of the troops heading their way must have been remarkable. One of the men peering across the landscape ventured that he saw the National colors. "Do you think so? Do you think so?" Thomas inquired anxiously, employing the habit under stress of repeating himself. Finally, Thomas had more than he could take of the mystery and sent an officer to gather the necessary intelligence at first hand.[68]

Only after what must have seemed an eternity to the anxious general, the staffer returned in the company of General James Steedman. As Steedman rode up to report, Thomas welcomed his arrival enthusiastically. "General Steedman, I have always been glad to see you, but never so glad as now." Then, practical matters being paramount under the circumstances, Thomas added, "How many muskets have you got?" The subordinate responded that he could bring 7,500 into the fray, and the Virginian noted gratefully, "It is a good force, and needed badly." There was no more time for pleasantries even if Thomas had been the type of leader to engage in them. He already had the notion as to just how these badly needed muskets could be employed. "General Steedman, the enemy are occupying that wood and have been annoying us very much. You will form your command on the left of General [Thomas J.] Wood's men and drive the enemy out of that timber."[69] A witness also noticed that Thomas reacted strongly to one of Steedman's inquiries about how the battle was proceeding. "The damned scoundrels are fighting without any system," he blurted, in reference to the Confederates. The subordinate offered the view that they might respond in kind, and Thomas quickly had the new arrivals deployed.[70]

In such situations, the general's reputation for stoicism on the battlefield was inspirational. One individual later recalled, "I see General Thomas, brave, bronzed, cool and unmoved, as he sat on his bay charger without any attempt at display or pomp—utterly alone in this very hell of battle."[71] In most instances the general would be surrounded by a retinue of staff, but in the heat of fighting, with some individuals racing off with messages and others seeing to the details of the command, it was not unusual for the Virginian to occupy a separate space while he assessed the fluid situation and contemplated his next actions. Thomas knew that in all instances he would be under scrutiny, but these circumstances were the perfect opportunity for the expression of personal characteristics that came naturally to him anyway and that he had assiduously cultivated through his years as a soldier.

During the course of the fighting, one of the aides Thomas had sent scrambling for assistance dashed up suddenly, gave his report, and, having received his instructions, turned sharply to scurry off. Thomas admonished him to lessen his pace so as not to give a negative impression to anyone who might be watching his demeanor for signs of distress. There was no need to promote any sense of panic among the hard-pressed Union defenders. Another courier, perhaps understanding the fluid nature of any combat, sought instruction as to where he could find the general when he returned from his mission. "Here, Sir, here," Thomas barked exasperatedly.[72]

Any exposure of dissatisfaction or concern dissipated rapidly. When at about the same time another subordinate appeared, hailing the general and inquiring, "How goes the battle?" Thomas remained poised, offering a hearty, "Very well, very well, sir!" But work remained to be done, and the commander added quickly, "Move your line forward!"[73] He was not one to be panicked easily, and as the Confederates threw the weight of their units at his line the Virginian found the means to react and adjust, while generally maintaining his composure and inspiring his men.

Just how well things might be going depended upon the circumstances that prevailed, but the presence of stout leadership from Thomas and his subordinates could not be discounted. One contemporary recalled the manner in which General Steedman prevented his wavering survivors from retreating. Despite determined resistance to repeated Confederate assaults, the command now "betrayed signs of breaking." The officer approached a flag bearer, grabbed the standard, and shouted out, "Go back, boys, go back, but the FLAG can't go with you!" The distressed soldiery responded as their commander had expected and returned to the fight with renewed gusto.[74]

Not every commander set such a stellar example. When Thomas left the vicinity of Snodgrass Hill to assess the realignment of men from Kelly Field, he left Gordon Granger in authority in his stead. The officer's performance at this point was subpar by any standard. "Granger, who had spent most of the afternoon serving as a cannoneer in the yard of the Snodgrass cabin, departed the field not long after Thomas, leaving subordinate commanders to their own devices," later students of the battle explained.[75] Described by one of his officers as "believed to be an incompetent man by everybody from colonels to privates," Granger would be subject to similar criticism later at Chattanooga.[76] However, on this occasion, Thomas took no disparaging official notice of his conduct.

Thomas had his favorites, although he did not tolerate sycophants, those who did not perform their duties in his estimation, or individuals who transgressed when it came to military protocols or the ill-treatment of vulnerable parties. He had certainly not made a habit of currying favors, but many associates came to admire him. Among these was James Garfield, who now hustled toward the battlefield with verbal instructions for Thomas from a shaken Rosecrans, admonishing the subordinate to withdraw from his embattled position immediately. Garfield would exploit his dramatic ride to Thomas for maximum personal and political benefit, but the breathless arrival was instantly calmed by the steady example the Virginian set. When Garfield had managed to blurt out his instructions, Thomas responded matter-of-factly, "It will ruin the army to withdraw it now. This position must be held until night."[77]

As reinforcements reached the field, Thomas sent them against the Confederate center, rather than use them simply to bolster the endangered flanks as conventional wisdom might suggest that he do. In this way, he

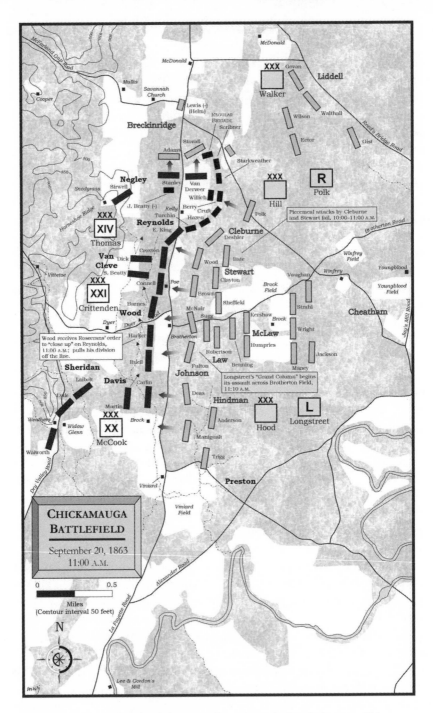

Thomas's hold on the Union left appeared tenuous as it absorbed repeated blows that increasingly found the flank north of Kelly Field and required the timely shifting of forces to sustain a viable defense, while James Longstreet began a critical assault against the Union center that jeopardized the entire Federal army. Situation on September 20, 1863, 11:00 A.M. © Mark W. Johnson.

forced the Southerners to concentrate on the center of their own lines, now threatened with giving way. The effort bought critical time to enable Thomas to hold on to the Snodgrass/Horseshoe Ridge defense line until the coming of night could allow him to pull back toward Chattanooga.

The Virginian was already preparing for the extraction of his men, even as they expended the last of their rounds and energy clinging to their positions. "Yes, he sent for me, and I went down into the hollow where he was," James Steedman recalled years later. "It was after sunset," he added. "He was sitting on a log, nervously picking off pieces of bark and biting them and throwing them away." Steedman did not say if Thomas was doing so deliberately or absent-mindedly, but the commanding general certainly had a great deal to ponder as the daylight slipped away. "Gen. Steedman, you know we must obey orders in war," he suddenly asserted. "I have received orders to fall back on Rossville." Fidgeting with what Steedman assumed were the instructions secreted in his blouse, Thomas opted not to display the document for his subordinate's perusal. Instead, he inquired if the officer had a regiment that remained "in any condition for fighting," and when Steedman responded affirmatively, Thomas instructed him to "put them in the rear."

General Thomas followed quickly with the query, "How are you situated for a retreat?" The answer would have a great bearing on the ability of the Union forces to effect a withdrawal, and Steedman assured his superior that both the ground and his available artillery cover would allow for such a retrograde movement. "All, right; do so," Thomas ordered with his accustomed economy of words. Steedman departed to carry out his orders and found that even under these extreme circumstances the Confederates seemed to have no desire to press their advantage. "They had got all they wanted and were glad to see us draw off," he surmised of his battered opponents, and consequently, "were in no mood to molest us."[78]

In the aftermath of the desperate defense, Thomas presented little publicly of the sense that he thought he had saved the command from complete destruction. To the casual observer he seemed once more lost in his own thoughts and oblivious to what was occurring around him. As he shared a cup of coffee with one of his colonels, he also apparently failed to notice that the officer had been hurt in the fighting. The conversation between the two men never reached a point above ordinary topics, as if they were passing a quiet meal at a restaurant. One of the men who watched the exchange recalled, "No one could have known from Thomas's remarks that a battle had been raging, or that his host had been wounded."[79] The recent events seemingly were just matters of course. The near destruction and the hard-fought salvation of the army apparently were factors now hardly worth mentioning.

Perhaps the explanation for Thomas's attitude concerning what was arguably his greatest battlefield performance in the war could be his belief that the soldiers themselves were responsible for any successes he enjoyed. "The brave fellows of that noblest military force the world ever saw made the Rock of Chickamauga, not I," he explained after the war. "On that sunny September afternoon as they stood in a half circle facing the enemy that again and again poured a superior force three lines deep upon our front, not a man of them but knew that our right had been shattered and our left disorganized, and yet the brave fellows plied their guns cool, firm and determined." It was almost as if he had been describing himself under those trying hours, but his conclusion was as sure as it was succinct. "They made success possible under all circumstances."[80]

Thomas's performance had secured the attentions of more than the participants in the action. Confiding his thoughts in his diary, Lincoln's secretary of the navy, Gideon Welles, observed, "The most reliable account of the battle leaves little doubt we were beaten, and only the skill and valor of General Thomas and his command saved the whole concern from a disastrous defeat."[81] The secretary continued to be positive in his assessment of the Virginian, communicating to President Lincoln in a Monday morning session on September 28, "I expressed a doubt if he had any one suitable for that command or the equal of Thomas, if a change was to be made. There was no one in the army who, from what I had seen, and known of him, was so fitted for that command as General Thomas." Considering the general "capable" and possessing "undoubted merit," Welles thought he held the characteristic most important of a commander at this moment when confidence needed to be reestablished, having demonstrated himself to be "a favorite with the men."[82]

Once the fighting was over and the recuperative period got under way, some of the staff officers found the opportunity to engage in other pursuits. George Flynt, whose punch had so delighted William Shanks at the general's breakfast mess, took the chance to visit Cincinnati. Among other items of business, he appeared to have been charged with the responsibility of monitoring and updating his superior's wardrobe. "I have purchased some under and linen shirts for the General," he wrote fellow staffer Andrew MacKay from Cincinnati, and had the items forwarded to the Galt House in Louisville. "The undershirts will suit the Genl., but I fear he will think the linen to[o] dark[.] I could not find any material that I thought would suit him better." The market for such goods in Cincinnati was "extremely feverish, and any style of merchandise advanced and advancing." But there were other compensations in the river city. "I have been feasted & invited every where. The unpleasant part of it all is no one would allow me to show the color of my money."[83]

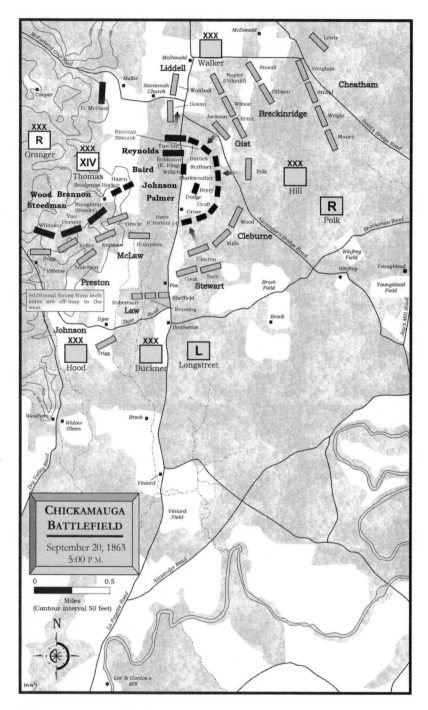

This was the scene of the crucial late-day action at Snodgrass Hill and Horseshoe Ridge that secured for George Thomas the sobriquet "Rock of Chickamauga." Situation on September 20, 1863, 5:00 P.M. © Mark W. Johnson.

Especially in later years, Confederate opponents recognized that George Thomas had played a critical role in the pivotal engagement. G. Moxley Sorrel, James Longstreet's staff officer, wrote of the Virginian after the war, "He was one of the ablest of their soldiers, perhaps none equaled him, and I heartily wish he had been anywhere but at Chickamauga."[84] In the context of the war itself, and particularly when assessing an outcome from a distance, even the basic facts were difficult to sort out, much less allow for credit or blame to be attached accurately. In Louisiana, a Confederate serving there tried to sift through the various rumors that flew around him. For a week in December he tried to sort out fact from fiction. "Hear one report to-day that Bragg has beaten Thomas desperately; & then hear that Thomas has beaten Bragg," he wrote on the seventh. Then he decided that the reports might as well cancel each other out. "An alkali & an acid, when mixed, neutralize each other."[85] Three days later there was more information, this time based on various newspaper reports. Even then, the intelligence was contradictory, with one holding that "Bragg has fallen back to Chickamauga after a hard contest with Thomas" and the other that "Bragg has beaten Thomas severely." It was enough to exasperate the soldier, who concluded simply and resignedly, "Some how, it seems to be hard to get the true history."[86]

George Thomas emerged from the crisis with a reputation firmly established as "the Rock of Chickamauga." Of course, as he knew well, there were plenty of heroics for the men who had stood with him and held as the rest of the army crumbled. Official Washington rewarded him with command of Rosecrans's remnant until Ulysses Grant could arrive. In the meantime, Thomas was left to assess the situation and begin to redress the problems that had ensued. His role in that future configuration of Federal forces would remain to be seen, but he had at last shaken any lingering doubts about his loyalty to the cause of the Union or his staunchness in her defense. At the critical moment, he had proven, in line with William T. Sherman's characterization, that he was "as true as steel."

10   Redemption at Missionary Ridge (October 1863–January 1864)

> *"Rosencranz has been superceded by Geo. H. Thomas, a good thing for us."*
> —J. E. B. Stuart to his wife

> *"I will hold the town till we starve."*
> —Thomas to U. S. Grant, Chattanooga

> *"I wish you would add also that I would not like to take the command of an army where I should be exposed to the imputation of having intrigued or of having exercised any effort to supplant my previous commander."*
> —Thomas to Charles Dana

> *"I cannot leave; something is sure to get out of order if I go away."*
> —Thomas to O. O. Howard

In the aftermath of Chickamauga, George Thomas had too much to do to savor any reputation that might have been won with the stand at Snodgrass Hill and Horseshoe Ridge. Thomas may have been responsible for saving Rosecrans's army from annihilation, but it was still "Old Rosy's" army. "Old Pap's" duty was to assist as much as possible in helping to hold a defense together while official Washington sorted out the situation and determined how best to proceed. He might also be given the authority of command if William Rosecrans would not or could not continue in that capacity. In any case, Secretary of War Edwin Stanton and General Ulysses S. Grant were the primary decision makers for filling that role, and neither wished to see Rosecrans continue.

An officer and future historian of the Army of the Cumberland, Henry Cist, noted that Rosecrans made his first priority in Chattanooga to prepare the command defensively, with earthworks and fortifications.[1] The effort to supervise this activity led to an awkward moment for the generals when Thomas accompanied Rosecrans to the front. "It happened that this was also General Thomas's first public appearance after the battle of Chickamauga," a contemporary recalled, "and wherever the two made their appearance, the troops threw down their spades and picks, gathered in tumultuous and noisy crowds" around the Virginian. The scene prompted "disgust" in the discomfited commander and "confusion" in his shy subordinate, but reflected the status to which Thomas had risen in the eyes of these survivors of Chickamauga.[2] Another observed grandiosely, "Genl. Thomas has always commanded the respect and confidence of the Army to a greater extent than any man in it. Today he is its idol." Then, adding that the general embodied "everything to inspire confidence," the infantryman concluded, "He is a soldier—Rosecrans [is] not, but is a seeker of popular favor."[3]

Secretary of War Stanton's man on the scene, Charles Dana, thought matters had progressed too far for Rosecrans to remain in place. He suggested keeping the commanding slot in the West, rather than bring in a general from outside with whom the army was unfamiliar, and thought Ulysses Grant would be the logical choice. Then, upon further thought, he turned to Thomas as a distinct possibility and began to express his feeling that the Virginian would prove to be a more popular selection with regard to the troops themselves. Stanton signaled his agreement by sending Dana to approach Thomas personally. "I wish you to go directly to see General Thomas, and say to him his services, his abilities, his character, his unselfishness, have always been most cordially appreciated by me," he explained, before applying the salve to the Virginian's tender ego by adding, "and that it is not my fault that he has not long since had command of an independent army."

Stanton knew his man well. The official's allusion to the undeserved deferral of recognition, despite the merit for it, and the possibility of "an independent army" would be enormously appealing to Thomas. Indeed, when Dana reached the headquarters and found the general just completing his evening meal, he presented the contents of the telegram. Dana recalled that the message left Thomas momentarily speechless. When at length he was able to speak the Virginian expressed his thanks and remarked that his genuine preference was for "command of an army that I could myself have organized, disciplined, distributed, and combined." Thomas further indicated that he did not want any assignment that others might construe as improper. "I wish you would add also that I would not like to take the command of an army where I should be exposed to the imputation of having intrigued or of having exercised any effort to supplant my previous commander."[4] Far from his taking the opportunity to advance his own fortunes, even the insinuation of having done so at someone else's expense was too much for him to bear. He could already hear the snickers and innuendo, which he squelched and silenced by refusing to accept the position under such circumstances.

Dana made no record of his immediate reaction to this sentiment, which he certainly recognized was more than a gesture made out of propriety or modesty. He described Thomas as "an officer of the highest qualities, soldierly and personally." The Virginian was "a man of the greatest dignity of character" and "a delightful man to be with; there was no artificial dignity about Thomas." But Dana also recognized that he was "very set in his opinions," albeit seemingly without impatience toward others.[5] Still, the

Washington official must have been perplexed by the reluctance to assume such an important role over concern for appearances.

Dana noted that several days later he received a confidant of General Thomas, who insisted that "he would gladly accept any other command, to which Mr. Stanton should see fit to assign him, [but] he could not consent to become the successor of General Rosecrans." The messenger reiterated Thomas's concern not to "do anything to give countenance to the suspicion that he had intrigued against his commander's interest," and for good measure pronounced Rosecrans fit to continue.[6]

Like so much of Thomas's complex personality, his loyalty remained among his most admirable of qualities, but his adherence to duty was equally so, and as developments unfolded in the aftermath of Chickamauga that trait would have to take precedence. Abraham Lincoln's secretary, John Hay, recorded in his diary of October 19, "The President told me this morning that Rosecrans was to be removed from command of the army at Chattanooga." Thomas was to take immediate control, and Grant would be called upon to "command the whole force" that was assembling there. "He says that Rosecrans has seemed to lose spirit and nerve since the battle of Chicamauga."[7] A few days later, Hay recorded Lincoln's famous assessment that ever since the fighting at Chickamauga Rosecrans had seemed "confused and stunned like a duck hit on the head."[8]

But John Hay was not prepared to provide the Virginian with an unqualified endorsement. In the initial conversation with the president, he observed bluntly, "I told him that I believed Thomas would fail in attack, like Meade and others." He felt that even the most significant of attributes that could be displayed under one set of conditions would likely become limiting in another to generals like George Thomas. "The *vis inertia* which prevents those fellows from running when attacked will prevent them from moving in the initiative."[9] This was a familiar indictment, and one that prompted the addition of Grant to the command mix at Chattanooga and that Thomas would continue to struggle to overcome in the months ahead.

Rosecrans received the official word of his removal and instantly sent for Thomas to pass leadership to him and make his intentions known about his departure. Rosecrans's biographer noted the awkward moment, made even more so by the Virginian's reluctance to appear that he was angling to assume command of the army and had in any way conspired or intrigued to get it. "Thomas came alone, sat down, and Rosecrans handed him the dispatch in silence," William Lamers explained. Rosecrans himself later described what transpired between the two men. "Slowly and solemnly," Thomas read the papers, "turning pale and drawing his breath harder as he proceeded." Rosecrans noted the personal distress that attended the moment for his loyal lieutenant and recalled that Thomas asserted, "General, you remember what I told you some two weeks ago." Rosecrans would not let him continue and quickly rejoined in an almost familial tone, "George, but we are in the face of the enemy. No one but you can safely take my place now; and for the country's sake, you *must* do it. Don't fear; no cloud of doubt will ever come into my mind as to your fidelity to friendship and honor."[10] Whatever his personal feelings, and there was no reason based upon his previous actions and relationship with his superior to assume that they were other than he articulated, George Thomas knew and accepted his duty as now laid out unequivocally for him.

In the higher echelons of Washington, sentiment for replacing Rosecrans was strong. But the desire to put Thomas in his stead was not unanimous. James Steedman recalled years after the war that he received a directive to travel to the nation's capital. Nerves had been so raw in Chattanooga following Chickamauga that he had experienced a heated exchange with Rosecrans and threatened to submit his resignation. Thomas was one of the officers who attempted to intervene in the squabble and settle the matter when the call came for Steedman's appearance. "That is equivalent to an order from the President," Thomas assured him, "and comes opportunely, and will probably settle your trouble."

Steedman met with Secretary of War Stanton briefly in Louisville, Kentucky, before proceeding to Washington. Three hours in the presence of the commander in chief allowed Lincoln also to query him about the leadership of the Army of the Cumberland. The chief executive wondered if the officer had an opinion about Rosecrans, and after Steedman insisted that Rosecrans would do fine as long as things went well, Lincoln thought the endorsement a decidedly lukewarm one. When Lincoln next asked the soldier whom he would recommend under the prevailing circumstances, Steedman suggested Thomas. "I am glad to hear you say that," Lincoln responded immediately, noting that he had been of the same opinion for some time. "I believe you are right, and that he is the man for the emergency."[11]

As news filtered out about the change in Union commanders, various Confederates took notice and offered their opinions. From his cavalry headquarters in Virginia, in October 1863, Jeb Stuart remarked pointedly to his wife, "Rosencranz has been superceded by Geo. H. Thomas, a good thing for us."[12] A Kentucky Confederate concurred with his Virginia counterpart in anticipating Thomas's elevation to command as a positive development for Southern fortunes in the Western Theater of operations. "Rosecrans removed & Thomas in command. Good for us," Edward Guerrant confided in his diary in late October as the news reached him. The soldier noted that "his army was defeated & is invested now, & a sacrifice was demanded," and concluded that the Federals had no choice but to say,

"Farewell 'Old Rosy.'" The transition he expected in his opponent's ranks presented Guerrant with the opportunity to assess the choices. Highlighting Thomas's name among those on the list for the "West," the Kentucky staff officer thought that the prospects for Northern success in both major theaters could be described simply as, "Going, going, gone."[13]

When Thomas assumed command on October 20, 1863, his first inclination was to assess the programs his former chief had already set in motion. Consistency and order being prized characteristics, it only made sense for him to continue such policies until he deemed a change necessary based upon his own observation and experience. Henry Cist explained, "One of the last subjects of conference between Generals Rosecrans and Thomas after midnight of October 19th, 1863, and after Rosecrans' order relinquishing the command had been written and signed, grew out of the request of General Thomas to General Rosecrans, 'Now, General, I want you to be kind enough to describe the exact plan for the taking of Lookout Valley as you proposed it.'" What followed was a sense of continuity, even as the command experienced a transition in leadership, as well as a degree of flexibility on the part of the Virginian.[14]

Thomas focused on the steps to be taken to secure a better system of supply for the beleaguered army. General William F. Smith had been out on the ground, surveying the area for potential operations under Rosecrans, when he returned to headquarters and learned that a change in leadership was about to take place. Also for continuity's sake, Thomas made the understandable decision to retain Smith as his chief engineer.

The next morning, Smith met with the new commander, and Thomas laid out his ideas for crossing the river. The engineer encouraged the general to defer any order for implementation until he had heard what Smith had learned on his reconnoitering mission. Over the next several days the men discussed the alternatives. Demonstrating open-mindedness rather than the rigidity of insisting upon the correctness of his plan simply because it was his, Thomas acceded to Smith's scheme for reopening the supply lines. Smith was quickly back at work, with Thomas's full support to back him.[15]

The most difficult challenge was to obtain sufficient resources to feed and maintain an army and restore morale in it, regardless of who eventually would assume responsibility in Chattanooga. If he were to prove successful in securing supplies the mind-set of the men would in many ways take care of itself, but the precarious state of supply was not an easy one to remedy. In later years, the Virginian paid an especially enthusiastic compliment to the man he considered instrumental in providing as much relief as possible to the troubled command. "Joining me at Chattanooga, at the period when all looked gloomy and foreboding," Thomas recalled to James L. Donaldson, "you unraveled the intricate meshes then surrounding the Quartermaster's

Department within my command, and restored system and order where confusion had triumphantly held sway."[16] Thomas could offer no higher praise, and an individual could not have provided more important service in his estimation than the establishment of "order" out of "confusion."

However, in the aftermath of the transfer of authority, not everyone was as anxious to move forward regarding the change in leadership as Rosecrans had demonstrated himself to be. On November 15, a disgruntled officer fired off a scathing letter of protest to his father. Frank Aldrich first articulated a defense of the departed officer, speculating that Rosecrans's personal popularity may actually have cost him support from Washington. He managed even to turn the defeat at Chickamauga into something amounting to victory when he observed, "These are the only reasons that I can give for this, in my opinion, most unfortunate removal of a general who was uniformly successful in every campaign." Finally, concerning the distasteful developments, he concluded, "Of one thing I am certain, Rosey has not lost one jot or tittle of the confidence of the officers of this army because of his late movements in the field, nor has his removal abated that confidence." Despite his feelings of betrayal, Aldrich was actually pleased with Rosecrans's successor. He recognized the Virginian as "universally respected and esteemed throughout this Department for his sterling qualities as a soldier and a great commander." Aldrich predicted, "Our men will fight under him with the greatest confidence wherever and whenever he will."[17]

Sergeant George Cram was angry for another reason. As he explained to his mother toward the end of October, "Our calculations are like chaff here, blown away by every new wind." This wind had produced a storm that left the soldier bitter. "I had my papers all made out for a furlough, all that was lacking was one man's name, the Adjutant Genl. of the Department," he reported unhappily, "but I was two days too late, for immediately upon Gen. Rosecrans' removal, Genl. Thomas issued orders to allow no more furloughs. So, having received my papers back, very respectfully disapproved, I proceed to make my visit home in the shape of a letter."[18]

The sergeant was hardly alone in harboring such feelings during this period. General Alpheus Williams wrote plaintively to his daughter in mid-November, "I shall try to get leave before Christmas, though Gen. Thomas is one of those officers who never leaves himself and thinks nobody should."[19] Thomas had faced similar circumstances before. But he under-stood that for all of the grousing and complaining there was important work to be done for an army that remained in a precarious position.

Others noted a change in the attitude and access to headquarters under the new commander, too. Journalist Henry Villard explained simply, "Thomas's staff followed his example, and was offish towards correspondents."[20] Looking back on the events from a considerable distance of time, Villard nevertheless professed to see Thomas as an outstanding choice for army command, with "longer military experience than any other general officer in the Army of the Cumberland." The Virginian had "a commanding presence," enhanced by his "soldier-like, erect bearing," and featuring "a sturdy, resolute character with the strongest sense of duty." Thomas was, according to Villard, "altogether, a thorough soldier."[21]

It was fortuitous for Grant that a "thorough soldier" was in place at Chattanooga while he traveled to the scene. He would do so painfully, ailing from a leg damaged in a collision of horses and a hard fall. Consequently Thomas was to be his man until he could reach the area himself. "Hold Chattanooga at all hazards," Grant wired, trying not to sound as if he expected a greater disaster than had already befallen the command to happen. "I will be there as soon as possible."[22]

Thomas received the news and girded himself for the task at hand. Chickamauga had underscored, if anything could, that he was not one to be intimidated. He was, in the words of one contemporary historian, "unflappable."[23] His message in response to Grant on October 19 demonstrated the strength of that characteristic in him. "I will hold the town till we starve."[24]

Despite his ailment, Grant hastened to take stock of the situation personally. James Harrison Wilson, who would later make a substantial contribution to Union success with the cavalry under Thomas, reached the beleaguered city first, found his way to Thomas's headquarters, and reported. The general left his subordinate with a favorable first impression, Wilson deeming Thomas a "Jove-like figure" who had an "impressive countenance, and lofty bearing." But Wilson's favorable initial introduction to the Virginian would be challenged when he returned after a brief departure to find that Thomas had new guests and seemed perplexed as to what to do with them. Ulysses S. Grant had ridden through the cold and wet weather while nursing his sore leg to reach Chattanooga late on October 23. He was now "sitting on one side of the fire over a puddle of water that had run out of his clothes; Thomas, glum and silent, was sitting on the other, while [John] Rawlins and the rest were scattered about in disorder."

Wilson recalled that he addressed the circumstances by gently upbraiding Thomas for the inconsiderate response shown thus far to his visitors. "General Thomas," Wilson recalled saying, "General Grant is wet and tired and ought to have some dry clothes, particularly a pair of socks and a pair of slippers. He is hungry, besides, and needs something to eat. Can't your officers attend to these matters for him?" Wilson's reminiscence of the moment was still strong when he composed a memoir years later, but whether he expressed himself at the time as forcefully as he recalled or not, he was certainly correct to suggest that cold and wet strangers ought to be provided with some relief. Biographer Edward Longacre concluded,

"Wilson was brash enough for any situation and had no fear of speaking out in front of the brass."[25]

When word reached Horace Porter of the need for his presence, the staff officer hastened through the elements "to the plain wooden, one story-dwelling occupied by my commander." Thomas was in the front room to the left of a hallway that led from the door, and Porter could see that he was not alone. "In an arm-chair facing the fireplace was seated a general officer," Porter recalled, "slight in figure and of medium stature, whose face bore an expression of weariness." At this point, the individual remained "carelessly dressed," clutching a cigar in his teeth, clothes still wet, "and his trousers and top-boots were splattered with mud." Thomas made a perfunctory introduction, and Grant offered his hand with a low-key but friendly greeting.

Porter's observation that Grant "had partaken a light supper immediately after his arrival" suggested that Thomas had already responded in a preliminary fashion to his superior's appearance by that point. But the officer recalled that it was only then that Thomas sent for his officers and staff and the room became busy with activity. In corroboration of Wilson's principal recollection, Porter noted that an unknown staff officer "quietly called" Thomas's attention to "the distinguished guest's" condition, arousing "all of his old-time Virginia hospitality." Grant declined the offers of conveniences, "except to light a new cigar." The staffer concluded that Thomas had meant no affront, but that his "mind had been so intent upon receiving the commander, and arranging for a conference of officers, that he entirely overlooked his guest's travel-stained condition."

Thomas was able to redeem the awkward situation. Within minutes, his chief engineer, William F. "Baldy" Smith, was familiarizing Grant with troop dispositions. Porter noted that Grant "sat for some time as immovable as a rock and as silent as the sphinx, but listening attentively to all that was said." A barrage of questions followed the report, revealing an impressively active and inquiring mind. Debate ensued, and when that had ended, Grant turned to the task of composing the telegrams that would set their discussions into motion before they could finally end their consultations for the night. The following day, Grant accompanied Thomas and Smith on a wide-ranging inspection tour that affirmed the circumstances they had discussed on the previous evening.

Much has been made of the discourtesy that Thomas's behavior appeared to show toward his superior. Wilson was less dismissive of Thomas's omission, but the secret to the Virginian's apparently churlish treatment may well be found in his tendency to retreat from awkward or uncertain personal moments. He had left the speechmakers at Camp Dick Robinson to seek solace in the deepest confines of his office. But the staff officer's suggestion of inadvertence certainly also fit the scenario that played out at headquarters as well as with regard to his commander's personality. Had Thomas anticipated Grant's momentary arrival, he would already have had every officer present whom he considered necessary and every amenity at hand. Grant had caught him ill-prepared, a mortifying experience for Thomas under any circumstance, and it clearly took him a few moments to recover his equilibrium.

Another explanation for the awkward situation that occurred in these opening moments of the collaboration between Grant and Thomas at Chattanooga lay less with the generals than their staffs. One source noted, "The General [Grant] and his aides took their first meals with Thomas. He welcomed them cordially, though his staff-officers were a little sore at seeing a superior placed over their chief."[26] Certainly, such a motive was possible, but the brusqueness of some of Grant's staffers over their perceptions of the treatment he had received suggested that sensitivity abounded all around.

As was plainly indicated in the headquarters incident between Thomas and Grant that occurred upon the latter's arrival, the contrasts between the styles and manners of the principal generals could be evidenced in numerous ways. James H. Wilson, who made something of a study of his commanders' natures and personalities, viewed both as "strong men with different points of view, habits of mind, and idiosyncrasies, and it is by no means strange that their prejudices and their preferences should have pushed them in different directions."[27] The generals even presented noticeable physical contrasts. Grant was clearly little concerned with appearance, while Thomas, who could be frugal enough to wear an older uniform rather than donning a newer one, nevertheless was always, as one contemporary noted, "scrupulously neat."[28] Even the most dominant trait that the men shared tended toward their personal estrangement. Contemporaries who knew them referred to each of them as "obstinate," and both had a reputation for stubborn adherence to positions, real and metaphorical, that allowed variations of terms like "tenacious" and "determined" to be applied to each of them. In Thomas's case, Wilson declared that Grant had "met his match" with an individual who could display "equal or greater obstinacy."[29]

Neither man was considered overly gregarious. Both were prone to become sullen and exhibit quiet moods. Grant could exhibit his own strong sense of detachment, especially when preoccupied. In a later moment of controversy between the men, in the difficult days of Nashville in December 1864, a staffer who journeyed with General Grant to Washington from City Point enroute to Nashville observed that the travelers indulged in "little or no conversation between us." Samuel Beckwith described the state as

"Grant's habit of silence" and thought his superior "never designed by the Creator for a sociable being, at least so far as I ever learned from observation and experience." The officer noted that he had "become accustomed" to Grant's "moods" and left the general "alone to his meditations."[30] On another occasion, the same officer and observer noted, "I believe that you would have a vain search to find two big men who could do more and say less than Grant and Thomas."[31]

In the case of the Grant-Thomas relationship, there was less rancor than retreat into a strictly professional interaction between them when it came to their personal connections. Each understood his role, and each preferred to keep his own counsel as a general rule. As James H. Wilson saw it, there was room to admire both "as entirely honorable in their personal and official conduct." Ultimately, he felt that the two men also held a similar position on the most important aspect of their personalities. "Whatever their personal feelings may have been towards each other," he concluded, "they were both beyond all question loyal in their sense of duty."[32]

Once in Chattanooga, Grant took up the plans that were already in the works and, finding them satisfactory, gave his approval to them. First among these and critical to the fate of Chattanooga was the plan to open a more substantial and supportable supply line. Despite the efforts of Thomas's quartermaster and commissary elements, the situation had deteriorated in that respect. Grant was hardly on the scene when he cleared the way for efforts to break the Confederate stranglehold along the Tennessee River. William Smith, who continued to have responsibility for developing the "Brown's Ferry" plan, later asserted, "there is not the slightest reason for doubting that Thomas would have made the same move with the same men and with the same results, had General Grant been in Louisville."[33]

As a preliminary, 1,500 troops and 100 oarsmen slipped along the Tennessee quietly on the night of October 26, so as to be in position to establish a bridgehead at Brown's Ferry. The next step was to bring more men under Joseph "Fighting Joe" Hooker to reinforce their colleagues and secure the tenuous supply route. Belatedly, on the night of October 28–29, the Confederates tested the new configuration with a daring and rare night attack that proved unsuccessful in driving off the Federals and reestablishing the Southern grip.

Typically, Ulysses Grant was not one to celebrate small victories. The "crackers" were finally coming in, and any resemblance to a siege was fading rapidly on the Southern side, but he remained aggressive in seeking more dramatic results. To that end he called for an assault against Braxton Bragg's right, anchored along Tunnel Hill and protecting the rail line that ran via Dalton to Atlanta. Grant was determined to press matters immediately. There were indications that Ambrose Burnside, dug in around the small East Tennessee town of Knoxville, could use the assistance of a strong diversion at Chattanooga. Consequently, on November 7, Grant issued an order to launch "an attack on the north end of Missionary Ridge with all the forces you can bring to bear against it, and, when that is carried, to threaten, and even attack if possible, the enemy's line of communication between Dalton[, Ga.,] and Cleveland[, Tenn.]." He expected the order to be carried out as soon as possible, by the officer who knew the local situation best. Grant was willing to offer General Thomas an unusual degree of autonomy in doing so. "The movement should not be made one moment later than to-morrow morning," Grant insisted. "You having been over this country, and having had a better opportunity of studying it than myself, the details are left to you."[34] When Smith approached the commander for clarification, Grant noted brusquely, "When I have sufficient confidence in a general to leave him in command of an army, I have enough confidence in him to leave his plans to himself." Smith took the message. There would be no further discussion and certainly no amelioration of the order.

Thomas understood the strategic implications of making an attack against Bragg's line, but he was doubtful that the effort that Grant wanted him to undertake had much chance for success. He sent for General Smith and explained to the engineer, "If I attempt to carry out the order I have received, my army will be terribly beaten." He hoped that the engineer might find a way to dissuade Grant, not realizing that this had already been tried, unsuccessfully. Smith did not divulge that he had seen Grant and that any subsequent attempt would likely be as futile and instead diverted the point by suggesting that Thomas and he reconnoiter the ground together. "We looked carefully over the ground on which Thomas would have to operate, noted the extreme of Bragg's camp-fires on Missionary Ridge," Smith reported, and the two soldiers determined that without the additional troops that William T. Sherman was bringing, the movement could not be made with any hope of success. When Smith returned and broached the matter once more with Grant, that general accepted the news less vehemently and issued instructions countermanding those that had called for the assault.[35]

The reference Grant had made initially to confidence in a commander may have been meant as a glancing blow at Thomas. Grant had moved almost instantaneously to assume overall command when the Virginian relieved Rosecrans, even with the assurance that the town would starve before it capitulated. Grant's initial insistence that "the movement should not be made one moment later than to-morrow morning" was evidence that he believed the order to be a viable one and expected it to be carried out as he had determined. The general felt that time was of the essence with regard to Burnside's situation in Knoxville and that any delay would be unacceptable. Yet, when the two subordinate officers scouted the ground and found the movement unlikely to succeed, Grant had the good sense to call off the operation until Cump Sherman, the person who he was certain shared his mind-set when it came to such matters, could arrive on the scene. A moment had passed for Thomas to win his superior's confidence that he would strike a decisive blow even at the risk of a setback rather than wait until all was in order. As understandable as it was under the circumstances, the choice did nothing to alter Grant's perceptions of Thomas in any appreciably positive way.

General Grant had communicated his plans to Henry Halleck on the afternoon of November 7.[36] The next day he had to inform that officer that the plans would have to be postponed. "General Thomas cannot make the movement telegraphed yesterday for several days yet," Grant explained without elaboration.[37] Then a few hours later he added with a hint of aggravation, "It has been impossible for Thomas to make the movement directed by me for Burnside's relief."[38]

Thomas always preferred adhering to orders rather than challenging or questioning them outright, but he was not above recommending that they be withdrawn or reconsidered if he felt the facts warranted such a reevaluation. His own tendency was to couch any critical comments only in the most professional terms in his official reports and let others sort out responsibility. In this regard, he later observed that at Chattanooga he had thought that an attack on the Confederate center was "premature; and that he believed his delay was not only justifiable but altogether correct, and 'that was the reason I expressed myself as I did in my report.'"[39]

By November 15, the Ohioan's troops were close at hand and Sherman himself even closer, arriving in Chattanooga to consult with his commander. The plan was for Sherman to take his men on a circuitous route around the town and reposition them for a thrust against the Confederate right flank in the vicinity of Tunnel Hill. The movement would take time to occur, especially since it was crucial that it be done without alerting the Southerners to it and allowing them the opportunity to anticipate the attack by stacking troops against it.

Braxton Bragg seemed willing to oblige. He had already sent a troublesome James Longstreet in the direction of Knoxville to see what might be done with Ambrose Burnside. Longstreet compelled Burnside to fall back into the city, but the Federals were located in strong earthworks spread over numerous small peaks and valleys and the meandering Holston River that made any approach a difficult one. Bragg thought the addition of more troops would help and made plans for others to follow that would further reduce his numbers at Chattanooga.

Although Grant had been disappointed at the initial postponement of an assault on Missionary Ridge, George Thomas had plenty of personal incentive for doing so when the time was right. In addition to the defeat of an opponent, he felt he had a score to settle with Bragg, his old battery commander from Mexico. When Sherman arrived and the men had a moment to reconnect themselves, Thomas confided that he had received a letter intended for an officer across the way and that as a courtesy he had made provision to send it over to him. "I put a slip of paper around it with a note asking Bragg to forward it to the [appropriate] address," he explained to Sherman. "The same parcel was returned with a flag of truce, with Bragg's endorsement." The individual who had once touted Thomas for positions of responsibility and counted him among what certainly must have been a limited number of genuine acquaintances, if not friends, had scribbled on the document, "Respectfully returned to General Thomas. General Bragg declines to have any intercourse or dealings with a man who has betrayed his State." Sherman recalled that the miffed Virginian spoke bitterly about his onetime friend and comrade. Apparently, Thomas vowed to get even with the haughty Confederate at the first opportunity, prompting the red-headed Ohioan to observe rather slyly of his colleague, "He was not so imperturbable as the world supposes."[40]

If powerful emotions boiled beneath the Virginian's composed public persona and he could be almost painfully locked into views about rank, seniority, and military protocol, Thomas nevertheless also demonstrated a willingness to embrace new concepts for which he could have genuine enthusiasm. One of these concerned the transitional nature of the institution of slavery in the crucible of rebellion and warfare. In a communication with the War Department, at about the same time he was contemplating ways of assisting General Grant in relieving the siege of Chattanooga, he articulated a clear statement of his views on the subject. "The Confederates regard them as property," he observed about the slaves. "Therefore the Government can with propriety seize them as property and use them to assist in putting down the Rebellion." The logical progression of thought Thomas displayed in his line of reasoning illustrated awareness, flexibility, and acceptance of changing circumstances. "But if we have the right to use the property of our enemies, we should also have the right to use them as we would all the individuals of any other civilized nation who may choose to volunteer as soldiers in our Army."

For Thomas the issue had moved from the realm of theory to one of reality. Men who had been enslaved were now to be considered no differently than those who came to military service through more traditional paths. Furthermore, he expected the school of the soldier to have the same positive effects upon these recruits as it had for any others, as well as affording even greater opportunities for the transition away from a slave society toward citizenship that the conflict also had come to represent. "In the sudden transition from slavery to freedom," Thomas explained, "it is perhaps better for the negro to become a soldier, and be gradually taught to depend on himself for support, than to be thrown upon the cold charities of the world without sympathy or assistance."[41] That such "assistance" remained necessary was the element of his paternalistic background and heritage he had never seen fit to forsake. The beneficiaries would be the former slaves themselves, who having once been brought under the expectations and training of military service would be capable of providing for themselves and their families once that service was complete.

Thomas continued to evolve in his thinking on the role of African Americans in the army and the place of such individuals in society, but current matters demanded his attention first. Ulysses Grant had wanted to revive his idea of attacking the north end of Missionary Ridge, but this time with Thomas acting in concert with Sherman. The Ohioan was indeed present, but weather had hampered the movement of enough of his men to participate in any attack on November 21. Nothing has emerged of the manner in which the commander demonstrated impatience or dissatisfaction with Sherman, but the fact remained that a delay of several days became necessary. Thomas used the time to improve his positions for the assault that he knew would be coming in the near future.

An important foundation for launching any attack against Bragg's main position atop the heights of Missionary Ridge could be found on a little eminence that lay between the city and the ridge called Orchard Knob. The Confederates held this advanced position, but the ground was tempting to the Federals, promising the benefit of a useful vantage point for anyone who possessed it. When word filtered through the lines that Bragg might be planning to withdraw from the vicinity of Chattanooga, Grant determined that a probe was in order. Accordingly, orders left Thomas's headquarters for General Gordon Granger to execute a reconnaissance meant to "discover the position of the enemy."[42]

At approximately 2 PM on November 23, Confederate defenders on the position began to notice unusual movement in their opponent's lines. Union troops were leaving their earthworks to assemble in formation as if on routine maneuvers. The sounds of drums, bugles, and shuffling troops cascading across the intervening ground suggested more of pageantry than more sinister purposes. Southern pickets and other onlookers took in the majestic scene as it unfolded, apparently uncertain as to intent. But the aim was soon clear. The grand movement was not part of an elaborate drill; it was to set in motion an effort to test the defenses of Orchard Knob. To accomplish this feat, Thomas committed four divisions from his Army of the Cumberland, a massive force designed to ensure the likelihood of a successful effort. As one modern historian noted, "George H. Thomas, careful, methodical, and conservative in his judgments, was not about to take lightly the matter of advancing against prepared enemy entrenchments, be it a reconnaissance or a major forward movement." Wiley Sword asserted that Thomas had thus "greatly overreacted," in an effort to ensure success.[43] Even so, neither Ulysses Grant nor George Thomas seemed overtly concerned about the operation. Both men observed the advance from Fort Wood in silence. According to one witness, Grant was "slowly smoking a cigar," while Thomas stood nearby, watching the movement through his field glasses.[44]

Under their generals' gaze, some 23,000 men surged forward, and the Confederates began to realize that a defense would be necessary. As the defensive fire mounted, it also became clear that there would be no stopping such an irresistible force. With Union flags showing through the battle smoke on the top of Orchard Knob, General Thomas J. Wood looked back across the expanse and saw Thomas atop the parapet following the developments. "I have carried the first line of the enemy's intrenchments," Wood ordered his signal officer to indicate in reference to Orchard Knob. Discerning the message and the significance of the moment, the Virginian immediately had one waggled out in reply. "Hold on; don't come back; you have got too much [to withdraw]; intrench your position."[45] Opportunities, whatever the original intention or design, were not to be discarded lightly. Granger observed succinctly, "The reconnaissance was a complete success. In making it we not only obtained the desired information, but had also successfully attacked the enemy and had driven him from a strong and important position."[46] "You should have seen that motley crew climb out as the splendid fire swept through, and scurry out of sight," a Northerner recalled. "It was their ditch, indeed, but they were not quite ready to die in it," he explained of the Southern defenders, and attributed the effectiveness of some of this fire to General Granger.[47]

Many of the new occupants in blue began using whatever means were available to "turn" the rifle pits, as one described it, in order to "throw the parapet to the other side of the trench so as to be between us and the rain of bullets and shells from the ridge."[48] Other Federals worked diligently to plant artillery on the ground to secure it further and maintain pressure on the Confederates. By early morning the placement of the guns offered the Union troops the promise of a longer-term residency.[49]

Within a couple of hours of the assault, conditions were settled to the point that Generals Grant and Thomas crossed over to the Union-held eminence. One of the soldiers recalled that Thomas "called for the officers of the regiment" and congratulated them for the success, which he termed "a very gallant thing."[50] Oliver O. Howard also expressed his satisfaction at the operation's success. "I know I felt freer to breathe when I placed my feet on that little advanced hill than I done since entering that beleaguered [town of] Chattanooga," he recalled.[51]

Granger did not impress everyone favorably with his leadership priorities during this period. Despite the preparations for moving out to strike at Orchard Knob, the general became fascinated by the pieces that crowned the parapets of Fort Wood and fixated on the impact they were having on the Confederate lines in the distance. "I found General Granger enjoying himself hugely," an officer recalled. "He always had the idea that he had a wonderful eye for artillery, so now I found him going from gun to gun of Fort Wood's great siege ordnance, sighting each at the ridge, and watching with much satisfaction the results of the shots." Initially, Thomas watched the spectacle in silence, but then grumbled at Granger, "Pay more attention to your corps, sir!"[52]

Another individual recalled that Granger, whom he described as "a rude, rough, and tough soldier," exhibited a "predilection for artillery." William Shanks thought the soldier "ought to have been an artillerist rather than an infantry-man, for he was devoted to the artillery" and would not "infrequently . . . abandon the direction of his corps to command a battery." Shanks noted that Granger "so disturbed Grant by his repeated firing of the monsters that the latter had to order him to the front." Even then, Granger's first inclination, or "ruling passion" as the newspaperman put it, was to have a battery mounted within "five minutes" and blazing "away at the rebels at a shorter range."[53] The visual effects of the heavy ordnance he had been firing must have been impressive indeed, for as another individual who watched the martial drama unfold later explained, "[Fort] Wood laid its shells about where it pleased, the little rolls of smoke lying on the Ridge like fleeces of wool."[54]

If Granger's neglect of his duty irritated him, Ulysses Grant could not help but be satisfied with the outcome of the action. Dutifully, he reported the results to Halleck, observing of Thomas's men, "The troops moved under fire with all the precision of veterans on parade." He promised that not only would these men remain in the positions they had taken, but they would join with Sherman in an attack in which "a decisive battle will be fought."[55] The stage was set for a frontal assault against Bragg on Missionary Ridge if the Federals chose, but work still remained to secure the flanks before initiating one.

An attack the next day on the Confederate defenders of Lookout Mountain was another precursor to lifting the siege that Braxton Bragg had put into place at Chattanooga. "The Battle above the Clouds" was actually an engagement encased in fog from the perspective of those who watched from below. But it too was successful. Thomas was with a contingent of officers, including General Grant, and their staffs as they watched the attacks unfold across the face of Lookout Mountain. One of the participants considered Thomas "even more inconspicuous" in his dress than Grant, and remembered that "an oilcloth cloak covered him from chin to boot and the only thing that indicated his rank was his hat with its little acorn tipped bullion cord about it." The officer remarked of the Virginian that anyone "might have mistaken him for a civilian spectator of events." Even so, because of the conditions, the observers caught only glimpses of the movement of troops and the effects of their fire amidst the swirls of fog.[56] Finally, when the appearance of a Union flag suggested the progress the attackers had made, George Thomas was among the spectators who reacted with what was for him a rare public display of jubilation.[57]

In the aftermath of the successes at Orchard Knob and Lookout Mountain, Grant's broader plan called for a concerted effort against the remaining defenders, largely located along the base and crest of Missionary Ridge. An initial thrust by Sherman on the opposite flank secured a foothold after a circuitous march and movement by pontoons across the Tennessee River, but revealed further ground over which any subsequent assault would have to take place and uncovered the presence of his command to the defenders. Hooker would work his way over from the vicinity of Lookout Mountain to Missionary Ridge and exert pressure on the Confederate left, while the main push came from Sherman's sector at Tunnel Hill on the Southern right.[58]

On November 25, several generals and their staffs rode over to Orchard Knob to take advantage of the central location and elevated ground from which to watch the fighting unfold on that day. Montgomery Meigs recorded the scene in vivid imagery. "Shot and shell screamed from Orchard Knob to Mission Ridge, from Mission Ridge to Orchard Knob, and from Wood's redoubt, over the heads of General Grant and General Thomas and their staffs, who were with us in this favorable position, whence the whole could be seen as in an amphitheater," he explained in his after-action report.[59] He noted the pyrotechnical effect of the Confederate fire on the visitors at Orchard Knob in a personal journal entry, but indicated that for all of the accompanying sound and fury the shelling failed to produce casualties at that point among the Union officers and staff.[60]

Grant was prepared to hold the troops at the center in abeyance until Sherman, primarily, and Hooker, secondarily, reached positions to threaten Confederate occupancy of the crest of the ridge. Thomas's initial role was little more than biding time for the moment when his troops would be needed, and this relative inactivity reduced him to being an impassive witness to the action. As the martial drama played out, he occupied his mind with such opportunities to contribute as came his way, and thus in an ironic twist given his earlier stance with Gordon Granger at Fort Wood, Thomas reverted to his training and experience as an artillerist, although not in terms of serving the pieces himself. At 9:00 AM he advised one of the subordinate commanders, "Do not fire any more from Fort Wood, except an occasional shot into the enemy's rifle-pits on their extreme right, and on top of the ridge, when the enemy show themselves in force."[61] A little over an hour later, movement in the woods in front of Orchard Knob caused him to direct, "Put a few Shells in there."[62] Then, to a different artillery commander fifteen minutes later, he communicated testily, "Your elevation is too small. Shells falling in front of our troops. Fire at the enemy's camp and top of ridge."[63] Finally, at 11:00 AM, he returned his attentions to Fort Wood. "You are firing in the wrong direction," he observed, redirecting the artillery in support of Sherman. "Fire near the tunnel north of Orchard Knob."[64]

General Thomas J. Wood had used the eminence on Orchard Knob as a headquarters since his men had secured it two days earlier. He watched as the various elements of the official entourage took their places and listened as Sherman encountered stubborn Confederate resistance by the superb fighter and Irish expatriate Patrick Cleburne. Wood recalled that the first hint of concern that matters were not progressing as planned came when Grant almost offhandedly remarked, "General Sherman seems to be having a hard time." Wood acknowledged that their comrades were "meeting with a rough time." "I think we ought to do something to help him," Grant noted, suggesting that Wood and Sheridan could be used against the Confederate rifle pits at the base of Missionary Ridge as a diversion. Wood assented. "General Grant walked immediately from me to General Thomas, distant about ten paces." Thomas had not heard the discussion, but was now brought into it by his superior. "Generals Grant and Thomas were in conversation a very short time, perhaps two or three minutes," Wood remembered, "when General Thomas called General Granger, who stood near him." These officers conversed briefly, and then Granger came over to tell Wood what he already knew. "You and Sheridan are to advance your divisions, carry the intrenchments at the base of the ridge, if you can, and, if you succeed, to halt there." The instructions called for the advance to be made when the six-gun battery atop Orchard Knob blazed forth. All of this effort had taken precious moments to pass down the chain of command. Wood estimated that about ten minutes had elapsed.[65]

An alternative version of events had the Virginian focusing on the ridge ahead with his usual quiet, but determined, focus. Unperturbed by events happening immediately around him, Thomas did not appear to notice Grant becoming increasingly anxious and Fourth Corps commander Gordon Granger playing artillerist while directing counter battery fire against the Confederates. An account that appeared shortly after the war illustrated the corps commander's inability to prioritize his duties appropriately. "He was

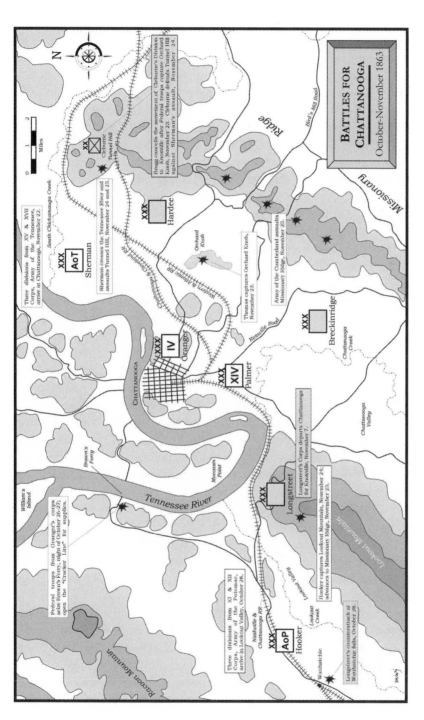

After retreating into the city from Chickamauga, Thomas became commander of the Army of the Cumberland and operated successfully in first holding Chattanooga and then contributing to the defeat of Bragg's besieging army at Orchard Knob and Missionary Ridge in November 1863. © Mark W. Johnson.

at the battery on Orchard Knob, in the zeal of the old artillerist, forgetting his soldiers, but sighting the guns, and shouting with delight when they did good execution."[66]

Finally, at around 3 PM, Grant signaled the end of his patience, although there were conflicting accounts as to on whom he focused his instructions. Toward the Virginian he was supposed to have observed, "General Thomas, order Granger to turn that battery over to its proper commander and take command of his own corps. And now order your troops to advance and take the enemy's first line of rifle pits."[67] Then, more abruptly, he demanded of Granger, "If you will leave that battery to its captain, and take command of your corps it will be a great deal better for all of us."[68] Howard remembered that "Grant took the cigar from his mouth, cleared his throat, and told Thomas to capture the entrenchments at the foot of Missionary Ridge." But, he insisted, a "patient Thomas had been ready all day" for such orders.[69]

Debate has persisted concerning the nature of the orders under which Thomas's men were meant to operate against the Confederates on Missionary Ridge and the degree to which the subordinate commander exhibited the requisite facility needed for communicating those orders to his troops. A modern biographer of the Virginian has suggested that Thomas behaved indifferently toward his commander at Orchard Knob. Describing their relationship as "quite poor," Christopher Einholf maintained that Thomas acted passively regarding orders to attack the ridge frontally of which he had not approved. The author insisted that the general had taken a more active role with previous commanders, but was surprisingly quiescent until Grant finally prodded him into action.[70] Certainly, such a view was a valid one, but the otherwise inexplicable behavior of both Thomas and Granger in the setting made sense in the context of orders given and current circumstances. Neither of the men was shirking his responsibilities or acting in an insubordinate manner as much as the two of them were keeping themselves occupied while the larger plan unfolded. Maintaining a presence through well-directed long-range fire was about all that either commander could do, much less was expected to do, until General Grant became convinced that other steps were necessary. Even then, no one anticipated that an assault meant to test the first line of Southern rifle pits would, or could, realistically do more than that.

The force being deployed here to capture the Southern rifle pits and assist Sherman through diversion constituted a similar one to that which had captured Orchard Knob so dramatically and efficiently. Absalom Baird and Richard W. Johnson formed on the left and right, respectively, of Wood and Sheridan, and the combination provided as many as 23,000 men to storm the Southern rifle pits. When the artillery pieces designated to signal the advance belched forth, the lines lurched into motion and entered a fire that had been triangulated to cover the open ground they now had to cross. Through the hail of shell and musketry, the men pushed forward and reached the Confederate works, taking prisoners of those who did not manage to scramble away. Above them was an intermediate line to which some of the Southerners retreated.[71]

The blue-coated soldiers hunkered down into rifle pits that were not designed to protect them from fire coming from above. The colonel of the Sixty-ninth Indiana, Frederick Knefler, reported that the situation was untenable as the men came under "terrible enfilading fire" from which the only true escape was to go forward. Another explained, "We first stuck to the Ridge like leaches, the shells would burst over head, some times they would come close in two feet of our heads and burst but we would hug the ground and stumps so close that they could not hit us at all."[72]

Historian T. Harry Williams has asserted that "Thomas's men were aware that Grant regarded them as inferior soldiers, and they were determined to show their mettle."[73] Certainly such speculations could be found around the campfires or after battles, but that type of motivation was not necessary for these men. The exposure to enemy fire was sufficient.

The example of the first men to surge forward became contagious, as others followed, and quickly more soldiers pulled themselves up the slope, anxiously trying to maintain their footing on shifting topsoil and rock.[74] Flags dipped and rose as the men carrying them fell, only to be replaced by others. Many of the exhausted soldiers paused momentarily behind stumps, rocks, and fallen trees to collect themselves before rising again to surge ahead toward the summit.[75] One of the witnesses to the effort recorded, "Not less than forty cannon poured an enfilading fire of grape and spherical case upon the troops as they ascended the ridge." In some ways the worst remained for them to encounter. As the men neared the crest, "they were greeted with hand grenades, extemporized by igniting shells with short time-fuses, and rolling them down on our lines." Although these blasts added to the casualties, they could not prevent the Federal troops from clawing their way forward and brushing aside the defenders, who desperately turned to bayonets to accomplish what the shells and musket fire had not. With a final push by the Union attackers these last lines now became theirs, too.[76]

Almost from the time the momentous charge took place there was conflicting evidence concerning the roles and states of mind exhibited by the commanding generals. By one account, when he could make anything out of the battle smoke, Grant seemed unconvinced that he was witnessing much more than a disaster unfolding before him. The terrain itself would surely work against an organized advance. The climb was bound to wear down the men, who would then have to find the fortitude to continue fighting as they closed with their opponents at the top. "Thomas, who ordered those men up the ridge?" Grant barked over the din of the struggle. "I don't know; I did not," came Thomas's quick reply. Grant rejoined that the matter might have to be considered later if not successful, but Granger expressed an earthy confidence: "When those fellows get started all hell can't stop them."[77]

Another version placed the uncertainty squarely on Thomas's shoulders. Newspaperman William Shanks noted that both Grant and Thomas "were standing together when the assaulting column had reached half way to the summit of Missionary Ridge, when a portion of it was momentarily brought to a halt, and when the stream of wounded retiring down the hill made the line look ragged and weak." Each watched the drama unfolding in silence, until Thomas turned to observe hesitatingly, "General, I—I'm afraid they won't get up." Grant remained focused ahead, digesting the scene and his subordinate's concern before removing his cigar. "Oh, give 'em time, general."[78]

After the war, Wood reflected on the significance of the sequence of events as he recalled them and the impulse of the men to continue on their own to the heights. "The gallant charge of my division was not only without orders from higher authority but had been positively prohibited by Genl Grant," he explained to a well-wisher in 1896, "hence the gratification caused by the grand success was all the more pronounced."[79] Joseph Fullerton, who carried messages for the assault "to push ahead," recorded that although neither Wood nor Sheridan were prepared to take responsibility for the effort that was under way, each considered success likely.[80] Undoubtedly, there was a sense of ambiguity about exactly what was expected, even with regard to which set of Rebel rifle pits an assault was intended to secure. As commanders, Thomas and Grant both failed to rectify that uncertain state of affairs or provide clear lines of communication to the subordinates charged with carrying them out.

Much would be made of the degree to which Grant dictated the nature of the final assault on Missionary Ridge. Several accounts suggested that he had intended the men to re-form after capturing the Confederate works at the base of the ridgeline before proceeding. Others maintained that no orders existed, or at least if they did the officers who carried out the initial assault were unaware of them, for anything more than taking the initial set of rifle pits themselves. Montgomery Meigs insisted that Grant considered the action as it unfolded "contrary to orders, it was not his plan—he meant to form the lines and then prepare and launch columns of assault, but as the men; carried away by their enthusiasm had gone so far, he would not order them back."[81] Another witness recalled that as the men surged forward up the slope, an audible "murmur of surprise arose from the little party of staff officers about me." But when a junior officer hastened to Grant with the assessment that the men had not stopped to reorganize as they were expected to do the commander noted plainly, "Let 'em go, Sheridan will come out all right."[82] A variation of this account had Thomas exhibiting concern regarding the likelihood of success for a subsequent advance up the slope. "Those fellows will be all cut to pieces," the Virginian supposedly announced, expressing the doubt that they would reach the summit. "Let us see what the boys will do," Grant retorted, and advised that the charging soldiers be left "alone" from any change in orders.[83]

Charles Dana helped to create the impression that the upper echelons of Union command in the field were little more than passive witnesses to the action. "Neither Grant nor Thomas intended it," he explained in reference to the final push. "Their orders were to carry the rifle-pits along the base of the ridge and capture the occupants, but when this was accomplished the unaccountable spirit of the troops bore them bodily up these impracticable steeps, over the bristling rifle-pits on the crest and the thirty cannon enfilading every gully."[84]

Whatever the precise exchange between the generals and regardless of whether or not developments played out according to expectation, the momentum remained nevertheless, and it would have been foolish not to capitalize on it, especially since there was realistically nothing else that anyone could do to alter it. Flexibility was always a hallmark for any successful commander as the capricious nature of the battlefield dictated, and both Grant and Thomas were more than capable of adapting to changing conditions. A staff officer watching them expressed awe at the "seeming indifference, or shall I say assurance, of these commanders in whose hands was the success or failure of combat, but I know that beneath the placid exterior were minds vigilant and masterful."[85]

In any event, as Thomas's men ascended the heights, the Confederate defenders began to crumble under the weight of an assault that they clearly had not anticipated. In a sense it was Orchard Knob all over, but on a grander and more decisive scale. One Indiana soldier observed that upon reaching the summit the attackers found that the defenders "Stampeeded and got in a terible hurry to get out." William Miller concluded, "The Slaughter was terible and the Rebel lines melted like snow under a July sun."[86] From his vantage point at Orchard Knob, Charles Dana was so exhilarated that he could hardly contain himself in informing Secretary of War Stanton, "The day is decisively ours. Missionary Ridge has just been carried by a magnificent charge of Thomas's troops, and [the] rebels routed."[87] General Thomas later asserted that his men assaulted the crest of the ridge and "carried [it] simultaneously at six different points."[88]

The moment also allowed a measure of revenge for the torment the Confederates had inflicted upon their counterparts since Chickamauga. One tendency was for the Southerners to call out across the lines derisively. "The Rebels on Picket after they drove Rosecrans in here [Chattanooga] used to hollow Chickamauga and called our Corps 'Thomases Pets.'" But now the tables were turned, and as the men in blue drove toward Missionary Ridge one of their number recalled, "our Boys retalliated by hollowing at the flying Johnies 'Here is your Thomases Pets and we give [you] Chickamauga.'" The soldier concluded slyly, with a sense of humor his commander would have appreciated, "Our Boys calls it the Battle of Mission run" in substitution of the name Missionary Ridge.[89]

At almost the turn of the century, the dramatic events of the day still resonated in General Thomas J. Wood's mind. To an inquiry for an autograph, the former soldier observed, "The proudest moment of a long and not uneventful life was when on the 25th November 1863, I saw the honored banner of my country floating in proud triumph on the crest of Missionary Ridge." He continued to strain for words to capture the event descriptively. "The sensation was more than exultation—*it was exaltation* of the profoundest type."[90]

Thomas was also elated by the unexpected result that came from what was supposed to have been the seizure of Confederate rifle pits at the base of the ridge. The Virginian was among a band of generals who left Orchard Knob to ascend Missionary Ridge to assess personally the dramatic developments that had just occurred there. He guided his mount to the top of the ridgeline, prompting cheers from the troops as they recognized him. The general found himself confronted by throngs of exuberant men, who, he observed, "always took liberties with me." They returned his compliments for their gallantry with their own expressions of appreciation for his generalship. "Why, general," one of them offered, "we know that you have been training us for this race for the last three weeks." Caught off-guard, Thomas responded self-consciously, "We have trained you as long as we want to." Then relief from the awkwardness of the moment came as he caught sight of a steamer approaching Chattanooga, and the general switched to a subject he knew would delight his battle-worn warriors: "Here come the rations."[91]

Officers and men alike were in understandably high spirits, not only for chastising Braxton Bragg's Confederates and exorcizing the demon of Chickamauga, but also for redeeming the months of short rations, in one dramatic dash to the summit of Missionary Ridge. The significance of the attack, given the obstacles presented, has not been lost on subsequent generations. Two modern historians, Herman Hattaway and Archer Jones, termed the carrying of Missionary Ridge as "the war's most notable example of a frontal assault succeeding against intrenched defenders holding high ground."[92]

In making his official report, Thomas chose his words carefully. "It will be perceived from the above report that the original plan of operations was somewhat modified to meet and take the best advantage of emergencies, which necessitated material modifications of that plan." As he rendered this statement it may have dawned on him that his words might also be interpreted as a veiled criticism of his chief. Thomas wanted no such interpretation. "It is believed, however, that the original plan, had it been carried out, could not possibly have led to more successful results."[93] In truth neither Grant nor Thomas could claim much credit for the spontaneous movement of the troops up Missionary Ridge and the sweeping victory they achieved from Bragg's demoralized army. As General Howard noted, "Thomas and Grant saw the conflict through their [field] glasses from Orchard Knob."[94] Although the account came from a disgruntled Joseph Hooker and thus must be taken accordingly, Grant was supposed to have been so disgusted with the ad hoc nature of the final assault that he observed angrily, "Damn the battle! I had nothing to do with it."[95]

General Grant may indeed have been frustrated. Dana was, his wave of euphoria having passed in the hours after the successful assault. "Grant gave the order at 2 p.m. for an assault upon their lines in front of Thomas, but owing to the fault of Granger, who devoted himself to firing a battery instead of commanding his corps, Grant's order was not transmitted to the division commanders until he repeated it an hour later," the official dutifully assessed for Stanton later in the evening of November 25. As far as he was concerned, the lateness of the hour and the lack of sufficient daylight for operations meant that the victory was not as complete as it otherwise would have been.[96]

Even with the cheers of victory resounding across the ridges outside of Chattanooga and the promise of fresh supplies, hard realities remained. Shortages of all types continued to be evident, and reorganization after the fighting was essential. Ulysses Grant wanted to keep pressure on the retiring Confederates and find a way to maintain the hard-won momentum. Thomas was prepared to undertake his associated duties, as he had done all others, with dedication and attention to detail, but he thought that refitting would take time. These dual approaches had plagued the relationship between the men before and would do so again as a restive Grant chafed at the means by which his more conservative and methodical subordinate seemed to engage in war making.

In the midst of all of the duties and requirements, there was time for tangential activities. One individual recalled that "some time after the battle of Missionary Ridge," General Grant "was anxious to ride over the battle-field of Chickamauga." On the morning set for the excursion, General Richard Johnson approached the man with an interesting invitation. "I am going with

Generals Grant and Thomas over to Chickamauga battle-field and would like to have you go along," the soldier explained to the delighted civilian. "We rendezvoused at General Thomas' headquarters, and rode via Rossville and through the gap, then down the Lafayette road. This route brought us first to the left of our lines where our division lay on that memorable Sunday." Grant had seen his share of battlefields, but was particularly impressed as he "gazed at the bullet riddled trees in front of that line, the only remark he made on the battle-field which I heard was, 'These trees would make a good lead mine.'"[97]

It is not known the reaction the Virginian had to revisiting the site of the most significant trial by combat he had endured as a commander in the Civil War, but he would make himself abundantly clear when it came to those who championed his cause for higher commander. On December 17, Thomas wrote to James Garfield from his headquarters in Chattanooga to thank his colleague for "the kind expressions of yourself and other friends on the success of the Army in the Battle of Chattanooga." But he was equally anxious to express his dismay at other possible developments. "You have disturbed me greatly with the intimation that the command of the Army of the Potomac may be offered to me. It is a position to which I am not in the least adapted," he explained candidly. Thomas was not particularly concerned with his "reputation," but he clearly preferred not to be "placed in a position where I would be utterly powerless to do good or contribute the least towards the suppression of the Rebellion." The Virginian remembered too well the badgering that had persisted in the early days of the conflict while he operated in Kentucky, and could read the fates of other commanding generals who had fallen afoul of official Washington. "The pressure always brought to bear against the commander of the Army of the Potomac would destroy me in a week without having advanced the cause in the least."

Thomas was convinced that even the position he now occupied was fraught with difficulties that only recent successful service had allowed him to overcome. "Much against my wishes I was placed in command of this Army," he explained. "I have told you my reasons," he added; "now however, I believe my efforts will be appreciated by the troops and I have reasonable hopes that we may continue to do good service." Thomas might not promote himself for another command, but he was not averse to offering another possibility. "If you will permit me I will suggest that a better commander for the Army of the Potomac can not be found than Genl. W. F. Smith, who is an imminent strategist, a man of firmness and energy, and whose *name is already* identified with that Army. His services with this Army richly entitle him to advancement."[98]

In the meantime, the press of business remained. Thomas adopted a noticeably different approach to the way he orchestrated affairs at headquarters in comparison to his predecessor. Joseph C. McKibben observed to a former colleague that the Virginian's staff offered a contrasting view. "You would hardly recognize Hd. Qrs.," he explained, "perfect order & system prevails & all the work done in office hours." The staffer was not dissatisfied with the changes, thinking them beneficial to "good soldiers." McKibben expressed the belief that the "solid estimate in which all hold Gen. Thomas will tell in future conflicts." He had particularly hoped to make a positive impact on the relationship he was establishing with this commander. "I never worked as hard in my life as the three days of the battle of Chatanooga. I was anxious to stand well with the General."[99]

Thomas remained proud of the contribution his command had made in driving Braxton Bragg from the heights at Missionary Ridge. At the end of the year, a former subordinate of the Virginian's observed in a letter to a friend, "General Thomas wrote me an account of the battle which he closes by saying was a brilliant success."[100] Not willing to press for public recognition of his achievements, Thomas was nevertheless aware of their scope and importance and willing to share his enthusiasm privately.

There always seemed to be a tenuous relationship between the army and the press. Often the zeal to report news did not mesh with the requirements of the armed forces. Sherman was becoming increasingly exasperated with the agents of the press. In the aftermath of the fighting around Chattanooga, Thomas was inclined to agree. In one instance, Sylvanus Cadwallader, correspondent to the *New York Herald*, had just completed a "full account of the battle of Lookout Mountain," but could not get it passed through Thomas's telegraphic connection. A staff officer had at first "demurred to some portions of the dispatch and finally declined to approve it on the ground that the line was already overloaded with military dispatches, and that mine could only be sent at the expense of more important matter." Sensing he was the victim of bureaucratic chicanery, the incensed correspondent raced to find General Grant, who, sight unseen, authorized the material to go through anyway. Undoubtedly pleased that he had circumvented the roadblock, Cadwallader asserted, "I never visited Gen. Thomas' quarters afterwards." Then he smugly concluded, "I no longer needed favors, but was rather in position to extend them to others." Presumably, the recipients of the newsman's largesse in the future would not include Thomas.[101] George Thomas later exhibited concern for what appeared in print, but he seemed not to desire to cultivate a base for disseminating information, even if it were to prove favorable for him to do so.

The year that was closing had been an eventful one, but Christmas Day 1863 was a sobering reminder that the conflict would continue and prevent the soldiers on both sides from enjoying the warm embrace of hearth and home. The solemnity of the day was not lost on George Thomas either as he considered an appropriate method of honoring those who had so recently fallen in the fighting around Chattanooga. The general was determined to set aside a portion of that field "to provide a proper resting-place for the remains of the brave men who fell upon the fields fought over upon those days, and for the remains of such as may hereafter give up their lives in this region in defending their country against treason and rebellion." The orders identified a location, with subsequent removal of the bodies of the slain and plans for the erection of a suitable monument, all work to be undertaken "exclusively" by members of the Army of the Cumberland.[102]

On January 8, 1864, General Orders No. 8 went out from headquarters, requiring commanding officers of Thomas's regiments to supply Chaplain Thomas B. Van Horne with pertinent data concerning the fallen. This "Mortuary Record" was to include "full information in regard to the full name, rank, company, native state, date, age, marital state, date of enlistment, address of nearest friends, numbers of engagements participated in, soldierly character, special circumstances of death, if killed in action, and whatever else is worthy of their history of record." Such a herculean effort to record and remember the individuals reflected Thomas's priorities as an officer and devotion to the persons under his command authority. Ultimately, those who perished elsewhere would also be included. But when asked if the men ought to be laid to rest in accordance with their state identification, Thomas balked. "No, mix them up," he commanded, "I've had enough of states' rights."[103]

The popular trend for such memorials had been to do so through some form of group identity or connection. The Civil War marked a period in which efforts would be made, whenever possible, to focus on the individual. Mass graves and unknown markers remained common practices, often due to circumstances that prevented more careful or identifiable interment.[104] Of this specific recognition of each soldier Chaplain Van Horne observed later, "In expression of the value of each citizen who fell in the war, the body of each was placed in a separate grave."[105]

In his history of the army, Van Horne concluded with a chapter devoted to "The Dead and Their Disposition." Although he celebrated the creation of the "first permanent National Cemetery for soldiers established by military order," at Chattanooga under General Thomas's direction, the chaplain lamented that the "exigencies of war" had "prevented the execution of all the work upon this cemetery by the troops of the Army of the Cumberland" and the lack of a monument as stipulated. "Neither was it subsequently practicable to obtain a brief history of the many thousands interred in this classic ground, as at first contemplated." Still, Van Horne later, and George Thomas before him, could be pleased to know that they had taken appropriate steps to honor the remains of "those who gave their lives to maintain the nation's life."[106]

The Virginian had other matters with which to contend as a new year broke upon the conflict as well. One of these involved determining the means of combating the scourge of guerrilla activity, or bushwhacking, as many termed it. Thomas considered these acts to be the most depraved, and his chief of staff, William Whipple, expressed the pervasive sense of outrage in the form of General Orders No. 6. "For these atrocities and cold-blooded murders, equaling in savage ferocity any ever committed by the most barbarous tribes on the continent, committed by rebel citizens of Tennessee," there was to be an assessment and monetary compensation for the families of the victims at the penalty of the seizure and public sale of their assets on noncompliance. Furthermore, Whipple explained on his commander's behalf, "The men who committed these murders, if caught, will be summarily executed, and any persons executing them will be held guiltless and will receive the protection of this army." Anyone who assisted the criminals could also expect to "be immediately arrested and tried by military commission."[107]

Thomas's approach to war mirrored others who thought the South brought ruin upon itself through a war it had inaugurated. "It is bad enough for us to demand that love of a restored Union at the point of a bayonet, but we can justify ourselves by claiming that what we do is from a sense of duty," he explained. However, it was the extreme application of the bayonet that concerned him. "The thing becomes horribly grotesque, however, when from an ugly feeling we visit on helpless old men, women, and children the horrors of a barbarous war." Thomas had seen enough of conflict to know that the steps one took to wage war could undermine the principles for which one fought. "We must be as considerate and kind as possible, or we will find that in destroying the rebels we have destroyed the Union."[108]

Many new and complex challenges lay ahead for Union leaders such as General Thomas as preparations continued for renewed campaigning in the spring. Yet, the demands associated with safeguarding what had already been accomplished through hard campaigning required the most immediate attention. On January 1, 1864, the appointment of W. E. Merrill as chief engineer of the Army of the Cumberland signaled Thomas's focus on defending the long rail system on which the flow of Union supply depended. Merrill later recorded proudly the herculean effort to construct a system of blockhouses meant to protect vulnerable bridges and trestlework against Confederate raids.[109]

A new year also brought with it promises of noticeable improvements that augured well for an upcoming campaign, but the workload of preparation and administration was significant. It was not until near the end of January that George Thomas was able to send a map he had asked to be made of the region to James Garfield. "There has been such a press of business on hand at the Engineer office, and as many changes necessarily made on the re-organization of the Army of the Cumberland that it has been utterly impossible to get it out sooner," he explained.[110] The state of affairs remained vivid in Thomas's memory nearly two years later when he contemplated assembling his papers for supporting a history of the army. "I am sorry to say that the condition of the papers in the [department] prior to the time I took command was not as it should have been," he confessed to former superior Don Carlos Buell.[111]

The Virginian was generally upbeat as he assessed the current conditions for his friend. "Affairs here assume a more encouraging aspect," he began. "We have the R.R, completed at last." The improvements represented a sea change from the time he had vowed to starve rather than submit. "We have been in that condition, since the day the Rebels opened their Batteries on us from Missionary Ridge & Lookout Mountain until to-day. Now we have full rations." Yet, even as Thomas expressed his gratitude for the developments, he noted with an evident pride how well they had operated under duress. "Whilst on short rations we managed to feed Sherman's Corps, about 10,000 destitute citizens, all the prisoners captured in the Battle of Chattanooga and upwards of eight thousand deserters who have all come in to this post since I assumed command of this Army." It had been virtually impossible to "accumulate any surplus here," and, accordingly, the general asserted, "With all these drawbacks the prospects for an advance towards Atlanta are certainly not very encouraging." Even so, Thomas remained hopeful that "eventually we shall overcome the immense difficulty" and be in a better position to commence a campaign into Georgia.[112]

For now, General George Thomas could look back at a period in which the fortunes of war could not have swung more abruptly. The disaster of Chickamauga, followed by the nerve-wracking days penned inside Chattanooga, had suggested that Union fortunes in the Western Theater were at their lowest ebb. True to form, Thomas clung tenaciously to his responsibilities and set matters in motion so that when Ulysses Grant arrived on the scene that general would have the prospects for a reversal of fortune. Their initial contact had hardly been one of Thomas's finest personal moments, but he had rallied to his duty under Grant. When the commander made a final push against the besieging Confederates, it was Thomas, not Sherman as Grant had anticipated, whose troops carried

Missionary Ridge and opened the way for a new phase of military operations in the spring. In the time since they had driven Braxton Bragg from the environs of Chattanooga, the Virginian continued to prepare himself and his men for what lay ahead, and the road appeared to be heading in the direction of Atlanta, Georgia.

11   The "Wheel Horse" Pulls for Atlanta (February–September 1864)

"He's my off-wheel horse, and knows how to pull with me, though he don't pull in the same way."
—William T. Sherman on George Thomas

"Keep everything in order, for the fate of a battle may turn on a buckle or a linch-pin."
—George Thomas

"Thomas . . . could move quickly enough when duty demanded it."
—O. O. Howard on Thomas

A significant evolution awaited the Union war effort in the nation in general, and in the Western Theater in particular. Ulysses Grant had proven his prowess and his mettle with astoundingly successful campaigns against the Confederate river fortress of Vicksburg and in breaking the erstwhile siege of Chattanooga. In the wake of such successes additional laurels seemed set to fall his way, and he was about to have the authority to attempt to achieve them on the grandest scale.

At the end of February, the president of the United States and the Congress cleared the way for the position of lieutenant general to be revived, and in short order Lincoln forwarded the name of Ulysses S. Grant for the post. With Senate confirmation, the nomination became a fact. Grant received his commission and the authority as commander of the Union armies, as Henry Halleck assumed the role of chief of staff. Fresh from an operation in Mississippi, highlighted by the wrecking of railroads and facilities in Meridian, William Tecumseh Sherman prepared to step into Grant's vacated place as the latter moved up to higher levels of responsibility. The fiery Ohioan would soon be poised to advance his portion of the larger program at the head of a three-army juggernaut that would aim its focus on Joseph E. Johnston's command and the terminal city of Atlanta, Georgia. For the time being he was engaged in the Meridian Campaign in Mississippi in conjunction with a cavalry raid in the northern part of the state designed to defeat Nathan Bedford Forrest.[1]

While Sherman was visiting destruction on the Southern infrastructure in Mississippi, Thomas ordered a probe at the Confederate works around Dalton, Georgia, that was to begin auspiciously enough on George Washington's birthday, but would have to be carried out without Thomas's direct involvement. Confined to bed temporarily with neuralgia, he placed General John M. Palmer in immediate command of the "demonstration."[2]

Thomas maintained contact from Chattanooga as Palmer led the operation through the next several days and felt sufficiently able to ride to the front himself on February 25.[3]

From the observations based on the effort came the suggestion of a campaign against Atlanta executed by the Army of the Cumberland. But Grant's promotion had changed the schematics for such an operation and now left them in the hands of William Sherman. Thomas was understandably disappointed. Publicly he said nothing, but to a fellow officer he admitted a frustration that went beyond the authorship of a campaign that he would have implemented. "I have made my last protest against serving under juniors. I have made up my mind to go on with this work without a word, and do my best to help get through with this business as soon as possible."[4]

Riding to the front, the Virginian was personally fortunate just to be in position to be angry about being passed over for command. While surveying the Southern positions and assessing their natural strengths through his field glasses, Thomas became aware of a round from an opposing sharpshooter passing uncomfortably close by to his right. In what must have seemed only an instant later, another round whistled past on the general's left side. Understandably assuming that the gray marksman was making sight adjustments, his subordinate Richard Johnson recalled, "Thomas coolly put up his glass and remarked that the next time he would probably hit him, and retired to another place."[5]

Grant's elevation in authority created the opportunity for concerted actions against the major Confederate armies in the field. In Georgia, the responsibility for tackling Joseph Johnston's Army of Tennessee fell to Sherman. George Thomas was responsible for the largest of the forces under Sherman's authority, the 72,000-man Army of the Cumberland. It would be teamed with the 24,000 troops of James B. McPherson's Army of the Tennessee and the 12,800 troops of the Army of the Ohio under John M. Schofield. The Confederates facing them initially could bring barely half of the soldiers arrayed against them. Those numbers would increase, but Joseph E. Johnston saw the advantage of the strong position he had taken near Dalton as easily neutralized if Sherman employed his full strength. Sherman had at least one distinct advantage besides numbers in waging war in this part of Georgia. He had spent some time in the region in 1844 as a young lieutenant and had the opportunity to register mentally the general features of topography with which he and his men now had to contend.[6]

During the lead-up to major campaigning, Sherman did what he could to sort through problems of command and control. Thomas had been contemplating changes in the Army of the Cumberland and passed his assessments along to his superior. He was particularly candid regarding the

Prussian-born orator and general Carl Schurz. "I do not think he is worth much from what I have seen of him," Thomas observed bluntly, "and should not regret to have him go."[7] The Virginian wanted the Army of the Cumberland in the best shape possible for the upcoming campaign. Sherman agreed. "Make up your command to suit yourself exactly," he informed Thomas on April 9.[8] There remained an unsettling discomfort on the part of Kentuckian John Palmer, but the matter did not seem pressing yet, and, as his colleague Richard Johnson put it, "Palmer was a great favorite with Thomas."[9] In any case, Sherman pronounced in his next communication with Grant that on the whole "Thomas is now well content with his command."[10]

General Sherman recognized and appreciated the extent to which Thomas had prepared the Army of the Cumberland for its duties. "General Thomas's army was much the largest of the three, was best provided for, and contained the best corps of engineers, railroad managers, and repair parties, as well as the best body of spies and provost-marshals." For the overall commander, this meant that the Army of the Cumberland, which had already proven indispensable, would likely do so again in the arduous campaigning to come. "On him," Sherman insisted of Thomas, "we were therefore compelled in great measure to rely for these most useful branches of service."[11]

In the course of the Atlanta Campaign, Sherman frequently employed General Thomas's command at the center of his advancing formations, maintaining contact with and pressure on the Confederates. Typical was a communication with James McPherson on May 18 in which Sherman noted that Thomas was to follow in the "broad, well-marked trail of Johnston's army."[12] Later, he recalled that in the course of the campaign, "I personally joined General Thomas, who had the centre, and was consequently the main column, or 'column of direction.'"[13] In assessing the reasons for the Army of the Tennessee's performance relative to its Union counterpart in Virginia, historian Richard McMurry noted Thomas's "thorough, consistent, and dependable" role as a field commander and concluded, "Together Sherman and Thomas made a very formidable combination leading the Western Yankees."[14]

George Thomas would be frequently chided for not moving as rapidly as Sherman expected in the campaign, but the Virginian might have pointed to the instructions he received from the outset of active operations in the field. In his directives for launching the campaign, the Ohioan explained specifically, "Thomas will aim to have forty-five thousand men of all arms, and move straight against [Joseph E.] Johnston, wherever he may be, fighting him cautiously, persistently, and to the best advantage."[15] The latter considerations of fighting "cautiously, persistently, and to the best advantage" were, of course, open to interpretation, but Thomas would have insisted that he obeyed the spirit as well as the letter of these opening orders.

Thomas was still tweaking his command as he prepared for active operations. He was convinced that efforts made in such moments as these would have dramatic payoffs when combat was joined. Consequently, the reviews and inspections continued unabated. One soldier observed to his sister in mid-April, "We had a grand review last Thursday by General Tommas, Hooker and Butterfield." But this was only one part of the readiness the commander expected of his men. "General Thommas is going to visit our camp tomorrow," he added. "I tell you what we have to put on the stile heare. Have to have our boots blacked when we go on guard or inspection, if we dont we catch fits."[16]

After an eventful period of duty, it certainly would have been understandable had the Virginian sought some relief from the accompanying stresses and strains. But such was not his inclination. Oliver O. Howard recalled riding over to visit with Thomas on March 29, 1864, and engaging in a conversation on the subject with the Virginian. Besides allowing the general to "visit his friends in the North," the rest would surely be invaluable in preparing for the spring campaigning to come. Thomas argued differently. "I cannot leave; something is sure to get out of order if I go away from my command." Then, after a moment of reflection, he added, "It was always so, even when I commanded a post. I had to stick by and attend to everything, or else affairs went wrong."[17] The lesson he had learned at Fort Mason in Texas, before the Civil War, when his absence from the post resulted in paperwork failing to be done properly by his subordinate, seemed to have remained with Thomas long after the fact.

In the spring, as the forces awaited a new campaigning season, Thomas grappled with old-style problems. One of these was the number of Confederate deserters accumulating and the debate over what should be done with them. Thomas saw the matter in terms of practicality and military reality. "I do not think it to the interest of the Government that they should remain in Tennessee or Kentucky," he explained to the governor of Ohio in early April, "as I believe many of them return to the enemy after recruiting their health and strength." He felt that such actions occurred for many reasons, ranging from "they are rebels by nature" to "because of family influence." Still others were motivated, he thought, "like the drunkard to his bottle, because they have not sufficient moral firmness to resist the natural depravity of their hearts." In all cases, and any other similar ones, he thought it best to "remove the poor wretches as far from the temptations of secessionism as possible, thinking by so doing that some of them at least might be reformed." For others there was the even more novel proposal floating in Thomas's mind of having the offenders shipped out to provide labor "on our Western farms," where they could "contribute somewhat in prosecuting the war in our favor."[18]

Another duty came to Thomas's attention about this time that proved to be anything but routine in its impact upon the sensitivities of the professional soldier that he prided himself on being. The complaint of a lieutenant colonel commanding a Wisconsin regiment who had served and been captured at Chickamauga reached his desk. Shuttled northward along the rail line to Richmond, the lower ranks of the prisoners of war found themselves systematically deprived of their personal property. The officer's insistence that the men were being subjected to "inhuman and cruel" treatment that operated "against the laws of civilized warfare" had fallen on deaf ears, but now drew Thomas's ire.[19]

In the initial endorsement of the document the general added a strongly worded condemnation for such activity by the Confederates by comparing their policies to his own with regard to captured troops. "I never have allowed prisoners of war to be treated in that way in this department," he explained. "They have always been allowed to retain whatever blankets and clothing they might have with them when captured." Thomas found such behavior reprehensible, but did not believe it to be unusual, having "frequently heard of such complaints of the Confederate authorities before."[20] Beyond questions of morality, to George Thomas the mistreatment of such prisoners made no sense. His approach to these individuals, as to anything else with which he was associated, was based on practical reality and common sense.

Even when confronted with the possibility that spies were infiltrating the ranks under the guise of deserters, Thomas maintained an overriding sense of practicality. One detainee brought in by the pickets shuttled from officer to officer as they sought to determine his legitimacy. Finally, the guards brought the man to Thomas. "The general looked him over and asked him a few questions," a witness recalled. Apparently the commander became convinced that the problem lay with language, and he summoned an officer who could speak German. That effort at communication also failed to produce a satisfactory result, but rather than become exasperated, Thomas instructed, "Turn him loose, follow him and see where he goes." The fellow wandered suspiciously through camp for awhile before finally some of the men recognized him and the mystery of his identity was solved to everyone's satisfaction.[21]

As he had expressed to members of his staff during the Tullahoma Campaign, General Thomas believed that proximity to the enemy would have tangible benefits for the state of his command's combat readiness. On April 24, 1864, he laid out his expectations and revealed a contradictory tendency to those who thought him too passive or cautious. "I am well aware that extreme outposts are always exposed, and for that reason they should be sleeplessly vigilant," Thomas observed to a subordinate. "If we do not run risks we never shall know anything of the enemy."[22] Vigilance would also decrease the likelihood of the type of unwelcome surprise by Confederate forces that Thomas had previously experienced, to his mortification, at the hands of John Hunt Morgan.

Thomas could certainly be unconventional in some ways, but he also remained mired in positions that reflected a more conservative nature and the traditions of his upbringing. Ever since President Lincoln's Emancipation Proclamation, the ranks of the United States armed forces had been opened to soldiers of African descent. White officers commanded these black units, and one of these recorded his interactions with Thomas on the subject. General Thomas Morgan argued that his superior, "though a southerner and a West Point graduate," was "a singularly fair-minded man." Morgan considered the factors of Southern birth and formal military education as usually debilitating when it came to the acceptance of African Americans as soldiers, but he thought that the Virginian would be able to transcend the barriers of paternity and professional elitism to consider the case of such troops on their own merits.

Even so, when Morgan organized black troops for combat service, General Thomas proved skeptical initially. "He asked me one day . . . if I thought my men would fight," the subordinate recalled. "I replied that they would. He said he thought, 'they might behind breastworks.'" Thomas had been around too many civilians learning to be soldiers, indeed had worked vigorously in helping them through the difficult transition, for him not to be wary of soldiers in the rawest state. "I said they would fight in the open field," the officer insisted. But, Thomas remained unconvinced. Morgan could only request an opportunity to change his mind.[23] When the men later performed well in parade drill, Thomas moved another step closer to accepting these men as soldiers. Morgan remarked that on one occasion after an exercise at which Thomas was present, the Virginian observed that he "never saw a regiment go through the manual as well as this one."[24] This represented progress, but he was still a long way from acknowledging the prowess of African American troops on the battlefield.

General Morgan was correct about his superior in one way. Thomas was unafraid of reassessing situations as they evolved and changing his positions based upon tangible evidence. Only if he had the sense of impropriety, undue pressure, or the concern that others might see unworthy motives in his actions would he revert to rigid adherence to orders or firmness in his duty as he saw it as the ultimate defense. The issue of the disgruntlement of white officers who commanded black troops was a case in point. When word filtered through channels that some of these individuals had professed their unwillingness to command men who would not be allowed to be tested in combat and that under those circumstances they preferred transfers, Thomas took the matter personally as well as professionally. He rode over to the camp, and according to one witness "did not dismount" as he summoned an "officer's call." When the subordinates appeared, the officer recalled that Thomas's demeanor in their presence was unmistakable. "There was lightning in his eye, and from out of his cropped beard came a sound lecture as to a good soldier's duty to obey orders and ask no questions and have no preferences, to leave others the direction of the campaign, to gain distinction by doing well our duty, not by choosing an assignment."[25] The moment was classic George Thomas, with the emphasis on adherence to duty without grumbling and the notion that any positive recognition would come only by following that course.

General Thomas also seemed to be reaching the point of having the lesson reinforced that the regulars that he frequently depended upon inserting in the most trying conditions were no longer uniquely essential for that duty. He had watched the volunteer farm boys and store clerks develop into the type of troops he expected his men to be. A scholar of the U.S. regular infantry that served with Thomas noted that the general "knew the value of regular troops and of what they were capable," but that he understood that their exposure to combat had reduced their numbers to "just a few score lucky survivors." For Mark Johnson, this forced the Virginian to accept that "fighting the regulars into extinction would not serve the nation's long-term interests." Of the general's evolution in this regard, Johnson concluded, "He also realized that many of his volunteers were now well-trained veterans themselves, much different from the armed mob he had commanded in Kentucky during 1861."[26]

In his initial report, filed on June 4, Thomas noted simply, "In obedience to instructions from the major-general commanding the military division, I got my command in readiness for a forward movement on Dalton, Ga., and was fully prepared to move on the 2d of May as directed."[27] In compact form these were his indications of the basis for "a forward movement": clear orders and sufficient time that allowed for complete preparation for an advance. With that foundation, Thomas was not only ready to proceed, but anxious to do so. Sherman later acknowledged that Thomas's troops "were already in position," when the campaign was set to begin and recalled that the Virginian "was in person at Ringgold" on May 4, after having spent much of the previous time based in Chattanooga.[28]

The grand offensive opened in the Eastern Theater with the movement of the Army of the Potomac against the vaunted Confederate Army of Northern Virginia of General Robert E. Lee. George Meade, who had defeated Lee at Gettysburg, was the nominal head of that Federal army, but Ulysses Grant, in his new capacity as general in chief, was present in that theater of action as well. Both Meade and Sherman had the same goal, outlined by Grant, of targeting the principal Confederate armies they faced. These campaigns were also set to be coordinated with actions on other fronts, too. The purpose was not only to maintain pressure on the Confederacy as broadly as possible but to prevent the various elements of the Southern defense from supporting each other.

In Georgia, Sherman planned to unleash his offensive as Grant indicated. Thomas suggested that he use the Army of the Cumberland to maneuver Johnston from his formidable defenses, primarily distributed along Rocky Face Ridge, by threatening the Confederate left flank and the communications and supply lines that wound back toward Atlanta. General David Stanley noted that the "scheme" for the movement through Snake Creek Gap "originated with General Thomas, who had, during the winter, a thorough examination of this defile made by his scouts."[29] Sherman agreed with the idea, but preferred to trust the turning movement to James McPherson instead. The Ohioan explained his preference in the terms he would employ whenever he compared his two largest commands. "The Army of the Tennessee are better marchers than the Army of the Cumberland and I am going to send McPherson." Upon hearing Sherman's decision, Thomas headed back to his headquarters to implement his superior's strategy, remarking resignedly to an aide that he did so because "I saw the game was up."[30]

The decision exposed a lack of trust in Thomas, and Sherman certainly expressed himself repeatedly on the subject of slowness with regard to his former West Point classmate. Yet, Thomas was a strong enough personality and had won sufficient recognition in the field that he could not be dismissed, even if Sherman had wanted to do so. The fact was that the Ohioan had a symbiotic relationship with McPherson that he did not with Thomas. McPherson would work in tandem with Sherman in ways that the Virginian could not. Even so, Sherman later remarked of Thomas, "He's my off-wheel horse, and knows how to pull with me, though he don't pull in the same way."[31] The old artilleryman would have appreciated the reference in which the wheel pair of horses, those closest to the limber, was responsible for providing both the driving energy and the brakes for the rest of the team. Still, if Sherman could dominate his subordinates, as one historian has asserted, the "sole exception" in the Atlanta Campaign at least would be the Virginian, "with whom his relationship was both unique and complex."[32]

Nevertheless, on May 9, when operations in Georgia got under way it was McPherson who made the push through Snake Creek Gap, while Thomas and Schofield launched diversionary assaults designed to draw Confederate attentions away from the main flanking movement. After some

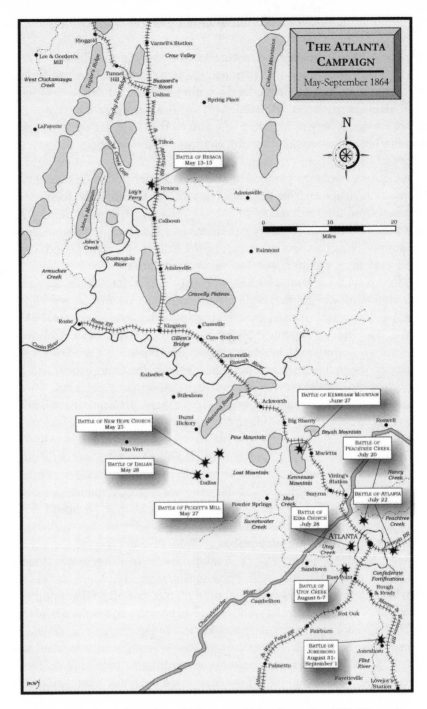

In the crucial Atlanta Campaign, which occurred May–September 1864, Thomas's Army of the Cumberland was one of three Union armies under William T. Sherman that forced Joseph E. Johnston steadily back toward the city and grappled with John Bell Hood over it. © Mark W. Johnson.

initial success, McPherson encountered sufficient resistance to prevent him from being able to reach his objective before pulling back to a more defensible position. Sherman was displeased with the failure to trap at least a portion of the Confederate army. "Well, Mac, you have missed the great opportunity of your life."[33] Left unsaid was the notion that by relying on that general Sherman might have missed his, too.

Belatedly, Sherman decided to provide the effort with more strength and punch his way through toward the Confederate rear. Johnston recognized that his opponent was not going to try to smash his way through the stout portion of his defenses and that it would be a matter of time before a flanking movement would succeed in isolating him. Rather than assume that risk, the Confederate commander opted to withdraw, abandoning the extensive defenses around Dalton and taking up new ones at Resaca.

A surgeon with one of the Michigan regiments noted Thomas's presence in this earliest phase of what would be a long and grueling campaign for Atlanta. "Gen. Thomas passed us on the way," John Bennitt wrote his wife, "and seems to have his eye on the whole movement here." The doctor was impressed with the physical bearing of a general not yet showing the wear and strain of the summer of maneuvering and fighting yet to come. "He is rather a fine looking man," the surgeon noted simply.[34] During the same campaign another participant observed, "How often I saw Thomas riding along close to, and inspecting the skirmish line on that campaign. He was slow of movement, large of body, six feet in height and rode a very large horse."[35]

By May 13, the Confederates had the happy news of reinforcements, under the fighting Episcopal bishop and general Leonidas Polk, but they also confronted Sherman's advanced units. Over the next couple of days, fighting roiled around the environs of Resaca, before Joseph Johnston again determined that his position could not be maintained and pulled his troops back to new positions across the Oostanaula River. In the sometimes stiff fighting that had occurred before the withdrawal, the Confederates had seen their number reduced by 2,800 casualties and the Federals by 2,747.

Johnston now had his choice of the next ground on which to challenge Sherman. He declined to make his stand at Calhoun and moved farther back to the area of Adairsville. Thomas moved forward, but preferred to hold up an assault until the Federals were in a better position to launch one successfully. In the meantime, Johnston assessed the situation and determined that the ground was not as suitable as he had thought. Once again, he pulled back. This time, the Confederate defense would rest near Cassville.

These early days of the Atlanta Campaign provided examples in which both Thomas and Sherman exhibited the habit of approaching as near to the front as possible to determine the state of affairs personally. But in doing so, both men put themselves in danger in ways that could have altered the outcome not only of the immediate campaign, but possibly of the war itself. In his *Memoirs*, Sherman vividly recalled being in the vicinity when, on the evening of May 17, near Adairsville, General Newton's division made contact with elements of the Confederate rear guard. "I was near the head of [the] column at the time," he recorded, "trying to get a view of the position of the enemy from an elevation in an open field." When his party of Union generals and aides "attracted the fire of a battery," the resultant close call scattered them to a safer location. Then at Cassville, Sherman and Thomas were out on the skirmish line evaluating the terrain when Confederate fire began "cutting the leaves of the trees thickly about us." Sherman could not recall which of them ventured to the other that "this was not the place for the two senior officers of a great army," so the generals rode back to a nearby battery rather than remain so dangerously exposed.[36]

Deeply committed to the duties Sherman had assigned to him, Thomas was unaware that he was about to receive a signal honor from another branch of the service. The United States government had authorized the construction of several steamers for service in the waters of the Western Theater. In May, Rear Admiral David Porter reported on their status to Secretary of the Navy Gideon Welles, noting that they were "almost ready for service." Seeing that the vessels would be shortly manned with crews and outfitted with weapons, he classified the four craft "as fine steamers in their class." Porter also took the liberty of recommending names to be considered for them, including George Thomas, in addition to Grant, Sherman, and Burnside, "in compliment to those gallant officers."[37] While the vessel's namesake was busily contesting the Confederates before Atlanta, the *General Thomas* remained active on patrol duty.[38]

Up to this point, Sherman had remained along the Western and Atlantic Railroad in his drive toward Atlanta. The plan allowed for the railroad to become a source of supply for the Federals as they moved forward and at the same time kept the remaining route targeted so that Johnston could not neglect to defend it. Once Sherman crossed the Etowah River, he faced the daunting prospect of striking at a strong defensive configuration at Allatoona Pass if he continued to use the railroad as the focus of his forward movement. Sherman now took the gamble of shifting westward toward the area of Dallas, Georgia, with McPherson on the right, Thomas in the center, and Schofield on the left. By pulling away from the rail line he hoped to avoid the difficult approach at Allatoona and compel another withdrawal by the Confederates. The engagements that resulted in the thick woods streaked with ravines were frequently bitter. By the time the three engagements that constituted this phase of the Atlanta Campaign had ended, the Federal losses amounted to 2,645 and the Confederates between 1,800 and 2,300.[39]

Union general William Carlin recalled that as his men faced stubborn fire from the Confederates at Little Pumpkin Vine Creek, Thomas came up to survey the conditions. "Some bullets struck the ground near General Thomas while he was inspecting the enemy's position and works in my front," Carlin observed. "He paid no attention to the bullets till he finished his inspection of the works through his spy-glass, when he deliberately turned to his left and gave a quizzical look at the ground where the bullets had fallen."[40]

Confederate fire had a different impact on the Virginian when one of the engagements at New Hope Church caused him to recognize and reevaluate the dispositions he made of his staff personnel while under enemy fire. Thomas had earlier ordered the relocation of his headquarters to a less exposed point. But in the process he became aware that the men on the firing line appeared to consider the realignment as less than inspiring. As one contemporary explained, "seeing that this movement made his troops a little nervous, he declared he would never do so again whatever the consequences might be to himself."[41] Many of the leading figures of the day understood the importance of personal example under duress, especially the appearance of calmness in the face of the storm of combat, as Thomas himself ordinarily demonstrated. But the Virginian now recognized that in the decision to remove his headquarters from danger he was not sending the message he intended to provide for the morale of his men.

Sherman once more altered his approach and returned to the line of the railroad. In early June, Johnston obliged by withdrawing to prepared defenses on a line of mountainous terrain in front of Marietta. Sherman used the respite to resupply his command. Part of this effort meant repairing the lines that had fallen into Union hands, and General Thomas's knack for levelheadedness and common sense that could take even the most novel ideas and make them practical and efficient came into use particularly in this aspect of the campaign.

As Sherman had already anticipated, the movement of this army group through North Georgia had produced a tremendous strain on the network of railroads that supported it. To solve the problem of rehabilitating the lines, the commander of the United States Military Railroads, General Daniel McCallum, suggested the expedient of completing a rolling mill begun by the Confederates near Chattanooga. Thomas supported the notion, but suggested that for the sake of security the mill ought to be relocated inside the Chattanooga defenses. He knew too well the possibility of Confederate cavalry raiders undoing in one quick strike what the Union military was trying to accomplish, and he wanted the vital plant to be at as secure a site as possible.[42]

Whatever Sherman may have thought about Thomas's efforts to keep the armies amply supported, he was frustrated by the slow progress his men were now making. Perhaps, Johnston's initial retreats gave the impression that a great deal of ground could be covered in a short period, but the Dallas–New Hope Church–Pickett's Mill clashes should have warned Sherman that as they moved closer to Atlanta their opponents would prove even more tenacious. But the Ohioan continued to feel vexed at the lack of progress. When word reached Generals Thomas and Hooker that trouble was brewing on their front, they took steps both to respond to the developments and to inform Sherman, who instead answered impatiently, "I don't see what they are waiting for in front now. There haven't been twenty rebels there today."[43] Sherman would have done well to recall a similarly misguided conclusion before Shiloh, when he insisted erroneously that hostile forces could not be present in any strength. Of course, the Confederates on this "front" would be happy to oblige by demonstrating their presence just as their counterparts had done on that previous occasion.

Union troops found the going most difficult in terrain heavily laced with ravines and thick woods. Against the Confederates holding the area of New Hope Church, members of Joseph Hooker's Twentieth Corps slogged it out in fighting that cost the Federals almost 1,700 casualties to their opponent's 550. An engagement against the Southerners in the vicinity of James Pickett's mill produced a similar disparity of losses as men under Thomas J. Wood and Benjamin F. Scribner clashed with those of Patrick Cleburne. The Federals had thought to be in position to turn the Confederate flank, only to learn in cruel fashion that the opposing line, while refused or bent back, was unquestionably intact. There would be additional fighting at Dallas, Georgia, as the Confederates there tried an ill-advised and ill-fated assault of their own, but the vicious fighting of May 25–28, 1864, and the resulting casualty lists did nothing to prevent Sherman from pressing his campaign against Atlanta.[44]

Subsequent action around Pine Mountain, in June, illustrated at least two factors relating to Thomas and Sherman. The first of these was the frugality of the Virginian. He had instructed subordinates to husband their artillery rounds, but Sherman saw an opportunity to harass the Confederates and maintain his own troops' morale by expending some of that ammunition. When the Ohioan caught a glimpse of a cluster of Southerners exposed in an open area he overrode the strictures Thomas had set in place. As things turned out, there was an even larger impact of this strategy. Sherman learned afterward that Confederate general Leonidas Polk had perished when a round slammed into him across the way.[45]

In the midst of his many frustrations in the Atlanta Campaign, Sherman seemed especially perturbed with George Thomas and the Army of the Cumberland. He was apologetic to his friend Grant in an intensely personal

June 18, 1864, communication in which he presented assessments of each of his principal subordinate commanders. "If our movement has been slower than you calculated I can explain the reason, though I know you believe me too earnest and impatient to be behind time." From the start, Sherman dredged up the factors that mitigated his actions, always assigning the responsibility to someone else and starting with an unusual source for his criticism. "My first movement against Johnston was really fine," he explained unabashedly, "and now I believe I would have disposed of him at one blow if McPherson had crushed Resaca." Instead, "Mc. was a little over cautious" and the great opportunity went by the boards. Still, comfort could be taken in his case. "With that single exception McPherson has done very well." Thomas would not be granted such latitude.

Sherman's evaluation of Schofield, whom he deemed had done as much as could be expected of such a small army, was brief. He saved his most elaborate criticism for the largest one, and by extension its commander. "My chief source of trouble is with the Army of the Cumberland, which is dreadfully slow. A fresh furrow in a plowed field will stop the whole column, and all will begin to intrench," he observed to Grant with a powerful sense of sarcasm. "I have tried again and again to impress Thomas that we must assail and not defend; we are the offensive, and yet it seems the whole Army of the Cumberland is so habituated to be on the defensive that, from its commander down to the lowest private, I cannot get it out of their heads."

Sherman saw the phenomenon as all-pervasive, even down to the baggage that accompanied the army. "I came out without tents and ordered all to do likewise," he explained, "yet Thomas has a headquarters camp on the style of Halleck at Corinth." Sherman knew that mention of that earlier campaign would have all of the necessary connotations for Grant of an absurdly slow and overwhelmingly encumbered operation that had almost represented the end of Grant's career at the hands of Henry Halleck.

Interestingly, Sherman was not content with the damning inference of that historical reference. He found disturbing trends throughout the Army of the Cumberland. Even Thomas's staff and aides reflected the attitude of their commander, "with a wall tent, and a baggage train big enough for a division." Hyperbole aside, Sherman looked at the issue symbolically. He was stripped down for action; Thomas was mired in traditional trappings and defensive-mindedness. "He promised to send it all back, but the truth is everybody there is allowed to do as he pleases, and they still think and act as though the railroad and all of its facilities were theirs." More importantly, Sherman argued, "The slowness has cost me the loss of two splendid opportunities which never recur in war." In one of these instances, argument over who should supervise an attack delayed it to the point that Sherman had to intervene personally. "I'm afraid I swore," he admitted, as David Stanley and T. J. Wood stood "quarreling [over] which should not lead."[46]

Compounding the situation was a series of days plagued with bad weather in the form of often torrential rains that had lasted from June 2 to 14. Sherman would later complain that the elements had "made the roads infamous," in justifying his sometimes slow progress.[47] But he was determined that nothing would prevent him from pushing on toward Atlanta. "You may go on with the full assurance that I will continue to press Johnston as fast as I can overcome the natural obstacles and inspire motion into a large, ponderous, and slow (by habit) army." Even so, apparently, like the weather, the Army of the Cumberland was a force that could not be controlled. "Of course it cannot keep up with my thoughts and wishes, but no impulse can be given it that I will not guide."[48]

There was no doubt that even under ordinary circumstances Thomas and Sherman operated in different fashions from each other. A contemporary noted the Virginian's propensity for order and confirmed the setting for the trappings of headquarters of which Cump Sherman had so vigorously complained. "Ten comfortable tents constituted the complement of the general and staff," J. Watts De Peyster noted of Thomas. "A large hospital tent served as an adjutant general's office, and he had the most complete headquarters' wagon for that office and his assistants to be found in the whole military services of the country." As a continuing reflection of Thomas's personality and preferences, the same individual observed, "Whenever he camped, his own tent stood at the head of a little street formed by those of his staff officers, five on each side." Reflecting not only symmetry but efficiency, the general also quite deliberately placed the tents of key subordinates in direct relationship and close proximity with his. "To the right of his own tent was that of his adjutant-general, to the left that of his chief of artillery."[49]

On another occasion, an individual not only witnessed the dispositions of Thomas's headquarters for himself, but offered the reasoning behind them. "Tents were pitched in a long row upon a small lawn in front of a frame house . . . for General Thomas preferred to sleep in his tent rather than turn a family out of their home, no matter how spacious it might be."[50]

Whatever his accommodations, George Thomas remained actively engaged in the campaign. He reported activities that suggested he was not merely operating defensively, and one of Sherman's aides responded with the commander's approval. At the same time that this aide indicated the satisfaction of the "general commanding," he also recognized "that it is probably impossible to do anything to-day during such a storm. Raining here [is] a perfect torrent."[51]

Within his own chain of command, Thomas's chief of staff, William D.

Whipple, passed along instructions to General Oliver O. Howard that illustrated his superior's desire for action. "The major general commanding thinks that every opportunity that occurs to annoy them [the Confederates] should be taken advantage of." Even so, these movements should not be made precipitously or ill-advisedly, and thereby expose the command to advantages that the Confederates might turn to their favor. Therein lay the rub. Both men championed a form of aggressiveness against the enemy, but Thomas saw risk first where Sherman saw opportunity. Thus, Sherman would have found Thomas's underlying message to Howard distressing. "This will not be construed into an order to attack unless an attack promises good results."[52]

Thomas was aware of Sherman's overall attitude toward him. On the same day he observed to Howard directly, "General Sherman is at last very much pleased," the Virginian added a note of acceptance to any annoyance his commander was also experiencing. "Our consciences approve of our work and I hope all will go right."[53] In the final analysis, Thomas was too sharp an old soldier not to know that if "results" were indeed "good," then "all things" would "go right" and any criticism would take care of itself.

Early the next morning, Thomas sent new instructions to Howard that reflected little of the single-minded adherence to the defensive thinking seen in Halleck's 1862 Corinth campaign, to which Sherman had alluded derisively. "If you find he has left your front," Thomas noted of reports that the Confederates had evacuated a portion of their lines, "push forward in pursuit, with the freshest troops in front." The implication was clear: "We must try to follow him up close."[54] Similar orders went out to Baird and Hooker as Thomas expressed his own desire to maintain the pressure on Johnston, rather than avoid it at all costs as Sherman indicated Thomas wanted to do.[55]

In the latter part of the month, Sherman's expression of frustration mirrored the position Thomas had taken with Howard. "Let them all hold fast to all we get, and be ready as soon as we can move with anything like life," he told the Virginian on June 21.[56] Sherman was about to reach a point at which his impatience would get the best of him. Certainly, both sides were demonstrating their proficiencies with digging equipment and the willingness to engage in that activity at every opportunity. They would have more chances to do so as the antagonists closed on Atlanta, already ringed with an impressive array of earthworks and fortifications that were being improved with each day.

Concerns of a different nature plagued the Union cause in the Western Theater in the summer of 1864. Major General William T. Sherman sent instructions to his principal subordinates, including Thomas, to take greater measures to combat "a class of people, who serve as spies and informants, and who encourage expeditions of the enemy's irregular cavalry, styled guerrillas."[57] For the Virginian this represented a return to the menace he had faced early in the conflict in Kentucky, as well as subsequently in Tennessee, but now found increasingly demanding upon his time, energies, and attentions.

Guerrillas and enemy raids, marches and the demands for sufficient rations, were all part of the recipe for frustration in what had turned into a long and grinding campaign. Ironically, while ensconced in a tent he had borrowed from George Thomas, Sherman laid out a more direct plan of attack that, if successful, could finally push open the door to Atlanta. He had determined to try to punch his way through the Confederate defenses. To David Stanley, Sherman simply observed, "Our flanking movements are ended; nothing comes of them. Now you have got to attack the enemy in front wherever you find him."[58]

None of the generals who were to carry out these instructions agreed with them. General Stanley recalled riding away from a meeting with Sherman in the company of the Virginian. "I said to General Thomas, as we broke up and were returning to our tents, 'General I am sorry this assault has been decided on, and I know it will fail.'" Thomas did not correct the impression or chide his subordinate for lacking appropriate confidence. Nor did he attempt to deflect his own doubts for success. "I fear it will be so," he explained softly, "but General Sherman has decided it, and we must do our best." Of course, there was always the chance that the outcome might exceed their expectations. "If we do possibly succeed it will lead to a great victory."[59]

Sherman had given Thomas discretion as to where he would assault the Confederate line. Thomas personally reconnoitered the front for any identifiable weakness, or at least a point at which some hope for success might be entertained. Once he had completed his scouting efforts, he instructed Palmer and Howard to select one division each from their corps for the attack. The divisions of Jefferson C. Davis and John Newton were relatively fresh, or at least unbloodied.

Early on June 27, a bombardment punished the Confederate line at Kennesaw as a prelude to the advance that would cover some 600 yards in the teeth of enemy fire. As historian Albert Castel contended, "Waiting for them are Cheatham's and Cleburne's divisions: unknowingly the Federals have chosen to attack the troops in Johnston's army that are the least likely to give way before any attack."[60] The Confederate positions themselves were formidably constructed, with obstructions to the front and well supported by artillery, so that by the time Thomas's men surged forward the odds for success were significantly weighted against them.[61]

Even for men conditioned to hard campaigning and inured to physically demanding activity, the climb toward the Southern position was exhausting. The maelstrom of fire descending upon them made it doubly so. Federal casualties mounted as commanders exhorted their men forward only to fall themselves. Acts of bravery and futility marked the day, perhaps best represented by a flag bearer who mounted a portion of the Confederate works, shot an enemy officer as he reached for the standard, and then fell himself under the horrific din of musketry. The battered Federals withdrew, still exposed to the firing as they did so, and Sherman's offensive faltered before the stoutly defended works.[62]

It took some time for Thomas to assess the situation. He had contradictory reports to sort through and pressure from Sherman, who was still hoping that the effort would pay the desired dividends. "I wish you to study well the position, and if it be possible to break the line," he instructed in the early afternoon.[63] Thomas responded glumly, "From what the officers tell me I do not think we can carry the works by assault at this point to-day," and then broached the unthinkable from the Ohioan's perspective by advocating a more methodical siege-oriented approach.[64] Sherman would have none of that sort of thing, but the Virginian was uncharacteristically blunt in observing that his division commanders considered the Confederate defenses "exceeding[ly] strong; in fact, so strong that they cannot be carried by assault except by immense sacrifice, even if they can be carried at all." He concluded soberly and succinctly, "We have already lost heavily to-day without gaining any material advantage; one or two more such assaults would use up this army."[65] Sherman was circumspect about the setback, despite his regret for the loss of gallant officers such as Brigadier General Charles Harker and Colonel Dan McCook. "Had we broken the line to-day it would have been most decisive," he explained to Thomas after Kennesaw, "but as it is our loss is small, compared with some of those East." The Virginian would have recognized the reference to the bloody slogging that represented the campaign in his native state between Generals Grant and Lee. Still, it was Sherman who summed up the cold reality as he had seen it. "At times assaults are necessary and inevitable."[66]

In the aftermath of the bloody effort to smash through the Confederate defenses at Kennesaw, Sherman and Thomas exchanged a series of telegraphic messages that at least one historian of the Atlanta Campaign has imputed to sarcasm from both men. As the two generals considered their options and contemplated the next steps that would be proper to take given the lessons so recently learned, Thomas resorted to his usual practice of asking from the commander every detail that he thought was necessary. Sherman knew the Virginian well and realized that he could indulge in what the Ohioan considered minutiae to a frustrating degree. Thus, when Sherman contemplated action that would force the issue on the Confederates, he understood that Thomas would want to know precisely how such action was meant to take place and what implementation of it would entail. Albert Castel has read into this exchange a sense of hostility on the part of Thomas toward Sherman, based upon what the historian labeled a "low opinion of the way in which Sherman has been conducting operations during the past two weeks."[67] But the tone on Thomas's part was less clear than this interpretation has acknowledged. When the Virginian asked the amount of force to be contemplated, he was not being frivolous or argumentative. "If with the greater part of the army, I think it decidedly better than butting against breastworks twelve feet thick and strongly abatised."[68] Practical experience had just reminded them of the hard lesson of such an approach and the costly expenditure of lives in following it. Both men wanted what Sherman termed as the best "chance of success."[69] They just saw that chance as coming in different ways.

Interpreting Thomas's characterizations as sarcastic does not mean that they were not, but his public expressions tended to reflect his respect for rank. Sherman certainly did not decline the opportunity to pay back any slight that he felt the Virginian had offered, intended or otherwise. "Go where we may we will find the breastworks and the abatis," Cump observed, adding pointedly, "unless we move more rapidly than we have heretofore."[70] Apparently, Sherman waited in vain for a reply, and when none came simply noted that he would see Thomas the following day.[71] "In the meantime" the Virginian was "to make such preparations as you can."[72] On June 28, in a much more civil tone, Sherman informed his subordinate, "I will ride over to see you to-day, and will explain fully the matter about which we conversed last night through the wires."[73]

Sherman seemed to be becoming more short-tempered than ever. He took a two-hour wait for Union cavalry under Brigadier General Kenner Garrard to reach Marietta, Georgia, especially hard. When Garrard finally appeared he received the brunt of his superior's frustration. Garrard had been one of Thomas's students at West Point, and the Virginian would attempt to mitigate criticism against him on several occasions as the Federals closed on Atlanta. But there was nothing that Thomas could do for the cavalryman here as he faced Sherman's invective. The tirade subsided with instructions to leave town immediately, but Garrard compounded his mistake by asking Sherman which direction he should take. "Don't make a damned bit of difference, [just] so you get out of here and go for the rebels."[74]

Thomas had continual intrusions of matters outside of the frontline struggles, too. As Union troops moved through the area of Marietta, Georgia, they found pockets of Southern sympathy among the abandoned homes and remaining Unionists. The McClatchey family, relatively recent arrivals from Tennessee and staunchly pro-Confederate, owned a farm a mile outside the town. Minerva McClatchey noted in her journal in July the departure of friendly soldiers and the arrival of pursuing Federals. Despite her inclinations, she received protection for a time from Joseph Hooker, but as his corps departed the guards went with them. Matters deteriorated quickly as personal effects and foodstuffs found new homes in marauding knapsacks. In desperation, the beleaguered matron looked for help once more from a Union patron. "Hearing that General Thomas camped at the [Georgia Military] Institute," McClatchey noted that she sent a son "with a note to him, asking for a guard." Thomas obliged the request, detailing two soldiers for the purpose. "They were a great protection and satisfaction to us," she observed and prevented the family from suffering further mischief for at least a couple of weeks.[75]

The Fourth of July offered one soldier an opportunity to pause and compose an update of the campaigning for his parents. "In a short time it [the Confederate rear guard] moved and Genl. Thomas' Splendid Columns were seen moving steadily down the roads, shelling as they went," Thomas Speed explained. These fireworks continued as the advance proceeded almost inexorably, according to the soldier, lending him a palpable sense of confidence. Retrospectively, he concluded of their recent opponents, "Their works on Kennesaw [are] said to be the very best. . . . But they do not seem to be able to hold any fortification however strong against our army."[76]

On July 10, Thomas sought direction regarding a unique set of captives. "The Roswell Factory hands, 400 or 500 in number have arrived at Marietta," he reported. "The most of them are women." Aside from the logical implication that such prisoners would not be treated as combatants, there was the need to determine a disposition of them that would not hinder Union operations or become viewed as inhumane. "I can only order them transportation to Nashville, where it seems hard to turn them adrift. What had best be done with them?"[77] Sherman thought that the "best" course should be to forward them to General Joseph D. Webster at Nashville, who would "dispose of them" by sending them on to Indiana.[78]

These types of concerns faced Union commanders like George Thomas as they advanced, penetrating new portions of the Confederacy, but they would not be dismissed wherever they occurred. General Thomas had consistently championed the downtrodden, but wartime considerations had to take precedence, and when situations arose that presented him with challenges he saw no choice in his course. Thus, when mechanics who were supposed to be working at the arsenal in Nashville opted to strike to secure the promise of overtime pay they had not received, the Virginian took drastic measures to bring the matter under control by sending some 200 of the workers packing and requiring the remainder to return to their stations by force at reduced wage levels.[79] The action was harsh from the perspective of labor relations and rights, but Thomas had felt it necessary under the exigencies of war.

Thomas could be less conservative when it came to other matters. He had supported Mary Walker, first as a civilian contract surgeon and then as the replacement for an assistant surgeon of the Fifty-second Ohio following the latter's death, despite the examining board's objections.[80] Still, the Walker case was less about gender equality than about effectiveness in meeting the critical needs of his men. The same practical considerations that drove him to drill and prepare his commands for battle caused him to take a personal interest in their care when they were wounded or killed in it. Hospitals frequently overflowed with the human refuse of combat and swelled when epidemics of disease swept through civilian and soldier populations alike. For example, Nashville hospitals remained busy, with increasing numbers of patients when combat flared or transportation to other facilities northward flagged, so that those who might be forwarded elsewhere remained in the city for treatment.[81]

Even in the midst of active operations and the myriad of concerns that piled on him, Thomas remained in contact with former associates as much as time and circumstances permitted. On July 16, he wrote James Garfield, "We are now so far down in Dixie that our letters etc. are very long in reaching us, which I regret very much on account of the letters, but not on account of being so far from home." The quixotic statement was not meant to disparage any personal connections so much as it was to serve as a commentary on the isolation of his present position and the necessity of campaigning in the remoteness of northern Georgia in order to reach Atlanta and shorten the war. To clarify this point, he added, "Probably the old saying, 'the longest way round the shortest way home,' may come true in my case as I do not at present see any [prospect] of getting into a land of civilization again but by driving ahead until we can get to the coast or by marching . . . [to] meet Grant somewhere between here and Richmond."

Thomas expressed his pleasure with the progress his command had made to this point, but mysteriously glossed over the setback Federal fortunes had endured at Kennesaw less than a month earlier. "We have reached this far without any repulse to any part of our Army, and all are in fine spirits." The advance had not stalled indefinitely, and the supply situation was improving considerably. "We shall in a few days have three months supplies of every thing in Chattanooga and at the front so that we will not now be disturbed or diverted from the main object of the campaign by any raids [Joseph] Johnston may send against our R. Roads or other means of communication." The changes gave Thomas a sense of supreme confidence. "If we are careful and keep our minds to the work before us securing what we get and moving to the other work with proper precautions and with a will to accomplish what we have to do I believe we shall be able to present to the Government by fall, the entire territory of the State of Georgia redeemed from the grasp of the Rebels." It is uncertain if he meant to include those areas beyond the northwestern portion of the state in which he was operating or assumed that all of Georgia would succumb when Atlanta did, but Thomas was obviously optimistic.[82]

On the day before he wrote to Garfield, Thomas had sent instructions to General Robert S. Granger at Decatur, Alabama, that expressed a sense of frustration with Confederate raiding and made his position clear on at least one other troublesome subject. "The major-general commanding says you have force enough to whip any force which may cross the river, and he expects you to do it," William Whipple began in the name of his chief. Then, "after you have driven them off arrest all sympathizers with the rebellion in your district and send them to Brigadier-General Webster, at Nashville, to be banished from the United States."[83] Thomas did not stipulate where such banishment might compel them to go, but he was clearly tired of confronting hostility among the civilian populations under his jurisdiction.

It was not surprising that he expressed similar views to Garfield concerning the state of white Southerners generally. "As for the people," he explained, "I think they will give less trouble than those of Ala. or some other State now in Rebellion." Thomas's litmus test was loyalty, and he believed that those who had money and property, and therefore ostensibly slaves, enjoyed the least of that commodity toward the Union. "All the wealthier class have left the region over which we have marched. Having left is sufficient evidence that they are rebels, and as such should not be permitted ever to return." What was worse, displays of loyalty were, according to his experiences, likely to only be momentary expedients. "We have seen enough of the Oath of allegiance and the game they play of taking [it]. I have never met a rebel who does not remain a rebel in spite of his oath of allegiance and for my part I no longer permit them to take it. The sooner they all leave the rebel territory the better for the peace, quiet and stability of the loyal parties of the State."[84] Such comments were uncharacteristic of the public persona that Thomas had worked so assiduously to present earlier in the war, but they anticipated the situation with which he would be confronted at the end of the conflict and the thinking that had already evolved with regard to the relations of white Southern civilians to Unionists and Northern sympathizers.

So much of Thomas's official communication reflected his professional character. His reporting seldom contained the editorializing that others could be susceptible to utilizing when describing events. But even the normally sedate Virginian could not resist the occasional comment that revealed a strong undercurrent of impatience. With regard to a raid by George

Stoneman, Thomas slipped in a postscript to an otherwise businesslike communication to Sherman on July 20. "The Stoneman raid turns out to be a humbug," he asserted. "It seems that when twenty-five of the enemy are seen anywhere, they are considered in force."[85] It is probably impossible to know what the Ohioan's reaction was to this comment, but he certainly must have smiled to think of such sentiments coming from the individual who he thought preferred entrenching to anything like aggressiveness.

Sherman was anxious to keep the Confederates from enjoying much of a respite. He had spent the day with Howard and Schofield, and detached a staffer to visit McPherson, assessing the situation on their fronts. His message once more was to prevent the enemy from constructing new defensive works. "We cannot pass Atlanta without reducing it," he observed, "and the more time we give them the harder it will be to carry." Sherman knew that even a supportive General Grant was watching over his shoulder, so that there could be no time for delay. "I wish you to press forward all the time, and thereby contract the lines," he wrote Thomas, with an eye to the first opportunity for a flanking movement. "We will tomorrow press at all points," he concluded. "I will push Schofield and McPherson all I know how." The clear implication was that Thomas was to consider himself already pushed.[86]

Thomas remained in the saddle, promising Brigadier General John Newton, "I will be over to see you in a few minutes on the Buck Head and Atlanta road."[87] He had insisted since his days on the frontier that he supervise as much activity personally as was possible, undoubtedly still harboring an underlying fear that when he left matters to others complications would arise that he would have to address anyway.

Surprises were in the offing, but they were first to be seen in the Southern ranks. The Union soldiers on the line began to get rumors that the Confederates had changed commanders, although the inquiry of one picket received an unexpected response. "Hello, Johnny," the fellow in blue sang out to his compatriot, "who's your commander now?" "Sherman," the butternut sentry replied. "How's that?" the Union soldier asked. "Well, when you move we move," he observed resignedly.[88]

Sherman later recalled that he learned of the replacement of Joseph Johnston with John Bell Hood through a spy brought to his headquarters by one of Thomas's staff officers. The citizen supplied the Union army commander with a copy of a newspaper that reported the change in Confederate leadership, and Sherman immediately sent for John Schofield, who had roomed with Hood at West Point. He thought Schofield might provide some insight into Hood's character from those early years, and the officer obliged by informing his superior that he assessed the Southerner as "bold even to rashness, and courageous in the extreme." It did not take much to conclude that given the character of his opponent, Sherman could expect a more combative approach than Johnston had thus far been able to produce in defense of Atlanta.[89]

By this point, Sherman had reached the outskirts of Atlanta and wanted to allow his men a brief rest before making a final push to capture or force the evacuation of the city. In addition to the Chattahoochee, other waterways provided continuing obstacles for Union forces and opportunities for the Confederates. An examination of the maps and what he knew of Federal dispositions convinced Hood that such a chance lay before him, just north of the city. If George Thomas wanted to move his command, now constituting the right of Sherman's line, in concert with the rest of the Union forces, he would have to cross Peachtree Creek. Hood planned to use William J. Hardee and Alexander P. Stewart as the fulcrum for pressuring the Federals into an untenable position that might secure the capture or destruction of a significant portion of the opposing forces.

On July 20, Thomas indicated to Sherman that he had been in the saddle, having "just completed an inspection of the lines from right to left." There was serious activity to evaluate, and he thought it best to cast a wary eye toward the opposing lines.[90] Sherman's initial response was to consider any enemy resistance as an indication that the Confederates were once again trying to buy time to build new fortifications.[91] The momentum had been in the direction of Atlanta from the beginning of the campaign. By evening, however, it was clear that something quite different was occurring.

Thomas later reported of the sudden action that transpired, "The enemy attacked me in full force at about 4 p.m., and has persisted until now, attacking very fiercely."[92] The Virginian was hard-pressed to prevent the Confederates from wedging him into a difficult situation. The Southern assault first hammered Newton's division, which, as Thomas reported, "gallantly stood its ground, repelling charge after charge." The engagement spread along the broken terrain as both sides groped for advantages against the other.[93]

In the heat of the combat at Peachtree Creek the Virginian reverted to his old artillery ways. "General Thomas happened to be near the rear of Newton's division," Sherman recalled, "and got some field-batteries in a good position, on the north side of Peach-Tree Creek, from which he directed a furious fire on a mass of the enemy, which was pressing around Newton's left and exposed flank."[94] A contemporary recalled that Thomas became more animated than usual in the course of the action. "He personally directed the placing of some of the guns," Henry Stone explained, "and with blows of his hand, urged on the horses as they dashed by him in position." Stone explained that on this occasion, the commander reverted to his "old skills and experience as an artillerist" and that these "stood him well" at

Peachtree Creek.[95] It may indeed have seemed like Buena Vista once more, as Thomas stood his ground and blasted the danger into oblivion. General Howard noted the alacrity with which the Virginian responded to the situation. "Thomas, who could move quickly enough when duty demanded it, hastened Ward's artillery to the proper spot near Newton's bridge where it could be most effective to sweep the Clear Creek bottom and the entangled woods that bordered it."[96]

At the conclusion of the fighting, Thomas could report that he and his men had "repulsed handsomely" the Confederate assault. Even so, "fierce" combat had taken place. "Our loss has been heavy, but the loss inflicted on the enemy has been very severe." Word was still filtering in, along with a handful of prisoners and "2 stand of colors" from the attacking Southerners, but a definitive report about the engagement would have to wait for fuller information.[97]

John Bell Hood continued to test Union resolve through trial by combat. In the course of another day of bitter fighting, James McPherson, one of Sherman's most trusted army commanders, wandered too close to the Confederate positions and lost his life. Despite the shock of McPherson's death, the reality of the situation demanded that action be taken to replace him on more than a temporary basis. "The sudden loss of McPherson was a heavy blow to me," Sherman confided to Halleck. "I can hardly replace him, but must have a successor."[98] Circumstances had elevated John Logan, a political general, into the command, but Sherman preferred to consult with his other principal generals before making a definitive decision. Thomas was instrumental in the choice that Sherman ultimately made, insisting that Oliver O. Howard be named to the post.

There was some evidence that Thomas believed that elevating Logan would produce unnecessary complications. "If he had an army I'm afraid he would edge over on both sides and annoy Schofield and me," the Virginian was supposed to have observed about Logan. He had already seen evidence of this disturbing tendency and recognized it as anathema to the standards expected of professionals. "Even as a corps commander," Thomas concluded, "he is given to edge out beyond his jurisdiction."[99] Thomas could be very protective of prerogatives, and if he already thought that Logan had acted unprofessionally he would not be averse to holding him responsible. Perhaps for personal reasons, Sherman attributed the intensity of feeling to something deeper. "If there was ever a man on earth whom Thomas hated, it was Logan."[100]

Joseph "Fighting Joe" Hooker, who had formerly served as the commander of the Army of the Potomac at Chancellorsville, and now led Thomas's Twentieth Corps, considered the elevation of Howard unacceptable, based upon his own availability. Sherman later remarked that neither

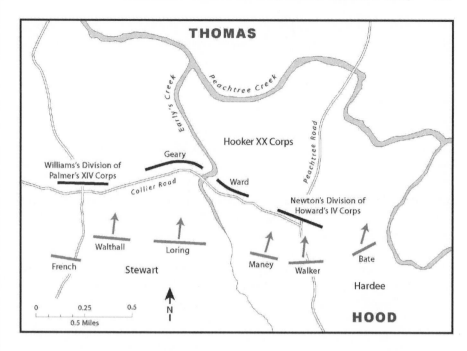

In an attempt to redeem the situation for the Confederacy in the vicinity of Atlanta, John Bell Hood launched an attack against Thomas that resulted in the Battle of Peachtree Creek, July 20, 1864. Map created by Heather Harvey.

he nor Thomas rated Hooker's "fighting qualities as high as he did," but the overall commander noted that in the final approaches to Atlanta he also wanted "a perfect understanding among the army commanders."[101] In typical high-handed fashion, Hooker vehemently protested the move. "Justice and self-respect alike require my removal from an army in which rank and service are ignored." Given his personal experiences, Thomas could hardly have agreed more with the sentiment, but the opportunity to reorder a corps was too great to pass up. He endorsed the request and Sherman forwarded it, with the observation that he could have "my place if the President awards it, but I cannot name him to so important a command as the Army of the Tennessee."[102] Hooker would be doubly chagrined to learn that Henry Slocum had replaced him in command of the Twentieth Corps.

One of the more interesting diversions for the general in the midst of active campaigning was his personal response to a rendition of the fighting that had occurred at Chattanooga the previous fall, created by a private from the Thirty-first Ohio. Apparently, Private A. E. Mathews, or someone acting on his behalf, had indicated to the general that the images existed. Thomas not only took the time to examine them, but wrote a short note in his own hand to the talented foot soldier. "Your paintings of scenery around Chattanooga and especially of the assault on Missionary Ridge are very accurate and lifelike, and reflect on your skill as an artist."[103]

Such respites from the current state of fighting and maneuvering were rare for Thomas and his compatriots. But the nature of warfare offered plenty of other distractions. One of these came when Andrew Johnson, in his capacity as military governor of Tennessee, offered his views regarding refugees with Southern sympathies who were currently being allowed to move northward to Nashville and beyond. The Tennessee chief executive recommended closing off this access and turning the civilians back from whence they had come. "The whole population in our front, instead of being sent this way, should be pressed back with the rebel army," he explained. "Let them hear the cries of suffering, and supply their stomachs and backs with food and raiment." The policy would be harsh, to be sure, but it would have a positive effect for the Federals and a deleterious one for the Confederates. "To the extent that we receive and feed their population, which is disloyal," Johnson observed dispassionately, "we relieve the Confederate Government." Furthermore, he concluded, the refugees "add to the rebel or Copperhead sentiment" and thereby increase opposition to the Union cause.[104]

Thomas responded that he had "always held the same opinion about sending the rebels and their sympathizers south instead of north that you do, and have had frequent conversations on that subject with General Sherman." However, to do so, he argued, would require the refugees to be sent across the lines under a flag of truce, which Sherman understandably did not wish to do "at this time." Such a practice might have alleviated the strains that most concerned the Tennessee politician, but the military imperatives of security would just as clearly be jeopardized by it, especially in a state of active operations. Thomas did not venture to elaborate on that issue with the governor, but assured him that he was of the opinion that such individuals would "probably all be sent south after the campaign is over."[105]

A short time later, Thomas and Johnson discussed matters of a different nature in a manner that revealed the Virginian's capacity for flexibility, even while adhering to system. In this instance the governor was concerned about East Tennesseans who had left the army without permission to attend to personal matters. After "hearing of the suffering and wants of their families" some of these otherwise loyal men felt "induced to return to extend whatever relief they could for the time [and] they did not intend to desert but to return to the service." Only the likelihood of facing charges prevented them from taking the risk of rejoining the ranks. Governor Johnson thought it might be expedient to give the men a grace period in which they could "return to duty without trial and punishment." Johnson offered the example of another officer who had taken a similar action.[106]

Thomas considered the proposal and a few days later responded with his assent for it. He thought there was no reason to object to allowing a period of "twenty days to return to duty and will issue the order." Such an unorthodox approach to a situation in the midst of combat might seem out of character for the professionally trained regular army officer, but he seemed to realize that extenuating circumstances prevailed that ought to be taken into consideration. If a degree of flexibility allowed men to reenter the ranks, then so much the better. Even so, Thomas's flirtation with laxity could only go so far, and he advised the governor that his order would not go into effect until the "application of the facts" from the officer Johnson had cited "come up regularly to these Hd. Qrs."[107] The system itself must be allowed to prevail. The result was Special Field Orders No. 240, delivered on August 31, which established the twenty-fifth of the following month as the date by which soldiers "now under charge of desertion" could choose to return to the ranks "without trial," and ostensibly without penalty.[108]

Ironically, at about the same time that Thomas was sorting these factors out, his superior, William T. Sherman, was becoming querulous about the way the Virginian was handling his cavalry commands. Kenner Garrard was particularly irksome to the Ohioan, and when Thomas tried to defend him, Sherman answered coolly, "I think I appreciate General Garrard's good qualities, but he is so cautious that if forced to make a bold move . . . I doubt if he would attempt it."[109] Indeed, Sherman was so exasperated that he informed both George Thomas and O. O. Howard, "I must have a better commander for General Garrard's cavalry," and suggested either Judson Kilpatrick "or some good brigadier for command."[110]

It is hard to know if Thomas recognized the same type of criticisms that had been leveled at him at various points in the campaign. That he may have could account for his reply to his commander's insistence: "I do not know of a better cavalry commander in the army than Garrard." Then Thomas's characterization of the cavalryman as "an excellent administrative officer" was bound to strike an unsettling chord in Sherman. "Garrard is much more judicious than Kilpatrick, who can knock up his horses as rapidly as any man I know," he explained, telling the Ohioan what practically everyone knew about "Kill-cavalry," as critics labeled derisively the cavalryman Sherman wanted to employ.[111] The debate among these officers, particularly over General Garrard, was hardly settled by the exchange.

Sherman was also complaining loudly to Secretary of War Edwin Stanton about the way the performance of a general in the field ought to be evaluated. "Our progress may be slow to you all at a distance," he explained, "but if you ever cross this ground you will not accuse us of being idlers."[112]

Thomas almost certainly would have given anything for Sherman to make the connection between the leeway he sought for himself and the demands he made of subordinates under similar circumstances.

Indeed, part of the mixed signals Sherman sent concerning the Virginian came in a communication with General Schofield, in which he used Thomas as an example of the kind of action he required on the part of his generals. "Now is the time for you to push," he asserted to Schofield. "General Thomas is hard at work well on the other flank."[113] Clearly, the Ohioan felt that in this instance at least Thomas was performing just as he expected and his example could be held up as a model for another to follow who was not.

Even in the midst of the attempt to seize Atlanta from her Southern defenders, there were those among the higher-ranking officer corps who seemed to prefer taking shots at each other. In early August, Sherman determined to send Schofield on a mission to wreck one of the Confederate rail lifelines leading into the city. To accomplish this he instructed General John M. Palmer to assist. Palmer brusquely declined, and Sherman spent a good deal of time and energy sorting out dates of commission and appropriate lines of authority rather than assaulting Hood's support system.[114] Sherman straightened the mess out to his satisfaction and insisted, "The movements of to-morrow are so important that the orders of the superior on that flank must be regarded as military orders, and not in the nature of cooperation."[115] Palmer should view his compliance as an imperative, not as an option.

The testy subordinate had already challenged Thomas's diplomatic skills by complaining about Absalom Baird and expressing a desire to have him removed. "Well, general, wait until we have a battle, then if you want Baird relieved, I will do it," Thomas had assured him at the time. Later, during the course of the campaign to take Atlanta, the Virginian had occasion to inquire of Palmer if he still wanted Baird out of his command. "No," Palmer rejoined, "Baird is a fighter—he devils the Rebs more than he ever did me."[116] But now it was General Palmer's turn to devil his comrades, and the solution became his own removal from command.[117]

Palmer's exit caused a shuffle in the vaunted Fourteenth Corps. In the process, Thomas demonstrated deftness in handling the situation while adhering to the military protocol he was anxious to uphold. The senior officer, and therefore the likely replacement, could be shifted elsewhere, as chief of cavalry in Nashville, opening the way for the next in line, Brigadier General Jefferson C. Davis. Sherman concurred and afterward maintained that the corps no longer demonstrated deficiencies in speed or activity. "It had been originally formed by General George H. Thomas," he explained, "had been commanded by him in person, and had imbibed somewhat his personal character, viz, steadiness, good order, and deliberation—nothing hasty or rash, but always safe, 'slow, and sure.'"[118] Even in a moment of supreme compliment to Thomas, Sherman could not resist the chance to gig the Virginian one more time.

As the war closed on Atlanta, Sherman determined that any price the city and its residents paid for their part in the conflict would be richly deserved. To Halleck, he noted, "whether we get inside Atlanta or not it will be a used up community by the time we get done with it."[119] Sherman was anxious to make the city and its inhabitants feel the war and hastened to instruct Thomas on August 8: "Orders for tomorrow, August 9: All the batteries that can reach the buildings of Atlanta will fire steadily on the town tomorrow, using during the day about fifty rounds per gun, shell and solid shot."[120] On the ninth, the Ohioan insisted that Thomas keep him informed about when the bombardment would begin so that he could ride down to observe it firsthand.[121] At about the same time, Sherman remarked to O. O. Howard, "Let us destroy Atlanta and make it a desolation."[122]

For Sherman, the war had entered a phase of destructiveness from which he seemed almost to derive personal pleasure. One of the general's biographers explained that as the missiles of war descended on the Southern city he "took considerable relish in all the destruction."[123] In his moral examination of "just and unjust wars" Michael Walzer devoted a section of his work to Sherman's attitudes regarding warfare and determined that the Ohioan laid responsibility for the "hell" of war on the rebels. For him, white Southerners had opened the way to whatever measures were necessary to extinguish their cause.[124] To Thomas there was no debate or equivocation about the fact that the Southerners had perpetrated the rebellion, but that was the point at which he departed from his comrade. He did not believe that such a line of reasoning justified all acts in response.

The same scene of violence that invigorated Sherman struck George Thomas in a different way. His superior might call on him to "hammer away," while he thought of the "next move" he and his armies would make, but the Virginian appreciated the precision and effect of what amounted to a firing exercise.[125] Perhaps he could not help reverting to his old army artillerist days as he watched the bombardment of Atlanta. "The 4½-inch guns have been firing every five minutes since 5 p.m.," he explained of the deliberate pace. Then, with only a hint of exuberance, Thomas added that these shells had "burst beautifully" over the city. He certainly experienced no love lost for the rebellion or those who were engaged in it, but his interest in this case was less with destruction for its own sake, or even for the accomplishment of the warlike ends such firing represented, than for the demonstration of technical prowess the effort exhibited against a fixed target.[126]

William T. Sherman had a particularly complex relationship with his old

West Point roommate. He seemed animated by both a competitive spirit and an affectionate one for his now subordinate general. A staff officer thought that the Ohioan was the only man Thomas would allow "to take the slightest liberty with him," and Sherman appeared to enjoy the indulgence when he could.[127] Sherman certainly had reasons to be exasperated with his comrade, and these did not abate with time. One particularly troublesome area was the degree to which these officers differed as to their conception of the role of cavalry in the operation. Thomas preferred to keep these units away from excessive exposure, while Sherman was not afraid to gamble and risk them to dangerous missions if the promise of a productive outcome seemed likely. When Edward McCook's slash at the Confederate rail lines around Atlanta proved initially successful, there was every reason to believe that Sherman had been correct. Then disaster struck. The Southern cavalry under Joseph Wheeler began to recoup some of the losses that had been inflicted and caused considerable damage to the raiding parties. Casualties reduced the command's effectiveness and quickly had remnants of the Union forces scrambling for safety. James P. Brownlow, a twenty-one-year-old officer and son of William G. "Parson" Brownlow, made his way back to Marietta, Georgia, in a shockingly disheveled condition that revealed the degree to which the operation had broken down, despite his protestations of success. Ultimately, more of the blue-coated horsemen resurfaced, but Thomas had the quiet, if unsettling, satisfaction of knowing that he had been wise to counsel prudence.[128]

Sherman related one instance that occurred in the late summer as the Federals moved to close the Atlanta Campaign. "I was with General Thomas that day," he recalled later of August 30, "which was hot, but otherwise pleasant. We stopped for a short noon-rest near a little church (marked on our maps as Shoal-Creek Church), which stood back about a hundred yards from the road, in a grove of native oaks." The infantry had taken advantage of the opportunity to halt and had "stacked their arms, and the men were scattered about—some lying in the shade of the trees, and others bringing corn-stalks from a large corn-field across the road to feed our horses, while still others had arms full of the roasting-ears, then in their prime." The hot air was soon filled with smoke as the men created small cook fires from the nearest fence rails, appropriated for the purpose, and were soon happily cooking the ears of corn over them. "Thomas and I were walking up and down the road which led to the church, discussing the chances of the movement, which he thought were extra-hazardous, and our path carried us by a fire at which a soldier was roasting his corn." Sherman marveled at the ingenuity and enterprise the soldier demonstrated as he attempted to cook not only his own corn cob, but dozens of others as well. Indeed, the infantryman was so intent on his operation that he did not notice the distinguished visitors nearby.

The Virginian was apparently equally absorbed in what he was considering. Sherman noted that his mind "was running on the fact that we had cut loose from our base of supplies, and that seventy thousand men were then dependent for their food on the chance supplies of the country (already impoverished by the requisitions of the enemy), and on the contents of our wagons." Finally, Thomas freed himself from the considerations to watch the soldier along with Sherman. At length he could not resist inquiring what the fellow was doing with all of that corn. "Why, general," the fellow replied with a smile, "I am laying in a supply of provisions." Unfazed, Thomas retorted, "That is right, my man, but don't waste your provisions."

Sherman chuckled at the comment from the austere warrior he knew so well. He recalled that as they "resumed our walk, the man remarked, in a sort of musing way, but loud enough for me to hear: 'There he goes, there goes the old man, economizing as usual.'" Sherman could only conclude that such "economizing" was unnecessary in this instance since the corn had been procured at the "cost of only the labor of gathering and roasting." He did not seem to grasp that Thomas was less concerned with the source of the supplies than with how they might be utilized effectively, in this case in the form of rations for another day.[129]

Surely Thomas's reaction to the soldier brought back to mind the dire circumstances the army had faced at Chattanooga after Chickamauga and his dramatic insistence that he and his men would hold that town or starve. He always knew that food and forage for a mighty army could easily be brought into short supply. It was most likely that the practical general was trying to teach this man, at least, the valuable lesson of husbanding their resources that he wanted all of them to know. His instinct to plan for another day overrode any desire he had to gratify more immediate urges.

Thomas's predilection for close attention to minute elements caught the attention of his friend James Garfield. "His reports and official correspondence were models of pure style, and full of valuable details," he explained. "Even during the exciting and rapid campaign from Chattanooga to Atlanta he recorded, each month, the number of rounds his men had fired."[130] Perhaps he harkened back to the days when as a subaltern he had to husband resources carefully or held authority in depots where waste could be watched and managed or it would be held to his account.

In any case, the general was not much different in that regard from the West Pointer whom his mathematics professor had praised for his thorough study of problems and desire for solutions. "He knew that the elements and forces which bring victory are not created on the battle field, but must be patiently elaborated in the quiet of the camp, by the perfect organization and outfit of his army," a contemporary noted. "His remark to a captain of artillery while inspecting a battery is worth remembering, for it exhibits his theory of success: 'Keep everything in order, for the fate of a battle may turn on a buckle or a linch-pin.'"[131] Another explained simply that to his estimation Thomas had been "Always a good student."[132]

Additionally, Sherman noted the bond that the Virginian had with his troops. "Between Thomas and his men there existed a most kindly relation, and he frequently talked with them in the most familiar way."[133] One of the men who had served on Thomas's staff put it another way. Despite the general's almost regal bearing and high standing in rank, "he was always approachable by any soldier in the ranks." The officer thought him "a most pleasant companion" as well. "He conversed easily and fluently." Then the subordinate noted the key ingredient to any good conversationalist when it came to interactions with others, again, regardless of station. "He was a good listener."[134]

Sherman continued to spar with his generals as much as with the Confederates. Once again, the use of cavalry was the sticking point. When Hood sent Wheeler northward on a run at the Union supply and communications lines, Thomas saw the threat and preferred to respond to it. Sherman believed that the same movement offered opportunity. "I think it better to pursue Wheeler with our cavalry than to attempt another raid with it on the enemy's communications during Wheeler's absence," the Virginian advised.[135] Again, the suggestion was the conservative, prudent one. But the same William Sherman who had seen the McCook debacle as "a bold and rash adventure, but I sanctioned it, and hoped for its success from its very rashness" was not likely to be less so now.[136] "If you think cavalry can destroy the Macon road sufficiently to force Hood to retreat, I think now would be a good time to raid against it," he explained, almost as if Thomas had not sent him the earlier advice.[137]

Thomas still lauded Garrard. "By not rashly pushing . . . he has preserved to us his fine division, with which I believe he will yet do good service."[138] But this advocacy for adopting a careful strategy clashed with Sherman's desire for a much more aggressive one. "I am willing to admit that General Garrard's excessive prudence saves his cavalry to us, but though saved, it is as useless as so many sticks." Sherman was haunted by the likelihood that the best chance to force Hood's hand in Atlanta was slipping away from his own grasp. "If we wait till Wheeler returns, of course an opportunity is lost, which never is repeated in war."[139]

Sherman offered an additional incentive to Thomas to make the removal of the cavalryman possible. He would see that Garrard received a posting that was more suitable to his talents, perhaps in Nashville.[140] With this the Virginian relented. He had made his effort, demonstrating loyalty to a subordinate, but the time had come to adhere to what his superior obviously wanted.[141] The Ohioan recognized the gesture and the difficulty his old West Point roommate would have in making it. "I don't want to act in this matter without your full and cordial consent," Sherman explained to Thomas, "as this cavalry is properly in your command, and it is for you to regulate it. I want that road broken bad, and I believe now is the time."[142]

As it turned out, the defense of Atlanta was drawing to a dramatic conclusion. Jonesboro, Georgia, proved the last blow against Hood's grip on the city. Ironically, it might also have proven to be detrimental to the existence of a sizable portion of the Confederate Army of Tennessee if a proposal Thomas broached with his superior had been given the go-ahead. In a dispatch sent out in the evening of August 31, the Virginian suggested using some of his troops to disable the critical rail line at Jonesboro while he took the bulk of his men in the direction east of Fayetteville to Lovejoy's Station with the goal of trapping a portion of Hood's forces. Sherman thought differently about what Hood's next move would be and withheld his approval. The Confederates had clung too tenaciously to Atlanta to give the city up easily, and Sherman expected the forces to converge for a continued defense there. His best move would be to have the supply lines completely compromised by the time the Southerners realized the untenable position they now held. In any case, the destruction of the railroad and the completion of movements already contemplated and under way should have precedence. "Clearly Sherman's prime objective remains what it has been since he crossed the Chattahoochee," historian Albert Castel explained, "isolate and take Atlanta by destroying the railroads that tie it to the rest of the Confederacy."[143]

Once more, however, things did not proceed as Sherman expected. He grew increasingly perturbed with what he perceived to be tardiness on the part of David Stanley, even as that officer fulfilled the instructions for wrecking the railroad that Sherman had given him and thus slowed his progress down considerably in the process. Thomas appeared to have sensed the necessity for hastier action and acted to achieve it. An officer observed that as the day slipped away, "Sherman, impatient and excited, turned towards the fast declining sun while he begged of Thomas to hurry up his army [before darkness fell]." He noted that Thomas did all in his power in compliance by dispatching couriers with the appropriate orders.[144] O. O. Howard recalled that the Virginian was unusually animated himself. "At Jonesboro, as his troops went into action by my side, just to the left of Logan's corps, his old stout horse, that hated to trot when laden with two hundred and twenty pounds, actually roused himself to a gallop; and his master was almost furious at a stupid officer who had failed to comprehend the situation."[145]

When it came, a final Union assault proved irresistible, even against the vaunted veterans of Patrick R. Cleburne. The Irish Confederate himself tried against astounding odds to stem to the tide, but the outcome was clear. The Federals had Confederate general Daniel Govan and some 600 of his men as prisoners.[146] Thomas labeled the assault "handsomely made" that netted two "field batteries of four guns each" and "1,000 prisoners," as well as "a number of small arms and battle-flags." He deemed the Southern losses to be "very severe."[147] Casualties for the Army of the Cumberland during the month of August were not inconsequential, with 256 officers and men listed as killed, another 1,384 wounded, and 300 missing or captured, for an aggregate of 1,940.[148]

More importantly, Union troops held the village, leaving Hood no choice but to pull away from Atlanta. A weak thrust at the fading Confederate column in the direction of Lovejoy's Station proved anticlimactic. Howard called the action a "minor combat" as they watched "Hardee slip away."[149] From Jonesboro one of the victorious bluecoats hurried a note off to his wife. "The long agony is over, and Atlanta is ours!" For the happy soldier the outcome was doubly significant after a decisive fight on September 1 that had convinced the Confederates to relinquish the city. "This Corps eclipsed their glories of Chickamauga and Mission Ridge, by its charge of day before yesterday."[150]

Redemption of a different sort awaited the command. John Schofield had been critical of the size and nature of the Army of the Cumberland from the outset of the campaign. Deeming Sherman's organization as "extremely faulty," Schofield considered Thomas's army to be "unwieldy and slow from being larger than one man could handle."[151] The Virginian was also aware that the term "Thomas's Pets" had come into vogue in some circles, as some of Bragg's men on Missionary Ridge had learned for themselves. In the aftermath of the fighting at Jonesboro, he turned the jest on Howard by observing, "Thomas' *pets* have [taken] several guns with Howard's mark on them. He can have them now, having probably loaned them to Hood, who has returned them."[152]

Thomas could not believe the initial reports, despite the one he heard first emanating from Sherman himself. The overall commander sent his chief lieutenant word that the city had fallen. Shortly afterward, Thomas appeared at headquarters personally to confirm that the prize they had so long sought was truly theirs. Glancing once more to be sure, the Virginian's face lit up. "The news seemed to him too good to be true," Sherman remembered. "He snapped his fingers, whistled, and almost danced."[153]

Even in the hour of triumph, shots continued to fall, although these came not from the weapons of the enemy, but from sources closer to home. Sherman wrote a private message to Halleck in which he complained, "I ought to have reaped larger fruits of victory. A part of my army is too slow." Although that assessment was not specific to Thomas, it was in the same communication that Sherman described the Virginian as both "slow" and "true as steel."[154] There was little doubt for whom the criticism was intended. William T. Sherman simply did not seem capable of resisting the chance to inflict another blow aimed at his comrade and friend.

Halleck took the moment to congratulate Sherman and offer his own assessments of several prominent Union generals in return. He was particularly harsh regarding Joseph Hooker, but agreed that O. O. Howard is "a true, honorable man." Then, Halleck turned to the Virginian. "Thomas is also a noble old war-horse. It is true, as you say, that he is slow, but he is always sure."[155]

Thomas might have chosen to return his superior's compliments by pointing out the ways in which Sherman had rebuffed his advice throughout the campaign. Historian Larry Daniel noted "five occasions" where the campaign commander "rejected" the Virginian's "tactical suggestions."[156] While there could never be any certainty that any of Thomas's proposals would have created different results, it was not in the Virginian's nature to dwell on what might have occurred at the expense of another.

Whatever credit might accrue to him and the other commanders for their achievements, Thomas knew where he felt the honors ought to be placed. "Your commander now desires to add his thanks to those you have already received," the Virginian instructed his aide to say to his men, "for the tenacity of purpose, unmurmuring endurance, cheerful obedience, brilliant heroism, and all those high qualities which you have displayed to an eminent degree, in attacking and defeating the cohorts of treason, driving them from position after position, each of their own choosing, cutting their communications, and in harassing their flanks and rear, during the many marches, battles, and sieges of this long and eventful campaign." As always the successes were tinged with the sense of loss for fallen comrades and for duty yet remaining to be done, but Thomas wanted the men who served so faithfully under him to understand his affection and appreciation for them, too.[157]

Morale was indeed high in the ranks. "The army is in excellent spirits," staffer Alfred L. Hough explained to his wife, "and only waiting for reinforcements to fill out the places of those we are mustering out."[158] This ability to replenish the battalions would ensure that the army that had captured Atlanta could remain in the field. But Hough also noted that an issue of a much more personal nature was bedeviling the Thomas headquarters these days. "The greatest subject of conversation and argument is that Genl. Thomas 'Old Pop' as they call him has sent for his wife to come and see him," he explained, adding, "he has not seen her since the war commenced, and can't find time to go and see her." But lest his own wife think less of the general because of this fact, Hough hastily continued, "You have no idea how he is beloved by the army."[159]

The staff officer was not alone in his exuberance. Over the next couple of weeks, James Connolly basked in "the bright glow of victory" and felt "ready to follow Sherman and Thomas to the ends of the Confederacy."[160] There would be time enough for dealing out responsibility for the missed opportunities and missteps that had occurred before the key Georgia city fell to Union forces. For now, the "glow of victory," was sufficient for all concerned.

12 Biding Time in Tennessee (September–December 1864)

"He who knows when he can fight and when he cannot will be victorious."
—Chinese theorist on war, Sun Tzu

"This looks like the McClellan and Rosecrans strategy of do nothing and let the rebels raid the country."
—Secretary of War Edwin Stanton to General U. S. Grant concerning George Thomas

"Wilson, the Washington authorities treat me as if I were a boy."
—Thomas to James Harrison Wilson

A welcome respite in the aftermath of the fall of Atlanta made the opportunity to savor the successful culmination of that campaign all the more sweet. Thomas used it to regroup, not only his command, but himself. Still, he was never far from considering the next steps to be taken. Sherman recalled an instance when the commanders had such a moment, and once again revealed the differences in their approaches that their discussions represented. "General Thomas occupied a house on Marietta Street, which had a veranda with high pillars. We were sitting there one evening, talking about things generally, when General Thomas asked leave to send his trains back to Chattanooga, for the convenience and economy of forage." Sherman thought the request betrayed a sense that the Virginian thought active operations were over. "I inquired of him if he supposed we would be allowed much rest at Atlanta, and he said he thought we would, or that at all events it would not be prudent for us to go much farther into Georgia because of our already long line of communication, viz, three hundred miles from Nashville." Sherman noted that his subordinate's point "was true; but there we were, and we could not afford to remain on the defensive, simply holding Atlanta, and fighting for the safety of its railroad. I insisted on his retaining all trains, and on keeping all his divisions ready to move at a moment's warning."[1]

In the aftermath of Atlanta's fall, the "slow" but "sure" "noble old warhorse" was already anticipating demands that would become common following the war. On September 23, he telegraphed Governor Andrew Johnson to query him about the state of "civil courts" in Tennessee. Were they ready for "full operation"? "I wish to know because I desire to dissolve the military commission now in session to assess damages upon rebel sympathizers for the act of guerrillas in their immediate neighborhood."[2]

Johnson replied that such civilian courts were already up and running in various parts of Tennessee. "We are going to organize the Courts as fast as practicable throughout the State," he assured the general, "but in many instances tis unsafe for Judges and jurors to attend and hold Courts." Such a revelation was not exactly what Thomas had in mind, but he surely found Johnson's next assertion heartening. "We are progressing as rapidly as possible in the rear of the Military to restore Civil authority."[3]

At about the same time, Thomas took up the cause of the assistant surgeon he had supported for her excellent work with the wounded. Mary Walker felt that her endeavors warranted a commission to the rank of major, commensurate with her position, and the Virginian concurred wholeheartedly. "Her services have no doubt been valuable to the government and her efforts have been earnest and untiring, and have been exerted in a variety of ways," he explained in his endorsement. He suggested that she might then be assigned to the Louisville Female Military Prison to supervise the medical needs of the individuals held there.[4]

By early October there began to be indications that the army was getting ready once more to take the field. Leaves were beginning to be curtailed under the admonition that no more would be granted, as one officer recorded, "on any account until further orders." The same fellow explained to his wife, "I am 'old soldier' enough to know what that means without any further explanation." Still there were mixed signals. Frances Thomas was supposed to be on her way from New York to join her husband in the company of at least one other general's wife. The "old soldier" was careful not to criticize his commanding general too seriously, although he suggested that in Union-held Atlanta "officers and soldiers may get along here very well, [but] it is not a *good* place for their wives."[5] Such concern was not ill-placed, for there would indeed soon be additional work for the victorious Union troops to do.

John Bell Hood was also searching for something of importance after his failed attempt to drive the Federals away in defeat. He wanted redemption. His pugilistic reputation and actions had not saved Atlanta. Now, he contemplated a gambit that was designed to lure William T. Sherman away from the city. If he could push northward, Sherman would surely have to follow in response to the threat to his supply and communications lines. Of course, if the Union commander chose to do something else, Hood would be free to move in ways that might prove more profitable than facing the formidable Union forces directly.

Consequently, on September 29, 1864, the Confederates crossed the Chattahoochee River on the mission of disrupting the Western and Atlantic Railroad, upon which Sherman would be expected to be dependent. The Southerners enjoyed some initial success, gobbling up small garrisons at various locations along the railroad and inflicting some damage to the line itself. Hood hoped to follow this promising beginning with a bolder strike against the defenders of Allatoona Pass, at which point a blockage of the railroad line could prove more substantial an inconvenience for the Federals. He could not know that with the aid of an intelligence coup from the most unlikely of sources—Confederate president Jefferson Davis had divulged the general scheme in speeches meant to bolster morale—Sherman recognized the threat. The Union commander promptly augmented the defenders with reinforcements under Brigadier General John M. Corse that brought the Union numbers to just over 2,000. They were still less than the approximately 3,200 Hood dispatched on the operation under Thomas's old Mexican War comrade Samuel French, but they would have the added benefit of strong defenses and improved weaponry. Nevertheless, on October 5, French was able to put himself in a position for success until an erroneous report reached him of additional Union troops that prompted his withdrawal. Both sides lost less than 1,000 men in the fighting, but the operation demonstrated the difficulty Hood would face as he sought to find some way to achieve more dramatic results. His options were certainly limited, although he was rewarded with a more positive result with the capture of a large garrison of predominantly African American troops at Dalton, Georgia, five days later. Still, with Sherman lingering relatively close on his heels he decided to turn for Alabama and more favorable ground from which to fight, all the while hoping to lure Sherman away from the ground that the Union general had so recently won.

For a time Sherman was left to determine what course he preferred to take. He could follow Hood, or turn toward the sea, via Mobile, Alabama, or Savannah, Georgia. He determined that he was not willing to pursue Hood to the extent that the Confederate desired, having long contemplated a more dramatic movement of his own. As a result, he gathered a powerful force under him and set out on the march that would establish his fame, and infamy. The movement of these Federals left George Thomas and whatever defenders he could scrape together to handle Hood's Confederates.

Even before Hood struck at Allatoona, Thomas was already in Nashville, anticipating the measures he would have to take to confront any Confederates who might come his way. He arrived in the city on October 3 and set about coordinating his troops by dispatching cavalry to key points and pulling back small detachments of infantry from exposed positions. He received authority over all of the troops who were not immediately with Sherman to defend Nashville as well as Chattanooga, and an enormous supply base at Fortress Rosecrans near Murfreesboro.[6]

Thomas also had to turn Nashville into the kind of supply center that could sustain large-scale numbers of troops, and for this he looked to his trusted quartermaster James Donaldson, who had already been working feverishly in the city for months. During this time, he supervised the construction of warehouses and other facilities, including barracks for his employees. He took steps to improve conditions for the sick and wounded convalescing in Nashville and worked on the waterfront to facilitate the delivery of troops and supplies by that route. Donaldson had even commandeered the printing presses of the Methodist Book Concern for Union army use. The quartermaster reported all of these developments dutifully to his superior on October 12, no doubt easing Thomas's concerns on that score.[7]

Engineer W. E. Merrill had tried to allay the department commander's worries as well by working diligently to fortify the rail lines that ran from Nashville and supported the many demands of Thomas's forces. Following a summer of heavy activity in Mississippi, Confederate cavalry raider Nathan Bedford Forrest was just as determined to add to Thomas's troubles. In late September the Southern horseman had brought a command of 4,500 troopers onto the Nashville and Decatur Railroad, capturing some of the blockhouse defenses that the Federals had designed to thwart such outcomes. Using a combination of guile and determination, Forrest wreaked as much havoc and wrecked as much trestlework as he could. Merrill termed his adversary's efforts "the most serious destruction" of the defenses he had constructed and noted that the Confederate managed to capture and destroy eleven of these works, even destroying a bridge with "bottles of a kind of Greek fire," or flammable substance, despite the refusal of the garrison holding the neighboring blockhouse to surrender as demanded.[8]

Thomas had no choice but to respond to the threat to his supply lines. He attempted to position forces so as to prevent further destruction and block the raiders' return to the safety of their lines. Indeed, Thomas was so confident in his measures that he observed to John Croxton, "I do not think we shall ever have a better chance at Forrest than this," having repeated essentially the same point to Lovell Rousseau.[9] Thomas insisted that in addition to pursuing "Forrest to the death," both subordinates should take care to keep their commands under their strictest control.[10] The wily Confederate might yet take advantage of opposing units that lost either tight cohesion or their vigilance. Testily, the meticulous commander also chided Rousseau for a "simple omission" in precision over identifying a locality "which has embarrassed me considerably." Consequently, Thomas insisted, especially in such fluid circumstances, "I would like to have all reports made as definite and concise as possible."[11]

When, despite the bravado, the discouraging word reached Nashville, "Forrest has escaped us," Thomas initially refused to accept that result without at least considering further action on his own part.[12] Within a few hours, he ordered Rousseau to weigh his options against the retiring Confederate raiders. "If you are sufficiently near to Forrest to lead you to hope you can capture him by crossing the river, you can do so and pursue him," the Virginian urged his subordinate, but then added cautiously, "but you must not venture too far from the river or so as to endanger your command."[13] When confirmation came that the Southerners were beyond reach, Thomas's reaction was understandable. He had anticipated greater results, demonstrating his "chagrin" to one officer, who concluded that since such "a large part of our force was mounted," the Federal pursuers "ought to have crowded that rebel into the river."[14] Forrest's successes had so bedeviled Thomas that the general named James R. Willett as "inspector of railroad defenses" and sent him through the department to improve the conditions among blockhouse garrisons, including the posting of instructions for "'No Surrender,' in capital letters."[15]

Despite what the most famous of Confederate raiders in the Western Theater might attempt to accomplish against their strategic imperatives, confidence remained at a high level in the Union ranks regarding George Thomas. On October 13, one Northern diarist recorded, "General Thomas again prominent," and spent a portion of the date's entry to cite the Virginian's qualifications. "Thomas never failed in any of his undertakings," the writer observed. "He is slow but sure; he does not aim at brilliancy, but never takes a false or backward step."[16] Such sure-footedness was bound to come in handy as a Confederate army closed on Tennessee.

Other significant national events coupled with Hood's approach to demand attention as well. From his new posting in Chattanooga, Gates Thruston wrote his father, in the context of an upcoming presidential election between Abraham Lincoln and George B. McClellan. The Lincoln ticket now included Andrew Johnson and campaigned under a National Union banner, while the Union general teamed with noted Democratic Ohio politician George Pendleton to unseat the incumbent. Thruston explained in a postscript what he perceived of the current political atmosphere of the department. "Neither Genl Sherman or Thomas would vote for McClellan if they had the opportunity." But if Thruston did not consider Sherman "particularly partial to Mr. Lincoln," he knew much better the Virginian's stance. "I have heard General Thomas say that the reelection of Mr. Lincoln was necessary to let the South know that the North was thoroughly in earnest."

Earlier in his November 2 letter, Thruston had hinted strongly at other military developments, suggesting that "certain changes" were in the air that promised to "work better results" than merely holding Atlanta would have achieved. Then he could not contain himself. "If General Sherman cuts loose, from us, upon his grandest raid of the war, General Thomas' command will be temporarily what Genl. S's has been, and though we shall lose two of *our* corps we will have from reinforcements as many men as before."[17]

With Ulysses Grant in Virginia, George Gordon Meade offered a short piece of speculation about the departure of Sherman for the sea. On November 11, he noted simply, "This is a bold move, the success of which will depend on Thomas's ability to keep Hood out of Kentucky and Ohio."[18] For Meade, whose record included turning back a major offensive by Lee's Army of Northern Virginia in Pennsylvania the previous year, the havoc that the Confederates might create could easily outweigh the impact of Sherman's dramatic operation, and he knew that it was up to George Thomas to prevent anything untoward from happening in Tennessee.

Soldiers in the rank and file understood the stakes as well. From the Rome area in North Georgia, an Indianan recorded on November 12 in his diary, "We received orders this evening to march to morrow morning and I suppose this is our last day here." There was no word from Hood or the Confederates they had been chasing, but there seemed to be an indication of what was to be expected in that regard. "We understand that Genl Thomas has force enough to look after him and that we will return to Atlanta from here."[19]

Sherman may have been thinking more of himself than of Thomas when he later insisted, "Of course, General Thomas saw that on him would likely fall the real blow, and was naturally anxious."[20] Lincoln confidants John Nicolay and John Hay maintained, The "Rock of Chickamauga" had not been especially pleased with his assignment to defend Tennessee, but he "accepted it as he did every duty ever confided him with modest confidence and devotion."[21]

A general who remained in Tennessee also likely stretched the point when he asserted, "Thomas was the only one who seemed to have no doubts in regard to the final issue."[22] Thomas had his doubts. He also had supreme confidence that he would find a way to be successful if given enough time. The question was not only if Hood would provide the necessary cushion of time, but whether the men who outranked Thomas would allow it. As Nicolay and Hay later explained, the atmosphere in which he would have to operate was an electric one. "Nothing exhibits more vividly the tension of spirit which had come with four years of terrible war" than the political pressure that now mounted for Thomas to move expeditiously against Hood.

Even the ordinarily composed field commander felt the strain. In an uncharacteristic and relatively public display, the Virginian allowed the emotional stress to enter into a dispatch to Wilson. Thomas had a comfort level with the cavalryman that would find expression in various ways throughout their collaboration. Just as the army was about to launch the attack that would redeem Thomas in the eyes of those who doubted, Wilson revealed some of the tension that had existed to General Cadwallader Washburn. "General Thomas directs me to say that he is being continually harried from

Washington to begin his operations against General Hood, and that it is of the greatest possible moment that the cavalry shall be put in an efficient basis, not only in the manner of equipment and organization, but in that of numbers."[23]

There was a lighter moment as Thomas's headquarters became connected via a telegraph post on Lookout Mountain outside Chattanooga. The station master sent greetings, and Thomas's chief of staff returned them from "Major-General Thomas and the rest of the world." Then in a takeoff on the name of the geographic feature, the officer added, "Long may it look out for and defend the interests of the United States of America and of all mankind."[24]

Thomas was doing all he could to expedite the collection of forces in Nashville while slowing the advance of the Confederates against them. Yet, too much of a holding action might itself lead to disaster. The correct balance had to be struck. Telegraph messages from headquarters in Nashville to John Schofield, still holding a forward position below the Tennessee capital, were an imperfect means of determining what was happening, but the best, in terms of speed of communication, that Thomas had available. "Have the pontoons arrived at Columbia[?]" he wanted to know in the late afternoon of November 13. "I still hear rumors of a portion of [Bedford] Forrest's command having crossed the Tennessee above Clifton and having advanced on the road between Waynesboro and Columbia." Such a course would put "that Devil Forrest," as Sherman had once called him, in an optimum position to impact the route along which Schofield would have to retire to reach Nashville. "Send out scouts in that direction and find out the truth," Thomas advised.[25]

From Chattanooga, a staff officer who had worked closely with the general and was now stationed at this critical supply point to carry out necessary commissary support was anxious about his commander's choice of strategy. "Thomas is quietly waiting for him," Alfred Hough explained of Hood's advance, and in the meantime "all goes on as usual in this department; the mails are regular." The emphasis was to be on continuing the ordinary flow of business and routine activity, despite underlying worries of any repetition of earlier shortages. As Hough explained to his wife, "we cannot help comparing our position with that of a year ago, when we were half starved, now we have plenty of everything, with as much force here as then and [yet] have sent 60000 men right into the heart of the Rebellion [under Sherman]."[26] Even with Thomas biding his time, prospects could hardly seem brighter from within the department itself.

The tenseness of the situation was not lessened by the fact that General Hood had several options available to him. On November 20, Hood's chief of staff instructed famed cavalry raider Nathan Bedford Forrest to "send forward at once small parties, under bold, reliable men, to break the enemy's railroad and telegraphic communications from Nashville to the north." Hood wanted to isolate Thomas and limit that commander's ability to dispose his forces freely, while maximizing the effective use of his own. "General Hood thinks that small parties, under the right men, would move more successfully than larger ones, and that we can't spare the larger ones."[27]

The Confederate commander also seemed to be motivated by the thought that he could overcome whatever force the Federals assembled against him, by either maneuver or direct assault. In an account that surfaced later in the year, a contemporary recalled Hood's assessment that Thomas had few dependable troops available to defend the Tennessee capital and that he felt he could force its evacuation. Even if called upon to assail the city, Hood was sure of success. "We have taken stronger places, and we will take Nashville."[28]

Of course, General Thomas knew that one of the most important means by which he could ensure victory over Hood would be if he was successful in assembling a sufficient quantity and quality of troops for the purpose. Reinforcements were on the way, but rather than serve as a source of comfort for the general they became one of additional worry instead. The reinforcements always seemed tantalizingly to be traveling toward Nashville, but Thomas could never quite be sure where they were or when they would reach him. His frustration was evident in messages sent back to the river town of Paducah, Kentucky, where some of these forces were to converge before moving by water to the Tennessee capital. "Have none of General [Andrew J.] Smith's troops left Paducah yet[?]" he inquired plaintively on the morning of November 25. "I thought that some of the regiments would leave last Wednesday."[29] He could not have been either much pleased or comforted by the terse response he received later that day: "Will start some time to-day."[30]

The next day, Thomas bypassed the post at Paducah and brought his concerns directly to his old commander, William S. Rosecrans, in St. Louis, Missouri. "Will you please inform me whether General Smith's troops have all embarked and started for this place, and if so when they left?"[31] Since so much of his preparation was predicated on these troops reaching him in time and having the opportunity to become incorporated in his defenses, Thomas's concerns seemed reasonable enough.

He was still hoping to employ Schofield as a means of delaying Hood to allow time for the concentration to be completed. For his part, Schofield had to be concerned about not reaching a point at which he became vulnerable to a flanking movement that would cut him off from Thomas in Nashville. Thomas needed Schofield intact as part of that collective defense force and naturally did not want to have him taken out of the equation either. Nevertheless, time remained of the essence. "If you can hold Hood in check until I can get Smith up, we can whip him," Thomas explained on November 27.[32]

But where was Smith? Fortunately for the Virginian, the vexing question was about to be answered. From Paducah, the telegraph whirred into action once more, this time with some welcome news. "I have just arrived at this point," Andrew Jackson Smith declared.[33] Paducah was not Nashville, but the much-needed reinforcements were finally within a reasonable distance, and Smith was bound to see that they moved forward rapidly.

In Chattanooga, the mood was equally testy. Gates Thruston lamented that Hood's advance meant "there is a probability that we may be cut off temporarily from Nashville." From that officer's perspective, it was also likely that any action would occur elsewhere in the vast department. "Genl Thomas' command now extends from Paducah to Western Virginia and therefore this is about the centre of it but our staff are much disgusted at our location here." For the disgruntled subordinate, Nashville would have been more centrally located to the business at hand and "would be a great deal pleasanter place to stay in, but he seems determined to keep us here . . . & has with him only his aides & a couple of adjutants." At length the unhappy officer remarked, "If I am to lose the glory and excitement of field service, and am to be confined to office work it would be some satisfaction at least to be where I could see something of society & have a good time." Indeed, Thruston was so frustrated by being relegated to what he termed "a sink pot of a town" that he momentarily thought it might be better, from a social perspective at least, to "be with *Rosecrans* or *Hooker*."[34]

As the Union officer trapped in the unexciting backwater of Chattanooga had suspected, the action was creeping closer to Nashville. Hood pushed first to Columbia, where he failed to flank Schofield and cut off his line of retreat to Nashville. Then a famously missed opportunity at Spring Hill prevented the same objective from being achieved and led a frustrated Hood to order a bloody and futile attempt to smash Schofield's command at Franklin. The losses for the attacking Southerners there were staggering, but did nothing to prevent either the safe arrival of the Federals to join their comrades in the Tennessee capital or Hood's battered command from following.

John Schofield had the responsibility for these preliminary actions on the part of the Federals. He afterward remembered that after a difficult night "sleeping quietly on my horse as we marched along," from Spring Hill, he arrived at Franklin in the early morning hours of November 30.[35] Schofield became testy toward his old commander for not supplying new pontoons to replace the ones he had been required to burn when pulling out of Columbia before Hood could cut him off on the road to Nashville. The subordinate worried that he might have difficulty moving his army across the Harpeth

River, especially with Hood pressing him, although the fighting at Franklin settled the matter satisfactorily.[36]

Ironically, on the day that the Southern forces smashed into the Union defenses, penetrating briefly in harsh hand-to-hand fighting around the Carter Gin and House, Thomas forwarded a plea for Schofield to try to hold Hood before Franklin for at least three days. "Genl. Smith reported to me this morning that one Division of his troops is still behind. We must therefore try to hold Hood where he now is until those troops can get up and the steamers [bringing them can] return. After that we will concentrate here, reorganize our Cavalry and try Hood again. Do you think you can hold Hood at Franklin for three days longer[?]" Thomas continued to weigh the possibilities and remained open to ideas outside his own. "Answer giving your views," he requested of Schofield, "and I should like to know what Wilson thinks he can do to aid you in holding Hood."[37]

Thomas remained concerned in his understated way, but the mood changed at headquarters in Nashville when two developments occurred almost simultaneously: news came of the outcome of the fighting at Franklin and the arrival of Andrew Jackson Smith and his troops in the area. James F. Rusling later recollected, "I dropped into General Thomas's headquarters (about nine o'clock) to inquire more about Franklin. Thomas, his hat up and face all aglow, handed me a telegram from Schofield, announcing that he had defeated Hood; putting *thirteen* of his *general officers* alone and over *six thousand* of his men *hors de combat*—a terrific blow to the Confederates—but was now falling back on Nashville in pursuance of orders." Even so, Thomas paused in his momentary revelry to ask if there was word of Smith yet. Thomas was worried that wounded as his army was, Hood would still muster sufficient strength to close the Cumberland River and prevent Smith from reaching Nashville.

Rusling had been on his way to a soiree when he paused at headquarters, and having satisfied his general's curiosity on the matter of these important subjects, he then proceeded on his way. Upon his return at approximately midnight, the officer "dropped in at Thomas's headquarters again, and there I found Schofield and T. J. Wood just arrived from Franklin, and all three in conference over what was to be done next day." After introducing the aide, Thomas asked once more on the status of Smith, and this time Rusling had better news. The noise along the river indicated that steamers were coming in, and the only appropriate conclusion was that Smith had reached the environs, and by implication Thomas and the Nashville defenders would now be "all right."

As if on cue, the officer recalled, "the door opened and in strode General A. J. Smith, a grizzled old veteran, but a soldier all through." No doubt worn by the exertions of travel, the soldier was nevertheless a welcome sight.

"They all four greeted each other eagerly," Rusling explained of the generals present, "but Thomas (undemonstrative as he was) literally took Smith in his arms and hugged him."

The unusually euphoric moment passed quickly as the men "first discussed Franklin, and rejoiced over it, and then Thomas spread his maps on the floor and pointed out his Nashville lines, explaining their bearings and significance." Rusling did not record individual elements of the discussions that followed, but noted, "I left them at 1 a.m., all four down on their knees and examining attentively the positions to be assumed next morning."[38] He went immediately out to examine the reinforcements and satisfy himself of their condition and appearance personally. "They were a rough-looking set, bivouacked all along the levee, and cooking coffee," Rusling pronounced, but "Smith's guerrillas" appeared prepared to do their duty.[39]

On December 1, Schofield's command reached Nashville. He watched as it moved along before riding ahead to converse directly with Thomas. The army commander had left headquarters to wait at the point in the lines that he had designated for Schofield's troops to occupy and was there when the general arrived in the city. "He greeted me in his usual cordial but undemonstrative way," Schofield recalled, "congratulated me, and said I had done 'well.'" The officer later offered a tinge of regret at the coldness with which he responded, but concluded, "I did not feel very grateful to him; but he gave no indication that he thought me unappreciative of his approbation." Thomas deduced that Schofield, who had spent many of the last hours in the saddle on the march or in battle, simply looked "tired." Schofield replied that he was and noted, "That was about all of the conversation we had that day."[40]

Of course, John Schofield had missed the anxiety Thomas was feeling and expressing in his own way over the fate of his subordinate's command. He was also understandably not present when the news reached Nashville of the victory at Franklin to which Thomas responded so enthusiastically. Now, the army commander demonstrated his concern for the personal welfare of a subordinate who had done his duty as he had expected, and Schofield reaped his largest reward by spending the next day and a half catching up on his sleep unmolested.

Another element that marked the first day of December was an extraordinary statement released by the headquarters of the Confederate Army of Tennessee. General Field Orders No. 38 might well have been meant to bolster morale in the wake of a tremendously costly battle, but it also served to illustrate the degree to which John Bell Hood had deluded himself about the outcome at Franklin. "The commanding general congratulates the army upon the success achieved yesterday over our enemy by their heroic and determined courage," the statement opened. "The enemy have been sent in disorder and confusion to Nashville, and while we lament the fall of many gallant officers and brave men, we have shown to our countrymen that we can carry any position occupied by our enemy." Hood instructed, through his assistant adjutant general, that each regiment be given the opportunity to hear the orders read to them.[41] All in all, it was a strange declaration of a victory that had cost him some 7,000 casualties, at least 1,750 of which had been killed, to Schofield's 2,326, compounded further by the deaths of talented generals such as the fighting Irishman Patrick Ronayne Cleburne.[42]

What resulted from the fight at Franklin was a sham siege of Nashville, as Hood's men reached the vicinity of the city and began to construct redoubts and rifle pits while Thomas scrambled to improve his defenses and prepare for an all-out assault. Either circumstance was likely to produce the blow to Hood's already decimated command that would decide the issue. But Thomas intimated to a postwar gathering that he had not despaired in allowing Hood to establish himself before the city. "The Government at Washington, and the general before Richmond could not know what we knew, that the Confederate Army was demoralized, and that the longer we held them at bay the weaker they became." For the Army of Tennessee it was a matter of subtraction that would ultimately tell against their chances for success. "While we in Nashville were comfortable, sheltered, well fed, and gaining every day in strength, poor Hood and his ragged, badly supplied men were lying out in the bleak hills about the place, being continually thinned out by sickness and desertion."[43]

Unhappily for George Thomas, Ulysses Grant was one of the key individuals who did not know about the circumstances in Tennessee directly. He remained adamant that Thomas deal with the Confederates regardless of what they might choose to do. "If Hood commences to fall back, it will not do to wait for the full equipment of your cavalry to follow. He should in that event, be pressed with such forces as you can bring to bear upon him."[44] Thomas replied that afternoon that he was "watching Hood closely" and would act when the Confederates committed themselves to follow Sherman or move elsewhere."[45]

The Virginian was already laying the groundwork for offensive operations, but he was painfully aware that he would enter any fight, unless allowed to address the matter, with one arm of the service in woeful condition. It must have troubled him considerably as an old horse soldier himself to admit that it was his cavalry that was currently deficient. Still, Thomas remained optimistic as he told Grant near the end of November, "The moment I can get my cavalry I will march against Hood, and if Forrest can be reached he will be punished."[46] It was bold talk, but the kind that the tenacious fighter "Sam" Grant most liked to hear.

Even with the tremendous success Union arms had won in the bloodbath of Franklin, the pressure mounted for an offensive against Hood's army. At mid-morning of December 2, Secretary of War Stanton stood next to a telegrapher who tapped out an imperative message to General Grant at City Point, Virginia. "The President feels solicitous about the disposition of Thomas to lay in fortifications for an indefinite period, 'until Wilson gets his equipments,'" he noted with as much frustration as undisguised sarcasm. "This looks like the McClellan and Rosecrans strategy of do nothing and let the rebels raid the country. The President wishes you to consider the matter."[47]

Thirty minutes later Grant had done enough contemplation to compose a note directly to Thomas. "If Hood is permitted to remain quietly about Nashville we will lose all the [rail]roads back to Chattanooga, and possibly have to abandon the line of the Tennessee River. Should he attack you it is all well, but if he does not you should attack him before he fortifies." Grant understood Thomas's concerns about a sufficient number of troops and proposed that his subordinate scour every available source. "Arm and put in the trenches your quartermaster employes, citizens, etc."[48]

The Confederates, at least those who rode with Bedford Forrest, were deploying "in sight of the capitol of Nashville" on December 2. The "Wizard of the Saddle" had his men out on either flank to offer some protection for the infantry units as they arrived. But a greater task awaited him than guarding an idle army. Hood detached him with the assignment to damage the rail system in the region as much as possible, and Forrest and his men "commenced operating upon the railroad, blockhouses and telegraph lines leading from Nashville to Murfreesborough."[49] The Southern cavalry commander had earned a stellar reputation for conducting such raids, his men lauded as being like infantry when it came to the level of destruction they could apply to railroads. Over the next several days, Forrest accomplished a great deal of what he had been sent to do, adding immeasurably to Thomas's concerns.[50]

Back in Virginia, George Gordon Meade was one of the visitors with whom Grant shared his frustration. One of Meade's staff officers accompanied him and reported, "The General went to City Point where Grant told him Thomas had fallen back to Nashville, which vexed the Lt. Gen. who telegraphed [Thomas] to attack."[51] The Union commander's answer to all challenges was to assume the offensive and wrest the initiative from an opponent. Thomas felt that the stakes demanded more prudence than Grant deemed was warranted and that the initiative could be seized when the appropriate measures for doing so had been undertaken.

When Grant wired a second communication to the Virginian that day, he referenced the recent events regarding the Confederate advance in a strange manner. "After the repulse of Hood at Franklin, it looks to me that instead of falling back to Nashville we should have taken the offensive against the enemy, but at this distance may err as to the method of dealing with the enemy." It is difficult to say if he failed to distinguish between Schofield's command that had defended Franklin and Thomas's in Nashville, or expected the Virginian to march out of the Tennessee capital for a rendezvous with Schofield's smaller force. Thomas was not falling back as Grant inferred, and the misunderstanding of the situation could not help but contribute to the subordinate's questioning of his distant superior's admonitions. The Virginian could be forgiven for wondering how accurate Grant's advice could be if that general did not understand what the actual dispositions of troops were in Middle Tennessee, especially given the rapidly developing situation there.

Grant still had in mind the conditions of the supply lines and repeated his prediction of trouble if Thomas did not act quickly. "You will suffer incalculable injury upon your railroads if Hood is not speedily disposed of. Put forth, therefore, every possible exertion to attain this end." The hope was that immediate Union action might prompt Hood to reevaluate his strategy, and if that happened Thomas would be in a prime condition to take advantage of the opportunity thus presented. "Should you get him to retreating give him no peace."[52]

Undoubtedly after a long day, Thomas had the opportunity to digest the communications from the East, and at 10:00 PM he sat down to provide a reply. He had considered the option of keeping a force at Franklin, however temporarily, indeed had instructed that Schofield make every effort to do so, although Grant did not know this, sitting at City Point in Virginia. His overarching concern of preserving as many troops for the defense of Nashville was his paramount principle in ordering Schofield's men back to the Tennessee capital. "The division of General Smith arrived yesterday morning, and General Steedman's troops arrived last night. I have infantry enough to assume the offensive if I had more cavalry, and will take the field anyhow as soon as the remainder of General McCook's division of cavalry reaches here, which I hope will be in two or three days." In almost exasperated fashion, the normally even-keeled general offered a litany of reasons for the delays, of most of which Grant would have been quite aware. Even so, he closed, "I earnestly hope, however, in a few days more I shall be able to give him a fight."[53]

Grant was beginning to take up a theme that would prove common in the days ahead. To Sherman he expressed the dissatisfaction that "Thomas has got back into the defenses of Nashville, with Hood close upon him." He wavered over whether such a move was necessary, but thought that "it did not look so, however, to me," and therefore was regrettable. The Virginian ought to have sufficient strength to confront the Confederates successfully. "I hope yet Hood will be badly crippled, if not destroyed."[54]

According to the general in chief, the problem lay as much in timing as anything else. "It seems to me," Grant explained directly to Thomas two days later, "while you should be getting up your cavalry as rapidly as possible to look after Forrest, Hood should be attacked where he is." Counter to the argument that Thomas would later make about Hood's steady weakening before Nashville, Grant had a different take on the situation. "Time strengthens him, in all probability, as much as it does you."[55] Even Thomas recognized that the Confederate might create a short-term irritation, but time was not on his side, at least as far as the Virginian was concerned.

In any case, Thomas was not going to remain inactive, whatever Hood might contemplate doing. "I have been along my entire line to-day," he told Halleck that evening. He felt reason to be encouraged by what he saw, but realized that more preparation was necessary before successful offensive operations got under way. Thomas wanted to convey that sense to the chief of staff as well and give him some notion of a viable timetable. "If I can perfect my arrangements I shall move against the advanced portion of the enemy on the 7th instant." The choice of date would prove to be unfortunate in that it became the yardstick by which progress could then be measured. Inadvertently and unwittingly, the Virginian had placed himself into a restricted time frame outside which any revision would appear to be unnecessary delay. Thomas did not realize that in trying to provide the command structure with a workable frame of reference he had created a pressure cooker for himself.

But if Thomas was thinking purely on the defensive as some in Washington and City Point, and others in subsequent years, thought, he did not entirely appear to have such a mind-set at the time. In his communication with Halleck, he urged that a force be prepared so that when Hood fell back before a pending Union offensive, the Confederate route of retreat could be hampered.[56] In planning for a successful defense, the Virginian was also preparing in his mind for what would follow it.

In the meantime, the soldiers in the impressively fortified town apparently felt less concern about their safety than did the upper echelons in Washington. A Kentuckian observed in a letter to his brother on the third of December, "We are now lying in the fortifications of Nashville. The rebel army in plain view south of the city." But lest his sibling be worried unduly, Thomas Speed insisted that under the circumstances, "We are resting delightfully, have plenty to eat, and get letters every day. What more could a soldier want[?]"[57]

A few days later, Speed informed another brother of the scenes he was witnessing in Tennessee. "Our regiment lies with the left resting on the Franklin pike just at the foot of Fort Negley. We go up very often to take a look at the grand sight that lies around us." The image was particularly impressive in the evenings. "[T]he rebel army is within 2 miles. at night their fires can be seen as plainly as our own." It was the kind of martial grandeur that made war seem so surreal when fighting was not occurring, generating as it did awe-inspiring scenes and unforgettable images. "I wish you could but take a look at these things," the Kentuckian observed unabashedly. Then, as if to enhance the visual impression he was trying to impart, Speed added, "Towards sundown every evening the bands begin to play and for an hour or two we hear the most delicious music."[58]

If the martial environment was unmistakably alluring for the moment, the natural elements were increasingly becoming less so. One soldier's early December weather prediction when he informed a brother on the seventh, "This is a very cold evening, it looks a great deal like snow," was about to be exposed as woefully understated.[59] Indeed, freezing rain, sleet, and snow were all destined to plague the troops on both sides, limiting movement along alternately slippery and soggy roads.

Grant seemed to be indifferent to the weather, preferring for the drama to end sooner rather than later, regardless of the circumstances. "Attack Hood at once, and wait no longer for a remount of your cavalry," he ordered abruptly on December 6. His concern was not so much to anticipate poor weather patterns, but to thwart any intention John Bell Hood might have for moving northward past the heavily fortified city. "There is great danger of delay resulting in a campaign back to the Ohio River."[60]

That evening Thomas fired off two messages. One went to City Point and Grant. In it, Thomas promised, "As soon as I can get up a respectable force of cavalry I will march against Hood." He had assigned James Harrison Wilson to the task and pushed him to accomplish it vigorously. "General Wilson has parties out now pressing horses, and I hope to have some six or eight thousand cavalry mounted in three days from this time. General Wilson has just left me, having received instructions to hurry the cavalry to remount as rapidly as possible." But until his cavalry commander had completed his work, Thomas was leery of committing his command to battle, influenced in part, as Sherman himself should have appreciated, by the presence of the famed Confederate Nathan Bedford Forrest. "I do not think it prudent to attack Hood with less than six thousand cavalry to cover my flanks, because he has under Forrest at least twelve thousand."[61]

In a second communication, this one to Henry Halleck, Thomas reiterated his need for additional horses to mount his cavalry and make it effective for the upcoming campaign. Although he would have served himself better to have stressed the need for mounted troops to harass a broken enemy, as indeed he would do when the circumstances permitted, he emphasized security first. Wilson needed mounts because the animals would allow him to put "a sufficient cavalry force" in the field "to protect my flanks."[62]

George Thomas had already experienced the debilitating effects of war on the animals that made up a central component of an army's support system. His time in the defenses of Chattanooga provided ample illustration for those who witnessed it. One Union surgeon recorded seeing the corpses of "a dozen or two dead horses and mules, their dead carcasses left where they fell, or at most dragged to one side of the road." That army had suffered mightily from what he deemed "a loss of not less than ten thousand mules and horses to Gen. Thomas' command."[63]

Now, a year later, a similar specter of potentially limited mobility and flexibility haunted the defenders of Nashville. Once again, General Thomas was doing his best to secure the animals necessary for his command to perform efficiently against his veteran opponents. This search extended to unsual sources, as one Illinois soldier recorded. "Howe and Norton's Circus in town," Chesley Mosman noted in early December. In the midst of active military operations he hoped to visit the show, "as I have not seen one for years." Mosman was struck by the poor quality of the performance, but not based on the high expectations of nostalgia. "It was a weak affair," he wrote, "as General Thomas pressed its horses into service to mount the cavalry." The Virginian was clearly tapping every available source for the critical resources. The soldier could only conclude sarcastically, "Mr. Howe was quite patriotic to bring horses to Nashville and tender them to the government in the same class with other conscripts."[64]

Almost as soon as his wires had left headquarters on December 6, Thomas read the preemptory message Grant had sent ordering an offensive. Once again he obediently signaled his intention to seize the initiative against the Confederates on his superior's terms. "I will make the necessary disposition, and attack Hood at once, agreeably to your orders," he told Grant, then displayed his continuing concern by adding, "though I believe it will be hazardous with the small force of cavalry now at my service."[65]

The question in Grant's mind was not whether the men were prepared to do their duty or not, but whether Thomas was going to do his. On December 6, he candidly explained the situation to Sherman as he saw it pertaining to their colleague. "Hood has Thomas close in Nashville," he observed, switching the order from an earlier communication that employed similar language. In doing so, Grant was not so subtly indicating that he viewed Hood as dictating the action at Nashville to Thomas and not the other way around. "I have said all I can to force him to attack," he observed of the Virginian, "without giving the positive order until to-day." The situation had reached a crisis point in his head and no longer called for deferring to a subordinate who did not seem to reflect his own priorities. "To-day, however," Grant declared, "I could stand it no longer, and gave the order without any reserve." The military terminology might as well have been deliberate.

Grant had thrown his full force into the effort. Even so, a sense of hesitation remained about whether the general in Nashville would act or continue to equivocate. "I think the battle will take place to-morrow," Grant observed, sounding as if he were actually trying to convince himself, not anticipate the immediate future.[66]

Sherman did not actually receive Grant's communication until the fifteenth of the month, but when he did he answered immediately and was sympathetic to his superior's plight. "I myself am somewhat astonished at the attitude of things in Tennessee," Sherman told him. He recalled the last communication that had passed between Thomas and himself before he set off on the "march to the sea." The Virginian had indicated that all would be well. Indeed, Sherman insisted that he did not depart until Thomas "had assured me he was 'all ready.'" Their last dispatch gave no hint of concern, Thomas rather boisterously telling his old West Point classmate that he would "ruin Hood" and imploring him to "give myself no concern of Hood's army in Tennessee."

Yet, instead of acting, Thomas pulled back to Nashville. "Why he did not turn on Hood at Franklin, after checking and discomfiting him, surpasses my understanding," Sherman asserted, repeating the mistaken mantra of Grant concerning Schofield and Thomas. There had been more than one chance for an offensive that should have settled matters before now. "I know full well that General Thomas is slow in mind and in action," he offered, "but he is judicious and brave, and the troops feel great confidence in him."[67] Other than those last few words on the subject, Sherman could offer Grant little to ameliorate his anxiety. Had the message reached City Point in a more timely fashion, it might have spurred the general in chief to act more abruptly in deciding on Thomas's fitness for command at Nashville. That delay, as much as any other factor, or combination of them, actually worked to the Virginian's benefit.

Another individual with Grant in Virginia shared his chief's sense of concern. General Meade built upon the speculation he had offered a few weeks earlier when he had initially learned that Sherman was separating from Thomas and leaving the Virginian to confront General Hood. "I feel some anxiety about Thomas in Tennessee," he candidly admitted. "I think I wrote you some time ago, when I first heard of Sherman's movement, that it's success would depend on Thomas's capacity to cope with Hood." He understood that many observers had expected Hood to pull back into Georgia, perhaps in pursuit of Sherman. But that had not been the case. Meade maintained that he had "anticipated just what he appears to be doing—a bold push for Kentucky, which, if he succeeds in, will far outbalance any success Sherman may have in going from Atlanta to the sea coast." Meade thought that Sherman's decision to take "the largest part of his army" with him and "leaving Thomas with the lesser force to confront and oppose Hood, with the whole of his organized forces" might be the cause of considerable trouble. It certainly was sufficient grounds for concern, which Meade summarized in an understated way. "I trust old Thomas will come out all right, but the news is calculated to create anxiety."[68]

Indeed, Hood had the troops and a degree of freedom of movement that Thomas did not for putting a larger-scale operation into motion. He had already envisioned using light cavalry forces to disrupt the flow of Union supplies and communications. Now, as an important element of his overall scheme, the Confederate commander planned to dispatch a force of mounted troops under Hylan B. Lyon to raid deep into Kentucky. If he could draw off Federal forces to defend against these threats, this would theoretically diminish his opponents' capabilities to safeguard Nashville.[69] Hood would never realize the degree to which he had achieved one of his purposes, for at the same time Thomas struggled to organize his cavalry arm, under mounting pressure from superiors, a portion of it had to be diverted to deal with Lyon and the near-constant threat of an appearance by Nathan Bedford Forrest.

Hood's expectations for Lyon's operation were reflected in his instructions for his lieutenant "to move up the north bank of Cumberland River, capture Clarksville, if practicable, tear up and destroy the railroad and telegraph lines running into Nashville, and to put all the mills in running order throughout that entire section for the use of the Government."[70] How Hood expected a Confederate cavalry raid to achieve the latter effect, while operating behind enemy lines with a limited force, was debatable, although Lyon possessed the aggressiveness that the army commander required for the key part of this ambitious assignment.

Consequently, General Lyon left the area of Paris, Tennessee, on December 6, with a force of some 800 men and two howitzers to accomplish the missions Hood had laid before him in conjunction with the Army of Tennessee's advance toward Nashville. As anticipated, his movements across the Cumberland River near Clarksville necessitated a countermove by General Thomas, who dispatched two brigades of Edward M. McCook's cavalry in pursuit. This shift in the vital cavalry support that would normally be available to him rendered Thomas's tendency toward caution all the more pronounced and helped to exacerbate the conditions under which the Virginian operated.[71]

To the southeast there was also Bedford Forrest with whom to contend. Having wreaked as much havoc as he could on the rail lines between Nashville and Murfreesboro, including the capture of a number of blockhouses and their garrisons that were supposed to prevent such mischief, Forrest finally received expected infantry reinforcements under General

William B. Bate. But even with infantry support and cavalry that had the reputation for fighting like foot soldiers, the Confederates faced formidable Fortress Rosecrans outside Murfreesboro. Although the inspection would be made several months later, a Federal officer speculated that the immense set of earthworks and lunettes constituted a difficult conquest under the best of circumstances. "This fortress could not be taken except by siege, if properly garrisoned and well defended," the engineer reported to George Thomas in the spring of 1865.[72] Of course, that condition of these defenses was exactly what the Confederate cavalryman wanted to explore.

Forrest gathered his own troopers and Bate's foot soldiers for a test of the stout Murfreesboro defenses and their defenders under Union general Lovell Rousseau. December 6 proved to be a day of probing defenses and receiving more infantry so that by nightfall Forrest could boast some 6,500 men. But if the Confederate cavalry commander counted on the numbers to intimidate Rousseau, as he had so often done with other opponents, he did not reckon with this one. A counterstroke by Rousseau reduced the enraged horseman to riding among the infantry, in an attempt to rally them, when their formation disintegrated. Nothing he did, including using the flat of his saber and shooting at least one of the panicked foot soldiers, could prevent the rout or lessen the panic until it ran its course. Finally, Forrest got the men into line, with timely assistance from his own horse soldiers, but it must have been clear to him, as it ought to have been to Hood, that many of the men were on the brink of collapse.[73]

While Lyon's horsemen rode off on their mission and Forrest's tested the defenses of Murfreesboro, Secretary of War Stanton picked up on the phraseology Thomas had employed in a recent communication to take another swipe at his general in Tennessee. "Thomas seems unwilling to attack because it is hazardous," he observed to Grant, "as if all war was any[thing] but hazardous. If he waits for Wilson to get ready, Gabriel will be blowing his last horn."[74]

Grant was beginning to have even deeper doubts that the situation outside Nashville could ever be resolved without the necessity of a change in command. On the eighth he reached a point at which such an alteration seemed the only viable course to undertake. "If Thomas has not struck yet, he ought to be ordered to hand over his command to Schofield," Grant noted to Halleck. Both men knew the record that the Virginian had established, and both agreed that in certain circumstances he was one of the best men available. "There is no better man to repel an attack than Thomas," Grant continued before offering the indictment, "but I fear he is too cautious to take the initiative."[75]

Halleck responded that Grant was certainly free to do as he desired with a subordinate position, but he wanted the army commander to take direct responsibility, not only for the decision, but for the action that would implement it. "If you wish General Thomas relieved, give the order. No one here will, I think, interfere. The responsibility, however, will be yours, as no one here, so far as I am informed, wishes General Thomas removed."[76]

Thomas continued to provide updates, particularly pointing to the excellent level of cooperation he was enjoying with the navy. The coordination of these forces was critical in many ways to Thomas's hopes for success.[77] But his references to the river and the importance of the navy may have actually backfired with regard to building confidence in Washington and City Point. Thomas undoubtedly meant to show the steps he had taken to keep matters in hand as much as possible. Grant, in particular, viewed the comments less as assurances and more as vulnerabilities that had to be addressed. His communication with Thomas on the evening of December 8 was a case in point. "It looks to me evidently the enemy are trying to cross the Cumberland, and are scattered. Why not attack at once?" The fear was not that Thomas would possibly lose an early confrontation with Hood, but that if he did not strike him, Hood might slip away for Kentucky. "By all means avoid the contingency of a foot-race to see which, you or Hood, can beat to the Ohio." Grant must have seen in such a "contingency" shades of Braxton Bragg's Kentucky Campaign and the largely ineffectual pursuit Don Carlos Buell had undertaken as the Confederates moved past. Grant knew that Thomas had been with Buell, even refusing to supersede him in command, claiming the ill wisdom of such a move in the middle of a campaign. What if Hood did the same as his predecessor? It would be Grant who was forced to answer to the president, the War Department, the newspapers, and, most importantly, public opinion. All could be settled with one bold move. "Now is one of the fairest opportunities ever presented of destroying one of the three armies of the enemy," he asserted. "Use the means at your command, and you can do this and cause rejoicing from one end of the land to the other."[78]

By that evening, Grant was uncertain enough that he had gotten his message through that he sought assistance once more from Henry Halleck. "I want General Thomas reminded of the importance of immediate action. I sent him a dispatch this evening, which will probably urge him on. I would not say relieve him until I hear further from him."[79]

Even in the midst of the hand-wringing that went on in the higher echelons beyond their ranks, the soldiers' confidence in their general apparently never wavered, if at least one individual's letter home was an indication. "Glorious old Genl. Thomas just rode by," one fellow explained. "Every man in the Army knows him. And he inspires confidence wherever he goes."[80]

But the situation, like the weather around Nashville, was deteriorating for

Thomas. At 10:30 on the next morning Halleck added his voice to that of Grant, calling upon Thomas to act for the good of the service and the nation. "Lieutenant-General Grant expresses much dissatisfaction at your delay in attacking the enemy," he advised. Then, paraphrasing the language that the secretary of war had used, Halleck prodded further, "If you wait till General Wilson mounts all of his cavalry, you will wait till doomsday, for the waste equals the supply." Finally, knowing his subject as well as he felt he did, Halleck offered a history lesson that Thomas was sure to understand, if not appreciate. If he did wait to secure all of the mounts he felt were necessary he would "be in the same condition that Rosecrans was last year, with so many animals he cannot feed them. Reports already come in of a scarcity of forage."[81]

Grant was becoming increasingly agitated and prepared to take the step of removing Thomas from command in Tennessee. In the late morning of December 9, he informed Halleck that by all reports the enemy forces were widely scattered in Middle Tennessee, "and no attack yet made by Thomas." There could be no further delay regarding a change in leadership. "Please telegraph orders relieving him at once and placing Schofield in command," Grant insisted. Thomas should be ordered "to turn over all orders and dispatches received since the battle of Franklin to Schofield."[82]

Accordingly, on December 9, 1864, the general orders specifying that John Schofield would replace George H. Thomas at Nashville became a reality, at least on paper. As Ulysses Grant had directed, the draft instructed Thomas to turn over to his successor all paperwork in making as smooth a transition in the face of the enemy as possible. What the Virginian had not deemed appropriate for him to do to Buell two summers earlier regarding the replacement of a commander in mid-campaign was now apparently going to happen to him.[83]

By mid-afternoon on the same day, Thomas sent out two messages. The first, to General Grant, insisted, "I have nearly completed my preparations to attack the enemy to-morrow morning, but a terrible storm of freezing rain has come on to-day, which will make it impossible for our men to fight to any advantage. I am therefore compelled to wait for the storm to break, and make the attack immediately after." Thomas wanted Grant to know that he was still keeping a tight rein on Hood, with the cooperation of other branches of the service. "Admiral [Samuel P.] Lee is patrolling the river above and below the city, and I believe will be able to prevent the enemy from crossing. There is no doubt but Hood's forces are considerably scattered along the river, with the view of attempting a crossing, but it has been impossible for me to organize and equip the troops for an attack at an earlier time." Finally, Thomas cut to the core of the matter. "Major-General Halleck informs me that you are very much dissatisfied with my delay in attacking. I can only say I have done all in my power to prepare, and if you should deem it necessary to relieve me, I shall submit without a murmur."[84]

The second went to Halleck. "I regret that General Grant should feel dissatisfied at my delay in attacking the enemy. I feel conscious that I have done everything in my power to prepare, and that the troops could not have been gotten ready before this." Ironically, Thomas wanted to assure Halleck that he was prepared to follow orders, whatever they might be, but that circumstances beyond his control had changed the situation drastically, and the Virginian told Halleck essentially what he had informed Grant. "And if he should order me to be relieved, I will submit without a murmur. A terrible storm of freezing rain has come on since daylight, which will render an attack impossible till it breaks."[85]

At 4:10 PM on the afternoon of December 9, 1864, Henry Halleck informed Grant in Virginia that all was in order if he wished to proceed with the dismissal of his troublesome lieutenant in Tennessee. "Orders relieving General Thomas had been made out when his telegram of this P.M. was received. If you still wish these orders telegraphed to Nashville they will be forwarded."[86] The situation was now back in Grant's hands. Author Stephen Ambrose has suggested that in such ways, "Old Brains" used his wits to delay Grant from taking action that could lead to Thomas's dismissal and thereby served to "save" the Virginian from such precipitous action. Yet, the evidence is less convincing that the chief of staff acted out of such a desire.

Halleck dutifully prepared the paperwork, but he could not overcome his fastidious nature. Adhering to details might buy Thomas additional time, but following bureaucratic procedure was to be done in any case. Besides, the preference to allow the general in chief to exercise his authority for such a momentous decision should provide a sufficient buffer against impulsiveness. Even if Grant followed through and removed Thomas, the responsibility would fall on him, particularly if circumstances should demonstrate that it had been premature or incorrect, or perhaps worst of all, unpopular in higher-level circles or the public mind.

At just a little over an hour later Grant wired Halleck: "General Thomas has been urged in every possible way to attack the enemy, even to the giving [of] the positive order." This was the point at which Thomas's own timetable came back to haunt him as Grant reminded the chief of staff, "He did say he thought he should be able to attack on the 7th, but he did not do so, nor has he given a reason for not doing it." The general in chief understood that this was no ordinary subordinate that he was taking to task. He was, after all, the "Rock of Chickamauga." "I am very unwilling to do injustice to an officer who has done so much good service as General Thomas has, however, and will therefore suspend the order relieving him until it is seen whether he will do anything."[87]

It was after dark when Grant wrote directly to the Virginian about this delicate matter. "I have as much confidence in your conducting the battle rightly as I have in any other officer," he observed, "but it seemed to me you have been slow, and I have had no explanation of affairs to convince me otherwise." New information was now available, and it had apparently reached City Point in the nick of time. "Receiving your dispatch to Major-General Halleck of 2 p.m. before I did the first to me, I telegraphed to suspend the order relieving you until we should hear further. I hope most sincerely that there will be no necessity of repeating the order, and that the facts will show that you have been right all the time."[88]

Thomas could not help but understand the directive, yet once more his answer to Grant's insistence could not have pleased that general. "I can only say in further explanation why I have not attacked Hood, that I could not concentrate my troops and get their transportation in order in shorter time than it has been done, and am satisfied I have made every effort that was possible to complete the task."[89]

The situation surely reminded the Virginian of the time when William Rosecrans faced similar pressure, including the potential for removal from command. Thomas had stood with his superior then. Now he summoned his subordinates to a council to lay out for them the broad parameters of the current circumstances. Thomas refused to divulge specifics, but one individual felt compelled to respond almost instantaneously. Although the procedure for such gatherings was to allow junior officers to express themselves first, apparently under the notion that they would be freest to do so before their seniors could set the tone, John M. Schofield asserted, "General Thomas, I will sustain you in your determination not to fight until you are fully ready."[90] Schofield would later claim that he had acted only as a show of support for his embattled chief, but the name of the replacement was his, and the next piece of his memoir was a recounting of the West Point court-martial for which he held Thomas largely responsible. "Time works legitimate 'revenge' and makes all things even," he noted before arguing that the steps he had taken, including this one, were not out of that motivation, but to demonstrate how he had risen above it.[91]

Also on December 9, Forrest got the situation more under control outside Murfreesboro, including replacing Bate's unreliable men with those of Colonel Charles Olmstead.[92] Further to the north, the Confederate cavalry raiding force of Hylan Lyon seized the town of Cumberland City on the Cumberland River, along with fifty prisoners. The Southern riders destroyed public property, including several vessels, estimated at approximately $1 million. Their positioning on the river also allowed them to move toward Clarksville, the initial target Hood had set for them, although the river town proved difficult for the Southerners to capture, protected as it was by troops in strong earthworks.

The Confederate raid then devolved into a twin struggle with the weather and the pursuing Union forces dispatched by General Thomas. Lyon achieved a reputation in the operation as "the courthouse burnin'est general" in the Confederate States, but the benefit to Hood and the threat to Thomas remained open to question.[93] Indeed, Lyon's initial success generated the kind of Federal response that Hood had sought, but with which the raiders now had to contend, in the form of McCook's two cavalry brigades, detached on December 14. By now the weather had turned quite cold, and conditions for the men and mounts of both sides were deteriorating.

In Nashville, the inability of the animals to move on the ice-coated ground was one of the reasons George Thomas cited in his communications for delaying an assault on Hood's army.[94] A mood to match the weather pervaded the Union headquarters. A staff officer recalled that the army commander remained busy, professing, "Not an hour, day and night, was he idle." At the same time, he admitted that the general would occasionally fall into an even quieter mood than was typical of him. "While the rain was falling and the fields and roads were ice-bound," the staffer remembered of Thomas, "he would sometimes sit by the window for an hour or more, not speaking a word, gazing steadily out upon the forbidding prospect, as if he were trying to will the storm away."[95] Another contemporary remembered seeing Thomas often in Nashville; "a cloud of anxious care rested always on his brow." The same individual noted, "Habitually, during all that period, he wore his military hat pulled down over his grave gray eyes—was reticent and gloomy."[96]

When not indulging in quiet introspection, Thomas kept himself occupied with numerous activities, including the hosting of delegations and guests on various matters. Officers marveled at his ability to consider the usually mundane complaints about seizures of animals, which his men had been doing regularly to prepare Wilson's cavalry for action, shortages of supplies, and the like. But Thomas almost certainly saw such routine duties as diversions from the more pressing issues that confronted him. Vice President–elect Andrew Johnson was apparently a frequent and vocal visitor, whom Thomas listened to patiently and impressed with his knowledge about matters relating to the law. For the Virginian, the activity was all in a day's work for a commander of a department, even in the face of the enemy.[97]

That opponent, or at least the cavalry portion of the enemy forces that Hood had sent raiding with Lyon, was also still lurking in nearby Kentucky. Union horse soldiers continued their pursuit, with McCook trying to catch the elusive Southerners by blocking possible escape routes and pressing the gray horsemen closely. Many of the Confederates managed to slip past the blocking forces by wearing captured apparel and dashing past before they could be recognized. Nevertheless, General Thomas reported some success from the effort. "After capturing Hopkinsville, Lyon was met by [Oscar H.] La Grange's brigade near Greensburg, and after a sharp fight was thrown into confusion, losing one gun, some prisoners, and wagons."[98] At the same time, telegrams raced across the wires as General Thomas and Admiral Samuel P. Lee sought to position their respective forces to challenge any Confederate crossing of the Cumberland River and create the conditions in which Lyon's command could be trapped.[99] The biographers of the Virginia-born Union admiral compared him favorably to his counterpart on land, but thought he suffered from the similar tendencies of superiors to view him as "overly cautious and lacking in aggressive leadership." The Nashville Campaign certainly offered a different perspective. "Now, in the waning months of 1864, these two Virginians were teamed to pull together for Union victory in one of the great closing campaigns of the war."[100]

Conditions around Nashville were certainly not cooperating with plans for an offensive. "The sleet and inclement weather still continue," Thomas explained to Halleck on the evening of December 10, "rendering offensive operations extremely hazardous, if not impossible."[101] The Virginian was no forecaster to be able to determine when those conditions might improve, but he knew that at present they were as formidable as any Confederate defenses.

Thomas had a great deal to consider, but he had faith in his subordinates to help provide a perspective that he might be too close to the situation to have for himself. Not one to pass responsibility, he nevertheless believed in consulting his lieutenants and benefiting from their views. At a council of officers he read the most recently received communications and the reply he had made earlier in the evening. As the junior officer present, James H. Wilson responded first, assuring his commander that conditions indeed warranted the message he had sent. An attack over such ground would prove ludicrously unproductive. The others chimed in with agreement, and Thomas, while undoubtedly buoyed by their concurrence, remained impassive to all outward appearances, thanking the officers for their views and dismissing them for the night.[102]

Wilson prepared to make his way out into the gloomy darkness, but Thomas called him back. The Virginian had come to see the young cavalry commander as something of a sounding board, and the astute horseman obliged his general with a willing ear. "Wilson, the Washington authorities treat me as if I were a boy," he blurted when out of earshot of any others. "They seem to think me incapable of planning a campaign or of fighting a battle, but if they will just let me alone till thawing weather begins and the ground is in condition for us to move at all I will show them what we can do." Thomas revealed confidentially that his only real concern was that Hood might depart before the blow could be delivered. "I am sure my plan of operations is correct," Thomas concluded, "and that we shall lick the enemy, if he only stays to receive our attack."[103]

Wilson reaffirmed his support for his commander and tried his best "to soothe Thomas's wounded feelings." He then led the general onto other paths of discourse and later recalled that "our discussion lasted till after supper." Whether it was a late meal, or the pleasant company of the officer, Thomas soon settled on more pleasant topics that his lieutenant soaked up eagerly.[104]

The evening left Wilson "with a higher opinion of Thomas and his character than I had ever had before." He was struck by the general's demeanor and rational process of thought for one under such enormous outside pressure. "He was calm during the whole interview, and as confident of victory as it was possible for a soldier to be," the cavalryman recalled. "Withal he made it clear that he would not permit himself to be hurried into battle, but would lay down his commission rather than fight against his judgment or before he had done all in his power to complete his preparation and to insure victory."[105]

On the afternoon of December 11, 1864, Grant sounded irrationally alarmist regarding the possibilities of what Hood might accomplish if Thomas did not dispense with him immediately. "If you delay attacking longer, the mortifying spectacle will be witnessed of a rebel army moving for the Ohio, and you will be forced to act, accepting such weather as you find. Let there by no further delay." Grant was correct in assessing that the Confederate leader had options, especially if the Virginian did not assume the offensive himself soon, but such speculation smacked more of desperation than reality. "Hood cannot stand even a drawn battle so far from his supplies of ordnance stores," he explained in one scenario. In another, "If he retreats and you follow, he must lose his material and most of his army." These were the most likely outcomes, as Grant saw them, if an outright Union victory had not occurred by then. "I am hoping of receiving a despatch from you to-day announcing that you have moved. Delay no longer for weather or reinforcements."[106]

As the commander on the scene who understood the situation as it existed on the ground, Thomas was caught between two difficult choices. If he acted, as he viewed it, precipitously, and elements beyond his control caused the effort to fail, he knew that he would be held responsible. The Virginian never shrank from challenges or shirked his genuine responsibilities, but he also preferred not to put himself or his command at serious risk when he could otherwise help doing so. Still, as a soldier, he recognized his duty to obey directives. "The weather continues very cold and the hills are covered with ice," he reminded Halleck, who could perhaps serve as a buffer for Grant's ire. "As soon as we have a thaw, I will attack Hood."[107]

An hour later, the beleaguered general in Nashville sent another message to Grant in Virginia. "I will obey the order as promptly as possible, however much I may regret it, as the attack will have to be made under every disadvantage. The whole country is covered with a perfect sheet of ice and sleet, and it is with difficulty the troops are able to move about on level ground." Since some of the most important Confederate defensive positions were atop steep rises that overlooked the city environs, Thomas knew that scaling heights, especially under fire and with uncertain footing, would be virtually impossible. Grant should know that he was not delaying or vacillating for no reason. "It was my intention to attack Hood as soon as the ice melted, and [I] would have done so yesterday had it not been for the storm."[108]

The next day, Thomas communicated again with Halleck. "I have the troops ready to make the attack on the enemy as soon as the sleet which now covers the ground has melted sufficiently to enable the men to march," he explained, "as the whole country is now covered with a sheet of ice so hard and slippery it is utterly impossible for troops to ascend the slopes, or even move on level ground in anything like order." Conditions were indeed abysmal. Therefore, delays were inevitable. But that was the least of his concerns. "It has taken the entire day to place my cavalry in position, and it has only been finally effected with imminent risk and many serious accidents, resulting from the numbers of horses falling with their riders on the road." With or without an advance the footing was treacherous. These conditions were like natural obstructions that would disrupt any attack and subject the advancing troops to insurmountable challenges to success. "Under these circumstances," Thomas concluded, "I believe that an attack at this time would only result in a useless sacrifice of life."[109]

Hood remained George Thomas's primary concern, but Forrest was causing his share of difficulties around Murfreesboro that could not be ignored by the department commander. On December 13, part of the Confederate's command captured a train loaded with military supplies. Two hundred prisoners made their way on to Forrest's parole lists, and a train and 60,000 rations, or at least those that could not be easily hauled off, went up in flames.[110]

The Union general also wanted the pesky Hylan Lyon "disposed of" and had confidence that he had set into motion the dispositions that would accomplish that task.[111] Late on the evening of December 13, 1864, Thomas informed his naval counterpart concerning Lyon, "I have ample force in pursuit of him to effectually destroy him, and I have no apprehension about the Louisville and Nashville Railroad."[112] The Virginian planned to rely on the river units to tighten the cordon and encouraged this support through calls for vigilance.

The Federal pursuit continued, although there was often little left besides smoldering ruins after the Confederates had departed. Thomas kept one eye on such activities and the other on the conditions prevailing around Nashville. "At length there are indications of a favorable change in the weather," he explained to Henry Halleck on December 13, "and as soon as there is I shall move against the enemy, as everything is ready and prepared to assume the offensive."[113]

The suspension of the order replacing Thomas with Schofield had put off that difficult duty and offered the Virginian something of a reprieve. But Grant's impatience would not allow him to endure delay much longer. Indeed, he crafted a reserve plan that called for Major General John A. Logan to go to Nashville and report on the status of circumstances there. If Thomas still had not moved against Hood, the proverbial ax would fall, this time wielded, on the general in chief's instructions, by Logan.[114] As one of Grant's staff officers recalled, the secret replacement order was to be considered "revoked" should Logan find that upon his arrival in Nashville "the battle was on."[115]

On the next day after Grant had set that second replacement plan into motion Henry Halleck wrote once more to Thomas himself to try to give that general a chance to understand, if he already did not, the larger strategic imperatives. "It has been seriously apprehended that while Hood, with a part of his forces, held you in check near Nashville, he would have time to co-operate against other important points left only partially protected." Such points as Fortress Rosecrans in Murfreesboro were large enough targets that should the Confederates succeed in capturing them the effect would be significant. "Hence, Lieutenant-General Grant was anxious that you should attack the rebel forces in your front, and expresses great dissatisfaction that his order had not been carried out." Halleck also pointed out the detrimental effect upon other areas of Union operations as well. "Moreover, so long as Hood occupies a threatening position in Tennessee, General Canby is obliged to keep large forces on the Mississippi River to protect its navigation and to hold Memphis, Vicksburg, etc., although General Grant had directed a part of these forces to co-operate with Sherman." The cumulative effect was that "Every day's delay on your part, therefore, seriously interferes with General Grant's plans."[116]

An early Thomas biographer recorded twenty-six separate communications pressing that general to act or criticizing him for not doing so quickly enough.[117] Grant's telegrapher recalled that as far as he could remember "no day went by that he did not place in my hands a despatch for Thomas" and that invariably when the word returned of further delays he resorted to the device of softening the blow for his worried commander by announcing "No battle yet, General," as he entered the room. Samuel Beckwith thought that Grant believed that Thomas "could and should conquer both the elements and the enemy."[118] Thomas's subordinate Richard Johnson described the situation as demonstrative of "how a commander may be compelled to fight front and rear at one and the same time."[119] James H. Wilson, who served under both Thomas and Grant and seemed to admire and appreciate each, was also defensive of the Virginian and the treatment he had received in the lead-up to the attacks at Nashville.[120]

Whatever the circumstances, clearly Ulysses Grant wanted action in Tennessee. "It was the expectation of Grant that his indomitable General would quickly overwhelm the enemy and bring another of his splendid triumphs to the Union arms," Samuel Beckwith observed. Even so, the staff officer thought that the overall commander's own difficulties outside Petersburg and Thomas's "hitherto uniformly successful career" offered a compelling context for assessing Grant's impatience with Thomas in Nashville. Beckwith explained that from his perspective, "the almost petulance displayed over the non-compliance with his orders, I am frank to admit, impressed me at the time as being rather strange."[121]

A later student of leadership in warfare concluded of Thomas's actions in the battle, "His adherence to the letter of his mission might have appeared to superiors like Grant or Sherman as sluggishness or obstinacy. In reality, his methodical procedures were only the outward signs of his determination to carry out his mission as he saw it—and it was characteristic of him that he never undertook an assignment until he was sure that he could see it through."[122]

Thomas was good enough a soldier and capable enough a thinker to appreciate strategic vision as well as tactical imperatives. He also felt tremendous responsibility for succeeding once he confronted Hood, for he knew that a setback, however unlikely that might be, would jeopardize Union plans far more than any delay on his part had already done. Besides, there really was still the weather to consider.

With all of these factors in mind, Thomas dictated a message to Halleck on the evening of December 14. "The ice having melted away to-day, the enemy will be attacked to-morrow morning. Much as I regret the apparent delay in attacking the enemy, it could not have been done before with any reasonable prospect of success."[123] A staff officer who remained noted that as he finished the first portion of the message, Thomas "drew a deep sigh of relief, and for the first time for a week showed again something of his natural buoyancy and cheerfulness." The general seemed to step more lively and, again true to his nature, worked diligently to close the necessary paperwork and other office requirements for the evening.

Another contemporary observed, "It was Thomas's habit, before starting on any considerable movement, to see that all pending matters of business were attended to, all papers properly arranged, his own signature affixed to every document that required it."[124] Such behavior could strike anyone assessing it as compulsive, but there was a method to his protocol that suited his personality perfectly. Clearing the items from an agenda that would normally require his time and energy would also free his mind to concentrate on the task at hand. There would have to be no nagging concern about mundane activities while his focus needed to be on more serious matters.

Tomorrow he planned to rise early so that the attack that had been delayed for so long could be launched. Now the soldier who said that he had disciplined himself "not to feel" turned out the lights and went to bed.[125] Thanks to his diligence and unceasing preparations, tomorrow would take care of itself.

13 The "Sledge" Hammers Hood (December 15–31, 1864)

"Dang it to Hell didn't I tell you we'd whip 'em?"
—Thomas to James H. Wilson outside of Nashville

"Thomas still-moving"—very good;
The cause is plainly understood—
He doesn't like his neighbor—Hood
—Epigram celebrating the defeat and pursuit of Hood
  in the 1864 Tennessee Campaign

George Thomas might not be blamed if he spent a rest-
less night awaiting a dawn that would bring the sounds of battle at last reverberating across the hills and fields surrounding Nashville. Yet, for someone
whose conscience was clear concerning what he felt he had been able to do
and when, he may never have slept more soundly. Still, in the early hours he
and the officers and men of his command began to stir. A heavy fog ob-
scured much that the predawn darkness did not already hide. It would not
lift for several hours, rendering an eerie sensation to the massive shifting
and sidling of soldiers into formation. Then, according to one witness,
"about 9 o'clock, the sun began to burn away the fog, [and] the sight from
General Thomas's position was inspiring."[1]

Even as he prepared to launch his offensive, Thomas remained a stickler
for details that others would have deemed irrelevant under the circumstances. As he rode over from his headquarters to the point at which he
planned to view the critical opening salvos of his long-awaited attack
against Hood, the staff officers who accompanied him watched as he suddenly stopped along the way. The general had thought of a last-minute item
he wanted cleared up. He was determined to address the matter before more
serious pursuits prevailed.

During the wintry weather that had plagued the army and prevented its
movement, he had depleted his personal store of coal. The shortage compelled him to borrow a quantity from a neighbor. He now wanted the debt
repaid and the supply scheduled for replenishment before the matter got lost
in the rush of greater affairs.[2] Clearly, it was not in his meticulous nature to
let even a minor matter go when he could resolve it before his attention
shifted elsewhere.

At last, General George Thomas felt free to unleash the juggernaut that
he had been collecting and perfecting for this moment. The general and his
entourage were soon in an excellent position for viewing the operations as
they unfolded. One of the staff officers recalled comparing the initial

advance to the one he had witnessed a year earlier at Missionary Ridge, based upon the spectacular view they had over the open ground that lay before them.

The Federals had constructed two lines of defenses along the southern and western approaches to the city, which narrowed to a single line on the eastern side. Significant fortifications crowned the works, situated on elevations that could easily command the ground in front of them. The Cumberland River completed the obstacles that had helped to keep Nashville in Union hands. For the Confederates there was a line that stretched from the Nashville and Chattanooga Railroad on the eastern side to the Hillsboro Pike on the western. An earthwork lunette and a series of redoubts anchored the defenses and, in the case of the latter, swung back along the pike to "refuse" the Confederate left flank or make it more difficult for the Federals to turn it if that was where they struck.[3]

The Virginian envisioned just such a turning movement for this occasion. Tradition called for a holding action to keep an opponent's attentions focused on one sector, while a heavier force hit the other. In Thomas's case this meant hurling troops against the main Confederate line, especially on their front-right, until the Southern left flank, with those redoubts, could be taken and the defense line compromised fatally. The cavalry command that he had worked so assiduously to develop was meant to be available to extend the offensive reach and threaten lines of retreat that could help to turn defeat into a rout, if not an outright surrender.

Major General James Steedman had the main responsibility of holding the Confederates in place with a direct assault on the Southern right. To accomplish this, his command, consisting of large numbers of black Union troops, had the difficult and unwelcome duty of drawing enemy fire as they crossed the open ground. Thomas had been dubious about the quality of such soldiers for duty outside of the earthworks and expressed these concerns, but received assurances that the men would fight. They were about to have that chance under his watchful gaze. In several subsequent works on Thomas, Nashville has served as the moment of epiphany for the Virginian regarding race and his accompanying change in attitude toward African Americans in uniform.[4] However, historian James McDonough made the excellent point that if Thomas had not already undergone some form of transformation in his thinking along those lines, "he would have simply left them manning fortifications around the city."[5] Their performances on this field would provide Thomas with the same type of evidence by which he applied his exacting standards to any troops he commanded. Such action would serve as the measure that he used for expressing praise or opprobrium, based not upon the racial makeup of the troops or their professional status, but on the results any of his men achieved while under fire.

Thomas positioned General Thomas J. Wood on the Union right with the largest corps in his army. The Virginian wanted the crucial blow to be struck by sufficient numbers to get the job done effectively, and his choice of Wood was significant. Wood was concerned with overcoming the sense that he had been responsible for the critical gap that the Confederates had exploited at Chickamauga on the second day of that engagement. Here was a moment of redemption, and he intended to make full use of it to punish the men across the way. Wood's men certainly understood the significance of what they were about to do, even with a victory like Missionary Ridge to their credit. "I rode along the corps from flank to flank," Wood observed. "The cry, which ran along the lines—'this is Old Pap's fight, and we are going to win it for him,'" reflected their determination and resolve.[6] Smith, Schofield, and Wilson were to extend the reach even farther, allowing Wood's punch to do its damage while the defenders swiveled to try to discern where the next blow would fall.

At about noon and for the next hour, the drama began to unfold. It had taken some time to put the units into place; it would take far less to cross the killing ground in front of them. Along the way the Federals had their share of missteps, but the Confederates lacked the strength to resist effectively and compounded that fact with a salient error of placing their defensive redoubts too far apart to support each other against a concerted assault. One frazzled Southerner spoke for many as he rushed past an earthwork, refusing to heed calls for rallying and defending the ground. "Captain, we can't do it," he called out as he raced by. "Their skirmishers alone outnumber us two or three to one."[7] While it is doubtful that he had stopped to count, the Confederate knew the mass in blue pouring down upon him was more than he and his comrades could resist, and his discretion proved superior to his valor.

The successes prompted an unusual experience for those watching the fight unfold. Confederate prisoners, consisting of those who had not been successful in escaping or who had fallen in combat, began to coalesce in such large numbers as to give the deceptive appearance of major active units. Several of Thomas's staff officers momentarily believed that a counterattack might actually be under way until they realized that the men they saw approaching were captives instead. Except for such instances of confusion and the usual obscurity of the battlefield from black powder smoke, the signs seemed to be pointing unmistakably to success.[8]

Wood had been skeptical about drawing the assignment of smashing the Confederate left-center salient. The works appeared especially formidable from a distance and must have looked daunting through his field glasses. When a staff officer brought orders for the movement forward, Wood was supposed to have responded, "You don't mean that we've got to go in here and attack the works on that hill? Why, it would be suicide, sir; perfect suicide." But those were indeed the orders, and the assault delivered shortly thereafter was far more successful than suicidal in its impact.[9]

In the wake of these successes, dejected Southern prisoners offered Thomas an opportunity for offering a lesson of a different sort near the end of this first day of the engagement. As the Federal commander passed a haggard group of captives, one of them called out, asserting the preference to perish rather than endure being held longer under the bayonets of black Union guards. Thomas accepted the comment without rancor, despite the obvious racial reference on the part of the disgruntled rebel. "Well, you may say your prayers and get ready to die," the Virginian observed straightforwardly, "for these are the only soldiers I can spare."[10] Practicality overrode all other considerations for General Thomas, however else the sensibilities of captured soldiers might be taken into account.

Another report had Thomas offering a generally positive, but less exuberant, assessment, almost as an aside. "So far, I think we have done pretty well," he observed. "Unless Hood decamps to-night, to-morrow Steedman will double up his right, Wood will hold his center, Smith and Schofield will again strike his left; while the cavalry work away at his rear."[11] Undoubtedly, he had gone over the details a hundred times in his head, pouring over the maps and consulting with his subordinates. He had reason to be pleased, and unlike the dreaded days when he stared out at the ice-covered landscape lost in thought, there was every good reason to anticipate the next day as a consummation of what had already been set in place, albeit as always on the battlefield, at the cost of so many good men's lives.

The Virginian was undoubtedly pleased to finally be able to report something positive to Henry Halleck. "I attacked the enemy's left this morning and drove it from the river, below the city, very nearly to the Franklin pike, a distance [of] about eight miles," he explained. "I shall attack the enemy again to-morrow, if he stands to fight, and if he retreats during the night, will pursue him, throwing a heavy cavalry force in his rear, to destroy his trains, if possible."[12]

Thomas also paused to inform the person who mattered most to him. "Mrs. F. L. Thomas, New York Hotel, New York," the opening read. "We have whipped the enemy, taken many prisoners and considerable artillery." The closing was typically routine and dignified. "Geo. H. Thomas, Major-General, U.S. Volunteers, Commanding."[13] It is not known what reaction Frances Thomas had when she learned that all was well on December 15. If she was indeed a match to her husband in temperament, any display would have been muted.

Grant was on his way to Nashville when the happy tidings of the

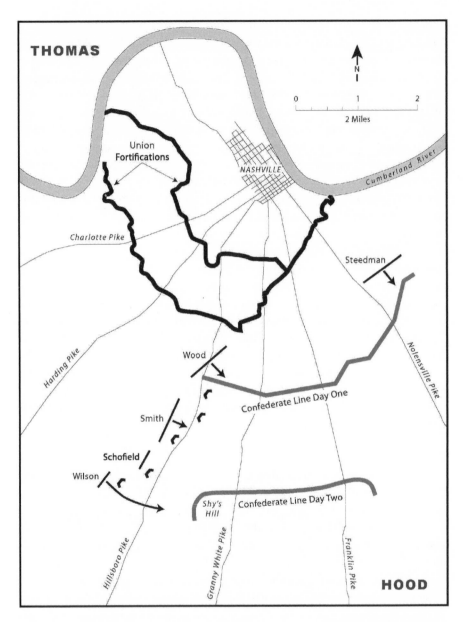

George Thomas won the name "Sledge of Nashville" for his dismantling of Hood's Army of Tennessee in fighting on December 15–16, 1864. Map created by Heather Harvey.

successful engagement there reached him and stopped him in his tracks. He had become so concerned with the inertia in Tennessee that late on the fourteenth he abruptly instructed an aide, "you've got just fifteen minutes to pack your knapsack and get on that boat. Hustle." By the afternoon of the next day, Grant and his aide were in Washington, based at the Willard Hotel, but unable to receive messages from Nashville temporarily. After a late-night conference that included the president in the war department, Grant returned to the hotel with a noticeably eased countenance. "Beckwith, I guess that we won't go to Nashville after all," he remarked to the anxious staffer who had waited for him there per instruction. "Thomas has licked Hood." For the remainder of the trip back to City Point, the tone was radically changed as a result of "a much more cheerful frame of mind."[14]

At 11:30 PM, Grant sent along his congratulations to Thomas for his "splendid success." Then, with a tangential reference to his aborted mission, the overall commander explained, "I shall go no farther." But the reputation the general had for never relaxing his grip on an opponent remained uppermost in his mind. "Push the enemy now, and give him no rest until he is entirely destroyed," he asserted. Then, with an eye to the tendency he felt his subordinate had for favoring planning over action, Grant admonished Thomas, "Do not stop for trains or supplies, but take them from the country as the enemy has done." Finally, the general closed, "Much is now expected."[15]

Secretary of War Stanton could be forgiven if when the news arrived of Thomas's initial day of battle against John Bell Hood outside Nashville, he thought he was hearing the sound of Gabriel's trumpet. Indeed, his reaction was downright rapturous. The midnight hour was tolling when he dictated a message that within five minutes would be racing its way along to Middle Tennessee. "I rejoice in tendering to you and the gallant officers and soldiers of your command the thanks of this Department for the brilliant achievements of this day, and hope that it is the harbinger of a decisive victory, and will crown you and your army with honor and do much toward closing the war." Almost as an afterthought, for the man who had just secured much of another army's pieces of artillery, Stanton, added, "We shall give you an hundred guns in the morning."[16] Thomas would have understood that a one-hundred-gun salute would peel through the Washington air in celebration, perhaps giving the uninitiated the sense that the final trump had indeed been sounded.

Only fifteen minutes earlier Grant had sent his second message of congratulations. Gone was any reference to the general's hasty journey toward Nashville for the purpose of finally taking control of the situation there if Thomas had not acted. Left in its place was a simple expression of praise and another veiled insinuation that even so thorough a victory as had been reported would not be enough.[17]

Hindsight enabled John Logan to be generous. He later recalled that he was in Cincinnati when December 15 dawned, delaying there "for some time, with the purpose of giving Thomas a fair opportunity to move if he intended to." This deliberately timed gesture from Logan apparently came despite the previous and repeated difficulties he had experienced with the Virginian in the Atlanta Campaign and in the face of a chance to assume command of an army over one of the usually favored West Pointers. By the time he reached Louisville, two days later, the issue was moot, for the Virginian had struck and averted the crisis in command. Logan returned to his command, now that the question of continuing on to Nashville had been settled in Thomas's favor.[18]

Another element of doubtful support came from the good offices of John Schofield and also had its public debut in postwar reminiscences. Schofield had always been prepared to offer his views, particularly in any manner that he thought might further his own interests. His was the helpful voice that had chimed in before Nashville, admittedly in violation of the protocol that called for junior officers to present their views first, by telling Thomas that he should adhere to his own schedule with regard to a battle. Now, with his chief apparently vacillating about the likely course for the next day, Schofield once more stepped forward selflessly to assist. "I told him I knew Hood much better than he did, and I was sure he [Hood] would not retreat."[19] Perhaps Thomas did not hear his subordinate's advice, for he did not react to the effrontery represented by the moment that surely would have prompted at least a stern rebuke from another commander.

In nearby Chattanooga, the news had not yet reached the headquarters when Alfred Hough sat down to write his wife concerning the latest developments as he knew them at the moment. "Genl. Thomas does not seem disposed to attack Hood, but still keeps on the defensive at Nashville," he groused discontentedly. Unlike Grant in distant Virginia, or the anxious War Department officials in Washington, he had reasons for wanting more immediate action that were much closer to home. "Well we must wait in patience I suppose," he explained to his wife resignedly, "but it is very hard on me, I had so impressed myself with the idea of spending Christmas with you, that my disappointment is almost like a child's."[20] Of course, such disappointment would be turned to elation when the word arrived that Thomas had struck so decisively, although subsequent events precluded a Christmas reunion for the war-weary soldier and his long-suffering spouse.

The Virginian was certainly proud of what his men had accomplished, but the task of destroying Hood's army remained unfinished. One of the officers with him that evening recalled, "As soon as General Thomas returned to his headquarters, he issued orders to his corps commanders to continue in the morning the movements against the enemy in the same order as before—i.e.

by attacking and if possible turning his left, if he awaited attack; if not, to pursue as rapidly as possible by the Franklin and Granny White Pikes."[21] Years later, Wilson intimated that Thomas had expressed regret that the engagement had not opened sooner, but did not seem to dwell on the matter. "He was well satisfied, however, with the day's work," the subordinate concluded, "and still more confident than ever that we should achieve a complete victory the next day."[22]

Another subordinate assessed the general's approach to the battlefield as unspectacular, but effective. William Shanks found that Thomas "originates nothing, but most skillfully directs his army on well-defined principles of the art."[23] Such efforts, he related, reflected the general's "methodical manner." His undertakings in campaigns strategically, and on the battlefield tactically, illustrated his professional mind-set and penchant for preparation before delivering the decisive blow. "There is little that is original in his plans or his mode of executing them," Shanks reiterated, "but all are distinguished for their practicality and completeness."[24] Hood would have reason both to experience and to rue that sense of completeness as another dawn broke over the war-scarred landscape outside Nashville.

Confidence in the Union ranks was understandably high. A soldier recalled that later in the day, when Thomas "appeared along our line of battle," the men met him with loud cheers. "He was an idol of the boys in blue," the fellow concluded as he offered a visual illustration of why this might be the case. As the soldier surged forward with his comrades he took an instant to glance back over his shoulder and saw "General Thomas sitting calmly on his tired horse."[25]

The next day Thomas followed his initial successes with the blows by which he hoped to complete the destruction of Hood's army. Yet, even after a day of pummeling the Southern forces, the task would not be so easy. If anything, the Confederates were in better shape, by virtue of their defensive configuration at least, than they had been on the fifteenth. The defensive line was more compact and anchored by heights on either flank. On the critical left where the Confederates had given way under Union pressure, Compton's Hill (later Shy's after a fallen Southern defender) offered an impressive geographical landmark that appeared daunting to would-be attackers.

One of the general's staff officers noted, "General Thomas left his headquarters in the town just after daylight." The occasion brought two thoughts to the subordinate's mind as he watched his commander that morning, both prompted by the sound of ordnance opening in the distance. The first of these impressions was the general's sudden haste of movement, as he "started his horse into a brisk trot, an almost unprecedented thing for him who always walked his horse, direct toward the sound of conflict."[26] The second observation, a corollary of the first, was that when the general "heard the cannonading," he moved, "as was his custom, [and] rode straight for the spot where the action seemed the heaviest."[27] The uncharacteristic pace that Thomas set paralleled a desire to watch events unfold personally and briefly exposed the inward anxiety he felt for completing the mission he had set for his command. The moment inspired an instance of humor in the midst of the drama of war as Thomas reacted to the nearby slamming of a window to catch a glimpse of a decidedly angry young girl staring out at him. The general looked over at his antagonist, offered her a brief smile, and rode on to the battle ahead.[28]

If Thomas has been disappointed that the previous day's fighting had been slow to develop, he would have had the same complaint on the following one. At midday, the general was with the troops facing Peach Orchard Hill (or Overton's Hill), explaining to General Wood there his intention to follow the pattern that had already worked so well of turning the Confederate left while holding the right in place. He expected the men in blue to press their opponents "vigorously," and once broken to "unceasingly harass" them as they withdrew. He left understood the possibility that developments might occur that would require initiative and advised Wood to be "on alert for any opening for a more decisive effort," although he should "bide events" for the time being.

Once Thomas had satisfied himself with the situation on this portion of his lines, he moved toward the opposite end to direct what he hoped would be a concerted effort from that point. But a combination of impatience and a liberal interpretation of the discretionary aspect of Thomas's instructions caused Wood to push his men forward prematurely. Thus, the earliest effort went against the Confederate right, with devastating consequences. Slipping and sliding across the wet ground, the attackers found themselves subjected to a withering fire that decimated their ranks. Soldiers, including a number of men of African descent, subsequently earned hard-won praise, but gained no success against the stubborn defenders.

Thomas was just reaching a position to view the lines around General Schofield's front when John McArthur sought permission to send his men against the Confederates on Overton's Hill. Schofield later claimed that Thomas borrowed his field glasses, "which he had occasionally used before and said were the only field-glasses he had ever found of much use to him."[29] The commander watched as the men surged forward, working rapidly across the intervening ground and up the slope in the face of heavy enemy fire. In the few instances where the haze of battle dissipated, the general could see the movement of the national standards to the top. Then, the sound of triumph echoed across the way to confirm that the advance had succeeded. Thomas turned aside and reflected on "the voice of the American people" that the cheering represented, but there was more work to be done, and he knew it better than anyone else.[30]

At one unspecified point in the fighting, newspaper correspondent Benjamin Truman approached the area where General Thomas was surveying the fighting. As he was wont to do, the general had reached a point in the line where he was relatively close to the action when "a shower of bullets rained in among his staff." His tendency was to treat such incidents as little more than annoyances, but this time, perhaps getting caught in the atmosphere of the combat raging around him, Thomas observed testily, "Why, I believe the scoundrels are shooting at me." It was impossible to know if the firing was indeed directed at him or just inadvertently in his direction, but the writer noticed that the Virginian remained where he was, "until duty called him to another part of the field."[31] At an earlier point, the correspondent had informed his readership of who this general was and the manner in which he approached the battlefield. "There can be no doubt of his exposing himself to danger," he argued, "but he always does it in the strict line of duty."[32]

Schofield remembered the moment as they came under fire from enemy shells as well as from Confederate small arms. He noted that as explosions occurred near Thomas and his horse the animal made "a slight start, and only a slight one,—for the nature of the horse was much the same as that of the rider,—the only change visible in the face or form of that stout-hearted soldier was a slight motion of the bridle-hand to check the horse."[33] Calmness behooved a leader at such a time, and Thomas exhibited that commodity in his usual portion.

Schofield may have seen little evidence of outward emotion in his superior, but beneath the surface welled up the pent-up frustration of weeks of building for combat and staring down foes in front and rear. At least one other outward demonstration of emotion came from General Thomas near the close of this second day. Richard Johnson recalled, "Thomas with his staff rode to the summit of Overton's Hill, and, scanning the grounds and the results, lifted his hat and said, 'Oh, what a grand army I have! God bless each member of it.'"[34] The raising of a hat in silent salute might have been enough for the Virginian on many occasions, but on this one, with the weight of the world seemingly lifted from his shoulders, the heartfelt verbalized observation was not entirely out of character either.

His exuberance continued, perhaps as much in the nature of being released from all of the pressure he had faced as anything else. One of A. J. Smith's staffers appeared with the news, "Gen. Smith presents his compliments, General, and requests me to say that the last charge was a grand success. He drove the enemy at all points, captured three general officers, two thousand prisoners and thirty pieces of artillery." Thomas could hardly contain himself as other members of the staff let out, "Hurrah!" "Hi! Hi!" The normally stoic commander "chuckled" at the reactions and returned the compliments. Then one of them thrust a bottle in his direction and, according to one witness, the general who seldom partook of such beverages "took a square drink." By this point, the sky had opened up with heavy rain. General Smith himself soon rode up, and the suddenly gregarious Thomas "tapped him on the shoulder" and pronounced, "Thank you, General, thank you. That finishes the battle of Nashville."[35]

There was still a great deal of confusion on the battlefield, perhaps made more so by the precipitous retreat Confederate defenders were making from their positions. Opposite the imposing Shy's Hill position, feisty Andrew Jackson Smith watched the action unfold. He became aware of the presence of another individual who had ridden up to see the situation for himself. "General, what is the matter, are your men being captured there?" George Thomas blurted out as he tried to grasp the shapes and forms of men and uniforms through the shroud of black powder smoke. "Not by a damn sight," the officer answered sharply. "My men are capturing them, those are Rebel prisoners you see." Perhaps Thomas had inured himself to a negative outcome, but the bluntness and the happiness of the assessment caused him to laugh demonstrably.[36] The day was indeed his.

As darkness prevailed on what had been another tremendous day of victory for the Union at Nashville, a heavy figure lumbered down the Granny White Pike. James H. Wilson had spent the day alternately urging his comrades forward and slashing into the Confederates. Now he strained through the murky blackness to distinguish who this fellow was that was approaching him. "Is that you, Wilson?" a familiar voice called and the cavalryman responded in the affirmative. Then the voice continued, "Dang it to hell, Wilson, didn't I tell you we could lick 'em, didn't I tell you we could lick 'em?" The outburst was a rhetorical expression of joy intermingled with relief that the cavalryman insisted was offered with "the vehemence of an old dragoon." Thomas wheeled his mount around in the darkness to return to Nashville without waiting for confirmation of his sentiments from the stunned subordinate. Over his shoulder he called out, "Continue the pursuit as far as you can tonight and resume it as early as you can to-morrow morning." With those instructions, George Thomas was gone.[37]

The shattering effect in the Confederate ranks was clear for all who wore gray or butternut to see, too. In his popular postwar memoirs, the chronicler of the private soldier's experience, Sam Watkins, offered his readers a stark picture of the devastating scene. "Hood's whole army was routed and in full retreat," he began in almost understated fashion. Everywhere men discarded the items that would otherwise impede their progress. Everything was "blended in inextricable confusion." All was chaos and terror, intermingled with exhaustion and despair.[38]

Now that the second strenuous day of fighting had concluded, the victorious Union Army commander was as susceptible to the taxing effects of battle as any of the other exhausted blue-coated warriors. Upon returning to his headquarters, Thomas made such final dispositions for the following day as he felt necessary, and soon fell into what an aide described as "a deep sleep." The need for his attention to a critical matter for facilitating the pursuit of the retreating Confederate forces prompted awakening Thomas from that rest; and in the state of rousing to full consciousness the Virginian made a glaring, if inadvertent, error: he ordered his pontoon train to take a road that led from Nashville to Murfreesboro instead of one that followed the more direct line of Union pursuit through Franklin. Even if the mistake was caught relatively quickly—as it indeed was—the diversion of the pontoon train over some fifteen miles down the wrong thoroughfare prevented the possibility of more effective action against the demoralized Southerners. A subordinate concluded harshly, "By this mistake we have been delayed about three days in the pursuit of the enemy, and have passed many splendid opportunities to inflict severe blows upon the enemy, perhaps to annihilate him."[39] While there was no doubt that the miscue impacted the best chance Thomas's men would have to overtake Hood, the presence of the pontoons at the appropriate time and place would have offered no guarantee of success either. The high water levels and swift currents that the men responsible for the utilization of the boats later faced proved problematic, as the same individual who criticized Thomas's "mistake" admitted when he observed, "the pontoon bridge is constantly breaking."[40]

In the meantime, the news of the developments in Middle Tennessee spread elsewhere. In Virginia, one of General Meade's staff officers recorded the update that had arrived by telegraph of events in far off Tennessee, announcing that "Thomas yesterday attacked Hood in his works and routed him entirely, taking a great deal of artillery & many prisoners." The next day, Theodore Lyman was equally elated. "This is fortune indeed! It was *the* point of the whole campaign, and crushes completely any rebel hopes of success to cheer them."[41]

Also from Virginia, George G. Meade expressed his appreciation for the news of Thomas's victory, sent to him via Brigadier General John A. Rawlins. "Your dispatch announcing General Thomas's success has been received with great satisfaction, as the situation of affairs at Nashville was much as to afford cause for anxiety." Meade, whose private expressions frequently matched his public ones, observed, "I had every confidence in the judgment and high soldierly qualities of General Thomas, and am truly rejoiced to hear of his brilliant success."[42]

Two days later, Meade remained almost euphoric regarding Thomas's recent successes. "We have all been greatly delighted at the good news from Tennessee," he explained to his wife. "Thomas is very much liked by all who know him, and things at one time looked unfavorable for him, it appearing as if he was giving Hood too much time; but it now turns out Old Thom, as we call him, knew what he was about, and has turned the tables completely."[43]

President Abraham Lincoln echoed the themes of both celebration and anticipation for greater achievements to come in a statement from Washington, with an even less muted reference to remaining expectations at the close. "Please accept for yourself, officers, and men the Nation's thanks for your good work of yesterday," the chief executive offered. "You have made a magnificent beginning. A grand consummation is within your easy reach; do not let it slip."[44]

When it came on December 16 in the form of General Orders No. 167, General Thomas's official congratulations to his men did not include any notice from the commander of the Union armies. Perhaps Thomas felt that the points made in the communications he included were sufficient to evoke a legitimate sense of pride and satisfaction among his men. He may also have been sensitive to the implication of why Grant had been on his way to Nashville and only turned back to City Point when word arrived of the long-awaited offensive and its initial success. In any case, it was enough for Thomas to add his brief words of "thanks to the troops for the unsurpassed gallantry and good conduct displayed by them in the battles of yesterday and to-day." It would not be lost on him that these soldiers had brought honor and distinction to themselves as well as to their commander, who now justifiably felt the mixture of collective and personal pride. "A few more examples of devotion and courage like these," he added, "and the rebel army of the West, which you have been fighting for three years, will be no more, and you may reasonably expect an early and honorable peace."[45]

The officers and men in the ranks certainly swelled with pride. On December 17 Colonel Emerson Opdycke informed his wife, "Two more days of battle have gone and two brilliant victories have crowned our arms." Although he tempered the feeling of success with gratitude for having passed through the storm of battle unscathed, the officer could judge the contest only in superlatives. "Thomas has stamped himself a far greater General than even I thought him," he confessed. "The enemy is badly beaten and demoralized, with light loss to ourselves, the result of Thomas' splendid Generalship."[46]

The next day, Colonel Opdycke returned to the scene of his greatest triumph when he reentered the ground over which he had fought so tenaciously at Franklin. This time the Federals were in pursuit of a routed foe and not in the act of falling back themselves. A few days later, from the proximity of Columbia, the officer explained to his wife, "The rain has been pouring ever since I wrote you; the roads are indescribable." Earlier during the fighting around Atlanta, Opdycke had scolded General Sherman for being slow in pressing his advantage against Hood. He had emphasized the importance of moving rapidly, but now offered no such criticism of Thomas. "We are pursuing Hood with all possible celerity," he observed. "Captured rebels and artillery are constantly passing to the rear, which keeps our wet, weary troops in good spirits."[47]

The actions of Thomas's cavalry on December 17 illustrated both the opportunities and the obstacles the Federals confronted in trying to run Hood's broken army to bay. Defeated Confederates were still scrambling to cross a pontoon bridge that spanned the Harpeth River at Franklin as the blue-coated riders approached. A Southern battery offered support, causing the Union horsemen to deploy in an effort to silence it by fording the river and outflanking the position. By the time this move could be attempted the Confederates had limbered their pieces and hastened away. "We swam the river," one of the blue-coated pursuers recorded, "killing four and capturing several, among them several sick and wounded." The battery had accomplished its purpose, and the relative handful of prisoners, including those incapacitated by disease and combat, was small compensation for the time lost in executing these maneuvers.[48]

Celebratory messages of various types soon emanated from numerous sources to pay homage to Thomas's decisive victory over Hood. Often these symbolized the spirit of success in Union arms that now pervaded in the wake of the fighting at Nashville:

> "Thomas still moving"—very good;
> The cause is plainly understood—
> He doesn't like his neighbor—Hood.
> Where Hood now is, it were not hard to tell;
> He said he'd go to Nashville or to hell.
> And hasn't gone to Nashville—very well.[49]

Such slightly ribald humor would be lost on the defeated general, his army, and their supporters. From distant South Carolina, diarist Mary Chesnut recorded her thoughts in the aftermath of the initial news from Middle Tennessee. "Yankees claim another victory for Thomas," she wrote on December 19. "Hope it may prove like most of their victories—brag and bluster."[50]

At the same time, the brother of Thomas's onetime commander, Robert Anderson, passed along his congratulations. Larz Anderson explained that not only did he feel the need to add his "applause and approbation" to the "plaudits of the Government & of the country," but that he wished to "assure" Thomas "that ever since your first appearance at our house, with Genl. Sherman and my brother—a time ever to be remembered by us with pride—we have not ceased to follow your career, with intense interest, and to rejoice in every successive step that has at length brought you to this height of glory."[51]

Secretary Stanton continued his change of heart with regard to Thomas in the afterglow of victory. To Major General John A. Dix, he lauded the minimal losses incurred and attributed them to "evincing, among other things the admirable skill and caution of General Thomas in his disposition of the battle."[52] Suddenly, the same tendency toward thoroughness and preparation could be seen as making a more bloodless victory possible, which must have been all the more stark when contrasted against the casualty lists from the 1864 Overland and Atlanta Campaigns and the fighting around Petersburg.

Of course, the losses were not nearly as light as the secretary of war had supposed. Thomas's force of approximately 50,000 men had lost 387 killed, 2,562 wounded, and 112 missing, for a total of 3,061.[53] As could be expected, Thomas's men had punished the Confederates severely. The general reported the captured Southerners over "the two days' operation" to be 4,462, "including 287 officers of all grades from that of major general, 53 pieces of artillery, and thousands of small-arms."[54] A Union participant in the fight recorded the butcher's bill in his diary, ostensibly from numbers he had read in the newspaper. When he tallied the figures from Nashville and combined them with those from Franklin and Murfreesboro, all "Since Dec. 1st 1864," the numbers were staggering. "From the above the loss of the rebel Army is 17,000 men and a complete demoralization in 20 days." The soldier concluded simply, "Good for 'Pap Thomas.'"[55]

Although Hood was no longer in Thomas's immediate front outside Nashville to harass him, other nuisances remained to demand his continuing attention. Hylan Lyon had managed to escape his Federal pursuers for a time, but the relentless pressure of the nearly constant movement and the extremely difficult wintry conditions had taken a severe toll on his unit's integrity. Rumors of General Hood's defeat at Nashville had caused significant desertion in Lyon's ranks and further diminished the capacity of the raiding force to do any more harm to the Federals.[56] The Southern horseman was reduced simply to watching the expedition dissolve around him.[57]

The results of Thomas's actions were obviously distressing to the Confederates and gratifying to Union arms, but the appearance on the retreat route of Nathan Bedford Forrest promised to make the Virginian's ability to inflict as much damage as possible on Hood's retreating army more difficult. The Confederate cavalry commander had been in the vicinity of

Murfreesboro, trying to penetrate the well-fortified Union supply depot there with little success. The first indication of trouble from Nashville was a call from Hood for Forrest "to hold" his command "in readiness to move at any moment."[58] The Confederates had maintained contact with the main body, and according to one officer, "kept in touch" through "a steady stream of couriers with dispatches reporting on the progress of the battle." One of these messengers brought the unhappy tidings "of the disaster at Nashville," and the effort began immediately to fall back so as to help cover the retreat of the army.[59]

General Grant could not quite bring himself to let the difficulty of prodding Thomas into action disappear entirely from his mind. In a confidential memo to Sherman, dated December 18, he was effusive in praise for the Ohioan, but less so their Virginia comrade. "It has been very hard work to get Thomas to attack Hood," he explained now three days after the desired offensive had gotten under way. "I gave him the most peremptory order, and had started to go there myself before he got off. He has done magnificently, however since he started," Grant admitted. Yet, despite the impressive haul of prisoners and captured ordnance and supplies, there was the nagging resentment of having had to expend so much energy to compel Thomas to act.[60]

The sensation was a very different one in Chattanooga, where staffer Alfred Hough declared, "Old 'Tom' has cleaned out Hood."[61] A few days later, buoyed by the holiday spirit of Christmas, the same fellow informed his wife, "The war news is very encouraging all round and another year I hope will end this war. How our 'Old Tom' has done things, how proud we all are of him."[62] Thomas had always been able to draw his subordinates to him, and Nashville gave them reason to celebrate his successes as if they were their own.

Never one to be prone to the extreme of emotions as they swung between short-term peaks and valleys, Thomas was nevertheless subject to the realities he faced. His intentions, reflected in his communications after Nashville, were to present explanations, not provide excuses. "The infantry has not been able to march to-day, in consequence of the heavy rain which set in last night and has continued all the day rendering all the streams impassable," Thomas wrote from "near Spring Hill." Missed opportunities by the Confederates had prevented Hood from sealing off Schofield from Nashville, and now similar conditions for the Federals threatened to assist the Confederates as they sought to retreat beyond Thomas's reach. Thomas could point to the capture of additional prisoners and the discomfiture of Hood's army as he and the weather pressed it, but Halleck, and more importantly Grant, wanted more decisive results. Finally, the Virginian offered what must have looked to him like a positive approach to a difficult situation, but which surely looked to the others like a further indication of what might have been done with the mired pursuit if Thomas had been so inclined. Instead of forcing the men ahead through a sea of churned-up roads and debris largely for appearance's sake, Thomas chose to engage in more productive measures. The infantry might not be able to move, but he reported that the "day has been profitably employed in concentrating and adjusting the trains of the different commands, [and] issuing rations and ammunition, preparatory to marching early to-morrow morning."[63]

For a soldier caught up in the pursuit itself, the conditions were difficult enough. Theodore Allen was one of the cavalrymen upon whom Thomas counted to keep the pressure on the retiring Confederates. On Monday, December 19, he reflected in his diary, "Today's ride was one of the hardest I ever experienced." He then recorded the dreadful circumstances of that ride. "Through a cold, very cold rain and we were passing troops and trains all the time. The roads were very bad." Allen had reason to lament the situation, but he was also aware of the plight of, and in a strange sense sympathetic to, those he was charged with following. "If we a victorious Army suffer now, what must be the sufferings of the rebel army, who beaten, demoralized and disappointed are retreating through storm and mud and through a naked and barren country."[64]

A newspaperman who slogged through the mud with the pursuers offered a vivid description of the conditions for his readers. "So violently was our cavalry urged, hundreds of horses perished from exhaustion," and "many of the riders fell off from sheer fatigue." The troops were pressing Hood's routed remnant, but the conditions had continued to deteriorate under a steady rainfall. "It is almost impossible to move. The whole country is one vast sea of mud." Even so, Benjamin Truman explained for the benefit of those who would follow the action from a comfortable distance, "In defiance of mud and rain, and cold, our fatigued, but enthusiastic, army, pursued the shattered columns of the enemy."[65]

Subsequently, the same writer continued his narrative. "This was the fifth day of the movement, and our troops were still buoyed up with the hope of bagging the one-legged chief and his army," Truman explained. "On account of the muddy state of the roads, made still more furious by the use of the rebels in their retreat, it was next to impossible to move our artillery and trains." The situation had been reduced, he observed plainly, into "one vast avalanche of mud in which the army floundered."[66] A Union soldier certainly concurred. "We have had two days of the severest fighting, and six of the hardest exposure, marching, starving and freezing I ever have yet seen." After a description the battle, the bluecoat from Kentucky closed, "we have slept on the ground in the mud and rain & had very little to eat besides. Roads awful, and hard times plentiful." Still, duty called, as he could "hear the bugle sounding strike tents. I must get ready to march."[67]

Halleck was less prone to be sympathetic. Indeed he seemed to prefer to return to his pre-Nashville mode in a communication to Thomas shortly before Christmas. "Permit me, general, to urge the vast importance of a hot pursuit. Every possible sacrifice should be made," he insisted. Halleck believed that the rewards to be derived would outstrip any of the hardships that the men were being called upon to endure and that they would do so gladly in any case to reap a "great result." Thomas needed to understand that he remained part of a bigger picture. "If you can capture or destroy Hood's army Sherman can entirely crush out the rebel military force in all the Southern states," the chief of staff continued. "A most vigorous pursuit on your part is therefore of vital importance. No sacrifice must be spared to attain so important an object," he repeated for the sake of reinforcing the main point in his subordinate's mind.[68]

Thomas could be forgiven if he recalled Halleck's own history before Corinth. He might also have become tired of being needled and lectured by those not present on the ground to understand the conditions as he saw them. If he thought that the victory at Nashville would provide him with a respite from such interference, Thomas was coming to see that he had been wrong. Instead the decisiveness of the success seemed to make matters worse.

As he read Halleck's latest message, his vaunted self-control gave way to the need for expression. "General Hood's army is being pursued as rapidly and as vigorously as it is possible for one army to pursue another," he observed pointedly. "We cannot control the elements," he noted. "I am doing all in my power to crush Hood's army, and, if it be possible, will destroy it; but pursuing an enemy through an exhausted country, over mud roads, completely sogged with heavy rains," and he might have added in the dead of winter, "is no child's play."[69] The Virginian had complained once to Wilson that he was being treated like a child, and the same thing seemed to be happening again despite his performance before Nashville and his dogged pursuit of Hood's broken command.

Had George Thomas known what Ulysses Grant had communicated to Secretary of War Stanton on the morning of December 20, his suppressed sense of personal outrage would have risen to even greater levels. The army commander had indicated that the Virginian's success at Nashville was worthy of reward as well as recognition, but thought the timing of any gesture should be considered carefully. "I think Thomas has won the major-generalcy," Grant explained, as he watched Thomas's pursuit of Hood unfold from City Point, Virginia, "but I would wait a few days before giving it, to see the extent of damages done."[70] The implication was that a promotion earned on the battlefield might still be used as an object lesson for a general who fell short of the army commander's expectations.

To a considerable extent, Stanton continued to try to reestablish a sense of trust with his general, still conducting active operations against Hood's remnant in the field. On the evening of December 22, he explained, "It is proper for me to assure you that this Department has the most unbounded confidence in your skill, vigor, and determination to employ to the best advantage all the means in your power to pursue and destroy the enemy." He deemed Thomas's actions as worthy of consideration that overrode any previous sense of doubt that might have existed. "No Department could be inspired with more profound admiration and thankfulness for the great deeds you have already performed," Stanton assured, "or [exhibit] more confiding faith that human effort could accomplish more than will be done by you and your gallant officers and soldiers of your command."[71] As further assurance of his esteem, the secretary of war followed his first communication with a second that sought from Thomas "such promotions as you desire to recommend." Stanton could offer little tangible opportunity beyond brevets and the occasional vacancy that might occur "by mustering out useless officers."[72]

From City Point, Grant wanted Thomas to know of his value in the wake of Nashville, too. "You have the congratulations of the public for the energy with which you are pushing Hood," he began. He hoped that the Virginian might be able to prevent the shattered Confederate army from escaping beyond reach. "If you succeed in destroying Hood's army, there will be but one army left to the so-called Confederacy capable of doing us any harm." Thomas would know that the army Grant was referencing was the one that general was facing. "I will take care of that," Grant assured, "and try to draw the sting from it, so that in the spring we shall have easy sailing." Grant always had the larger strategic implications in mind, and he wanted Thomas to be reminded of them, too. "You now have a big opportunity, which I know you are availing yourself of. Let us push and do all we can before the enemy can derive benefit either from the raising of negro troops or the concentration of white troops now in the field."[73]

Pushing ahead was what many of the exhausted blue-coated pursuers were still trying to do to their fleet-footed foes. On the twenty-second, Thomas Speed paused to write his impressions of the aftermath of the battle. "I have seen and talked with a great many prisoners," he explained, "and they all seem to think their army is ruined."[74] Even then, the state of mind of the defeated Southerners could be a matter of semantics. "I confess I'm horribly whipped and badly demoralized," one straggler was supposed to have observed, "but blame if I'm scattered."[75] Another later recalled a condition that could not have been unique to him among these dejected Confederates. "My feet were bleeding [when] we got back near Columbia," Russell Brown remembered. "I left the army and came home."[76]

The roads were not much better, subjected as they had been to "an immense deal of rain," so that even "the turnpikes between this [Spring Hill] and Nashville are litterally ruined." He had also viewed ample evidence of death and disintegration along the way, but the opposing force was not all that had been impacted. "I tell you it is desolation for two large Armies to play 'base' through any country," Speed observed.[77] One Union soldier remembered that even these improved roads created misery for the foot soldiers under the circumstances. "We were on a macadamized road made of broken rock. This was hard on our shoes," Elisha Stockwell concluded.[78]

Not only was Ulysses Grant prepared to bestow praise, he was finally ready to offer more tangible recognition. "I think it would be appropriate now to confer on General Thomas the vacant major-generalcy in the Regular Army," he wrote Stanton just before Christmas. Although he no longer made the promotion contingent on subsequent actions, Grant obviously had continuing expectations of the Virginian. "He seems to be pushing Hood with energy, and I doubt not but he will completely destroy that army."[79]

Secretary of War Stanton's subsequent December 24th letter of praise and promotion did not have the initial effect on Thomas that one might have expected. An individual who was present with him at the time noted that upon opening the message and reading its contents, "he was for some time silent, lost in thought and seemingly forgetful of his promotion and the tenor of Secretary Stanton's language." Then Thomas turned to Surgeon George E. Cooper, his departmental medical director, and handed him the document. "What do you think of that?" he inquired, giving the officer a chance to peruse it. Cooper then replied, "Thomas, it is better late than never," to which Thomas simply answered, "I suppose it is better late than never, but it is too late to be appreciated; I earned this at Chickamauga." Chaplain Van Horne, who related the story, added, "His emotion, as he uttered these words, became too strong for his self-poise in this unguarded moment, and he gave way to the strongest possible indication of intense feeling."[80]

From his headquarters in the field at "McKane's Church, Pulaski Road," Thomas paused on Christmas Day to acknowledge his promotion officially. The response mirrored the nature of the man making it. As a professional soldier, he understood well that one's level of rank in the regular army was significant, but the Virginian wanted Secretary Stanton to know that he attached a deeper meaning to the elevation in position. "I beg to assure the President and yourself that your approbation of my services is of more value to me than the commission itself," Thomas explained.[81] For the soldier who had once been expected to "wait" for such recognition of his worth to the Union cause, the choice of wording was meaningful.

General Sherman, located in distant Savannah, Georgia, was only learning of the success Thomas had enjoyed against Hood at Nashville. On

Christmas Day, he expressed his satisfaction, and not a considerable amount of relief, at the circumstances. "I do not believe your own wife was more happy at the result than I was," he offered, assuring the Virginian that had "misfortune" occurred instead, "I should have reproached myself for taking away so large a proportion of the army and leaving you too weak to cope with Hood." Thomas's victory had rendered such an outcome moot, and now the Virginian had only to "go on and pursue your advantage to the very uttermost." On a more pleasant personal note, Sherman's current location reminded him of "the old barracks around which cluster so many of our old memories," although he expressed a hint of guilt that "whilst you are freezing to death in Tennessee we are basking in a warm sun." Then Sherman added, "I fear I did you personal injustice in leaving you behind whilst I made my winter excursion," but promised "next time I will stay at home and let you go it."[82]

The rank and file of Union troops, especially those who had been under Thomas's command at one point or another, rejoiced at the news of the Nashville victory. One Indiana noncommissioned officer wrote in his diary on the twenty-third, "We got the news that 'Old Pap Thomas' had given hood a terrible drubbing at or near Nashville Tenn and captured a great many of his men and Hood was retreating again." For Sergeant Miller, the best news was that all of the successes that Union arms were enjoying might mean "we will soon go home."[83]

Northern newspapers continued to trumpet the achievements of the Southern-born Union general. "Look at the glorious career of George H. Thomas!" one proclaimed. "He won the first battle in the Southwest," referring to Mill Springs, "which will ever be remembered as one of the cleanest battles on record. He is the hero of the last battle in the Southwest [Nashville], which is one of the largest of the war." Such victories could be accomplished only by a commander who was "always successful, always on hand, never excited, and perfectly at home in the thickest of the fight, he sits his steed like a grim old warrior whom neither disaster nor success can move." After offering a physical description and noting that there were "very excellent photographs of him," Benjamin Truman insisted that the illustrated newspapers "do not do him justice," before concluding that "resolution" was *his peculiar quality*."[84]

Under the circumstances that now prevailed, Thomas could only do so much. Forrest's appearance had helped to stabilize the retreat and slow the pursuit, through leapfrog defensive stands and ambushes. Despite the constant grating of the withdrawals, the casualties and desertions that continued to mount, and the wounding of one of his best subordinates in Abraham Buford, Forrest largely accomplished this critical task.[85] Even so, the Federal commander sought to maintain the impetus in his favor. "We pressed them on day after day, fighting them some every day, capturing prisoners," one of the jaded pursuers observed. Abandoned arms and equipment discarded by the demoralized Southerners littered the roadways, providing moot testimony of Union success, but the momentum of the pursuit was slowly disappearing.[86]

Conditions continued to be abysmal for the troops on both sides as they slogged through mud and combated fatigue as much as any other foe. The situation was particularly acute for the Southerners, but Thomas had to take care not to press his own exhausted troops too hard. Tired men could march only so far and endure only so much and still remain in fighting trim. George Thomas was not about to make a mistake that would allow the Confederates to recoup their losses. He drove his men to the degree that he felt he could under the circumstances.

For at least one Union commander on the ground the success was plain enough for anyone to see. Emerson Opdycke wrote his wife on December 29 to say that despite the inclement weather the army had pushed forward. Both the "pursuit" and the "rain" were unabated, although mail from home relieved some of the distress. "We do not move today," the officer observed, but reminded his spouse that Thomas's reports on the successes they had achieved against Hood "do not exaggerate at all." The Confederate commander "has gone back with the remnants of his army utterly demoralized. Thomas is a great general. What has Sherman ever done that equals this?"[87] If George Thomas had such rhetorical questions on his mind he kept them to himself.

A subtle shift in priorities in the minds of many of Thomas's subordinates began to indicate that they thought active campaigning was about over for a time, too. Having been cooped up in Nashville and then bound by the pursuit of Hood, some of these officers now sought permission from their commanding officer for leaves of absence. Thomas had frequently turned down such requests, but as duties in the field subsided, those with more confidence in their chances or powers of persuasion chose the moment to approach the general. One of these was a staff officer named Watkins. "General, you know I have a sweetheart," he announced boldly and offered that he had not seen her for some months. Thomas quickly retorted, "Watkins, I've been there, and the truth is that I too have a sweetheart, and I have not seen her for more months than you have yours for so many weeks. And, what is more, I have been married to my sweetheart, and want to see her as much as you do yours, and it is likely more."

But Thomas could not let the matter drop just on his example alone. There were practical measures for such matters. "But I won't let her come to camp. A camp is no place for a wife. She is out of her element, and it softens [a] man." Then, perhaps anticipating the anxious subordinate's suggestion that the general visit her instead, just as he was now requesting to do, Thomas added, "And I won't go to see my wife till my duty is ended and the war over. What I will not do myself I will not allow you to do."[88]

Thomas spent a portion of the latter part of the month visiting other locations in the department. He was in Lexington, Kentucky, for a brief time before making his way back to Nashville. While there, he spoke to a man he would tap six months later for the special duty of assisting African Americans in much of Tennessee. Reuben D. Mussey recorded some of the conversation that passed between them in a letter to Andrew Johnson. In this account, Mussey observed the Virginian's views on conditions relating to these individuals. "General Thomas tells me that the Slaveholders of this State who have had their male Slaves enlist [in the Union army] have, in many cases, turned the women and children out of doors, pulled their cabins down etc. etc.—and that there is a great deal of suffering and hardship among the Colored people in consequence."[89] Thomas did not seem to respond to the incident because of the race of the individuals involved as much as he sympathized with the plight of the families affected by cruel retaliatory measures. The general was clearly concerned about the price that some individuals were paying as society transitioned from slave to free. But his views were certainly consistent with the position he had taken with regard to returning white East Tennesseans who had temporarily deserted the ranks to succor their families suffering from abuse at home. These situations appealed directly to Thomas's paternalistic instincts and background. Such circumstances deserved attention and remedy. Furthermore, the behavior of the "Slaveholders in the State" would have to be held to account, too.

Thomas had not always been so quick to intervene in such matters, but he would brook no breach of protocol. When Mussey was particularly outspoken about the willingness of generals to accept the role of African American men as soldiers, he received a quick reprimand. The expression of such sentiments was "in violation of the spirit and letter of the regulation of the army." Then, when another officer continually agitated for the opportunity for his regiment of United States Colored Troops to be sent into combat, the reply came down, "The Major General commanding directs me to say that when you shall have learned cheerfully to perform your duty to the best of your abilities in such positions as may be assigned to you, then shall you have learned the first lessons of that discipline, which apparently, you are so anxious should be taught your regiment."[90] Soldiers were expected to behave like soldiers, and recruits of all types could be expected to become soldiers only if their officers performed their duties rigorously and professionally.

General Thomas was in Pulaski by the end of the year and paused in his routine duties to communicate again with Johnson. He had already broached the subject of civil authority with Tennessee's military governor, but now that the Confederates had been "driven out" of the state he was prepared to return to that subject once more. "I would Respectfully suggest that immediate measures be taken for the reorganization of the Civil Government of the state as it is desirable if possible to place as large a force of the army beyond the Borders of the State and as close to the Enemy as we can and I should be very happy to be assured that I could leave the state in the hands of the Citizens[.]" He was convinced that "all should Certainly now feel that the Establishment of Rebel authority in the state of Tennessee is hopeless and their own interests should induce them to return to their allegiances to the United States & Restore Peace to their state without further quibbling."[91]

If Johnson minded the comments on the part of the soldier he did not indicate as much in his response. He assured Thomas that action was being taken to reorganize the state apparatus. "The Courts are all being established, & so far are working well," he explained in a nod to the earlier conversation that had passed between them on that subject. Then, with the deftness of a savvy politician's hand, he stroked the general's ego gently. "The effect of the great victory over Hood's army at Nashville is being seen & felt in every part of the State. Its withering influence upon Rebels is more decided than anything which has transpired since the beginning of the Rebellion." As if that were not enough, Johnson thanked Thomas for his suggestions. "I think the work can now be undertaken with greater prospects of success, than at any former period, & no efforts on my part shall be omitted in trying to accomplish so desirable an end." The war governor and vice president–elect closed once more with a demonstration of appreciation that the sensitive warrior could not fail to miss. "It is not necessary for me to say that you have the Nations gratitude, for what you have done in preserving the Government of the United States—but my prayer is that all your future efforts in preservation of the Union may, as the past have been, be crowned with success & unfading honor."[92]

Reports were part of the routine, and late on December 29 General Thomas provided Henry Halleck with one. Much of what he had to say was good, including the outstanding cooperation between land and riverine units. But the old issue of weather had returned to the operations. "In consequence of the terribly bad weather, almost impassable condition of the roads, and exhausted country, the troops and animals are so much worn down by the fatigues of the last two weeks that it becomes necessary to halt for a short time to reorganize and refit for a renewal of the campaign." Hood might stop at Corinth or move on to Meridian, but in either case Thomas thought it "best for the troops to be allowed [a rest] till early spring, when the roads will be in a condition to make a campaign into the heart of the enemy's country." He had already begun gathering information on possible approaches for an offensive that "would be practicable in the spring and summer, but are altogether impracticable at this season of the year."[93]

Halleck was not the same general he had been at Corinth in 1862. The war was not the same either. Grant expected movement to continue regardless of the conditions of the troops or the roads. "Old Brains" had now worked with Sam Grant long enough to understand this, and Thomas seemed to be lapsing into his pre-Nashville mode of behavior. Such an old-school military approach and mind-set just would not do. "I think, from the tone of General Thomas' telegram of last night," he explained to Grant, "that there is very little hope of his doing much further injury to Hood's army by pursuing it." Halleck had to know the reaction that such a comment would prompt from the commanding general, but he added for effect, "You will perceive that he is disposed to post-pone further operations till spring. This seems to me entirely wrong. In our present financial condition we cannot afford this delay." The simple solution would be to shift some of Thomas's troops elsewhere to be employed more efficiently, and effectively.[94]

Ironically, it was now Halleck who was calling for more aggressiveness while Grant suggested a different course. "I have no idea of keeping idle troops in any place," Grant asserted, "but before taking troops away from Thomas it will be advisable to see whether Hood halts his army at Corinth." In a sense Hood would again dictate the action if Thomas chose not to do so. "Let Thomas collect all troops not essential to hold his communications at Eastport, [or] if he chooses a part of them at Tuscumbia, and be in readiness for their removal where they can be used."[95]

As a most eventful year drew to a close, Thomas paused, again through the good offices of his assistant adjutant general, to provide a measure of perspective in the form of General Orders No. 169. These orders emanated from the little town of Pulaski, not far from the Tennessee border over which Hood's defeated troops had retreated. "The major-general commanding announces to you that the rear guard of the flying and dispirited enemy was driven across the Tennessee River on the night of the 27th instant." Wintry weather prevented further action "for the present," but the men could take tremendous pride in what they had accomplished. With soaring rhetoric that seemed uncharacteristic for the normally taciturn commander, the statement reminded the soldiers that they had engaged a "veteran rebel army" that "invaded Tennessee, buoyant with hope," only to find itself "hurled back from the coveted prize upon which it had only been permitted to look from a distance, and finally sent flying, dismayed and disordered, whence it came, impelled by the instinct of self-preservation, and thinking only how it could relieve itself for short intervals from your persistent and harassing pursuit." Along the way, the "shattered, diminished, and discomfited" foe had left the symbols of its martial pride, in the form of "artillery and battleflags in your victorious hands, [as] lasting trophies of your noble daring and lasting momentoes of the enemy's disgrace and defeat." Even these tangible elements did not include the vast number of prisoners and deserters that had "diminished the forces of the rebel army" and would prevent the Southern forces from realistically having any continued "hope of bringing Tennessee again within the lines of the accursed rebellion." Thomas and his men had shattered their opponents, and following a "short time" to rest and recuperate, he planned for them "to prepare to continue the work so nobly begun."[96]

Halleck passed Grant's wishes along to Thomas and did so without a great deal of varnish. The Virginian was to collect "all of your available forces, not essential to hold your communications" and "be ready for such movements as may be ordered." Some of these men might be "availed of for active operations elsewhere. They should be made ready for that purpose." More information on Hood's current dispositions would be helpful, but only as a prelude to "a continuance of the campaign." At any rate, Grant and Halleck agreed that there were no circumstances under which it was intended that "your army shall go into winter quarters; it must be ready for active operations in the field."[97]

Thus, in the aftermath of a pursuit that had failed to net him the remnant of the army he had virtually destroyed outside Nashville, Thomas underwent another sudden and distressing development. He expected to have time to allow the men the opportunity to rest and refit, as was usually the case after a grueling campaign. Soldiers and animals alike had been pushed to their limits of endurance. Restoring unit cohesion and obtaining replacements for casualties among the officers and the men in the ranks were necessities, not luxuries. Yet, Thomas had no sooner issued the order for the command to stand down and go into winter quarters than word arrived that General Grant did not intend for him to follow that course. The irony was that to satisfy his superior, Thomas would have to make his usual preparations while engaged in active campaigning, a notion that represented a violation of every tenet of command Thomas valued.[98]

As the commanding officer, Thomas felt compelled to reply, not only to signal his compliance with orders, but to register what he saw as very real concerns that might jeopardize the overwhelming success he and Union arms at Nashville had obtained thus far. Therefore, "to continue the campaign without rest, I fear, will cost us very heavy losses from disease and exhaustion," he explained. Weakened men could hardly be counted on to give their best in the field and would be all the more vulnerable due to the conditions they would face, even against a seriously depleted enemy. "I do believe it is much the best policy to get well prepared before starting on an important campaign," he reminded General Halleck.[99]

Halleck and Grant saw in the response not only the continuity of thought it represented, but the contrast with the style of command and warfare they found most desirable, particularly at this stage of the contest. Once more, Thomas, whose offensive prowess had been demonstrated with sensational results, was exasperating his superiors. The crucial difference was that now Grant intended to do something about it. He could simply bypass the troublesome Virginian if Thomas did not want to cooperate. Thus, he agreed to transfer Schofield elsewhere, a move he explained to Sherman: "I was induced to do thus because I did not believe Thomas could possibly be got off [into active operations] before spring."

Sherman's tendency to file his reports "in the field" was precisely the attitude Grant wanted from Thomas, and Henry Halleck, whose personal history had undergone its own evolution, concurred. Thomas would be well advised to heed the message, but none of the other generals was inclined to believe that he could or would. Sherman undoubtedly agreed based upon his own experience. But more troublesome was Grant's determination that the Thomas who was usually present with the lead elements in his command had not been at that point in this recent phase of the campaign. "The command of the pursuit was left to subordinates," he observed, "whilst Thomas followed far behind." He felt that this left the Virginian out of touch, and what was worse, caused the command to be in position to prevent Hood from taking his shattered command across the Tennessee River to relative safety. Compounding this lapse was Thomas's apparent contentment with what he had already accomplished rather than the aggressiveness expected of him.

In short, to some in the higher echelons of Union command, Thomas seemed to be incapable of understanding the broader strategic role he was supposed to play, much less implementing it. Grant knew that Thomas had tremendous personal and soldierly qualities, but he was not convinced that the Virginian was up to the task he had currently set for him. "He is possessed of excellent judgment, great coolness, and honesty," Grant reminded Sherman, "but he is not good on a pursuit." Thomas's report on the strained condition of his command coupled with a strong desire on Grant's part to "give the enemy no rest determined me to use his surplus troops elsewhere." Thomas would still be left with an adequate command, although any further action in this season would require the services of "an energetic leader." The Union commander's greatest indictment of Thomas came with the dismissive observation to Cump Sherman: "His pursuit of Hood [out of Nashville] indicated a sluggishness that satisfied me that he would never do to conduct one of your campaigns."[100] There was no mention of the success these same generals, Thomas and Sherman, had experienced together a year earlier against the Confederates in the Atlanta Campaign.

In the process of determining the disposition of Thomas's command, Grant had the assistance of John M. Schofield. This was not the first time that Thomas's lieutenant had taken steps designed to benefit himself at his superior's expense. One scholar observed, "Schofield's relations with Thomas had always been correct, but never cordial." Yet, the correctness of the relationship was in doubt, too. The same ambition that prompted the subordinate to question his superior during the recent campaign now encouraged his anxiety to be elsewhere, on a more active field under more important eyes than those of the "Sledge of Nashville," despite the blows the two commanders had struck together to Confederate fortunes in the West. Thus, Schofield biographer Donald Connelly conceded, "Beyond the purely personal, Schofield had professional reasons for the transfer."[101]

Thomas had chafed under reports that unauthorized communications were going out and felt sufficiently concerned to investigate the matter while simultaneously trying to defeat John Bell Hood. After the war and his death, the general's widow remembered what her husband had shared with her. "I know that Genl Thomas fully *believed* Genl Schofield was trying to get his command away from him for he told me so, in telling me about matters which occurred at that time."[102]

Schofield was one of the individuals who had stood to benefit if Thomas stepped down or was relieved. Now that the matter of command was settled with victory, Schofield expressed his preference for a transfer to the person he felt best suited to respond to it when a couple of days after Christmas he communicated directly with Ulysses Grant. He preferred service "in Virginia, or elsewhere, where decisive work is to be done." Sweeping up the remnants of a defeated army and preparing his men for winter quarters under Thomas did not qualify, whatever the Virginian might feel compelled to do in the following traditional spring campaigning. If Robert E. Lee's Army of Northern Virginia were "virtually all that is left of the rebellion," Schofield understood that the troops who finally brought that Confederate force to bay would win new accolades. The possibility of additional promotion was not far from his mind either. "Nominally, I command both a department and an army in the field," he explained to the man who ought to have known these facts as well as anyone, before he complained, "in fact, I do neither." A shift in command could rectify that situation as well.[103]

Regrettably for Thomas, the message Schofield employed in a communication the following day was even more insidious. The disgruntled subordinate passed along what he had said to Grant about the desirability of a transfer, while simultaneously generating doubt about the Virginian's competence. The basic element of this piece of the puzzle was to put himself forth as the hero of the Nashville Campaign who had allowed Hood's Confederates to spend themselves, particularly at Franklin, so that there was nothing left of consequence for Thomas to do at Nashville. The two-day engagement that shattered the Confederates earlier in the month was hardly worth mentioning and certainly brought no independent credit to the overall commander.[104] The insufferable subordinate would make it crystal clear in his memoirs that Thomas had been fortunate to have Schofield as one of "the few educated soldiers" who was also "anxious to aid him and save him from personal defeat."[105] In short, Thomas had needed Schofield to save the Virginian from himself, but now the disgruntled colleague determined he could do better elsewhere and presumably Thomas would have to fend for himself.

It is difficult to assess all of the influences at work on Ulysses Grant when it came to George Thomas. Apart from their differences in personality and martial styles, there were undoubtedly the intriguing voices of men such as John Schofield. The rebel newspapers may also have goaded the Union chief with their hopeful insistence that all was not as bad as it seemed in the West. Admitting that they were dependent upon their Northern counterparts for information, Richmond newspapers, like the *Daily Dispatch* and the *Sentinel,* attempted to put matters in the best light. In reports "From Hood's Army" on December 19 there was the suggestion that Thomas's success at Nashville might have come only when Hood made a "move towards Murfreesboro," and "Thomas dashed into his evacuated lines and pursued his retreating columns."[106] Two days later, the speculation was that "It is not impossible that matters have taken a turn, at once unexpected and unpleasant to Thomas." This hope was predicated on the notion that "General Forrest, with his splendid cavalry, have turned up in the right place and put a sudden change upon the aspect of affairs." The editorial expressed supreme confidence in such a scenario. "He has a way of turning up unexpectedly and always make[s] his presence felt." There was the hope that Hood had not been "crushed" as Northern accounts proclaimed and that "Forrest's sword and presence" could turn matters around in any account.[107]

Then, as the news continued to paint a stark picture for Hood's fate, the *Daily Dispatch* editorialist tried a new tack. "Having failed to catch Hood," Thomas and his cohorts were providing "wonderful stories of what damage they have done him" to bolster their claims of success.[108] A day later, the writer insisted, "Notwithstanding this 'utter rout' as other Yankee accounts state it, Hood falls back only twenty-two miles in two days!" As for his supposedly battered and demoralized command, the writer explained, "The very fact of its continued existence is proof positive against their statements."[109] Unfortunately for General Thomas, this last sentiment was certainly one with which General Grant would have concurred.

The following day, the Richmond *Sentinel* added its own brand of a favorable assessment of otherwise dire reports. Labeling "the movements of our army" since the fighting at Nashville as still "more deliberate, self-confident and defiant," the editorialist admitted that Hood's next movements were unclear. "He is, however, master of them," the writer insisted before concluding that the recent engagement had actually only been a "drawn battle."[110] Of course, no amount of wistful speculation was going to reverse the setback that the Confederates had suffered, but doubt, reasonable or otherwise, was not going to accrue to Thomas's favor either.

Nevertheless, George Thomas had to report matters to his superiors as he saw them from his vantage point. In his final communication with the chief of staff, Thomas reiterated his themes of watchfulness, poor weather, lack of supplies, and the worn condition of the troops after an interminably long season of campaigning. To this last point he added emphasis and predicted that for him to "continue the campaign without any rest, I fear, will cost us very heavy losses from disease and exhaustion." He had never been one to squander the lives of the men needlessly, even if he called upon them to sacrifice those lives in battle. "I had already taken steps, before receiving your telegram of to-day, to refit the troops under my command as soon as possible, so as to commence the campaign again at the earliest possible moment," Thomas offered, as he hoped, reassuringly.[111]

Later in the spring, Grant once more confided in General Sherman. Thomas had exasperated him to the extreme, and he felt justified in taking the actions he had at the end of 1864. "Knowing Thomas to be slow beyond excuse," Grant noted matter-of-factly, "I depleted his army."[112] The Virginian had remained lethargic, despite the prodding and the interest Grant had taken personally in his command. By contrast, other commanders acted. "Sheridan has made his raid, and with splendid success, so far as heard."[113] This comparison remained in Grant's head. Well after the war, he insisted that "Thomas was an inert man," and firmly believed that this "inertness" not only "affected him as a commander," but contributed to his untimely death.[114]

That Ulysses Grant seemed inordinately preoccupied with his subordinate's "slowness" was reflected in his conversations with other individuals as well. Although she did not cite a specific time frame for her observation in her postwar writings, General John Logan's wife, Mary, recalled, "I often heard General Grant and General Logan discuss Thomas and his heroism as a soldier, but they expressed regret that his temperament was so obstinate and that he shrank from responsibility."[115]

Two other old comrades may have captured Thomas's character at this time as well as anyone. A former colonel in a Kentucky regiment offered the view: "General Thomas was a greater man at the close of the war than he was at the beginning, not more in the public estimation than in intrinsic worth." The individual with whom he shared these thoughts agreed. "The patience and self-restraint which he was called upon to exercise, I have no doubt, had a wonderful influence upon his after life."[116]

Thomas's vast reservoir of patience would continue to be tested by the army commander who now felt compelled to chip away at the forces that had operated so successfully under the "Rock of Chickamauga" in the aftermath of arguably his greatest moment of triumph. A participant explained, simply, "The battle of Nashville was the only instance during the war in which two armies, of nearly equal force, met in battle, and one was destroyed by the other."[117] Yet, the rebellion persisted, and when the Virginian did not act promptly to grasp the opportunity to assert himself into the post-Nashville equation, Grant chose not to defer the matter on the grounds of recent success. Consequently, he broke up Thomas's command and sent portions of it where it could be employed more effectively in the final strategy that he hoped would bring the Confederacy to its knees. For George Thomas, the commander who had added fresh laurels to his record, this was now another time when "the Virginian" would be called upon to "wait."

14　A Different Kind of War (January–May 1865)

"You know he is as reticent as a mole, though full of kindness and good feeling."
—Quartermaster J. L. Donaldson on Thomas

"Write nothing but the truth."
—George Thomas to Army of the Cumberland historian
　Thomas B. Van Horne

"I have not been treated by the authorities as though they had confidence in me."
—Thomas to Secretary of War Stanton

For once the sound of artillery must have come as a welcome sign for the war-weary soldiers who served under Pap Thomas. During the mid-morning hours of April 3, 1865, word reached the general from Washington "announcing the evacuation of Petersburg and probably of Richmond." The retreat of Robert E. Lee's defenders and the consequent fall of the Confederate capital were certainly most welcome developments. From the Nashville headquarters of the Department of the Cumberland came the reply, "I have ordered a salute of 100 guns at all the principal points in this department in honor of the glorious and encouraging news."[1] The news also meant that the end of the war George Thomas and his comrades had been fighting was finally in sight.

But that welcome day was still months ahead when the new year dawned and the Virginian faced the grim reality that even in the aftermath of the resounding victory he had achieved outside Nashville much work remained to be done. The close of 1864 had proven anything but smooth for him as he found his command divided and dispersed to more active theaters, and the same threats and demands appeared to be nagging him. Yet, even with his old commander Sherman on the Georgia coast and the general in chief and the War Department looking broadly over his shoulder, Thomas focused on the tasks at hand of maintaining his department and fulfilling his obligations in the field.

Hindsight proved particularly valuable to William Tecumseh Sherman at the dawn of a new year. He forwarded a long report from Savannah, Georgia, the town he had presented to Abraham Lincoln as a sort of Christmas present. In it he laid out the larger scheme that he had sought to implement with regard to Hood and the Confederate Army of Tennessee and in which Thomas had played a role. Gone was any sense of the anxiety that had beset him or the general in chief concerning the Virginian. All had worked as it was expected to do, including the decision to split his command into two elements: one offensive to march to the sea and ravage the "enemy's resources" and the other defensive, which was meant to "invite the enemy to attack, risking the chances of battle." Hood had taken the latter challenge, and all that transpired vindicated Sherman in his strategic vision and wisdom. "In this conclusion," as he explained it, "I have been singularly sustained by the results." Hood had taken on Thomas, who "wisely and well fulfilled his part of the grand scheme in drawing Hood well up into Tennessee until he could concentrate all his own troops and then turn upon Hood, as he has done, and destroy or fatally cripple his army." There was no reference to the inability of the Virginian to attack Hood at an earlier location or time. Sherman now professed that he trusted the command "with perfect confidence, its management and history to General Thomas."[2]

On the second day of the year, James Harrison Wilson was in Huntsville, Alabama, working hard to create a cavalry force that could act either independently or in conjunction with Thomas if the Virginian chose to push any additional advantage against his Confederate adversaries. Wilson explained to his friend Adam Badeau, recovering from an illness in the East, that he had urged Thomas to concentrate the cavalry at Eastport several times and was endeavoring diligently to meet the needs of the command, including obtaining sufficient horseshoes from Nashville. Still, for the aggressive Wilson, the roads and the wintry conditions were as much a deterrent to immediate movement as his commander had seen them at the end of the year.[3] Nevertheless, the cavalryman would have an extensive role to play in the months to come as the Federals sought to strike the final blows against the Confederate infrastructure and its capability to sustain a war.

Thomas also received a telegram on January 2 from Admiral S. P. Lee, who was seeking his advice and once more demonstrating a willingness to act in a manner "consistent with your plans and views." The naval officer thought it best to rid the region of western Tennessee and Kentucky of the nuisance of Nathan Bedford Forrest, probably not fully realizing that defending Hood's retreat had sapped the strength of that Confederate force, too. Admiral Lee wanted approval for reconstructing the works that Forrest had destroyed just a few months prior in a daring attack on the Union depot at Johnsonville, on the Tennessee River.[4]

Thomas responded the same day with a report that he was concentrating his men at Eastport "preparatory to a continuance of the campaign" and promised, "I shall be there myself at the latter part of this week or the beginning of the next week, going by water from Nashville." He requested that Lee do what he could "to keep the river open if possible" and signaled his agreement for the contemplated improvements at Johnsonville.[5] The cooperation that had marked the relationship through the month of December during the crisis of Hood's Campaign clearly was continuing in its aftermath and into the new year.[6] Admiral Lee forwarded the report to Secretary Welles a day later, including Thomas's appreciation for the "cordial cooperation of the Navy during the last thirty days."[7]

Hood might be done as far as Thomas was concerned, but not everyone was prepared to call the Confederate cause lost just yet. Not surprisingly, the reports of the Union forces' success found skeptical eyes and ears in Richmond and other parts of the floundering Confederacy. The Confederate war clerk, John B. Jones, famed in later years for his wartime journal, noted in a January 1 entry, "The new year begins with the new rumors that Gen. Hood has turned upon Gen. Thomas and beaten him." Jones did not offer the source from which he derived such incredible intelligence, offering only that the fantastic story "is believed by many." He knew that Hood had suffered a defeat before Nashville, but was convinced that "Federal accounts of his disaster were probably much exaggerated."[8] What he did not seem to fathom was that the same exaggeration he believed bolstered Union accounts was more than present in the Confederate ones, too.

Local newspaper accounts undoubtedly helped to influence the thinking of the war clerk and anyone else who gleaned them for scraps of information about what was happening in distant Tennessee. "From our own part," one editorial writer asserted demonstrably, "we have arrived at the conclusion that the bulletins of Thomas are a tissue of lies, such as nobody but a yankee, unless it be a *renegade* could possibly weave together." The obvious slap to the Virginian and his victory over Hood fulfilled at least two purposes: bolstering sagging Confederate morale and once more excoriating a Southern traitor. "The lies are as gross as the father who begot them," the newspaperman concluded.[9]

"From Thomas's Army." "Where is Hood?" The *Cincinnati Daily Commercial* inquired on behalf of its readers. The correspondent offered explanations about how it would be reasonable to assume that the Army of Tennessee could hardly have crossed its namesake river. "The heavy and continuous rains which set in immediately after the battles of Nashville" surely must have caused the river to swell sufficiently to trap the Southern remnant. Then, the essay turned to the reasons why just such an outcome might have been reached after all. Citing factors that ranged from the retreating troops having greater motivation to escape than the pursuers to catch them to the opportunity to utilize the churned-up roads first and obstruct their tormentors, the writer attempted to make the case for the uncertainty that prevailed over the Confederate army's fate.[10]

Of course, it did not really matter what others might think or say, the reality was that Thomas had dealt a critical blow to the Confederacy's fortunes in the Western Theater. He was also about to deliver a final one to the raiders Hylan Lyon had led against his supply and communications lines in conjunction with Hood's Campaign. In an after-action report, Thomas followed the pursuit in detail, including a final engagement in which Lyon was initially captured in his bedclothes, before he managed to escape after killing a Union sergeant who had tried to accommodate his prisoner by allowing him to put on warmer apparel.[11] In addition to almost "capturing Lyon himself," the Federal force took "his one piece of artillery, and about 100 of his men, with their horses."[12] The dramatic series of events left Lyon's command broken and demoralized. Of the effectiveness of the expedition, Union colonel William Palmer observed simply, "I do not think Lyon's command will give much more trouble as an organization."[13] Strategically, the Confederate actions had caused Thomas to siphon off some of his cavalry from the defense of Nashville for the purpose of engaging in the pursuit. Even with Hood forced from Middle Tennessee Thomas was not able to bring the full complement of his cavalry to bear against that retreating army.[14] One student of the operation concluded that whatever else Lyon's efforts had accomplished, "there is no question but that the raid was an effective diversion."[15]

An atmosphere of celebration for the larger achievements continued to pervade the department. Union general Gates Thruston was in Chattanooga as the new year unfolded. In the middle of the month he wrote his sister that "our grand party on Thursday in honor of General Thomas has given all other matters a regular back seat and now I find it difficult to catch up, and get back into the regular routine." The dilemma was one that was surely welcome, but business was not about to be slackened greatly, with the Virginian quickly returning to the saddle. As Thruston noted, "General Thomas is up the Tennessee River."[16]

The new year brought reflections from a number of individuals concerning the state of the nation, the war, and the primary figures in it. A great deal of assessment was making its way into the record one way or another. In a candid exchange of letters between them, James H. Wilson and Adam Badeau outlined their personal evaluations of Thomas. Wilson offered a mitigating view of his superior, although he was by no means sycophantic, but Badeau was unimpressed. "I can't say I admire his slowness, although 'twas afterwards so gloriously redeemed," Badeau observed. "Neither do I think it soldierly in any General to be unwilling to submit to detachments from his army when the good of the service require it, nor unwilling to be hurried in his preparations." He was convinced that Grant would leave Thomas no choice but to comply. "I imagine he will have to submit to these very things whenever the Lieut. General deems it advisable." Badeau admitted that he could not understand "the idea of his feeling hurt" when called upon to redistribute troops, then concluded rather pointedly, "I don't see that purity and disinterestedness here that distinguished Grant and Sherman himself and Sheridan." Badeau thought it might be helpful to "hint at Thomas's feeling to the General" and promised that he could do so in a manner "so as not to injure Thomas, and perhaps have the effect you deem desirable."[17]

Upon reading his friend's response, Wilson thought better of what he had shared with him concerning his superior's expressions and attitudes. Although he agreed substantially with the conclusions Badeau had drawn, he did not want to betray Thomas's confidences or offer an overly negative view of a man he had come to admire. Wilson had to admit, "I have no hesitation in saying my estimate of the *selfish* element in Thomas's character is no new discovery." As the foundation for this position, Wilson recalled the incident at Chattanooga after the battle of Chickamauga and upon Grant's initial arrival in that embattled city. "This however is nothing new," Wilson explained of Thomas's apparent hostility to Grant, "as the General himself could tell you if he remembers a cold rainy dismal winter night over a year ago when he first arrived at Chattanooga as the guest of the former and commanding officer of the Military Division of Mississippi." The cold reception, and Wilson's sharp recollection of chiding Thomas for it, remained indelibly marked in the cavalryman's mind. "I *shall never* forget the occasion to which I allude," he assured his friend, but then hastily added, "It would be an injustice however, to leave even upon your mind any doubt of Thomas's honesty or zeal. He is strictly conscientious in his duty and I am sure would never hesitate to obey a legitimate order." Wilson emphasized what he perceived of Thomas's views on Grant: "It may be well for you to remember that Thomas feels quite mollified by his Major Generalcy but I can scarcely believe him well disposed towards the General."[18]

Once again any assessments largely depended upon the individuals making them. An officer indicated to Union general Montgomery Meigs that Thomas was not especially satisfied with his promotion under the circumstances. "He feels very sore at the rumored intentions to relieve him and the major generalcy does not cicatrize the wound." For this person, at least, the general's reaction was not surprising. "You know Thomas is morbidly sensitive and it cut him to the heart to think that it was contemplated to remove him." In assigning responsibility for the treatment, the observer only said that the Virginian thought that as "a fair and just man," Secretary of War Stanton was blameless in the matter.[19]

There was no doubt that the Virginian's relationships could be strained, but he developed strong and positive working associations with individuals both within and outside of his branch of the service. His connection with Admiral Lee had already done much to contribute to the success of the Nashville campaign. Indeed, the naval commander was effusive in his evaluation of their professional partnership. "The intercourse between the military and naval branches of the service during the recent campaign has been of a most pleasing and cordial character," Lee explained to Secretary Welles in late January.[20] Biographers of the admiral concluded, "It is difficult to find anywhere in the history of the American Civil War a better demonstration of combined operations in which the army and the navy worked together with fewer problems and more impressive results."[21]

Cooperation of another sort was also forthcoming. This time the combined effort was to be between the forces of Edward R. S. Canby and George Thomas. Henry Halleck discussed the idea with Grant as he inquired of the general whether or not accessions to Thomas's command, particularly with regard to horses for the cavalry, should continue at the pace that had been set prior to the fighting around Nashville. The chief of staff thought that an aggressive operation, cooperatively carried out, could net the Federals control of the cities of Selma and Montgomery in Alabama.[22]

Grant was unsure of just how this effort might unfold, since he saw Thomas as being in no position to capture these cities if he had to come at them from his present location. Grant reiterated some of his earlier criticisms: "He is too ponderous in his preparations and equipments to move through a country rapidly enough to live off it." In such a case, the general in chief thought his subordinate could "do without horses for some time," and some of his men could be detailed to serve with any independent operation Canby might undertake. Grant seemed prepared to leave the choice of a course of action to his subordinate, although he hastily concluded, "Thomas must make a campaign or spare his surplus troops."[23]

From the Georgia coast, Sherman offered a detailed campaign plan. He anticipated making a "dive into the interior" of the Carolinas shortly and wanted the Virginian to know what he expected of him in the meantime. Demonstrations with cavalry toward North Carolina from Knoxville would be useful, as would the buildup of small forces and provisions for protecting the region from Chattanooga to Rome, Georgia, but the key effort should be made in the direction of the remaining Confederate industrial infrastructure located at Selma and Montgomery, Alabama. The destruction occurring from such an expedition should be comprehensive, with the troops Thomas designated to undertake it prepared to do "all the damage possible; burning up Selma, that is the navy yard, the railroad back to the Tombigbee [River], and all iron foundries, mills and factories." Moving from that point to Montgomery, the Union troops should "deal with it in like manner." He thought that such a punitive expedition would prove "perfectly practicable, and easy, and that it will have an excellent effect." If carried out properly, the raid would demonstrate the incapacity of the Confederate government to protect its people and secure their safety and property. Almost as an aside,

Sherman threw in a preference concerning his long-standing nemesis. "I would like to have Forrest hunted down and killed, but doubt if we can do that yet."[24]

From Eastport, Thomas indicated a different set of priorities than those outlined by Sherman, and ostensibly approved by Grant. It must have seemed like a repetition of Nashville from both perspectives: the weather dogging the activities and plans of the one and the resulting delays frustrating the schemes of the others. Thomas explained to Henry Halleck that troops on the ground reported the roads to be "in an impassable condition for wagons and artillery, and that it would be impossible to make a move of any magnitude until the weather becomes more favorable." Thomas was aware of the similarities of the situation. "Awaiting a more favorable change in the weather, I am doing everything possible to organize General Smith's command for a long march," Thomas offered as mitigation, "and also equipping and mounting the cavalry as thoroughly as possible, which I am confident I shall be able to accomplish by the time the roads become passable."[25]

Thomas still planned to use James H. Wilson for a major expedition to achieve the outcome in Alabama that Sherman desired. "General Wilson has a fine location for thoroughly organizing and disciplining his command, which he can accomplish in a few weeks. He will then have a force which the enemy will be utterly unable to resist." Still, an unnerving element, at least in the eyes of those who would read his dispatch, remained. "I earnestly recommend that I may be permitted to put my command in thorough shape before being again ordered to take the field." Thomas's next assertion suggested that he continued to be oblivious to the message he was sending. "You may rest assured I will not delay matters, but will be fully prepared before the roads are practicable, if sufficient horses can be furnished to remount the cavalry."[26]

If George Thomas was not setting his sights on further penetrations of the Confederate States of America as Halleck and Grant might want him to do, he was nevertheless thinking of what the close of the war would mean to the defeated region. Part of this consideration arose when a "deputation of citizens of Northern Alabama" met with him for advice as to "the best mode of bringing their section back into the Union." Thomas explained that he thought a convention might accomplish the task and offered them a novel approach that he uncharacteristically did not appear to clear with the War Department or his superiors first:

> I advised them to call a convention of the people living in north of the Tennessee River, and adopt the necessary measures in convention for re-establishing civil law in their district, and then to make a petition to the

President to be admitted into the Union as a section of Alabama, prepared in all respects to perform their duties as loyal citizens of the Government of the United States, acknowledging the practical abolition of slavery, and expressing a desire that the institution may never be restored; then to send a delegation to Washington with a copy of the proceedings of their convention and their petition to lay before the President.

Thomas expressed a belief in his visitors' sincerity and the "hope that they may be encouraged to reorganize civil authority in their district, believing it will greatly facilitate any future efforts that may be made to re-establish civil authority in the State of Alabama, and its restoration to the Union."[27]

In the meantime, the general had other matters to consider that would require him to disperse a portion of his command to accomplish. Troops were needed to secure the reconstructed post of Johnsonville, ravaged in a spectacular raid by Nathan Bedford Forrest just prior to the Nashville Campaign. Others would be needed for more onerous duty. "The major general commanding directs also that you will use every means to permanently and thoroughly clear the country of the guerrillas now infesting it," a directive went out from headquarters to the commander at Eastport, "and for this purpose you are authorized to mount from 200 to 500 of the men of your command upon horses taken from the rebel sympathizers along the line of the railroad and the surrounding country." Such measures would simultaneously accomplish many tasks by providing for the security of the region, the deprivation of resources ordinarily available to the guerrillas and Confederates by their friends, and the procurement of the needed mounts without materially affecting the effort to obtain them for Wilson's impending cavalry force.[28] To Thomas this could not be a clearer indication of his good faith in fulfilling his obligations. To Sherman, Grant, and Halleck, it must have seemed as if it amounted to the type of subdued energy they had come to expect from their colleague.

Halleck continued to make dispositions according to the needs of the army and the war effort at the expense of General Thomas's command. When the need for more personnel to "guard prisoners of war at Chicago" arose, the chief of staff turned to the Virginian. "None [are] available except from your command," he explained, and passed along the request for him to "send a small regiment for that purpose."[29] The notion that Thomas would have to use his men in active campaigning or lose them was taking on new meaning.

Yet, it was not as if Thomas did not finally realize what was happening. He felt that it was his duty to report conditions as they were, just as he had done at Nashville, and daily reports indicated that the country he would have to operate in was in horrendous condition. "I therefore think that it will be impossible to move from the Tennessee River upon Montgomery and Selma with a large force during this winter." It had been his "purpose," he insisted, that once conditions improved in spring he would take up such an offensive, but for the moment no expedition could set out with "any reasonable chance of complete success."

Astonishingly, Thomas revealed his awareness of the situation by offering portions of his troops for other campaigns. "Should Lieutenant-General Grant determine upon a winter campaign from some point on the Gulf I could send General Canby Maj. Gen. A. J. Smith's command and all of the cavalry now here, except two divisions, feeling able to securely hold the line of the Tennessee," he explained to Halleck. Badeau's indictment notwithstanding, Thomas was prepared to transfer some 24,000 men to a theater outside his jurisdiction if called upon to do so.[30]

It could be argued that Thomas made such an offer only because he realized that it was likely to occur anyway. But if his motive had been to hold as substantial a command as he could for as long as possible, he certainly would not have had to make the process of transfering his troops easier. Thomas also felt he deserved consideration for his tremendous successes, including those most recently accomplished against Hood, but rather than make that case, or simply complain of ill-treatment, he took the larger perspective of the national good, especially if the men could better serve the cause of the Union elsewhere. What one general might have seen as an intolerable and insulting diminution of his authority and responsibility, the Virginian saw as another indication of the duty he had sworn to uphold when he chose to follow the Old Flag. In this attitude he reflected the spirit of one of his own subordinates who observed, "My rule is . . . to perform to the best of my abilities whatever duties my superiors assign to me; this is consistent with self respect and the dignity of an officer; the other course is not."[31]

Routine matters returned to the forefront as the men constructed and settled into winter quarters. Thomas included requests for promotion among his official paperwork. "I want to do something for you," he explained to General Thomas J. Wood, "[as well as] for Opdycke and something for Col. [Philip Sidney] Post." The Virginian knew that timing was significant, with the efforts and achievements on recent battlefields still fresh. Consequently, he instructed Wood, "please send me items and dates and be very prompt while everything is warm."[32]

Andrew Johnson was among those who were helping to keep the memories "warm." On January 12, 1865, he delivered an extensive and pointed set of remarks before the Union State Convention. The military governor and vice president–elect recalled the stirring defense of Nashville and Thomas's reassuring presence. But the time had come to face the work ahead, and for those who wished to continue in the path of rebellion, Johnson declared, "treason must be made odious, and traitors punished and impoverished—[I] mean the leaders. The rank and file must be treated leniently when they give proof of penitence. Men must be made to realize the enormity of treason."[33]

Johnson believed George Thomas shared such views with him and was determined to link their fortunes together in these turbulent times. To President Lincoln, the Tennessean forthrightly expressed the "hope the President will include all Tennessee in the Department of the Cumberland when placed under Genl. Thomas['s] command. We can have consort and unity with the Civil & Military Authorities, and [this] is very important at this time. I hope the President will have no hesitancy in placing Memphis and the Western part of the State in Genl Thomas['s] Dept[.]"[34]

Favorable expressions continued to pour forth from a grateful citizenry. One prompted a public response from the general and illustrated the priorities he hoped that well-wishers would follow. From his headquarters at Eastport, Thomas communicated with the editor of a Cincinnati newspaper, saying that he had read of the desire to "raise a sum of money for the purpose of presenting me with a suitable testimonial of their appreciation of my services." Thomas was duly grateful for "the high compliment," but preferred "that any sum which may be raised for that purpose may be devoted to the founding of a fund for the relief of disabled soldiers, and the indigent widows and orphans of officers and soldiers who have lost their lives during this war." Here, for him, lay the crux of the matter. The soldiers had made any reputation he enjoyed. A return for their sacrifice was small recompense indeed. "I am amply rewarded," he closed, "when assured that my humble services have met with the approbation of the Government and the people."[35]

Post-Nashville developments presented decidedly mixed signs, as Gates Thruston explained in a letter home just before leaving Chattanooga to go to Nashville. "The Department of the Cumberland has been much increased of late by an order from the War Department adding the Dept. of the Ohio and other territory to it." But, while the area of responsibility had grown, the number of men needed to secure it had actually diminished rather considerably. "We have so much territory to protect now and so few troops to do it with that at present, Genl Thomas' command will be upon the defensive entirely. Nothing is left us but the 4th Corps a corps of cavalry and a few detached divisions."[36]

Thomas was doing everything in his power to bring hostilities to a conclusion and reassert Federal authority wherever he found it to be under question or threat. In February, he identified one such source in Rome, Georgia, where outward displays of Confederate loyalty persisted. The mayor and other prominent citizens wrote protesting "the arrest of certain citizens of Rome, Ga., for being concerned with the display of the flag of the late Southern Confederacy in that city, and asking that justice may be done and the prisoners be released." The leaders claimed that "no disrespect was intended to the United States Government by the exhibition of the Confederate flag, and that the parties who displayed it have accepted in good faith the present state of affairs and do acknowledge the jurisdiction of the United States Government." The challenge was unmistakably clear and the answer to it had to be as well.

Thomas's response was characteristically firm. "If that is the case, it can only be supposed, assuming that they possess ordinary intelligence that they misunderstand the present 'state of affairs' which is that the rebellion has been decided to be a huge crime, embodying all of the crimes of the decalogue, and that it has been conquered." As such, "the very name and emblems [of the Confederacy] are hateful to the people of the United States and he must be indeed obtuse who expects without offense to parade before the eyes of loyal people that which they execrate and their abhorrence of which they have expressed in the most emphatic language in which it is possible for a great nation to utter its sentiments."[37] The situation called for more than cosmetics, and Thomas was convinced that a stoutly delivered object lesson would prove most useful.

Thomas subsequently explained his typical response to such matters. "My usual course was to call immediately upon the local civil officers to act in the matter, and they failing, I sent troops to arrest the perpetrators." The Rome incident involved "some indiscreet young rebels [who] made public demonstrations of their patriotism by hoisting the rebel flag." The Virginian could not help revealing a sense of personal satisfaction with the actions he had taken. "Desiring to enable them still further to show their devotion to 'the cause' I caused their arrest and deportation to jail at Atlanta, from which place of confinement they were afterwards released at the insistence of the Mayor of Rome and other citizens, who stated the young men did not intend any demonstration of disloyalty by their action, etc." Nevertheless it troubled him that an underlying defiance remained in areas that were supposed to have been pacified. Thomas noted that his efforts in the Georgia town prompted public excoriation in the press, which he saw as "additional evidence of the disloyal spirit of the people," although he thought these actions still "had a most wholesome effect in preventing similar demonstrations."[38]

Thomas's duties as department commander kept him regularly on the move overseeing his large sphere of responsibility. The Virginian had never been one to remain strictly behind a desk directing operations in that detached manner in any case and was not about to implement a change in his policy at this stage of his career. From Nashville, Gates Thruston reflected the active tone in a letter, "Our Hd Qrs are of course here tho Genl. Thomas is travelling about in the Department & field Hd. Qrs. are wherever he goes."[39] A week earlier, on February 12, Alfred Hough noted having arrived "safely last night" in the Tennessee state capital. "My arrival was very opportune Genl. Thomas having reached here only an hour before me, and had business for me this morning." There was to be no rest for the weary staffers and their chief. "I have just left him," Hough added concerning Thomas. "I find myself plunged into an abyss of work."[40]

Of course, Thomas could not be everywhere at once, which was precisely why he had worked so hard to hone an effective staff. Still, his skills were well suited to a multiplicity of simultaneous responsibilities. A contemporary observed of the general, "His mind, given to the details of the several departments of his command, whether a division, a corps, or an army, took in every particular."[41] One of these details reflected another passion of his: having official Washington render appropriate recognition for his men. Thus, when General Wilson recommended a promotion to brevet brigadier general for John Henry Hammond and Thomas endorsed the same, word of intrigue drew the Virginian's attention and ire. "I learn that strong influences are about to be used to prevent the confirmation of Bvt. Brig. Genl. J. H. Hammond whose name is now before the Senate," Thomas wrote Senator Henry Wilson of Massachusetts from his headquarters in Nashville on February 16. "General Hammond is one of the most energetic, intelligent and faithful young officers in the service," he noted, adding indignantly, "I should regret exceedingly if he should lose his confirmation in consequence of private political opposition."[42]

Thomas had reason to believe that his expressions of support might have some effect. Examples of public esteem were already forthcoming. Another important and personally gratifying form of this recognition came his way when, on March 3, 1865, the United States Senate and House of Representatives issued a joint resolution that expressed "the thanks for Congress" for "the skill and dauntless courage, which the Rebel Army under General Hood was signally defeated and driven from the State of Tennessee."[43] Had such laurels come with a requirement for public expression, the Virginian would have been discomfited, but within the deep reservoir of ambition that drove him, there had to have been a sense of gratitude and satisfaction over the distinct honor the gesture represented.

In the meantime, Thomas anticipated being back in the field in a new campaigning season. General Grant was anxious for the Virginian to unleash his cavalry on raids against the Confederate infrastructure, informing him on February 16 that he was to dispatch George Stoneman on such a mission "without delay." Grant seemed particularly concerned that Thomas would repeat what had happened prior to Nashville and wait until all of his cavalry was in hand before he sent them out. Stoneman was to "go without waiting," and the rest of the horsemen could remain with Thomas's command as they arrived.[44]

Unfortunately, the approach of another spring did not offer an end to the weather complications that had plagued operations in the region. Thomas dutifully informed Ulysses Grant at City Point, "We have had a very heavy storm which had retarded the commencement of operations in this department by swelling the streams and distroying RR bridges but I am in hopes Wilson has started by this time." In addition, Thomas had a second mounted force under General Stoneman ready to move toward Knoxville "by Saturday next with his expeditionary force and will start from there immediately." Thomas planned to supplement this movement with "the available Infantry force" and use it also to "repair the E. Tennessee & Virginia R.R. as far as the Watauga bridge for the present." General Hatch was to remain in Eastport where the command could be mounted and would constitute a "strong enough" force "to hold that point for the present." In the meantime, the Union commander would "await the developments of events in Miss & Ala." before committing another of his relatively meager units.[45]

On March 20, 1865, Thomas's quartermaster, J. L. Donaldson, reported to his boss, Montgomery C. Meigs, from Nashville. He and Thomas had just reached that city from Knoxville "this morning," he explained, laying out the general state of affairs in the department. The only negative was that many of the resources gathered at Eastport to sustain the troops had been lost to rapidly rising waters and the attendant flooding that occurred there. "More forage was accumulated there than was desired," Donaldson admitted, "and it could not be saved." Still, the command remained well situated, and he deemed the men charged with the operations generally competent at their duties.

Donaldson paused to cover speculation concerning Thomas's plans for East Tennessee, but confessed that the general "has said nothing to me on the subject." Then, in a remarkable moment of candor in an official communication, the quartermaster added of the Virginian, "You know he is as reticent as a mole, though full of kindness and good feeling." He did not venture into any other personal observations and, after a short digression on his activities, concluded, "I believe I have written you an unreasonable, gossipy letter, and will stop." Then it was back to business. "I go with General Thomas on Thursday, 24th [23rd] instant, to Memphis and thence to Eastport."[46]

Thomas made a thorough inspection and an overhaul of the department in the month of March. Quartermaster Donaldson noted in a broad report just at the beginning of April, "During this month [March] I have also made a general tour of the department, visiting Eastport, Knoxville, and Memphis, with you in succession."[47] Thomas also had his inspector general of fortifications, the aptly named Zealous B. Tower, out on a widely encompassing tour that produced several reports on the state and condition of fortifications throughout the department.[48] Brigadier General Tower had helped to improve the Nashville defenses before Hood's army tested them during the latter part of 1864.[49]

In Virginia, rumors were rampant that Thomas was doing more than riding the circuit of his department. Confederate general James Longstreet's men brought in a Union deserter who insisted that the Union general was no longer in the Western Theater. General Robert E. Lee replied the next day that he did not place much credence in the intelligence. "I doubt the correctness of the deserter's report," the Confederate commander explained. "I know of no part of Thomas' army that has come east except that under Schofield in N. Carolina. All of the northern papers and our own reports from the south agree that Thomas with the rest of his force is in Mississippi."[50]

Concern about Thomas's location and actions was a matter Ulysses Grant seemed to share with his Confederate counterpart. He spent a long communication complaining to Sherman about the Virginian's apparent contentedness with delaying active operations on his part until a later, and ostensibly better, time in the year. The example of the cavalryman James Wilson was enough to make the point. Grant had ordered him out in the direction of Selma, Alabama, "as soon after the 20th of February as possible." Now it was mid-March and Wilson "had not at last advices" begun to move. The same was true of George Stoneman, whom Grant wanted to sweep into South Carolina so as to cooperate with Sherman in that state. Failing that, Grant insisted that cavalryman be sent to Virginia to damage or destroy Confederate infrastructure and resources. That, too, had not been done, and Grant laid the responsibility as it should have been, on the overall commander, George Thomas.[51]

Compounding the demands on the Virginian's energies and attentions were the indications of difficulties that awaited him in the postwar period that was approaching. From Memphis, a Federal treasury agent saw some positive economic signs, but felt that a general sense of uncertainty and insecurity also remained. W. R. Hackley found it safer to remain at his office or in his home, "where I am after dark as I am not in the street more than I can help after night." Although the city was no longer subject to Confederate raids as it had been, lawlessness prevailed in and around Memphis. "There are a few scattering robbers (called Guerrillas, deserters from both sides who rob and murder on the Highways) but they will soon be cleared out," Hackley explained to his wife. Even so, he felt he had reason to be optimistic. "The country people are tired of the war and want rest and the opportunity to cultivate their fields."[52]

Parts of the South might be pacified and emerging into a transition period toward peace, but other Confederate forces remained. The jockeying for units that had so significantly diminished Thomas's command also continued. But this time the pressure came not from Sherman or Grant in the east, but E. R. S. Canby and Benjamin Grierson from the west. Grierson had established himself as a cavalry raider in 1863 with a spectacular expedition that ran the length of the state of Mississippi and ended in Baton Rouge, Louisiana. Although he subsequently experienced difficulties against Bedford Forrest at Brice's Cross Roads the following summer, Grierson was now the commander of the cavalry in Canby's department, and the latter anticipated additional active campaigning for which he required a sufficient mounted force. To that end, Canby ordered General Cadwallader Washburn in Memphis to release cavalry for this use. As Washburn's superior, Thomas turned to the chief of staff, Henry Halleck, in Washington for guidance. Halleck gave the Virginian permission to act "as you may deem proper" in the matter, and Thomas responded to his subordinate with a definite refusal of the Canby/Grierson request. "At the same time I informed General Halleck that this cavalry could not be spared from your district and that you were authorized by me to detain it until I heard from him." Having done so, Thomas saw no reason to reverse his position. He also promised to travel to Memphis shortly, "to visit you."[53]

A struggle for control over troops and limited resources was certainly not anything new. Nor was Thomas's insistence upon instructions in the matter. But for once the Virginian was using fairly open-ended authority to hold on to troops he might have agreed to transfer earlier. Thomas had concerns of his own regarding continuing resistance in his department. To Edward Hatch, the general wrote at the end of March, "Rumors reach me that there is smuggling going on across the line. Take steps to ascertain and arrest all parties engaged in the business." As long as Bedford Forrest ranged free, there was also the likelihood of mischief from that source. "You will have to keep a sharp lookout for Forrest," Thomas warned. "He is, as you know, a tricky fellow."[54]

On the same day, the Virginian instructed Washburn to "endeavor to restore confidence to the people of West Tennessee, and encourage them in any desire they may express to enforce civil laws against the outlaws and guerrillas who infest their counties." Such a return to prewar conditions would be manifestly beneficial to all. "Encourage all the counties of West Tennessee to organize their county courts and administer the civil laws, assuring them that they will not be interfered with by the military authorities as long as they conduct themselves in a manner loyal to the Government of the United States."

The litmus test for these individuals as far as Thomas was concerned would be loyalty, and they could demonstrate this best by getting back to work on their farms, "with the assurance that no more arbitrary seizures of private property of any kind, particularly horses, mules, and oxen will be permitted." Furthermore, the farmers were free to market "whatever products of their farms they may have to dispose of without molestation." Of course, there could be no trade in "contraband of war," but he wanted it clearly understood that "it is expected that they will at least make an effort to redeem themselves from their present miserable condition and exhibit to the world that they are worthy of the leniency which has been shown them." No aiding or abetting the enemy would be tolerated, and "to avoid sending troops into the interior as much as possible it is expected that the people of each county will take care to preserve peace and quiet within its limits, as it will be held responsible for the same."[55] This was the outline for George Thomas's policy regarding a reconstruction of the South in the closing days of the conflict.

News of developments from different points began to arrive at a furious pace. Word of the Confederate capital's fall was quickly followed with erroneous reports of the "capture" of General Lee, although there was no specific reference made about the Confederate commander's army. Still, Thomas was pleased to issue the order to various subordinates, "Fire a salute of 100 guns in honor of the capture of Richmond."[56]

But a familiar dispute returned to tarnish the luster of the moment when one of General Canby's inspectors arrived in the department to insist upon the transfer of Thomas's Memphis-based cavalry. "I have just received General Thomas' answer," the officer reported glumly. "He says that as he is informed that that cavalry belongs to the District of Tennessee [and therefore] it cannot go."[57] On the following day the officer conceded, "As Thomas has refused to allow this cavalry to go I do not see that I can do anything more in the matter."[58]

Thomas received welcome news from Wilson's horsemen in Alabama. At mid-morning on April 4, the cavalryman informed his superior that he had defeated Bedford Forrest and captured Selma. "My corps took this place by assault late on [the] evening of the 2d," Wilson explained. In addition to thousands of prisoners and a "large quantity of military stores of all kinds," the Federals had secured "arsenals and foundaries with their machinery."[59] The Confederates had sought to build an industrial complex that could support the war effort, which Wilson and his men were now busily doing their best to dismantle.[60] The strategic implications were enormous, as were the psychological benefits of besting one of the Confederacy's best horse soldiers.

Positive news continued to spread from the east, and Thomas dutifully passed it along to his subordinates. There were "reports that Lee has surrendered his army to General Grant: that is the Army of Virginia."[61] Now the celebratory volleys could be fired to honor another critical development. From Nashville, headquarters sent out a message for all of the commanders in the department: "Fire a salute of two hundred guns at Meridian tomorrow at each post within your command . . . in honor of the capture of the rebel Army of Northern Virginia and of the raising of the old flag over Fort Sumpter."[62] On the same day, Thomas learned that Wilson's men had taken "possession" of the original Confederate capital of Montgomery, Alabama, on the previous day.[63] The rebellion was collapsing on all sides.

As the major operations of the war wound down, the atmosphere in Nashville changed dramatically. One officer assigned there passed word of the new circumstances to the folks at home. "Mrs. Thomas will be here in a day or two & nearly all of the married officers on the staff have their wives here now, so army society abounds. Next week there is to be a grand party here, 300 invitations out," he explained. "I shall go to see the *show* if for no other reason." Experiencing a period absent of active campaigning also allowed Thomas to take greater interest in spiritual matters, too. Gates Thruston observed in correspondence with his family, "For the past two Sundays I have been going to church with Genl. Thomas. He sent for me each day, to go with him, as his aides have been absent, and church goers are scarce upon our staff."[64]

The general had never been one to be demonstrative when it came to religious expressions. In all things he went by the rule that he should avoid public displays. But in this case at least, he appeared to have had a keen understanding of the power of the pulpit to convey messages to the congregants and undoubtedly felt his presence was an important symbolic one to send. Even more, he wanted to know what the assembled worshippers were hearing from their religious leaders, and he took the sermons seriously as political, as well as religious, statements. He would shortly become engaged in a struggle with some of these religious practitioners, who insisted upon using their positions to promote political agendas antithetical toward the Union in general and the United States government in particular. If Thomas was not going to let citizens express such views openly, he was not likely to find restrictions on clergy to be more troublesome for him to impose either.

As the army prepared for a period in which wartime honors would have to be balanced against regular army positions, Thomas took up a new type of duty designed to help bring order to the process. The issue involved the proliferation of brevet ranks that the war had unleashed. In order to guard against abuses Thomas agreed to serve on a board of officers that would "decide upon a given date for each general officer by brevet." The service could not have picked a better officer, whose only concern was the legitimacy of the individual for the claim he made and the good of the service and the nation.[65]

In the midst of these mundane duties, Thomas learned, as did a shocked nation, that an assassin had struck down the president of the United States. John Wilkes Booth deprived Abraham Lincoln of the opportunity to see the war to its full conclusion and to take a place in helping to rebuild the nation. That task now fell to Vice President Andrew Johnson. On April 15, Thomas passed along his condolences in a solemn expression of the "profound sorrow for the calamity which has befallen the nation." Recognizing the role Johnson would have to play in filling the place so suddenly and tragically vacated, the Virginian offered his new commander in chief "assurances of my profound esteem and hearty support."[66]

Thomas also communicated with the secretary of war, erroneously repeating the news that Secretary of State Seward had been killed as well. He explained that the word had arrived in Nashville, "just before the ceremonies in commemoration of the fall of Richmond and the surrender of Lee's army were about to commence." The sad tidings had dampened the positive atmosphere that prevailed. "The whole community, military and civic, is profoundly affected at this terrible national calamity," he explained. "The flags displayed at the different military offices have been draped in mourning, and minute guns will be fired until sundown."[67] Duties continued to demand attention, but a much more somber aspect cast its pall over the Virginian and his command in what was becoming increasingly clear was their moment of triumph.

President Johnson replied two days later with a short expression of his appreciation for the sentiments that the general had expressed. Theirs already was a complicated relationship and would remain so, but it also was one based upon a long period of service in their respective spheres that had often brought them into contact with each other. Indeed, their communications had often displayed ample grounds for agreement between them. Once more Johnson expressed the wish that Thomas "will communicate with me fully in reference to all that pertains to the public interest."[68]

Complications of a different sort soon arose. In late April, Thomas informed Wilson that the terms upon which Joseph Johnston had surrendered to William T. Sherman in North Carolina "are disapproved and repudiated by the President of the United States, and orders have been accordingly issued that all U.S. commanders push to the utmost all military operations in which they were engaged at the time of the armistice above referred to." He forwarded the new terms to be offered, based upon those already accepted by Generals Grant and Lee in Virginia.[69]

Thomas was also concerned with the apprehension of the Confederate president, who had fled when Richmond fell. His intelligence suggested that Jefferson Davis was attempting to make his way to Texas, and he requested that General Canby replace Wilson's cavalry occupying Selma and Montgomery, Alabama, with infantry. This would free the cavalry commander "to move in any direction with his whole force." Thus, even if Davis emerged with a considerable escort, Wilson could track and overtake the rebel chieftain and bring about his surrender.[70]

At the same time, Thomas sent instructions to his principal commanders in the field to watch for Davis. "Keep scouts out in your front," he admonished, "and if he should attempt to pass near your command intercept and capture him if possible."[71] To Stoneman in Tennessee, Thomas offered an additional incentive. Troops ought to be dispatched to "capture Jeff Davis or some of his treasure. They say he is making off with from two to five millions in gold."[72] Finally, to his counterpart in the navy, Admiral S. P. Lee, Thomas explained his dispositions and objectives with a degree of satisfaction. "All West N.C., Middle and N. Ga., and North Alabama are virtually under my control," he observed confidently. Then, with a parting shot at their adversaries, he asserted, "If Davis escapes through my lines, Canby's and yours, he will prove himself a better general than any of his subordinates."[73] Thomas knew well that the slim thread of hopes for any continued Confederate resistance rested upon the shoulders of the ousted president reaching a point beyond the Mississippi where he could attempt to rally troops. It was imperative to deny even that possibility.

Better news arrived shortly after when Thomas learned that Johnston's surrender had at last been consummated. He informed several of his field commanders of this development and instructed one of them with an eye to the future and his vision for it. "I wish you to do everything in your power to aid the Civil authorities in restoring Civil Law," he ordered one subordinate in Tennessee.[74] At the same time, he passed along the position taken by the secretary of war that further "recruiting of men in the loyal states for the Volunteer forces be stopped," and that the same directive should include "colored men in all states."[75]

On May 1, Thomas notified General Grant that he had ordered his department commanders to bring a halt to hostilities. "I have directed all my local commanders to send under flag of truce a summons to all bands of armed men operating near their commands, or who may be nearer to them than to any other Federal command, to come in and surrender on the same terms made by General Lee and Johnston." Thomas also reiterated his desire to capture Jefferson Davis, or at least prevent him from escaping through his area of responsibility. He informed Grant that he had given his subordinates explicit orders to "be prepared to pursue him on the first information of his whereabouts and use every exertion to capture him."[76]

Aside from the concern about apprehending Davis, Thomas identified another danger in the form of bands "of armed men." These roving forces had long operated in the nebulous regions between the armies. He wanted them neutralized, voluntarily if possible through surrender, but by force if necessary should the offer of terms be rejected. "If they disregard your summons and continue acts of hostility, they will therefore be regarded as outlaws," he explained forthrightly, "and be prosecuted against, pursued and when caught treated as outlaws."[77]

On the following day, Thomas sent Edward Hatch a second communication and directed a portion of it to the man who had served as a nemesis for many Union commands in the Western Theater of the war. At his directive, Hatch was to "send under flag of truce a summons to Forrest to surrender upon the same terms given by General Grant to Lee and Johnston." As the commander most associated with an April 1864 assault on African American and Tennessee Unionist troops at Fort Pillow that had led to excessive killings and branded him the "Butcher of Fort Pillow," Forrest might have been judged reluctant to lay down his arms. In addition, concern abounded that the Confederate cavalryman would continue his resistance. "Inform him at the same time of the rumors that have reached you, and that you are prepared for him" Thomas explained, "and that if he attempts such a reckless and bloodthirsty adventure, he will be treated thereafter as an outlaw, and the States of Mississippi and Alabama will be so destroyed that they will not recover in fifty years."[78]

The Virginian was reaching a point at which the tactics employed in conventional warfare had to be adapted to new conditions. He had always adhered to military protocol, or at least seriously attempted to do so. Some contemporaries and later historians interpreted this tendency as excessive caution, but failed to understand his adherence to the system in which he had long been a participant. It was not out of an abundance of caution that he operated, but due to his respect for the process and the chain of command that Thomas sought orders for authorization or instruction on every major initiative he was called upon to undertake. His requests were certainly not indicative of any lack of confidence or want of personal direction or incentive. The disposition of paroled Southerners was a case in point.

With the overriding desire to return affairs to as close to prewar norms as possible outside of the existence of slavery, Thomas hoped to be able to let former Confederates return to their civilian lives and pursuits. Wartime considerations made the movement of these soldiers to their homes, if those homes were in loyal areas, problematic. Now that active operations were winding down, Thomas sought guidance on the government's policy. On May 3, 1865, he used the son of the editor of the *Louisville Journal* as an example. He had been "an officer of rank in [the] Rebel Army, recently paroled, is at Chattanooga wishing to return to Louisville his father's home." For now he was being detained, unless clarification of any change in policy allowed him to continue on to his desired destination.[79] In another communication with Grant, Thomas sought specific instructions regarding captives. "Have I authority to release or parole prisoners of war, in prison or hospitals in this Department upon their taking the oath of allegiance?"[80]

On the same day, he informed a concerned Unionist in Ringgold, Georgia, who had inquired about the political process available to people in the defeated states, "To assist and encourage the people in their efforts to restore civil authority, I will act until a military governor can be appointed, upon all such cases as require the action of the governor by the laws of the State which were in force before the rebellion, (my action being subject of course to the approval of the President, or my superiors in office.)" As such, Thomas encouraged the election of persons to political offices and called upon them "to perform the functions of office, under the laws of the State which were in force before the rebellion, except in such cases as may have any bearing on the former status of the negro." This latter point was a significant caveat. "In all civil proceedings hereafter, the negro must, whenever concerned, be regarded and treated as a free man."[81]

Thomas believed the "people of all Georgia will be encouraged and sustained in all honorable efforts to restore the civil law, and peace and confidence throughout the State." To the commander who had authority in the state, he continued to insist that active military operations be suspended as much as possible, "unless you hear of guerrilla bands committing depredations." In that case, he ordered General Steedman in Chattanooga, "Pursue and destroy all guerrillas, who refuse the terms offered them."[82]

With regard to the former Confederate chief executive, Thomas thought that the net that would lead to his capture was tightening nicely. To his counterpart E. R. S. Canby, he outlined the latest intelligence on "Jeff Davis with his treasure" and offered a new likely destination. "I do not believe he can escape between Vicksburg and Memphis, nor do I see how he can cross below, I therefore believe he will attempt to escape into Florida, and from thence by the coast into Cuba." He requested Canby's assistance in conveying this supposition to Wilson, who was in the best position to intercept the party that Thomas now thought consisted of "two thousand picked Cavalry under [George G.] Debrill, and accompanied by Breckenridge, [Confederate secretary of the treasury George C.] Trenholm and Wade Hampton."[83]

As a general rule, the regularly constituted units of the Confederacy were rapidly breaking down, in the aftermath of surrenders, into individuals who simply wanted to return to their homes and get on with their lives. The transition from wartime to peacetime was bound to be imperfect given the way the conflict was ending. On the one hand, the formula for treating formally surrendered troops was clear, but on the other there remained technicalities that had to be addressed. "Paroled prisoners surrendered by Lee & Johnston, and others entering into the same arrangement, will be allowed to return to their homes if within any of the states which Seceded," Grant informed Thomas on May 6. "If belonging to other states they must take the oath of Allegiance first under the decision of the Attorney Gen." The War Department would continue to have jurisdiction over captives taken in battle, presumably until such time as they were released and allowed to go home.[84]

Such instructions clarified the status of the regular Confederate troops, but unconventional forces also concerned Thomas and plagued the Federals at various points in his jurisdiction. In particular, one Southerner raised the Virginian's ire, and he authorized his chief of staff to forward explicit orders. "The general hopes you will Kill Meade and his party, not capture them."[85] Four days later Thomas similarly instructed General R. S. Granger at Huntsville, Alabama, to "hunt Meade down." There was to be no mercy for such individuals. "Give him no quarter, he is an outlaw."[86]

Thomas continued to define for himself the parameters of his authority in a rapidly changing environment. He wrote extensively concerning his desire to restore civilian authority and the prewar laws upon which that authority had been based as well as about the changing status of blacks, who were now "relieved from the requirements of all laws heretofore enacted in Georgia, which held and considered him as a slave." When it came to the state itself, he explained, "I consider more than half the State under my Military control, and therefore have the right, in the absence of a military Governor, duly appointed to issue such orders."[87]

The general continued to evolve in his thinking with regard to those who had participated in the rebellion. He found it difficult, if not impossible, to absolve those who bore responsibility for the war. He was convinced that the common soldiers were under the influence of officers who now sought to behave, and expected to be treated, as if no conflict had actually taken place. Consequently, Thomas instructed his commander in Memphis, "You are authorized to administer the amnesty oath to rebel soldiers, but not to officers or citizens. It is now too late for them to be reaping the benefit of the amnesty proclamation, after having maintained an attitude of hostility for four years."[88] Even in matters as basic as mobility he took the opportunity to ease the restrictions that a state of war had rendered necessary. Thus, when President Johnson wired to ask if passes for travel from Louisville,

Kentucky, to Nashville, Tennessee, might "not be dispensed with," Thomas immediately obliged and dispatched orders to ease that policy accordingly.[89]

Thomas had spent a considerable part of his correspondence with Washington during this period seeking direction or attempting to juggle the evolving command as discharges occurred and troops shifted in and out of his department. There were vast shortages of forage, and the absence of mounted forces to cover a wide range of territory concerned him constantly. Telegraphic messages raced back and forth across the wires to address these many challenges. Thomas probably would not have seen the volume of communication itself as disturbing; such was the existence of a departmental commander.[90] But he was increasingly looking for official confirmation of any steps he wanted to take.

If George Thomas found himself harried he did not show it, and Nashville itself was soon the scene of one of the more pleasant experiences he would have in the waning days of the war. The general had designated May 9 for a "grand review," and the subordinate commanders formed their troops for that purpose. Emerson Opdycke offered an extensive assessment the following day in a letter. "Each regiment was formed in mass by division and even in that order the line must have been a mile long." The Virginian rode along the face of these commands to make his way to the point from which he would conduct the review. Opdycke noted, "As the immortal Thomas approached the troops rent the air with spontaneous cheers." Brigade musicians soon added to the chorus, the men snapping smartly to attention. "The Genl. returned the salute by taking off his hat," Opdycke explained, and then Thomas offered a few personal pleasantries before proceeding along the line.[91]

One of the participants recorded in his diary that on the morning of May 9, he had ridden to a point, "half [a] mile West of the city" to the location of "the Review ground, [w]here the 4th Corps was formed." He noted that upon General Thomas's arrival "a salute of thirteen guns was fired, [and] as he passed in review he was received with deafening cheers by the brave soldiers." The troops then assembled and "marched by the Gen. in review," presenting him with what this witness deemed the "finest display ever in the department."[92]

Historian of the Army of the Cumberland Larry Daniel termed the event "a spectacular review; his farewell to the IV Corps." He noted that David Stanley led the procession of veterans as they passed before their honored chieftain.[93] Stanley recalled the scene vividly. The day was "bright and cool" as "General Thomas and his numerous staff rode down the front, passed by the rear and took the reviewing stand." The men whirled into formation before their chief, and Stanley recalled that from his perspective at least, "It was a very fine review and not a mistake or a hitch occurred."

Over the course of the two hours it took for the columns of veterans to cross before them, Stanley thought Thomas to be "highly pleased" and recalled he was "very complimentary." The officer was impressed himself, expressing the belief that the number of participants represented "a larger muster than the corps could show at any time since its organization in 1863," and attributed the numbers to the conscripts and returnees who had recently joined the ranks. Food, drink, and speeches followed to mark what had turned quickly into a festive occasion.[94]

Before all of the men could retire to the camps, Thomas requested an additional display of martial prowess. Expressing the desire to see one more charge on the part of some of his men, the commander turned to General Opdycke to oblige. "Look[,] look wife[!] Genl. Opdycke is going to show us how to fight," Thomas was supposed to have observed gleefully to Frances. Although her reaction was not recorded to this admonition or the display that prompted it, the exercise impressed her husband. "Ah! That was first rate[,] first rate," he was overheard repeating "with evident satisfaction."[95]

Thomas expressed his own views on the occasion in the form of General Orders No. 30, disseminated the next day. "The general commanding the department takes pride in conveying to the Fourth Army Corps the expression of his admiration, excited by their brilliant and martial display at the review of yesterday," Thomas's assistant adjutant general wrote on his behalf. Then, betraying a sense of understanding of how Thomas could sometimes be perceived, William Whipple noted, "As the battalions of your magnificent corps swept successively before the eye the coldest heart must have been warmed with interest in contemplation of those men who had passed through the varied and shifting scenes of this great modern tragedy." The general knew that these were the men "who had stemmed with unyielding breasts the rebel tide threatening to engulf the landmarks of freedom" and that their features bore "the enobling marks of the years of hardship, suffering, and privation, undergone in the defense of freedom and the integrity of the Union." The Virginian had watched as the men followed the banners "all shred and war worn" that they carried on the fields of battle.[96]

Finally, on May 14, Thomas also had some significant positive news to forward from the field. "General Wilson reports to me the capture of Jeff Davis, his family, Mr. Reagan Postmaster General, Col. Johnson Aid de camp, at Irvinwille Ga. at daylight on the morning of the 10 inst." Adding to the fugitives now brought into the custody of the Federal government was the Confederate governor of Georgia, Joseph Brown.[97]

Thomas was strong in his praise for Wilson and the command, offering his "entire satisfaction with its operations." The capture of Davis had been just the final achievement for a force that had swept through the South, wreaking destruction to the Southern infrastructure and now denying its fugitive leader his final refuge. "They have the proud satisfaction of Knowing that they have imminently done their part towards the suppression of this gigantic rebellion, and that their deeds will be rewarded among the honorable and glorious in the history of their Country."[98] He also celebrated the news with his counterpart, Admiral Lee, observing with satisfaction, "So it seems the Southern Confederacy and Georgia are done for."[99] A subordinate noted simply in a letter to his family, "That cheif of sinners Jeff Davis passed through Nashville last night. No one saw him not even Genl. Thomas himself."[100]

Another chief among the sinners was about to be brought to justice for his vengeful actions. A subordinate of Lovell Rousseau's in Nashville forwarded the characterization of "the major-general commanding the Department of the Cumberland" that designated the notorious guerrilla Champ Ferguson "and his gang of cut-throats" as "outlaws" for apparently having refused to surrender themselves to Federal authorities.[101] Thomas had always had little patience with behavior that breached the protocols of civilized warfare. The Union commander was prepared to take extraordinary measures to halt the depredations. By the end of the month, Ferguson was in custody and would face justice at the end of the rope before the year was out.[102]

As active military operations wound down, the consideration of some for postwar pursuits became the topics of discussion. Emerson Opdycke observed, "Gen. Thomas spoke to Gen. Wood about recommending me for an appointment in the regular army and I had an interview with Gen. Thomas about it." The officer referred to his commander as "very kind and appreciative," but then noted a hint of the Virginian's character. "He thought a good position in the Regular Army [to be a] very desirable one in which a man can be true to his own highest ideal better than in business pursuits."[103] Thomas did not indicate politics as a career outside of the army, but clearly thought that such worlds beyond his own were fraught with a peril that ought to be avoided.

The push for postwar austerity measures also began to take place. Admiral Lee contacted Thomas to ascertain if the need existed for "continuing [the] naval expense of four gunboats." If no "military necessity" required their further service, the Navy Department was prepared to "turn them over to the Quartermaster Department." In a demonstration of his respect for the general, Lee closed, "Your opinion wanted."[104] Thomas quickly and succinctly replied, "I think there is no longer a military necessity for keeping up the gunboats on the Upper Tennessee River."[105] As far as Thomas was concerned, the vessels and their vigilant crews were free to stand down from the duty they had been conducting. By summer the transfer was complete, and the combat career of the *General Thomas* was at an end.[106]

The Richmond-born Treasury agent W. R. Hackley still did not trust the ever-changing environment in which he worked and lived. Although he believed the fact that "Confederates are coming in daily" represented a positive development, and included in his assessment that the dreaded Nathan Bedford Forrest was among those "paroled" and now "on his farm," he feared the worst. There were bound to be new troubles because so many of the men who had laid down their arms had not ceased their former allegiances. "The Confederates have the same *feeling* they ever had and have only given up their arms because they cannot longer fight but they hate the men who have staid at home and will fight them upon small provocation. They hate them even more than they do the Yanks." Hackley did not raise the specter of race in his evaluation, but that factor was liable only to exacerbate matters.[107]

Thomas had to adapt himself to the conditions that prevailed in the department for which he was responsible. He also wanted to assure that those who had sacrificed to achieve victory over the rebellion would secure a place in posterity. In a conversation with a former member of the Army of the Cumberland, the Virginian shared his pride with the command's accomplishments. Then he seemed to understand that a more tangible form of recognition was in order. "I wish you to write a *narrative* history of the Army of the Cumberland," he explained to Chaplain Thomas B. Van Horne. The would-be author momentarily recoiled at the responsibility that this effort would entail, but agreed to try. "Write nothing but the truth," Thomas insisted. Even so, the Virginian had learned painfully that such honesty often ran counter to the prevailing sentiments and positions of others. "You will contravene received opinions," he warned, "and you must fortify yourself." The advice was vintage George Thomas, and it was the full extent of instruction that he would offer Van Horne before setting him out on his task.[108]

Van Horne noted that Thomas's propensity for meticulous record keeping proved of immeasurable benefit in the work that lay ahead. "It is not known when it first occurred to General Thomas to have the history of his army written, but had it been his purpose from the beginning of his connection with it, in the organization and command of its first brigade, he could not have been more exhaustive in collecting the materials upon which it was based."[109]

As for the personal role that Thomas took with the project, the writer explained, "From the time the composition of the history was begun until his death, I was in constant communication with him, and he knew fully its scope and the pivotal facts which would constitute its framework and determine its purview." Van Horne observed that in the relatively short period remaining to him, Thomas availed himself of the opportunity "to examine and approve several completed chapters relating to campaigns and battles in which he was a prominent actor," although the writer did not specify which of these accounts Thomas reviewed.[110]

George Thomas had endured one of the most difficult periods of his life. He felt that the recognition he had earned not only failed to be forthcoming, but seemed to be positively ignored in the ways he perceived himself to be treated by official Washington. Yet, there was a genuine affection for those with whom he served, even if he often was unable to demonstrate such emotions publicly except under the most extraordinary circumstances. Only toward the men themselves was he able to express himself openly, and then it often appeared in an awkward, though genuine, form that the soldiery seemed to appreciate and those closest to him adored. Perhaps it was the sense of vulnerability that they recognized and found endearing in one who ought to have been the most supremely confident among them. The general, after all, as one of his aides had suggested, was both reticent and bighearted, neither characteristic seeming to overwhelm or outweigh the other, and yet both were present to more than one observer. Thomas, the quiet but resolute patriot, would find his nature further tested in the months to come as the nation transitioned from wartime to peace. It had already become a different kind of war from what he had experienced at Mill Springs or Chickamauga, Missionary Ridge or Nashville, and evolving circumstances were only going to compound that difference going forward.

15   An Exasperating Peace (May 1865–December 1866)

"I have required all commanding officers to keep their commands under good discipline and as a general rule I believe they have."
—Thomas on the African American troops under his command.

"The people of the States lately in rebellion are each day growing more and more insolent and threatening in their demeanor."
—Thomas to Grant, August 1866

If his earlier service, particularly at Chickamauga and Missionary Ridge, had not captured the popular imagination concerning George Henry Thomas, Nashville certainly did. Writers scrambled to present portraits of the general that assessed his character as well as his military career. In May 1865, *Harpers New Monthly Magazine* featured a large spread on the Virginian under "Recollections of Thomas." The writer, William Shanks, offered additional views on Thomas and others in a subsequent publication the following year, but the germ of his assessment first appeared here. Emphasizing Thomas's "deliberation" and "mature reflection," the writer stressed that the general uniformly thought before he spoke and embraced "exceedingly regular habits." One of these "habits" reflected his attention to detail and exhibited itself when straggling began to occur. "He has been known to halt in the march and spend ten or fifteen minutes in directing stragglers to their commands."[1]

In addition to the increased journalistic coverage, George Thomas was set to reappear on an important national stage. Plans were under way for a grand celebration that would feature veterans converging on the nation's capital from various points to participate in festivities that included speeches, reunions, and a grand review. Once these ceremonial tasks were complete, the soldiers often became tourists, visiting the important sites of a Washington, D.C., they had so valiantly defended through a bloody war. These would be the final official ceremonies for the volunteers who were preparing to be mustered out of the service. For Thomas and his men of the Fourteenth Corps, the most poignant of these exercises took place on June 3, when the troops gathered to bid their former commander adieu. Emotions were intense and the parting bittersweet, yet necessary for the men to return to their civilian lives and the professionals, like their esteemed general, to continue with their duties.[2]

As the exigencies of war subsided, the reorganization of the army also became a priority. Word filtered through to Thomas that he might have difficulty securing a role commensurate with his service and standing. For once, the professional soldier who disdained politicians recognized that he would be wise to seek help in every quarter. Just as he had gathered disparate forces on the ground to defeat Hood before Nashville, so he now sought aid to carry his personal battle to the halls of Washington if need be. Consequently, Thomas dispatched a subordinate to the nation's capital to take up his cause directly with President Andrew Johnson. As was typical of the Virginian when his patience had been tested, he informed the emissary that this would be a case of success or nothing. Either he would be suitably recognized through his appointment or there would be no need to attach his name to any recognition at all.

As things turned out, the Virginian needed no advocate, for when the officer representing Thomas's interests took up the issue with the chief executive, Johnson responded by pointing to the area of the South that stretched from Kentucky to Florida. "There is his military division." Then, drawing closer, he pointed out the town that Thomas had defended so valiantly and successfully against Hood and that Johnson himself had inhabited while war governor of Tennessee. "There are his headquarters," he observed of Nashville.[3] As much as the president could control such decisions, Thomas would have his command.

Alpheus Williams, who had served in Georgia with Thomas, wrote from "Near Washington, June 5th, 1865," that "our old commander of the Army of the Cumberland, is here." The men met briefly, and the Virginian inquired into his subordinate's interest in a command of "one of the Southern states." Thomas assured Williams of his high regard and promised to do what he could to secure a position. He had advocated for him to receive command of the Twentieth Corps during the 1864 campaign. There was a hint of the tension that had existed when Williams noted, "He did not doubt that Gen. Sherman had acted for what he supposed was in the best interests of the service, etc., etc."[4]

Williams considered Thomas to be an "officer of great purity and most devoted to his duties, so much so that for four years he has never left the field and never seen his family, until he went back to Nashville just before the battles with Hood." Word had filtered to Williams that Thomas had shared positive assessments of his performance during the campaign, and Williams deemed the compliments "an unsual thing to be heard by his staff, as he talks but little and seldom with his staff generally." Thomas was "here to see the President on special summons." Although the former subordinate hoped to serve once more under his chief, such was not to be the case.[5]

George Thomas and Andrew Johnson had already enjoyed a complex relationship that was both contentious and cooperative, as indicated by exchanges in Kentucky over an expected movement into East Tennessee early in the war and later with regard to the defense of Nashville. That complexity continued in the postwar period as the general and the president dealt with issues of persistent Confederate sympathy and questions of military versus civilian authority and racial antipathy versus equality. The president became exasperated with his field commander on several levels, including the personal one of a failure to protect Johnson's property in Greeneville, Tennessee, from vandalism and abuse. Thomas always responded to the pressure and queries with assurances that he would follow orders and fulfill his duties.[6]

As had been indicated informally, Thomas received notification from the War Department on June 7, 1865, that he was being given command of a new Division of the Tennessee, with headquarters in Nashville. The division consisted of five distinct departments, each commanded by a major general: the Department of Kentucky, based in Louisville, under John M. Palmer; Tennessee, under George Stoneman, with headquarters in Knoxville; Georgia, under James B. Steedman, operating out of Augusta; Alabama, headquartered in Mobile, under Charles R. Woods; and Florida, under Andrew A. Humphreys, with headquarters in Tallahassee.[7] Thomas's would be a broad geographic responsibility.

The new division commander enjoyed comfortable quarters and a measure of peace and quiet that must have been particularly welcome as the heat of summer threatened to engulf Nashville. A contemporary recalled, "His residence was in a block, and on every pleasant evening he and the other occupants of the same building were in the habit of sitting on the front stoop or porch to enjoy the cool pleasant breezes."[8]

There was also the pleasant diversion of plans that some of the officers were drawing up of honoring the Army of the Cumberland with a specially designed badge. Thomas did not expect such recognitions for himself, but he was zealous with regard to his men. This was especially true since, according to the resolutions supporting the act by a special committee, "many of the soldiers of the Army of the Cumberland are about to abandon the profession of arms and again mingle in the peaceful pursuits of home." The men had shared an association that bound them together inextricably, represented by this distinctive badge, which could be worn by anyone currently serving "and in good standing," or those who had received honorable discharges. An acceptable design quickly emerged that featured a five-pointed star with a triangle and an acorn in the center, connected by a red, white, and blue ribbon to a pin that would allow it to be affixed. The oval of the pin, featuring a laurel wreath, would carry the name "Army of the Cumberland."[9]

Thomas notified Secretary Stanton that he would shortly have the paperwork associated with the transfer from departmental to divisional status completed, although he wanted clarification from the War Department that Mississippi was included in his jurisdiction.[10] Early in the morning of the twenty-third Stanton sent Thomas a confirmation that assured him the "omission" of Mississippi constituted "a clerical mistake."[11] But matters were not destined to remain so simple for the soldier. Even as Thomas announced his new staff configuration, consultations in Washington were reaching a different conclusion with regard to the parameters of the Virginian's division.[12] Within a matter of days a high-level meeting occurred between Stanton and Grant that altered Thomas's area of authority. "I find that I was mistaken in the belief that the State of Mississippi formed part of your command." It was to go instead to General Sheridan "so as to give him command on both sides of the [Mississippi] river," he explained. "No other changes are made," Stanton concluded.[13]

General Orders No. 118 confirmed all of the new arrangements. Thomas would lead one of three new divisions, along with Generals George G. Meade (Atlantic), William T. Sherman (Mississippi), Philip H. Sheridan (Gulf), and Henry W. Halleck (Pacific). The Virginian's was "to embrace the Department of the Tennessee, Department of Kentucky, Department of Georgia, and Department of Alabama; headquarters at Nashville."[14] These assignments linked the principal commanders of the Union armies in the war in ways that reflected their prominence in the service and significance to the postwar army structure.

Duty soon took the commander of the Division of the Cumberland once again to Washington in answer to a summons for his presence there. Thomas had never been one for public self-promotion, or self-congratulations for that matter, and he was as reluctant a visitor this time as might have been expected by those who knew him best. He remained wary as he now heard superlatives personally from Secretary Stanton, who insisted, despite Thomas's previous questioning of it, that the confidence now being expressed toward him was genuine. "Nevertheless," Thomas retorted, "I have not been treated by the authorities as though they had confidence in me."[15]

Whatever Thomas may have felt of his treatment from the chief official of the War Department, he was unaware of the esteem being offered by a person with whom he had experienced occasional difficulties. On June 8, under the mistaken impression that Thomas was about to be transferred from the division, Governor William G. Brownlow communicated with President Johnson. "We are all sorry that the noble old Thomas is to leave us," he explained. "He is vastly popular with loyal men in Tennessee, and respected by rebels, for his ability, integrity, and manly bearing."[16] Another wartime friend of the president's made the same point, but with the knowledge that Thomas would be staying put. "I am glad Thomas is to remain," Lizzie Young observed. "He is Just. That is better than anything else."[17]

Governor Brownlow had made himself anathema in many circles, not only because of his agenda with regard to equality for former slaves, but due to an undisguised disgust toward former Confederates. The result was strong feeling against the Tennessee government as long as Brownlow held the reins of power. Still, Thomas thought that publicizing support from a fellow Southerner might help and implored the president to release his communications on the governor's behalf. He believed this statement would "do much good in satisfying many obtuse minds in this state [that] Gov. Brownlow is approved by you." In any case, no gesture could be too small, given the resistance that was beginning to grow in Tennessee. Thomas concluded rather ominously, "The Rebel element of this state is very restive under the present state of affairs."[18]

Additional public recognitions were also forthcoming for the soldier. The state legislature of Tennessee adopted a resolution on June 12, 1865, expressing satisfaction that Thomas was to be assigned to the military division that embraced the state. "That we do most heartily congratulate our citizens upon the appointment of this model soldier, possessing as we do the most unbounded confidence in his ability and judgment, and believing that under his rule, early peace and quiet and Unionism will prevail in every section of our State."[19]

The nature of these comments suggested a balanced view on the part of the Virginian in the aftermath of war. Undoubtedly because of his insistence upon the impartiality of the professional soldier and his practice that such views remain confined to private spheres, even relatively close compatriots could only speculate as to Thomas's positions on the politics of the day. Chaplain and biographer Thomas Van Horne described Thomas as having "entertained radical views of reconstruction" that aligned him "in sympathy with the higher aims and wisest measures of the Republican Party."[20] But the authors of the Tennessee resolution came closer to describing him accurately as a "model soldier" whose desire for "peace and quiet and Unionism" overrode all else. Unlike Thaddeus Stevens, George Thomas did not consider the Southern states to be "conquered provinces" that demanded vindictive punishment following their defeat. He differed from Charles Sumner in wanting to restore civilian governments without necessarily having considered them as having committed "state suicide" by virtue of secession and rebellion. Thomas hailed the rights of African Americans, but did not advocate the redistribution of plantation property on their behalf.[21] In short, he did not insist that Union authority had to come from a rifle barrel. But if a recalcitrant rebel had to go to jail, be denied opportunities for the unfettered expression of treasonous beliefs, or otherwise be held accountable for continuing to defy the realities of war or for endangering the lives and welfare of others, then so be it.

In any case, practical realties informed his decisions. Thomas found that the austerity measures he was suddenly being called upon to make greatly limited his ability to react to trouble spots with rapid and sufficient force. On July 17, Grant notified him that he was to phase out "all of the Cavalry in your Division that can be spared and [execute] the sale of their horses where they now are." Even some of the troopers who remained would find themselves unceremoniously dismounted if held for garrison duty and would have to submit to the auctioning of their mounts, too. "A very limited number of mounted men in each state is all that is necessary," Grant concluded from Washington, insisting that Thomas send him the numbers so affected.[22]

In August, the focus on belt-tightening measures intensified. General Grant stressed to Secretary of War Edwin Stanton his preference for Thomas to divest himself of cavalry, where the expenses being borne by the government included horses as well as riders.[23] From Galena, Illinois, Grant informed that general, "It is now the desire of the Government to reduce the military force of the Country and expenses of the Government, all that is possible." Thomas should promptly "muster out of service any organization you deem dispensable." Grant thought that the Virginian might be able to make do with two regiments of cavalry "for the whole State of Tennessee, and one for the rest of the division," although he did not believe Kentucky warranted any such force. The infantry could be culled as well, and African American troops could do the work in place of the men who thus left the service. Grant also suggested that the number of posts should be reduced, with the remaining men concentrated at the most likely locations "where they may be required either to suppress hostilities or to aid the civil laws."[24]

Thomas handled the situation as always, methodically, practically, and systematically. Instead of designating certain units for discharge arbitrarily, he communicated with his subordinate commanders and instructed them to provide him with reports of "the smallest number of white troops they can get along with."[25] From that point, decisions could be made that reflected the requirements commanders on the ground had determined for themselves. Such an approach had the twofold benefit of bringing these men into the discussion and of limiting the amount of difficulty that might be experienced when the number of troops under each declined. A commander could hardly complain as much, or at least as successfully, when he had provided the formula for the reduction in his area of authority himself.

Thomas also remained alert to other issues that were arising. It had disturbed him enormously that some Southern Whites did not seem prepared to accept the verdict of the war. But there was the less easily detected subterfuge of appearing to exhibit contrition under false pretenses. A case in point concerned John Overton, a Tennessean with extensive landholdings who had found refuge behind Confederate lines during the war, but now wanted to return to his property. Overton's attempt to take the "oath of allegiance" as an indication of his good faith ran into difficulty with General Thomas. The general questioned the sincerity of the act, in part due to its taking place in Kentucky rather than in Overton's home state of Tennessee. The Southern landowner pleaded his case to President Johnson. "I took it in good faith," he argued of the oath, "and so help me God I intend hereafter to be governed by it." Overton insisted that he had not acted in Kentucky "under any apprehension that I would not be allowed to take it at Nashville, or with any intention of treating the Comg. Genl. here [Thomas] disrespectfully."[26] Advocates for Overton continued to bring the case to the president's attention and ultimately proved successful in obtaining satisfaction for him.[27]

Two factors appeared to have rankled Thomas regarding the Overton case. The first of these was the taking of the oath in a state where the sworn party was not a resident. For Thomas this was not a matter of technicality, it was one of propriety. There were important measures and appropriate procedures for which no shortcuts or exceptions could be tolerated. The second was that such oaths of allegiance were meant to be taken seriously, not as pro forma steps for the purpose of securing personal benefits. Thomas revealed something of his position on such grounds when he warned a subordinate "to look sharp for these pretended pardoned Rebels."[28]

Thomas spent a portion of the busy summer reorganizing his new department. The shift in personnel brought individuals through Nashville for instructions and consultations. Benjamin Grierson was one of the soldiers who passed through on his way to New Orleans and a new assignment as commander of the cavalry in Louisiana. He had expected to be under General Canby, but learned that he would now answer to Thomas under the new configuration. While he regretted what appeared to be a reduction in his responsibilities, Grierson recalled a most pleasant evening with the Virginian. "I found the general looking healthy and vigorous, and like all other officers who had taken an active part in the war, greatly rejoiced at its close." Grierson and Thomas shared dinner and a conversation that the subordinate observed "was extremely agreeable."[29]

Such pleasantries could not mask the concern that remained for securing ample forces to maintain order. From Nashville, Thomas directed a communiqué that sounded an almost desperate tone for the usually sure-handed and cool-headed commander. "Your telegram of the 4th instant [is] just received, directing the withdrawal of the negro troops from East

Tennessee," he explained to President Johnson. "I have given the necessary orders but have to report that I have no white troops to send to East Tennessee to preserve the peace." Thomas wanted it understood that strict compliance to instructions was one thing, implementation of them another. "Complaints reach me almost daily of difficulty between the returned Rebels and loyal citizens either in defiance of the civil authorities or that the civil authority is inefficient or does not act." The latter concerned him most, for it amounted to complicity in tolerating, if not outwardly supporting, acts of civil disobedience among the population. To further complicate the situation, many of the white troops "are clamorous to be mustered out of service," and thus were likely not to prove to be a meaningful answer for Thomas in any crisis.[30]

Secretary Stanton underscored the Virginian's position in such endeavors in a communication with President Johnson. Offering his "observations," the secretary of war noted, "That in Genl. Thomas's command, and wherever there is any loyal sentiment, there appears to be no difficulty in regard to the presence of colored troops—complaint being confined chiefly to the most rebellious States—South Carolina and Mississippi."[31] Stanton's characterizations of two former Confederate states did not reflect the similar sentiments that existed elsewhere. Thomas's reference to East Tennessee and earlier concerns about Rome, Georgia, and Alabama, suggested that at least in pockets, these states could prove problematic for him as well.

President Johnson was also anxious to see that civil law and authority received respect, whatever political persuasions might exist otherwise. He knew that words alone would not be enough and sought stronger measures to support state governments. "I hope that you will have it understood that whatever amount of military force is necessary to sustain the Civil authority and enforce the law, will be furnished," Johnson explained to Thomas. But he need not have worried on that count, for the Virginian was a firm believer in law and order and was more than willing to do his part in maintaining it. Johnson thought that the mere possibility of military intervention might serve to "exert a powerful influence throughout the State" and prevent the necessity of calling upon it at the same time.[32] Thomas could hardly have agreed with such a position more and stood ready to implement his commander in chief's orders to that effect as he always did.

The general's concerns had been as ever of a practical nature. He wanted to do what he could to ensure that he had the means of accomplishing whatever mission might be assigned to him without challenging legitimate civil authority or worsening tensions between the former adversaries. The response his communication from Washington generated suggested that the president did not see matters in the same way. Johnson placed the onus for potential trouble on the same black troops Thomas wanted to utilize to keep the peace. Johnson's answer was to muster out the African American troops if "there are too many of them in the service," a point that Thomas had not raised. Johnson revealed his largest concern by noting that if difficulty came, "it is feared that the colored troops, so great in number, could not be controlled." Once more, the president intimated, the problem was not with the returning rebels, but with "mischevious persons, acting as Emissaries, inciting the Negro population to acts of violence, revenge, and insurrection." Johnson wanted this aspect "carefully looked to" and trusted that in doing so, "all conflict between whites and blacks should be avoided as far as practicable." To the man who had seen so much difficulty from those who persisted in defying the government, the president's next observation must have produced incredulity, if not dismay. "There would be no danger of this kind if this description of persons could be expelled from the country— whose business it is to excite and originate discontent between the races."

President Johnson openly considered expanding Thomas's jurisdiction and argued that the Virginian was one of the few who might be able to "renew their former relations with the Federal Gov't." Then, with a politician's stroke of vanity toward the esteemed warrior, he added, "You can do much in the consummation of this great end." As if that were not enough to win Thomas's support and assistance, Johnson asserted, "The whole South has confidence in you, & any move you make in that direction, will inspire confidence & encourage them in the work they have undertaken."[33]

The day after receiving the president's communication, Thomas replied with one by which he undoubtedly hoped to dampen the concerns relating to racial conflict and the deportment of the black troops under his command. The chief executive need not worry on the first count, he noted: "I do not believe that there is the least foundation for fearing an insurrection" or any other difficulty from the the black troops who remained in the service. "As a general rule the negro Soldiers are under good discipline," he explained, but these demands were true of anyone in uniform under him. "I have required all commanding officers to keep their commands under good discipline and as a general rule I believe they have."

Thomas expected the men in his command and the officers with authority over them to perform as duty required, but he genuinely believed that potential difficulties lay elsewhere. "I believe in the majority of cases of collision between whites and negro Soldiers that the white man has attempted to bully the negro, for it is exceedingly repugnant to the [white] Southerners to have negro Soldiers in their midst & some are so foolish as to vent their anger upon the negro because he is a Soldier." His own early experiences in a slaveholding society offered him insight into such views and behaviors. Now he was seeing fresh evidence of the difficulties created from a transitioning world.

Thomas realized that race played a factor in both North and South. White troops serving under him often held antagonistic views toward the blacks who served with them. That fact, and the positions expressed by the president on questions of race, further complicated matters. But as he always sought to do, Thomas searched for the path that would simultaneously allow him to fulfill his obligations to the country and follow the most pragmatic course. "I have always endeavored to observe a just & concilia-tory course towards the people of the States within my command & believe they are as a mass Satisfied." He had seen enough of human nature to know that there would always be malcontents. Such "evil-minded persons" were "always ready to misrepresent and exaggerate every event however trifling that does not in some manner benefit them."[34] By mid-September, Thomas was able to report that he had moved well toward accomplishing his mission. "All the white Vol troops in Ky and Ten., are being mustered out." At the same time, he had "ordered the Black troops concentrated, at the most convenient points to meet emergencies," as Grant had directed.[35]

Grant had promised a visit with Thomas in Nashville on his way back to Washington, and the Virginian replied inquiring if the army commander planned to do so before the end of September. "If Not," he explained, "I desire to go to N. York to bring my wife out to Nashville which will take 2 weeks."[36] Grant was so pleased with the dispositions Thomas had assured him he was carrying out that he decided not to stop in Nashville and added, "You are authorized to go to New York at your pleasure."[37]

It was during this period that issues of a more ecumenical nature came to General Thomas's attention. Perhaps it was inevitable that strong-willed persons would clash in the still-heated atmosphere of the months following the Civil War. Thomas expected that with the close of active hostilities any reasonable individual would happily embrace peace. Thus, he was surprised, and not a little perturbed, when Reverend Richard Wilmer, bishop of the Episcopal Church in Alabama, used his position to make a statement regard-ing current political realities. Wilmer had undertaken his office in the early days of the existence of the Confederate States and maintained strong sympathies for that cause.[38] He had already come under fire for adhering to the liturgical requirements of the Episcopal Church in the South that substituted "Confederate States" for "United States" and stipulated the same for prayers traditionally offered for those in political authority. The reaction included the use of Union troops to shut down offending churches.[39]

At the end of the war, Wilmer maintained that although "the God of battles" had "given his decision against us" and it was no longer necessary for the clergy to offer prayers to a Confederate president, he could not forgo the instructions by which he felt bound. Conveniently, that interpretation meant that until revisions occurred in the language of the liturgy, he construed that omitting prayers for the president of the United States was perfectly acceptable. Wilmer professed only to be interested in religious matters, but the bishop was not troubled by the political undertones of the message either. Thomas considered these instructions to be "utterly incongruous under the present state of affairs" and suspended Bishop Wilmer.[40]

The matter was not so much one of tackling constitutional issues such as freedom of expression or freedom of religion as it was what he deemed to be the irresponsible behavior of a public figure from a respected profession. Acting as he was contrary to the public interests, Wilmer was forfeiting his right to espouse his views in Thomas's opinion. The soldier himself had subordinated his personal views and any partisan positions he might harbor for the good of the service and expected the cleric to exhibit the same restraint and decorum. When Wilmer could not, Thomas believed that he had no alternative but to intervene by suspending him and closing offending churches.

Thomas did not handle recalcitrance well, and his reaction to it in this case matched his degree of impatience and disdain. In the aftermath of his successful assault on Missionary Ridge, the Virginian had confronted the notion of desertion in the Confederate ranks and the manner in which such men should be treated. Among other possibilities, he had concluded that some of these men were similar to "the drunkard to his bottle," in that they lacked "sufficient moral firmness to resist the natural depravity of their hearts." This was the bishop's greatest crime, as Thomas saw it, for the minister continued to encourage the weaknesses in those susceptible to the poor example he set for them. Rather than help his wayward brethren wean themselves from the bottle of rebellion, the prelate seemed anxious to encourage them to continue to drink. The Virginian had acted to squelch the problem at the source. The dilemma for Thomas was that now he had to deal with the backlash that came from those who saw his measures as extreme.[41]

Finally, three days before Christmas 1865, Thomas issued General Orders No. 40 from Nashville. He maintained that in variance with President Johnson's wishes for reconciliation based upon a respect for the government and its representatives, "an individual, styling himself Bishop of Alabama, forgetting his mission to preach peace on earth and good will towards man," propagated the instructions that omitted the president from Episcopal prayers on the basis that he could not do so as long as military rule prevailed. As such, the cleric had taken advantage "of the sanctity of his position to mislead the minds" of his followers and "attempted to lead them back into the labyrinths of treason." These were the reasons that he had been stripped of authority, and only the fact that so many of his fellow citizens were seeking to "reinstate civil authority" and "repudiate their acts of hostility during the past four years" allowed Thomas to reconsider the punishment imposed. In removing the restrictions, the soldier insisted that he took satisfaction in having left the bishop to the "remorse of conscience." Wilmer could boast that he had prevailed over the hosts of error, but on Christmas Day he reversed his position and instructed the clergy to pray on behalf of the president of the United States.[42]

A later account of the collision between Bishop Wilmer and General Thomas posited the notion that the common ingredient of Virginia birth lay at the heart of the matter for the two men. William Stevens Perry insisted in his history of the American Episcopal Church written in the mid-1880s that the military officer had exhibited the "peculiar bitterness of feeling which is commonly exhibited in family feuds." Despite the distance of two decades, emotions remained taut for the writer. Stevens felt that in Bishop Wilmer's case General Thomas "assumed a judicial right to interpret the canons of the Church, a more than episcopal right to enforce them, and an entirely papal prerogative of discipline." Of course, George Thomas had no intention of establishing or interpreting church canon. But, he insisted that pulpits were not the appropriate places for engaging in politically motivated nuance, especially when it came to Wilmer's insistence that he would encourage the resumption of the appropriate prayers "as soon as civil authority should be restored" to Alabama.[43]

In the midst of the Wilmer controversy, Thomas demonstrated his consistency by applying similar expectations and standards to a religious tiff in Georgia. John H. Caldwell had gotten himself in trouble with the Methodist powers in the state when he condemned the institution of slavery from the pulpit. In this instance, Thomas stepped in to bring relief to the minister for his dismissal over the incident. Once again, irate correspondence reached President Johnson on the subject, but this time the president left the matter to his general to resolve. Thomas did not indicate if he thought his measures had been sufficient to make his point, but he pressed this particular matter no further.[44]

Much more pleasant developments awaited Thomas in Nashville as the anniversary of his battle against Hood approached. The Tennessee General Assembly tendered its official thanks and called for the fashioning of a special "Gold Medal" to be struck "in commemoration of the great and decisive event," whose central features would include a bust of the general on one side and the state capitol on the other. Crowning the state building would be the words that the Virginian had used at Chattanooga and made immortal for the Union cause in Tennessee: "I will hold the town till we starve."[45]

But even with such moments to savor, at least in his quiet way, Thomas still had much work to do. On December 12, 1865, he reported to Secretary of War Stanton concerning a recent tour through his division. The general had returned to Nashville after stopovers in Mississippi, Alabama, and Georgia. "The prevailing sentiment seems to be a desire to restore the rebel States to their old relations and functions," he explained of the attitude he found awaiting him there. But Thomas knew that simmering beneath the surface was a discontent with the outcome of the recent conflict that would take longer to resolve. He saw this attitude reflected in the ways in which "many of the people are unfriendly to the people of the loyal States, and to those who have continued loyal to the Government of the United States in the South." Thomas took a hands-on approach in Mississippi, meeting with the individuals who would take the reins of power and encouraging them to "cooperate cordially together."

Thomas was even more pleased with the actions of the legislative body of Alabama. "The people of Alabama are either more practical or more loyal than the Mississippians," he observed. "The Legislature is a dignified body, and seems ready to meet the emergency and to act on the various questions presented fully, and seems sincerely desirous of the reconstruction" of their state, "in complete harmony with the policy of the President." But if Alabama politicians could be reconciled, there remained important pockets of defiance that were as yet untouched from Thomas's perspective, with special reference to the Wilmer incident. "The last symptom of open rebellion in Alabama is exhibited by the self-styled Bishop of Alabama and the women."[46]

Not everyone connected with the South tried Thomas's patience in this regard. Only a short time earlier he had received a communication concerning a group of "Union men" who had held a meeting in Lexington, Kentucky, that passed a resolution supporting the policies of the president and calling for a military force to remain in the state so as to prevent a resurgence of Confederate sympathizers. The expression of loyalty must have been most welcome at a time when so much rhetoric seemed to be taking a very different tone.[47]

Perhaps Thomas's experiences with recalcitrant Southern sympathizers intensified his desire to ensure that the story of his command be told. Only a day after he lifted his edict against Wilmer, the Virginian wrote an old commander, Don Carlos Buell, from his Nashville headquarters. "As I have been with this Army from its organization to the end of the war I feel it to be especially my duty to arrange the official papers so that an impartial history can be written, believing that when the work is done that its Record will be second to that of no other army engaged in the recent struggle."[48] Reminiscences of the achievements of these men on past battlefields surely softened the onerous duties he now faced in peacetime.

George Thomas ended 1865 in sessions with a committee of the Thirty-ninth Congress anxious to discover the nature of conditions in the postwar South. The Virginian was one of a relatively few general officers to provide testimony. He assessed Tennessee as deserving readmission to the Union because "that State, on her own accord, has complied with every instruction of the President, and has done all that it was believed it would be necessary for her to do in order to gain admission into Congress." Furthermore, Thomas offered, the acceptance of Tennessee back into the national political fold could serve as a valuable model for other states to follow.[49]

The balance between civil and military authority remained a delicate one even if the line that separated them seemed clear enough to George Thomas. Cases constantly cropped up that placed the two elements at odds with each other, and increasingly the general had less resources with which to make an impact on developments as they arose. Understandably many of the volunteers who had risked their lives and sacrificed so much to win the war were anxious to return to their homes and their civilian lives. A military system that no longer needed to sustain major armies in the field at taxpayer expense was only too glad to oblige.

At a point during this legislative session, Thomas made the rounds himself, including acceding to pressure from friends to appear before the United States House of Representatives. The Virginian's well-known reticence at such public occasions did not prevent him from attending, but kept him from finding much personal joy in the experience. "He was escorted to the Speaker's desk, and received from all the most enthusiastic greeting," one account contended. But House Speaker Schuyler Colfax would later say of the ordeal: "I noticed as he stood beside me that his hand trembled like an aspen leaf." The politician concluded of the soldier, "He could bear the shock of battle, but shrank before the storm of applause."[50]

In his report for 1866, Thomas noted that the year opened with a command, designated the Military Department of the Tennessee, which consisted of the states of Kentucky, Tennessee, Georgia, Alabama, and Mississippi. The sprawling area contained numerous important towns and rail centers. Thomas distinguished between the areas he expected to have difficulty controlling and those that ought to pose fewer problems, but developments would contest his generally optimistic view.

Compounding the matter of command and control for the general was the increasingly limited pool of manpower available to him. For the state of Kentucky, the only one under his jurisdiction that had remained in the Union, he set his number of effectives at 3,121. The former Confederate state of Tennessee held 8,908, Georgia 2,429, Alabama 7,000, and Mississippi 4,224. Altogether, these numbers amounted to 25,682, still "mostly Volunteers, white and colored," and a combination that seemed far from adequate to cover the wide geographical scope over which they had to operate. These limited troop totals alone would have given many commanders pause, but Thomas faced even more upheavals as additional volunteers left the service and shrank the pool of troops to less than what had been available in Mississippi alone at the beginning of the year. The conversion of army property to other agencies as cost-cutting measures went into effect promised only to complicate matters even more.

Outside of the internal adjustments expected of him in his department, Thomas could sense a much different type of war than the one in which he had only recently engaged. "At the beginning of the year 1866 the feeling of the people in the States comprising my Department was more that of disappointment in the realization of the hopes they had of establishing a Confederacy, than of real love for the Supreme Power of the land, they were tired of war, and seeing the bitter results of their error, were willing to accept the situation of affairs and endeavored with more or less good will to recover all they could from the wreck surrounding them."

Lawmakers in the "respective Legislatures" had "complied with the requirements of Congress with a view to the Reconstruction of the State Governments, lately in Rebellion." But Thomas also began to identify a worrisome fracture that could unravel any progress before it fairly got started. On the one hand, "in more educated communities peace and order reigned to a great extent." However on the other, "in unsettled districts, lawless characters were at large oppressing the freedmen, persecuting and murdering Union-men, threatening those who had lately emigrated from the North to settle in their midst." Most disturbing of all, instead of responding, the civil authorities "seemed either unwilling or incompetent to act in suppressing violence and depredation."[51]

Thomas had much to consider as the year 1866 opened. Ulysses Grant wanted Thomas, along with Generals Sherman and Meade, to hasten to the nation's capital "with as little delay as practicable."[52] Grant had imperatives of his own. In addition to reconfiguring the army for its new peacetime status, he had to watch closely any pending legislation that might come from Congress. The meeting of the veteran army commanders was meant for just such a purpose.[53]

On the first of February, after reading and discussing proposed Senate legislation, Grant forwarded to Senator Henry Wilson of Massachusetts the amended document, "which you were kind enough to submit to me for such remarks as I might wish to make on it." He included the interlined comments of "three Major Generals of the Regular Army, distinguished for their services in the field, Maj. Generals Sherman, Meade and Thomas." Grant also indicated his concurrence with their assessments.[54] At his behest, the three major generals also authored a detailed description of their responses and suggested modifications to the bills to Brigadier General John

A. Rawlins, so that the army would have a record of their proceedings. All combined, the effort represented an impressive collection of wisdom and military experience.[55]

While the three veteran army officers remained in Washington, Grant availed himself of their assistance in other matters, too. New and improved infantry accoutrements and equipment for the troops required testing in the field. Grant signaled his request for Thomas to receive one thousand sets of these items for his command, among the five thousand to be distributed, "in order that their merits may be thoroughly tested by actual service in the field."[56]

Guarding the army's interests through the labyrinth of Washington, D.C., and keeping the troops in the field amply equipped were time-consuming efforts. But other developments were taking place that required attention as well. Throughout the early part of the year, requests went out from officials in at least two states for the withdrawal of Federal troops from them. General Grant was inclined to defer such matters on the grounds that the civil authorities were not prepared to "execute the laws and good order." Grant informed President Johnson in reference to Mississippi, "When however the civil authorities prove themselves amply sufficient to fairly and justly execute the laws among all her citizens and to perpetuate their loyalty, the troops will not be permitted to interfere in civil matters."[57]

These policy directives also applied to Thomas and his command. Already the governor of Alabama had requested assistance from the Federal government in arming the state militia in anticipation of the departure of the regulars. Thomas passed along his endorsement to Grant. The Virginian seemed to believe the pledge that Governor Robert M. Patton had made to use the weapons only in "Sustaining the laws, and Constitution of the state of Alabama and of the Federal Union." But in addition to documenting the official's assurance "that these arms shall be used solely for the maintenance of equal justice to all classes in the state and to sustain the authority of the United States," Thomas appended an important caveat. "I further recommend the withdrawal of the troops from the interior of the state as soon as there can be a perfect understanding between the Freedmens Bureau and the Civil authorities as to the civil rights and duties of the Freedman."[58]

Grant accepted the general principle that Thomas had espoused for Alabama, but he altered the timetable for its implementation. Federal troops would remain for now, "until there is full security for equitably maintaining the right[s] and safety of all classes of citizens in the states lately in rebellion." Reductions in troop levels might occur, but enough men should be left in place to "insure tranquility should be retained," and for the time being, it was best not to supply the state forces with arms.[59]

From his headquarters in Chattanooga, one officer brought a case to the attention of President Johnson. Several men had been accused of murder and subjected to a court-martial. All except two of these individuals received acquittals on the grounds that they had been following orders at the time. The two officers were slated to be hanged when the commander of the department, George Stoneman, intervened. But no sooner had the men in question mustered out of the service than civilian authorities stepped in, rearrested all, and sent some of them to jail. The incarcerated men appealed to Thomas "on the ground of having been already tried for the offence," and the Union general apparently agreed. He ordered the sheriff to have the men released, but that officer refused. A detail sent to accomplish the same task met with some 100 men, who prevented them from carrying out their orders, and only the dispatch of a larger force completed the task.[60]

In April the issue was reversed, with an individual's case dispensed through a military tribunal when it should have been left to the civilian process, if any process at all, according to the complainant. The defendant was a newspaperman and railroader from Louisville, and the issue over which he was being charged was his failure to adhere to an army contract. Judge Bland Ballard maintained to the president that "Neither the certificate nor the orders of Gen. Thomas show any cause for the arrest or detention of [Isham] Henderson, nor that he is guilty of any offence subject to military jurisdiction—nor, indeed, that, he is guilty of any offence whatsoever." Thomas subsequently suspended the military proceedings and bound Henderson over to civilian control.[61]

Thomas had been operating under the assumption that those Southern whites who accepted the outcome of the struggle should be left alone while those who insisted upon continuing to demonstrate resistance should be dealt with more severely. He allowed common sense to determine when transgressions were inadvertent, but did his best to limit even those. Thomas was particularly cognizant of the sacrifices men in Union service had endured to obtain victory, and more than a part of his sensitivity on such issues related to honoring those fallen comrades. He knew that soldiers slain in battle often had not received the benefit of interment where their final resting places could be cared for and watched appropriately. On February 13, 1866, his office released orders in which he admonished those engaged in agricultural pursuits to take care not to "mutilate or obliterate the traces of such graves" in the course of their planting and ploughing.[62] The goal was clearly not to deprive Southern farmers of their livelihoods or peaceful farming pursuits, but to ensure the proper respect for Union war dead.

Thomas's focus on appropriate treatment for the fallen dated to his efforts in that regard just after the fighting at Chattanooga, Tennessee, had ended in 1863. He now continued that program by ordering the establishment of a national cemetery near Pittsburg Landing on a portion of the ground over which the combatants had contended in April 1862. He had arrived too late to participate in the main portion of that engagement, but his attachment to the field and to the men themselves was undiminished by the lack of a significant role in the fighting there.[63]

Remembering soldier sacrifice was an important legacy of the conflict, but in many ways a reunited country had to find ways to move forward rather than just looking back. A reordering of the apparatus for waging war was also becoming more of a necessity. On April 10, the headquarters for the division released General Orders No. 8 requiring all commissary, quartermaster, and ordnance stores "not required for the immediate use of the troops" be forwarded to the respective authorities for disposition. In a sign that the full-scale mobilization of wartime was no longer considered to be either necessary or financially expedient, the instructions also called for the identification of surplus staff officers for mustering out of the service.[64]

Thomas was committed fully to scaling the military structure back to something much closer to a peacetime configuration, but he knew that in the aftermath of the type of destructive war the nation had just experienced more would have to be done to get the defeated South in a position to restore its viability as a region. In May 1866, the Virginian did something that might have ordinarily seemed anathema to him: he accepted an elected office. In this case, the position, which he obtained, was as president of the Colonial and Immigration Society, whose charge and charter from the state legislature called for "its object [to be] the promotion of immigration to Tennessee." The organization's vice president was Thomas's compatriot, R. W. Johnson, although neither he nor any of the other of the general's future biographers mentioned the organization or its success or lack thereof.[65]

Certainly, Tennessee could benefit from those who wanted to settle in the state and add to its productivity and economic advancement, but the transitional period that Southerners, white and black, were undergoing was also fraught with fear and uncertainty. It increasingly began to look as if it would entail violence. Early in the month of May, Memphis, Tennessee, erupted in disorder that lasted for several days. A seemingly petty incident unleashed pent-up frustrations and racial hostilities among Memphians when a collision on the street and subsequent attempts at arrest generated a volatile reaction. For several days, white laborers and policemen clashed with discharged black soldiers and their families, with city officials either unwilling or unable to exert control or openly advocating violence. The streets of the river town erupted in paroxysms of shooting and burning that left forty-six black and two white citizens dead, as well as resulting in substantial property destruction.[66]

In the aftermath of the outburst, General Grant instructed Thomas to have the local commander obtain information concerning "the principal actors in the late disgraceful Memphis riots" so that arrests could be made at an appropriate time.[67] Later in the year, the Virginian issued a report that lay responsibility squarely on one faction. "On the 1st of May at Memphis an outbreak occurred," he explained, "occasioned by an assault of the base white population on the colored people." When the mayor turned to Major General George Stoneman, commander of the Department of Tennessee, headquartered in the city, "for the assistance of the troops to quell the riot," that officer became involved in the situation. Thomas maintained rather simplistically, "Military assistance was furnished and in co-operation with the police force, restored order."[68] But, in fact, with a minimal number of troops at his disposal and the racial composition of the force itself to consider, there was little that Stoneman could do until the wave of violence and destruction subsided.[69]

Just at the time that it began to appear that more troops would be needed to attend to disturbances and protect vulnerable citizens, Thomas faced his lowest numbers to meet those needs. The last volunteer organization, the Fifth Colored Heavy Artillery, mustered out of service on May 20, and Thomas was left with "an entire force at my disposal numbered [at] only 4047 men." Although these men constituted regulars, mostly in the form of infantry, they were of necessity widely scattered. A detachment of cavalry remained in Nashville, a central location from which the commander could dispatch them wherever they might be required. But Thomas's fraction could easily find the situation beyond their capabilities.

Whatever irritation he might have experienced from the unhappy Tennessee solons, Thomas became even more exasperated with the state of affairs in the South generally. With that motivation, he apparently considered a radical proposal of his own. If incentive could help create more amenable conditions, then why not use it to treat white Southerners as in a very real sense they had insisted they be treated when they advocated secession and independence: make them reapply for American citizenship. "Genl Thomas thinks that all the inhabitants of the Southern States should be declared by act of Congress aliens [and] that those who could establish their loyalty should be admitted to citizenship at once, that all others with a few designated exceptions should be compeled to take the ordinary course of naturalization in the same manner as foreigners." The individual who informed President Johnson of the proposal thought it unwise on several grounds, not the least of which being that those affected would have more reason for hostility toward the government and the country. "Why keep a wound open five years that can be sooner healed[?]" he observed. "Would the southern people of the south come back to their duties with any better feeling after a five years punishment[?]"[70] It is difficult to say what the context of the discussion had been that prompted Thomas to divulge such views. But his idea was no doubt born more from frustration than anything else.

The Virginian handled the situation as best he could by insisting upon clear instructions and following what largely amounted to a noninterference policy championed by President Andrew Johnson. Another racially based confrontation challenged that philosophy in New Orleans in July.[71] It must have looked to many like a continuation of what had recently occurred in Memphis and now might happen at any point throughout the former Confederacy.

In the wake of increased violent activity, General Grant issued General Orders No. 44, on July 6, 1866. It stated unequivocally that "Commanders in the States lately in rebellion are hereby directed to arrest all persons who have been or may hereafter be charged with the commission of crimes and offences against officers, agents, citizens and inhabitants of the United States, irrespective of color, in cases where the civil authorities have failed, neglected, or are unable [to act]." Lest there be any misinterpretation of the imperative, Grant added at the close, "A strict and prompt enforcement of this order is required."[72] Far from being viewed negatively, these were the type of peremptory orders that Thomas desired so that he could be sure that he was adhering to the policies and procedures of the army and the government.

Grant immediately set about the implementation of these orders. On the same day that he announced General Orders No. 44, Grant directed Thomas to send several companies of cavalry to be based in Memphis, where they could be dispatched more easily to the northern portion of Mississippi. "The object to be attained is to suppress violence that is now being committed by outlawry in North Mississippi," Grant explained. "If the Civil Authorities fail to make arrests for past violence let the troops make them and hold the parties in confinement until they, the Civil Authorities, give satisfactory evidence that justice will be done, or until you receive orders more clearly defining the course to be pursued."[73]

Closer to his own area of responsibility, General Thomas confronted a resistance of a different kind. In order to thwart radical measures a number of state legislators in Tennessee deliberately absented themselves in a parliamentary procedure to deny the body sufficient numbers for a quorum. Thomas hastily wired Grant concerning the gambit on July 14, informing him, "Some of the members of the House of Representatives of the Tennessee General assembly conduct themselves in a very refractory manner." Their efforts at obstruction were serious enough that Governor William G. "Parson" Brownlow had turned to the Army for assistance. "Shall I furnish it?" Thomas inquired.[74]

Gideon Welles was in a cabinet meeting when the word arrived. "Stanton read a strange dispatch from Gen. George H. Thomas at Nashville, stating that some of the Tennessee members of the legislature would not attend the sessions and asking if he should not arrest them." Welles noted in his diary entry that President Johnson impatiently replied to the request by observing, "if General Thomas had nothing else to do but to intermeddle in local controversies, he had better be detached and ordered elsewhere."[75]

The president's exasperation could not translate into action for his subordinate in Nashville because of the time that had already elapsed since his initial communication, but Secretary of War Stanton sent Grant explicit instructions to pass on to Thomas that reflected the continued reluctance that existed in official circles for the United States Army to play such an active role in state affairs. "The administration of the laws and the preservation of the peace in Nashville belong properly to the State Authorities and the duty of the United States forces is not to interfere in any controversy between the political authorities of the State; and General Thomas will strictly abstain from any interference between them."[76]

Grant's telegraphic reply consisted only of one sentence based upon the instructions he gleaned from the message he had received from the secretary of war. "The facts stated in your despatch of the Fourteenth do not warrant the interference of Military authority." Grant must also not have thought that additional elaboration was necessary.[77] Ironically, the pace of martial bureaucracy proved beneficial to Brownlow's contingent, permitting in the interim the detention of two legislators and the establishment of a quorum that allowed the body to conduct its business.[78]

Historian Brooks Simpson has postulated that these circumstances provided an indication that Thomas was "afraid as usual to act on his own."[79] He insisted not only that the Virginian failed to show "initiative" but that "Grant was often embarrassed by his requests for advice, which served only to alert Johnson to a delicate situation."[80] Grant certainly did not seem "embarrassed" by Thomas's requests for clarification in July 1866, when it appeared that regional difficulties might require the employment of Federal troops. In this instance, Grant's orders left more than enough room for Thomas to await further orders before taking action that might be judged precipitous.

As an individual who had trained his whole life to follow the chain of command, Thomas exhibited less a fear to act than a hesitation to act without the appropriate authority and risk censure for his independence or recklessness. The Virginian felt that his actions ought to include an adherence to the Constitution and obedience to the Federal government and did what he could to promote these tenets. He was less sensitive than others about alienating white Southerners in the process. With the heat of summer in the South intensifying, the overall situation was also becoming increasingly volatile. "The people of the States lately in rebellion are each day growing more and more insolent and threatening in their demeanor," he explained to Grant in August 1866, "as they find themselves relieved from punishment by military authorities." Then, he added the assurance, "No troops will be furnished unless some overt act be committed, when the parties committing it will be arrested and held for trial under General Orders No. 44."[81]

At the same time, Thomas experienced another shift in the order of things regarding his division. On August 6, 1866, the War Department issued General Orders No. 59 that changed the status of Thomas's command from a division to a department, although, as he later explained, "the territory embraced therein remaining unchanged in extent."[82] He had based his headquarters at Nashville, Tennessee, but now shifted to Louisville, Kentucky. Thomas took a brief leave of absence, using it to travel in the North and to tour Canada as well. In the meantime, his staff completed the transfer of his official papers so that he would be prepared to assume his new duties when he returned from his trip.[83]

If the maps did not change appreciably with the new designation, the attitudes of some of the commanders were undergoing an evolution. Grant sounded a great deal like George Thomas when he observed of Reconstruction, "The best way, I think, to secure a speedy termination of military rule, is to execute all the laws of Congress in the spirit in which they were conceived, firmly but without passion." That combination of being firm without allowing emotion to get in the way was exactly the manner in which Thomas consistently operated with regard to his public discourse and actions. Underneath the surface there was a much stronger tendency toward passion than Thomas generally allowed others to see, but ultimately both he and Grant agreed that military force, or at least the threat of it, remained a necessary component of life in the postwar South.[84]

Thomas continued to tread carefully on a line between civil and military authority. When complaints found their ways to his desk, his first inclination was to seek approval for any action he might take rather than act independently. One of the by-products of Nashville and the period that followed was that Thomas now adhered closely to the course prescribed for him. Deviations from the expectations of those in authority had left him hammered and battered, even when the situation had played out as desired. Still, the current circumstances were murky at best as to which authority in the national government to follow. As one historian of the army's role in Reconstruction observed, "During 1866, as at other times during Reconstruction, the fact that local conditions varied from place to place and over periods of time made it difficult for Washington to formulate general instructions for the field commanders."[85] The lack of clear instructions ran counter to the Virginian's preferred mode of operation. "System and method are absolutely necessary to Thomas's existence," explained one contemporary.[86] But the system that was in place was dysfunctional.

One point of clarity finally emerged in the latter part of 1866. Generated initially by Andrew Johnson on April 2, but disseminated through General Orders No. 84 on October 4, a presidential proclamation declared the "insurrection" of the Confederate States to be "at an end, and is henceforth to be so regarded."[87] The order had the effect of rendering military action on behalf of Unionists more problematic. Thus, when a Mississippi planter sought to protect his black workers by arming them, Thomas insisted that he ought to follow a more conventional path. Vigilantism, even in the cause of justice, amounted to a state of chaos that the Virginian could not tolerate, much less condone. He would certainly not allow depredations to intimidate him or prevent him from taking necessary measures to prevent them from occurring or to punish the perpetrators. But there were reasonable and legitimate ways to demonstrate the "firmness and discretion" that he called on those beset by violence and threats to exhibit.[88]

Among the most pressing matters continued to be lawless disturbances, often associated with guerrilla bands or other extralegal organizations. The president of the Louisville and Nashville Railroad became so beset by such activities that he appealed to Thomas for relief. When the general hesitated to act on his own authority, the railroad executive took his case directly to President Andrew Johnson. He detailed the host of crimes to which his line and his passengers had been subjected, then, citing Thomas's reluctance to act without authorization, called for the president to intervene personally. "Some prompt and energetic action is absolutely necessary," he explained. "The people of the State of Ky. & Tenn. would support any measures you would adopt to make them secure in their homes" and presumably train travels. "They are now at the mercy of these robber bands."[89]

James Guthrie's clout was sufficient to warrant action. Secretary Stanton notified Thomas that he could station troops in such a manner as to combat the guerrilla activities, although he should remain cognizant of the potential for abusing military power, even in the face of such provocation.[90] For Thomas, it was the authorization he had sought and a reflection of the policy he supported in maintaining law and order while carefully avoiding damaging or disregarding civil authority.

Nevertheless, there were those who were convinced that Thomas represented the hand of tyranny in their midst. A farmer from the little Tennessee community of Woodbury felt so desperate as to cause him to address his complaint to the president, too. "My subject is the grievances of our downtrodden people," the farmer explained, "and knowing you to be an ardent friend of the people I feel encouraged to inform you of military despotism, under the regime of [Governor William G.] Brownlow that we are forced to live under." Samuel Franks particularly noted the presence of a small detail of Federal troops, "sent here by Gen. Thomas from Nashville, at the urgent request of Brownlow, for no other purpose than to intimidate the people." Although only a small contingent, the troops had already committed "all manner of depredations on private property" and were apparently aided in their behavior by "Genl Thomas and Brownlow, [who] are radicals, and exult in the miseries of our people, supposing you to be ignorant of the continuation of martial law, after your Peace Proclamation [of April 2]."[91]

Thomas found that action was no guarantee of achieving positive results. "Guerrilla depredations in Tennessee and Northern Georgia continue to occur from time to time," he observed. "I have on several occasions sent detachments of troops to scour the Country infested by these marauders, although with indifferent success in apprehending them, from the fact that in most cases, on the appearance of troops the friends and sympathizers of these bad men secrete them so successfully as to prevent their arrest, and throw every possible obstacle in the way of obtaining information as to their whereabouts."

This was guerrilla warfare that Thomas confronted. Unchecked, it left "the law abiding Citizens in such dread of retaliation that even were they willing to aid the Military Authorities in suppressing violence they do not dare to do so from fear of harm to their persons or to their families." Moreover, "the Civil authorities of the sections in question" had demonstrated themselves to be "utterly inefficient, in the discharge of their duties, being either active sympathizers with the Guerrillas, or have from fear become indifferent to the interests of their respective localities."

Thomas's annual report spelled out the steps he had taken over a year of transition from a wartime footing to a peacetime one. The prognosis was guarded, but promising for the area over which he had responsibility, and he had worked hard to adhere to the general policy of noninterference with strictly civil matters. Thomas felt that he had been largely successful in achieving his duty of maintaining law and order. "With the exception of the Memphis Riot quiet has been most generally observed throughout my command," he observed. "The people make no public exhibition of feeling, possibly because they find it will militate to their disadvantage," he explained, but the Virginian was under no illusion that all was well in the so recently defeated South. He readily admitted that "no one living in their midst can fail occasionally to observe, unmistakeable evidences of animosity to the Government, which if unchecked at the outset will easily fan into open defiance."[92]

There may have seemed to be reason for optimism as George Thomas assessed the year 1866, but a subsequent inspection carried out by a subordinate undoubtedly dulled any sense of enthusiasm the general's report generated. Thomas dispatched William D. Whipple on an extensive fact-finding mission that resulted in a "tour through the States of Mississippi, Alabama, and Georgia for the purposes of ascertaining the best permanent locations for troops, visiting on his route, Vicksburg, Mobile, Montgomery & Macon." When Whipple reported his findings, he advised that the retention of troops "in the late insurrectionary States" was indeed necessary because "the bitter animus of the people fully warrants it, for he found everywhere in his route, in hotels and railroad cars, the general theme of conversation to be the hated yankee, and anything representing loyalty to the Union, and this bitter state of feeling on the part of the more ignorant is fanned into a continual glow by the local newspaper writers, most of whom are ex-rebel officers of intelligence and accomplishments." Unfortunately, as the Union officer had learned, the anger of Southern whites who remained loyal to their lost cause was expanding in its scope. "Not confining themselves to threats, mutterings or curses, Union men were murdered in their beds in cold blood, or were driven off from their farms; soldiers and government employees were assaulted or shot at by unknown persons whilst in the performance of their duties; and when application was made to the civil authorities for redress, either through incompetency or the fact of a man's loyalty to the government, no action would be taken." Some states were thus afflicted worse than others, but such sentiments were general and tainted the hope that reconciliation would lead the way quickly to a meaningful reunification of the nation.[93]

Thomas had honed this type of personal intelligence gathering during the war. In one instance, he and Whipple had traveled along the East Tennessee and Virginia Railroad to ascertain routes of march for the command. Interestingly, the fact finding came with a degree of deception that mirrored the Virginian's private personality. Throughout the circuit, Thomas moved about inconspicuously, as one contemporary recorded, "with no mark of military rank" beyond "a simple blouse and slouch hat," while Whipple garnered attention from the crowds dressed "in full uniform." Although the general "talked with the citizens at every stop," none seemed to be aware of his identity, and the effort allowed him to collect unvarnished information.[94] Whipple's approach to the citizenry in the postwar tour was not indicated, but the frankness of their expressions in some of these conversations suggested that, like his chief had done formerly, he traveled incognito for at least a portion of the journey.

As these inspection tours and the role of chief of staff indicated, Thomas enjoyed a close professional relationship with Whipple. Their association dated from the latter part of 1863, forged through the field operations of the Atlanta, Chattanooga, and Nashville Campaigns. Through the process, the men established a tandem marked by a mutual sense of trust. Yet, the degree of influence the subordinate may have had as a result troubled at least some onlookers. When the subsequent discussions of the possibility of Thomas being assigned to a command in New Orleans, replacing General Philip Sheridan, a Union officer and friend of the general's expressed his concerns directly to President Andrew Johnson. It was not that John G. Parkhurst believed his friend and former commander was incapable of exercising effective leadership in the troubled district. It was not even that Thomas's health might be more at risk in the warm climate of the Deep South. Parkhurst was singularly worried that if the Virginian went into the new department with his current chief of staff he would be heading into trouble. "I feel it my duty to you, to say, that Genl. W. D. Whipple, A.A.G. & Chief of Staff for Genl. Thomas is one of the rankest radicals in the country." Parkhurst's clear but confidential message to the president was that any charges leveled at Thomas for radicalism would be more appropriately placed on his chief of staff and implied that the subordinate's influence had been considerable on a man whose tendencies were not nearly prone to exhibit themselves in the same way. Whipple "would delight in exhibiting his radical propensities as chief of Staff in the N.O. [New Orleans] district & in attempting to give direction to Genl. Thomas['s] administration. I believe that if Genl. Thomas should be sent to relieve Genl. Sheridan, Whipple should be detailed on some other duty."[95]

Another subordinate, William P. Carlin, whose admiration for the Virginian bordered on the excessive, termed the general's ability to select staff personnel among his highest attributes. Noting that Thomas "had the good sense to select a staff that was really a support and help to him," Carlin thought Whipple to be "an officer who combined great ability with unusual zeal for the cause."[96] The degree to which Thomas was vulnerable to such influence is probably impossible to know, but the information he had received following Whipple's tour either reflected or confirmed his statements concerning the postwar South. Certainly, John M. Schofield believed that the Virginian was susceptible to poisonous messages, although he tended to be convinced that the prejudices involved were aimed especially at him.[97]

Thomas was once more undergoing a transformation in his thinking. He had always been a champion of those who he believed could not fend for themselves. It was an effect of his paternalistic upbringing that he could never entirely eliminate. He had also seen enough abuse to shake his confidence in the ability of human nature to overcome its fears and baser instincts. Rebel rascality, racial prejudice, or a combination of both required that people of goodwill be vigilant to see that excesses would be held in check.

But even in the midst of these struggles, there were reminders of the value of his services in some eyes. Work on the commemorative medal that honored Thomas's service in Tennessee was finished, and with another anniversary of the Battle of Nashville approaching, it could now be bestowed. On December 6, 1866, the *New York Times* reported that Governor William G. Brownlow would present it, with the kind of pomp, circumstance, and speechmaking that Thomas usually tried to avoid. Describing the item for its readership, the writer of the short piece thought the Union general would "well be proud to receive it."[98]

The medal George Thomas accepted was symbolic of his stubborn defense of the Union and the esteem in which many held him for this service. He had reached an important stage in his life and career, and had finally witnessed the end of the war he had waged for the preservation of the Union and in defense of the government for which he had taken his oath as an officer. In the aftermath he engaged in a different kind of struggle as the transition from war to peace got under way. He learned quickly that on the one side there were those who could not accept the verdict of the battlefield and on the other those who insisted that their defeated opponents be reminded of that fact at every opportunity and regardless of the consequences. Thomas fell between these extreme poles. He could not tolerate rebellion and could not fathom treasonous expressions, but seemed willing to accept those who had rebelled and were now anxious to embrace the nation and laws they had once flouted. He could not allow individuals who had supported, much less served, the Union to be mishandled or mistreated, regardless of their status prior to the war or the animus that their presence engendered after it. His was simply the practical mission of a soldier who sought to enforce the peace. Defending the nation, as well as its most downtrodden citizens, was the calling he had chosen to answer.

16   Final Stages (1867–1868)

"You all know that I am a modest man, and never speak unless I am forced to."
—Thomas before the Society of the Army of the Cumberland

"I have no taste whatever for politics."
—George Henry Thomas

"I want to die with a fair record, and this I will do if I keep out of the sea of politics and cling to my proper profession."
—General Thomas

For a time in 1867 it must have seemed to Ulysses Grant as if he were once again in Virginia in 1864, waiting for George Thomas to act against Hood before Nashville. This time the threat came not from a Confederate army, but from political challenges within the state of Tennessee in Memphis and Nashville. The leadership now in authority in the state had been consistently supportive of the Union, but Thomas had to act in a manner that reflected new political realities, especially with regard to the role of the army in connection to civil affairs. U. S. Grant shared a concern that Thomas might dally rather than take timely steps to prevent outbreaks of violence, but it remained to be seen if he felt his presence was necessary to motivate the subordinate to his duty.[1]

By the latter part of 1867 Thomas would be able to submit a report that reflected the tenor of his response to the crisis and the balancing act that he recognized he had been called upon to execute. "Anticipating trouble at the period of the August elections for Governor of Tennessee, I disposed of my troops at central points, particularly at Memphis and at Nashville, that they could be on hand to render all the assistance in their power to the civil authorities in suppressing riot or violence, should any occur."[2]

Fortunately for the general, these troubles lay in the future. At the start of the year, an opportunity awaited for him to visit with old comrades and cherished subordinates. In February 1867, he appeared before the first gathering of the Society of the Army of the Cumberland in Cincinnati, Ohio. George Thomas could hardly have asked for a more favorable setting, yet his reticence to speak publicly always weighed heavily upon him. Biographer and colleague Richard Johnson was present when the attendees offered a toast to their former commander and he rose to accept it. "I thank you for the toast," he recalled an emotional George Thomas remarking. "At the same time, it is too personal for me to attempt to reply." The soldier complained that the previous speakers had "anticipated" his comments and thus covered the ground quite thoroughly. "You all know that I am a modest man, and never speak unless I am forced to."

Whatever his initial emotions might have been, Thomas was not about to let the moment pass. "I don't know how I shall draw out. Nevertheless I will try to do so; I will make the attempt." What followed was as effusive an expression of affection and personal attachment as he was capable of making in a public setting. His comments were extensive and heartfelt, highlighted by a simple recounting of the army's accomplishments on the various fields in which they had been engaged in the recent conflict.

"Now, gentlemen, my time is very near up," he explained, but his parting words would be in many ways the most important ones for him to make. He took especial delight in the impact the Army of the Cumberland had exhibited on the South. "We have not only broken down one of the most formidable rebellions that ever threatened the existence of any country, but the discipline of the Army of the Cumberland alone has civilized two hundred thousand valuable patriots and citizens." This was not an observation that came from reports, but the personal investigation of the general himself. "I have travelled a little since the war was over," he explained. "Wherever I have been, whether on steamboat or rail, I have either seen on the steamboat, engaged in peaceful occupation of merchant sailors, or I have seen in the fields, along the railroads, engaged in peaceful following the plough, and setting an example of industry worthy to be followed by all in the country, men innumerable dressed in blue."

Thomas was convinced that the great tragedy of war would actually have positive results for the shaken nation. "I hope that such sentiments, and such civilizing influences as have been produced by this war, will serve for all time to inspire this nation with such a feeling of patriotism that no enemy can ever do us the least harm." A witness to this presentation and a subsequent biographer insisted that these words constituted "the longest" speech "he ever made."[3] Although his association with this organization was brief, it was a significant institution for him. As Chaplain Van Horne explained, "General Thomas was greatly interested in the Society of the Army of the Cumberland from its organization in February, 1868, until his death. He was its first president, but was present only at the meetings in Cincinnati and Chicago."[4]

One matter was certain: the Virginian was prepared to take extraordinary measures to prevent the insertion of any political agenda into the meetings of the Society. When some attendees made an attempt to present a political resolution Thomas deemed the matter out of order. As he explained, "This association was organized for the purpose of a renewal of our fraternal relations to each other, and not for the purpose of engaging in political discussions." Yet, the general was determined to do so as ever in a civil manner, with respect toward those with whom he happened to disagree and against whom he was now ruling. "At the same time that I decide the gentleman out of order, I return him thanks for giving me this opportunity of expressing my views on the subject."[5]

It was his reluctance to speak outside of the settings in which he felt most comfortable that had so long characterized Thomas and limited any political effectiveness his battlefield successes might have offered him. Yet, even on the topics in which his knowledge and experience were indisputable, he was often disinclined to express himself. Newspaperman Alexander McClure once complained, "it required exhaustive ingenuity to induce him to speak about any military movements in which he was a prominent participant. Any one might have been in daily intercourse with him for years and never learned from him that he had won great victories in the field."[6]

McClure would have advised against trying, but as a presidential election year loomed some individuals sought to convince General Thomas to allow them to advance his name and candidacy. He rebuffed each overture with a passion he seemed to reserve especially for such matters. When a Union Convention gathering adopted such a resolution in a meeting on February 22, 1867, Thomas learned of the effort and responded hastily. In a March 4 letter to Senator Dewitt C. Senter in the Tennessee state capital Thomas was unequivocal in his message. While he "felt free to acknowledge my high appreciation of your friendship as well as the complimentary manner in which the resolution was conceived and adopted by the Convention," the general did not consider himself qualified for "the high and responsible office for which I find myself nominated so unexpectedly," and requested that his name not be "used in connection therewith." Thomas was acutely aware that his talents lay in the profession he had practiced throughout his adult life. "Having been educated as a soldier, and served for many years in the army, I am better qualified to continue my duties as a citizen of the United States in that department of the Government than in any other." He closed with the wish that these views be passed along to any others with similar intentions.[7]

At about the same time, General Henry M. Cist raised the possibility of a run for the presidency of the United States with Thomas. Cist may have acted out of courtesy to the people who had convinced him to speak on their behalf, for as a wartime associate he surely knew of the Virginian's disdain for things political. Indeed, in a response as methodical as any military campaign he might wage, the general outlined the "many reasons why I cannot consent to be a candidate for the Presidency." Foremost among these was his perception of his own shortcomings in "the science of statesmanship." A second reason was more personal. "I have not the necessary control over my temper, nor have I the faculty of conforming to a policy and working to advance it, unless convinced within myself that it is right and honest." But, Thomas insisted, the years of military service and his "habits of life" severely hampered any personal political ambitions. "I have no taste whatever for politics," he maintained. Recent congressional actions had also weakened the office, further limiting its attractiveness, especially for a man who had preferred not to command an army unless he could mold and lead it unfettered. "I could name many more equally valid reasons for not wishing the office," he continued. "I will name only one more, and that not the least: I am poor and could not afford it."[8]

Despite Thomas's strenuous objections, Cist remained adamant. He pushed the subject once more, perhaps hoping that his friend would reconsider. The persistence proved futile. "I still do not see why I, as an American citizen, can not be allowed to exercise my choice of a course in life," Thomas stated firmly, even testily, before adding for good measure, "I think I mentioned in my last that I had no taste for politics." The course he had chosen was "a military life," and Thomas insisted that he preferred "to remain in the army as long as I can be of use to the country." The latter point put him again in mind of the general principle he had espoused as a member of the armed forces, that he should keep "free from political complications and adhere strictly to its appropriate sphere of duties under the Government." In closing this second letter on the subject he promised to "decline in a more formal manner, which if nominated I shall certainly do."[9]

Thomas followed these letters with another one to J. Watts De Peyster on April 20, 1867. In each one he revealed a bit more about his motivations for avoiding political office. "I will here state, and hope you will repeat for me whenever you hear my name mentioned in connection with the Presidency of the United States, that I never will consent to being brought before the people as a candidate for any office." Although he might have forgone any further explanation, Thomas could not resist. "I have too much regard for my own self-respect to voluntarily place myself in a position where my personal and private character can be assailed with impunity by newspaper men and scurrilous political pettifoggers and demagogues."[10] This was an argument similar to the one in which he had deflected efforts to name him as commander of the Army of the Potomac during the war, and he meant the sentiment now as he had meant it then.

Thomas's focus on the differences in his public and private spheres increased in this latter stage of his life. "All that I did for my government are matters of history," he observed with a hint of self-conscious pride, "but my private life is my own and I will not have it hawked about in print for the amusement of the curious."[11] Even the attempt to appeal to his sense of duty by noting that he ought not to decline the call of the people if and when it came made no headway with him. "I will have nothing to do with politics," he averred. "I am a soldier, and I know my duty; as a politician I would be lost." Thomas understood so well his propensity for preparing the ground on which he would have to stand and offer battle. The political battleground was beyond his ken. "No, sir," he continued, "not even if I were elected unanimously would I accept." Then, in a moment of final reflection on the matter, Thomas added insightfully, "I want to die with a fair record, and this I will do if I keep out of the sea of politics and cling to my proper profession."[12]

This attitude placed some in a quandary. On the one hand there was the desire to extend the highest honors to their chieftain; on the other the unmistakably clear position Thomas took on such matters and the need to respect that decision. It may well have been that his close aide, Alfred Hough, captured the overriding sentiment long before the measure was raised. While still in the midst of the conflict that would eventually raise the general's name to such lofty possibilities, Hough quietly admitted in a letter home, "I would not go against Pop Thomas' wishes for a million."[13] Thus, nothing more needed to be said on the subject once Thomas expressed his mind. Even so, James A. Garfield, who developed a strong attachment to Thomas that dated from the solid stand on Snodgrass Hill and Horseshoe Ridge at Chickamauga, did not understand Thomas's wishes in this regard. One of Garfield's biographers noted simply, "Had Thomas only lived longer, Garfield later claimed, he would have been President of the United States."[14]

The general's refusal to be considered for the nation's highest office did not diminish the devotion of his comrades and associates toward him. The officers and men of the Army of the Cumberland held their former commander in an almost sanctified esteem. Alfred Hough had found it necessary to explain why he would not even approach General Thomas for a leave of absence that might look like he was taking advantage of his position. "Genl. Thomas has highly honored me, and I shall ask no favors," Hough observed, for fear that this would cause him "to lose thereby his good opinions, [since] he has never left his post since the war began."[15] As difficult as Frances Thomas might have found at times the example of devotion to duty her husband represented, it explained the intense feeling subordinate officers had for their commander.

Thomas might have professed not to be savvy when it came to politics, but he had long been sensitive to the prerogatives of rank and service, and these feelings now seemed to intensify. He began to suspect that much more than seniority was going on behind the scenes when it came to assignments and duties. At the end of April, Grant replied to a communication that Thomas had written relating to cavalry general Philip St. George Cooke. "I do not think Gen. Cooke has any secret enemy here working against him," Grant observed candidly. "His last removal was not in consequence of any fault committed by him but because it was thought that Gen. [Christopher C.] Augur, being a much younger man, would be much better able to conduct an active campaign in person than Gen. Cooke. Hostilities were and are threatened in the Dept. from which he was relieved." Grant explained that he had not known the reason for Cooke's removal from duty at the time, but insisted that the "right to select commanders for important armies was acted upon."[16] Thomas could read into this last statement as he wished, but the implication was, as it had been for him during the war, that officers served at the pleasure of their superiors and their removal could occur whenever those superiors chose and for whatever cause they deemed appropriate.

Even as Thomas sought to clarify issues that mattered to him concerning wartime colleagues and army protocol, the tremulous political ground of Tennessee was issuing troubling signs that could not be ignored. The river town of Memphis once again appeared ready to erupt in violence. The Virginian had Grant's support in taking stern measures for securing the peace. "I directed Gen. Thomas to give orders for the most vigorous use of the Military to preserve order on election day and not wait until people are killed and the mob beyond controll before interfering," Grant informed Secretary of War Edwin Stanton. "I will direct Gen. Thomas to go directly to Memphis in person but do not think there is any need of my going to Nashville."[17] To Thomas directly, Grant explained, "Go to Memphis in person and remain there until after the election. Let it be felt that where the military is [the] law must prevail and the guilty punished. Do not wait for a riot to take place but use the military vigorously to prevent one commencing."[18] Thomas wired his acceptance of the charge and promised "to be in Memphis before [the] election takes place."[19] After the fact, Thomas explained that per "the direction of the General in Chief, I went in person to Memphis, as there was more probability of an outbreak there than elsewhere."[20]

Thomas was still not completely sure of his authority in the netherworld between civilian and military rule. "Complaints are constantly made to me of oppression and maltreatment of union men and negroes by returned paroled rebels. Am I authorized to arrest and punish them for violation of their parole?"[21] Despite any uncertainties, Thomas sorted everything out satisfactorily, reporting, "Everything went off quietly however and to the satisfaction of the defeated party as well as to the elected," at least in terms of the way the contest had been conducted, if not, understandably enough, its outcome.[22] Thomas had understood his mandate well, and the absence of trouble in the streets attested as much as anything to the effectiveness of the measures he took.

Even greater personal matters now arose. A flurry of official communications took place through the midpoint of August that affected George Thomas's career. President Andrew Johnson contemplated relieving General Sheridan of command over the Fifth Military District and replacing him with Thomas. Sheridan had fallen afoul of President Johnson by virtue of the tone he set in his official correspondence. The directness that made him a favored lieutenant with Grant and a nemesis for Confederate opponents came across as insubordinate and hostile to Johnson. Biographer Roy Morris noted, "Again, it was Sheridan's language, as much as his actions, that gave offense."[23] Offense toward this president, who had proven prone to brawl with critics in past election cycles, was bound to have serious negative repercussions for even former war heroes.

In seeking some political cover by approaching the matter through the popular war hero Ulysses S. Grant on the propriety for making this move, Johnson undoubtedly did not expect either the haste or the vehemence of his army commander's reply. Grant had tried to walk a fine line in dealing with two important branches of government, including the one run by his commander in chief. One Grant biographer has labeled the soldier "magnificently cagey at not tipping his hand."[24] But Johnson was getting more suspicious of Grant's motives and was anxious to hem him in, if not connect their fortunes and fates together. Thomas would become caught in the middle, despite his disdain for politics and his best efforts to steer clear of such power struggles.

Grant informed the president that he would be "pleased to avail myself of this invitation to urge, earnestly urge, urge in the name of a patriotic people who have sacrificed Hundreds of thousands of loyal lives, and Thousands of Millions of treasure to preserve the integrity and union of this Country that this order be not insisted on." Grant explained that Thomas's transfer was not the issue, since his service "in battling for the union entitles him to some consideration," but that Sheridan should not be removed from his post.[25] As additional support for this position, Grant insisted of Thomas, "He has repeatedly entered his protest against being assigned to either of the five military districts, and especially to being assigned to relieve Gen. Sheridan."[26]

Two days later, Johnson responded to Grant's impassioned communication. The president's reply seemed couched more in the promotion of Thomas than in the demotion of Sheridan, although he insisted that it "would be unjust to the army to assume that, in the opinion of the nation, he alone is capable of commanding the States of Louisiana & Texas, and that were he for any cause removed, no other General in the military service of the United States would be competent to fill his place."

Johnson focused more positively on Thomas, calling him "well known to the country." The president observed, "Having won high and honorable distinction in the field, he has since, in the execution of his responsible duties of a departmental commander, exhibited great ability, sound discretion, and sterling patriotism. He has not failed, under the most trying circumstances, to enforce the laws, to preserve peace and order, to encourage the restoration of civil authority, and to promote as far as possible a spirit of reconciliation." Perhaps unwittingly, Johnson left Grant one significant opportunity to negate the Thomas factor in the equation. "No one, as you are aware, has a higher appreciation than myself of the services of General Thomas, and no one would be less inclined to assign him to a command not entirely consonant with his wishes." Still, Johnson thought his subordinate would answer this call to duty as he had always done. "Knowing him, as I do," the president noted, "I cannot think that he will hesitate for a moment to obey any order having in view a complete and speedy restoration of the Union, in the preservation of which he has rendered such important and valuable services."

President Johnson remained adamant that Sheridan should be replaced, reminding Grant that he had initially held misgivings about the appointment. "Time has strengthened my convictions upon this point, and has led me to the conclusion that patriotic considerations demand that he should be superseded by an officer who, while he will faithfully execute the law, will at the same time give more general satisfaction to the whole people, white and black, North and South."[27]

On the surface Grant seemed prepared to implement the president's instructions, but he had anticipated Johnson's position well and was already taking steps to undermine it. On the same day Grant had written to Johnson, he dashed a telegram off to Thomas. "Please mail a copy of your last letter to Sec. of War objecting to assignment to 5th Military District." In so doing, Thomas would bolster Grant's argument that matters should remain as they were with regard to Sheridan.[28]

Just in case the Virginian should remain in the equation, Grant laid a restriction on him that he must have known Thomas would find intolerable: to continue all measures currently in force unless and until ordered to do otherwise. New commanders often left a status quo in place while they assessed the new authority, but then were ordinarily allowed on their own initiative to implement whatever changes they saw fit. "The best explanation seems to be that Grant wanted to make certain that Sheridan's vigorous interpretation of the laws would be continued," one scholar of the period observed, "and that he was not certain Thomas would adopt that policy."[29]

At least one contemporary saw the act for what it was and shared his strong opinion with the president. R. King Cutler latched onto the statement that required Thomas, as Sheridan's would-be successor, to continue all orders already set in place before he arrived. "If you please, what is the benefit of the removal of Gen. Sheridan, if Gen. Thomas—a man of whole soul, an independent, honorable man, a man of energy, nerve and education, a man who is thoroughly skilled in military affairs—is to be dictated to by your Secretary-of-War, or by the General commanding." If the same policies were to be maintained, then the government might as well leave the original commander in place to carry out his radical agenda.[30] Of course, Cutler's diatribe only confirmed the wisdom Thomas exhibited in wanting to avoid such political pitfalls altogether.

In the meantime, the general traveled to West Virginia to attend to departmental matters. His surgeon and medical director informed Grant that the general was "under medical treatment this summer for an affection of his liver and it would be a great risk for him to go South at this time."[31] While undergoing treatment, Thomas kept abreast of developments through newspaper reports. What he read in an August 20 edition prompted him to write to Grant personally. "Why I should have been assigned to the command of the Fifth Military District I cannot conceive," he explained. "I cannot hope to be of any more service in executing the Reconstruction of the states composing that District than Genl. Sheridan nor can the citizens of those states be in the least benefited by substituting me for General Sheridan; on the contrary knowing my sentiments I fear that the reconstruction of those states will be very much retarded, if it does not fail altogether, by appointing me to Command."[32]

Ulysses Grant remained firm in his support of Sheridan, while Andrew Johnson took the extraordinary view that the news of Thomas's fragile health was divinely ordained to enable him to implement his preferred scheme. Johnson's private secretary, W. G. Moore, recalled, "The President thought that this was a favorable indication that Providence was aiding him—his desire, in the first instance, having been to send [Winfield Scott] Hancock to relieve Sheridan, but Thomas having been finally selected, because he was know[n] to be a Radical in his views, and one to whom that party could offer no objection."[33] Hancock, a Democrat and former Union general with an enviable war record of his own, met Johnson's requirements better than Thomas would have done.

Fortunately for Thomas, and in substantial measure because of his refusal to be caught up in the whirlwind of politics, he remained detached from the drama. President Johnson informed General Grant on August 26, "In consequence of the unfavorable condition of the health of Major General George H. Thomas, as reported to you in Surgeon Hasson's despatch of the 21st instant, my order dated August 17, 1867, is hereby modified, so as to assign Major General Winfield Hancock to the command of the Fifth Military District."[34] Johnson had already telegraphed Thomas three days earlier with his instructions.[35]

Thus, in the end, Sheridan left for the post now vacated by Hancock and that officer proceeded to New Orleans. Thomas's assignment in the reorganization was the easiest, remaining where he was "until further orders," in command of the Department of the Cumberland. For him, it was another instance of managing to avoid becoming mired in a morass that he preferred to view from a distance anyway. But the incident raised another difficulty that seemed to follow the Virginian in almost every aspect of his life and that plagued him tremendously in this one. References to the state of his health suggested that it was for that reason that he had not received the post that Sheridan vacated and Hancock secured. The validity of that explanation concerned him to the point of wanting to clarify the matter to at least those in his closest circles.

To his friend and former staff officer Colonel Robert A. Ramsey, Thomas explained in great detail on September 7, 1867, that the state of his health really was not in question after all. True, he was under doctor's orders after he had experienced "a peculiar sensation which I had on my right side." But medicine had brought relief, and he continued to conduct "official business" as required. "It so happened that while on that trip [to Lewisburg, West Virginia] the President issued his order for me to relieve Sheridan." His own protest had followed, but not because of his health or concerns about the potential for threats to it, "but because of the hostility of the people toward me, making it impossible for me to be of any service in endeavoring to reconstruct the Southern States." He had made the same argument earlier in another instance, a bow to the consistency on which he prided himself for his actions. "I presume, to ease off the withdrawal of the order, it was stated that, owing to the unfavorable condition of my health, as reported by the Medical Director of the Department of the Cumberland, I was released from the operation of General Orders No. 77, and Hancock was detailed to assume command of the Fifth Military District."[36] Of course, for the old soldier, such maneuverings were only further proof of his wisdom in remaining aloof of politics, even with regard to the service.

Thomas was not unaware of the implications of his decisions for his own future. In another letter to Ramsey, he pointed out, "I am happy to inform you that it is my intention to be at home all this month unless I am ordered to go somewhere by Genl. Grant or the President. The latter contingency I do not feel any apprehension about now as I expect A.J. is altogether disgusted with my obstinacy in not complying with his desire for me to go to N. Orleans for which I return him my sincere thanks as I have no desire to enter into politics." As for the army commander, Thomas could conceive of "no reason why Genl. Grant should order me on duty elsewhere and consequently feel pretty secure."[37]

Even so, any sense of calm that Thomas may have felt was about to be tested on another front. This situation arose when conflicting proclamations for municipal elections emerged from the offices of the mayor of Nashville and the governor of the state of Tennessee. Thomas anticipated trouble and sought to have his role clarified for responding if such disagreements turned to violence in the streets and required greater force than existed through civilian agencies to suppress. There did not appear yet to be any need for a military force to intervene, but the Virginian's experience encouraged him to be prepared. The standing instructions from the War Department were "to assist the civil authorities in preserving the peace," and Thomas planned to turn to Governor Brownlow as the state's chief executive. "I am of the opinion, that if called upon, I shall be compelled to aid him in enforcing his decree with the forces of my command. Such will be the action taken unless ordered to the contrary, and instructions by telegraph are requested if this is not approved of."[38]

Knowing that the realities of numbers favored their opponents, Nashville Conservatives, led by Mayor W. Matt Brown, offered an interesting gambit. Instead of forcing a single tainted election, there should be two, or at least two counts that could be sorted out later. "It was a shrewd ploy that made the Conservatives appear conciliatory," a later student of the election concluded.[39] The army commander on the scene, Thomas Duncan, thought he could "protect both parties in a quiet election" by allowing both to proceed with competing tallies that could then be "settled by the proper tribunal" as the mayor had suggested.[40] Thomas was disinclined to follow such a convoluted path that might still result in violence at the polls. He instructed Duncan, "In the absence of any requisition upon you for troops prior to the day of the election, you will, on that day, hold your command in readiness for immediate action, as you may be called on at any moment to assist in quelling riots."[41]

It had become increasingly clear that neither the mayor nor the governor wanted to give ground to the other on the question of whose election authority should hold forth in Nashville. Thomas hoped for clarifying instructions from Washington, and early on September 25th, a delayed "cipher telegram" arrived from Grant. "Go to Nashville tomorrow to remain until after the election to preserve the peace," the general in chief instructed Thomas. "If you think more troops necessary for that purpose order them there from the most convenient points in your Command." Grant wanted the Virginian to be vigilant in preventing violence, but not to try to involve the U.S. Army beyond that point. "The Military cannot set up to be the judge as to which set of election judges have the right to control. But must confine their action to putting down hostile mobs." Grant's final word was a gesture to peace as well as to his belief that the Virginian possessed the skills to secure it. "It is hoped however by seeing the Governor and city officials here referred to your presence and advice may prevent disturbances."[42]

Thomas immediately wired back his compliance with the orders. "I start for Nashville this afternoon and will do what I can to preserve the peace."[43] Historian Ben Severance offered the Virginian a deliberate motivation in this new Nashville campaign. "Clearly Thomas favored the Radicals," he noted, suggesting that it was Grant who had to hold the reins tightly on his partisan subordinate.[44] But the subordinate's interactions with the army chief suggested a much different interpretation. Far from being anxious to support the Brownlow candidate and agenda or become the dispenser of justice for the cause of racial equality, Thomas was determined to be the guarantor of peace and order.

George Thomas continued to battle with perceptions of his political leanings that failed to take into account his determination to remain out of political equations as much as possible. As Gideon Welles recorded in his diary, there was at least the sense in some circles that war and the early phases of Reconstruction had caused an evolution in Thomas's personal political positions. "Thomas inclines to the Radicals," he observed on September 27; "at the beginning of the Rebellion he inclined to the Secessionists."[45]

As quickly as transportation allowed, the general was in the state capital and took up temporary residence in the familiar confines of the St. Cloud Hotel. Thomas found that Governor Brownlow was absent in Memphis, and thus could not be interviewed personally about matters, but Mayor Matt Brown and a delegation of city officials were anxious to meet with him. The city solons presented their positions, the mayor making the point that he intended to proceed "unless prevented from doing so by the U.S. authorities." General Thomas listened attentively and then suggested that the parties "settle their differences amicably" after "discussing the points of difficulty in a calm and dispassionate manner." Such a procedure might work well with the cool-headed Thomas, but the mayor and the governor, who was now expected back in the city at any time, would be another matter.

Thomas was certainly not sanguine of success. Following the meeting with Mayor Brown, the general reported to Grant in a manner that must have perplexed his superior. "If both parties persist in holding their elections there will be great danger of collision. In such contingency am I to interfere and allow both elections to go on, or are my duties simply to prevent mobs from aiding either party[?]" Thomas had already asserted, in no uncertain terms, the requirement to side with Brownlow if he became involved at all. Now he seemed to equivocate. But Grant offered precious little clarification of his own. "I neither instruct to sustain the Governor nor the Mayor but to prevent conflict; the Governor is the only authority that can legally demand the aid of the United States troops & that must be by proclamation declaring invasion or insurrection exists beyond the control of other means at his hands." Grant remained optimistic that a quieter resolution could be achieved. "It is hoped your presence and good judgment and advice will prevent collision," he observed to his subordinate.

Thomas was not the type to panic, but he was convinced that trouble might not be able to be avoided. "I cannot preserve the peace without interfering in case of a collision," he replied.[46] Grant hastily wired back, "You are to prevent conflict. Your mission is to preserve peace and not to take sides in political difference until called out in accordance with law. You are to prevent mobs from aiding either party. If called upon legally to interfere your duty is plain."[47] The frenetic pace of communications continued late into the evening.[48] Grant's last message of the day reinforced the basic approach. "Nothing is clearer than that the Military cannot be made use of to defeat the Executive of a State in enforcing the laws of the State. You are not to prevent the legal State force from the execution of its orders."[49]

Early on the twenty-seventh Thomas met with Mayor Brown and apprised him of the current instructions. Brown agreed to take the matter under advisement.[50] But not much time elapsed before the answer came. Founded on the premise that he had no intention of resisting legitimate state statutes, Mayor Brown insisted, "I have only designed if not prevented by armed violence to hold a strictly legal election, in a perfectly peaceable manner, and in full accordance with the provisions of the charter of this city." He would "yield to the authority of the Government of the United States" if required, albeit under protest "against the signal and deplorable mistake which I must consider to have been made in this case, and with the expression of that profound regret which I cannot but feel, in view of the deplorable and ruinous consequences now plainly in store for this devoted city, whose chartered interest I have so long and earnestly labored to protect."[51]

Johnson's cabinet officials assembled to assess the crisis and offer advice. "The apprehension of a collision at Nashville was the principal topic of discussion in the Cabinet," Gideon Welles observed. Grant read the messages that had thus far passed between them on the matter, and the president instructed him to tell Thomas to use regulars to preserve the peace and avoid interfering except at the direct request of the governor.[52] The Nashville mayor also communicated directly with President Johnson, obviously hoping to override Thomas's intended course. Citing Grant's telegram, Brown noted that he had "asked of Gen. Thomas in writing" whether he felt committed by his orders to "uphold the lawless attempt" of "the Unconstitutional Military forces" to "prevent the strictly legal election heretofore ordered from proceeding." Mayor Brown obviously hoped that Johnson would order the general to refrain from any interference, assuring the president that if Thomas adhered to Grant's orders, "I then yield up the city to a state of organized anarchy never paralleled."[53]

Thomas had left the morning session under the impression that Brown would not press the matter further.[54] But the mayor's subsequent letter disavowed any progress and forced Thomas to reiterate his intention to sustain Brownlow if violence between the factions occurred. "It is not left to me to decide the question of legality or illegality of the election ordered by you," he explained, surely feeling that he had indicated in writing a sufficiently clear statement of his intentions.[55]

Additional troops were beginning to reach the city, and Thomas issued instructions directing their commanders "how to post the troops for the preservation of order." But complications threatened to inflame the situation to the point of a conflagration when word reached Thomas that Brownlow's militia "had taken possession of the polls . . . for the purpose of preventing the City authorities from attempting to open the polls under the charter."[56]

Governor Brownlow had issued strict orders to militia commander Joseph A. Cooper for the state troops to watch the polls to prevent the competing elements from attempting to run their own election alongside the one that he considered legitimate.[57] Cooper had served under Thomas during the Nashville campaign against John Bell Hood and the two seemed to have a positive relationship. Yet, while suggestions that the militia commander deferred to his former superior were legitimate given their connection, there was nothing to indicate that Thomas performed in any way other than he had said he would once the polls opened at 9 o'clock the next morning. Indeed, the presence of the soldiers, now bolstered by a thousand new arrivals to 1,400, was apparently enough to satisfy the governor, and the militia voluntarily stepped down.[58]

Mayor Brown was livid concerning the outcome of the standoff. In a publicly released statement he withdrew his candidacy in protest and insisted that General Thomas had assisted "in preventing a peaceable election."[59] Thomas could not allow the imputation to stand and responded the next day, denying that he had ever indicated anything other than the path he had followed. "I will further say that the troops under my command will not be used to prevent a peaceable election. On the contrary they will be used to preserve peace. And with that view the troops are here to preserve order, peace and quiet at the polls."[60] Brown would not be mollified. The election had come off quietly, but the mayor angrily stated his intention not "to recognize its validity."[61]

Under those circumstances, it is difficult to say why Thomas felt that he could not let the matter drop. He reiterated his position, taking exception to the implication that he had done anything to "use the military power of the

United States in sustaining the Governor of the State in *forcibly preventing a peaceable election.*" The question was more than one of semantics or interpretation. Brown might not like the outcome, but Thomas had followed orders to prevent violence, not to affect the election. "How these words can be construed as meaning that I intended to use the troops to prevent a *peaceable election* I confess I cannot understand." Thomas was convinced that both he and the militia commander had their instructions from their superiors and that the mayor himself had insisted that he would "hold said election in defiance of all power except that of the United States." The municipal leader might take his words to mean that he intended to go forward unless prevented, but Thomas considered them indications that Brown would not defy the United States government position that he believed he had made clear.

By the end of the potentially tumultuous day, Thomas felt secure enough to make the brief statement, "The election over all quiet."[62] His final report concluded in similarly anticlimactic fashion. "The elections having closed without any disturbance and there being no other cause of excitement, at 4 P.M. the troops were ordered to their various stations, and I returned to Louisville on the morning of the 29th."[63] The Radical candidate, A. E. Alden, had powered to an easy, lopsided victory of 2,423 to 258. Thomas would be chided as acting in an "unmilitary" fashion in the affair by disgruntled Conservatives, but he had achieved his real purpose of preventing violence in the streets.[64]

The Nashville contretemps had required Thomas's attentions, but now that it was settled he turned to private affairs. The general had always been interested in obtaining a measure of financial security, and he used the opportunity of the communication with a former staffer to discuss financial matters and offer an investment opportunity to his friend. "The Gentlemen interested with me in the marble of E. Ten. have affected an arrangement for quarrying & sending to market which I fear will absorb all of the shares," Thomas explained to Robert Ramsey, "but if I can secure any for you & after talking the matter over you would wish to take an interest I shall be glad to aid you."

The soldier/entrepreneur also had another opportunity in his mind. "I have another interest which I think is as good as the marble business," he offered. "I own one fourth of fifty thousand acres of land on the Cumberland plateau almost in Virgin forest timber of the very best quality, and underplayed with an inexhaustible supply of the best quality of Bituminous Coal. Also an abundance of iron." Here the Virginian melded his military service in the region that had made him acquainted with its resources with his scientific interests and his fiduciary desires. The prospects were good. "The Geologist reports that the timber alone would sell in the forest for ten dollars the acre," he happily noted. "After completing the boundary surveys

& plaits we propose to put the land on the market at two dollars & fifty cents the acre and we want to get some of your Pa. farmers, coal miners, and lumber cutters to take it off our hands at the price I have named."[65]

At the same time he discussed business ventures, Thomas demonstrated the eclectic interests of a busy and varied life through a communication with his friend George Gibbs in Washington. Although he had more than enough to occupy his attentions, the scientist in George Thomas was never more strongly present. "I have lately been assembling my notes on the Colorado River Indians," he told his friend and promised that at some point in the near term he hoped to "send you a Vocabulary of names as complete as I can make it." Including a catalog of such terms as an example, Thomas demonstrated a fascination with the Native language and culture to which he had been exposed prior to the Civil War.[66] Were such matters refuges from the more disturbing cascade of daily events, or simply the continuation of a lifelong interest in learning, it is not possible to say with certainty, but Thomas's intellectual curiosity remained as sharp as ever.

If personal pursuits occupied some of his energies, Thomas could count on public matters intruding as well, even if he was not always aware of it directly. In one case, John Tyler Jr., the son of the former president, expressed his concern about the possibility of "*the Nomination & probable election of Major General George H. Thomas*." Although Tyler conceded that the fellow Virginian "is a member, through my own marriage, of my own family" and possessed a "marked character—a solid intellect, immoveable nerve, and enviable abilities, with his passions & feelings under command," he was concerned that his kinsman had become too closely associated with the Radical Republican agenda. Tyler felt that only prompt action on Johnson's part, perhaps in conjunction with General Grant, could thwart a Thomas presidency and retain the office for Conservatives.[67] As things turned out, Tyler should have worried more about Grant than Thomas, for the "Rock of Chickamauga" had no intention of being rolled into the political arena.

With rare exceptions, the Virginian's public pronouncements tended to be short and heavily tinged with a sense of duty and pride reflected in the performances of his men. Thomas aimed any criticism that might creep in toward himself rather than others. When he expressed his views more openly, he did so with friends and associates. On one such occasion, J. Watts De Peyster took the rare opportunity to obtain the Virginian's position on a controversial matter. He wanted to know if the general attached any blame to William Rosecrans over the fighting and outcome of Chickamauga. "No farther than this," Thomas began, insisting that Rosecrans "should have acted as I did [later at Nashville]—he should have paid no attention to Halleck or Stanton, or the pressure from Washington."

Thomas had paid attention to the criticism then, too, although he responded to the pressure in his own fashion. But his larger point dealt with the confidence that he believed came with his prior service and success. "The 'Army of the Cumberland' had done a good nine month's work in driving the Rebels out of Tennessee, and getting a foot-hold south of the river," he explained. "Rosecrans should have waited to get another 'good ready' before he pushed forward again." If that record did not suffice to offer some relief from pressure, Thomas insisted that as Rosecrans, "I would have asked to be relieved sooner than act on compulsion contrary to my judgment." This was consistent with Thomas's views of generalship, as he concluded strongly, "When a general commanding an army is ordered to do what he feels he ought not to do, he should act upon his own opinions, and let things take their course." The assessment was vintage George Thomas. Hold your ground and follow only the course you feel to be correct. His conclusion blended the perspectives tellingly. "Rosecrans was only blameable for his blind obedience to orders which I knew to be wrong."[68]

In Washington, D.C., President Andrew Johnson arrived at the office on February 21, 1868, with instructions for the preparation of official papers that would have a profound effect on the state of the nation and the military command structure. The chief executive ordered the creation of documents ordering the removal of Edwin Stanton as secretary of war, the nomination of George McClellan to an ambassadorship, and a "nomination for the appt. of George H. Thomas as a Lieutenant General by brevet, and a General by brevet."[69]

Thomas was back at his headquarters in Louisville when he addressed the matter of promotion that had found its way into the public press, and did so directly to the chief executive. "The War Department dispatches of yesterday to the Louisville Journal mention my name as having been sent to the Senate recommended for the Brevet of Lieutenant General and Brevet General," he informed President Johnson on February 22. But the Virginian had no intention of celebrating the birthday of another popular soldier with an elevation of himself. So often compared to George Washington from the earliest days at West Point, first by physical stature and later by demeanor and attitude, Thomas was disdainful of advancement for its own sake or at the expense of others. "Whilst sincerely thanking you for the proposed compliment," the soldier explained, "I earnestly request you to recall the nomination." His final expressions on the subject would be his most telling. "I have done no service since the war to deserve so high a compliment, and it is now to[o] late to be regarded a compliment if conferred for services during the war."[70] He forwarded a similar pronouncement to Benjamin F. Wade, as president of the Senate. "For the battle of Nashville I was appointed major general United States army," he explained, adding essentially the same rationale that his postwar service did not "merit" the promotion and that it was past the time for anything done based on wartime achievements. "I, therefore, earnestly request that the Senate will not confirm the nomination."[71]

Thomas could be prickly when it came to timing. He did not so much reject the offer outright, but rather as if it were conferred for the wrong reason. The transparent political machinations associated with the maneuver did not encourage him to accept, but he had shown that gestures made "too late" might as well not be made at all as far as he was concerned. To a Confederate neighbor in postwar Nashville, who had purposely ignored his presence on the front stoop of their adjacent residences, Thomas was curt when the Southerner finally deigned to offer his hand as a token of friendship. "Too late, too late, sir; you have sinned away your day of grace."[72] Slow to anger in that instance, George Thomas demonstrated that he would nevertheless have been an unforgiving deity.

Frances Thomas later referred to the progression of events in Washington as evidence of her husband's magnanimity toward General Grant. In a letter to Alfred Hough, she observed, "when President Johnson sent Genl Thomas' name to the Senate for Brevets of Genl. & Lt. Genl. which Genl. Thomas declined, as he did not wish to be used against Genl Grant which could have been done by his being put in his just rank." In presenting this assessment of the situation, she wanted her correspondent to understand that her views were based on evidence, not conjecture. "That I *know*," Frances explained, "for I saw the messages he sent to President Johnson & the Chairman of the Military Committee of the Senate, *before* they were sent, and the reason he told me." She concluded testily, "Genl Grant *never appreciated that* in Genl Thomas."[73]

At about the same time, word reached Thomas that his aide Colonel Ramsey had welcomed a new addition to the family. George and Frances did not have children of their own, but that fact did not prevent him from having affection for little ones and a willingness to express advice concerning them that would have surprised those who knew the general only superficially. "Don't let him tyranise over your household," Thomas gently teased his friend, "but such advice is useless for I know the more he lords it over you the more implicitly you and the good mother will submit and praise his gentleness and conduciveness. But Babies always rule the house where they belong especially the first who came and I have yet to see either the Father or the Mother who could be convinced of it."

Ramsey had not been able to be in Cincinnati for the first gathering of the Society of the Army of the Cumberland, but in the same letter the Virginian assured him, "Our reunion was most enthusiastic and cordial and the organization of the Society of the Army of the Cumberland was a complete success." A second meeting was set for December in Chicago, and Thomas expressed the hope that Ramsey might be able to join them this time. Thomas was genuinely excited about what had taken place. "We had over four hundred at the Banquet and over a thousand signatures to the Constitution and Bylaws," he recalled warmly, expressing the belief that as long as the veterans could do so "we shall always have a full attendance."[74] Thomas's enthusiasm for the creation of the Society of the Army of the Cumberland reflected his deep affection for that command. He was vastly proud of its accomplishments and preferred any light of recognition to fall on it directly rather than on himself.

The general and his former aide and current business associate Robert Ramsey continued to exchange letters in the spring. Heavily focused on business affairs, Thomas's letter of March 7, 1868, also revealed genuine anxiety concerning the likelihood that duty would uproot him once more. "I intended to have written you several days since about our Ten[ant] Lands, or rather about my fourth interest in them. I have been three times suddenly upset here, and ordered away within a twelve month [period], but have been fortunate enough to escape moving." He did not think that this settled aspect of his life would continue indefinitely. "I cannot expect the same good luck to follow me & have therefore concluded to dispose of my interest in the Manning Lands."

With this pressing business concluded, Thomas turned briefly to politics, with particular reference to the difficulties that President Andrew Johnson was currently confronting. "I am very happy to see that the impeachment trial makes but little excitement in the Country." He used as a barometer the stabilized price of gold and the indications that "trade is being attended to as if all went smoothly at Washington." Things might not indeed be going so smoothly, but the Virginian was optimistic. His conservative nature called for a return to more contented and potentially prosperous times. "I sincerely hope this political strife may be set at rest soon."[75]

Thomas's position on President Andrew Johnson might be clear to his friend, but others suspected the Virginian's motives and politics. At the end of July, two gentlemen from Gallatin, Tennessee, excoriated Thomas for allowing the state to become essentially a "land of tyranny and oppression." Robert Bennett and William Wright implored the president to act in his capacity as commander in chief of the Army and Navy of the United States and "for God's sake relieve this Department from the command of General Thomas." They deemed the soldier to be "the tool of [Governor] Brownlow" and declared him "the most vindictive Radical we know of; for our people to be oppressed, robbed and murdered during this campaign by a set of degraded negroes, backed by General Thomas is a shame to humanity and civilization."[76]

It is difficult to know how President Johnson reacted to such strong sentiments, except to say that he did not comply with the request to remove Thomas from command. But the unhappy Tennesseans were not alone. A short time later a less vehement, but similar, communication reached the president's desk. John Leftwich wrote from Memphis requesting "the presence in Tenn of a sufficiency of National Troops to supercede the necessity of militia," calling the substitution of the forces "our only hope." He added firmly that if such a change took place the troops "ought to be under command of some one not so prejudiced against the masses of our people as Genl. Thomas has on all occasions shown himself to be."[77]

Thomas was oblivious to these specific objections, but he had already demonstrated that he was generally aware of such sentiments on the part of many Southern whites when he discussed the inadvisability of his replacing Sheridan in Louisiana. Even so, he also had his friends and supporters. Among these was Robert Ramsey, with whom he continued a rather extensive correspondence in early August. In this instance, the Virginian seemed to be preparing for the possibility of a transfer to other duty. Thomas recognized that "my stay here is dependent upon the contingencies of the service," and consequently he thought it best to divest himself of the assets he accumulated. Thomas was convinced that the shares he owned had considerable value. The timber, which he explained "consists of primitive forests of Prime" oak, cedar, poplar, and walnut, "all large and well-grown trees" would provide an ample return to an investor by itself. Aside from this resource, there was "good grazing & farming lands, the whole underlined with a fine quality of coal and contains large quantities of iron ore," waiting for profitable development and therefore attractive to any buyer.[78]

It was also in one of the letters to his friend Ramsey that Thomas offered a glimpse at the routine he and his wife had established for their hectic lives. Thomas lamented that in the brief time that Ramsey and his wife would be guests in his home Frances would be away. "I am very sorry that Mrs. Thomas will not be home to receive Mrs. Ramsey, but one of her last injunctions to me before leaving was that I must be sure to tell Mrs. R. how much she regretted the necessity for her going to N. York during this month." Thomas added, "I suppose you know that both she and her sister have to go to N. York every spring & fall, generally in the months of May and September or October," But he assured his friend that he would "have every thing ready" for their visit.[79]

The general took time in mid-August to compose letters that addressed the most contentious arguments raised about him. One person had alerted him to a damning piece in a Kentucky newspaper that impugned Thomas's motives, from embracing secessionism and flirting with Confederate service to acting as he did in remaining loyal to the Union solely for the sake of ambition.[80] The Virginian responded strongly to the implications by denying that he had ever "belonged to the States Rights Party," offered to assist in taking Virginia out of the Union, or made contact with any representative of the Confederacy for obtaining "a Commission either civil or military under their Government."[81] A later historian suggested a level of disingenuousness in the statement, suggesting Thomas cast his answer in "a less than fully candid fashion" by omitting facts. Francis MacDonnell maintained that by avoiding references to his correspondence with Virginia officials prior to the war Thomas "only offered a terse, legalistic and misleading explanation of his actions on the brink of the Civil War."[82] Thomas may well have been obfuscating, but it is much more likely, given the approach he had on many troubling matters, that he chose precision to make his point without intending to mislead or misdirect. Whatever his private sympathies, he had not joined a political movement and certainly did not embrace secession. He also had not made contact with anyone who was then involved with the Confederate government in any capacity, and these facts were sufficient, as he saw it, to make his larger point.

On the same day, he responded to a citizen from Chicago to dispel once more any sense of a desire for personal involvement in the realm of politics. Apparently, William Plum had asked the general questions concerning his political views. As gracious as ever, and as equally blunt, the Virginian dipped his pen into ink to reply that he had "considered the matter deliberately" before arriving "at the conclusion not to give my consent to the publication of my views of political affairs written in a private letter." By way of explanation, he continued, "I take no part in politics. It is neither to my taste, nor in my judgement is it becoming in an Officer of the Army or Navy especially to muddle in politics. They are both that is army & navy conservative Departments of the Government and the officers should therefore especially refrain from giving public expression to their political sentiments."

For Thomas, the "Government" was no longer in "immediate danger," the people had "put away their implements of war," and the time had come for the citizen to enjoy "the exercise of his Constitutional rights" while guarding "the best interests of the Government according to his individual views." The old soldier seemed genuinely optimistic. "My confidence in the general intelligence of the people is so firm that I have no fears but they will want the best men & best measures to insure the peace and prosperity of the country." At the close of the letter he still felt so passionately about the stance he had taken earlier that he repeated his distaste of politics, emphasizing that for officers "it is their duty to sustain the Government whether one party or another happens to have charge of office."[83] George Thomas offered these sentiments sincerely and without rancor. The nation should bind its wounds and soldiers should continue to do their duty.

Some still felt as if the binding of the nation's wounds could not be possible if left to George Thomas, based upon the proclivities he had demonstrated thus far. Mary Furguson of Mount Hope, Tennessee, added her voice to the chorus of those who wrote to President Andrew Johnson to complain about the general. She repeated the notion that white Southerners only wanted peace, but associated such a peace with the success of the Democratic Party. Even so, she maintained that if the government put "wisely tempered conservative *military commander[s]* over the different departments," affairs would be better and "*relief would* be immediate and order preserved." As she saw it, such was not the case for her home state. "Partizans such as Genl. George H. Thomas who commands the United States forces in this department are not calculated to aid in [the] restoration or sustain authority."[84]

Thomas also remained focused on consummating his land deal with Robert Ramsey, but he was particularly troubled with a pending lawsuit over another parcel. The most disturbing aspect was the allegation that Thomas had "fraudulently" gotten possession of the other property "by using Military intimidation to force people to dispose of them to us." He understood that the legal matter would compel a change in his approach concerning any pending sale. "Of course, our negotiations will have to stop now, at least until the suit is decided. I shall insist on a thorough investigation so far as I am concerned, for there are no grounds whatever for charging me with using military intimidation or any other means of getting possession of these lands [other] than by a legitimate way." In the meantime, Thomas needed for Ramsey to return some transactional papers he had lent to him in order to further bolster his case.[85]

General Thomas was susceptible to the charge of military connivance in part because his partners in these investment ventures he had undertaken were former military associates. Ramsey and Andrew J. MacKay were one-time members of his staff, Sanford Kellogg was a soldier and relation by marriage, and J. G. Parkhurst was a former subordinate who had also served briefly as the general's provost marshal.[86] Their connections to the enterprise were legitimate and understandable, but the Virginian bristled at any suggestion of impropriety in his affairs, even by way of appearance.

Thomas thought he had better news to share with Ramsey when he communicated with him in early October. "I have also heard from [Gates] Thruston that it was extremely doubtful if the United States Court could take cognizance of the suit initiated by the Littons against us," he explained, representing the views of another of his former wartime subordinates. "But to be prepared for such an emergency," Thomas had gotten his papers in order to be ready to "make the necessary answer" to the charges in any court proceeding. Still, the dispositions he wanted to make within the department had to take precedence in his mind over any legal concerns. As always, duty came first, and any other personal matters would have to wait. "I shall have to delay here until the last moment to see the troops ordered to Ten. properly stationed and instructed as to their duties in the approaching elections," he explained.[87]

In December, the proposed transaction and the lawsuit remained as items to be addressed. Thomas finalized an arrangement with Ramsey by forwarding him "a Draft on NY for the one thousand dollars I owe you." Thomas still had his lawsuit hanging over him and told his friend that he had been "engaged all day Saturday with Otis drawing up my answer to the Bill brought in the U.S. Circuit Court against me by the Littons and I think we were successful—very—in our answer." Thomas expressed his gratitude for Ramsey's suggestion that the legal representative point out that the original offer made by the investors for the land was actually substantially higher than the appraisal of it and therefore unlikely to sustain any charge of "undue pressure" for the sake of financial gain.

Thomas shifted the topic to the current state of affairs in Louisville and the impact that deterioration in law and order there was having on his own family circle. "On my arrival home I found the ladies well," he observed of Frances and her sister, "but somewhat demoralized by fear of Robbers." Perhaps as department commander too many other distractions had put his focus elsewhere, but Thomas appeared to be struck by the extent of the lawlessness and the powerlessness of local authorities to do anything about it. "It seems that class of Gentry have been doing business in Louisville for the last six weeks on a very large scale. None have been caught yet, but the police are after them."[88]

The Thomases were apparently not directly impacted by the crime spree that plagued their city, beyond a vague level of concern, but the tranquility of the holiday season received a jolt when the thousand-dollar draft Thomas had sent Ramsey proved to be drawn on a bank that unexpectedly shuttered its doors. A distraught George Thomas informed his friend of the unhappy development. "Much to my surprise I find this morning that Tucker & Co. Bankers of this place have suspended [business transactions]." Thomas noted that he had engaged the firm in good faith. "Having perfect confidence in their solvency I purchased the one thousand dollar draft I sent you Monday from them & I fear it is gone." The sequence of events was distressing on many levels for the man who took such pride in his honest dealings with others. "I write to ask you to present it for collection as soon as you receive it," he advised Ramsey of the check, "& let me know the result at once as I want to save as much as I can out of their wreck."

Obviously, he hoped that the aide might still find that the paper retained its value, but Ramsey should be prepared for any eventuality. "Should the draft be protested, I shall have to get you to trust me for another month or two longer, but I hope you may be able to collect on the draft already sent you." Thomas would have chosen any path other than one that would put his connection with his former staffer at risk. The whole business was as galling as it was embarrassing to him.[89]

On the day after Christmas another letter left Louisville for Robert Ramsey in Pennsylvania. Thomas was already making plans to travel to meet with his associate personally. "I really feel mortified that I should have been caught so inocently on my part, but I had dealt so much with Mr. Tucker and always found him so accommodating that I went to him on this occasion with as much confidence in his solvency as I could have had in any body in the world," he offered as background for the unsavory situation. Then, when the crisis arose, Thomas scrambled to make matters right, as much as it was in his power to do so. "I found since writing you last that I will be able to pay you five hundred dollars when I see you & hope to be able to pay the balance on the 1st of February." Thomas wanted Ramsey to know that the payment did not represent a hardship for him. "I have been assured by one of Mr. Tucker's partners that I shall not be much of a loser in the end, but just at this time he can not pay me." But despite the debacle the Virginian displayed the grace and equanimity for which he was famous among friends and associates. "I have always believed him an honest man & therefore shall wait with as much patience as I can command hoping he will be able to settle with me in the course of the spring." This letter, like the one that had preceded it, was a very difficult one for Thomas to write. "What I regret most about it is that I should have disappointed you in not being able to return you the money you loaned me at the time I engaged to do so."[90]

The end of a year that represented so many challenges in areas as disparate as politics and finance must not have been unwelcome for Thomas. He had taken up the peacetime challenges represented by race and reconstruction in the former Confederate states after helping to bring the Civil War to a successful conclusion. Now he would spend the next phase of his life confronting different issues, in other settings. As an army man Thomas accepted his duty as it came, even if it meant distancing himself from the fields on which he had won so much glory, as long as he could be of service to the nation. In one sense he would soon be moving back in time, to some of the places that had marked his prewar regular army days. It was almost as if his life after West Point were coming around full circle.

17   Thomas's Last Battles (1869–1870)

"History will do me justice."
—George Henry Thomas to Thomas B. Van Horne

"All civil honors and duties I shall continue to decline."
—Thomas concerning any postwar ambitions

George Thomas appeared to have had at least some faith that time and distance would allow his story to be told and his service appreciated. "History will do me justice," he explained to Thomas B. Van Horne, the former chaplain of the Army of the Cumberland whom the general tapped to write a history of the command that would cement its reputation, and by extension his own.[1] He had admonished the soldier/historian to undertake the task honestly, even if his account challenged the "received opinions" of others.[2]

Thomas certainly had much of which he could be proud. He also remained ever sensitive to the criticisms leveled against him. He often internalized his frustration and remained silent, if nevertheless seething over the insult he felt that had been foisted upon him. Yet, in some ways, the Virginian could be his own worst critic. During a visit to a social club meeting, he agreed to provide the gathering with a description of the battle of Nashville that included a candid assessment of his conduct of the engagement. An attendee later sent his recollection of the session to an individual who was gathering information for a lecture on the general. In it, L. F. S. Foster noted that Thomas observed that "he ought to have detached a force and sent it around to the rear of the enemy, and cut off his retreat. Had he done so, he would have captured nearly or quite the whole of Hood's army." The witness added that he tried to offer the general alternative explanations that would account for the judgment that he made being the best that could have been undertaken at the time. Thomas rejected the effort and insisted, "a general must be prepared to take some risks," before concluding definitively "that Hood's army ought all to have been captured."[3]

Thomas's willingness to assess himself critically also fit well with his desire to provide credit to others for his successes. He always seemed to place himself in the sphere that would serve the public interests rather than his own. But, unlike his wartime superior, Ulysses Grant, such spheres would not be political ones. Grant was busily engaged in waging a campaign for the presidency of the United States under the standard of the Republican Party. His status from the recent conflict offered a great appeal for the electorate, as opposed to the former governor of New York, Horatio Seymour, who carried the Democratic banner in the contest. A solid majority of electoral votes propelled Grant into the high office and promised a shift in the chain of command that would undoubtedly affect George Thomas, too. Grant's likely successor at the top of the military command structure would be William T. Sherman, but the ripple effect of these elevations opened the prospects for others to rise to fill any vacancies.

Ulysses Grant had not yet assumed the presidency when Thomas traveled to Washington, D.C., to supervise a court of inquiry of fellow Virginian and regular army veteran Alexander B. Dyer, who had most recently served in the capacity of chief of army ordnance. Dyer's otherwise stellar reputation had come under question, and he was now under scrutiny due to a high volume of complaints about abuses related to army contracting. Thomas was among those required to sort the matter out and determine the validity, if any, of the charges posed against his colleague.[4]

William T. Sherman, who liked to affirm his affection for the Virginian, recalled that Thomas, "whose post was in Nashville, was in Washington on a court of inquiry investigating certain allegations against General A. B. Dyer, Chief of Ordnance." That general had taken a room near the residence of Senator John Sherman. Accordingly, General Sherman noted that it became his "habit each morning to stop at Thomas's room on my way to the office in the War Department to tell him the military news, and to talk over matters of common interest." Much of this discussion seemed to center on what Sherman recollected as Thomas's private obsession with regard to appointments and seniority. The men had been close, Sherman calling them "intimately associated as 'man and boy' for thirty-odd years," and the Ohioan described his friend as considered widely to be "the embodiment of strength, calmness, and imperturbability." Some of the emotion that remained generally unseen to the public spilled forth in these private settings. "Yet of all my acquaintances Thomas worried and fretted over what he construed [as] neglects or acts of favoritism more than any other." Sherman had never been afraid to be frank about his comrade, especially in communications with General Grant, and continued this trend in his memoirs.[5]

General Thomas also had the duty to appear before a congressional committee to provide information for austerity measures that body was considering. The lawmakers wanted individuals who had the experience and knowledge to provide answers primarily connected to staff structures and arrangements. Thomas settled into his chair and laid out his credentials. "The principal part of my service has been in the line," he began, "although whilst a subaltern I was post quartermaster and commissary, and a short time after the Mexican war I was depot commissary at Brazos Santiago." The general felt that these assignments and the ones he had engaged in since were ample to meet the purposes of the hearing. "I have had considerable experience in the working of all the staff departments by virtue of being in command of important posts before the war of the rebellion; during and since that time I have been in command of troops, and have had a good deal of supervision over the working of all the staff departments."[6]

With the framework laid for his expertise in such matters, he patiently responded to inquiries, including what he deemed as the wisdom of keeping quartermaster and commissary duties separate if possible. When it came to assessing the paymaster's responsibilities he exposed an understanding of human nature as well as common sense. "If you could insure honesty in all men you might do it," he replied to a question about letting quartermasters handle soldiers' pay, "but in the matter of handling money I would confine it to as few as possible."[7]

Thomas tended to emphasize a preference for retaining structures as they already existed, although he was particularly enthusiastic about one technical system. "The advantage of a signal corps has been so thoroughly demonstrated during the last war that a knowledge of signaling should be preserved."[8] But he was troubled by the implications of a question relating to the level of rank for staff members who had served in the war. "I do not think it ought to be done," he answered strongly regarding the idea of having those individuals revert to their prewar ranks. "These officers having performed their duties faithfully and received their promotions, they should not now be deprived of their rank."[9] This was a fundamental question for Thomas, of not only fairness, but appropriate gratitude for duties faithfully executed.

One of these staffers, Alfred Hough, accompanied the general for at least a time in Washington, and he had such men in mind for the work they had done and the occasions when those tasks brought them under enemy fire. Thomas had his own need to engage in his departmental duties from afar, and he did so through communications with his staff. High on the list of concerns was the possibility that public officials in Tennessee would request the intervention of regular army troops, and Thomas wanted to make sure that such action was warranted if it occurred. Thomas was perturbed at the interruption the service in Washington created in his normal administrative routines. "If no inspection is made of my department in the first half of the Current year it is not my fault," he complained to Hough on February 1, 1869. Then thinking better of the point, he suggested, "as there is no particular necessity of making one before the summer you need not undertake a regular tour." His current duty was impacting everything else, causing Thomas to observe almost painfully, "We are getting along very slowly with our court business and really I can form no idea when we shall get through, certainly not before the fourth of March next."[10]

Times were difficult for the army that had so recently won a war. "The

Army is in such a bad odor in Congress and there has been considerable squabbling over the various bills before the House of Representatives on military affairs," he explained to Hough in February.[11] Indeed, old comrades in arms were proving quite problematic. Benjamin Butler, the former Union general universally despised in Southern circles, was apparently also willing to make his share of enemies among old friends. Anxious to gain political plaudits by reducing the size of the army, Butler went to considerable trouble to lobby support. Thomas made an appearance at one affair, whose lavish appointments struck the Virginian as contradictory to the soldier-turned-politician's calls for public fiscal restraint. The setting presented an appearance that Thomas described as "very fine" to his aide but that he thought was more than tinged with "a strong and disagreeable odor of dirty greenbacks." For George Thomas there was nothing worse than a hypocrite, especially one who seemed so bent upon presenting himself in a righteous cast. "Ben cant crush the army though," he concluded. Indeed, Thomas's sense of the matter led him to think that Butler's efforts would ultimately prove counterproductive. "The more he attacks us, the more friends we find."[12]

At an unspecified point not long before President Grant's inauguration, Thomas dutifully made the rounds with members of the incoming administration. Alfred Hough was back in Washington when he did so and accompanied the general on these important social visits. When the officers sat with the Grants, the casual conversation turned to the need to ascertain Thomas's desires for a posting when the president-elect assumed office. "Thomas, there has got to be a change on the Pacific coast," Grant ventured, "and either you or Sheridan will have to go there; how would you like it?" The Virginian responded thoughtfully. "As for myself I would have no objection to serving there, but on Mrs. Thomas' account I would not want to take her any further away from her friends in the East." Then Grant's wife interjected that since Thomas was already married and Sheridan was not, the prospects for that general's chances for matrimony dictated that he ought to remain in the East instead. The awkward moment passed, but not its effect on Thomas, who quietly observed to his staffer as they left, "Hough, we are going to California, that was settled tonight."[13]

While in the capital, Thomas kept a watch over the situation that prevailed in his department. Reading the newspapers, he gleaned items of interest and drew what he saw to be appropriate conclusions from the intelligence he had thus gathered. "The Courier-Journal is showing its hand & making a desperate effort to revive & keep up the spirit of the Rebels," he observed to Hough, "but I think I can clearly see the day Rebel respectability is over." Such wishful thinking did not prevent the need for further measures, and with the new president's inauguration pending, Thomas thought, "If Grant does not put them in their proper place Congress is clearly determined to do it." Such considerations put him in mind of the Fifteenth Amendment, which was now circulating in the states for ratification. He seemed pleased that the measure "disqualifies all who participated in the Rebellion from holding office."

Annoying elements plagued him, ranging from office seekers who sought his assistance to the historical accounts of the late war that were beginning to come forth. Of the former, Thomas was so exasperated that he threatened to put any new ones "in the fire . . . unless the case is very meritorious." Of the latter, he was particularly perturbed by one version of Mill Springs that seemed to elevate the role of Albin Schoepf and by the characterization that Ulysses Grant had replaced Rosecrans in Chattanooga. Displaying sensitivity for setting the record straight, Thomas requested that Hough address both matters in the interests of clarifying these inaccuracies. "In one sense the author is not altogether incorrect when he says Grant relieved Rosecrans at Chattanooga, because he took command of the troops, but it would be more correct for him to say that Rosecrans was relieved by Thomas in the command of the Army of the Cumberland & that the troops of the Army of the Cumberland and Tennessee were united together and Grant assigned by the War Department to command the whole."[14] This was typical of Thomas in that it relied on a strict recitation of the facts. Grant had assumed command, but not until it devolved on Thomas first.

The stresses and strains associated with these matters and the seemingly interminable Dyer Court proceedings consumed a great deal of time in addition to a substantial quantity of the general's patience. It was about this time when the Virginian exposed some of the raw feeling he harbored toward the new president. That moment came in answer to a request for his assistance with an appointment. "I could not possibly have any influence, because General Grant is not a friend of mine," Thomas concluded with uncharacteristic public bluntness, employing the term of office with which he was most comfortable regarding the new president, "and would not be disposed to accommodate me in any way, if public opinion did not compel him to do so."[15] This was a stark admission that Thomas was now willing to express openly.

Duties required someone to fulfill them, and so the general surveyed the possibilities for assignments that he felt he had earned through his service and seniority, casting his gaze on the Division of the Atlantic. The "hero of Gettysburg," George Meade, had the stronger claim to that post, and Sheridan obtained another that Thomas had considered in the Division of Missouri. President Grant mulled the possibility of sending Schofield to the Division of the Pacific, but Thomas's objection procured him the assignment instead.

Sherman later explained regarding Thomas's attitudes on the subject, "At that time he was much worried by what he supposed was injustice in the promotion of General Sheridan; and still more that General Meade should have an Eastern station, which compelled him to remain in Nashville or go to the Pacific." Thomas indicated that his long and faithful service had entitled him to consideration and "claimed that all his life he had been stationed in the South or remote West, and had not had a fair share of Eastern posts, whereas that General Meade had always been there." Sherman recalled inviting him "to go with me to see President Grant and talk the matter over frankly, but he would not, and I had to act as a friendly mediator." At that session, Grant apparently offered unvarnished assurances "that he not only admired and respected General Thomas, but actually loved him as a man." Sherman received permission "to do anything and everything to favor him," except the one thing that the Virginian had expressed himself as desiring. There was to be no rescission of the appointments of Generals Sheridan and Meade, even for George Thomas.[16]

Thomas would have to look elsewhere for satisfaction, but suitable remaining choices were limited. "I gave General Thomas the choice of every other command in the army," Sherman recalled, "and of his own choice he went to San Francisco, California."[17] Perhaps as a salve to the Virginian's wounds, in retrospect the Ohioan suggested a gesture that Congress did not choose to make. "The truth is, Congress should have provided by law for three lieutenant-generals for these three pre-eminent soldiers, and should have dated their commissions with 'Gettysburg,' 'Winchester,' and 'Nashville.'" He thought that Thomas might have been mollified somewhat and concluded, "It would have been a graceful act," but as circumstances remained, the Virginian was left "feeling that [he] had experienced ingratitude and neglect."[18]

Sherman certainly knew that aspect of his friend's personality well. Almost as confirmation, another acquaintance summed up the silent, brooding manner in which Thomas endured the slights that never seemed to end from within his military family. "I doubt whether anyone ever heard him utter a single complaint but it was obvious to those who knew him well that he felt humiliated and heart sore at the treatment he had received from the military power of the Government."[19]

A letter to Alfred Hough from Washington, dated March 16, 1869, came as close as George Thomas could to condemning the actions of the man under whom he had served so faithfully in the previous war. Insisting that he had been too busily occupied to respond to a letter immediately, including the time spent "sitting for my portrait," Thomas reserved the final portion of the communication for providing his staffer with a description of the process by which he had ended up assigned to the Military Division of the

Pacific. The literal order came in the form of "Genl Order No. 18 of this date," but the fact of the assignment was nothing compared to the manner in which it had occurred. "The way in which this thing was managed was that assignments were being made & it was given out that Halleck was to be relieved & ordered East, & the next day the papers stated that Schofield was to go to the Pacific." Ever sensitive to the prerogatives of rank and service, Thomas felt that matters were amiss. "Very naturally I came to the conclusion that I was being intentionally slighted & so informed Genl. Sherman."[20]

In this instance the slight came with regard to the difference in status between a department and a division. Thomas currently commanded a department. Schofield's assignment to a division would mean putting "a junior" in rank, as the Virginian explained it, into a higher-level post. Consequently, Thomas insisted to Sherman that his service and position "should not be degraded," and his resolution to "publicly protest against it," if the decision persisted, caught Sherman's attention and caused him enough anxiety to work to ameliorate the situation. An early biographer and close associate concluded, "General Thomas did not want to go West, but would rather go than have his rank degraded. Schofield was to be elevated at his expense, and only his vigorous protest prevented it."[21]

Thomas informed his friend Colonel Hough that Sherman had listened intently to the complaint. "He replied that between him and me it did not appear so," the Virginian explained regarding the perception of a slight. But Thomas was not content solely to speak with Sherman on the matter or accept his assessment at face value. "Then I determined to see if the President so intended & applied to be assigned according to my rank." If Grant complied, then no insult had been meant; if not, the message would be clear and Thomas could determine any recourse he might have available to him in the interests of personal honor.

What Thomas did not seem to realize until it was too late was that the president had another option open to him and one that he was apparently happy to take. In doing so, Ulysses Grant outmaneuvered George Thomas as deftly as he had once done to John Pemberton before Vicksburg. The moment exposed Thomas's weaknesses with regard to a new type of campaign for which he was not suited, or certainly not as much as the man who had worked his way into the presidency. The Virginian's letter to his trusted friend and aide revealed that Thomas figured out what had happened to him, but only after it was already an accomplished fact. "Grant protested he had no intention of the kind & had me assigned to the Pacific," Thomas explained.[22] Then, with the ink hardly dry on the orders, Grant created the Military Division of the South for Henry Halleck. What had been a department for Thomas was now a division for someone else.

While the redesignation was hardly inappropriate for Halleck, it had not been done when Thomas held command in the area subsequently reconstituted. Thomas had not transferred to the Pacific because he preferred that posting, but because under the circumstances that prevailed at the time a junior officer would have held higher status based upon the nature of their respective commands. Creating a new "division" for Thomas where he already was located would have meant satisfying his concerns without presenting him with the conditions that dictated a reassignment. Chaplain Van Horne assessed the situation plainly regarding the general's feelings on the sensitive subject. "He always felt that, at least, he should have been left at Louisville to command the new division. This was all there was to the matter."[23] The disappointed Virginian professed not to be disillusioned, but his sense of propriety regarding the president's actions was shaken. "The whole transaction only confirms me in my previous estimate of the paltry mind we have at the head of affairs," he closed the matter disdainfully.[24]

John Schofield had reemerged in Thomas's life in such a way as to have a significant negative impact upon it. The men were bound to clash on numerous grounds. "Both were ambitious and jealous of their reputations," one historian assessed, "yet Thomas would silently fume about slights, while Schofield actively politicked."[25] Historian James L. McDonough insisted that Schofield generally mellowed with age, experience, and greater authority, describing him as "becoming less 'touchy' about matters involving him personally—with the notable exception of General Thomas."[26] Schofield later claimed that he treated Thomas respectfully, even deferentially, during this period, including inviting him to a high-profile Washington dinner and making him "president of a very important military court," referring to the Dyer inquiry.[27] In any case, there was no mistaking the antagonism that marked the relationship.

Throughout these internal army tussles, Thomas tried to maintain his public equilibrium. In response to a letter from a former officer he observed, "I was not at all disappointed that Genl. Sheridan was nominated as Lt. General instead of myself, his commission as Major General was older than mine and being a personal friend of his I always supposed the President would exercise the right to appoint his friend to an office in preference to another who he did not particularly like." At this point in his career, Thomas stuck to his guns when it came to mixing his profession and politics. He noted his regret at not being able to make a recommendation for a postmaster position. "I was very sorry I had to decline to act," he explained. "I have made it a rule not to meddle in the least in politics especially in recommending for places under the Government. I therefore felt that to be consistent I must decline to make his case an exception."[28]

The wearing circumstances were not confined to politicking for professional assignments. Thomas was still dealing with a pending hearing over the Litton lawsuit, although his attorney professed to be "very confident of success." He also had other business matters to attend to, but the time was drawing near for him to take up his new assignment on the West Coast. "I shall start for Cal. in a few days," Thomas explained to Robert Ramsey, "& will be glad to hear from you at all times."[29]

Although distracted by the ordinary activities of his official duties, including participation in the seemingly interminable Dyer hearings, General Thomas spent the better part of April making arrangements for his relocation to the West Coast. In the early part of the month, he asked Alfred Hough to inquire into the possibility "of sending my bay horse across the country by rail."[30] He followed that with a more urgent message to have the papers of the Army of the Cumberland appropriately assembled and forwarded to Washington, D.C., as well as entertaining the differences between the relative costs of shipping "two grays" or selling the horses "for $500." In the meantime, the Dyer Court "still hangs on, but I hope to be able to start back after the 25th."[31]

Whatever his internalized disappointments, the Virginian left the region of the country in which he had lived and served for most of his years to return to an area he had worked in briefly while in the old army. He arrived to considerable local praise; a San Francisco newspaper lauding him as "a man of uncommon executive ability."[32] Indeed, his stature as a result of the late war was unquestioned in the public mind. Even so, Thomas seemed not to anticipate remaining at this post for an indefinite period of time. A stint of four or five years would be sufficient for him to seek another assignment to a more desirable location.

In the order that announced Thomas's succession, the current commander of the Military Division of the Pacific, Henry Halleck, struck a high-sounding tone. "In compliance with General Orders No. 18, current series from Head Quarters of the Army, the command of this Military Division is hereby relinquished to Major General *George H. Thomas*," the announcement opened. "It is gratifying to the Divisional Commander to know that he is succeeded by one of the ablest and most accomplished Generals in the Army."[33] Thomas promptly assumed the command and issued instructions that all of Halleck's "existing orders" were to "remain in force until countermanded."[34]

Thomas had set such actions in place to ensure the smooth transition of one commander to another, but there was some question as to the nature of the farewell contact between the Virginian and his departmental predecessor. In what was meant to serve as a banquet to honor his successor, Halleck was supposed to have spoken openly about the fate that Grant and official Washington had in store for Thomas during the Nashville Campaign. This led to the disclosure of Schofield as a chief culprit in the drama, with John Logan playing a significant role as well. Thomas biographer Donn Piatt insisted, "General Thomas had never known the names of those with whom it was determined to supercede him, in fact, he did not know of the second attempt with Logan at all."[35]

Later, Halleck explained that he had only told Thomas privately how close the Virginian had come to being replaced by John Schofield. "Old Brains" had not expected any of these remarks to be expressed in print and described himself as being "surprised that so much had been made out of so little" when the matter appeared in the newspapers. Halleck made it clear that he and Thomas had not dined together "since they left West Point Academy" and any reports to the contrary were a mere "sensation," since, as he explained it to his newspaper interlocutor, the dinner and the alleged speech attributed to him never actually happened.[36] Still the sensitive Virginian could not help but be affected by confirmation of his suspicions. Apparently, Halleck had attempted to be coy by initially refusing to name the individual specifically. Then, he relaxed and divulged Schofield's name. "I knew it," Thomas reacted with an uncharacteristic open display of emotion. "I knew he was the man."[37]

Whatever Halleck's intentions in making his disclosures concerning Nashville, George Thomas was already showing the strain of the years of service and the squabbles that he had endured since the war. An old comrade, Erasmus Keyes, recalled seeing him at this point in his life and made special note of his careworn appearance. "After the Rebellion, when he arrived in San Francisco to assume command of the Division of the Pacific, I met him and was shocked to observe the effect which war and change of climate had wrought in his countenance." The general had aged considerably, and the friend explained, "White lines bordered his lips and his eyes had lost their wonted fires." True to form, Thomas did not complain about his state of health or any other aspect of his affairs to Keyes, "but applied himself with his customary strictness to duty."[38]

Thomas's first task was to set in place a staff structure, comprised of people with whom he had implicit faith, including Captain Alfred L. Hough and Lieutenant Sanford C. Kellogg.[39] But the Virginian was not looking for the assignment to be a sinecure or a semiretirement for himself or his aides. Whether it was his devotion to duty or a renewed spirit once he had taken up his new post, Thomas embraced his responsibilities with zeal. He was also bound to display his usual thoroughness in assessing them regardless, but the opportunity seemed to reinvigorate him.

He immediately implemented changes that he believed would bring improvement to the ways in which the system that existed prior to his arrival functioned. In the Department of California he demanded that all purchasing matters be carried out appropriately, with due public notice "to be given of all purchases of supplies, and contracts for freighting to be made in this market, that all markets and freighters in this city may have an opportunity to compete for the same." He had long been a champion of equal opportunity in this sense, but found that when there had not been "sufficient time to advertise for bids in the usual manner," purchases and contract awards had tended to be made to the benefit of a favored relatively few individuals.[40] Certainly, the manner of purchasing that formerly prevailed did not constitute "best practices," in modern parlance.

The commander clearly wanted an efficiently run division that reflected good military order. General Orders No. 27 reassigned employees of the chief paymaster in the division to "the city of San Francisco"; even if living expenses might prove to be more difficult for the personnel themselves, Thomas deemed the configuration to "best subserve the public interests."[41] The flurry of initial orders also included steps to close two posts in Arizona and open another for the purpose of establishing a more efficient organization of his jurisdiction.[42]

Thomas could be excused for thinking that he might finally be allowed to enjoy the laurels he had won in combat. He was no longer competing with unreconstructed Southerners. The distance from the intrigues and manipulations of the nation's capital must also have made the move to California appear less onerous. Nevertheless, critical battles remained, and Thomas was determined to make his contribution regarding them. One of these was a product of the austerity movement that had been afoot in Congress. In this case, the political volunteer general John A. Logan, who seemed to delight in discomfiting his former regular army colleagues, led the charge. The effort called for the reduction of the number of generals and the extinction of brevet ranks, but it also targeted the salaries of general officers, not only with the intention of limiting the number of general officers, but with the immediate effect of lowering them in economic status. Thomas's service on the panel that considered brevet ranks had been meant to head off such drastic measures. As usual the action served to sweep too broadly and impact those who had a legitimate claim to such honors. According to one contemporary, "Thomas threw the weight of his influence in favor of this, but he failed to have his cherished plan carried out."[43]

Such measures met with a howl of discontent among the officers affected. It meant that as a major general, Thomas would have his pay capped at just under $10,000, a princely sum to be sure in comparison to other officers, but one that had been established at a higher level and would now have to be implemented by adjustment downward. "The military leadership was enraged," Logan's biographer explained. "General George H. Thomas, commanding at San Francisco, wrote Sherman to ask if passage could not be prevented. He called it 'more heartless' than he thought Congress capable of." But the measure, despite some minor changes that did not address the salary aspect of the legislation, passed through the body in Washington.[44]

Sherman expressed strong concern over the measure, referencing Thomas in his appeal in ways that would have made the Virginian blush, even if he could agree with the overall sentiments. The general insisted that his current position and compensation bore connection to his past services. "I will say the same for Generals Sheridan, Meade, and Thomas," he explained. Reminding Congress of the inadequacy of any payment for Gettysburg, Winchester, and Five Forks for the architects of those crucial Union victories, Sherman added, "What [is owed] Thomas for Chickamauga, Chattanooga, or Nashville?" Perhaps reflective of the pessimistic mood that the measure had created for even the most senior generals, the Ohioan observed of the ultimate costs "of the late war": the greater mortality rate among those who had served in the field versus the "civilians of like age and conditions, who staid at home."[45]

Thomas's refusal to meddle deeply in politics had already cost him at several turns, but he tried to find ways to protect others as best he could. In the aftermath of the Army Appropriations Bill of 1869, entities known as "Benzine Boards" for their responsibility to cleanse the service based upon legislative requirements sprang into operation. While serving on one of these boards in San Francisco, George Crook received notice of an opening in the command of the Department of Arizona. Crook demurred, and Thomas promised, "as far as he could control," to allow the soldier to stay where he was. The Virginian felt that the long-standing service of his colleague meant that officer ought to have some choice in such matters.[46]

Thomas had made a habit of conducting his business outside of the confines of an office as well as within it. Some of these matters could be handled behind a desk; others required him to be in the saddle. It was also clear to him that he should inspect as much of the geographic limits of his divisional responsibility personally as he could muster, which would require an extraordinary effort to cover vast distances over a wide-ranging and diverse territory. By one account, in order to view this territory the Virginian would have to cross approximately 14,000 miles of territory in his travels over a single year.[47] It was bound to be a monumental feat by any calculation, especially for one whose health had been in question for some time.

On June 15, 1869, Special Orders No. 100 detailed the requirement for two of the staff officers, including Brevet Colonel Hough, A.D.C., to "accompany the Major-General Commanding on a tour of inspection, to Portland, Oregon, via Camp McDermit, Nevada, and Fort Boise, Idaho."[48] Camp McDermit had been established in August 1865, while Fort Boise dated from 1863. Both protected travel routes and were supposed to enable the army to control the Paiutes and Shoshonis in their areas, respectively. In his reorganization and assessment, Thomas phased out Fort Churchill in Nevada as no longer needed and therefore an unnecessary expense for the military.[49] Additionally, the new commander investigated charges of "irregularities" attributed to some of the officers in the department.[50] Indeed, one newspaper editor cheerily announced, "It is expected that salutary changes will be made by Gen. Thomas."[51]

Such endeavors required a demanding effort from Thomas and his staff officers. Hough recorded the progress of the entourage through the frontier region for posterity and in letters to his wife, beginning with a departure from the divisional headquarters in San Francisco on June 15. It took a few weeks for the party to reach Portland, Oregon, from which the new division commander wrote to his friend Colonel Ramsey back in Pennsylvania. Much of the July 7 letter related to the dismissal of agents who had been privately speculating with investors' money, a conflict of interest that Thomas found unacceptable. "I have for some time had an idea that they may have been using our funds for private speculations, and although we may not have suffered any material injury yet it is too great a risk to run to keep an agent who may be induced to use money necessarily entrusted to his management to speculate in any venture." Thomas hoped to obtain representatives who would not be tempted to use such funds as venture capital. The general was also pleased with the journey thus far. "I am now on my trip through the territory I have supervision over & so far have had a delightful trip though exceedingly warm." He promised to write again when he returned to his headquarters in San Francisco.[52]

Even as he traveled for professional purposes, George Thomas gave many indications of his varied interests and intellectual pursuits. Although occasionally depicted as studious if not brilliant, he had a tendency to engage in multiple pursuits at the same time, which indicated an active and inquisitive mind. Among the notes in his aide's papers, presumably left from the time that the two men traveled across the general's new responsibility, was a brief essay on the habits of ravens and crows and their significance for coastal tribes of Northwestern Native Americans. He was particularly drawn by the habit of ravens to pick shellfish at the shoreline, "which they carry up into the air for several hundred feet and let them fall on certain spots for the purpose of breaking the shells," to enable them to consume the contents.[53] In other instances, Thomas not only demonstrated practical skills of observation, but specific scientific knowledge relating to species, which he freely shared with interested parties, including the Smithsonian Institution.[54]

Hough noted a nostalgic stopover in California. "After visiting all other forts he paid a flying visit to his old post, Fort Yuma, where, as captain, he had been stationed, and where he had suffered so much from the heat and other causes incident to the climate." Although Thomas was not prone to pretentiousness, he was cognizant of rank and the status that accrued to it. The visit "filled him with pleasant memories, and those were intensified in a recollection that his rank now would forever exempt him from continuous service there."[55] Thomas was clearly happy to have the days of a struggling subaltern behind him and honored to have the officers and men of the post turned out to receive him.

The next day, following these brief glimpses back at earlier days, the travelers boarded the vessel *Fideleter* and set out for Alaska, arriving at Sitka on July 22. Former wartime colleague Jefferson C. Davis met the party at the dock on their initial stop, and they remained in Sitka for several days.[56] The opportunity to rekindle acquaintances among old army comrades, enjoy the wonders of the natural elements, and satisfy himself personally of the nature of his command helped to make the trip easier for Thomas to endure, at least initially.

The travels were not as easy for Thomas's aide. During the excursion, Alfred Hough suffered from numerous bouts with seasickness during what proved to be an exhaustive voyage for all. While the staffer offered no specific record of any ill effects on the part of General Thomas, he provided a glimpse at the wear the travelers exhibited in August. To his wife, Mary, Hough noted that cold nights and generally rainy conditions made everyone miserable. "The General seems tired and suffers from the cold weather," the aide explained in August, but indicated that at the same time both of their fellow travelers appeared to feel the effects to a greater extent than their chief.[57]

The significant portion of the mission from a professional standpoint was the opportunity to obtain vital intelligence. Gaining an understanding of the nature and conditions of the indigenous peoples in this part of the division was important. "They are very peaceable and quiet except when they get whiskey," Colonel Hough recorded of local residents with whom they made contact, "when they quarrel among themselves." As he was wont to do, Thomas not only observed, but acted on the basis of what he had learned. Hough attributed the difficulties with alcohol to the "Russians," who, as that officer explained to his wife, "have always sold them whiskey, and as yet our folks have not entirely stopped it, but Genl. Thomas has forbidden any further shipments of whiskey here."[58]

Thomas had two occasions to meet with Native American leaders, each of which Hough described as a "big talk." Aided by interpreters, the first of these conversations proved lengthy and productive, with "the General" offering practical advice. With this first set of leaders Thomas informed his hosts of the desire of the "great Chief at Washington" to use troops to protect the local population "from bad white men." Following the adjournment of that session, the visitors retired to dinner and "celebrated the Generals 54th birthday," with everyone having, as Hough recorded, "a pleasant time."[59]

In a subsequent second meeting, this time with representatives of the Aleuts, Thomas again provided "his usual good advice and information." The army commander warned his counterparts about the dangers of "believing all the stories that were told them by unscrupulous adventurers." With his own experiences to inform him, the Virginian observed, "I suppose you have, like us, some bad mean men among you who will lie and steal." Even so, Thomas surely could not have been prepared for the response he received. "We have none," the chief explained in a nonplussed manner concerning such bad influences; "we are Christians, and are very sorry to hear you have them." Hough must have looked straight at his commander, for he noted, "The General blushed and humbly acknowledged the unfortunate truth."[60]

While on the Alaska excursion, General Thomas was not above participating in some of the activities that others might have considered beneath the dignity of his office. On one occasion he agreed to become the unofficial "coxswain" of their row boat, with the remainder of the party serving as "oarsmen," as they transported themselves to and from the larger vessel.[61]

By the end of August, the exhaustive inspection was complete. As Thomas and his companions prepared to take their leave of the region, the general offered his observations for the benefit of a local newspaper. He was "much pleased with Alaska," he explained.[62] Nor were the words meant solely for public consumption. Thomas had been enormously impressed with the new territory he had traversed. His long and varied military service had taken him to a wide variety of settings and locations, each with its own distinct features and awe-inspiring elements. While pausing in a subsequent trip at West Point in October 1869, Thomas recalled his summer tour of the Pacific region. "I had a very interesting trip to Alaska last summer," he observed to his friend Fitz John Porter. "It is a beautiful country, but too far North ever to be of any use to us except as a fur producing region." He explained that he considered the purchase of Alaska "as judicious if made for the purpose of crowding England out of British Columbia" and expressed the belief that the individuals who currently resided there "begin to realize that we will have them in our hands before many years." Thomas was convinced that "the most energetic of them are anxious to come under the Government of the United States."[63] The trip had been active, enervating, and educational. Once more, as he done years earlier while stationed at Fort Yuma, Thomas forwarded samples to the Smithsonian Institution, including examples of walrus bones and a box of coal specimens, as "Additions to the Collections."[64]

The time spent in Alaska as recorded by Alfred Hough offered a few telling glimpses of the character of the commanding general. At one location, younger Native American leaders had sent word of a desire to meet with him, and when Thomas determined that the request was being made for the purpose of showing their independence from their chiefs, he rejected the proposal.[65] There was no point in alienating established leaders for the purpose of cultivating those who sought an audience only for their own purposes. Thomas seemed to be able to sense political gamesmanship in many forms.

At another point, Thomas assessed the hunting of seals by the local populace with a comment that might have applied in another day to some of his earliest recruits. "If the manner of killing seals is left to the natives," he explained to Alfred Hough with a hint of sarcasm, "there is no fear of their overdoing it."[66] He had seen a great deal, satisfying himself with a better understanding of this portion of his division, and was back in San Francisco on September 16. Even then he was not destined to remain desk-bound there for long.[67]

A trip to the East Coast required another extensive journey for the fellow who bragged as he paused in Chicago that his recent Alaska venture had proven pretty "fast traveling for a slow man."[68] The Virginian attended the marriage of a daughter of his old army comrade Erasmus Keyes. "Thomas, I notice no change in our social relations now, when in Florida, New Orleans and Charleston I used to order you to go and drill the company," the soldier recalled of his former subordinate. The general, whose rank and reputation had moved well beyond in the intervening years, replied frankly, "There is none, and why should there be?"[69] In short, Thomas felt that he remained in his essence the same as he had been those many years ago.

While visiting the larger metropolitan communities east of the Mississippi, Thomas availed himself of various other social opportunities. Newspaperman Alexander McClure recalled one of these pleasant diversions with the general while in Washington. "We spent the evening together at the opera, and afterward sat until late in the night conversing on topics of general interest." McClure thought that his famous companion still "felt humiliated and heartsore at the treatment he had received from the military power of the government," but incongruously concluded that he doubted anyone had ever heard Thomas "utter a single complaint" on the subject.[70]

One of the interesting elements of George Thomas's personality was that for all of his disdain of public demonstrations and displays, he appeared to enjoy conversations among friends. He continued to prefer not to interject himself heavily into what was being said, but he had a reputation for listening carefully and speaking concisely. Thomas had opinions. He did not mind sharing them with others, but would never have ventured to dominate

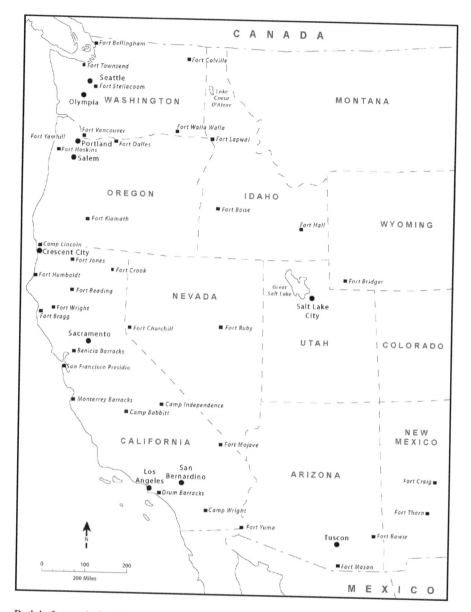

Both before and after the Civil War, George Thomas served in various posts on the Pacific Coast. His final headquarters assignment was at the Presidio in San Francisco, where he died on March 28, 1870. Map created by Heather Harvey.

discussions or attempt to lead or direct them. Even if he did not express himself as frequently as the others, he was not averse to inserting his views when he deemed them appropriate to the occasion.

The Thomas humor could creep in, usually in ways that would not seem to fit initially into his professional demeanor. When he repeatedly goaded a friend over the years for having so many children, Thomas finally determined that if they were going to continue, "I think you might name one of your children for me." Apparently despite the light sarcasm, the fellow determined to honor the soldier in just such a manner. While in Washington, General Thomas received a surprising notice that "George Henry Thomas Scribner has this day reported in person for duty." The proud father recalled that the general hastily replied "by return of mail" with a "document bearing all the official marks of special orders, with the following extract: 'George Henry Thomas Scribner having reported in person for duty, is hereby assigned to the care of his mother until further orders.'"[71]

Perhaps not surprisingly, given the exertions he had undergone in assuming command of the division, the Virginian also struck an almost tired tone. While visiting briefly in the East, he told a former Union colleague that he planned to return to the West Coast shortly and hoped to be able to enjoy "a pleasant sojourn for the next three or four years."[72] The idea of such a "sojourn" must have been appealing for a soldier whose duty had carried him to the far corners of the nation's territory and called on him to battle opponents in diverse areas of the North American continent over several decades. The grueling inspection tour he had felt compelled to make was also completed.

Of course, divisional demands continued to require his attention. Just prior to Christmas 1869 he took up another thorny issue that must have caused consternation in some circles. This action came from a matter that Thomas had seen many times in the old army of pre–Civil War days, when the small number of regular officers available compelled post commanders to improvise to meet their needs. In this case, the situation must have been acted upon in the extreme, for it warranted strong measures, as reflected in General Orders No. 42.

These instructions were intended to address the issue of "the proper assignment of Recruits skilled as clerks and mechanics, to the Companies in this command where they are most needed." In order to get a better idea of the number of skilled personnel available for the division as a whole, Thomas "directed that Post Commanders report to these Head Quarters, on monthly extract from Post Returns, the number of clerks, carpenters, saddlers, blacksmiths, tailors, shoemakers and masons, if any, at their respective Posts."

Having determined these craft persons in uniform, Thomas insisted that "every effort will be made to properly distribute all clerks and mechanics that may be required," but in any case he wanted "the frequent practice" of hiring civilian employees to cease forthwith. In disapproving of the hiring of civilian clerks, Thomas insisted that "it is expected that troops will do all the necessary current work at the Posts, and where there are not men skilled for the purpose they should be taught."

Through his many years of service Thomas had written more than his share of post returns and official reports. He understood the necessity for the duty and considered it the appropriate purview of the individual in authority. "Officers are responsible for the preparation of their own papers, and where they cannot find clerks in the command they can educate them for such duty or must perform it themselves." Part of the necessity for such measures came from the need for frugality in the face of congressional cutbacks. "A rigid economy should be practiced by Officers in the administration of their duties, and no expenditure of money will be authorized or approved that can be obviated by the proper performance of their legitimate duties by both Officers and men."[73]

The Christmas holiday offered little respite from the toils and cares that weighed so heavily on the general. Former subordinate G. P. Thruston wrote from Nashville to tell his old commander of a proposal to remove Thomas's portrait from the state capitol building. Remarking that the effort seemed to be part of a "general overturning of old landmarks here," and thus less likely to have been a measure aimed specifically at Thomas, Thruston added ominously, "it is possible" that "some mean thing" might occur "in relation to your picture." Of course, such an eventuality, the officer assured, would "require the prompt intervention of your friends."[74]

Thruston followed the letter with another that suggested that the speaker of the Tennessee House, William O'Neil Perkins, was "said to have been a Union man before the war but like most of his neighbors about Franklin Tenn, has not much unionism to boast of since that time." Still, Thruston was convinced that there would be insufficient support in the legislative body to remove the portrait in any case.[75] Such an outcome could hardly be comforting, and Thomas did not wait long to express himself on the matter.

Although he usually avoided public demonstrations, Thomas undoubtedly believed that once they had been made any further consideration, or reconsideration, would only be personally insulting. He had to believe that it would have been better never to have received the honor in the first place. In that context, Thomas wrote what for him was a scathing letter at the close of the year. He offered to refund the state for the costs of commissioning and procuring the portrait and expected it to be moved from the capitol. "I will premise by stating although I regretted at the time, the Legislature of 1866 had ordered, by joint resolution, a portrait of me, to be painted and placed in the State Library, yet being convinced it was done through motives of friendship and esteem,—the joint resolution having been passed without my knowledge,—I felt a natural delicacy in declining a compliment so unexpected, assured as I was of the sincerity of the act."

Now, circumstances were decidedly different. New political realities prevailed, and the sentiments that originally attached to the portrait and its subject were no longer the same. Thus, impelled primarily by "self-respect" and a sense of loyalty to the earlier legislature, the general insisted that he wanted to prevent the "possibility of seeing a disagreeable picture" in the presence of the new body of lawmakers by its removal. He also planned to return the medal that had been cast as soon as he secured it from New York, where he had left it for safekeeping before coming to the Pacific.

Thomas explained that he did not view his decision as a repudiation of the sentiments expressed earlier, but as recognition that the current environment created the impression that "a wrong [had been] perpetrated by a former Legislature on the people of that state in my behalf." Interestingly, the letter and the sentiments he had expressed in it forced the acknowledgment that the proposal to sell the likeness had actually been an effort to gain attention for other causes and was not intended to exact the removal of them.[76]

Thomas's wrangling with the Tennessee legislature suggested that in the new year he faced some of the same old issues and challenges. He had returned to the West Coast and settled back into his routine, but matters that had proven difficult for him in the past resurfaced. One of these was the determination of some that he ought to be involved in national politics. As he had indicated so often before, nothing could be further from his desires. But much of that impetus had existed during the 1868 presidential election and had dissipated once that campaign season ended. A new presidential election cycle loomed only a scant two years in the future, and probes already were evident concerning Thomas's potential placement on a political ticket. In this case, the individual pressuring the general to consider entering the national political arena was his cousin by marriage, John Tyler Jr. Tyler had formerly opposed a Thomas presidency to then-president Andrew Johnson, condemning his kinsman as having become too radicalized in his social and political views. Now, he thought differently on the matter.

George Thomas remained unmoved. In a March 8, 1870, letter he reiterated some of the arguments he had employed before successfully. "My services are now, as they have always been, subject to the call of the Government in whatever military capacity I may be considered competent and worthy to fill, and will be cordially undertaken whenever called upon to render them." But the caveat as ever was "whatever military capacity," and a run for any political office did not fit under that criterion. "All civil honors and duties I shall continue to decline," he reiterated.

But Thomas was not without an understanding of the motivation that existed for such a summons to public service. "Is it not rather early to begin to look for another Republican candidate for the next Presidential term?" he asked pointedly. Ulysses Grant and the Virginian had experienced at best a strained relationship in the past, but Thomas did not deem it sufficiently flawed to act now, any more than he had acted before, in such a way as to distress his comrade deliberately. "Grant is still young," he insisted, "has not, as yet, committed any serious mistake, and if he continues steadfast to the principles enunciated at his inaugural, will be entitled to the second term, or at least to the nomination, as an expression of the approbation of the party for his past services."

This was a fundamental part of George Thomas's being, not only to refuse a challenge to someone who had not yet "committed any serious mistake," but to believe that loyal service entitled one to "approbation" because of it. The Thomas who would not supplant Don Carlos Buell in mid-campaign and only reluctantly did so when William S. Rosecrans stumbled badly after Chickamauga was not about to challenge Ulysses Grant simply because he could. The reticence was his shield and buckler against such temptations, and his political sword remained in its scabbard. Circumstances would prevent Thomas from having to consider such matters further, but his consistency in responding to what had to be flattering indications of his stature was as clearly evident in 1870 as it had been previously in 1868.

In the meantime, George Thomas faced a renewed rhetorical assault that threatened his peace of mind in a way that recalcitrant rebels or lukewarm Unionists could not have done. The matter once more dealt with one of his greatest and proudest moments of triumph—the defense of Nashville in December 1864. The antagonist in this new campaign was not John Bell Hood or another former Confederate opponent, but one of the subordinates who had assisted in that same campaign. An anonymous letter published in the *New York Tribune* on March 12, 1870, purported to offer "Secrets of History—the Battle of Nashville—Was Grant's Order a Blunder?" The tone of the piece was clearly favorable to John M. Schofield and critical of George H. Thomas.

It is unclear precisely when Thomas became aware of the article, but he was an avid reader of newspapers with a large circle of friends who could inform him of what he might have otherwise missed. Thomas tried to dismiss the article, telling his aide that it represented "funny reading." But the surface bravado hid the deeper trouble the document engendered. The general's wife realized the toll that the situation took on her husband better than anyone else. To a query about the matter she replied bluntly, "I will say that it preyed upon him and affected his health."[77]

Thomas found the assault on his character astonishing. Having prided himself on never doing anything that might remotely resemble an intrigue against a superior, he had expected similar behavior from those who had served under him. That he should have known better is an understandable criticism of Thomas's failure to recognize the degree of such unsavory aspects of human nature in others. But the public forum in which the case was made rendered it all the harder for Thomas to accept. "I am now satisfied that what I have suspected for some time is true," he explained to Colonel Hough, "that is, that General Schofield intrigued for my removal, to enable him to get my command." Thomas professed not to understand all of what he knew had happened in the aftermath of Nashville. But now that the motive was clear, any mystery dissolved in a rising tide of rage over the betrayal.

In addition to posterity, there were other battles for the Virginian to fight. He sent a strongly worded message on March 14 to General Sherman relating to action pending in the U.S. Congress. "Can nothing be done to prevent the passage of the bill now before Congress for the reduction of the officers of the army?" he inquired. From what he could discern from such a distance, a number of the army's "most deserving officers, who, in consequence of wounds and disability from exposure in the discharge of their duties have been placed on the mustering order list, and will by the provisions of the present bill, be mustered out of service, whenever it becomes law."

For Thomas there was no crime quite so great as ingratitude, and if the government sought to impose frugality measures they ought not to be done at the expense of those who had sacrificed so much in the preservation of the Union. Thomas expressed the hope that what he was reading in the public press might have been misrepresented, but he feared the worst. In his opinion, the bill as it was currently conformed "exhibits more hardness than I supposed our Congress guilty of." The Virginian saw little to redeem the measure. "The fact is, it is even in a worse shape than the bill originally offered by Logan, for there appears to be no promise for returning officers who have been disabled by their devotion to the service."[78]

It is difficult to know the extent to which Thomas sought to internalize his outrage before finally allowing it to vent. There were still indications of levity, too. The last special order that issued from his office under his signature touched on his unique sense of humor. The case involved one David Lyons, "Music Boy" of the Twelfth Infantry, who had apparently received his position without much of an audition and had been since found woefully lacking in his ability to carry out his official duties. Special Orders No. 53 noted that the young man "being incapable of learning music," a prerequisite for the position of "Music Boy," no doubt, was to be "discharged from the service of the United States upon the receipt of this Order at the Post where he may be serving." In the language of what would traditionally be a pro forma order, there is a hint that Thomas's wry humor remained, even under the strain he no doubt otherwise felt.[79]

Yet, on the same day that he ended both young Lyons's military and budding musical career, March 28, 1870, the Virginian remained so disturbed by the public assault on his Nashville legacy that he went to his office to compose a response. He would set the record straight with an unvarnished narrative, referring to himself in such a manner as to establish an air of objectivity. Nevertheless, the words came in torrents as he scribbled out sentence after sentence, his mind racing to the next point that he wanted to make. There was the disposition of troops to discuss and the wayward pontoon train that "could not have reached Franklin, under any circumstances, in time to place a bridge for crossing of the troops when the infantry reached that point." There was the situation that developed after the battle of Nashville when high water in the numerous rivers and watercourses limited avenues of pursuit. Even so, the infantry and cavalry performed as well as circumstances permitted and caused the Confederate retreat to be undertaken "with such haste, as to get beyond the reach of the main column before all of the infantry could cross Duck River." Then it was back to the gathering of reinforcements pursuant to General Sherman's orders and the urgent measures he had taken to prepare these men for likely combat.

Thomas had poured much of his soul and energy into the response to this point and now came full circle back to Schofield and the lead-up to Franklin. He felt once more the urge to reiterate why he had remained in Nashville while action occurred elsewhere. "To attend to the equipping of this force, as well as to be able to correspond with General Sherman, Thomas was compelled to remain in Nashville," he explained, "whilst he placed Schofield in immediate charge of the troops engaged in watching the movement of Hood, and retarding his advance on Nashville." He noted ironically that his absence had offered Schofield the chance for personal achievements that would not have been possible if he had been present and supervising the operations personally. "This necessity existing until the army fell back to Nashville, gave Schofield the opportunity to fight the battle of Franklin." Knowing the spirit that never took deliberately from another the laurels that the individual had won, Thomas spoke favorably of Schofield's victory. "This was a very brilliant battle, most disastrous to the enemy, and as the writer in the Tribune says, no doubt contributed materially to the crowning success at Nashville." From there, the pen scratched but a few more illegible words before tapering off.[80]

In his agitated state it is impossible to say precisely if or when Thomas felt the pain. According to one witness, "I want air" was all that he could manage as the massive frame thrust its way through the door before he collapsed. Those present laid him out on a lounge while summoning medical attention.[81] Thanks to the attendance of physicians and their ministrations, Thomas lingered through the day. Occasionally he rallied, at one point apparently able to rise to his feet briefly before being once more overcome. This battle was to be the toughest he had ever faced. In the end, the strength that he had evinced on many battlefields and critical situations in a long and storied career was not enough. One contemporary recorded the final moments. "Partial unconsciousness advanced to entire insensibility. The pupils dilated, and his breathing became more and more labored and apoplectic."[82] The general never regained consciousness after mid-afternoon, and by early evening he was in his last throes. At approximately 7:25 PM, General George Henry Thomas convulsed slightly and then simply stopped breathing. The man whose service to the nation had so significantly marked his life and career was gone.[83]

The news stunned associates. "I am afraid old Tom is gone," Ulysses Grant remembered Cump Sherman saying as he brought the news to the White House "in a state of deep emotion." Grant observed simply, "The news was a shock and grief to us both."[84] In the earlier world of Reconstruction politics, that general had employed reports of Thomas's illness to outmaneuver President Johnson's attempt to replace Phil Sheridan in New Orleans, but the sudden demise of the soldier now caught Grant by surprise.

So much remained to be done, even as the great warrior lay in death. Arrangements had to be made for transporting the remains from the California coast. William T. Sherman sent immediate instructions to Captain Hough, Thomas's adjutant. "Order in my name Colonels Kellogg and Willard to Troy, New York, with the body and family of General THOMAS, thence to report to me for orders."[85] Hough cut the orders that sent "Brevet Lieutenant-Colonel John P. Willard, U.S.A., and Brevet Lieutenant-Colonel S.C. Kellogg, U.S.A.," on the sad duty. He further instructed, "The Quartermaster's Department will furnish the necessary transportation for the body and four members of his family."[86]

The first, and shortest, part of the journey was to be conducted by water. As the vessel carrying the coffin ventured across San Francisco Bay, the batteries of Fort Alcatraz blazed forth in salute. The weapons of a visiting British warship, *Zealous*, joined the chorus, the booming of all the guns providing a requiem of tribute. Thomas was then placed in a specially designated railcar for the much longer journey across the nation to a final resting place in Troy, New York. Frances Thomas had spent so much of her married life apart from her husband and would do so again here as she stayed behind temporarily to attend to the last duties required of her. However, at least one of the general's aides remained with him throughout, even when the honor guard that accompanied the procession had to be rotated.

Thomas's old friend and West Point roommate William T. Sherman contemplated having the burial take place at the United States Military Academy. On this issue Frances Thomas would not budge. If she were going to relocate to her home in Troy, the general would have to be laid to rest nearby. "I feel that I must bury General Thomas in my family lot at the cemetery there," she explained. The arrangements for an appropriate funeral could now be left to Sherman.[87] These matters would have to proceed without her, for Frances had determined to remain in California to attend to her late husband's affairs. Alfred Hough assisted her in the difficult duty, sorting through papers to determine what was official and would have to remain and what could be turned over to her as personal in nature.

Frances Thomas was not be able to start her journey eastward until April 5, only days before the funeral was scheduled to occur, and subjected to the strictures of distance and transportation did not arrive in Troy until April 14, just under a week after the general had been laid to rest.[88] In another of those supreme ironies that life casts people's way, on the day she began the trip, President Ulysses Grant approved a resolution of Congress that extolled the virtues and service of her husband and lamented his passing.[89]

The widow understood well that she had to share her grief with the nation and especially the veterans who had served under her husband and for whose welfare he had always taken such a devoted interest. Among the pallbearers were former superior William Rosecrans and army commander colleagues George Meade and Joseph Hooker, as well as subordinates such as William Hazen, Granger, and even Thomas's nemesis, John Schofield. The solemn procession was to be a lengthy one as those who traveled to attend offered the fallen comrade this final public honor. The burial was set to occur at Oakwood Cemetery, amidst the Episcopal rites and volleys of arms and taps.[90]

A train brought the general's remains to what one contemporary termed "his adopted home" and that of his wife and family: Troy, New York. A special correspondent who recorded the scene for readers of the *New York Times* praised the citizens of that community for their outpouring of grief and affection. "It is not, then, to be wondered at that the Trojans should in a special sense, lament his untimely decease, nor that they should manifest their sorrow with more than ordinary solemnities," the writer averred.[91]

Distinguished visitors flocked to the city to pay their respects to the fallen warrior and to extend their support to the grieving widow. The luminaries came from the general's extended military family and included Ulysses Grant and William T. Sherman. Notably absent was Philip Sheridan, who was in Philadelphia to attend a gathering of the Society of the Army of the

Potomac. The news writer covering the event did not allow the moment to pass without mention. "The comments on this remarkable absence were not complimentary to the hero of Winchester, and more than once the intimation was thrown out that the proceeding on his part could not be reconciled with the correct idea of what was proper on such an occasion."[92]

A steamer pulled in early on the morning of the funeral with soldiers to serve as an honor guard, and a train carried President Grant and cabinet officials. Delegations from the House of Representatives and the U.S. Senate added further to the entourage that descended upon the town. Thomas had been placed in St. Paul's Episcopal Church, the casket adorned with flags and bunting that alternated between the national colors and those of mourning. A simple inscription marked the coffin, with name, occupation, and birth and death dates, but without further elaboration. The casket also held a photograph of the general and the sword he had carried during the war. On the day of the final services, crowds of mourners began to gather by mid-morning, with the dignitaries taking position in the front pews. At 11:30 AM, the officiating clergy opened the proceedings. The *New York Times* correspondent reported that Frances Thomas made the "special request" that there be "no panegyric or eulogy pronounced over the remains." Once the services ended, a procession brought the general to Oakwood Cemetery amidst tolling church bells and the firing of "minute-guns." Thomas's final resting place was to be in the Kellogg family vault. The commitment ceremony, including "the customary burial salute" fired by the honor guard, closed the occasion.[93] It would not be until later in the year, on October 26, 1870, that the monument of white marble that would mark the area of the general's gravesite was in place. An eagle clutching a sword and a garland of victory adorned the work.[94]

As the complex person that he had been in life, George Thomas would have appreciated the national trappings and military elements, but he would not have missed the speeches. Although born, and raised in his early years, in Virginia, he had spent so much of the greater portion of his adult and professional life elsewhere. He had embraced the community of Troy and cherished it as the home of his beloved spouse and her family. His would not be an uneasy rest there. The time for encomiums followed as former comrades, friends, and soldiers expressed their emotions in the manner they believed would best reflect the admiration and respect he had won from them in his country's service. "Gen. George Henry Thomas, U.S. Army," would have asked for nothing more.[95]

Epilogue: What History Has Done

George Thomas died while making an effort to ensure that history had its facts correct if it was going to render him and his men a just verdict. Yet, his relatively early passing left many behind to sketch that legacy in a manner to fit their own agendas. Some of these were contemporaries, whose affections for "Pap Thomas" surpassed all else. Others were anxious to advance themselves, such as John McAllister Schofield. In one of the last bitter ironies, Thomas's death opened the way for his disgruntled former subordinate to assume his post as commander of the Division of the Pacific. Winfield Scott Hancock had hoped to secure the position, feeling entitled to it by virtue of his seniority, but Sherman responded to the matter with less deference than he would have shown to Thomas and with an insistence that the Virginian would have recognized. "The President authorizes me to say to you," Sherman asserted coldly to Hancock, "that it belongs to his office to select the Commanding Generals of Divisions and Departments, and that the relations you chose to assume towards him, officially and privately, absolve him regarding your personal preferences." Winfield Hancock, as Thomas had done often in such circumstances before him, decided to let the matter stand at that.[1]

At the time of Thomas's death, a *New York Times* account bore out the same tendency in the general. "The steps he successively mounted in rank and fame do not mark, as in so many cases, merely the deficiencies of other commanders, but his own superlative merits."[2] The *Chicago Times* made the case even more fervently. "Full of simple integrity, and fidelity to a single-eyed sense of duty, he never permitted himself to be made an instrument in the tangled imbroglio of politics, but kept himself aloof, and took the straight and narrow path which his conscience pointed out to him."[3] George Thomas would not have wanted these views to be presented in any other way and would have been pleased, if admitted openly, that such a selfless trait could be so easily recognized and widely identified with him.

On the other hand, the Virginian might well have found the superlatives that appeared in the Louisville *Courier-Journal* to mark his passing more difficult to embrace. Many of the anecdotes featured friends and associates who recalled elements of his professional life that reflected his strength of personality and record of success. Others focused on traits that spoke to Thomas's character and individual interests. Among these was Governor Thomas E. Bramlette of Kentucky, whose recollection of Thomas included indications of a wide-ranging intellect that challenged critics who had questioned the general's capabilities. "As a conversationalist on every subject he was unexcelled," Bramlette asserted, "being familiar with and having a love for the sciences, literature and art." Although Thomas could hardly be considered gregarious, the governor's remarks made clear the expanded scope of the soldier's store of knowledge. "He combined [the] powers of observation of men and things to an eminent degree," Bramlette concluded.[4]

Another aspect of this period would have pleased the professional soldier in Thomas, who sought to place the army and the nation above all other interests. The moment came in a very simple communication from the headquarters of the Military Division of the Pacific in San Francisco, over which Thomas had exercised authority for such a short time. At the beginning of April, and with the general's passing still painfully fresh, staffer Alfred Hough put in a request for new duties. "My position as aide de camp to Maj Genl Geo H Thomas being vacated by his death," he explained succinctly to Adjutant General E. D. Thompson, "I respectfully request to be assigned to an Infantry Regiment and ordered back for duty."[5] Such a routine element reflected the general's values and character as loudly as any eulogy. The service would go on without him.

At least initially, Ulysses Grant proved magnanimous in the wake of Thomas's death. To Frances Thomas, he offered his "heartfelt sympathy for you, the Army and the Nation," and assured her, "No eulogy of mine can add to the nation's knowledge of the goodness, and virtues of your deceased husband nor of the loss sustained by a grateful people in his death."[6] Not long afterward he observed to a comrade, "No more conspicuous or beloved soldier has gone to his final rest than your late commander." The president also predicted that the fallen soldier's memory "will be kept green in history."[7]

The general's widow returned the sentiment with a demonstration of her appreciation for the steps President Grant had taken to assist her and her husband's immediate staff members in their time of loss. From Troy, New York, she wrote on April 30, 1870, to express her "many thanks for your very kind reply to my letter sent by Col. Willard and also yours of yesterday's enclosing a note from Genl Cooke which I have forwarded to my nephew Col. Kellogg who is now at Detroit for a few days." She was well aware of her husband's difficulties with her correspondent over the years, but in a spirit that reflected the larger nature of his character Frances asserted sincerely, "Your kindness in so promptly providing for the officers of

Genl. Thomas' staff is most deeply appreciated by me," adding the same for Grant's "deep interest in my welfare," which she explained would "always be most sincerely prized."[8]

From her home in Troy, Frances Thomas also wrote the general's aide, Alfred Hough, to express her appreciation for his assistance through the difficult period. Admitting that she continued to feel the terrible effect of her loss as evidenced by "the incoherence of this letter," she noted that "my head and hand are still so unsteady that I find it difficult to guide my pen." Frances was anxious to secure the contents of that "book you used to copy letters of Genl. Thomas which were not exactly official." Provided that regulations did not prohibit the removal of such items, she preferred to have Hough forward the material to her. "I do not care to leave *any writings* of Genl. Thomas which were not purely official to fall into the hands of the person appointed to succeed him in command of the Division of the Pacific, or of his personal staff. *You* understand the reason."[9] Clearly, she valued the privacy that had marked their personal lives and sought to maintain it, but she also recognized the corrosive effect John Schofield could still have on a Thomas legacy. Frances Thomas was always prepared to guard her husband's name and reputation jealously, and was still extraordinarily sensitive over the circumstances that she believed had contributed to his premature death and the person she held in large measure responsible for it.

In a more practical sense, Frances realized that she had to continue despite the void that had entered her life. The general's place in the Union pantheon provided at least a measure of stature for her, but she existed for a time through her own resources. He had died intestate, without a legal will, and it took some time to sort through the process of placing her in the position he would have wanted for her with regard to the estate.[10] The obligation of the nation toward Thomas's service was reflected in sustaining his widow through a pension when she determined the time was right to access it. In 1879, Frances Thomas applied for the sum of $30.00 per month, which she then received until Congress voted in 1885 to allow her to receive $2,000 per year.[11]

Even in the absence of his former commander and inspiration, Thomas Van Horne completed his examination of the Army of the Cumberland in December 1872. Interruptions would prevent his seeing it set into galley sheets for another three years. Finally, in September 1875, he added his preface, and the publisher printed the volume for a public audience.[12] However, the chaplain soon arrived at the conclusion that the history he had written at Thomas's behest had not been sufficient to establish indisputably the general's reputation. He confessed that the Virginian had "overestimated the suggestive force of such a narrative to effect his own vindication, and it is certain that he did not anticipate the disparaging tenor of histories published since his death." Unlike the notion that had guided Thomas in setting the record straight, "Justice has not been done him," Van Horne concluded. The "need" existed, he maintained, of writing a volume that would project Thomas as the "very great man and general" that many believed him to be.[13]

Fittingly, in the field, Thomas's colleagues found tangible means of honoring their fallen associate. From his post in the Dakota Territory, a soldier wrote to his mother in early May. "We have been firing guns every fifteen minutes to day in honor of the memory of Genl. Thomas," he observed.[14] Two posts, a camp in northeastern North Dakota and another in eastern Arizona, received names in honor of George Thomas. The former took its designation upon the general's death, but changed later that same year to Fort Pembina, and the latter ultimately became known as Fort Apache, after being called Camp Thomas.[15]

Nearly a decade after the general's death, his name and reputation remained alive in the minds of those with whom he had served and fought. As Republican and former Union general Rutherford B. Hayes moved into the White House following a contentious and controversial election, fellow Republican Carl Schurz offered a familiar comparison in a letter to a colleague. "Hayes is a general like old Thomas; wants to have his wagons together when he marches, but loses no battles."[16] Thus, even after his death, George Thomas remained notable for the twin elements of preparation and military success.

For the rest of his years, Ulysses Grant was unswerving in his views on his former colleague. "I yield to no man in my admiration of Thomas," he observed of the memory of his friend and compatriot. "He was a fine character, all things considered—his relations with the South, his actual sympathies, and his fervent loyalty—one of the finest characters of the war." But Grant was equally adamant concerning Thomas's martial qualities. "As a commander he was slow. We used to say laughingly, 'Thomas is too slow to move and too brave to run away.'" The superior who had nearly executed his subordinate's removal thought Nashville to have been a "vindication, even against my criticisms," but noted that only his suppression of part of a "final report at the close of the war," consisting of some "fourteen or fifteen pages criticising Thomas," had spared that general a more official reckoning. "I have it among my papers and mean to destroy it," Grant insisted. "We differed about the Nashville campaign, but there could be no difference as to the effects of the battle."[17]

Another of Thomas's former commanders, and the man whom he had replaced following Chickamauga, also held firm to his opinion of the Virginian. When asked confidentially what he thought of Thomas being labeled the "Rock of Chickamauga," William Rosecrans answered hastily and unequivocally. "Of course he was the Rock, he was my rock, and he would not have been intrusted with the command of my army on the field after my return to Chattanooga, if he had not been a rock, and a solid rock at that."[18]

Other postwar reminiscences were less generous to the Virginian who chose to remain faithful to the Union. One of the most troubling, from the standpoint of coming from the hand of one who had a long association with and professed unquestioned devotion toward Thomas, was the memoir of William T. Sherman that appeared in 1875. Assailed in subsequent years for its patent inaccuracies, the work became the means by which the general who had taken Atlanta and marched to the sea, among other things, undermined his loyal subordinate and friend. The effort may have lacked malicious intent, as some scholars have argued, but it reflected a deep level of personal insecurity and smacked of disingenuousness at its best. Historian Albert Castel labeled Sherman's attempt at the "denigration of Thomas" as "devious," and argued that the author sought to diminish the stature of his able lieutenant as a means of elevating himself.[19] If, as Thomas biographer Christopher Einholf has insisted, Sherman had convinced himself that what he was writing was true, it did not prevent others from taking him to task for the fabrications.[20]

The "truth" as they saw it was very much on the minds of Thomas's long-time staffer Alfred Hough and his wife, Frances. At about the same period, each strove to correct the statements that were reappearing concerning the general's alleged dalliances with the Confederacy and motivations for remaining with the Union. The debate had flared at various points, but in the years surrounding the nation's centennial the discussions seemed to reemerge with a vengeance. Hough was so determined to record his views that he generated an extensive private statement on the subject of Thomas's fidelity, and only adherence to the widow's insistence that he refrain from releasing these views publicly prevented him from doing so. Composing his thoughts originally in January 1876 from his post at Fort Mackinnac, Michigan, Hough was able to append an addendum to his document when a newspaper clipping came into his possession in March of the same year. The author of that letter, Frances Thomas, had written it from her home in Troy, New York, on December 31, 1875, and forwarded it to the editor of the *New York Herald*. She repeated the accounts of her husband's debilitating railroad injury, his subsequent uncertainty about his future active career, and her insistence that no outside influences had been brought to bear on what was ultimately his decision to remain loyal to the Union. Frances chided those who had chosen to renew the controversy after the general could no longer respond to them personally. In the comments he added to the page that contained his copy of this published letter, Hough joined her in hoping that the "questions" regarding General Thomas's motivations would finally be "settled."[21]

Another significant and more pleasant form of remembrance and commemoration for Thomas, certainly from the standpoint of his friends and admirers, occurred in the nation's capital in 1879 with the unveiling of an equestrian statue of the general. Although she lamented the fact to one of her husband's closest colleagues, Frances Thomas would not be among the number in attendance. On the day before the ceremony was set to take place she explained her disappointment that none of Thomas's personal staff would be able to travel to Washington. "As to myself, it was *utterly impossible*" for her to participate, although she assured Alfred Hough, "at some future time I will go to Washington quietly and see it." Despite the pain of an absence that was not yet a decade old, she expressed gratitude for "the beautiful tribute the survivors of the Army of the Cumberland are paying to the memory of Genl Thomas." Her decision to remain away was obviously an intensely personal one for her and not meant to suggest her approval or disapproval of anyone else's actions in such affairs. Frances, like husband George, preferred to keep these matters to herself. "No one *could* appreciate it *more* than I do," she noted simply. "Any woman who has gone through what I have, I know can appreciate my feelings at this time."[22]

The dedication of the statue on November 19, 1879, allowed for numerous expressions of appreciation and affection for the general by those who served with him or had studied his life and career closely. In the flowing oratory of the day, Stanley Matthews observed, "To-day, Art summoned to its proper work, lifts aloft the dignity and majesty of his person, as the Society of the Army of the Cumberland, by these public acts and solemn ceremonials, dedicates to the people of the United States the form and presence of its beloved commander."[23]

William T. Sherman presented his thoughts as well. Noting his long association with the general, he defined their relationship as "more of a social character than of the commander and the commanded." He professed to have seen too much of Thomas, and on too personal a level, to view him "to be a hero." Sherman explained that he knew the man, understood his strengths and weaknesses, and recognized his "noble qualities." His was also meant to be a fuller understanding of the person. "You men only saw him in his military dignity," he remarked, "you did not, could not love him as we did." Sherman observed that he was less concerned with reflecting on the accomplishments of the soldier than on the virtues of the man. As the Virginian moved forward in the ranks from cadet to major general there was only evidence of his "noble character" and the determination to advance on the basis of merit and performance, to the point that "nothing could prevail against that powerful element in his character that forbade him to jump over intermediate grades of command."[24]

Like his friend Grant had done at the time of the Virginian's death, Sherman predicted that Thomas's reputation would flourish over the years. He anticipated that it would experience rehabilitation even among the Southerners who remained distant toward their regional compatriot. "The day is coming, gentlemen of Virginia," and the rest of the South, he asserted, "when you and your fellow-citizens will be making their pilgrimage to this magnificent monument . . . and say that there was a man who, under the tumult and excitement of the times, stood true and firm to his country, and he is the hero, and that brave George Thomas will become the idol of the South." Sherman suggested bluntly that he did not expect to be alive then, but reiterated that the day would come nevertheless.[25] Even old "Fighting Joe" Hooker, whose wartime association with Thomas had ended so abruptly during the latter part of the Atlanta Campaign, was reported to have offered praise for his comrade and the statue in the nation's capital as one of the last sentiments he expressed before his own death.[26]

The quiet opportunity Frances Thomas sought for visiting Washington came in the following April. After what was apparently a very short but pleasant trip, she subsequently noted, "I had a fine opportunity of examining the Statue in every point, and although I was prepared to find it excellent from letters I had received from many old friends, some of whom have very critical tastes, yet, it far exceeded my expectations, in every way." She had been extraordinarily moved by what she saw. "The likeness is excellent, the figure & position of Genl. Thomas life like to a degree I did not suppose the Artist could get." Labeling the craftsmanship "superb," Frances could not help but return to what impressed her most about the piece. "The position is life like," she reiterated, "as Genl Thomas so often in driving out, would on going up an elevation, take off his hat & look over the country; it was the first thing that struck me as I approached the Statue."[27]

However, Thomas's statue had not risen long over the capital he had striven to defend through a lifetime of service to his country when another type of civil war erupted. This one featured former comrades in arms who used a variety of means to present history in their own light and for their own purposes. Perhaps not surprisingly, given the contentious nature of such postwar posturing, any sense of decorum among the contending parties that had prevailed initially began rapidly to dissipate. George Thomas would be at the center of the storm, championed by his defenders and challenged by his detractors. Ironically, the strongest of these public outbursts occurred over the general's greatest wartime triumph: Nashville.

The general's widow became increasingly vocal in expressing her views on controversies that touched upon her husband. Throughout the period she communicated frequently with former members of the general's staff. In an intense flurry of correspondence with Alfred Hough she exposed a sensitivity to slights and injuries that would not have been alien to the general himself. Nor, as the subject matter of the letters indicated, would the culprits, as she identified them, have been surprising to him.

Like her husband, Frances Thomas intended to be prepared for the battle. In early 1881, she explained to Hough that her nephew, Sanford Kellogg, the staff officer who had been "with Genl T. from before Murfreesboro where he joined him, until Genl T.'s death in San Francisco," would be in a unique position to assist her. "He is clear-headed and not rash in his actions," she noted in language that reflected her husband's demeanor while he had lived, "and of course, can take a clearer view of such things than I."[28]

Kellogg responded readily to the call for action. "I have made a careful study of the Schofield doc. and have consulted with friends about it, and have also supplied myself with the materials for a reply to it," he informed Hough several months later. There was no question that partisanship toward the general's memory fed his passion, but he expressed the determination to "demonstrate much of the 'true inwardness' of the Nashville campaign," and felt that in doing so he would "show up not only Schofield's but Grant's and Sherman's behavior to Thomas, who were all far from friendly to him." Kellogg's tasking of Sherman and Grant did not include the nefarious motives he attributed to Schofield. Kellogg's assertion that "Sherman's selfishness blinding his other feelings,—Grant's anger at not being consulted by Thomas regarding the minutia of his [Thomas's] plans," compared favorably to "Schofield's falsity to Thomas all the way through." The tone clearly suggested that defense of the deceased George Thomas was a matter of urgency and importance.[29]

The controversies swirling around Thomas's memory reinforced the conclusions that Frances Thomas had reached regarding the impact of associated stresses and strains on her husband during his lifetime. "While I am not prepared to say the great wrong which Genl. Thomas considered done him during and after the battle of Nashville was the direct cause of his death," the aggrieved widow maintained, "I *will say* that it preyed upon him & affected his health, which Genl. Schofield's base attack on his military reputation added to & which was the cause of the fatal attack [of] March 28th, 1870." It was distressful in the extreme to have to revisit those difficulties, especially as the general was no longer able to answer any challenges directly. She was also adamant concerning another of the individuals she held responsible for the continuing problems the general's reputation faced. "I have ever felt that Genl Grant has not treated Genl Thomas since his death, with the same generosity Genl Thomas treated him

(Genl Grant) while living." She certainly felt that Grant's attitude had hardened toward her husband over time, noting that his recent comments represented "a different tone from the telegram he sent me at the time of Genl Thomas['s] death."[30]

The dissension in the postwar ranks reached crescendos at various points as parties from different camps hurled printed barbs through the newspapers or in published personal memoirs. Throughout the early 1880s few exchanges matched the vituperation expressed regarding the Schofield/ Thomas relationship. Frances Thomas undertook a running correspondence with former staff officer Alfred Hough in which she offered her views on various subjects, but she saved some of her sharpest fire for John Schofield and his associates. It was clear that the general's widow read as much as possible of the published material that related to her husband's reputation and career. "I was rather surprised to hear that Genl. [Jacob D.] Cox had written *all* the articles in the Schofield interest against Genl Thomas," she told Hough, "though his two books on the campaigns of the Civil War rather prepared me by their tone to hear it." Noting her belief that the truth would eventually work its way out, she observed, "One thing has solaced me in this contemptible work of Genl Schofields—it cannot hurt Genl Thomas *now*, he was spared from a great deal of Genl Schofields malignity."[31]

Schofield's communications with Cox no doubt aided in the degree to which this postwar controversy intensified. In December 1881, Schofield insisted sarcastically that other subordinates surrounding Thomas deserved the "credit" for supporting any delays at Nashville, far more than he. "What I do claim is very different," he added defiantly, "viz: that when the crisis came in which I alone could give him [Thomas] the effective support he needed to save him from impending humiliation, I promptly and emphatically gave him that support without waiting for the advice or opinion of anyone."[32] Schofield's compatriot ensured that on the subject at hand, this interpretation reached a public audience. Nevertheless, a later historian concluded that while Cox was "a prolific writer in military topics connected with the Civil War," some of his work "reflected little credit" on him on account of its bias.[33]

A new source of difficulty emerged when the United States moved to address the court-martial findings against Fitz John Porter for disobedience of orders. In the course of supporting speeches, Simon Cameron, formerly secretary of war under President Lincoln and now a member of the U.S. Senate from Pennsylvania, invoked Porter's name as a person asserting influence over General Thomas's decision to remain with the Union at the beginning of the conflict. "That brave officer, Mr. Cameron maintained," according to the newspaper report, "would have gone with the rebellious South if Porter had not won him to the Union side."[34]

As innocuous as such an assertion might seem, presented as it was for the purpose of supporting Porter's case before the legislative body for the restoration of his rights, the statement disturbed Frances Thomas and many of the general's wartime associates profoundly. Reading into the statement a slur on her husband, she not only expressed her profound gratitude "to Genl Thomas' old officers & friends coming to the rescue of his good name," but took direct steps to refute the assertion Cameron had made to the senator himself. "Of course I feel indignant," she admitted freely to Alfred Hough, "and at once cut out the paragraph stuck it in a letter, and wrote to Mr. Cameron saying referring to it, 'Allow me to say that Genl Thomas did not require the influence of Genl Porter or any one else to secure his adhesion to the Union Cause.'"

Frances Thomas reiterated what she had said before, maintaining consistency with her earlier statements on the subject. "In Genl Thomas' own words from a letter he wrote me at the time of the attack on Fort Sumpter every time he thought of the matter his duty to his Country was uppermost." The widow added that she had contacted Porter himself, whom she declared "an old friend of mine" of long standing, with "a very *plain* letter" advising him of her feelings on the matter. Even before her communication had reached him, Porter sent his own message to her denying any connection to the statements made on the floor of the Senate regarding any influence he was supposed to have had over the Virginian. Frances apologized for the letter to Hough going longer "than I intended, but I wished to impress you with the truth, that Genl Thomas has been wholly, willfully & falsely slandered which slander I hope I have silenced."[35] On Christmas Eve 1889 she "passed a delightful evening with her family and a few friends," by one contemporary account. Retiring for the night, Frances Kellogg Thomas fell into a sleep from which she did not awaken.[36] Her death, on December 25, 1889, brought an end to the fight she had waged on her husband's behalf. Her interment would be at his side in Troy, New York.[37]

Heated discussions continued among the fading warriors and their patrons, but ultimately many of the surviving veterans came to appreciate the sacrifices endured on both sides. The oratory of the day shifted from focusing on "bloody shirts" and "damn Yankees," even if a "Lost Cause" mentality remained, toward an emphasis on reconciliation.[38] Already a plethora of volumes had appeared that touted the career and character of George Thomas, mostly in laudatory fashion, highlighted by the work of Chaplain Van Horne, published in 1882. But the appearance of Ulysses Grant's memoirs in 1885–1886, and later those of John Schofield (1897), prompted renewed efforts to bring the pro-Thomas view to the forefront once more. Journalist Donn Piatt and General Henry Boynton took the greatest responsibility for these efforts, addressing the manner in which the Virginian was supposed to have suffered slights and slanders despite a stellar wartime record. One of the best illustrations of the era's emphasis on the nobility of the subject and the nationality of his appeal came from a former staff officer in 1899. "In General George H. Thomas we have one of the grandest figures in the war, one that will grow brighter as the years go by," Byron A. Dunn asserted. "His modesty, his bravery, his patriotism, his nobleness of character, place him among the greatest of Americans."[39]

Philip Sheridan did his part in helping to perpetuate the memory of his colleague through the naming of an installation situated in northern Kentucky and overlooking the Cumberland River. Fort Thomas provided one of the ways in which the Virginian who had fought to save the Union decades earlier became associated with the Spanish-American War at the close of the century, with the post serving as a mustering point, and later as a hospital facility, for American troops.[40] That conflict also resurrected the general's name at the site of one his greatest accomplishments in the Civil War when Major General John R. Brooke chose to gather troops on the grounds of the recently established National Military Park at Chickamauga, Georgia. He had a name in mind for the camp that would be placed there. On April 24, orders came down. "The U.S. troops assembled in the Chickamauga Park will form an encampment, to be known as Camp George H. Thomas, and will constitute temporarily, an army corps, under the command of Maj. Gen. John R. Brooke."[41] Within a short time, the camp hosted 7,300 regular army men, including the Ninth and Tenth U.S. Cavalry, regiments of African American "buffalo soldiers."[42] By mid-May the regulars had moved on, but waves of volunteers soon swelled the camp to staggering proportions that approached numbers that had not gathered in such a manner since the Civil War itself.[43] Now aging veterans of that earlier conflict such as Henry V. Boynton, the Chickamauga Park Commission head, could not help but make nostalgic comparisons with the old days. "I believe there was more food left over in that army at Camp Thomas, every day of its existence, than the Army of the Cumberland had to eat during the entire siege of Chattanooga," he observed somewhat sardonically.[44] Thomas would likely have agreed, as both the former subaltern with quartermaster and commissary responsibilities and the field general who always preferred efficiency at the highest level possible. Waste was akin to disloyalty or ingratitude on the list of transgressions that had most grieved him during his lifetime.

Sadly, the facility's namesake would have been disappointed to learn of its longer-term reputation, too. According to historian Gregory Dean Chapman, "Camp Thomas, more than any other cantonment, became the nation's symbol of the government's ineptitude in running the war." Disease and illness so affected the volunteers stationed there that 752 of the camp's personnel lost their lives. "As its legacy," Chapman concluded, "Camp Thomas claimed more victims than any other camp or battlefield of the war."[45]

He would have been more pleased to know that some of the lessons that subordinates attributed to their service under him found application to later conflicts. Arthur MacArthur had adamantly agreed with his superior's notions of the importance of drill and discipline, even with veteran troops in the latter stages of the Civil War. He carried these notions into the Philippines, where American forces engaged in a brutal guerrilla-style struggle following the Spanish-American War. MacArthur's biographer noted, "He knew that parade ground drills did not make a combat soldier, but he believed as General George Thomas had taught that parade drills instilled discipline and obedience."[46]

At the turn of the century, debate flared once more regarding Thomas's motivations for choosing the Union over his state. J. William Jones renewed the controversy with an article in *Confederate Veteran* at the end of 1903 that declared Thomas "a strong secessionist," and offered a number of examples as proof of his true intentions of loyalty to Virginia and the South.[47] Even without the strong voice of Frances Thomas to refute them, these allegations were bound to stir responses from those who could still be heard on the general's behalf.

In March 1908, a strong denunciation of the charge that Thomas had ever communicated with Confederate authorities for the purpose of obtaining a position in the service of the Confederacy appeared in print. "It would take something more than a mere assertion to make the people believe the great Virginian, George H. Thomas, would betray a trust or tell a lie," William Repert of Culpeper, Virginia, asserted. The editor could only retort in a short aside, "In printing the foregoing it is not intended by any means to commend the expressions. There would have been no 'slander' if General Thomas had served in the Confederate army from first to last, even as a private soldier."[48]

By the next issue, North Carolinian B. F. Grady offered the Thomas letter to Governor John Letcher once more as proof of the Virginian's genuine intentions. This letter, he believed, represented "a counter 'assertion'" to that made in the previous edition. Without further elaboration, Grady used the correspondence to illustrate Thomas's desire to continue in the United States service only as long as Virginia remained in the Union. "Within less than six weeks after the date of this letter Virginia withdrew from the Union, and the world knows the rest," he noted caustically.[49]

Memory was increasingly becoming the issue as war veterans passed from the scene and the nation reached important anniversary landmarks. Historian David Blight has noted, "The semicentennial of the Civil War stimulated a flood of memories and commemorative activities."[50] During the period, a Virginia-born Democrat, Woodrow Wilson, took occupancy of the White House and *The Birth of a Nation* filled seats in movie houses. The darker elements of Jim Crow segregation and lynching could not obscure the more comforting and ubiquitous evidences of a clasping of hands by former opponents. Honoring the shared sacrifices of the soldiers and their loving families at home became the paramount theme that suggested neither side in the conflict had enjoyed a monopoly on honor and virtue. In such an atmosphere, any emphasis on Thomas the stalwart patriot had to be done in a manner that did not also threaten the boys in gray and butternut who had opposed him. Increasingly, references to the "Late Unpleasantness" thus became a matter less of emphasizing rebellion than reunion.

In the aftermath of the First World War and the Great Depression, the nation remembered George Thomas in ways that reflected those new conditions. During the Second World War his name was one of a number of public figures' selected for designation for a Liberty Ship. The Oregon Shipbuilding Corporation, out of Portland, produced the 422-foot vessel in 1942.[51] The wave of construction was ultimately responsible for the production of 2,695 such vessels bearing famous titles from personalities that ranged from presidents, politicians, and generals to preachers, writers, and musicians. The *George H. Thomas*, number 569 in hull number sequence, also found a varied career after the war, including sale and renaming under Panamanian and Danish registry.[52]

Recognitions of the Civil War general were less forthcoming outside of these wartime contexts, but the centennial of the conflict brought renewed attention to the period itself. Thomas's cultural moment came with the release in 1963 of a two-part Walt Disney presentation focusing on the exploits of Johnny Clem.[53] Young John Lincoln Clem had won renown, first at Shiloh, and then at Chickamauga, for his tenacity and courage. He had subsequently come to the general's attention, and Thomas took more than a passing interest in the lad, referring to him at one point as "my manly little friend." Thomas assisted with Clem's education and praised him for "improvement" in his letter writing with regard to penmanship and spelling. Admonishing his protégé to "study hard" and "fill your head with knowledge," the general seemed inordinately pleased to share his own intellectual curiosity and quest for personal enrichment.[54] One biographer suggested that the approach Thomas took with Clem not only reflected the mores of nineteenth-century parenthood, but implied the values he would have sought to instill in children of his own if circumstances had allowed.[55]

George Thomas had gone through a cycle of recognition that moved from the heights of emphasis on his patriotic stance and service to the Union to the low points of questions regarding the same. As the veterans left the scene and the war faded, to be replaced by new national and international imperatives, Thomas's reputation experienced eclipse. Then, as if to demonstrate that it could not be contained indefinitely, the warrior's record found a new champion from what might have been considered an unlikely source. In a program in which he was the featured speaker, former governor of Virginia, president of the University of Virginia, and fellow Southampton County native Colgate W. Darden Jr. offered his support for the maligned neighbor in the national bicentennial year of 1976.

Reminding attendees of his own connection to and affection for the county in which he had spent "a happy childhood," Darden explained that "the courage and fine spirit which I knew as a child still obtain here." His address contained a number of historical references, but the popular former governor extended his longest remarks on behalf of General Thomas. Darden offered a brief outline of the general's background and provided his own thoughts concerning the choice that Thomas had made in adhering to the Union. Then the modern-day Southampton Countian offered a final pointed observation about the warrior's stature. "As the years have gone on and a more temperate appraisal of his situation can be made there are many Virginians, among whom I am one, who believe that the bitter condemnation of this countryman was unjust and that the officer who became known as the 'Rock of Chickamauga' and to whom Southampton County gave a beautifully engraved sword to mark his services in combat in Mexico and other theaters of action deserves far better treatment than he has received from the states south of the Potomac."[56]

The extent to which such views impacted the audience that had gathered before the former governor would be impossible to assess. Certainly, his sentiments did not eradicate ill will toward Thomas in all circles where it had existed. At least one twenty-first-century area newspaper writer felt obliged to offer observations of the general that reflected this divided opinion in an article entitled "Southampton's Civil War Hero, Like Him or Not."[57] Nor have modern discussions of Thomas failed to elicit attitudes that might be termed, at best, as dismissive of him.[58]

In any case, George Thomas has still struggled to get his due. In 1997, Edward L. Ayers produced a volume of "a century of great Civil War quotations," to which Thomas apparently had nothing to contribute.[59] In a subsequent publication of *The Oxford Dictionary of Civil War Quotations*, however, his two entries were superior in number to Don Carlos Buell's (0), but fewer than John Pope's (4) and William Rosecrans's (5). The loquacious George McClellan had 48 and Ulysses Grant 99, but even these found themselves passed considerably by William T. Sherman (158) and Robert E. Lee (190). Understandably, given his eloquence and prominence, Abraham Lincoln topped them all, with 537 quotations attributed to him.[60] Happy to avoid speaking and hardly likely to be accused of being a wordsmith in any case, George Thomas remained as silent in the sphere of memorable oral associations with the war as he tended to be in person in the company of others during the conflict and in its immediate aftermath.

On another level of public analysis and awareness, two individuals, Victor Brooks and Robert Hohwald, offered grades for the generals they studied and invited readers to do the same. Thomas was one of a handful of commanders on both sides to receive the highest marks. "The authors believe that the Union-loyal Virginian is one of the most underrated generals of the Civil War," they concluded. "He scored the first significant Union victory of the war at Fishing Creek, saved the Army of the Cumberland from possible annihilation at Chickamauga, performed superbly during the Atlanta campaign, and then won one of the most lop-sided battles of the war at Nashville." Marking as his sole "blemish" his relationship with Grant, Brooks and Hohwald offered the Virginian "an outstanding 'A' rating."[61] Whatever might be thought of such ratings, the authors were certainly sound in observing, "Grant, Sherman, Thomas and Sheridan were all extremely minor figures in the earliest stage of the war, and yet by the autumn of 1864 these four men were operating a juggernaut that was tearing the Confederacy apart."[62]

Whatever their legitimacy, comparisons between the leaders on either or both sides occurred from the time of the war itself. Contemporaries made these judgments in reminiscences and orations frequently. Later students of the Civil War have done likewise. On occasion these efforts have produced intriguing points of analysis. For instance, one historian has asserted that while "their tactical and personal styles differed radically," neither Sherman nor Thomas possessed "a killer instinct."[63] Of course, one would be hardpressed to think that Confederate general John Bell Hood would agree in either case or that their joint service in the decisive Western Theater of the Civil War was not significant to the outcome of the demise of the Confederacy.

Yet, in some important ways, George Henry Thomas could be said to stand alone. Dan Crofts, a scholar who has written extensively about Southampton County, pointed out that in a war replete with ironies, Thomas was unique. "No other southerner inflicted such heavy blows on his home region." For his contributions to the preservation of the nation in the turmoil of civil war, the Virginian "is now recognized as one of the ablest Union generals."[64] Albert Castel, who examined Thomas's role closely in connection with the Atlanta Campaign, observed in a subsequent volume that the Virginian and Ulysses Grant deserved the labels "great." Of Thomas, the historian explained, "A Southerner, he contributed more to Union victory than any Northern-born general except Grant." Then, he concluded with an observation that would have brought a wry smile from both. "Thomas never committed a serious mistake and, like Grant, always sought to annihilate the enemy."[65]

In many ways, Nashville has come to serve as the template for assessing the Virginian, his generalship, and his level of social consciousness. Two modern historians in particular considered the culminating battle as a prime example of the decisive engagement that leaders in the war sought. Herman Hattaway and Archer Jones noted the combination of factors, including those outside of the Virginian's control, that resulted in victory at Nashville. "With the help of the weather and the low morale of Hood's army, Thomas came close to fighting the battle of annihilation which had for so long existed in the minds of the public, politicians, and journalists."[66] W. J. Wood offered a similar conclusion. "The fact remains, however, that Nashville was the only Civil War battle where the objective of annihilation was made possible by the victor's deliberate intent being carried through to its end."[67]

The Battle of Nashville has stood as the prime indicator of Thomas's determination and prowess in the field. The engagement had a textbook quality to it. "Indeed, Nashville was the cleanest and completest campaign and battle of our great Civil War on either side," contemporary observer Benjamin Rusling wrote, "and it stamped Thomas henceforth as a really great commander." The brilliance of the affair, Rusling noted, was in its planning, preparation, and precision. "He had worked it all out like a problem in mathematics, and executed it like a fine piece of engineering."[68] Clearly, the engagement offered a powerful counterpoint to those who, like John Schofield, questioned Thomas's mental capacity and martial capability.

Of course, the question has remained of Thomas's dalliance or reluctance before launching the final assaults that drove the Confederate defenders into wholesale retreat. Hood occupied the positions he did before Nashville because he wanted the Federals to seize the initiative. Apparently he hoped to do to his opponents what they had allowed him to do to himself at Franklin as he propelled his troops against the Union defenses, producing massive casualties, including costing him some of his best officers. The strong points of high ground that had to be assailed must have given the illusion of impregnability. Thomas was wise to be sure of his command before unleashing it. The fact that Hood felt confident to send Lyon's men raiding into Kentucky and Forrest's cavalry, plus some infantry additions, to test the formidable Union defenses around Murfreesboro only indicated the Confederate commander's lack of understanding of the precariousness of his position. Historian Archer Jones has argued that through the prescriptions of "traditional generalship" Thomas could have "let Hood's army waste away in the open in the winter," but because of the "political embarrassment of a rebel force in a position abandoned almost three years before," the circumstances compelled him to become more aggressive.[69] Of course, the Virginian hardly believed he had that luxury, even if it had not been for the continual prodding from the general in chief and the War Department.

A student of the battle chastised Thomas for his flawed intelligence estimates, but noted that he "suffered more from an inadequacy of the collection of intelligence than from his evaluation of it." W. J. Wood thought that the general's constant demand for better prepared mounted units demonstrated that "as an old cavalry officer, he was acutely aware of the weakness of his cavalry arm" and "the resulting weakness in the intelligence that was provided for him." Of course, Thomas's interest lay as much in being able to employ these mounted forces to threaten the Confederate flanks or pursue troops if they retreated as in gaining information on Southern dispositions. Even so, Wood maintained that Thomas was at fault for overestimating the enemy.[70]

Poor intelligence could have its price, but adequate planning was critical in any case. In his examination of the trench warfare of the Overland Campaign in Virginia that Grant carried out against Robert E. Lee, Earl Hess explained: "Those many Union attacks often were characterized by inadequate planning and a lack of coordination, especially by a failure to coordinate supporting troops." Hess felt that the lack of support "was the most important in understanding why they generally failed," an accusation that would not normally be made against Thomas. He concluded, "Grant had a tendency to set a timetable that did not allow subordinates ample opportunity to prepare."[71] Certainly, debate has ensued as to what constituted "ample opportunity to prepare," and such a schedule would be very different for a general such as Thomas, who was so meticulous in his preparations. But the problem lay with the tendencies of both men: Grant for pressing so relentlessly and Thomas for preparing so thoroughly before attacking. Ironically, in the end, it worked for both as Grant finally got the Virginian moving and Thomas's excellent preparations, including his use of the troops he had so painstakingly gathered, such as A. J. Smith's command and Wilson's cavalry, paid off handsomely in a tremendous and overwhelming victory.

One modern scholar captured the dilemma of Thomas's command style for the general and his superiors. "Yet, though rock-solid in appearance and seemingly reserved in manner, behind that solid shell was a mind whose keenness was enhanced by a calm reasoning and a tenacity of purpose that could be mistaken for inflexibility—a mistake once shared by Grant and Halleck, to their later chagrin," W. J. Wood explained.[72] Horace Porter's assessment of the strained relationship between General Grant and the commander of the army in Nashville was generous to both men. "When General Thomas did not obey the instructions repeatedly sent him, the general in chief did not treat the case as one of insubordination or defiance, and act hastily or arbitrarily in taking steps immediately to enforce his orders, but exercised a patience which he would not have done under other circumstances or toward any other army commander."[73] Regarding Thomas, Porter asserted, "He believed that he was right, and that he was acting for the best interests of the service, and evidently felt so thoroughly convinced of this that he was willing to run the risk of assuming responsibility, and to submit to being displaced from his command, rather than yield his judgment."[74] As a third party to the drama between the two commanders whom he admired and respected, Porter not surprisingly concluded that other men placed in the same circumstances would not have fared so well. Indeed, he insisted that as far as he was able to determine, in the associations Thomas and Grant had in the aftermath of the war there was no discernible "lack of cordiality on either side."[75]

Another intriguing aspect of the fighting at Nashville involved Thomas's views on race and war. In his post-action assessment, the Virginian came to what looked to some to be a singular conclusion concerning the performance of the African American troops under his command. "The question is settled; the negro will fight," he observed almost introspectively.[76] A contemporary and biographer of the general noted that Thomas found the actions of these men impressive. "This proves the manhood of the Negro," Chaplain Van Horne recorded Thomas as saying.[77]

At least two modern scholars, John Cimprich and Christopher Einholf, have determined that such statements represented a fundamental shift in Thomas's attitudes on race and equality. Both saw the participation of black troops at Nashville as bringing about this significant alteration. "Everything changed with the Battle of Nashville," Cimprich explained. "Nationalism and a career officer's habitual obedience to superiors had made Thomas a nominal supporter of new federal policies on race relations, but the battle forced him to rethink private attitudes that he had accepted as correct from his upbringing."[78] Likewise, Einholf asserted that Thomas underwent a transformation with Nashville and that the African American performance there served as the catalyst. For the Thomas biographer, the effect of the battle "challenged a lifetime of assumptions about black inferiority" in the general and set him on a road to embracing equality.[79]

Both scholars emphasized the finality in Thomas's description and the nature of his actions afterward to suggest such a dramatic reordering of the Union general's personal views. Yet, George Thomas was only articulating another milestone in the development, which had been occurring since childhood and accelerated through his professional career, of his attitude toward all fellow human beings, and especially those who served under him. In this case, his sense was of the "settlement" of a question of the fighting capability of any new set of troops. Mill Springs had accomplished such a degree of recognition for the men he had drilled and trained so diligently in 1861 Kentucky. Other battles were necessary for newer units or conscripts who subsequently came under his authority to demonstrate their mettle. The Army of the Cumberland won its stripes for Thomas through hard service and amidst the harsh crucible of combat, both in the face of extreme adversity and victory.

Actually, the Virginian did not emerge from Nashville so much as a champion of a race as he did a commander who felt his troops had proven themselves in action to his satisfaction. White volunteers, and then conscripts, had settled these matters previously because they had earlier chances to do so on the spot. Although he had earlier doubted the possibility, black volunteers did so in this engagement, and Thomas acknowledged the fact forthrightly.

Thomas's development with regard to race and the institution of slavery mirrored the broader changes he had witnessed across the wide spectrum of his wartime experiences. In another context, W. J. Wood argued, "Perhaps the most pertinent observation that could be made about Thomas' command abilities would be that he *grew* in command. His record shows that he not only learned from personal experience," but from others' mistakes, enabling him ultimately to demonstrate that "he had gained mastery of his own art at the highest operational level of command."[80]

A Thomas revival has allowed the Virginian's name and reputation to enjoy resurgence in recent years. Larry J. Daniel's 2004 volume on Thomas's beloved Army of the Cumberland offered fresh insights into the general's role that contained a usually fair mix of praise and criticism. Three years later, Christopher Einholf published a well-researched and thoughtful study with a major emphasis on placing George Thomas in a more modern context as an early champion of civil rights. Benson Bobrick's 2009 examination not only reviewed the general's reputation as a "master of war," but did so in a fashion that would have pleased his wartime and postwar comrades and biographers with its celebration of his generalship and strident condemnation of Ulysses Grant and William T. Sherman.

Thomas's latest biographers have joined in the broadly positive portrayal of the man and the soldier. Einholf noted, "Most military historians place Thomas either second or third in the pantheon of Union generals, behind Grant, and sometimes behind Sherman." But his assessment of Thomas's progression with regard to slavery and race, which established the Virginian as "the war's most prominent Southern Unionist" and "one of the few white Southerners whose views on race and slavery changed as a result of the war," was more open to question.[81] Bobrick asserted, "Only a razorlike judgment combined with an incredibly sure and prompt capacity for action could have rescued the Union army from calamity at Stones River,

Chickamauga, and Peachtree Creek. There was absolutely nothing in the careers of either Grant or Sherman that remotely compares to it." Of Nashville, the writer concluded simply, "And there we see that he was not slow but wise."[82]

In the sesquicentennial of the American Civil War, George Thomas will undoubtedly receive further ado. Individuals wishing to visit the battlefields over which he fought and the sites associated with his life have greater interpretation to guide and assist them. In addition to state historical markers, Civil War Trails signage has enhanced information available at these locations, including Thomaston, the general's home. A revised guide to Civil War sites in Virginia has added and updated features on Newsoms and Courtland, Virginia, to encourage awareness, although the home itself remains in private hands.[83]

Those who have become familiar with him or will do so find the Virginian who chose the Union in the Civil War to be more complicated than traditional views usually have allowed. His complex views embraced the worlds of professional military service to his country and scientific inquisitiveness, attention to detail and compassion to those for whom he felt a paternalistic responsibility, love of nation and of family that transcended borders and knew no other bounds. A meticulous and sensitive individual, he often seemed impervious to danger in combat and could understand nothing less than a total commitment to one's duties. His flaws, including a sharp, if frequently disguised, temper and an adherence to personal loyalties that could blind him to the motivations and weaknesses of others, were hardly sufficient to overshadow the strengths of his character and his capabilities as a professional soldier. Thomas had a rare ability to inspire his men and generate a familiarity with officers and staff that not only rendered them effective in their duties, but created a powerful and long-lasting bond that extended beyond wartime service.

As a commander, George Thomas could become excessively concerned with the circumstances that confronted him. This attitude came from his training and the desire to let those with greater authority and responsibility focus on issues on a broader scale. He understood strategic implications and the contributions he could make to them, but his professional gaze lay more often than not on the immediate landscape. On several occasions, such as the engagement of Perryville in 1862 and his famous stand at Chickamauga, his sharp focus on his duty limited his effectiveness or threatened to eliminate it from the field altogether. In the Atlanta Campaign, Thomas failed to convince Sherman that he could be as effective as James McPherson in implementing the goals of the campaign against Joseph Johnston's Confederates. Sherman's exasperation with the Army of the Cumberland was something that the Virginian seemed powerless to alleviate. At Chattanooga and Nashville, Grant became frustrated with Thomas because he was not William Sherman, and the Virginian bore the burden stoically from the outside while seething from within. George Thomas carried the responsibility for not being able to adapt to the expectations of these commanders, but Grant himself acknowledged that the results were generally unquestioned. Just as was true of any general, Thomas was not always at his best in every encounter simply because he had been, or would be, so effective in the vast majority of them. His performances were not as consistently flawless as his most vehement apologists have suggested, but they tended to be the most significant at critical junctures.

Methodical and experienced, Thomas often succeeded in moments of crisis because he was less interested in experimenting or setting military precedents than he was in obtaining control of the situation at hand and providing a steady example of leadership in the face of the turmoil and chaos of the battlefield. Consequently, when faced with the elements of the "fog of war" that transpired suddenly, and often unexpectedly, Thomas could be counted on to lend a sense of solidity to fluid or disintegrating circumstances. His dependability and usually sound judgment found a place at headquarters as well as on the battlefield. Conditions that often confounded others were less likely to intimidate him, as attested at Stones River and Chickamauga. Thomas, the imperturbable, came in handy when all else appeared unsettled and uncertain.

Thomas's positive contributions to the Union war effort were considerable. At Mill Springs he fed troops into a developing engagement that culminated in a devastating defeat for the opposing force and the unraveling of the Confederate defense line in the Western Theater. At Stones River, whatever the debate over his exact words at an evening council of war, Thomas's actions were unquestionably crucial to holding the vital center, while other commands faltered or shifted around him to gain their footing. Chickamauga represented the best example of the Virginian's prowess as a defensive commander. Faced with powerful thrusts on both September 19 and 20, 1863, Thomas understood the pivotal role his command played in securing the Union left, particularly on the second full day of battle after the Union right and center had collapsed. The Atlanta Campaign demonstrated the capabilities the Virginian had in cooperating with comrades in a fluid operation that combined maneuver and aggressive punches. Nashville also illustrated the ways in which Thomas could unleash a powerful offensive thrust of his own after working feverishly to gather sufficient forces and resources to do so.

On the opposite side of the ledger, sure-footedness could devolve into something akin to plodding. The Virginian's tendency to devote his energies to preparation caused him at the minimum to appear less than anxious to channel that effort into the active campaigning that would yield the results that he and his superiors intended. His desire to minimize the risk inherent to battle as much as possible stymied his ability to move more aggressively. Yet, if Thomas took too long to strike against a foe, such as John Bell Hood, once he did so his assaults proved irresistible.

George Thomas had proven himself on the nation's battlefields, but he demonstrated less effectiveness in battles of another sort. He could have done more to advance his own prospects had he been willing to go outside proper military channels. While commendable in its own right, all the thoroughness he practiced in paperwork to report this service could not surmount those who cultivated political contacts more directly or who bypassed the niceties when it suited their purposes to do so. Thomas seemed to think that his actions would speak for themselves and was often befuddled and angered when they did not. It was understandable in one sense for him to downplay machinations and disdain politics, but his dismissal of such efforts hurt his cause as much as it reflected positively on his character. There was no one else to press his claims, even if it could be said that he had not advanced his own prospects through injury to another's. The actions of many of his contemporaries and compatriots, including his wife after his death, were greater than those he undertook for himself during his lifetime.

One factor that lay beneath the success of Union arms was the effective combination of the aggressiveness of Generals Sherman and Grant with the thoroughness of General Thomas. Grant later assessed a Confederate icon harshly while suggesting the ways in which Thomas and others had evolved successfully through the course of the war. "The tactics for which ["Stonewall"] Jackson is famous, and which achieved such remarkable results, belonged entirely to the beginning of the war and to the peculiar conditions under which the earlier battles were fought," Grant explained. "They would have insured destruction to any commander who tried them upon Sherman, Thomas, Sheridan, or Meade, in fact any of our great generals."[84]

In the final analysis, Union general George Thomas became noted for his improvisational skills and tenacity on the battlefield. Although he achieved a tremendous victory at Mill Springs in January 1862 through his own means, perhaps his greatest contribution to Union victory was bringing his very different talents and approaches to work in tandem with those of Grant and Sherman. By late 1863, even with some setbacks and disappointments, the combination proved irresistible at Chattanooga, and in the Atlanta and Nashville campaigns. Thomas very nearly found himself removed during the latter, a situation he made worse himself by relying so heavily on preparation and by exhibiting poor communication skills with his superiors.

But his achievements placed him then, and now, as one of the Union's finest field generals, exemplary in defense, but more than capable of assuming the offensive in a fashion devastating to his opponent.

George Henry Thomas's life and service exemplified as well as anyone's the motto that has come since his death to be so closely associated with the United States Military Academy at West Point, where he received his education: "Duty, Honor, Country."[85] As a professional soldier he lived under the rule that if one failed to prepare one should be prepared to fail, and he did not countenance failure. In the process, he demanded of himself and the officers and men under his command that all be done that reasonably could be to offer the greatest chances for success. In the process, each would have the opportunity to respond to challenges as they arose with the confidence that the system he had encouraged and perfected would prepare them for those contingencies. Each could then enter the fray free to focus on the demands of duty and the desire to perform as capably as possible. No greater glory could come to them, or to him, than the performance of that duty. Yet, for all of these measures, historian Wiley Sword captured George Thomas's essence superbly when he observed, "Great men are distinguished not only by their deeds, but equally so by what is in their hearts. There perhaps never beat a heart more worthy and true than that of the outcast Virginian who had triumphed over mind and matter at Nashville, George H. Thomas."[86] The historian might have added that at the heart of the soldier and the man was the pulse of a patriot and a nature whose devotion to duty and his ideals made him "as true as steel."

Appendix A: Military Milestones and Principal Responsibilities

Second Lieutenant, Third Artillery, July 1, 1840
Brevet First Lieutenant, November 6, 1841
First Lieutenant, Third Artillery, April 30, 1844
Brevet Captain, September 23, 1846
Brevet Major, February 23, 1847
Captain, Third Artillery, December 24, 1853
Major, Second Cavalry, May 12, 1855
Lieutenant Colonel, Second Cavalry, April 25, 1861
Colonel, Second Cavalry, May 3, 1861
Brigadier General, U.S. Volunteers, August 17, 1861
Major General, U.S. Volunteers, April 25, 1862
Brigadier General, U.S. Army, October 27, 1863
Major General, U.S. Army, December 15, 1864
(Adapted from Cullum, *Biographical Register*.)

Appendix B: George Thomas's Military Divisions and Departments, Post–Civil War

June 27, 1865
Division of the Tennessee—George Thomas
Department of Alabama—Charles R. Woods
Department of Georgia—James B. Steedman
Department of the Tennessee—George Stoneman
Department of Mississippi (after Oct. 7)—Peter J. Osterhaus

May 19, 1866
Division of the Tennessee—George Thomas
Department of the South (Ga., Ala.)—Charles R. Woods
Department of Tennessee—George Stoneman (became Department of the Cumberland, June 5)
Department of Mississippi—Thomas J. Wood

August 6, 1866
Department of the Tennessee (Tenn., Ga., Ala., Miss.)—George Thomas

March 12, 1867
Department of the Cumberland (Tenn.)—George Thomas

July 28, 1867
Department of the Cumberland (Tenn.)—George Thomas

March 16, 1869
Department of the Cumberland (Tenn.)—George Thomas

June 1, 1869
Division of the Pacific—George Thomas
(Adapted from Sefton, *U.S. Army and Reconstruction*, 255–257; Cullum, *Biographical Register*, II, 35.)

Notes

Abbreviations

DUL	Perkins Library, Duke University, Durham, N.C.
EU	Woodruff Library, Emory University, Atlanta, Ga.
HL	Huntingdon Library, San Marino, Calif.
MOC	Eleanor S. Brockenbrough Library, Museum of the Confederacy, Richmond, Va.
NA	National Archives, Washington, D.C.
OR	*The War of the Rebellion: The Official Records of the Union and Confederate Armies in the War of Rebellion*
ORN	*Official Records of the Union and Confederate Navies*
SHC-UNC	Southern Historical Collection, University of North Carolina, Chapel Hill
USMA	United States Military Academy, West Point, N.Y.
USMAL	United States Military Academy Library, West Point, N.Y.
UVA	Alderman Library, University of Virginia, Charlottesville
UCBL	University of Colorado at Boulder Libraries
VHS	Virginia Historical Society, Richmond
VSL	Virginia State Library, Richmond
West Texas	*West Texas Historical Association Year Book*

Introduction: Embattled Virginian

1. Benjamin F. Taylor, *Pictures of Life in Camp and Field* (Chicago: S. C. Griggs, 1875, 1888), 193.

2. Ezra J. Warner, *Generals in Blue: Lives of the Union Commanders* (Baton Rouge: Louisiana State University Press, 1964), 500.

3. Marcus Woodcock, *A Southern Boy in Blue: The Memoir of Marcus Woodcock, 9th Kentucky Infantry (U.S.A.),* edited by Kenneth W. Noe (Knoxville: University of Tennessee Press, 1996), 214.

4. General Orders No. 31, Washington, March 29, 1870, Headquarters of the Army, copy in James A. Garfield, *Oration on the Life and Character of Gen. George H. Thomas Delivered before the Society of the Army of the Cumberland* (Cincinnati: Robert Clarke, 1871), 50–51.

5. Bruce Catton, *U. S. Grant and the American Military Tradition* (Boston: Little, Brown, 1954), 114.

6. Bruce Catton, *The Hallowed Ground: The Story of the Union Side of the Civil War* (Garden City, N.Y.: Doubleday, 1956), 369.

7. R. E. Lee to Jefferson Davis, September 23, 1863, *OR*, vol. 29, pt. 2, 743; William F. G. Shanks, *Personal Recollections of Distinguished Generals* (New York: Harper & Brothers, 1866), 79. Shanks added "Old Pap Safety" and "George H." to the mix as well, ibid.

8. John Calvin Hartzell, *Ohio Volunteer: The Childhood and Civil War Memoirs of Captain John Calvin Hartzell, OVI*, edited by Charles I. Switzer (Athens: Ohio University Press, 2005), 116 and 128 as examples.

9. Joseph Allan Frank, *With Ballot and Bayonet: The Political Socialization of American Civil War Soldiers* (Athens: University of Georgia Press, 1998), 45.

10. George W. Cullum to Gentlemen, 315 Fifth Avenue, New York, November 15, 1879, quoted in Richard W. Johnson, *Memoir of Maj.-Gen. George H. Thomas* (Philadelphia: J. B. Lippincott, 1881), 276.

11. Quoted in "General George H. Thomas," *Knoxville Whig and Rebel Ventilator*, June 11, 1864.

12. T. Harry Williams, *Lincoln and His Generals* (New York: Alfred A. Knopf, 1952), 341.

13. Stephen E. Ambrose, *Halleck: Lincoln's Chief of Staff* (Baton Rouge: Louisiana State University Press, 1962), 192.

14. Donn Piatt and Henry V. Boynton, *General George H. Thomas: A Critical Biography* (Cincinnati: Robert Clarke, 1893), 342. See also Francis F. McKinney, *Education in Violence: The Life of George H. Thomas and the History of the Army of the Cumberland* (Detroit: Wayne State University Press, 1961), 207–208; Peter Cozzens, *This Terrible Sound* (Urbana: University of Illinois Press, 1992), 422–423; and Glenn Tucker, *Chickamauga: Bloody Battle in the West* (Indianapolis: Bobbs-Merrill, 1961), 328.

15. Quoted in Donn Piatt, *Memories of the Men Who Saved the Union* (New York: Belford, Clarke, 1887), 183.

16. Shanks, *Personal Recollections,* 72; Richard W. Johnson, *Memoir of Maj.-Gen. Thomas*, 236.

17. Richard W. Johnson, *Memoir of Maj.-Gen. Thomas*, 236.

18. Carl Sandburg, *Abraham Lincoln: The War Years* (New York: Harcourt, Brace & World, 1939), 2:435.

19. William T. Sherman to Henry Halleck, In the Field, near Lovejoy's twenty-six miles south of Atlanta, September 4, 1864, *OR*, vol. 38, pt. 5, 793.

20. W. T. Sherman to Dear Phil, Camp 5th Divn. Moscow, Tenn, July 13, 1862, *Sherman's Civil War: Selected Correspondence of William T. Sherman, 1860–1865*, edited by Brooks D. Simpson and Jean V. Berlin (Chapel Hill: University of North Carolina Press, 1999), 253. In the same letter he termed Don Carlos Buell "our best soldier" and Henry Halleck "the ablest man," while calling Ulysses Grant "very brave, but not brilliant," ibid.

21. Shanks, *Personal Recollections,* 71.

22. Ibid., 75.

23. Piatt and Boynton, *General Thomas*, 334.

24. B. H. Bristow to Donn Piatt, 20 Nassaw St., New York, n.d., Bristow Papers, Filson.

25. Shanks, *Personal Recollections,* 73–75.

26. McKinney, *Education in Violence*, 206.

27. Shanks, *Personal Recollections,* 80.

28. J. Henry Haynie, *The Nineenth Illinois: A Memoir of a Regiment of Volunteer Infantry Famous in the Civil War Fifty Years Ago for Its Drill, Bravery, and Distinguished Service* (Chicago: M. A. Donohue, 1912), 308–310.

29. Ibid., 65.

30. Thomas B. Van Horne, *The Life of Major-General George H. Thomas* (New York: Charles Scribner's Sons, 1882), 460.

31. Ibid., 457.

32. Ibid., 372.

33. John Russell Young, *Around the World with General Grant*, edited by Michael Fellman (Baltimore: Johns Hopkins University Press, 2002), 303.

34. Albert D. Richardson, *A Personal History of Ulysses S. Grant, Illustrated by Twenty-six Engravings; Eight Fac-similies of Letters from Grant, Lincoln, Sheridan, Buckner, Lee, etc.; and Six Maps* (Hartford, Conn.: American Publishing, 1868), 326.

35. John M. Schofield, *Forty-Six Years in the Army* (New York: Century, 1897), 242.

36. McKinney, *Education in Violence*, x.

37. Catherine Ann Devereaux Edmonston, *"Journal of a Secesh Lady": The Diary of Catherine Ann Devereaux Edmonston, 1859–1866*, edited by Beth G. Crabtree and James W. Patton (Raleigh: North Carolina Division of Archives and History, 1979), 601.

38. Joshua Wolfe Shenk, *Lincoln's Melancholy: How Depression Challenged a President and Fueled His Greatness* (Boston: Houghton Mifflin, 2005), 214.

Chapter 1: Young George (1816–1840)

1. Freeman Cleaves, *Rock of Chickamauga: The Life of George H. Thomas* (Norman: University of Oklahoma Press, 1948,) 7–8; Christopher J. Einholf, *George Thomas: Virginian for the Union* (Norman: University of Oklahoma Press, 2007), 14–15; Francis F. McKinney, *Education in Violence: The Life of George H. Thomas and the History of the Army of the Cumberland* (Detroit: Wayne State University Press, 1961), 3–4; Wilbur Thomas, *General George H. Thomas: The Indomitable Warrior* (New York: Exposition Press, 1964), 45–46.

2. Einholf, *George Thomas*, 14–15.

3. Thomas family genealogical notes, 2, VSL.

4. McKinney, *Education in Violence*, 47.

5. Ibid., 331.

6. J.E.B., "The Late Gen. Thomas," *New York Times*, April 9, 1870.

7. "Widow's Declaration for Additional Bounty Laws," Thomas family genealogical notes, Accession no. 25436. There has been some discrepancy concerning the date of John Thomas's death. McKinney also placed it on "February 19, 1829," *Education in Violence*, 3. Einholf cited "April 1829," *George Thomas*, 15; and Wilbur Thomas used the year "1829," *Indomitable Warrior*, 48; Cleaves placed the death "in 1830," *Rock of Chickamauga*, 8.

8. Erasmus D. Keyes, *Fifty Years' Observation of Men and Events Civil and Military* (New York: Charles Scribner's Sons, 1884), 166.

9. Oliver Otis Howard, "Sketch of the Life of George H. Thomas," in *Personal Recollections of the War of the Rebellion: Addresses Delivered before the New York Commandery of the Loyal Legion of the United States, 1883–1891*, edited by James Grant Wilson and Titus Munson Coan (New York: Published by the Commandery, 1891), 287. Einholf has raised questions concerning Howard's motivation for the story. "Howard wanted to explain Thomas's Unionism in terms of an antipathy toward slavery and so looked for early indications of sympathy toward African Americans in Thomas's childhood." Ironically, as he did throughout a fine study, Einholf seemed anxious to impute motives rather than recognize that Thomas simply liked being around boys his own age and these were the ones in the closest proximity to him outside of his siblings. Einholf, *George Thomas*, 12.

10. Thomas B. Van Horne, *The Life of Major-General George H. Thomas* (New York: Charles Scribner's Sons, 1882), 3–4.

11. Van Horne's placement of Thomas as being in his "twentieth year" at the time suggested that he generalized the young man's age, ibid., 2. W. H. T. Squires, who visited the area for a volume on Virginia, was probably closer to the mark, Squires, *The Days of Yester-*

Year in Colony and Commonwealth: A Sketch Book of Virginia (Portsmouth, Va.: Printcraft Press, 1928), 186.

12. Squires, *The Days of Yester-Year*, 186.

13. Van Horne, *Life of General Thomas*, 2.

14. McKinney, *Education in Violence*, 6; Wilbur Thomas, *Indomitable Warrior*, 54.

15. Quoted in Frank A. Palumbo, *George Henry Thomas: The Dependable General* (Dayton, Ohio: Morningside House, 1983), 7.

16. Donn Piatt and Henry V. Boynton, *General George H. Thomas: A Critical Biography* (Cincinnati: Robert Clarke, 1893), 56.

17. Daniel W. Crofts, *Old Southampton: Politics and Society in a Virginia County, 1834–1869* (Charlottesville: University Press of Virginia, 1992), 23.

18. Thomas genealogical notes, 17, VSL.

19. Keyes, *Fifty Years' Observation*, 166. The *Official Register* for June 1837 set his age at 19 years, 11 months, at the time of his admission to the Academy. *Official Register of the Officers and Cadets of the U.S. Military Academy, West Point, New York*, 2:15.

20. Cleaves, *Rock of Chickamauga*, 9; Ezra J. Warner, *Generals in Blue: Lives of the Union Commanders* (Baton Rouge: Louisiana State University Press, 1964), 524.

21. The *Official Register* for June 1837 listed Sherman as 16 years, 6 months, and Vliet at 20 years, 10 months. *Official Register of the Officers and Cadets*, 2:14.

22. Lloyd Lewis, *Sherman: Fighting Prophet* (New York: Harcourt, Brace, 1958), 57.

23. Quoted in Palumbo, *The Dependable General*, 9.

24. "Gen. Van Vliet," unidentified newspaper clipping in the Thomas Papers, Filson.

25. Henry Coppée, *General Thomas* (New York: D. Appleton, 1893), 322–323. See also Van Vliet letter, quoted in Palumbo, *The Dependable General*, 10.

26. William T. Sherman, *Memoirs of General William T. Sherman* (New York: Charles L. Webster, 1892), 1:16.

27. Jeffry D. Wert, *General James Longstreet: The Confederacy's Most Controversial Soldier—A Biography* (New York: Simon & Schuster, 1993), 31.

28. Squires, *The Days of Yester-Year*, 186.

29. James L. Morrison Jr., *"The Best School in the World": West Point, the Pre–Civil War Years, 1833–1866* (Kent, Ohio: Kent State University Press, 1986), 66.

30. Coppée, *General Thomas*, 322–323; Thomas J. Fleming, *West Point: The Men and Times of the United States Military Academy* (New York: William Morrow, 1969), 100.

31. That West Pointer was Thomas's future student, Jeb Stuart. James to My Dear Cousin, Camp Gaines U.S. Military Academy West Point, N.Y. July 8th 1850, Stuart Papers, VHS.

32. Stephen E. Ambrose, *Halleck: Lincoln's Chief of Staff* (Baton Rouge: Louisiana State University Press, 1962), 147.

33. Howard, "Sketch of the Life of George H. Thomas," 346.

34. W. H. Scott, "An Enlisted Man's Estimate," 97, United States Army Military History Institute, Carlisle Barracks, Carlisle, Pa.

35. J.E.B., "The Late Gen. Thomas," *New York Times*, April 9, 1870.

36. Oliver Otis Howard offered this description in *Autobiography of Oliver Otis Howard, Major General United States Army*, 2 vols. (New York: Baker & Taylor, 1908), 1:46.

37. J. E. B. Stuart, "J. E. B. Stuart's Letters to His Hairston Kin, 1850–1855," edited by Peter W. Hairston, *North Carolina Historical Review* 51, no. 3 (July 1974): 263. Stephen Ambrose noted the schedule of Henry A. du Pont in the summer of 1856. It was a rigid regimen that the harried cadet termed "too much like slavery to suit me." Ambrose, *Duty, Honor, Country*, 148.

38. Morrison, *"The Best School in the World,"* 70–71.

39. Ewell to Dear Ben, Military Academy, West Point, November 6, 1836, in Richard S. Ewell, *The Making of a Soldier: The Letters of General R. S. Ewell*, edited by Percy Gatling Hamlin (Richmond, Va.: Whittet & Shepperson, 1935), 22.

40. George W. Cullum, *Biographical Register of the Officers and Graduates of the U.S. Military Academy at West Point, N.Y., from Its Establishment, in 1802 and 1890, with the Early History of the United States Military Academy,* 2 vols. (Boston: Houghton, Mifflin, 1891), 1:489.

41. Ewell to Dear Ben, Military Academy, West Point, November 6, 1836, in *The Making of a Soldier*, 22.

42. Morrison, *"The Best School in the World,"* 73.

43. *Official Register of the Officers and Cadets*, June 1837, 21.

44. James I. Robertson Jr., *Stonewall Jackson: The Man, the Soldier, the Legend* (New York: Macmillan, 1997), 33.

45. McKinney, *Education in Violence*, 15.

46. Lloyd Lewis, *Captain Sam Grant* (Boston: Little, Brown, 1950), 91.

47. *Official Register of the Officers and Cadets*, June 1838, 11.

48. *Official Register of the Officers and Cadets*, June 1839, 8.

49. Robertson, *Stonewall Jackson*, 33.

50. John F. Marszalek, *Commander of All Lincoln's Armies: A Life of General Henry W. Halleck* (Cambridge, Mass.: Belknap Press of Harvard University Press, 2004), 25–26.

51. Einholf, *George Thomas*, 14.

52. Cullum, *Biographical Register*, 1:110. DeRussy's term as superintendent began on July 1, 1833, ibid., 21.

53. Ewell to Dear Ben, Military Academy, West Point, N.Y., January 10, 1840, in *The Making of a Soldier*, 32.

54. Donald C. Pfanz, *Richard S. Ewell: A Soldier's Life* (Chapel Hill: University of North Carolina Press, 1998), 23–24; Robertson, *Stonewall Jackson*, 32–33.

55. Ewell to Dear Ben, Military Academy, West Point, N.Y., January 10, 1840, in *The Making of a Soldier*, 32.

56. GHT to Dear Brother, West Point Feby 16th 1839, Thomas Papers, VHS.

57. Cullum, *Biographical Register*, 1:183.

58. GHT to Dear Brother, West Point, April 23d 1839, Personal Collection of Wiley Sword.

59. *Official Register of the Officers and Cadets*, II, 1840, 9. Louisianan Paul Hebert led the class, George Getty stood at fifteenth, Henry Whiting at seventeenth, and Bushrod Johnson at twenty-third, ibid.

60. Circulation Records, Thomas, USMAL, 1836–1841.

61. GHT to Dear Brother, West Point Feby 16th 1839, Thomas Papers, VHS. Ruffin, whose later fame would consist of such intense support for the Confederacy that he killed himself rather than exist under "Yankee rule," established the *Farmers' Register* in the 1830s, in which he reprinted Davy's publication and other works relating to science and agriculture. Avery Craven, *Edmund Ruffin Southerner: A Study in Secession* (Baton Rouge: Louisiana State University Press, 1966), 61–62 and 259.

62. Circulation Records, Thomas, USMAL, 1836–1841.

63. Ibid.; Edwin C. McReynolds, *The Seminoles* (Norman: University of Oklahoma Press, 1957), 231.

64. Keyes, *Fifty Years' Observation*, 167.

65. GHT to Dear Brother, West Point, April 23d 1839, Personal Collection of Wiley Sword.

66. Demerits, Thomas, George H., 1836–1837, USMAL.

67. Ibid., 1837–1838.

68. Ibid., 1839–1840.

69. GHT to Dear Brother, West Point, April 23d 1839, Personal Collection of Wiley Sword.

70. William B. Skelton, *An American Profession of Arms: The Army Officer Corps, 1784–1861* (Lawrence: University Press of Kansas, 1992), 349.

71. Marszalek, *Commander of All Lincoln's Armies*, 22.

72. Van Horne, *Life of General Thomas*, 457.

73. Ambrose, *Duty, Honor, Country*, 163; Wert, *Longstreet*, 27–28.

74. Emory M. Thomas, *Robert E. Lee: A Biography* (New York: W. W. Norton, 1995), 55.

75. Robert Utley, *Frontiersmen in Blue: The United States Army and the Indian, 1848–1865* (New York: Macmillan, 1967), 33.

76. Morrison, *"The Best School in the World,"* 101.

77. "Gen. Van Vliet," unidentified newspaper clipping in the Thomas Papers, Filson.

Chapter 2: First Duties (1840–1845)

1. George W. Cullum, *Biographical Register of the Officers and Graduates of the U.S. Military Academy at West Point, N.Y., from Its Establishment, in 1802 and 1890, with the Early History of the United States Military Academy,* 2 vols. (Boston: Houghton, Mifflin, 1891), 2:33.

2. Francis Paul Prucha, *A Guide to the Military Posts of the United States, 1789–1895* (Madison: State Historical Society of Wisconsin, 1964), 67.

3. Erasmus D. Keyes, *Fifty Years' Observation of Men and Events Civil and Military* (New York: Charles Scribner's Sons, 1884), 166.

4. GHT to Dear Brother, Fort Columbus Sept. 27th 1840, Thomas Papers, VHS.

5. Post Returns for October and November, 1840, Returns for U.S. Military Posts, 1800–1916, Fort Lauderdale, Florida, M617, Roll #604.

6. GHT to Dear Brother, Fort Columbus Sept. 27th 1840, Thomas Papers, VHS.

7. GHT to Dear Brother, Fort Wood Bedlow's Island New York Oct. 19th 1840, Thomas Family Papers, VHS.

8. Post Returns for December, 1840, Returns for U.S. Military Posts, 1800–1916, Fort Lauderdale, Florida, M617, Roll #604.

9. Edwin C. McReynolds, *The Seminoles* (Norman: University of Oklahoma Press, 1957), 231.

10. Ibid.

11. GHT to Dear Brother, Fort Lauderdale E.F. Jany. 25th 1841, Thomas Family Papers, VHS.

12. Letter quoted in Henry Coppée, *General Thomas* (New York: D. Appleton, 1893), 7–8.

13. Ibid., 7.

14. Ibid., 9.

15. Post Returns for May and June, 1841, Returns for U.S. Military Posts, 1800–1916, Fort Lauderdale, Florida, M617, Roll #604.

16. July, 1841, Ibid.

17. Unidentified newspaper clipping, Thomas Papers, Filson.

18. Post Returns for August, 1841, Returns for U.S. Military Posts, 1800–1916, Fort Lauderdale, Florida, M617, Roll #604.

19. September and October, 1841, ibid.

20. John T. Sprague, *The Origin, Progress and Conclusion of the Florida War,* facsimile reproduction (Gainesville: University Press of Florida, 1964), 392–393.

21. Cullum placed the total at 70, *Biographical Register*, 2:33; McReynolds put the number at 55, *The Seminoles*, 232.

22. Francis F. McKinney, *Education in Violence: The Life of George H. Thomas and the History of the Army of the Cumberland* (Detroit: Wayne State University Press, 1961), 25.

23. John K. Mahon, *History of the Second Seminole War, 1835–1842* (Gainesville: University Press of Florida, 1967), 309.

24. Edward M. Coffman, *The Old Army: A Portrait of the American Army in Peacetime, 1784–1898* (New York: Oxford University Press, 1986), 67.

25. Thomas B. Van Horne, *The Life of Major-General George H. Thomas* (New York: Charles Scribner's Sons, 1882), 18.

26. Keyes, *Fifty Years' Observation*, 166. Thomas's eyes remained a notable feature as a writer observed: "blue eyes, with depths to them," Benjamin F. Taylor, *Pictures of Life in Camp and Field* (Chicago: S. C. Griggs, 1875, 1888), 193.

27. Mahon, *Second Seminole War*, 321.

28. Ibid., 322. Among the lessons this scholar contended the conflict offered its military participants was exposure to guerrilla warfare, ibid., 325.

29. Commission of Brevet First Lieutenant George H. Thomas, March 6, 1843, Thomas Papers, VHS; Cullum, *Biographical Register*, 2:33.

30. Cullum, *Biographical Register*, 2:33.

31. Post Returns for July, August, September, October, November, and December 1842, Returns for U.S. Military Posts, 1800–1916, Fort Moultrie, South Carolina, M617, Roll #815.

32. Wayne Wei-siang Hsieh, "'I Owe Virginia Little, My Country Much': Robert E. Lee, the United States Regular Army, and Unconditional Unionism," in *Crucible of the Civil War: Virginia from Secession to Civil War,* edited by Edward L. Ayers, Gary W. Gallagher, and Andrew J. Torget (Charlottesville: University Press of Virginia, 2006), 39–40.

33. William T. Sherman, *Memoirs of General William T. Sherman* (New York: Charles L. Webster, 1892), 1:29.

34. Unidentified newspaper clipping, Thomas Papers, Filson.

35. Samuel G. French, *Two Wars: An Autobiography of Gen. Samuel G. French* (Nashville, Tenn.: Confederate Veteran, 1901), 24; Wilbur Thomas, *General George H. Thomas: The Indomitable Warrior* (New York: Exposition Press, 1964), 77.

36. Post Returns for January, February, and March 1843, Returns for U.S. Military Posts 1800–1916, Fort Moultrie, South Carolina, M617, Roll #815. The February report merely listed him as present.

37. September, October, and November, 1843, ibid. The first appointment lasted only a week, from September 2–9. The second was for an unspecified time that seemed to have begun in October and ended on November 4, when he was relieved of the assignment. The April–August reports had Thomas present for duty, ibid.

38. December, 1843, ibid.; Post Returns for December 1843, Returns for U.S. Military Posts, 1800–1916, Fort McHenry, Maryland, M617, Roll #675. Thomas was listed as present in January and February 1844, ibid.

39. French, *Two Wars*, 26.

40. McKinney, *Education in Violence*, 28.

41. Norma Lois Peterson, *The Presidencies of William Henry Harrison and John Tyler* (Lawrence: University Press of Kansas, 1989), 201–203.

42. Post Returns for April, 1844, Returns for U.S. Military Posts, 1800–1916, Fort McHenry, Maryland, M617, Roll #675.

43. July and September 1844, ibid. May, June, and August listed him as present, ibid.

44. GHT to Dear Brother, Ft. McHenry Md. Oct. 17th 1844, Thomas Family Papers, VHS.

45. October, 1844, ibid. Thomas left Fort McHenry on October 19. He was listed on the Fort Moultrie report for the same month and remained on the rolls there until April 1845. Post Returns for October, November, and December 1844, and January, February, March, and April 1845, Returns for U.S. Military Posts, 1800–1916, Fort Moultrie, South Carolina, M617, Roll #815.

46. GHT to Dear Brother, Ft Moultrie S.C. Nov. 8th 1844, Thomas Papers, DUL.

47. GHT to Dear Brother, Fort Moultrie S.C. January 11th 1845, Thomas Papers. DUL.

48. Post Returns for February, March and April 1845, Returns for U.S. Military Posts, 1800–1916, Fort Moultrie, South Carolina, M617, Roll #815.

Chapter 3: "Under Fire" in Mexico and Virginia (1845–1848)

1. Thomas M. Anderson, *General George H. Thomas: His Place in History, A Paper Read before Oregon Commandery of the Military Order of the Loyal Legion of the United States, March 7, 1894* (Portland, Ore.: A. Anderson, 1894), 11–12.

2. James M. McPherson, *Battle Cry of Freedom: The Civil War Era* (New York: Oxford University Press, 1988), 4; McPherson included Thomas in his brief review of these future adversaries, ibid., 5.

3. Unidentified newspaper clipping, Thomas Papers, Filson.

4. Thomas B. Van Horne, *The Life of Major-General George H. Thomas* (New York: Charles Scribner's Sons, 1882), 5.

5. Francis F. McKinney, *Education in Violence: The Life of George H. Thomas and the History of the Army of the Cumberland* (Detroit: Wayne State University Press, 1961), 31.

6. Daniel H. Hill, "Chickamauga—The Great Battle of the West" in *Battles and Leaders of the Civil War*, edited by Robert Underwood Johnson and Clarence Clough Buel (New York: Century, 1887), 3:639. Grady McWhiney noted Bragg's presence in the mess there, *Braxton Bragg and Confederate Defeat*, vol 1: *Field Command* (New York: Columbia University Press, 1969), 53.

7. McKinney, *Education in Violence*, 32.

8. Lloyd Lewis, *Captain Sam Grant* (Boston: Little, Brown, 1950), 152.

9. Grady McWhiney observed that officers in the fort voted unanimously to continue their defense, in *Field Command*, 61.

10. Maurice Matloff, *American Military History* (Washington, D.C.: Office of the Chief of Military History, United States Army, 1969), 164–166.

11. American participant Samuel French offered a description of Monterrey in his memoirs, calling the Citadel "the Black Fort," and the other major work, "Fort Tanaria." Samuel G. French, *Two Wars: An Autobiography of Gen. Samuel G. French* (Nashville, Tenn.: Confederate Veteran, 1901), 61. For a general discussion, see also K. Jack Bauer, *The Mexican War: 1846–1848* (New York: Macmillan, 1974), 81–105; Robert Selph Henry, *The Story of the Mexican War* (Indianapolis: Bobbs-Merrill, 1950), 138–155; Justin H. Smith, *The War with Mexico* (Gloucester, Mass.: Peter Smith, 1963), 239–261.

12. Bauer, *The Mexican War*, 93.

13. McKinney, *Education in Violence*, 36.

14. John Pope, *The Military Memoirs of General John Pope,* edited by Peter Cozzens and Robert I. Girardi (Chapel Hill: University of North Carolina Press, 1998), 94.

15. French, *Two Wars*, 62.

16. Ibid., 65.

17. Jefferson Davis to J. A. Quitman, Letters Received, AGO, M567, Roll No. 361, NA.

18. Zachary Taylor Report, Camp before Monterey, Sept. 23rd, 1846, Letters Received, AGO, M567, Roll No. 361, NA.

19. French, *Two Wars*, 66.

20. Jefferson Davis to J. A. Quitman, Letters Received, AGO, M567, Roll No. 361, NA.

21. French, *Two Wars*, 66.

22. Ibid.

23. Ibid., 67.

24. Bauer, *The Mexican War*, 100. Edward Mansfield listed 8 officers and 47 men killed, one officer and 8 men mortally wounded, for 64 total among the regulars at Monterrey, Edward D. Mansfield, *The Mexican War: History of Its Origins, and a Detailed Account of the Victories Which Terminated in the Surrender of the Capital; With the Official Despatches of the Generals* (New York: A. S. Barnes, 1849), 359.

25. George W. Cullum, *Biographical Register of the Officers and Graduates of the U.S. Military Academy at West Point, N.Y., from Its Establishment, in 1802 and 1890, with the Early History of the United States Military Academy,* 2 vols. (Boston: Houghton, Mifflin, 1891), 2:33.

26. Jeanne Twiggs Heidler, "The Military Career of David Emanuel Twiggs," doctoral dissertation, Auburn University, 1988, 178–179.

27. Wilbur Thomas, *General George H. Thomas: The Indomitable Warrior* (New York: Exposition Press, 1964), 101.

28. Cadmus M. Wilcox, *History of the Mexican War* (Washington, D.C.: Church News Publishing, 1892), 118.

29. McKinney, *Education in Violence*, 40.

30. Some of the harshest criticism came from the politically connected and highly charged Tennessee volunteer Gideon Pillow. See, for example, Nathaniel Cheairs Hughes Jr. and Roy P. Stonsifer Jr., *The Life and Wars of Gideon J. Pillow* (Chapel Hill: University of North Carolina Press, 1993), 48.

31. For a general discussion of Buena Vista, see Bauer, *The Mexican War*, 201–231; Henry, *The Story of the Mexican War*, 238–257; and Smith, *The War with Mexico*, 370–400.

32. Wilcox, *History of the Mexican War*, 219.

33. French, *Two Wars*, 78.

34. Letters Received, AGO, M567, Roll No. 362, NA.

35. Wilcox, *History of the Mexican War*, 222.

36. W. H. L. Wallace to Dear George, Camp Taylor, 20 miles south of Saltillo, Mexico, March 1, 1847, in Isabel Wallace, *Life and Letters of General W. H. L. Wallace* (Chicago: R. R. Donnelley, 1909), 48.

37. Ibid., 49–50.

38. French, *Two Wars*, 80.

39. James Henry Carleton, *The Battle of Buena Vista, with the Operations of the "Army of Occupation" for One Month* (New York: Harper and Brothers, 1848), 85.

40. Wilcox, *History of the Mexican War*, 226.

41. Bauer, *The Mexican War*, 216.

42. Wilcox, *History of the Mexican War*, 231–232.

43. Ibid., 233.

44. Ibid.

45. McKinney, *Education in Violence*, 44; Bauer, *The Mexican War*, 216; Henry, *The Story of the Mexican War*, 252–253.

46. Biographer Grady McWhiney called the popular version that included a call for "more

grape" at best an exaggeration and most likely, as one participant insisted, inaccurate since there was no grape shot actually used in the engagement. See McWhiney, *Field Command,* 90–92.

47. Henry, *The Story of the Mexican War,* 253.

48. Carleton, *The Battle of Buena Vista,* 85.

49. Abner Doubleday, *My Life in the Old Army: The Reminiscences of Abner Doubleday from the Collections of the New-York Historical Society,* edited by Joseph E. Chance (Fort Worth: Texas Christian University Press, 1998), 113.

50. Ramon Alcaraz, "Description of the Battle of Buena Vista," in Ernesto Chavez, *The U.S. War with Mexico: A Brief History with Documents* (Boston: Bedford/St. Martin's, 2008), 108–109.

51. Bauer, *The Mexican War,* 217. French put the U.S. toll at the same with one additional man wounded, *Two Wars,* 84; Wilcox tabulated the American deaths slightly lower (267), and wounded and missing slightly higher (456 and 23, respectively), Wilcox, *History of the Mexican War,* 236. Henry concurred with Wilcox, *The Story of the Mexican War,* 253. Mansfield listed only deaths among the regulars and placed that number at 8, Edward D. Mansfield, *The Mexican War,* 359.

52. Carleton, *The Battle of Buena Vista,* 191–192.

53. French, *Two Wars,* 81.

54. Edward D. Mansfield, *The Mexican War,* 138–139. The entire report was found in ibid., 125–143.

55. Letters Received, AGO, M567, Roll, No. 362, NA.

56. W. H. L. Wallace to Dear George, Camp Taylor, 20 miles south of Saltillo, Mexico, March 1, 1847, in Wallace, *Life and Letters,* 40.

57. [GHT to] Captain, Camp Cooper, Tex. September 21st 1859, Thomas Papers, HL.

58. Cullum, *Biographical Register,* 2:33.

59. McKinney, *Education in Violence,* 45.

60. GHT to Dr. Duncan, Buena Vista Mex., March 18th 1847, James Duncan Letter in Cullum File, Manuscripts Collection, USMA.

61. Daniel William Cobb 1847 Diary, "Munday, 19 July" entry, Cobb Papers, VHS; Daniel William Cobb, *Cobb's Ordeal: The Diaries of a Virginia Farmer, 1842–1872,* edited by Daniel W. Crofts (Athens: University of Georgia Press, 1997), 58–59.

62. James Maget to Dear Miss Judith, Southampton Va July 20th/47, Thomas Papers, VHS.

63. James Maget to Dear Madam, Southampton County Feby 8/48, Thomas Papers, VHS. Another letter went to Thomas's brother William, James Maget to Dear Sir, Thomas Papers, VHS.

64. GHT to Dear Sir, Buena Vista Mex., March 31st 1848, Thomas Papers, VHS. The ornate presentation sword and scabbard have been housed in the collections of the Virginia Historical Society in Richmond.

65. Daniel W. Crofts, *Old Southampton: Politics and Society in a Virginia County, 1834–1869* (Charlottesville: University Press of Virginia, 1992), 187.

66. Ibid., 23–24. Crofts explained, "Mason's success gradually eroded his ties to Southampton. During the last two decades of his life, he rarely set foot in the county." Ibid., 24.

67. Bragg to Jones, November 22, 1847, in McWhiney, *Field Command,* 94.

68. Braxton Bragg to Col., Camp near Monterey, Mexico 22d November 1847, Braxton Bragg Papers, DUL.

69. Eugene C. Tidball, "A Subaltern's First Experiences in the Old Army," *Civil War History* 45, no. 3 (Sept. 1999): 197–222, 206.

70. GHT to Dear Brother, Brazos Island, Texas Oct. 25th, 1848, VHS.

71. Braxton Bragg to Dear sir, Mobile 17 Novr. /48, Bragg Papers, DUL.

72. Kevin Dougherty, *Civil War Leadership and Mexican War Experience* (Jackson: University Press of Mississippi, 2007), 110.

Chapter 4: New Frontiers (1848–1854)

1. Post Returns for August and September, 1849, Returns for U.S. Military Posts, 1800–1916, Fort Adams, Rhode Island, M617, Roll #3, NA.

2. Post Returns for July, August, September, October, and November, 1850, Returns for U.S. Military Posts, 1800–1916, Fort Myers, Florida, M617, Roll #827, NA. For a brief description of Fort Myers, see Francis Paul Prucha, *A Guide to the Military Posts of the United States, 1789–1895* (Madison: State Historical Society of Wisconsin, 1964), 93.

3. GHT to Dear Brother, Ft. Vinton E. Fla, April 28th 1850, VHS. The letter did not actually go out until May 4.

4. Post Returns for September, October, and November, 1850, Returns for U.S. Military Posts, 1800–1916, Fort Myers, Florida, M617, Roll #827, NA.

5. Thomas B. Van Horne, *The Life of Major-General George H. Thomas* (New York: Charles Scribner's Sons, 1882), 9–10; Freeman Cleaves, *Rock of Chickamauga: The Life of George H. Thomas* (Norman: University of Oklahoma Press, 1948), 47.

6. Post Returns for January, 1851, Returns for U.S. Military Posts, 1800–1916, Fort Independence, Massachusetts, M617, Roll #508, NA.

7. GHT to Dear Brother, Ft. Independence, Boston Harbour, Feby 8th, 1851, Thomas Papers, VHS. An envelope indicated that the letter routed from Boston to Jerusalem at a cost of ten cents, VHS.

8. GHT to Dear Brother, Ft. Independence Boston Harbour Mar 23 51, Thomas Papers, ibid.

9. Post Returns for March, 1851, Fort Independence, Massachusetts, NA.

10. February, 1852, ibid.

11. Various Post Returns to June, 1853, for Fort Independence, Massachusetts; Post Returns for July and August, 1853, Returns for U.S. Military Posts, 1800–1916, Fort Adams, Rhode Island, M617, Roll #3, NA.

12. Coppée, *General Thomas*, 22–23.

13. Ibid., 182–183.

14. Joseph B. Mitchell, *Military Leaders in the Civil War* (New York: G. P. Putnam's Sons, 1972), 218.

15. Dabney Herndon Maury, *Recollections of a Virginian in the Mexican, Indian, and Civil Wars* (New York: Charles Scribner's Sons, 1897), 61–62.

16. Emory M. Thomas, *Robert E. Lee: A Biography* (New York: W. W. Norton, 1995), 152–161.

17. John M. Schofield, *Forty-Six Years in the Army* (New York: Century, 1897), 241–242; Donald B. Connelly, *John M. Schofield and the Politics of Generalship* (Chapel Hill: University of North Carolina Press, 2006), 17–18.

18. Richard W. Johnson, *Memoir of Maj.-Gen. George H. Thomas* (Philadelphia: J. B. Lippincott, 1881), 26.

19. Frank A. Palumbo, *George Henry Thomas: The Dependable General* (Dayton, Ohio: Morningside House, 1983), 51; Cleaves, *Rock of Chickamauga*, 50.

20. Wilbur Thomas, *General George H. Thomas: The Indomitable Warrior* (New York: Exposition Press, 1964), 105.

21. Richard W. Johnson, *Memoir of Maj.-Gen. Thomas*, 27.

22. Ibid.; Francis F. McKinney, *Education in Violence: The Life of George H. Thomas and the History of the Army of the Cumberland* (Detroit: Wayne State University Press, 1961), 55; Christopher J. Einholf, *George Thomas: Virginian for the Union* (Norman: University of Oklahoma Press, 2007), 65. Cleaves recorded the vows as being taken in the home of the uncle, Daniel Southwick, in Troy, *Rock of Chickamauga*, 50. Piatt and Boynton noted the date as November 7 in an obviously unintentional typographical error, *General George H. Thomas: A Critical Biography* (Cincinnati: Robert Clarke, 1893), 71.

23. McKinney, *Education in Violence*, 55; Cleaves, *Rock of Chickamauga*, 50–51.

24. Coppée, *General Thomas*, 23.

25. Quoted in Einholf, *George Thomas*, 66.

26. Piatt and Boynton, *General Thomas*, 71.

27. See, for example, the reference in GHT to My dear Fanny, Fort Belknap Tex December 22, 1858, Thomas Family Papers, VHS.

28. Cleaves, *Rock of Chickamauga*, 51.

29. R. E. Lee to Tho. S. Jesup, U.S. Mil: Acady, West Point 17 March 1853, *The Daily Correspondence of Brevet Colonel Robert E. Lee Superintendent, United States Military Academy September 1, 1852 to March 24, 1855*, edited by Charles R. Bowery, Jr. and Brian D. Hankinson, Occasional Papers 5 (West Point, N.Y.: United States Military Academy Library, 2003), 68–69.

30. R. E. Lee to Jos: G. Totten, U.S. Mil: Acady, West Point 8 Oct: 1853, ibid., 130.

31. Geo. W. Cullum to General, U.S. Military Academy West Point, N.Y. August 18, 1853, ibid., 113–114.

32. McKinney, *Education in Violence*, 59.

33. U.S. Military Academy West Point 21 January 1854, Lee Letterbook [Mss1 L51c 735], 309–312, VHS.

34. Herman Hattaway, *General Stephen D. Lee* (Jackson: University Press of Mississippi, 1976), 5.

35. Edwd. Hartz to Dear Father, Military Academy West Point N.Y., April 10th, 1854, Hartz Papers LOC.

36. *Official Register of the Officers and Cadets*, 1854, 7. Hattaway noted the friendship of Lee and Pender, *Stephen D. Lee*, 6.

37. *Official Register of the Officers and Cadets*, 1854, 7.

38. Edwd. Hartz to Dear Father, Military Academy West Point N.Y., April 10th, 1854, Hartz Papers LOC.

39. J. E. B. Stuart [to Bettie Hairston], U.S. Military Academy, West Point, N.Y., Feby 9th 54, quoted in J. E. B. Stuart, "J. E. B. Stuart's Letters to His Hairston Kin, 1850–1855," edited by Peter W. Hairston, *North Carolina Historical Review* 51, no. 3 (July 1974): 307–308.

40. Monday, June 14 [1852], Report of Board of Visitors, in *Executive Documents, Senate, Second Session, Thirty-Second Congress, 1852–'53*, 209.

41. Tuesday, June 15, in ibid., 210.

42. R. E. Lee to Jos: G. Totten, U.S. Mil. Acady, 13 April 1854, *Daily Correspondence of Superintendent*, 178.

43. R. E. Lee to Jos: G. Totten, U.S. Mil. Acady, 21 April 1854, ibid., 180.

44. *Official Register of the Officers and Cadets*, 1854, 4. Lee's directive was in R. E. Lee to Jos: G. Totten, U.S. Mil. Acady, 28 April 1854, *Daily Correspondence of Superintendent*, 182.

Chapter 5: The West Beckons (1854–1860)

1. Francis F. McKinney, *Education in Violence: The Life of George H. Thomas and the History of the Army of the Cumberland* (Detroit: Wayne State University Press, 1961), 56.

2. Joseph King Fenno Mansfield, *Mansfield on the Condition of the Western Forts, 1853–54*, edited by Robert W. Frazer (Norman: University of Oklahoma Press, 1963), 182–183.

3. Unidentified newspaper clipping, Thomas Papers, Filson.

4. Post Returns for July, 1854, Returns for U.S. Military Posts, 1800–1916, Fort Yuma, California, M617, Roll #1488, NA.

5. Francis Paul Prucha, *A Guide to the Military Posts of the United States, 1789–1895* (Madison: State Historical Society of Wisconsin, 1964), 118.

6. Joseph King Fenno Mansfield, *Condition of the Western Forts*, 146–149. Quotation on 148.

7. GHT to My Dear Brother, Fort Yuma Cal Sept 11, 1854, Thomas Papers, VHS. As he had promised, Thomas enclosed a check, dated "Fort Yuma Cal. Sept. 2, 1854 on National Bank, New York, for $208, which had been made payable to Maj. Geo. H. Thomas 3rd Artly, USA.," ibid.

8. Thomas B. Van Horne, *The Life of Major-General George H. Thomas* (New York: Charles Scribner's Sons, 1882), 18. See also Gilbert C. Kniffin, "The Life and Services of Major General George H. Thomas," in *War Papers Being Papers Read before the Commandery of the District of Columbia Military Order of the Loyal Legion of the United States*, vol. 1, *Papers 1–26. March 1887–April 1897* (Wilmington, N.C.: Broadfoot Publishing, 1993), 26.

9. GHT to My Dear Mr. Gibbs, Louisville, Ky., Nov. 18, 1867, Yale.

10. William H. Goetzmann, *Exploration and Empire: The Explorer and the Scientist in the Winning of the American West* (New York: Alfred A. Knopf, 1966), 303.

11. *Executive Documents, House of Representatives of the United States, Third Session, Thirty-Fourth Congress,* "Annual Report of the Board of Regents of the Smithsonian Institution Showing the Operations, Expeditions, and Conditions of the Institution, for the Year 1856," 49, 51, 57–58, and 67.

12. *Executive Documents, House of Representatives of the United States, Second Session, Thirty-Third Congress,* "Reports of Explorations and Surveys to Ascertain the Most Practicable and Economical Route for a Railroad from the Mississippi River to the Pacific Ocean," 4 (1856), 125 and 134.

13. *Executive Documents, House of Representatives of the United States, Third Session, Thirty-Fourth Congress,* "Annual Report of the Board of Regents of the Smithsonian Institution Showing the Operations, Expeditions, and Conditions of the Institution, for the Year 1856," 49, 51, 57–58, and 67.

14. Michael Fellman, *Citizen Sherman: A Life of William Tecumseh Sherman* (New York: Random House, 1995), 5.

15. GHT to My dear Friend, Fort Yuma, Cal., November 30, 1854, Sherman Papers, LOC.

16. McKinney, *Education in Violence*, 59.

17. See numerous articles in the *New York Times* related to the disaster, ranging from September 1854 to November. The abandonment of the crew was highlighted in "The Wreck of the Arctic," November 13, 1854, and limited lifeboats in "The Arctic," November 17, 1854.

18. GHT to My dear Friend, Fort Yuma, Cal., November 30, 1854, Sherman Papers, LOC.

19. John F. Marszalek, *Sherman: A Soldier's Passion for Order* (New York: Free Press, 1993), 57 and 93–94.

20. Fellman, *Citizen Sherman*, 42.

21. K. Theodore Hoppen, *The Mid-Victorian Generation, 1846–1888* (New York: Oxford

University Press, 2000), 178; John Shelton Curtiss noted that the Russians suffered severe losses of 12,000 men and 6 generals at Inkerman, *The Russian Army under Nicholas I: 1825–1855* (Durham, N.C.: Duke University Press, 1965), 335–337.

22. GHT to My dear Friend, Fort Yuma, Cal., November 30, 1854, Sherman Papers, LOC.

23. Hoppen, *Mid-Victorian Generation*, 179–182.

24. GHT to My dear Friend, Fort Yuma, Cal., November 30, 1854, Sherman Papers, LOC.

25. GHT to My dear Friend, Fort Yuma, Cal., March 15, 1855, Sherman Papers, LOC.

26. Thomas was not alone. As biographer Michael Fellman observed, "Sherman failed to notice the contradiction between his negative moral view of the mad dash speculations of others and how he himself was behaving." Fellman, *Citizen Sherman*, 27.

27. GHT to My dear Friend, Fort Yuma, Cal., March 15, 1855, Sherman Papers, LOC.

28. Ibid.

29. Richard W. Johnson, *Memoir of Maj.-Gen. George H. Thomas* (Philadelphia: J. B. Lippincott, 1881), 28–29.

30. GHT to My dear Friend, Fort Yuma, Cal., April 29, 1855, Sherman Papers, LOC.

31. GHT Field Report, Head Quarters Fort Yuma Cal. February 15, 1855, Letters Received AGO, M567, Roll #528, NA.

32. Post Returns for July, 1855, Returns for U.S. Military Posts, 1800–1916, Fort Yuma, California, M617, Roll #1488, NA.

33. GHT to My dear Brother, Jefferson Bks Mo, October 10, 1855, Thomas Papers, VHS.

34. Richard W. Johnson, *Memoir of Maj.-Gen. Thomas*, 30–31. Johnson was listed as a first lieutenant and regimental quartermaster at Fort Mason in the May 1856 report. During several of Thomas's absences, he assumed command of the post. Post Returns for May 1856, and April and May 1857, Returns for U.S. Military Posts, 1800–1916, Fort Mason, Texas, M617, Roll #1488, NA.

35. Robert Utley, *Frontiersmen in Blue: The United States Army and the Indian, 1848–1865* (New York: Macmillan, 1967), 126.

36. Ibid., 127.

37. Post Returns for January, 1856, Fort Mason, Texas, M617, Roll #759, NA.

38. Post Returns for September, October, November, and December, 1856, and January, February, March, and April, 1857, Fort Mason, Texas, M617, Roll #759, NA.

39. George Meade, *The Life and Letters of George Gordon Meade, Major-General United States Army*, edited by George Gordon Meade, 2 vols. (New York: Charles Scribner's Sons, 1913), 2:253.

40. Lee Diary, VHS.

41. R. E. Lee, Fort Brown, Texas, 8, Nov. 1856, Lee Papers (Mss1 L51c 174), VHS.

42. R. E. Lee, Fort Brown, Texas, 19th Nov 1856, Lee Papers (Mss1 L51c 176), VHS.

43. R. E. Lee, Fort Brown, Texas, 27 Decr. 1856, Lee Papers (Mss1 L51 181), VHS.

44. Lee Diary, VHS. See also Emory M. Thomas, *Robert E. Lee: A Biography* (New York: W. W. Norton, 1995), 170, which noted the amount of traveling he was called upon to make. The biographer noted that for an eight-month period, from September 2, 1856, to May 5, 1857, "Lee underwent his own species of trial by court-martial," ibid.

45. Post Returns for February, March, April, and May, 1856, Fort Mason, Texas, M617, Roll #759, NA.

46. R. E. Lee, San Antonio, Texas, 7 March 1857, Lee Papers (Mss1 L51c 189), VHS.

47. Lee Diary, VHS.

48. R. E. Lee, Indianola, Texas, 20th March 1857, Lee Papers (Mss1 L51c 192), VHS; R. E. Lee, Indianola, Texas, 28th March 1857, Lee Papers (Mss1 L51c 196), VHS.

49. R. E. Lee, Indianola, Texas, 28th March 1857, Lee Papers (Mss1 L51c 196), VHS.

50. Van Horne, *Life of General Thomas*, 16.

51. Post Returns for February, March, April, and May, 1856, Fort Mason, Texas, M617, Roll #759, NA.

52. R. E. Lee, Camp Cooper, Texas, 26 Apr. 1857, Lee Papers (Mss1 L51 c202), VHS.

53. F. L. Thomas to My dear Col Hough, Troy NY, May 1st 1883, Hough Papers, UCBL.

54. Quoted in Van Horne, *Life of General Thomas*, 218.

55. Richard W. Johnson, *Memoir of Maj.-Gen. Thomas*, 32–33.

56. Post Returns for May, June, and July, 1857, Fort Mason, Texas, M617, Roll #759, NA.

57. GHT to Colonel, Fort Mason Texas, July 7, 1857, Yale University.

58. Post Returns for August, 1857, Fort Mason, Texas, M617, Roll #759, NA.

59. GHT to Sir, Hd Qrs Fort Mason Tex Aug 11 1857, in Post Returns for Fort Mason, Texas, M617, Roll #759, NA.

60. Post Returns for June, 1858, Fort Mason, Texas, M617, Roll #759, NA. Post Returns for July, 1858, Fort Belknap, Texas, M617, Roll #95, NA.

61. Freeman Cleaves read more into the Twiggs-Thomas imbroglio than other biographers, *Rock of Chickamauga: The Life of George H. Thomas* (Norman: University of Oklahoma Press, 1948,) 57–58. McKinney thought the lesson that Thomas took away from the clashes was that courts-martial could be "used for a weapon about as frequently as for a shield," *Education in Violence*, 73.

62. Richard W. Johnson, *Memoir of Maj.-Gen. Thomas*, 35.

63. Robert G. Hartje, *Van Dorn: The Life and Times of a Confederate General* (Nashville, Tenn.: Vanderbilt University Press, 1967), 63.

64. Arthur B. Carter, *The Tarnished Cavalier: Major-General Earl Van Dorn, C.S.A.* (Knoxville: University of Tennessee Press, 1999), 16.

65. Hartje, *Van Dorn*, 64.

66. GHT to My dear Fanny, Fort Belknap Tex December 22, 1858, Thomas Family Papers, VHS.

67. Prucha, *Military Posts*, 60.

68. GHT to Sir, Camp Cooper Tx Feby 27, 1859, Zabriskie Papers, VHS.

69. Van Horne, *Life of General Thomas*, 13–14.

70. Kniffin, "Life of Thomas," 26.

71. McKinney, *Education in Violence*, 77–78.

72. Post Returns for July and August, 1859, Returns for U.S. Military Posts, 1800–1916, Camp Cooper, Texas, M617, Roll #253, NA.

73. Kenneth F. Neighbours, "Indian Exodus Out of Texas in 1859," *West Texas Historical Association Year Book* 36 (Oct. 1960): 80–97.

74. Kenneth F. Neighbours, "The Assassination of Robert S. Neighbors," *West Texas Historical Association Year Book* 34 (Oct. 1958): 38–49.

75. Post Returns for November, 1859, Camp Cooper, Texas, M617, Roll #253, NA.

76. Ibid.

77. General Orders No. 11, New York, November 23, 1860, *Adjutant General's Office, General Orders, 1849–61*, USMAL.

78. George W. Cullum, *Biographical Register of the Officers and Graduates of the U.S. Military Academy at West Point, N.Y., from Its Establishment, in 1802 and 1890, with the Early History of the United States Military Academy*, 2 vols. (Boston: Houghton, Mifflin, 1891), 2:33; Richard W. Johnson, *Memoir of Maj.-Gen. Thomas*, 80–82; Utley, *Frontiersmen in Blue*, 140.

79. General Orders No. 11, New York, November 23, 1860, *Adjutant General's Office, General Orders, 1849–61*, USMAL.

80. Post Returns for September, October, and November, 1860, Camp Cooper, Texas, M617, Roll #523, NA.

81. Donn Piatt and Henry V. Boynton, *General George H. Thomas: A Critical Biography* (Cincinnati: Robert Clarke, 1893), 75–76.

82. Van Horne, *Life of General Thomas*, 16.

83. Piatt and Boynton, *General Thomas,* 75.

84. Contents of letter quoted in Henry Coppée, *General Thomas* (New York: D. Appleton, 1893), 35–36. Van Horne erroneously placed the accident "near Norfolk," *Life of General Thomas*, 19; which W. H. T. Squires used as his source, *The Days of Yester-Year in Colony and Commonwealth: A Sketch Book of Virginia* (Portsmouth, Va.: Printcraft Press, 1928), 189, as did Frank A. Palumbo, *George Henry Thomas: The Dependable General* (Dayton, Ohio: Morningside House, 1983), 56. McKinney correctly noted Lynchburg as the location of the mishap, *Education in Violence*, 85; as did recent biographers, Christopher J. Einholf, *George Thomas: Virginian for the Union* (Norman: University of Oklahoma Press, 2007), 80, and Benson Bobrick, *Master of War: The Life of General George H. Thomas* (New York: Simon & Schuster: 2009), 55. Bobrick offered the unusual suggestion that Thomas's distraction over the coming crisis and his place in it contributed to the accident, ibid.

85. McKinney, *Education in Violence*, 87.

86. Coppée, *General Thomas*, 28–29.

87. Van Horne, *Life of General Thomas*, 20.

88. Coppée, *General Thomas*, 29.

Chapter 6: Duty Calls (1860–1861)

1. Francis F. McKinney, *Education in Violence: The Life of George H. Thomas and the History of the Army of the Cumberland* (Detroit: Wayne State University Press, 1961), 90.

2. Erasmus D. Keyes, *Fifty Years' Observation of Men and Events Civil and Military* (New York: Charles Scribner's Sons, 1884), 166.

3. Daniel H. Hill, "Chickamauga—The Great Battle of the West" in *Battles and Leaders of the Civil War*, edited by Robert Underwood Johnson and Clarence Clough Buel (New York: Century, 1887), 3:639. Grady McWhiney noted Bragg's presence in the mess there, *Braxton Bragg and Confederate Defeat,* vol 1: *Field Command* (New York: Columbia University Press, 1969), 53.

4. Keyes, *Fifty Years' Observation*, 167–168.

5. Quoted in Thomas B. Van Horne, *The Life of Major-General George H. Thomas* (New York: Charles Scribner's Sons, 1882), 25–26.

6. See, for example, discussions in chapters 2 and 3 in Emory M. Thomas, *The Confederate Nation: 1861–1865* (New York: Harper and Row, 1979).

7. Quoted in Van Horne, *Life of General Thomas*, 26.

8. Henry Coppée, *General Thomas* (New York: D. Appleton, 1893), 36.

9. Quoted in Van Horne, *Life of General Thomas*, 26.

10. [Frances Thomas] to My dear Col., Troy, NY, January 21st, 1876, Hough Papers, UCBL.

11. Ibid.

12. Quoted in McKinney, *Education in Violence*, 86.

13. Francis H. Smith to My dear Madam, Virginian Military Institute, Feb. 8, 1876, VMI.

14. Quoted in McKinney, *Education in Violence*, 87.

15. Frank A. Palumbo, *George Henry Thomas: The Dependable General* (Dayton, Ohio: Morningside House, 1983), 58.

16. F. N. Boney, *John Letcher of Virginia: The Story of Virginia's Civil War Governor* (Tuscaloosa: University of Alabama Press, 1966), 106.

17. Palumbo, *The Dependable General*, 58.

18. GHT to My dear Friend, Nashville, Ten, March 22, 1865, Thomas Letters, USMA.

19. John Letcher to My Dear Sir, Richmond, Va., Feb: 12th: 1861, VMI.

20. [Frances Thomas] to My dear Col., Troy, NY, January 21st, 1876, Hough Papers, UCBL.

21. F. L. Thomas to My dear Col Hough, 3 Park Place, Troy NY, Jany 20th 1883, Hough Papers, UCBL.

22. Fannie C. Thomas [to John Allan Wyeth] Newsom P.O., Southampton, Va., November 2, 1900, in John Allan Wyeth, *With Sabre and Scalpel: The Autobiography of a Soldier and Surgeon* (New York: Harper & Brothers, 1914), 261–262.

23. Frances Thomas offered Benjamin Thomas's perspective in her letter to Alfred Hough. [Frances Thomas] to My dear Col., Troy, NY, January 21st, 1876, Hough Papers, UCBL.

24. F. L. Thomas to My dear Col Hough, 3 Park Place, Troy NY., Jany 20th 1883, Hough Papers, UCBL.

25. Francis Smith to Frances Thomas, February 8, 1876, VMI.

26. Francis MacDonnell, "The Confederate Spin on Winfield Scott and George Thomas," *Civil War History* 45, no. 4 (Dec. 1998): 255–266, 263.

27. John Russell Young, *Around the World with General Grant*, edited by Michael Fellman (Baltimore: Johns Hopkins University Press, 2002), 303. See also Gamaliel Bradford, *Union Portraits* (Boston: Houghton Mifflin, 1915), 107.

28. McKinney, *Education in Violence*, 91.

29. Bradford, *Union Portraits*, 106.

30. F. L. Thomas to My dear Col Hough, Washington DC, Nov 5th 1884, Hough Papers, UCBL.

31. [Frances Thomas] to My dear Col., Troy, NY, January 21st, 1876, Hough Papers, UCBL.

32. F. L. Thomas to My dear Col., Troy NY, Aug 29th 1881, Hough Papers, UCBL.

33. Bradford, *Union Portraits*, 107.

34. Wilbur Thomas, *General George H. Thomas: The Indomitable Warrior* (New York: Exposition Press, 1964), 118.

35. Emory M. Thomas, *Robert E. Lee: A Biography* (New York: W. W. Norton, 1995), 190.

36. James I. Robertson Jr., *Stonewall: The Man, the Soldier, the Legend* (New York: Macmillan, 1997), 213.

37. Quoted in Donn Piatt and Henry V. Boynton, *General George H. Thomas: A Critical Biography* (Cincinnati: Robert Clarke, 1893), 359–360.

38. James H. Wilson, *Under the Old Flag: Recollections of Military Operations in the War for the Union, the Spanish War, the Boxer Rebellion, etc.*, 2 vols. (New York: D. Appleton, 1912), 2:88.

39. Emory M. Thomas, *Bold Dragoon: The Life of J. E. B. Stuart* (New York: Harper and Row, 1986), 61–62.

40. Brian Steel Wills, *Gone with the Glory: The Civil War in Cinema* (Lanham, Md.: Rowman & Littlefield, 2007), 65. Hollywood has undertaken no treatment of Thomas comparable to other figures, North or South, from the Civil War.

41. Wilbur Thomas, *Indomitable Warrior*, 136–137.

42. Thomas to Wm. R. Plum, Louisville, Ky., August 11, 1868, Thomas Papers, HL.

43. Piatt and Boynton, *General Thomas*, 502.

44. Quoted in ibid.

45. Hough statement, "Genl Geo. H. Thomas & Fitzhugh Lee," Fort Mackinnac, Mich., Jan. 8, 1876, Hough Papers, UCBL.

46. F. L. Thomas to My dear Col. Hough, 3 Park Place, Troy N.Y., Jany. 20th, 1883, Hough Papers, UCBL.

47. McKinney, *Education in Violence*, 87.

48. [Frances Thomas] to My dear Col., Troy, NY, January 21st, 1876, Hough Papers, UCBL.

49. Post Returns for April 1861, Carlisle Barracks, Pa., M617, Roll #184, NA.

50. F. J. Porter to Major Thomas and Major Graham, April 20, 1861; GHT to Porter, York, April 24, 1861; GHT to Porter, York, April 24, 1861, Porter Papers, 3, LOC.

51. F. J. Porter to Colonel H. L. Scott, Harrisburg, April 20, Porter Papers, 2, LOC.

52. GHT to F. J. Porter, Carlisle Barracks, Pa., April 20 1861; GHT to Porter, Carlisle, April 21, 1861, Porter Papers, 2, LOC.

53. E. D. Townsend to GHT, Washington, April 22, 1861, *OR*, vol. 2, 587–588.

54. L. P. Graham to Major, Carlisle Barracks, April 22, 1861, Porter Papers, 2, LOC.

55. F. J. Porter to Colonel Charles Thomas, April 24, 1861; Porter to Commanding Officer, Pittsburg Arsenal, Harrisburg, Pa, April 24, 1861; and Porter to GHT, Harrisburg, April 24, Porter Papers, 3, LOC.

56. GHT to F. J. Porter, York, April 24, 1861, Porter Papers, 3, LOC.

57. GHT to F. J. Porter, York, April 24, 1861, Porter Papers, 3, LOC.

58. Richard W. Johnson, *A Soldier's Reminiscences in Peace and War* (Philadelphia: J. B. Lippincott, 1886),158.

59. Ibid., 159.

60. Porter Report, Philadelphia, May 1, 1861, Porter Papers, 3, LOC.

61. Richard W. Johnson, *A Soldier's Reminiscences*, 161; Richard W. Johnson, *Memoir of Maj.-Gen. George H. Thomas* (Philadelphia: J. B. Lippincott, 1881), offered a variation of the wording that nevertheless fit the spirit here, 38.

62. McKinney, *Education in Violence*, 101.

63. Ibid., 470.

64. George W. Cullum, *Biographical Register of the Officers and Graduates of the U.S. Military Academy at West Point, N.Y., from its Establishment, in 1802 and 1890, with the Early History of the United States Military Academy,* 2 vols. (Boston: Houghton, Mifflin, 1891), 2:33; GHT report to the Committee on the Conduct of the War, Nashville, Tennessee, March 9, 1866, 3.

65. Joseph H. Parks, *General Edmund Kirby Smith, C.S.A.* (Baton Rouge: Louisiana State University Press, 1954), 128.

66. The other was Joseph Abercrombie. Quoted in McKinney, *Education in Violence*, 98.

67. GHT report to the Committee on the Conduct of the War, Nashville, Tennessee, March 9, 1866, 3.

68. William T. Sherman, *Sherman's Civil War: Selected Correspondence of William T. Sherman, 1860–1865,* edited by Brooks D. Simpson and Jean V. Berlin (Chapel Hill: University of North Carolina Press, 1999), 100–101.

69. Alexander McClure, *Old Time Notes of Pennsylvania: A Connected and Chronological Record of the Commercial, Industrial and Educational Advancement of Pennsylvania, and the Inner History of All Political Movements Since the Adoption of the Constitution of 1836* (Philadelphia: John C. Winston, 1905), 1:492.

70. Alexander McClure, *Lincoln and Men of War-Times: Some Personal Recollections of War and Politics during the Lincoln Administration* (Philadelphia: Times Publishing, 1892), 369–370. Historian Edward L. Ayers used the incident as an illustration of attitudes being ex-

hibited on the eve of war in *In the Presence of Mine Enemies: War in the Heart of America 1859–1863*. (New York: W. W. Norton, 2003), 186–187.

71. Henry Stone, "Major-General George Henry Thomas," in *Critical Sketches of Some of the Federal and Confederate Commanders* (Boston: Houghton Mifflin 1895), 199.

72. Samuel H. Beckwith, "Samuel H. Beckwith 'Grant's Shadow,'" edited by John Y. Simon and David L. Wilson, in *Ulysses S. Grant: Essays and Documents,* edited by David L. Wilson and John Y. Simon (Carbondale: Southern Illinois University Press, 1981), 102.

73. McClure, *Lincoln and Men of War-Times*, 369–370.

74. Wilbur Thomas, *Indomitable Warrior*, 135.

75. [Frances Thomas] to My dear Col., Troy NY, January 21st 1876, Hough Papers, UCBL.

76. A. T. Caperton to GHT, Near Monroe Co. House Va May 10th/62, Caperton Papers, VHS.

77. A. T. Caperton to GHT, Near Monroe Co. House Va May 31st/62, Caperton Papers, VHS.

78. Circular, F. J. Porter, Chambersburg, Pa., June 12, 1861, *OR*, vol. 2, 679. [All are Series I, unless otherwise identified.]

79. Thomas B. Buell, *The Warrior Generals: Combat Leadership in the Civil War* (New York: Crown, 1997), 189.

80. William T. Sherman, *Memoirs of General William T. Sherman* (New York: Charles L. Webster, 1892), 1:205.

81. GHT report, July 3, 1861, *OR*, vol. 2, 180.

82. D. D. Perkins report, July 4, 1861, *OR*, vol. 1, 180–181.

83. GHT report, July 3, 1861, *OR*, vol. 2, 180.

84. T. J. Jackson report, Darkesville, July 3, 1861, *OR*, vol. 2, 186.

85. "Hoke's Run," in Frances H. Kennedy, ed., *The Civil War Battlefield Guide*, 2nd ed. (Boston: Houghton Mifflin, 1998), 11.

86. Jeb Stuart to My darling Wife, The Old Oak Tree, June 11th 1861, Stuart Papers, VHS.

87. Minutes Of Council of War, Martinsburg, Va., July 9, 1861, *OR*, vol. 2, 163.

88. GHT to Dear Colonel, Camp Near Hyattstown, Md., August 25, 1861. Quoted in Piatt and Boynton, *General Thomas*, 99.

89. GHT to Patterson, Before Atlanta, Ga., August 8, 1864, quoted in Piatt and Boynton, *General Thomas,* 101–102.

90. Ibid., 102.

Chapter 7: Keeping the Blue in the Bluegrass (August 1861–January 1862)

1. Francis F. McKinney, *Education in Violence: The Life of George H. Thomas and the History of the Army of the Cumberland* (Detroit: Wayne State University Press, 1961), 107.

2. Larry J. Daniel, *Days of Glory: The Army of the Cumberland, 1861–1865 (*Baton Rouge: Louisiana State University Press, 2004), 35.

3. R. S. [Anderson] to Dearest, Washington, DC Fri. Aug 6 1861, Anderson Papers, LOC.

4. William T. Sherman, *Memoirs of General William T. Sherman* (New York: Charles L. Webster, 1892), 1:221.

5. Special Orders No. 57, August 15, 1861, *OR*, vol. 4, 254. The announcement of Anderson's assumption of authority came in General Orders No. 1, Louisville, Ky., September 24, 1861, ibid., 273. A note indicated that Anderson had exercised his duties since September 4, ibid.

6. Special Orders No. 141, Washington, Aug. 24, 1861, in Anderson Papers, LOC.

7. GHT to Dear General, Camp near Hyattstown, Md August 26th 1861, Thomas Papers, USMAL.

8. [Frances Thomas] to My dear Col., Troy, NY, January 21st, 1876, Hough Papers, UCBL.

9. Special Orders No. 3, September 10, 1861, *OR*, vol. 4, 257.

10. John F. Fisk and Rich'd A. Buckner to GHT, September 14, 1861, ibid., 258.

11. G. W. Berry to GHT, September 14, 1861, ibid.

12. Garrett Davis to General GHT, September 16, 1861, ibid., 259–260.

13. R. M. Kelly, "Holding Kentucky for the Union," in *Battles and Leaders of the Civil War*, edited by Robert Underwood Johnson and Clarence Clough Buel (New York: Century, 1887), 1:382.

14. Gilbert C. Kniffin, "The Life and Services of Major General George H. Thomas," in *War Papers Being Papers Read before the Commandery of the District of Columbia Military Order of the Loyal Legion of the United States,* vol. 1, *Papers 1–26. March 1887–April 1897* (Wilmington, N.C.: Broadfoot Publishing, 1993), 23.

15. Donn Piatt and Henry V. Boynton, *General George H. Thomas: A Critical Biography* (Cincinnati: Robert Clarke, 1893), 61.

16. Ibid., 333.

17. Bruce Catton, *The Hallowed Ground: The Story of the Union Side of the Civil War* (Garden City, N.Y.: Doubleday, 1956), 75.

18. Robert Anderson to GHT, September 17, 1861, *OR*, vol. 4, 260.

19. Freeman Cleaves, *Rock of Chickamauga: The Life of George H. Thomas* (Norman: University of Oklahoma Press, 1948,) 69–70.

20. Scully to My Dear Wife, November 10, 1861, Scully Papers, DUL.

21. Daniel, *Days of Glory*, 111.

22. Ibid., 22; Cleaves, *Rock of Chickamauga*, 81–84.

23. Kniffin, "Life of Thomas," 24.

24. Gamaliel Bradford, *Union Portraits* (Boston: Houghton Mifflin, 1915), 118–119.

25. Cleaves, *Rock of Chickamauga*, 84.

26. Kniffin, "Life of Thomas," 14..

27. Alfred Lacey Hough, *Soldier in the West: The Civil War Letters of Alfred Lacey Hough*, edited by Robert G. Athearn (Philadelphia: University of Pennsylvania Press, 1957), 27.

28. Quoted in Thomas B. Van Horne, *The Life of Major-General George H. Thomas* (New York: Charles Scribner's Sons, 1882), 218.

29. Kniffin, "Life of Thomas," 25–26.

30. GHT to Col. Garrard, Sep 23d 1861, Thomas Papers, HL.

31. Cleaves, *Rock of Chickamauga*, 84.

32. GHT to Col. Garrard, Sep 23d 1861, Thomas Papers, HL.

33. Kelly, "Holding Kentucky for the Union," 382.

34. Daniel, *Days of Glory*, 18.

35. Abraham Lincoln to Orville H. Browning, Washington, Sept. 22d 1861, *Collected Works of Abraham Lincoln*, edited by Roy P. Basler (New Brunswick, N.J.: Rutgers University Press, 1953), 4:532.

36. Kniffin, "Life of Thomas," 26.

37. General Orders No. 7, Louisville, Ky., October 8, 1861, *OR*, vol. 4, 297.

38. Daniel, *Days of Glory*, 16.

39. GHT to O. M. Mitchel, October 11, 1861, *OR*, vol. 4, 303.

40. Daniel, *Days of Glory*, 17.

41. Wilbur Thomas, *General George H. Thomas: The Indomitable Warrior* (New York: Exposition Press, 1964), 163.

42. Quoted in Richard W. Johnson, *Memoir of Maj.-Gen. George H. Thomas* (Philadelphia: J. B. Lippincott, 1881), 39.

43. Friedrich Bertsch and Wilhelm Stangel, *A German Hurrah!: Civil War Letters of Frederich Bertsch and Wilhelm Stangel*, translated and edited by Joseph R. Reinhart (Kent, Ohio: Kent State University Press, 2010), 232.

44. Wilbur Thomas, *The Indomitable Warrior*, 164.

45. S. Cooper to F. K. Zollicoffer, July 26, 1861, *OR*, vol. 4, 374.

46. GHT to George B. McClellan, September 30, 1861, ibid., 284.

47. Kenneth Hafendorfer examined the campaign minutely in *The Battle of Wild Cat Mountain* (Louisville, Ky.: KH Press, 2003).

48. Zollicoffer reports, October 24 and October 26, 1861, *OR*, vol. 4, 206; GHT report, October 22, 1861—4 AM, ibid., 205 and Scheopf report, October 22, 1861, ibid., 210. Hafendorfer corrected the reported casualties to 12 and 45 C.S. and 5 and 20 U.S. in *Wild Cat Mountain*, 239 and 275–278.

49. T. T. Garrard to GHT, Camp Wildcat, October 25, 1861, *OR*, vol. 4, 319.

50. GHT report, October 23, 1861, ibid., 206.

51. T. T. Garrard to GHT, Camp Wildcat, October 25, 1861, ibid., 319.

52. GHT to A. Schoepf, October 29, 1861, ibid., 323.

53. GHT to Sherman, October 23, 1861, ibid., 206.

54. Wm. Blount Carter to GHT, October 27, 1861, ibid., 320.

55. W. T. Sherman to GHT, October 25, 1861, ibid., 318.

56. GHT to W. T. Sherman, November 3, 1861, ibid., 329.

57. W. T. Sherman to GHT, November 5, 1861, ibid., 335–336.

58. Noel C. Fisher, *War at Every Door: Partisan Politics and Guerrilla Violence in East Tennessee: 1860–1869.* (Chapel Hill: University of North Carolina Press, 2002), 54–56.

59. W. T. Sherman to GHT, November 11, 1861, *OR*, vol. 4, 350.

60. Fisher, *War at Every Door*, 56–57.

61. F. K. Zollicoffer to Mackall, November 20, 1861, *OR*, vol. 7, 687.

62. F. K. Zollicoffer to S. Cooper, November 22, 1861, ibid. 7, 690.

63. J. P. Benjamin to W. B. Wood, November 25, 1861, ibid., 701.

64. Henry Fry and Jacob M. Hinshaw died at Greeneville at the end of November, Jacob and Henry Harmon and Christopher Haun at Knoxville in mid-December.

65. GHT to Sherman, November 5, 1861, *OR*, vol. 4, 338.

66. GHT to Sherman, November 5, 1861, ibid., 338–339.

67. A. Schoepf to George E. Flynt, November 6, 1861, ibid., 341.

68. S. P. Carter to GHT, November 12, 1861, ibid., 356.

69. S. P. Carter to GHT, November 14, 1861, ibid., 359–360.

70. W. T. Sherman to GHT, November 16, 1861, ibid., 359.

71. GHT to S. P. Carter, November 17, 1861, ibid., 361.

72. Carter to GHT, Camp Calvert, November 22, 1861, *OR*, vol. 7, 445.

73. See S. P. Carter to Horace Maynard, Camp Calvert, near London, Ky., November 21, 1861, ibid., 468–469, and S. P. Carter to Horace Maynard, Camp Calvert, November 25, 1861, ibid., 469–470, as examples of the communications between the two.

74. GHT to Andrew Johnson, November 7, 1861, *OR*, vol. 4, 342–343.

75. Daniel, *Days of Glory*, 26.

76. Quoted in ibid.

77. D. C. Buell to Mr. Maynard and Governor Johnson, December 8, 1861, *OR*, vol. 7, 483.

78. GHT to General Schoepf, November 7, 1861, *OR*, vol. 4, 343.

79. A. Schoepf to GHT, November 8, 1861, ibid., 347.

80. W. T. Sherman to GHT, November 8, 1861, ibid., 347.

81. S. R. Mott to Dear Sir, Camp Near Somerset, Jan 5th 1862, *The Papers of Andrew Johnson*, edited by Leroy P. Graf and Ralph W. Haskins (Knoxville: University of Tennessee Press, 1979), 5:92.

82. Special Orders No. 39, December 6, 1861, *OR*, vol. 7, 479.

83. Daniel, *Days of Glory*, 50.

84. Buell to GHT, December 28, 1861, *OR*, vol. 7, 519.

85. Buell to GHT, December 29, 1861, ibid., 78. A similar communication occurred on the same date, ibid., 522.

86. Scully to My very Dear Wife, Camp near Campbellsville, Ky., January 5th 1862, Scully Papers, DUL.

87. GHT to Buell, January 13, 1862, *OR*, vol. 7, 550.

88. Scully to My Dear Wife, Camp on Somerset road, January 13 1862, Scully Papers, DUL.

89. Buell to GHT, January 17, 1862, *OR*, vol. 7, 558.

90. Thomas Speed, *The Union Cause in Kentucky, 1861–1865* (New York: G. P. Putnam's Sons, 1907), 196.

91. Scully to My Dear Wife, Camp 5 miles from the "Enemy" Jany 17th 1862, Scully Papers, DUL.

92. G. B. Crittenden to Assistant Adjutant-General, January 18, 1862, *OR*, vol. 7, 103.

93. Crittenden report, Camp Fogg, Tenn., February 13, 1862, ibid., 108.

94. The battle took additional names, including that of nearby Fishing Creek. Kenneth A. Hafendorfer, *Mill Springs: Campaign and Battle of Mill Springs, Kentucky* (Louisville, Ky.: KH Press, 2001), 17.

95. Scully to My Beloved Wife, Sunday night 11 oclock Jany 19th 1862, Scully Papers, DUL.

96. William F. G. Shanks, *Personal Recollections of Distinguished Generals* (New York: Harper & Brothers, 1866), 66.

97. Scully to My Beloved Wife, Sunday night 11 oclock Jany 19th 1862, Scully Papers, DUL.

98. John Watts De Peyster, *Sketch of George H. Thomas from Representative Men* (New York: Atlantic Publishing, 1875), 552.

99. Thomas B. Buell, *The Warrior Generals: Combat Leadership in the Civil War* (New York: Crown, 1997), 158.

100. Scully to My Beloved Wife, Sunday night 11 oclock Jany 19th 1862, Scully Papers, DUL.

101. Kelly, "Holding Kentucky for the Union," 391.

102. GHT report, Somerset, Ky., January 31, 1862, *OR*, vol. 7, 82.

103. Crittenden report, Camp Fogg, Tenn., February 13, 1862, ibid., 110. See also Hafendorfer, *Mill Springs*, 460–467 and 471; Raymond E. Myers, *The Zollie Tree: General Felix K. Zollicoffer and the Battle of Mill Springs* (Louisville, Ky.: Filson Club, 1964; reprint, 1998), 107.

104. Speed, *Union Cause in Kentucky*, 198.

105. Kelly, "Holding Kentucky for the Union," 390; Hafendorfer, *Mill Springs*, 468.

106. Kelly, "Holding Kentucky for the Union," 391.

107. Thomas's easiest arguments could have been those posited by P. G. T. Beauregard regarding Shiloh. Years after the war, when asked why he had not pressed his advantage at the end of the first day of the battle, Beauregard maintained that his men "were worn out" and disorganized, but also admitted, "I thought I had Grant just where I wanted him, and could finish him in the morning." Douglas Putnam Jr., "Reminiscences of the Battle of Shiloh," in *Sketches of War History 1861–1865, Papers Presented for the Ohio Commandery of the Military Order of the Loyal Legion of the United States, 1880–1890*, edited by Robert Hunter (Cincinnati: Robert Clarke & Co., 1890), 3:210–211.

108. GHT report, Somerset, Ky., January 31, 1862, *OR*, vol. 7, 81.

109. GHT to Buell, Somerset, Ky., February 3, 1862, ibid., 83.

110. GHT report, Somerset, Ky., January 31, 1862, ibid., 82; Wolford report, January 22, 1862, ibid., 100; Crittenden report, Camp Fogg, Tenn., February 13, 1862, ibid., 108.

111. GHT report, Somerset, Ky., January 31, 1862, *OR*, vol. 7, 81.

112. Steven E. Woodworth, *Jefferson Davis and His Generals: The Failure of Confederate Command in the West* (Lawrence: University Press of Kansas, 1990), 70.

113. Buell testimony, *OR*, vol. 16, pt. 1, 25.

114. Buell, *Warrior Generals*, 159.

115. Scully to Dearest, Monday morning Jany 20, 7 oclock, Scully Papers, DUL.

116. Frances Peter, *A Union Woman in Civil War Kentucky, The Diary of Frances Peter*, edited by John David Smith and William Cooper Jr. (Lexington: University Press of Kentucky, 2000), 5.

117. Ibid., 6.

118. Ibid., 6–7.

119. Buell to McClellan, January 20, 1862, *OR*, vol. 7, 76.

129. General Orders No. 4b, January 23, 1862, ibid., 78.

121. Congratulatory order from the President, January 22, 1862, ibid., 103.

122. Horace Maynard to GHT, February 4, 1862, ibid., 582.

123. Henry M. Cist, *The Army of the Cumberland* (New York: Charles Scribner's Sons, 1882), 19.

124 Gerald J. Prokopowicz, *All for the Regiment: The Army of the Ohio, 1861–1862* (Chapel Hill: University of North Carolina Press, 2001), 62.

125. GHT to David Tod, February 4, 1862, *OR*, vol. 7, 581–582.

126. James A. Ramage, *Rebel Raider: The Life of General John Hunt Morgan* (Lexington: University Press of Kentucky, 1986), 51–52.

127. Bell Irvin Wiley, *The Road to Appomattox* (Memphis, Tenn.: Memphis State College Press, 1956), 49–50.

Chapter 8: A Difficult Interlude (February 1862–January 1863)

1. Buell testimony, *OR*, vol. 16, pt. 1, 28.

2. See Richard W. Johnson, *Memoir of Maj.-Gen. George H. Thomas* (Philadelphia: J. B. Lippincott, 1881), 65.

3. See Wiley Sword, *Shiloh: Bloody April* (Dayton, Ohio: Press of Morningside Bookshop, 1988), for an outstanding treatment of Shiloh.

4. Chas. L. Fitzhugh to GHT, April 6, 1862, *OR*, vol. 10, pt. 2, 96.

5. Chas. L. Fitzhugh to GHT, Savannah, April 6, 1862, ibid., 96.

6. In addition to Sword, *Shiloh: Bloody April*, see James Lee McDonough, *Shiloh—in Hell before Night* (Knoxville: University of Tennessee Press, 1977), and Larry J. Daniel, *Shiloh: The Battle That Changed the Civil War* (New York: Simon & Schuster, 1997).

7. Albert D. Richardson, *A Personal History of Ulysses S. Grant, Illustrated by Twenty-six Engravings; Eight Fac-similies of Letters from Grant, Lincoln, Sheridan, Buckner, Lee, etc.; and Six Maps* (Hartford, Conn.: American Publishing, 1868), 254.

8. Wm. S. Hillyer to GHT, Pittsburg, April 7, 1862, *OR*, vol. 10, pt. 2, 96.

9. The earliest account has Thomas reaching the area on April 8, Frank A. Palumbo, *George Henry Thomas: The Dependable General* (Dayton, Ohio: Morningside House, 1983), 105. The consensus is April 9. See Freeman Cleaves, *Rock of Chickamauga: The Life of George H. Thomas* (Norman: University of Oklahoma Press, 1948), 104, and Francis F. McKinney, *Education in Violence: The Life of George H. Thomas and the History of the Army of the Cumberland* (Detroit: Wayne State University Press, 1961), 137.

10. Special Field Orders No. 35, Pittsburg Landing, Tenn., April 30, 1862, *OR*, vol. 10, pt. 2, 144 and 185. These orders indicated an arrangement of two wings and a reserve, dated on May 13, but the approach of the forces took place in three formations as delineated in Buell's report, August 1, 1862, *OR*, vol. 10, pt. 1, 672.

11. Buell report, August 1, 1862, *OR*, vol. 10, pt. 1, 672.

12. William T. Sherman, *Memoirs of General William T. Sherman* (New York: Charles L. Webster, 1892), 1:278.

13. Scully to My Dear Wife, Camp Shiloh, Tenn April 14th 1862, Scully Papers, DUL.

14. Stephen E. Ambrose, *Halleck: Lincoln's Chief of Staff* (Baton Rouge: Louisiana State University Press, 1962), 51.

15. John Pope, *The Military Memoirs of General John Pope,* edited by Peter Cozzens and Robert I. Girardi (Chapel Hill: University of North Carolina Press, 1998), 88.

16. GHT report, Camp, near Corinth, Miss., June 3, 1862, *OR*, vol. 10, pt. 1, 739.

17. GHT report, Camp, near Corinth, Miss., June 3, 1862, ibid., 740.

18. Sherman report, Camp near Corinth, Miss., May 30, 1862, ibid., 742.

19. GHT report, Camp, near Corinth, Miss., June 3, 1862, ibid., 740.

20. Halleck to Buell, Pope, and Thomas, Corinth, Miss., May 30, 1862, *OR*, vol. 10, pt. 2, 231. Subsequently, Halleck indicated in a communication with the secretary of war that John Pope was engaged in a vigorous pursuit. Halleck to Stanton, Halleck's Headquarters, June 4, *OR*, vol. 10, pt. 1, 669. In May 1865 Pope wrote Halleck denying that he had issued such a report and requesting a copy of it, which Halleck could not supply at the time. Pope to Halleck, Washington, D.C., July 3, 1865, *OR*, vol. 10, pt. 2, 635; Halleck to Pope, Washington, July 5, 1865, ibid., 635; and Pope to Halleck, Washington, D.C., July 5, 1865, ibid., 636–637.

21. GHT report, Camp, near Corinth, Miss., June 3, 1862, *OR*, vol. 10, pt. 1, 740.

22. Special Field Orders No. 89, Corinth, Miss., June 5, 1862, *OR*, vol. 10, pt. 2, 262.

23. Special Field Orders No. 90, Corinth, Miss., June 10, 1862, ibid., 288.

24. Richard W. Johnson, *Memoir of Maj.-Gen. Thomas*, 67.

25. GHT to Halleck, *OR*, vol. 16, pt. 2, 657.

26. F. L. Thomas to My dear Col., Troy NY, Aug 29th 1881, Hough Papers, UCBL.

27. Wilbur Thomas, *General George H. Thomas: The Indomitable Warrior* (New York: Exposition Press, 1964), 219–220 and 226.

28. Leonard Erwin report, July 3, 1862, *OR*, vol. 16, pt. 1, 729–730; Minor Milliken report, July 9, 1862, ibid., 729.

29. GHT report, July 3, 1862, ibid., 728.

30. Buell testimony, ibid., 31.

31. George C. Bradley and Richard L. Dahlen, *From Conciliation to Conquest: The Sack of Athens and the Court-Martial of Colonel John B. Turchin* (Tuscaloosa: University of Alabama Press, 2006), 144.

32. Salmon P. Chase, *The Salmon P. Chase Papers*, edited by John Niven (Kent, Ohio: Kent State University Press, 1993), 355.

33. GHT report, August 7, 1862, *OR*, vol. 16, pt. 1, 839.

34. Ibid.

35. Ferdinand Van Derveer Report, August 9, 1862, ibid., 840–841.

36. Michael Walzer, *Just and Unjust Wars: A Moral Argument with Historical Illustrations* (New York: Basic Books, 1977), 23–24.

37. For an assessment of the evolution of the response to this incident, see Clay Mountcastle, *Punitive War: Confederate Guerrillas and Union Reprisals* (Lawrence: University Press of Kansas, 2009), 64–67.

38. GHT to Johnson, August 16, 1862, HL.

39. Ibid.

40. GHT to Buell, Altamont, August 25, 1862—5 PM, *OR*, vol. 16, pt. 2, 421.

41. GHT to Colonel Fry, McMinnville, August 29, 1862, ibid., 445–446.

42. GHT to Buell, McMinnville, September 2, 1862, ibid., 471.

43. GHT testimony, *OR*, vol. 16, pt. 1, 182, 185, 188, 189, 202–203. Buell disputed Thomas's recollections, suggesting that the Virginian might not have remembered correctly what he had advocated at the time, given the events that transpired subsequently. Buell was careful not to suggest malice on his colleague's part, believing Thomas to be genuinely misguided by a poor memory. See Buell testimony, ibid., 41–43.

44. "Honor to Gen. Thomas," Louisville *Courier-Journal*, March 20, 1870, Thomas Papers, Filson.

45. Buell, "East Tennessee and the Campaign of Perryville," in *Battles and Leaders of the Civil War,* edited by Robert Underwood Johnson and Clarence Clough Buel (New York: Century, 1887), 3:44.

46. GHT to Halleck, Louisville, Ky., September 29, 1862—11:45 AM, *OR*, vol. 16, pt. 2, 555.

47. Stephen D. Engle, *Don Carlos Buell: Most Promising of All* (Chapel Hill: University of North Carolina Press, 1999), 300–302.

48. Christopher J. Einholf, *George Thomas: Virginian for the Union* (Norman: University of Oklahoma Press, 2007), 132–133.

49. Quoted in Larry J. Daniel, *Days of Glory: The Army of the Cumberland, 1861–1865* (Baton Rouge: Louisiana State University Press, 2004), 136.

50. GHT to Halleck, Louisville, Ky., September 29, 1862—11:45 AM, *OR*, vol. 16, pt. 2, 555. Buell's dispatch went to Halleck at 2:30 PM, D. C. Buell to H. W. Halleck, Louisville, Ky., September 29, 1862—2:30 PM, ibid., 554.

51. Quoted in Thomas B. Van Horne, *The Life of Major-General George H. Thomas* (New York: Charles Scribner's Sons, 1882), 76.

52. Halleck to GHT, Washington, September 29, 1862, *OR*, vol. 16, pt. 2, 555.

53. Halleck to D. C. Buell and GHT, Washington, September 29, 1862, ibid., 555.

54. Special Orders No. 158, Louisville, September 29, 1862, ibid., 558–559.

55. Daniel, *Days of Glory*, 132–133 and 137.

56. Ibid., 138. The order assigning Thomas to second in command came the next day, Special Orders No. 159, Louisville, September 30, 1862, *OR*, vol. 16, pt. 2, 560.

57. Donn Piatt and Henry V. Boynton, *General George H. Thomas: A Critical Biography* (Cincinnati: Robert Clarke, 1893), 172.

58. Quoted in ibid., 175.

59. Daniel, *Days of Glory*, 148.

60. GHT testimony, *OR*, vol. 16, pt. 1, 187.

61. Lieut. C. L. Fitzhugh testimony, ibid., 667.

62. Ibid., 669.

63. GHT testimony, ibid., 193. Thomas insisted under questioning that he had felt he was sufficiently connected to his superior. "Whenever we met General Buell was always communicative," ibid., 189.

64. Buell testimony, ibid., 670 and 676.

65. GHT testimony, ibid., 188.

66. See Kenneth W. Noe, *Perryville: This Grand Havoc of Battle* (Lexington: University Press of Kentucky, 2001), xiii and 215. Noe referred to the atmospheric condition "more properly" as "sound refraction," ibid., 215.

67. Thomas biographers were uniformly at a loss to explain the Virginian's lethargic response to the developing conditions at Perryville. See, for example, Piatt and Boynton, *General Thomas*, 175–176, and McKinney, *Education in Violence*, 163–164.

68. GHT to Buell, October 12, 1862—10 AM, *OR*, vol. 16, pt. 2, 608.

69. William F. G. Shanks, *Personal Recollections of Distinguished Generals* (New York: Harper & Brothers, 1866), 65–66.

70. "The Late Gen. Thomas," *New York Times*, April 9, 1870.

71. Michael H. Fitch, *Echoes of the Civil War as I Hear Them* (New York: R. F. Fenno, 1905), 326.

72. H. W. Halleck to D. C. Buell, Washington, October 24, 1862, *OR*, vol. 16, pt. 2, 642.

73. Edwin M. Stanton to Governor Tod, October 30, 1862—3:40 PM, ibid., 652.

74. Buell to GHT, October 30 [1862], ibid., 654.

75. Quoted in Piatt and Boynton, *General Thomas*, 198. Piatt was present when Stanton returned from the heated session. "Well, you have your choice of idiots; now look out for frightful disaster," ibid.

76. Thomas B. Buell, *The Warrior Generals: Combat Leadership in the Civil War* (New York: Crown, 1997), 186–187.

77. GHT to Halleck, Camp near Campbellsville, Ky., October 30, 1862, *OR*, vol. 16, pt. 2, 657.

78. Halleck to GHT, Washington, November 15, 1862, ibid., 663.

79. GHT to Halleck, Gallatin, Tenn., November 21, 1862, ibid., 663.

80. Peter Cozzens, *No Better Place to Die: The Battle of Stones River*. Urbana: University of Illinois Press, 1990), 23; Wilbur Thomas, *The Indomitable Warrior*, 275.

81. Van Horne, *Life of General Thomas*, 76.

82. GHT to Rosecrans, Gallatin, December 7, 1862, *OR*, vol. 20, pt. 1, 41.

83. Rosecrans to GHT, Nashville, December 7, 1862, ibid., 41.

84. GHT to Rosecrans, Gallatin, December 7, 1862, ibid., 41.

85. Rosecrans to Halleck, Nashville, Tenn., December 7, 1862—11 PM, ibid., 41.

86. Buell, *Warrior Generals*, 187. Sherman was particularly complimentary of this aspect of Thomas's capabilities in his discussions of the Atlanta Campaign. See Sherman, *Memoirs*, 2:9.

87. J. R. D. to Dear Sister, Near Gallatin Tennessee December 8th/62, Dow Family Papers, Filson.

88. GHT testimony, December 18, 1862, *OR*, vol. 16, pt. 1, 182–204.

89. See, for example, ibid., 197.

90. Engle, *Don Carlos Buell*, 336.

91. Cozzens, *No Better Place to Die*, 21.

92. GHT to Rosecrans, Murfreesborough, Tenn., March 12, 1863, *OR*, vol. 20, pt. 2, 383.

93. General Orders No. —, *OR*, vol. 20, pt. 1, 183.

94. Alfred Pirtle, "Stone[s] River Sketches," in *War Papers Being Papers Read before the Commandery of the State of Ohio, Military Order of the Loyal Legion of the United States* (Wilmington, N.C.: Broadfoot Publishing, 1992), 6:96–98.

95. GHT report, Murfreesboro, Tenn., January 15, 1863, *OR*, vol. 20, pt. 1, 373.

96. Ibid.

97. Cozzens, *No Better Place to Die*, 155.

98. Quoted in Daniel, *Days of Glory*, 217.

99. William Henry Bisbee, *Through Four American Wars: The Impressions and Experiences of Brigadier General William Henry Bisbee as Told to His Grandson William Haymond Brisbee* (Boston: Meador Publishing, 1931), 127.

100. Vance, *Stone's River*, quoted in Wilbur Thomas, *The Indomitable Warrior*, 306.

101. GHT report, Murfreesborough, Tenn., January 15, 1863, *OR*, vol. 20, pt. 1, 373.

102. GHT report, Murfreesborough, Tenn., May 16, 1863, ibid., 376.

103. Quoted in Piatt and Boynton, *General Thomas*, 334.

104. Oliver Otis Howard, "Sketch of the Life of George H. Thomas," in *Personal Recollections of the War of the Rebellion: Addresses Delivered before the New York Commandery of the Loyal Legion of the United States, 1883–1891*, edited by James Grant Wilson and Titus Munson Coan (New York: Published by the Commandery, 1891), 341.

105. John Lee Yaryan, "Stone River," *War Papers Being Papers Read before the Commandery of the State of Indiana, Military Order of the Loyal Legion of the United State* (Wilmington, N.C.: Broadfoot Publishing, 1992), 174. For their assessment of this critical moment, see Cozzens, *No Better Place to Die*, 173; James Lee McDonough, *Stones River: Bloody Winter in Tennessee* (Knoxville: University of Tennessee Press, 1980), 160; Van Horne, *Life of General Thomas*, 97; McKinney, *Education in Violence*, 195; Wilbur Thomas, *The Indomitable Warrior*, 299; Cleaves, *Rock of Chickamauga*, 131–132. Thomas's most recent biographers split on the efficacy of including both of the quotations. Christopher Einholf chose to focus on the one that advocated not retreating, *George Thomas*, 150, while Benson Bobrick offered both accounts as plausible for the occasion, *Master of War: The Life of General George H. Thomas* (New York: Simon & Schuster: 2009), 154–155.

106. John Beatty, *Memoirs of a Volunteer, 1861–1863*, edited by Harvey S. Ford (New York: W. W. Norton, 1946), 155.

107. Steven E. Woodworth, *Six Armies in Tennessee: The Chickamauga and Chattanooga Campaigns* (Lincoln: University of Nebraska Press, 1998), 3.

108. Cozzens, *No Better Place to Die*, 176–198; McDonough, *Stones River*, 182–201, and 202.

109. Report of Casualties of the Center, *OR*, vol. 20, pt. 1, 375.

110. GHT report, Murfreesborough, Tenn., January 15, 1863, ibid., 375.

Chapter 9: "The Rock of Chickamauga" (February–October 1863)

1. General Orders No. 9, Murfreesborough, Tenn., February 2, 1863, *OR*, vol. 23, pt. 2, 36.

2. GHT endorsement, Murfreesborough, Tenn., February 11, 1863, ibid., 57.

3. Halleck to Rosecrans, Washington, D.C., March 5, 1863, ibid., 107.

4. Circular, Camp Winford, July 6, 1863, ibid., 517.

5. GHT to Rosecrans, Murfreesborough, Tenn., March 12, 1863, *OR*, vol. 20, pt. 2, 383.

6. J. J. Reynolds report, Murfreesborough, Tenn., April 30, 1863, *OR*, vol. 23, pt. 1, 269–270.

7. GHT endorsement, Murfreesborough, Tenn., May 4, 1863, ibid., 271.

8. Quoted in Donn Piatt and Henry V. Boynton, *General George H. Thomas: A Critical Biography* (Cincinnati: Robert Clarke, 1893), 333–334.

9. William Bluffton Miller, *Fighting for Liberty and Right: The Civil War Diary of William Bluffton Miller, First Sergeant, Company K, Seventy-fifth Indiana Volunteer Infantry* (Knoxville: University of Tennessee Press, 2005), 97. Miller also placed Thomas at a brigade drill on June 17, ibid., 98.

10. Quoted in Piatt and Boynton, *General Thomas*, 342–343.

11. J.R.D. to Dear Father, Murfreesboro Tenn. Feb. 20th [1863], Dow Family Papers, Filson.

12. John Beatty, *Memoirs of a Volunteer, 1861–1863*, edited by Harvey S. Ford (New York: W. W. Norton, 1946), 225.

13. Alfred to My Dearest Mary, Dechard Tenn. Aug. 10th 1863, in Alfred Lacey Hough, *Soldier in the West: The Civil War Letters of Alfred Lacey Hough*, edited by Robert G. Athearn (Philadelphia: University of Pennsylvania Press, 1957), 123.

14. William F. G. Shanks, *Personal Recollections of Distinguished Generals* (New York: Harper & Brothers, 1866), 72–73.

15. B. H. Bristow to Donn Piatt, 20 Nassaw St., New York, n.d., Bristow Papers, Filson. Bristow insisted that Piatt's rendition of the popular tale was less than true to the spirit of the incident as he recalled it. Piatt and Boynton, *General George H. Thomas*, 334. See also Robert L. Kimberly and Ephraim S. Holloway, *The Forty-first Ohio Veteran Volunteer Infantry in the War of the Rebellion, 1861–1865* (Cleveland: R. H. Smellie, 1897), which recorded the soldier's response as, "Well, General, me and my wife ain't that kind of folks," 58.

16. Freeman Cleaves, *Rock of Chickamauga: The Life of George H. Thomas* (Norman: University of Oklahoma Press, 1948), 140. See also Francis F. McKinney, *Education in Violence: The Life of George H. Thomas and the History of the Army of the Cumberland* (Detroit: Wayne State University Press, 1961), 205–206, and Frank A. Palumbo, *George Henry Thomas: The Dependable General* (Dayton, Ohio: Morningside House, 1983), 127.

17. [Frances Thomas] to My dear Col., Troy NY, January 21st 1876, Hough Papers, UCBL.

18. Beatty, *Memoirs of a Volunteer*, 172.

19. Bearss noted, "On April 30, General Grant had transported 22,000 men across the Mississippi—the greatest amphibious operation in American history up to that time," Edwin C. Bearss, *The Campaign for Vicksburg* (Dayton, Ohio: Morningside Press, 1985–1986), 2:346. Ed Bearss's three-volume work has remained the definitive study of the campaign. See also Michael B. Ballard, *Vicksburg: The Campaign That Opened the Mississippi* (Chapel Hill: University of North Carolina Press, 2004).

20. Halleck to Rosecrans, June 2, 1863, *OR*, vol. 24, pt. 3, 376. Herman Hattaway and Archer Jones, *How the North Won* (Urbana: University of Illinois Press, 1983), 387.

21. GHT to Rosecrans, June 9, 1863, *OR*, vol. 23, pt. 2, 413–415.

22. Sheridan to Goddard, June 9, 1863, ibid., 411.

23. "To Correspondents," *Southern Illustrated News*, June 13, 1863.

24. Cozzens, *This Terrible Sound*, 14.

25. Ibid., 2.

26. James A. Connolly, *Three Years in the Army of the Cumberland: The Letters and Diary of Major James A. Connolly*, edited by Paul Angle (Bloomington: Indiana University Press, 1959), 94.

27. Lewis [to Miss Nettie Cooper], June 25th 1863, 4½ o'clock PM, Hanback Letters, Filson.

28. Quoted in Piatt and Boynton, *General Thomas*, 347–348.

29. Ibid., 358.

30. Ibid., 359.

31. Hough, *Soldier in the West*, 102.

32. Thomas Report, *OR*, vol. 23, pt. 1, 433.

33. Halleck to Grant, Washington, D.C., July 11, 1863, *OR*, vol. 24, pt. 3, 498.

34. Grant to Lincoln, Vicksburg, July 22, 1863, ibid., 540–542.

35. George W. Cullum, *Biographical Register of the Officers and Graduates of the U.S. Military Academy at West Point, N.Y., from its Establishment, in 1802 and 1890, with the Early History of the United States Military Academy*, 2 vols. (Boston: Houghton, Mifflin, 1891), 1:491.

36. W. J. Wood, *Civil War Generalship: The Art of Command* (Westport, Conn.: Praeger, 1997), 103–104.

37. Steven E. Woodworth, *Six Armies in Tennessee: The Chickamauga and Chattanooga Campaigns* (Lincoln: University of Nebraska Press, 1998), 48.

38. Thomas Lawrence Connelly, *Autumn of Glory: The Army of Tennessee, 1862–1865* (Baton Rouge: Louisiana State University Press, 1971), 166–175.

39. Cleaves, *Rock of Chickamauga*, 155.

40. Shanks, *Personal Recollections*, 76.

41. Ibid.

42. Ibid. Shanks notes that two unnamed "aids" usually ate with the general, ibid.

43. Glenn Tucker, *Chickamauga: Bloody Battle in the West* (Indianapolis: Bobbs-Merrill, 1961), 118.

44. Woodworth, *Six Armies in Tennessee*, 85.

45. Michael H. Fitch, *Echoes of the Civil War as I Hear Them* (New York: R. F. Fenno, 1905), 134.

46. Gilbert C. Kniffin, "The Life and Services of Major General George H. Thomas," in *War Papers Being Papers Read before the Commandery of the District of Columbia Military Order of the Loyal Legion of the United States*, vol. 1, *Papers 1–26. March 1887–April 1897* (Wilmington, N.C.: Broadfoot Publishing, 1993), 28–29.

47. John M. King, *Three Years with the 92d Illinois: The Civil War Diary of John M. King*, edited by Claire E. Swedberg (Mechanicsburg, Pa.: Stackpole Books, 1999), 129–130.

48. Fitch, *Echoes of the Civil War*, 135–136.

49. Tucker, *Chickamauga*, 340–341.

50. McKinney, *Education in Violence*, 388.

51. Quoted in Piatt and Boynton, *General Thomas*, 334–335.

52. William M. Lamers, *The Edge of Glory: A Biography of General William S. Rosecrans, U.S.A.* (New York: Harcourt, Brace & World, 1961), 334; Allan Peskin, *Garfield: A Biography* (Kent, Ohio: Kent State University Press, 1978), 204.

53. Steven E. Woodworth, *A Deep Steady Thunder: The Battle of Chickamauga* (Fort Worth, Tex.: Ryan Place Publishers, 1996), 41.

54. The descriptions of the fighting are composites drawn from Tucker, *Chickamauga*, and Cozzens, *This Terrible Sound*.

55. Shanks, *Personal Recollections*, 67.

56. Ibid., 70.

57. Larry J. Daniel, *Days of Glory: The Army of the Cumberland, 1861–1865* (Baton Rouge: Louisiana State University Press, 2004), 332. See also ibid., 323.

58. Cozzens, *This Terrible Sound*, 422.

59. William Glenn Robertson, Edward P. Shanahan, John I. Boxberger, and George E.

Knapp, *Staff Ride Handbook for the Battle of Chickamauga, 18–20 September 1863* (Fort Leavenworth, Kans.: Combat Studies Institute, U.S. Army Command and General Staff College, 1992), 134.

60. Unidentified newspaper clipping, Thomas Papers, Filson.

61. William Wirt Calkins, *The History of the One Hundred and Fourth Regiment of Illinois Volunteer Infantry: War of the Great Rebellion, 1862–1865* (Chicago: Donohue & Henneberry, 1895), 143 and 520.

62. Ibid., 422. Similarly, Emerson Opdycke was supposed to have responded to Thomas's "You must hold this position at all hazards," with "We will hold this ground or go to Heaven from it," ibid.

63. Cozzens noted plainly that Negley "lost his will to fight," Cozzens, *This Terrible Sound*, 423; Robertson et al., *Staff Ride Handbook, Chickamauga*, 134.

64. Quoted in Terry L. Jones, *The American Civil War* (New York: McGraw-Hill, 2010), 397.

65. Quoted in "General George H. Thomas," *Knoxville Whig and Rebel Ventilator*, June 11, 1864.

66. Shanks, *Personal Recollections*, 273.

67. Ibid., 69.

68. J. T. Woods, *Steedman and His Men at Chickamauga* (Toledo: Blade Printing & Paper, 1876), 49.

69. Shanks, *Personal Recollections*, 64.

70. Woods, *Steedman and His Men*, 119.

71. Quoted in Daniel, *Days of Glory*, 332.

72. Woods, *Steedman and His Men*, 117.

73. Benjamin F. Taylor, *Pictures of Life in Camp and Field* (Chicago: S. C. Griggs, 1875, 1888), 201.

74. Robertson et al., *Staff Ride Handbook, Chickamauga*, 140.

75. Quoted in Daniel, *Days of Glory*, 236.

76. Tucker, *Chickamauga*, 359.

77. "Talk with Gen. Steedman," *New York Times*, November 4, 1879.

78. Shanks, *Personal Recollections*, 70.

79. Piatt and Boynton, *General Thomas*, 61.

80. September 26, Saturday [1863], Gideon Welles, *Diary of Gideon Welles, Secretary of the Navy under Lincoln and Johnson,* 3 vols. (Boston: Houghton Mifflin, 1911), 1:444.

81. Ibid., 1:447.

82. G.E.F. to Dear Mack, Cincinnati Oct 18/63, MacKay Papers, Filson.

83. G. Moxley Sorrel, *Recollections of a Confederate Staff Officer*, edited by Bell Irvin Wiley (Jackson, Tenn.: McCowat-Mercer Press, 1958), 186.

84. William Henry King, *No Pardons to Ask, nor Apologies to Make: The Journal of William Henry King, Gray's 28th Louisiana Infantry Regiment*, edited by Gary D. Joiner, Marilyn S. Joiner, and Clifton D. Cardin (Knoxville: University of Tennessee Press, 2006), 128.

85. Ibid.

Chapter 10: Redemption at Missionary Ridge (October 1863–January 1864)

1. Henry Cist, "Comments on General Grant's 'Chattanooga,'" in *Battles and Leaders of the Civil War*, edited by Robert Underwood Johnson and Clarence Clough Buel (New York: Century, 1887), 3:717.

2. William F. G. Shanks, *Personal Recollections of Distinguished Generals* (New York: Harper & Brothers, 1866), 262.

3. Quoted in Mark W. Johnson, *That Body of Brave Men: The U.S. Regular Infantry and the Civil War in the West* (Cambridge, Mass.: Da Capo Press, 2003), 435.

4. Charles A. Dana, *Recollections of the Civil War: With the Leaders at Washington and in the Field in the Sixties* (New York: D. Appleton, 1902), 125.

5. Ibid., 124–125.

6. Ibid., 125–126.

7. John Hay, *Inside Lincoln's White House: The Complete Civil War Diary of John Hay,* edited by Michael Burlingame and John R. Turner Ettlinger (Carbondale: Southern Illinois University Press, 1997), 94.

8. Ibid., 99.

9. Ibid., 94.

10. Material included quotations credited to Rosecrans in William M. Lamers, *The Edge of Glory: A Biography of General William S. Rosecrans, U.S.A.* (New York: Harcourt, Brace & World, 1961), 392.

11. "Talk with Gen. Steedman," *New York Times*, November 24, 1879.

12. J. E. B. Stuart to My Darling Wife, Hd Qrs Cav Corps, Oct. 25, 1863, Stuart Papers, VHS.

13. "Thursday 29h. Oct. 1863," in Edward O. Guerrant, *Bluegrass Confederate: The Headquarters Diary of Edward O. Guerrant,* edited by William C. Davis and Meredith L. Swentor (Baton Rouge: Louisiana State University Press, 1999), 359.

14. Cist, "Comments on General Grant's 'Chattanooga,'" 717.

15. William Farrar Smith, "Comments on General Grant's 'Chattanooga,'" in *Battles and Leaders of the Civil War*, edited by Robert Underwood Johnson and Clarence Clough Buel (New York: Century, 1887), 3:714.

16. GHT to Bvt. Major-General J. L. Donaldson, Nashville, Tenn., October 28th 1866, in George W. Cullum, *Biographical Register of the Officers and Graduates of the U.S. Military Academy at West Point, N.Y., from its Establishment, in 1802 and 1890, with the Early History of the United States Military Academy,* 2 vols. (Boston: Houghton, Mifflin, 1891), 1:640.

17. Francis T. Sherman, *Quest for a Star: The Civil War Letters and Diaries of Colonel Francis T. Sherman of the 88th Illinois,* edited by C. Knight Aldrich (Knoxville: University of Tennessee Press, 1999), 75–76.

18. George F. Cram, *Soldiering with Sherman: Civil War Letters of George F. Cram,* edited by Jennifer Cain Bohrnstedt (DeKalb: Northern Illinois University Press, 2000), 58.

19. Williams to My Dear Daughter, Tullahoma, Nov. 11, 1863, in Alpheus S. Williams, *From the Cannon's Mouth: The Civil War Letters of General Alpheus S. Williams,* edited by Milo M. Quaife (Detroit: Wayne State University Press, 1959), 270.

20. Henry Villard, *Memoirs of Henry Villard Journalist and Financier 1835–1900* (Westminster, UK: Archibald Constable, 1904), 2:212.

21. Ibid., 214.

22. Grant to GHT, Louisville, October 19, 1863—11:30 PM, *OR*, vol. 30, pt. 4, 479.

23. Larry J. Daniel, *Days of Glory: The Army of the Cumberland, 1861–1865* (Baton Rouge: Louisiana State University Press, 2004), 361.

24. GHT to Grant, October 19, 1863, *OR*, vol. 30, pt. 4, 479.

25. Edward G. Longacre, *From Union Stars to Top Hat: A Biography of the Extraordinary General James Harrison Wilson* (Harrisburg, Pa.: Stackpole, 1972), 90.

26. Albert D. Richardson, *A Personal History of Ulysses S. Grant, Illustrated by Twenty-six Engravings; Eight Fac-similies of Letters from Grant, Lincoln, Sheridan, Buckner, Lee, etc.; and Six Maps* (Hartford, Conn.: American Publishing, 1868), 354–355.

27. James H. Wilson, *Under the Old Flag: Recollections of Military Operations in the War*

for the Union, the Spanish War, the Boxer Rebellion, etc., 2 vols. (New York: D. Appleton, 1912), 1:276.

28. Gilbert C. Kniffin, "The Life and Services of Major General George H. Thomas," in *War Papers Being Papers Read before the Commandery of the District of Columbia Military Order of the Loyal Legion of the United States,* vol. 1, *Papers 1–26. March 1887–April 1897* (Wilmington, N.C.: Broadfoot Publishing, 1993), 26.

29. Wilson, *Under the Old Flag*, 2:93. Wilson quoted Grant's wife as describing her husband as "a very obstinate man," ibid.

30. Samuel H. Beckwith, "Samuel H. Beckwith 'Grant's Shadow,'" edited by John Y. Simon and David L. Wilson, in *Ulysses S. Grant: Essays and Documents,* edited by David L. Wilson and John Y. Simon (Carbondale: Southern Illinois University Press, 1981), 117.

31. Ibid., 102.

32. Wilson, *Under the Old Flag*, 1:276.

33. Smith, "Comments on General Grant's 'Chattanooga,'" 714.

34. Grant to GHT, Chattanooga, Tenn., November 7, 1863, *OR*, vol. 31, pt. 3, 73.

35. Smith, "Comments on General Grant's 'Chattanooga,'" 715–716.

36. Grant to Halleck, Chattanooga, Tenn., November 7, 1863—1:30 PM, *OR*, vol. 31, pt. 3, 74.

37. Grant to Halleck, Chattanooga, Tenn., November 8, 1863—9:30 AM, ibid., 84.

38. Grant to Halleck, Chattanooga, Tenn., November 9, 1863—2:30 PM, ibid., 92.

39. John Watts De Peyster, *Sketch of George H. Thomas from Representative Men* (New York: Atlantic Publishing, 1875), 572.

40. Lloyd Lewis, *Sherman: Fighting Prophet* (New York: Harcourt, Brace, 1958), 316.

41. Quoted in Frank A. Palumbo, *George Henry Thomas: The Dependable General* (Dayton, Ohio: Morningside House, 1983), 201.

42. Orders of November 23, 1863, included in Granger report, February 11, 1864, *OR*, vol. 31, pt. 2, 128.

43. Wiley Sword, *Embrace an Angry Wind: The Confederacy's Last Hurrah: Spring Hill, Franklin, and Nashville* (New York: HarperCollins, 1992), 178.

44. Oliver Otis Howard, "Grant at Chattanooga," in *Personal Recollections of the War of the Rebellion: Addresses Delivered before the New York Commandery of the Loyal Legion of the United States, 1883–1891,* edited by James Grant Wilson and Titus Munson Coan (New York: Published by the Commandery, 1891), 250.

45. Thomas J. Wood, "The Battle of Missionary Ridge," in *War Papers Being Papers Read before the Commandery of the Ohio Military Order of the Loyal Legion of the United States* (Wilmington, N.C.: Broadfoot Publishing, 1991), 4:29. The exact circumstances in this instance are not clear. According to General Howard, orders for holding the ground came only after John Rawlins approached Grant to insist that having the men go over the same ground a second time at some undetermined future date would have "a bad effect" on them. Accordingly, Grant directed, "Intrench them and send support," and the appropriate orders went out. Howard, "Grant at Chattanooga," 250.

46. Granger report, February 11, 1864, *OR*, vol. 31, pt. 2, 129.

47. Benjamin F. Taylor, *Pictures of Life in Camp and Field* (Chicago: S. C. Griggs, 1875, 1888), 36.

48. Michael V. Sheridan, "Charging with Sheridan up Missionary Ridge," in *Battles and Leaders of the Civil War,* edited by Peter Cozzens (Urbana: University of Illinois Press, 2002), 5:455.

49. Granger report, February 11, 1864, *OR*, vol. 31, pt. 2, 130.

50. Robert L. Kimberly and Ephraim S. Holloway, *The Forty-first Ohio Veteran Volunteer Infantry in the War of the Rebellion, 1861–1865* (Cleveland: R. H. Smellie, 1897), 65–67.

51. Howard, "Grant at Chattanooga," 250.

52. Sheridan, "Charging with Sheridan," 458–459.

53. Shanks, *Personal Recollections*, 268–271.

54. Taylor, *Pictures of Life in Camp and Field*, 36.

55. Grant to Halleck, *OR*, vol. 31, pt. 2, 24.

56. Beckwith, "Grant's Shadow," 102.

57. Peter Cozzens noted the rumor that Thomas "tossed his hat in the air," although the gesture would appear to be greater than the Virginian usually made, even under exceptional circumstances. *The Shipwreck of Their Hopes: The Battles for Chattanooga* (Urbana: University of Illinois Press, 1994), 200.

58. Ibid., 146–149. Cozzens argued that a disgruntled Thomas "chose to flout Grant's directive" for Hooker to carry the summit of Lookout Mountain on November 25 and that the Virginian modified the order to suit his own purposes, largely of protecting his right flank. Once the day's action began, a "sullen" Thomas remained focused on Hooker's progress, while nursing a silent grudge against Grant for the lack of respect shown the Army of the Cumberland and convinced that Sherman's efforts would be thwarted, ibid., 200–201 and 203. Craig L. Symonds has provided an outstanding picture of the confusion over terrain that left Sherman in a less than advantageous position for the November 25 assault, in *Stonewall of the West: Patrick Cleburne and the Civil War* (Lawrence: University Press of Kansas, 1997), 163–164.

59. Meigs report, *OR*, vol. 31, pt. 2, 78.

60. Montgomery C. Meigs, "First Impressions of Three Days' Fighting: Quartermaster General Meigs's 'Journal of the Battle of Chattanooga,'" edited by John M. Hoffmann, in *Ulysses S. Grant: Essays and Documents,* edited by David L. Wilson and John Y. Simon (Carbondale: Southern Illinois University Press, 1981), 72–73.

61. GHT to Commanding Officer, Fort Wood, Orchard Knob, November 25, 1863—9 AM, *OR*, vol. 31, pt. 2, 114.

62. GHT to Commanding Officer, Fort Wood, Orchard Knob, November 25, 1863—10:30 AM, ibid., 114.

63. GHT to Battery North Side of River, Orchard Knob, November 25, 1863—10:45 AM, ibid., 115.

64. GHT to Commanding Officer, Fort Wood, Orchard Knob, November 25, 1863—11 AM, ibid., 115.

65. Wood, "The Battle of Missionary Ridge," 4:33–34.

66. Richardson, *Personal History of Ulysses S. Grant,* 365.

67. Quoted in Steven E. Woodworth, *This Grand Spectacle: The Battle of Chattanooga* (Abilene, Tex: McWhiney Foundation Press, 1999), 82.

68. Richardson, *Personal History of Ulysses S. Grant,* 365–366.

69. Oliver Otis Howard, *Autobiography of Oliver Otis Howard, Major General United States Army,* 2 vols. (New York: Baker & Taylor, 1908), 1:485.

70. Christopher J. Einholf, *George Thomas: Virginian for the Union* (Norman: University of Oklahoma Press, 2007), 215.

71. Granger set the signal at "twenty minutes before 4 PM." Granger report, London, East Tenn., February 11, 1864, *OR*, vol. 31, pt. 2, 132.

72. Quoted in Johnson, *That Body of Brave Men*, 449.

73. T. Harry Williams, *The History of American Wars: From 1745 to 1918* (New York: Alfred A. Knopf, 1981), 293.

74. Knefler report, Chattanooga, Tenn., November 27, 1863, *OR*, vol. 31, pt. 2, 304–305.

75. Dick report, November 27, 1863, ibid., 306–307.

76. A. J. Phelps report, Chattanooga, Tenn., December 15, 1863, ibid., 140.

77. Joseph S. Fullerton, "The Army of the Cumberland at Chattanooga," in *Battles and Leaders of the Civil War*, edited by Robert Underwood Johnson and Clarence Clough Buel (New York: Century: 1887), 3:725; William Wirt Calkins, *The History of the One Hundred and Fourth Regiment of Illinois Volunteer Infantry: War of the Great Rebellion, 1862–1865* (Chicago: Donohue & Henneberry, 1895), 180.

78. Shanks, *Personal Recollections*, 118.

79. Th. J. Wood to My Dear Sir, Dayton, Ohio, Feby. 26, 1896, Wood Papers, Filson.

80. Fullerton, "The Army of the Cumberland at Chattanooga," 725.

81. Meigs, "First Impressions," 74.

82. Beckwith, "Grant's Shadow," 103.

83. Richardson, *Personal History of Ulysses S. Grant,* 367.

84. Dana to Stanton, November 26, 1863—10 AM, *OR*, vol. 31, pt. 2, 69.

85. Ibid., 102. Beckwith did not quibble over the extent to which Grant ordered the assault or the manner in which the men carried it out. But most closely to the point of ultimate responsibility and authority, he termed the attack "the brightest page of Grant's military history," ibid., 103.

86. William Bluffton Miller, *Fighting for Liberty and Right: The Civil War Diary of William Bluffton Miller, First Sergeant, Company K, Seventy-fifth Indiana Volunteer Infantry* (Knoxville: University of Tennessee Press, 2005), 171.

87. Dana to Stanton, November 25, 1863—4:30 PM, *OR*, vol. 31, pt. 2, 68.

88. GHT report, Chattanooga, Tenn., November 25, 1863—12 PM, ibid., 90.

89. William Bluffton Miller, *Fighting for Liberty and Right*, 171.

90. Th. J. Wood to My Dear Sir, Dayton, Ohio, Feby. 26, 1896, Wood Papers, Filson.

91. Quoted in Richard W. Johnson, *Memoir of Maj.-Gen. George H. Thomas* (Philadelphia: J. B. Lippincott, 1881), 242, with a differing account and phraseology on p. 131. Major F. H. Loring also offered a slight variation for this response, in "General George A. [*sic*] Thomas," in *War Papers Being Papers Read before the Commandery of the State of Iowa, Military Order of the Loyal Legion of the United States* (Wilmington, N.C.: Broadfoot Publishing, 1994), 290.

92. Herman Hattaway and Archer Jones, *How the North Won* (Urbana: University of Illinois Press, 1983), 461.

93. GHT report, *OR*, vol. 31, pt. 2, 96–97.

94. Howard, *Autobiography*, 1:487.

95. Quoted in Clarence Edward Macartney, *Grant and His Generals* (New York: McBride, 1953), 15.

96. Dana to Stanton, November 25, 1863—8 PM, *OR*, vol. 31, pt. 2, 68.

97. Michael H. Fitch, *Echoes of the Civil War as I Hear Them* (New York: R. F. Fenno, 1905), 187.

98. GHT to Dear General, Chattanooga, Tenn Dec. 17, 1863, Garfield Papers, LOC.

99. Jos. C. McKibben to Old Fellow, Dec. 19th 1863, Garfield Papers, LOC.

100. Alvan C. Gillem to My dear General, Nashville, Dec. 27, 63, Garfield Papers, LOC.

101. Sylvanus Cadwallader, *Three Years with Grant*, edited by Benjamin P. Thomas (New York: Alfred A. Knopf, 1956), 155. Cadwallader preceded this story with a scathing critique of Thomas, although one whose motive subsequently became clear, ibid., 154–155.

102. General Orders No. 296, Chattanooga, Tenn., December 25, 1863, *OR*, vol. 31, pt. 3, 487.

103. Francis F. McKinney, *Education in Violence: The Life of George H. Thomas and the History of the Army of the Cumberland* (Detroit: Wayne State University Press, 1961), 303.

104. Timothy B. Smith, *The Golden Age of Battlefield Preservation: The Decade of the*

1890s and the Establishment of America's First Five Military Parks (Knoxville: University of Tennessee Press, 2008), 18–20.

105. Thomas B. Van Horne, *History of the Army of the Cumberland Its Organization, Campaigns, and Battles, Written at the Request of Major-General George H. Thomas, Chiefly from His Private Military Journal and Official and Other Documents Furnished by Him* (Cincinnati: Robert Clarke, 1875), 2:379.

106. Ibid., 377–379.

107. General Orders No. 6, Chattanooga, Tenn., January 26, 1864, *OR*, vol. 32, pt. 2, 37.

108. Quoted in Donn Piatt and Henry V. Boynton, *General George H. Thomas: A Critical Biography* (Cincinnati: Robert Clarke, 1893), 502.

109. W. E. Merrill, "Block-Houses for Railroad Defense in the Department of the Cumberland," in *Sketches of War History 1861–1865, Papers Presented for the Ohio Commandery of the Military Order of the Loyal Legion of the United States, 1880–1890*, edited by Robert Hunter (Cincinnati: Robert Clarke, 1890), 3:391 and 395.

110. GHT to Garfield, Chattanooga, Tenn., Jany. 17, 1864, Garfield Papers, LOC.

111. GHT to Dear Buell, Nashville, Tenn., Decr 13 1865, Buell Papers, Filson.

112. GHT to Garfield, Chattanooga, Tenn., Jany. 17, 1864, Garfield Papers, LOC.

Chapter 11: The "Wheel Horse" Pulls for Atlanta (February–September 1864)

1. A timeline for these events is easily accessible from E. B. Long, *The Civil War: Day By Day: An Almanac 1861–1865* (Garden City, N.Y.: Doubleday, 1971), 460–467.

2. Mark W. Johnson, *That Body of Brave Men: The U.S. Regular Infantry and the Civil War in the West* (Cambridge, Mass.: Da Capo Press, 2003), 464; Palmer designated as leader of the expedition, *OR*, vol. 32, pt. 1, 419.

3. GHT to Palmer, Chattanooga, February 22, 1864, *OR*, vol. 32, pt. 2, 445; GHT to Hooker, Chattanooga, February 25, 1864, ibid., 466; GHT to Grant, Tunnel Hill, February 26, 1864, ibid., 480.

4. Quoted in Donn Piatt and Henry V. Boynton, *General George H. Thomas: A Critical Biography* (Cincinnati: Robert Clarke, 1893), 519.

5. Richard W. Johnson, *Memoir of Maj.-Gen. George H. Thomas* (Philadelphia: J. B. Lippincott, 1881), 136.

6. William T. Sherman, *Memoirs of General William T. Sherman* (New York: Charles L. Webster, 1892), 2:42.

7. GHT to Sherman, Chattanooga, Tenn., April 8, 1864, *OR*, vol. 32, pt. 3, 292.

8. Sherman to GHT, Nashville, April 9, 1864, ibid., 306.

9. Richard W. Johnson, Memoir of Maj.-Gen. *Thomas*, 153.

10. Sherman to Grant, Nashville, Tennessee, April 10, 1864, *OR*, vol. 32, pt. 3, 313.

11. Sherman, *Memoirs*, 2:9.

12. Sherman to McPherson, In the Field, near Kingston, May 18, 1864—10:30 PM, *OR*, vol. 38, pt. 4, 244.

13. Sherman, *Memoirs*, 2:43.

14. Richard M. McMurry, *Two Great Rebel Armies: An Essay in Confederate Military History* (Chapel Hill: University of North Carolina Press, 1989), 34.

15. Sherman to Grant, Nashville, Tennessee, April 10, 1864, *OR*, vol. 32, pt. 3, 313.

16. Laforest to sister, Lookout Station, Tennessee, April 17, 1864, in Alburtus A. Dunham and Charles Laforest Dunham, *Through the South with a Union Soldier*, edited by Arthur H. DeRosier Jr. (Johnson City: East Tennessee State University, 1969), 114–115.

17. Oliver Otis Howard, *Autobiography of Oliver Otis Howard, Major General United States Army,* 2 vols. (New York: Baker & Taylor, 1908), 1:495.

18. GHT to Governor John Brough, Chattanooga, Tenn., April 7, 1864, *OR*, vol. 32, pt. 3, 287–288.

19. H. C. Hobart to Southard Hoffman, Camp on Lookout Mountain, Tenn., April 16, 1864, *OR*, ser. 2, vol. 7, 60–61.

20. First Indorsement, Chattanooga, April 17, 1864, ibid., 61.

21. Michael H. Fitch, *Echoes of the Civil War as I Hear Them* (New York: R. F. Fenno, 1905), 106–107.

22. Quoted in John D. Wright, *The Oxford Dictionary of Civil War Quotations* (New York: Oxford University Press, 2006), 403.

23. Thomas J. Morgan, *Reminiscences of Service with Colored Troops in the Army of the Cumberland, 1863–1865* (Providence: Soldiers and Sailors Historical Society of Rhode Island, 1885), 21–22.

24. Ibid., 22.

25. Elvero Persons, "General George H. Thomas," *Christian Advocate* (1866–1905), April 19, 1894, 249. http://www.proquest.com.

26. Johnson, *That Body of Brave Men*, 438.

27. GHT report, In the Field, near Dallas, Ga., June 5, 1864, *OR*, vol. 38, pt. 1, 139.

28. Sherman, *Memoirs*, 2:31.

29. David S. Stanley, *Personal Memoirs of Major-General D. S. Stanley, U.S.A.* (Cambridge, Mass.: Harvard University Press, 1917), 163.

30. Quoted in Frank A. Palumbo, *George Henry Thomas: The Dependable General* (Dayton, Ohio: Morningside House, 1983), 219.

31. William F. G. Shanks, *Personal Recollections of Distinguished Generals* (New York: Harper & Brothers, 1866), 58. Union general Howard used similar terminology, calling Thomas "Sherman's wheel-horse," in the Atlanta Campaign. Oliver Otis Howard, "Sketch of the Life of George H. Thomas," in *Personal Recollections of the War of the Rebellion,* edited by A. Noel Blakeman (New York: G. P. Putnam's Sons, 1907), 299.

32. Albert Castel, *Articles of War: Winners, Losers, and Some Who Were Both in the Civil War* (Mechanicsburg, Pa.: Stackpole Books, 2001), 231.

33. Quoted in John F. Marszalek, *Sherman: A Soldier's Passion for Order* (New York: Free Press, 1993), 265.

34. John Bennitt to My Dear Wife, Camp 19th Regt. Mich. V.I. 2nd Brid. 3rd Div. 20th A.C., Pea-Vine Church, Ga., 7 miles S.W. Ringold, in *"I Hope to Do My Country Service": The Civil War Letters of John Bennitt, M.D., Surgeon, 19th Michigan Infantry,* edited by Robert Beasecker (Detroit: Wayne State University Press, 2005), 273.

35. Fitch, *Echoes of the Civil War*, 321.

36. Sherman, *Memoirs*, 2:37 and 38.

37. Rear-Admiral Porter report, May 26, 1864, *ORN*, 26, 326. The *General Thomas* was the smallest of the vessels that Porter mentioned. The craft measured 165 feet in length and 26 feet across the beam. It displaced 184 tons and carried five guns. Lieutenant-Commander Fitch report, September 23, 1864, ibid., 566, and Acting Rear Admiral Lee report, February 21, 1865, *ORN*, 27, 56.

38. Fitch report, July 14, 1864, *ORN*, 26, 476. The commander of the Mississippi Squadron, Lieutenant Commander LeRoy Fitch, reported, "The *General Thomas* has been patrolling the river for some weeks, but not regularly in commission." The gunboat's paperwork came several months later. See Fitch report, September 23, 1864, ibid., 566.

39. Frances H. Kennedy, ed., *The Civil War Battlefield Guide*, 2nd ed. (Boston: Houghton Mifflin, 1998), 335.

40. William Passmore Carlin, *The Memoirs of William Passmore Carlin, U.S.A.*, edited by Robert I. Girardi and Nathaniel Cheairs Hughes Jr. (Lincoln: University of Nebraska Press, 1999), 125.

41. John Watts De Peyster, *Major General George H. Thomas* (New York: Atlantic Publishing, 1875), 9.

42. Russell F. Weigley, *Quartermaster General of the Union Army: A Biography of M. C. Meigs* (New York: Columbia University Press, 1959), 292. Weigley noted that the relocation raised the cost of reopening the facility and delayed its operation until April 1, 1865, but "the project more than paid for itself" and the government was able to sell it later in the year, ibid.

43. Quoted in Albert Castel, *Decision in the West: The Atlanta Campaign of 1864* (Lawrence: University Press of Kansas, 1992), 223. See also ibid., 221–222.

44. For descriptions of these engagements, see ibid., 223–241.

45. Sherman, *Memoirs*, 2:52–53.

46. Sherman to Grant, In the Field, June 18, 1864, *OR*, vol. 38, pt. 4, 507–508.

47. Sherman, *Memoirs*, 2:50.

48. Sherman to Grant, In the Field, June 18, 1864, *OR*, vol. 38, pt. 4, 507–508.

49. De Peyster, *Major General George H. Thomas*, 19.

50. Alfred Pirtle, "Stone[s] River Sketches," in *War Papers Being Papers Read before the Commandery of the State of Ohio, Military Order of the Loyal Legion of the United States* (Wilmington, N.C.: Broadfoot Publishing, 1992), 6:97.

51. L. M. Dayton to GHT, In the Field, June 18, 1864, *OR*, vol. 38, pt. 4, 510.

52 Wm. D. Whipple to O. O. Howard, Near Big Shanty, June 18, 1864, ibid., 512.

53. GHT to Howard, June 18, 1864, ibid., 513.

54. GHT to Howard, June 19, 1864—6:30 AM, ibid., 521.

55. GHT to Baird, Near Big Shanty, Ga., June 19, 1864, ibid., 521, and GHT to Hooker, Near Big Shanty, Ga., June 19, 1864, ibid., 522.

56. Sherman to GHT, In the Field, June 21, 1864, ibid., 546.

57. W. T. Sherman to Major-General Rousseau, In the Field Big Shanty, June 21, 1864, *OR*, vol. 39, 133.

58. Stanley, *Personal Memoirs*, 173.

59. Ibid.

60. Castel, *Decision in the West*, 313.

61. Christopher Losson, *Tennessee's Forgotten Warriors: Frank Cheatham and His Confederate Division* (Knoxville: University of Tennessee Press, 1989), 154; Craig L. Symonds, *Stonewall of the West: Patrick Cleburne and the Civil War* (Lawrence: University Press of Kansas, 1997), 217.

62. Castel, *Decision in the West*, 313–314.

63. Sherman to GHT, In the Field, June 27, 1864—11:45 AM, *OR*, vol. 38, pt. 4, 609.

64. GHT to Sherman, June 27, 1864—1:40 PM, ibid., 609.

65. GHT to Sherman, In the Field, June 27, 1864, ibid., 610.

66. Sherman to GHT, Near Kenesaw Mountain, June 27, 1864, ibid., 611.

67. Castel, *Decision in the West*, 318.

68. GHT to Sherman, June 27, 1864, *OR*, vol. 38, pt. 4, 612.

69. Sherman to GHT, In the Field, near Kenesaw, June 27, 1864—9:45 PM, ibid., 612.

70. Ibid.

71. Castel, *Decision in the West*, 319.

72. Sherman to GHT, In the Field, near Kenesaw, June 27, 1864—9:50 PM, *OR*, vol. 38, pt. 4, 612.

73. Sherman to GHT, In the Field, near Kenesaw, June 28, 1864, ibid., 630.

74. David Evans, *Sherman's Horsemen: Union Cavalry Operations in the Atlanta Campaign* (Bloomington: Indiana University Press, 1996), xxi–xxii and 5.

75. Minerva Leah Rowles McClatchey, "A Georgia Woman's Civil War Diary: The Journal of Minerva Leah Rowles McClatchey, 1864–65," edited by T. Conn Bryan, *Georgia Historical Quarterly* 51, no. 2 (July 1967): 197–216, 203.

76. Thomas Speed to Dear parents, Hd. Qrs. 3rd Brig. 3rd Div. 23rd AC July 4th 1864, Speed Letterbook, Filson.

77. GHT to Sherman, July 10, 1864, *OR*, vol. 38, pt. 5, 104.

78. Sherman to GHT, In the Field, near Chattahoochee, July 10, 1864, ibid., 104.

79. David Williams, *A People's History of the Civil War: Struggles for the Meaning of Freedom* (New York: New Press, 2005), 123–124.

80. Elizabeth D. Leonard, *Yankee Women: Gender Battles in the Civil War* (New York: W. W. Norton, 1994), 130.

81. Walter D. Durham, *Reluctant Partners, Nashville and the Union, 1863–1865* (Knoxville: University of Tennessee Press, 2008), 146–147.

82. GHT to Dear General, July 16th 1864, Garfield Papers, LOC.

83. William D. Whipple to General Granger, In the Field, July 15, 1864, *OR*, vol. 38, pt. 5, 148.

84. GHT to Dear General, July 16th 1864, Garfield Papers, LOC.

85. GHT to Sherman, July 20, 1864—12 m., *OR*, vol. 38, pt. 5, 196.

86. Sherman to GHT, In the Field, near Atlanta, Ga., July 20, 1864—6:10 [PM], ibid., 196–197.

87. GHT to Brig. Gen. J. Newton, July 20, 1864—10:30 AM, ibid., 199.

88. Quoted in Marszalek, *Sherman*, 276.

89. Sherman, *Memoirs*, 2:72.

90. GHT to Sherman, July 20, 1864—12 m., *OR*, vol. 38, pt. 5, 196.

91. Sherman to GHT, In the Field, near Atlanta, Ga., July 20, 1864—6:10 [PM], ibid., 196–197.

92. GHT to Sherman, July 20, 1864—6:15 PM, ibid., 197.

93. GHT report, August 17, 1864, *OR*, vol. 38, pt. 1, 156–157.

94. Sherman, *Memoirs*, 2:73.

95. Henry Stone, "The Siege and Capture of Atlanta, July 9 to September 8, 1864," in *The Atlanta Papers*, no. 3 (Dayton, Ohio: Press of Morningside Bookshop, 1980), 112.

96. Howard, *Autobiography*, I, 619.

97. GHT to Sherman, July 20, 1864—6:15 PM, *OR*, vol. 38, pt. 5, 197.

98. Sherman to Halleck, Near Atlanta, Ga., July 24, 1864—3 PM, *OR*, vol. 38, pt. 1, 241.

99. Quoted in Castel, *Decision in the West*, 611. Castel dismissed the likelihood that Thomas would offer "such a silly reason" for opposing Logan or that he threatened to resign if the recommendation were made for such an appointment, ibid.

100. Quoted in Larry J. Daniel, *Days of Glory: The Army of the Cumberland, 1861–1865* (Baton Rouge: Louisiana State University Press, 2004), 417. Ironically, Howard came close to losing the appointment when he suggested Hooker had seniority. A testy Sherman responded, "Hooker has not the moral qualities that I want—not those adequate to command; but if you don't want promotion, there are plenty who do," ibid.

101. Sherman, *Memoirs*, 2:85–86.

102. Sherman to Halleck, *OR*, vol. 38, pt. 5, 272–274.

103. GHT to Sir, Chattanooga Tn July 24 1864, Thomas Papers, HL.

104. Andrew Johnson to GHT, Nashville, July 29, 1864, *OR*, vol. 39, 210.

105. GHT to Governor Andrew Johnson, In the Field, July 30, 1864, ibid., 211.

106. Johnson to GHT, Nashville, Tenn., Aug. 16th, 1864, *The Papers of Andrew Johnson*, edited by Leroy P. Graf (Knoxville: University of Tennessee Press, 1986), 7:98.

107. GHT to Johnson, August 19, 1864, ibid.

108. Special Field Orders No. 240, August 31, 1864, *OR*, vol. 39, pt. 2, 325.

109. Sherman to GHT, In the Field, near Atlanta, Ga., July 31, 1864, *OR*, vol. 38, pt. 5, 309–310.

110. Sherman to GHT and Howard, In the Field, near Atlanta, Ga., July 31, 1864, ibid., 310.

111. GHT to Sherman, July 31, 1864—8:30 PM, ibid., 311.

112. Sherman to Stanton, In the Field, near Atlanta, Ga., August 5, 1864, ibid., 367.

113. Sherman to Schofield, In the Field, near Atlanta, Ga., August 5, 1864, ibid., 378.

114. Sherman to Palmer, In the Field, near Atlanta, Ga., August 4, 1864, ibid., 354; Palmer to Sherman, In the Field, August 4, 1864, ibid., 355; Sherman to Palmer, In the Field, near Atlanta, Ga., August 4, 1864, ibid.; Palmer to Sherman, August 4, 1864—1 PM, ibid.; Schofield to Palmer, Before Atlanta, Ga., August 4, 1864—3 PM, ibid., 355–356.

115. Sherman to Palmer, In the Field, near Atlanta, Ga., August 4, 1864—10:45 PM, ibid., 356.

116. John M. Palmer, *Personal Recollections of John M. Palmer: The Story of an Earnest Life* (Cincinnati: Robert Clarke, 1901), 199.

117. Ibid., 209–221.

118. Sherman, *Memoirs*, 2:100–101.

119. Sherman to Halleck, August 7, 1864—8 PM, *OR*, vol. 38, pt. 5, 409.

120. Sherman to GHT, August 8, 1864, ibid., 431.

121. Sherman to GHT, In the Field, near Atlanta, August 9, 1864, ibid., 435.

122. Sherman to Howard, In the Field, near Atlanta, August 10, 1864, ibid., 452.

123. Michael Fellman, *Citizen Sherman: A Life of William Tecumseh Sherman* (New York: Random House, 1995), 176–177.

124. Michael Walzer, *Just and Unjust Wars: A Moral Argument with Historical Illustrations* (New York: Basic Books, 1977), 32–33.

125, Sherman to GHT, In the Field, near Atlanta, August 10, 1864, *OR*, vol. 38, pt. 5, 448.

126. GHT to Sherman, August 10, 1864, ibid., 448.

127. Gilbert C. Kniffin, "The Life and Services of Major General George H. Thomas," in *War Papers Being Papers Read before the Commandery of the District of Columbia Military Order of the Loyal Legion of the United States*, vol. 1, *Papers 1–26. March 1887–April 1897* (Wilmington, N.C.: Broadfoot Publishing, 1993), 26.

128. See chapters 11–20 in Evans, *Sherman's Horsemen*, which also covered concurrent operations under George Stoneman.

129 Sherman, *Memoirs*, 2:106–107.

130. James A. Garfield, *Oration on the Life and Character of Gen. George H. Thomas Delivered before the Society of the Army of the Cumberland* (Cincinnati: Robert Clarke, 1871), 37.

131. Ibid., 28–29.

132. James M. Woolworth, "George H. Thomas," in *Civil War Sketches and Incidents. Papers Read by Companions of the Commandery of the State of Nebraska, Military Order of the Loyal Legion of the United States* (Omaha: Published by the Commandery, 1902), 147.

133. Sherman, *Memoirs*, 2:106–107.

134. Kniffin, "Life of Thomas," 26–27.

135. GHT to Sherman, August 14, 1864, *OR*, vol. 38, pt. 5, 489.

136. Sherman to Halleck, Near Atlanta, Ga., August 3, 1864—9 PM, ibid., 340.

137. Sherman to GHT, August 16, 1864, ibid., 524.

138. GHT to Sherman, August 16, 1864—10 AM, ibid., 526.

139. Sherman to GHT, In the Field, near Atlanta, Ga., August 16, 1864, ibid., 526.

140. Sherman to GHT, In the Field, near Atlanta, Ga., August 16, 1864, ibid., 526.

141. GHT to Sherman, August 16, 1864, ibid., 526.

142. Sherman to GHT, August 16, 1864, ibid., 527.

143. Castel, *Decision in the West*, 507.

144. Charles Dana Miller, *The Struggle for the Life of the Republic: A Civil War Narrative by Brevet Major Charles Dana Miller, 76th Ohio Volunteer Infantry*, edited by Stewart Bennett and Barbara Tillery (Kent, Ohio: Kent State University Press, 2004), 202.

145. Howard, "Sketch of the Life of George H. Thomas," 300.

146. Symonds, *Stonewall of the West*, 240–241.

147. GHT report, Atlanta, Ga., September 19, 1864, *OR*, vol. 38, pt. 1, 166–167.

148. Consolidated report of casualties in Army of the Cumberland for August, 1864, ibid., 168.

149. Howard, "Sketch of the Life of George H. Thomas," 299.

150. James A. Connolly, *Three Years in the Army of the Cumberland: The Letters and Diary of Major James A. Connolly*, edited by Paul Angle (Bloomington: Indiana University Press, 1959), 256–257.

151. John M. Schofield, *Forty-Six Years in the Army* (New York: Century, 1897), 122–123.

152. F. H. Loring, "General George A. [*sic*] Thomas," in Papers Read before the Commandery of the State of Iowa, Military Order of the Loyal Legion of the United States (Wilmington, N.C.: Broadfoot Publishing, 1994), 291.

153. Sherman, *Memoirs*, 2:109.

154. Sherman to Halleck, In the Field, near Lovejoy's twenty-six miles south of Atlanta, September 4, 1864, *OR*, vol. 38, pt. 5, 792 and 793.

155. Halleck to Sherman, Washington, September 16, 1864, *OR*, vol. 38, pt. 5, 857.

156. Daniel, *Days of Glory*, 426. Daniel's list included the missed opportunity at Snake Creek Gap and several chances to outflank the Confederates, *OR*, vol. 38, pt. 5, 426–427.

157. General Orders No. 134, Atlanta, Ga., September 9, 1864, ibid., 843.

158. Alfred to My Dearest Mary, Atlanta, Ga. Sept. 18th 1864, in Alfred Lacey Hough, *Soldier in the West: The Civil War Letters of Alfred Lacey Hough*, edited by Robert G. Athearn (Philadelphia: University of Pennsylvania Press, 1957), 214.

159. Ibid., 214–215.

160. Connolly, *Three Years with the Army of the Cumberland*, 257–262; quotation on 261.

Chapter 12: Biding Time in Tennessee (September–December 1864)

1. William T. Sherman, *Memoirs of General William T. Sherman* (New York: Charles L. Webster, 1892), 2:130. The standard early work on the Nashville Campaign and battle of December 15–16, 1864, was Stanley F. Horn, *The Decisive Battle of Nashville* (Nashville: University of Tennessee Press, 1956). Sword's *Embrace an Angry Wind* offered an outstanding assessment, particularly of the last phases of the campaign. McDonough's *Nashville,* and his earlier *Five Tragic Hours* on Franklin with Thomas Connelly, covered those engagements. All of these sources provided the basis for this composite discussion. Wiley Sword, *Embrace*

an Angry Wind: The Confederacy's Last Hurrah: Spring Hill, Franklin, and Nashville (New York: HarperCollins, 1992); James Lee McDonough, *Nashville: The Western Confederacy's Final Gamble* (Knoxville: University of Tennessee Press, 2004); James Lee McDonough and Thomas L. Connelly, *Five Tragic Hours: The Battle of Franklin* (Knoxville: University of Tennessee Press, 1983).

2. GHT to Johnson, September 23, 1864, *The Papers of Andrew Johnson*, edited by Leroy P. Graf (Knoxville: University of Tennessee Press, 1986), 7:194.

3. Johnson to GHT, Nashville, Tenn., September 26th, 1864, ibid., 193–194. See also in *OR*, vol. 39, pt. 2, 482.

4. Elizabeth D. Leonard, *Yankee Women: Gender Battles in the Civil War* (New York: W. W. Norton, 1994), 141–142.

5. James A. Connolly, *Three Years in the Army of the Cumberland: The Letters and Diary of Major James A. Connolly*, edited by Paul Angle (Bloomington: Indiana University Press, 1959), 264–265.

6. An April 28, 1865, inspection report noted the dimensions of Fortress Rosecrans as "inclosing 200 acres on either side of Stone's River," noted the formidable construction and impressive fields of fire, covered at the time of the inspection by fifty-seven guns, Tower report, Nashville, Tenn., April 28, 1865, *OR*, vol. 49, pt. 2, 502–503.

7. Walter D. Durham, *Reluctant Partners, Nashville and the Union, 1863–1865* (Knoxville: University of Tennessee Press, 2008), 116–118.

8. W. E. Merrill, "Block-Houses for Railroad Defense in the Department of the Cumberland," in *Sketches of War History 1861–1865, Papers Presented for the Ohio Commandery of the Military Order of the Loyal Legion of the United States, 1880–1890*, edited by Robert Hunter (Cincinnati: Robert Clarke, 1890), 3:410. In addition to inflating his forces and using the light artillery pieces he brought with him effectively, Forrest also used the captured commander of one post to induce the surrender of another, ibid.

9. GHT to J. T. Croxton, October 4, 1864, *OR*, vol. 39, pt. 3, 82; GHT to Rousseau, October 4, 1864—9:30 PM, ibid.

10. GHT to Rousseau, October 4, 1864—11:50 AM, ibid., 81; GHT to Croxton, October 4, 1864, ibid., 82.

11. GHT to Rousseau, October 4, 1864—11:50 AM, ibid., 81.

12. J. D. Morgan to Captain Ramsey, West side of Shoal Creek, Ala., October 7, 1864—7 AM, ibid., 140.

13. GHT to Rousseau, October 7, 1864—10:30 PM, ibid., 142.

14. J. C. Van Duzer to Maj. T. T. Eckert, Nashville, Tenn., October 8, 1864—10:30 PM, ibid., 153. Thomas gave several commanders explicit orders to round up as many of Forrest's stragglers as possible. See, for example, GHT to Rousseau, Nashville, October 8, 1864, ibid., 155, and GHT to Starkweather, Nashville, October 8, 1864, ibid.

15. Merrill, "Block-Houses for Railroad Defense in the Department of the Cumberland," 3:413. In the course of his inspections, Willett exposed other concerns as well. In one instance, all but two men, neither of whom seemed to Willett to be alert themselves, were absent in the nearby forest cutting wood for the locomotives to use as fuel since they would perform the task more cheaply for the railroad executives than hired hands, ibid., 414.

16. Adam Gurowski, *Diary: 1863–'64–'65*, edited by Charles Richard Williams (New York: Burt Franklin, 1886; reprint, 1968), 372.

17. GPT to My dear Pa, Chattanooga Tenn November 2d, 1864, Thruston Papers, Filson.

18. George Meade, *The Life and Letters of George Gordon Meade, Major-General United States Army*, edited by George Gordon Meade, 2 vols. (New York: Charles Scribner's Sons, 1913), 2:241.

19. William Bluffton Miller, *Fighting for Liberty and Right: The Civil War Diary of William Bluffton Miller, First Sergeant, Company K, Seventy-fifth Indiana Volunteer Infantry* (Knoxville: University of Tennessee Press, 2005), 273.

20. Sherman, *Memoirs*, 2:108.

21. John G. Nicolay and John Hay, *Abraham Lincoln: A History* (Chicago: University of Chicago Press, 1966), 310.

22. Henry M. Cist, *The Army of the Cumberland* (New York: Charles Scribner's Sons, 1882), 179.

23. J. H. Wilson to C. C. Washburn, Nashville, Tenn., November 16, 1864, *OR*, vol. 45, pt. 1, 919.

24. Lewis W. Leads to Whipple, Lookout Mountain, November 16, 1864—6 PM, ibid., 915.

25. GHT to Maj. Gen. Schofield, Nashville Nov 13 186[4] 5 PM, Thomas Papers, HL.

26. Alfred to My Dearest Mary, Chattanooga Nov 20th 1864, in Alfred Lacey Hough, *Soldier in the West: The Civil War Letters of Alfred Lacey Hough*, edited by Robert G. Athearn (Philadelphia: University of Pennsylvania Press, 1957), 230.

27. A. P. Mason to Forrest, Florence, Ala., November 20, 1864, *OR*, vol. 45, pt. 1, 1227.

28. *Daily Dispatch*, December 27, 1864.

29. GHT to Lieut. M. J. Kelly, Nashville, November 25, 1864—11 AM, *OR*, vol. 45, pt. 1, 1055.

30. M. J. Kelly to GHT, Paducah, November 25, 1864, ibid., 1055.

31. GHT to Maj. Gen. W. S. Rosecrans, Nashville, November 26, 1864—12 m., ibid., 1057.

32. GHT to Schofield, Nashville, November 27, 1864—8:00 AM, ibid., 1085.

33. A. J. Smith to GHT, Paducah, November 27, 1864, ibid., 1104.

34. GPT to My darling Mother, Chattga, Tenn November 26th 1864, Thruston Papers, Filson.

35. John M. Schofield, *Forty-Six Years in the Army* (New York: Century, 1897), 174.

36. Ibid., 175–176.

37. GHT to Maj. Gen. Schofield, Nashville Nov 30th 1864, Thomas Papers, HL.

38. James F. Rusling, *Men and Things I Saw in Civil War Days* (New York: Eaton & Mains, 1899), 86–87.

39. Ibid., 87–88.

40. Ibid., 226–227.

41. General Field Orders No. 38, Near Franklin, December 1, 1864, *OR*, vol. 45, pt. 2, 628.

42. McDonough and Connelly, *Five Tragic Hours*, 157, 160, and 168.

43. Quoted in Donn Piatt, *Memories of the Men Who Saved the Union* (New York: Belford, Clarke, 1887), 191.

44. U. S. Grant to GHT, City Point, November 15, 1864—11 AM, *OR*, vol. 45, pt. 1, 895.

45. GHT to Grant, Nashville, November 15, 1864—4 PM, ibid., 895.

46. GHT to Grant, Nashville, November 25, 1864—11 AM, ibid., 1034.

47. Stanton to Grant, December 2, 1864—10:30 AM, *OR*, vol. 45, pt. 2, 15–16.

48. Grant to GHT, December 2, 1864—11 AM, ibid., 17.

49. Forrest Report, January 24, 1865, *OR*, vol. 45, pt. 1, 754.

50. Brian Steel Wills, *A Battle from the Start: Nathan Bedford Forrest* (New York: Harper Collins, 1992), 286–287.

51. Theodore Lyman, *Meade's Army: The Private Notebooks of Lt. Col. Theodore Lyman*, edited by David W. Lowe (Kent, Ohio: Kent State University Press, 2007), 302.

52. Grant to GHT, December 2, 1864—1:30 PM, *OR*, vol. 45, pt. 2, 17.

53. GHT to Grant, December 2, 1864—10 PM, ibid., 17–18.

54. Grant to Sherman, City Point, Va., December 3, 1864, *OR*, vol. 44, 612.

55. Grant to GHT, December 5, 1864—8 PM, *OR*, vol. 45, pt. 2, 55.

56. GHT to Halleck, Nashville, December 5, 1864—10:00 PM, ibid., 55.

57. T. Speed to Dear Horace, Hd. Qrs. 12th Ky. Inf., Nashville, Tenn., Dec. 3rd 1864, Speed Letterbook, Filson.

58. T. Speed to Dear Will, Hd. Qrs. 12th Ky. Vol. Inf., Nashville, Tenn., Dec. 7th 1864, Speed Letterbook, Filson.

59. Ibid.

60. Grant to GHT, City Point, Va., December 6, 1864—4 PM, *OR*, vol. 45, pt. 2, 70.

61. GHT to Grant, December 6, 1864—8 PM, ibid., 70.

62. GHT to Henry Halleck, Nashville, December 6, 1864—8:00 PM, ibid., 70.

63. "Same Nov. 8, 1863, Sunday," in Daniel Garrison Brinton, "Dr. Daniel Garrison Brinton in the Army of the Cumberland," edited by D. G. Brinton Thompson, *Pennsylvania Magazine of History and Biography* 90, no. 4 (Oct. 1966): 478–479.

64. "December 7 [1864]," in Chesley A. Mosman, *The Rough Side of War: The Civil War Journal of Chesley A. Mosman, 1st Lieutenant, Company D, 59th Illinois Volunteer Infantry Regiment,* edited by Arnold Gates (Garden City, N.J.: Basin Publishing, 1987), 317.

65. GHT to Grant, December 6, 1864—9 PM, *OR*, vol. 45, pt. 2, 70.

66. Grant to Sherman, City Point, Va., December 6, 1864, *OR*, vol. 44, 636–637.

67. Sherman to Grant, In the Field, near Savannah, December 16, 1864, ibid., 728.

68. To Mrs. George G. Meade, Headquarters Army of the Potomac, December 6, 1864, in Meade, *Life and Letters*, 2:250.

69. B. R. Roberson, "The Courthouse Burnin'est General," *Tennessee Historical Quarterly* 23 (Dec. 1964): 372–378. A short account of Lyon's life and military career may be found in Brian Steel Wills, "Brig. Gen. Hylan Benton Lyon," in *Kentuckians in Gray: Confederate Generals and Field Officers of the Bluegrass State,* edited by Bruce S. Allardice and Lawrence Lee Hewitt (Lexington: University Press of Kentucky, 2008), 180–186.

70. H. B. Lyon report, January 3, 1865, *OR*, vol. 45, pt. 1, p. 803.

71. Sword, *Embrace an Angry Wind*, 289.

72. Tower report, Nashville, Tenn., April 28, 1865, *OR*, vol. 49, pt. 2, 502.

73. Forrest report, January 24, 1865, *OR*, vol. 45, pt.1, 755; Wills, *A Battle from the Start,* 287–288. Forrest had enjoyed one of his earliest successes in a lightning raid on Murfreesboro in July 1862, ibid., 72–76.

74. Stanton to Grant, December 7—10:20 AM, *OR*, vol. 45, pt. 2, 84.

75. Grant to Halleck, December 8, 1864—4 PM, ibid., 96.

76. Halleck to Grant, December 8, 1864—9 PM, ibid., 96.

77. GHT to Halleck, December 7, 1864—10 PM, ibid., 96.

78. Grant to GHT, City Point, Va., December 8, 1864—8:30 PM, ibid., 97.

79. Grant to Halleck, December 8, 1864—10 PM, ibid., 96.

80. T. Speed to Dear Will, Hd. Qrs. 12th Ky. Vol. Inf., Nashville, Tenn., Dec. 7th 1864, Speed Letterbook, Filson.

81. Halleck to GHT, December 9, 1864—10:30 AM, *OR*, vol. 45, pt. 2, 114.

82. Grant to Halleck, City Point, Va., December 9, 1864—11 AM, ibid., 115–116.

83. General Orders No. —, December 9, 1864, ibid., 114.

84. GHT to Grant, Nashville, December 9, 1864—1 PM, ibid., 115.

85. GHT to Halleck, December 9, 1864—2 PM, ibid., 114.

86. Halleck to Grant, December 9, 1864—4:10 PM, ibid.116.

87. Grant to Halleck, December 9, 1864—5:30 PM, ibid., 116.

88. Grant to GHT, December 9, 1864—7:30 PM, ibid., 115.

89. GHT to Grant, December 9, 1864—11:30 PM, ibid., 115.

90. Schofield, *Forty-Six Years in the Army*, 237–238.

91. Ibid., 241.

92. Forrest report, January 24, 1865, *OR*, vol. 45, pt. 1, 756.

93. Roberson used the quotation for his article and in the text, pp. 372 and 378, which he attributed to Hall Allen in *Center of Conflict* (Paducah, Ky.: n.d.), 146. Hylan Lyon's later justification for these incendiary activities was that "The Court Houses in all these towns had been used by the Federal Troops as forts and prisons for Confederate sympathizers" and consequently they bore military importance that warranted their destruction, Roberson, "The Courthouse Burnin'est General," 373–374. Lyon marked the litany of destruction proudly in his reminiscences, Hylan B. Lyon, "Memoirs of Hylan B. Lyon, Brigadier General, C.S.A.," edited by Edward M. Coffman, *Tennessee Historical Quarterly* 18 (March 1959): 47–48.

94. Thomas biographer Francis McKinney noted the combination of inadequate cavalry and poor weather as factors for Thomas's reluctance to attack Hood in early December, Francis F. McKinney, *Education in Violence: The Life of George H. Thomas and the History of the Army of the Cumberland* (Detroit: Wayne State University Press, 1961), 402.

95. Henry Stone, "Repelling Hood's Invasion of Tennessee," in *Battles and Leaders of the Civil War*, edited by Robert Underwood Johnson and Clarence Clough Buel (New York: Century, 1887), 4:455.

96. Rusling, *Men and Things I Saw*, 86.

97. Stone, "Repelling Hood's Invasion of Tennessee," 455.

98. GHT report, January 20, 1865, *OR*, vol. 45, pt. 1, 45.

99. See, for example, various communications, *ORN*, Series I, 26, 661, 667, 671, and 672.

100. Dudley Taylor Cornish and Virginia Jeans Laas, *Lincoln's Lee: The Life of Samuel Phillips Lee, United States Navy, 1812–1897* (Lawrence: University Press of Kansas, 1986), 142.

101. GHT to Halleck, Nashville, Tenn., December 10, 1864—8:30 PM, *OR*, vol. 45, pt. 2, 130.

102. James H. Wilson, *Under the Old Flag: Recollections of Military Operations in the War for the Union, the Spanish War, the Boxer Rebellion, etc.*, 2 vols. (New York: D. Appleton, 1912), 2:100–101.

103. Ibid., 102.

104. Ibid., 102–103.

105. Ibid., 104.

106. Grant to GHT, December 11, 1864—4 PM, *OR*, vol. 45, pt. 2, 143.

107. GHT to Halleck, December 11, 1864—9:30 PM, ibid., 143.

108. GHT to Grant, Nashville, December 11, 1864—10:30 PM, ibid., 143.

109. GHT to Halleck, December 12, 1864—10:30 PM, ibid., 155.

110. Forrest report, January 24, 1865, *OR*, vol. 45, pt. 1, 756.

111. GHT to Samuel P. Lee, December 14, 1864—8 PM, *ORN*, 26, 665.

112. GHT to S. P. Lee, December 13, 1864—9 PM, ibid., 663.

113. GHT to Halleck, Nashville, Tenn., December 13, 1864—9 PM, *OR*, vol. 45, pt. 2, 168.

114. Special Orders No. 149, City Point, Va., December 13, 1864, ibid., 171.

115. Samuel H. Beckwith, "Samuel H. Beckwith 'Grant's Shadow,'" edited by John Y. Simon and David L. Wilson, in *Ulysses S. Grant: Essays and Documents,* edited by David L. Wilson and John Y. Simon (Carbondale: Southern Illinois University Press, 1981), 117.

116. Halleck to GHT, Washington, D.C., December 14, 1864—12:30 PM, *OR*, vol. 45, pt. 2, 180.

117. Richard W. Johnson, *Memoir of Maj.-Gen. George H. Thomas* (Philadelphia: J. B. Lippincott, 1881), 194.

118. Beckwith, "Grant's Shadow," 116.

119. Richard W. Johnson, *Memoir of Maj.-Gen. Thomas*, 194.

120. Throughout his postwar memoirs, Wilson provided evidence of his esteem for both individuals, although he soured in his relationship with Grant in later years. For example, see Wilson, *Under the Old Flag*, 1:276, and 2:66 and 104. Of course, any criticism of the cavalry was a veiled criticism of Wilson, too.

121. Beckwith, "Grant's Shadow," 116.

122. W. J. Wood, *Civil War Generalship: The Art of Command* (Westport, Conn.: Praeger, 1997), 228.

123. GHT to Halleck, Nashville, Tenn., December 14, 1864—8 PM, *OR*, vol. 45, pt. 2, 180.

124. Gamaliel Bradford, *Union Portraits* (Boston: Houghton Mifflin, 1915), 115.

125. Stone, "Repelling Hood's Invasion of Tennessee," 455.

Chapter 13: The "Sledge" Hammers Hood (December 15–31, 1864)

1. Henry Stone, "Repelling Hood's Invasion of Tennessee," *Battles and Leaders of the Civil War*, edited by Robert Underwood Johnson and Clarence Clough Buel (New York: Century, 1887), 4:455.

2. Gamaliel Bradford, *Union Portraits* (Boston: Houghton Mifflin, 1915), 115.

3. James Lee McDonough, *Nashville: The Western Confederacy's Final Gamble* (Knoxville: University of Tennessee Press, 2004), 162 and 220 (present-day Nashville area); 161 and 219 (antagonist's defensive lines).

4. See, for example, John Cimprich, "A Critical Moment and Its Aftermath for George H. Thomas," in *The Moment of Decision: Biographical Essays on American Character and Regional Identity*, edited by Randall M. Miller and John R. McKivigan (Westport, Conn.: Greenwood Press, 1994), 173–187, and Christopher J. Einholf, *George Thomas: Virginian for the Union* (Norman: University of Oklahoma Press, 2007).

5. McDonough, *Nashville*, 159.

6. Wood, "Address to comrades," n.d., Wood Papers, Filson.

7. McDonough, *Nashville*, 183.

8. Stone, "Repelling Hood's Invasion of Tennessee," 459.

9. Ibid., 459–460.

10. Quoted in Smith, *In the Lion's Mouth*, 68.

11. James F. Rusling, *Men and Things I Saw in Civil War Days* (New York: Eaton & Mains, 1899), 96.

12. GHT to Halleck, Nashville, Tenn., December 15, 1864, *OR*, vol. 45, pt. 2, 194.

13. GHT to Mrs. F. L. Thomas, Nashville, December 15, 1864, ibid., 195.

14. Samuel H. Beckwith, "Samuel H. Beckwith 'Grant's Shadow,'" edited by John Y. Simon and David L. Wilson, in *Ulysses S. Grant: Essays and Documents,* edited by David L. Wilson and John Y. Simon (Carbondale: Southern Illinois University Press, 1981), 117–118.

15. Grant to GHT, Washington, D.C., December 15, 1864—11:30 PM, *OR*, vol. 45, pt. 2, 195.

16. Stanton to GHT, Washington, D.C., December 15, 1864—midnight, ibid., 195; also found in pt. 1, 50.

17. Grant to GHT, Washington, D.C., December 15, 1864—11:45 PM, ibid., 195; also found in pt. 1, 50.

18. John A. Logan, *The Volunteer Soldier in America* (Chicago: R. S. Peale, Publishers, 1887), 67.

19. John M. Schofield, *Forty-Six Years in the Army* (New York: Century, 1897), 245.

20. Alfred to My Dearest Mary, Head-Quarters Department of the Cumberland, Office of Commissary of Musters, Chattanooga Dec. 15th 1864, in Alfred Lacey Hough, *Soldier in the West: The Civil War Letters of Alfred Lacey Hough*, edited by Robert G. Athearn (Philadelphia: University of Pennsylvania Press, 1957), 233.

21. Henry Stone, "The Battle of Nashville, Tennessee December 15 and 16, 1864," in *Campaigns in Kentucky and Tennessee Including the Battle of Chickamauga 1862–1864. Papers of the Military Historical Society of Massachusetts* (Boston: Military Historical Society of Massachusetts, 1908), 7:524–525.

22. Wilson, *Under the Old Flag*, 2:113.

23. William F. G. Shanks, *Personal Recollections of Distinguished Generals* (New York: Harper & Brothers, 1866), 61.

24. Ibid., 78.

25. Isaac R. Sherwood, *Memories of the War* (Toledo, Ohio: H. J. Chittenden, 1923), 47.

26. Stone, "The Battle of Nashville," 525–526.

27. Stone, "Repelling Hood's Invasion of Tennessee," 461.

28. Ibid.

29. Schofield, *Forty-Six Years*, 250.

30. Stone, "Repelling Hood's Invasion of Tennessee," 463.

31. "The New Campaign—Union Convention—Tennessee Clear of Rebels," *New York Times*, January 9, 1865.

32. Benjamin C. Truman, "The War in Tennessee," *New York Times*, January 1, 1865.

33. Schofield, *Forty-Six Years*, 250.

34. Richard W. Johnson, *Memoir of Maj.-Gen. George H. Thomas* (Philadelphia: J. B. Lippincott, 1881), 195.

35. "The New Campaign—Union Convention—Tennessee Clear of Rebels," *New York Times*, January 9, 1865.

36. Wiley Sword, *Embrace an Angry Wind: The Confederacy's Last Hurrah: Spring Hill, Franklin, and Nashville* (New York: HarperCollins, 1992), 379–380.

37. James H. Wilson, *Under the Old Flag: Recollections of Military Operations in the War for the Union, the Spanish War, the Boxer Rebellion, etc.* (New York: D. Appleton, 1912), 2:126–127.

38. Sam R. Watkins, *"Co. Aytch": A Confederate Soldier's Memoirs* (New York: Collier Books, 1962), 240.

39. Journal of the Fourth Army Corps, Pulaski, Tenn., *OR* 45, pt. 1, 161.

40. Ibid., 163. Historian Wiley Sword postulated that Thomas was "so embarrassed over this matter that he apparently attempted to cover up his involvement in the episode." Sword, *Embrace an Angry Wind*, 400. But Thomas's focus on the absence with Sherman of the "splendid pontoon train properly belonging to my command with its trained corps of pontoniers" was less an attempt to avoid or deflect criticism than what the Virginian would have deemed a lamentably necessary statement of fact under the circumstances. GHT report, Eastport, Miss., January 20, 1865, *OR* 45, pt. 1, 41.

41. Theodore Lyman, *Meade's Army: The Private Notebooks of Lt. Col. Theodore Lyman*, edited by David W. Lowe (Kent, Ohio: Kent State University Press, 2007), 310.

42. Geo. G. Meade to Brig. Gen. Rawlins, December 16, 1864—10 AM, *OR*, vol. 45, pt. 2, 212–213.

43. To Mrs. George G. Meade, Headquarters Army of the Potomac, December 18, 1864, in George Meade, *The Life and Letters of George Gordon Meade, Major-General United States Army*, edited by George Gordon Meade, 2 vols. (New York: Charles Scribner's Sons, 1913), 2:253.

44. A. Lincoln to GHT, Washington, D.C., December 16, 1864—11:30 AM, *OR*, vol. 45, pt. 2, 210; also in *Lincoln Papers*, VIII, 169.

45. General Orders No. 167, Near Nashville, Tenn., December 16, 1864, *OR*, vol. 45, pt. 1, 50.

46. Franklin, Tenn. Dec. 17th 1864, in Emerson Opdycke, *To Battle for God and the Right: The Civil War Letterbooks of Emerson Opdycke*, edited by Glenn V. Longacre and John E. Haas (Urbana: University of Illinois Press, 2003), 260.

47. Near Columbia, Tenn. Dec 21st, 1864, in ibid., 261.

48. James Alex Baggett, *Homegrown Yankees: Tennessee's Union Cavalry in the Civil War* (Baton Rouge: Louisiana State University Press, 2009), 308.

49. Undated newspaper clipping in Thomas Papers, Filson. A popular version of Hood's failed campaign appeared in the form of lyrics set to the tune of "Yellow Rose of Texas."

> "You may talk about your Beauregard
> And sing of General Lee,
> But the gallant Hood of Texas
> Played hell in Tennessee!"

Quoted in Charles P. Roland, *An American Iliad: The Story of the Civil War* (New York: McGraw-Hill, 1991), 241.

50. Chesnut, *Mary Chesnut's Civil War*, 694.

51. Anderson to My dear Genl., Cincinnati, Dec. 19th 1864, Anderson Papers, Filson.

52. Stanton to Maj. Gen. Dix, Washington, D.C., December 17, 1864—8:35 AM, *OR*, vol. 45, pt. 2, 227–228.

53. E. B. Long, *The Civil War: Day By Day: An Almanac 1861–1865* (Garden City, N.Y.: Doubleday, 1971), 611.

54. GHT report, January 20, 1865, *OR*, vol. 45, pt. 1, 40.

55. "Dec. 20, Thursday, [1865]," Allen Diary, Filson.

56. Lyon report, January 3, 1865, *OR*, vol. 45, pt. 1, 805.

57. Hylan B. Lyon, "Memoirs of Hylan B. Lyon, Brigadier General, C.S.A.," edited by Edward M. Coffman, *Tennessee Historical Quarterly* 18 (March 1959): 48 and 50; GHT report, January 20, 1865, ibid., 45–46.

58. Forrest report, *OR*, vol. 45, pt. 1, 756.

59. Charles H. Olmstead, "Rear Guard Service in Tennessee," 1, Charles H. Olmstead Papers, Georgia Historical Society, Savannah, Ga.

60. Grant to Sherman, Washington, D.C., December 18, 1864, *OR*, vol. 44, 740.

61. Alfred to My Dearest Mary, Chatt. Dec. 20th 1864, in Hough, *Soldier of the West*, 235.

62. Alfred to My Dearest Mary, Chattanooga Tenn. Christmas Morn, 1864, in ibid., 236.

63. GHT to Halleck, Near Spring Hill, December 19, 1864—8:30 PM, *OR*, vol. 45, pt. 2, 265. The conditions were indeed abysmal. One commander noted the deaths of two men who tried to cross a swollen watercourse on rafts. Nathan Kimball to Lieut. Col. J. S. Fullerton, December 18, 1864, ibid., 270.

64. "Dec. 19, Monday, [1865]," Allen Diary, Filson.

65. Benjamin C. Truman, "The War in Tennessee," *New York Times*, December 20, 1864.

66. "The New Campaign—Union Convention—Tennessee Clear of Rebels," ibid., January 9, 1865.

67. Tom to Dear Will, Hd. qrs. 12th Ky. V.V. Inf., Near Springhill Tenn Dec 21st 1864, Speed Letterbook, Filson.

68. Halleck to GHT, Washington, December 21, 1864—12 m., *OR*, vol. 45, pt. 2, 295.

69. GHT to Halleck, In the Field, December 21, 1864, ibid., 295–296.

70. Grant to E. M. Stanton, City Point, Va., December 20, 1864—10:30 AM, ibid., 283.

71. Stanton to GHT, Washington, December 22, 1864—9 PM, ibid., 307.

72. Ibid.

73. Grant to GHT, City Point, Va., December 22, 1864, ibid., 307.

74. T. Speed, Head Quarters 12th Ky V.V. Inf., Near Springfield Tenn Dec. 22nd 1864, Speed Letterbook, Filson.

75. Quoted in Thomas J. Morgan, *Reminiscences of Service with Colored Troops in the Army of the Cumberland, 1863–1865* (Providence: Soldiers and Sailors Historical Society of Rhode Island, 1885), 48.

76. "Brown, Russell Lasetor," in *Tennessee Civil War Veterans Questionnaires*, compiled by Gustavus W. Dyer and John Trotwood Moore, 5 vols. (Easley, S.C.: Southern Historical Press, 1985), 1:401–402.

77. T. Speed, Head Quarters 12th Ky V.V. Inf., Near Springfield Tenn Dec. 22nd 1864, Speed Papers, Filson.

78. Elisha Stockwell Jr., *Private Elisha Stockwell, Jr. Sees the War,* edited by Byron R. Abernathy (Norman: University of Oklahoma Press, 1958), 135–136.

79. Grant to Stanton, City Point, Va., December 23, 1864—6 PM, *OR*, vol. 45, pt. 2, 318.

80. Thomas B. Van Horne, *The Life of Major-General George H. Thomas* (New York: Charles Scribner's Sons, 1882), 371–372.

81. GHT to Edwin M. Stanton, McKane's Church, Pulaski Road, December 25, 1864—8 AM, *OR* 45, pt. 2, 342.

82. William T. Sherman, *Sherman's Civil War: Selected Correspondence of William T. Sherman, 1860–1865,* edited by Brooks D. Simpson and Jean V. Berlin (Chapel Hill: University of North Carolina Press, 1999), 779–780.

83. William Bluffton Miller, *Fighting for Liberty and Right: The Civil War Diary of William Bluffton Miller, First Sergeant, Company K, Seventy-fifth Indiana Volunteer Infantry* (Knoxville: University of Tennessee Press, 2005), 293.

84. Benjamin C. Truman, "The War in Tennessee," *New York Times*, January 1, 1865.

85. Brian Steel Wills, *A Battle from the Start: Nathan Bedford Forrest* (New York: Harper Collins, 1992), 291–293.

86. Quoted in Baggett, *Homegrown Yankees*, 310–312.

87. Near Lexington Alabama December 29th 1864, in Opdycke, *To Battle for God*, 264–265.

88. "Pap Thomas," undated newspaper clipping in Thomas Papers, Filson.

89. Reuben D. Mussey to Johnson, Lexington Ky Dec 29/64, *The Papers of Andrew Johnson*, edited by Leroy P. Graf (Knoxville: University of Tennessee Press, 1986), 7:366–367.

90. Quoted in Noah Andre Trudeau, *Like Men of War: Black Troops in the Civil War, 1862–1865* (New York: Little, Brown, 1998), 334–335.

91. GHT to Johnson, Hd Qrs D C [Pulaski] Dec 30 1864, *Johnson Papers*, 7:369.

92. Johnson to GHT, Nashville Tenn. Dec. 31st 1864, ibid., 371.

93. GHT to Halleck, Pulaski, Tenn., December 29, 1864—9 PM, *OR*, vol. 45, pt. 2, 402–403.

94. Halleck to Grant, Washington, December 30, 1864—1:30 PM, ibid., 419–420.

95. Grant to Halleck, City Point, December 30, 1864, ibid., 420.

96. General Orders No. 169, Pulaski, Tenn., December 29, 1864, *OR*, vol. 45, pt. 1, 50–51.

97. Halleck to GHT, Washington, December 31, 1864—11:30 AM, *OR*, vol. 45, pt. 2, 441.

98. Halleck to GHT, Washington, December 31, 1864—11:30 AM, ibid., 441.

99. GHT to Halleck, Pulaski, Tenn., December 31, 1864—8 PM, ibid., 442.

100. Grant to Sherman, Washington, D.C., January 21, 1865, *OR*, vol. 47, pt. 2, 101.

101. Donald B. Connelly, *John M. Schofield and the Politics of Generalship* (Chapel Hill: University of North Carolina Press, 2006), 148.

102. F. L. Thomas to My dear Col., Troy NY., Aug 29th 1881, Hough Papers, UCBL.

103 Schofield to Grant, Columbia, Tennessee, December 27, 1864, in *Forty-Six Years*, 253–254.

104. Schofield to Sherman, Columbia, Tennessee, December 28, 1864, in ibid., 254–255.

105. Ibid., 242.

106. *Daily Dispatch*, December 19, 1864.

107. Ibid., December 21, 1864.

108. Ibid., December 27, 1864.

109. Ibid., December 30, 1864.

110. "Hood's Campaign," *Sentinel*, December 28, 1864.

111. GHT to Halleck, Pulaski, Tenn., December 31, 1864—8 PM, *OR*, vol. 45, pt. 2. 441–442.

112. U. S. Grant to Sherman, City, Point, Va., March 16, 1865, *OR*, vol. 47, pt. 2, 859.

113. U. S. Grant to Sherman, City, Point, Va., March 16, 1865, ibid., 860.

114. John Russell Young, *Around the World with General Grant,* edited by Michael Fellman (Baltimore: Johns Hopkins University Press, 2002), 304.

115. Mrs. John A. Logan, *Reminiscences of a Soldier's Wife: An Autobiography* (New York: C. Scribner's Sons, 1913), 188.

116. Gilbert C. Kniffin, "The Life and Services of Major General George H. Thomas," in *War Papers Being Papers Read before the Commandery of the District of Columbia Military Order of the Loyal Legion of the United States,* vol. 1, *Papers 1–26. March 1887–April 1897* (Wilmington, N.C.: Broadfoot Publishing, 1993), 26.

117. Wood, "Address to comrades," n.d., Filson.

Chapter 14: A Different Kind of War (January–May 1865)

1. E. M. Stanton to GHT, Washington City, April 3, 1865—10 AM, *OR*, vol. 49, pt. 2, 197–198. The message contained the telegraphic message of President Lincoln. GHT to Stanton, Nashville, April 3, 1865—12 m., ibid., 198.

2. Sherman report, In the Field, Savannah, Ga., January 1, 1865, *OR*, vol. 44, 13.

3. Your friend and Left Arm to My Dear Ad, Huntsville, Ala., January 2, 1865, Wilson Papers, LOC. Thomas had already indicated his support of such a move to Wilson. See, for example, GHT to Wilson, Pulaski, January 1, 1865—5 PM, *OR*, vol. 45, pt. 2, 477.

4. S. P. Lee to GHT, Eastport, Miss., via Paducah, January 2, 1865, *ORN*, 27, 9.

5. GHT to S. P. Lee, Pulaski, January 2, 1865, ibid., 10.

6. Dudley Taylor Cornish and Virginia Jeans Laas, *Lincoln's Lee: The Life of Samuel Phillips Lee, United States Navy, 1812–1897* (Lawrence: University Press of Kansas, 1986), 150.

7. S. P. Lee to Gideon Welles, Clifton, Tenn., January 3, 1865, *ORN*, 27, 11.

8. John B. Jones, *A Rebel War Clerk's Diary at the Confederate States Capital* (Philadelphia: J. P. Lippincott, 1866), 471.

9. *Daily Dispatch*, December 30, 1864.

10. Q.P.F., "From Thomas's Army Where is Hood? Nashville, December 20," *Cincinnati Daily Commercial*, January 2, 1865.

11. GHT report, January 20, 1865, *OR*, vol. 45, pt. 1, 45–46; Hylan B. Lyon, "Memoirs of Hylan B. Lyon, Brigadier General, C.S.A.," edited by Edward M. Coffman, *Tennessee Historical Quarterly* 18 (March 1959): 35–53, 48. See also John Allan Wyeth, *Life of General Nathan Bedford Forrest* (New York: Harper & Brothers, 1899), 400–401, and Huntsville Alabama Jan 20th 1865, in Emerson Opdycke, *To Battle for God and the Right: The Civil War Letterbooks of Emerson Opdycke*, edited by Glenn V. Longacre and John E. Haas (Urbana: University of Illinois Press, 2003), 274.

12. GHT report, January 20, 1865, *OR*, vol. 45, pt. 1, 45–46.

13. William J. Palmer report, January 17, 1865, ibid., 800.

14. H. B. Lyon report, January 3, 1865, ibid., 806.

15. B. R. Roberson, "The Courthouse Burnin'est General," *Tennessee Historical Quarterly* 23 (Dec. 1964): 378.

16. GPT to Janet, Chattanooga Jany 16th 1865, Thruston Papers, Filson.

17. Ad to Dear Harry, 102 Madison Avenue, New York, Jan. 8, 1865, Wilson Papers, LOC.

18. Your friend to My Dear Ad., Gravelly Springs, Ala., Jan. 26, 1865, Wilson Papers, LOC. Both Wilson and Badeau were thoroughly enamored of Grant. "Grant is *sui generis*—has no equal, no successful imitator among his lieutenants in unselfish, true hearted devotion to duty. He excels them all in magnanimity and truthfulness. You must not look for the same virtues everywhere," ibid. See also James H. Wilson, *Under the Old Flag: Recollections of Military Operations in the War for the Union, the Spanish War, the Boxer Rebellion, etc.*, 2 vols. (New York: D. Appleton, 1912), 1:273–276.

19. Quoted in Larry J. Daniel, *Days of Glory: The Army of the Cumberland, 1861–1865* (Baton Rouge: Louisiana State University Press, 2004), 433.

20. S. P. Lee to Gideon Welles, Mound City, January 22, 1865, *ORN*, 27, 28.

21. Cornish and Laas, *Lincoln's Lee*, 150.

22. Halleck to Grant, Washington, D.C., January 18, 1865—4:30 PM, *OR*, vol. 45, pt. 2, 609.

23. Grant to Halleck, City Point, Va., January 18, 1865—9 PM, ibid., 609–610.

24. Sherman to GHT, In the Field, Savannah, Ga., January 21, 1865, ibid., 621–622.

25. GHT to Halleck, Eastport, Miss., January 21, 1865—noon, ibid., 620–621. Thomas would reiterate this same basic message three days later to Halleck. See GHT to Halleck, Eastport, Miss., January 24, 1865, ibid., 627–628.

26. GHT to Halleck, Eastport, Miss., January 21, 1865—noon, ibid., 620–621.

27. GHT to C. A. Dana, Eastport, Miss., January 21, 1865, ibid., 622.

28. Henry M. Cist to Col. C. R. Thornton, Eastport, Miss., January 22, 1865, ibid., 626.

29. Halleck to GHT, Washington, D.C., January 23, 1865, ibid., 627.

30. GHT to Halleck, Eastport, Miss., January 24, 1865, ibid., 627–628.

31. Chattanooga, Tenn. September 28th, 1864, in Opdycke, *To Battle for God*, 230–231.

32. Huntsville Al. January 11th 1865, in ibid., 271. Post later received the Medal of Honor for his actions at Nashville, ibid., 272.

33. Johnson Speech to Union State Convention, January 12, 1865, *The Papers of Andrew Johnson*, edited by Leroy P. Graf (Knoxville: University of Tennessee Press, 1986), 7:398.

34. Andrew Johnson to His Excellency A. Lincoln Prest U.S., Nashville Tenn Feby 7th 1865, ibid., 464.

35. "Letter from Gen. Thomas—A Testimonial Declined," *New York Times*, February 2, 1865.

36. Gates to My darling Mother, Chattanooga Feby 5 1865, Thruston Papers, Filson.

37. GHT to Charles H. Smith, Mayor of the City of Rome, Ga., James J. Winder, of the City Council, Rome and others, Louisville, Ky., February 9, 1865, RG 393, Entry 909, Dept. of the Cumberland, Letters Sent, NA.

38. GHT Report, Louisville, Ky., Sept. 30th 1867, AG, General's Papers, RG 94, Box 18, NA.

39. G.P.T. to My dear Mother, Nashville, Feby 28th 1865, Thruston Papers, Filson.

40. Alfred to My Dearest Mary, Nashville Sunday Feb 12/65, in Alfred Lacey Hough, *Soldier in the West: The Civil War Letters of Alfred Lacey Hough*, edited by Robert G. Athearn (Philadelphia: University of Pennsylvania Press, 1957), 238.

41. Gilbert C. Kniffin, "The Life and Services of Major General George H. Thomas," in *War Papers Being Papers Read before the Commandery of the District of Columbia Military Order of the Loyal Legion of the United States,* vol. 1, *Papers 1–26. March 1887–April 1897* (Wilmington, N.C.: Broadfoot Publishing, 1993), 17.

42. GHT to Senator Wilson, Nashville, Tenn., Feby 16th 1865, Hammond Papers, Filson. Also in *OR*, vol. 49, pt. 1, 726. General Wilson's February 3 recommendation of Hammond and Thomas's February 5 endorsement of it were included, Hammond Papers, Filson. See also *OR*, vol. 49 pt. 1, 638, without Thomas's endorsement recorded, and 661, which contained Wilson's letter of February 6 to the adjutant general of the Army. Thomas's appeal was successful as evidenced by documents in the *OR*. See, for example, Special Orders No. 56, Louisville, Ky., April 28, 1865, *OR*, vol. 49, pt. 2, 509.

43. George W. Cullum, *Biographical Register of the Officers and Graduates of the U.S. Military Academy at West Point, N.Y., from its Establishment, in 1802 and 1890, with the Early History of the United States Military Academy,* 2 vols. (Boston: Houghton, Mifflin, 1891), 2:35.

44. Grant to GHT, City Point, Va., Feby. 16th, 1865, Ulysses S. Grant Papers, Series 3, Box, 26, Folder 57, Ulysses S, Grant Papers, Mississippi State University, Starkville, Miss.

45. GHT to Grant, Hd. Qr. DC Nashville Mar 6 1865, Thomas Papers, DUL.

46. J. L. Donaldson to M. C. Meigs, Nashville, Tenn., March 20, 1865, *OR*, vol. 49, pt. 2, 35–36.

47. Donaldson to William D. Whipple, Nashville, Tenn., April 2, 1865, ibid., 187.

48. Z. B. Tower to GHT, Nashville, Tenn., April 4, 1865, ibid., 213–216; April 18, 1865, ibid., 390–393; April 28, 1865, ibid., 499–503; May 15, 1865, ibid., 775–781; May 25, 1865, ibid., 898–901; and June 10, 1865, ibid., 977–981.

49. Frank A. Palumbo, *George Henry Thomas: The Dependable General* (Dayton, Ohio: Morningside House, 1983), 277–278; James L. McDonough, *Nashville: The Western Confederacy's Final Gamble* (Knoxville: University of Tennessee Press, 2004), 133.

50. R. E. Lee to Lt. Gen. J. Longstreet, Hd. Qrs. ANV 11th March 1865, Lee Papers, VHS.

51. Grant to Sherman, City Point, Va., March 16, 1865, *OR*, vol. 47, pt. 2, 859–860.

52. WR Hackley to My Darling, Memphis Mch 12th 1865, in William Beverley Randolph Hackley, "The Letters of William Beverley Randolph Hackley: Treasury Agent in West Tennessee, 1863–1866," edited by Walter J. Fraser Jr. and Mrs. Pat C. Clark, *West Tennessee Historical Society Papers* 25 (1971): 102–103.

53. Halleck to GHT, Washington, D.C., March 19, 1865—11:30 AM, *OR*, vol. 49, pt. 2, 28; GHT to C. C. Washburn, Nashville, March 20, 1865—11 AM, ibid., 40.

54. GHT to E. Hatch, Nashville, March 31, 1865, ibid., 156.

55. Wm. D. Whipple to C. C. Washburn, Nashville, March 31, 1865, ibid., 168–169.

56. GHT to R. S. Granger, Nashville, April 3, 1865—3 PM, ibid., 204.

57. C. J. Walker to J. E. Harrison, Louisville, Ky., April 3, 1865, ibid., 206.

58. C. J. Walker to J. E. Harrison, Louisville, Ky., April 4, 1865, ibid., 225.

59. J. H. Wilson to GHT, Selma, Ala., April 4, 1865—10 AM, ibid., 217.

60. Emory M. Thomas, *The Confederacy as a Revolutionary Experience* (Englewood Cliffs, N.J.: Prentice-Hall, 1971), 87–88.

61. GHT to D. S. Stanley, Nashville, April [10], 1865, *OR*, vol. 49, pt. 2, 310.

62. Wm. D. Whipple to J. B. Steedman, Nashville, April 13, 1865, HL. See also *OR*, vol. 49, pt. 2, 345, with the same message sent to Knoxville and Memphis as well; Whipple to L. H. Rousseau, Nashville, Tenn., April 13, 1865, Thomas Papers, 346.

63. J. H. Wilson to GHT, Montgomery, Ala., April 13, 1865, ibid., 347.

64. G.P.T. [to Mother], Head-Quarters Department of the Cumberland, Nashville, April 7th, 1865, Thruston Letters, Filson.

65. Richard W. Johnson, *Memoir of Maj.-Gen. George H. Thomas* (Philadelphia: J. B. Lippincott, 1881), 236.

66. GHT to Johnson, April 15, 1865, *Johnson Papers*, 7:575. See also *OR*, vol. 49, pt. 2, 359.

67. GHT to E. M. Stanton, Nashville, April 15, 1865, *OR*, vol. 49, pt. 2, 359.

68. Johnson to GHT, Washington, April 17/65, *Johnson Papers*, 7:575. See also *OR*, vol. 49, pt. 2, 375.

69. GHT to Major General Wilson, Nashville, April 26, 1865, Telegrams Sent, RG 94, AG, Thomas, Box 3, NA.

70. GHT to Hon. E. M. Stanton, Nashville, April 27, 1865, ibid.

71. GHT to Major General Steedman, Chattanooga, Major General Washburne, Memphis, Brig. General Hatch, Eastport, Miss., Nashville, April 27, 186[5], ibid.

72. GHT to Major General Stoneman, Knoxville, Nashville, April 27, 1865, ibid.

73. GHT to Admiral S. P. Lee, Nashville, April 27, 1865, ibid.

74. GHT to Brig. Genl. R. W. Johnson, Nashville, April 29, 1865, ibid.

75. J. B. Fry to GHT, Washington D.C., April 29, 1865, in GHT to Major General J. B. Steedman, Chattanooga, Tenn., Major General Stoneman, Knoxville, Tenn., Major General Washburne, Memphis, Tenn., Nashville, April 30, 1865, ibid.

76. GHT to U. S. Grant, May 1, 1865, *ORN*, 27, 176.

77. GHT to Major General Stoneman, Knoxville, Major General Steedman, Chattanooga, Major General Washburne, Memphis, Major General Rousseau, Nashville, Brig. Genl. Ed. Hatch, Eastport, Miss., Brig. Genl. Meredith, Paducah, Ky., Colonel Smith, Clarksville, Tenn., Major General Palmer, Louisville, Ky., Brig. General Granger, Huntsville, Ala., and Colonel Gelfillin, Gallatin, Tenn., Nashville, May 1st 1865, Telegrams Sent, RG 94, AG, Thomas, Box 3, NA.

78. GHT to Brig. General Hatch, Nashville, May 2nd, 1865, ibid.

79. GHT to Adjutant General, Nashville, May 3rd, 1865, ibid.

80. GHT to Lieut. General U. S. Grant, Nashville, May 3rd, 1865, ibid.

81. GHT to Asa Seward, Nashville, May 3rd, 1865, ibid.

82. GHT to Major General Steedman, Nashville, May 5, 1865, ibid.

83. GHT to Major General E. R. S. Canby, Nashville, May 3rd, 1865, ibid.

84. U. S. Grant to GHT, Washington, May 6th/65 [1:00 PM], in Ulysses S. Grant, *The Papers of Ulysses S. Grant,* edited by John Y. Simon (Carbondale: Southern Illinois University Press, 1988), 15:17.

85. Wm. D. Whipple to Brig. Genl. R. W. Johnson, Nashville, May 6, 1865, Telegrams Sent, RG 94, AG, Thomas, Box 3, NA.

86. GHT to Brig. General R. S. Granger, Nashville, May 10, 1865, ibid.

87. GHT to Major General Steedman, Nashville, May 5, 1865, ibid.

88. GHT to Major General Washburne, Nashville, May 6, 1865, ibid.

89. Andrew Johnson to George H. Thomas, Washington May 6th 1865, and reply, *The Papers of Andrew Johnson*, edited by Paul H. Bergeron (Knoxville: University of Tennessee Press, 1989), 8:40.

90. See, for example, various telegrams between GHT and U. S. Grant, noted in *Grant Papers*, 15:67–69, and 81–84.

91. Camp Harker near Nashville, Tenn., May 10th 1865 in Opdycke, *To Battle for God*, 290.

92. "May 9th Tuesday, [1865]," Tilford Diary, Filson.

93. Daniel, *Days of Glory*, 433.

94. David S. Stanley, *Personal Memoirs of Major-General D. S. Stanley, U.S.A.* (Cambridge, Mass.: Harvard University Press, 1917), 226–227.

95. Camp Harker near Nashville, Tenn., May 10th 1865 in Opdycke, *To Battle for God*, 291.

96. General Orders No. 30, May 11, 1865, *OR*, vol. 49, pt. 2, 699–700.

97. GHT to Lieut. General U. S. Grant, Nashville, May 14, 1865, Telegrams Sent, RG 94, AG, Thomas, Box 3, NA.

98. GHT to Bvt. Maj. Genl J. H. Wilson, Nashville, May 14, 1865, ibid.

99. GHT to S. P. Lee, Nashville, May 16, 1865, *ORN*, 27, 203.

100. Camp Harker May 16th 1865, in Opdycke, *To Battle for God*, 292.

101. H. C. Whittemore to Major-General Milroy, Nashville, May 16, 1865, *OR*, vol. 49, pt. 2, 806.

102. Wm. D. Whipple to Stoneman, Nashville, May 30, 1865, ibid., 933. Ferguson was hanged in Nashville on October 20, 1865. For a complete treatment of Ferguson, see Brian D. McKnight, *Confederate Outlaw: Champ Ferguson and the Civil War in Appalachia* (Baton Rouge: Louisiana State University Press, 2011).

103. Camp Harker May 28th 1865, in Opdycke, *To Battle for God*, 292.

104. S. P. Lee to GHT, Mound City, May 19, 1865, *ORN*, 27, 213.

105. GHT to S. P. Lee, Nashville, May 20, 1865, ibid., 214.

106. S. P. Lee to Gideon Welles, Flagship Tempest, Mound City, June 29, 1865, ibid., 283. By the end of the next month the navy had settled the books with regard to the accounts of "the late U.S. steamers, *General Grant, General Sherman, General Thomas* and *General Burnside*," establishing their value at "an invoice price of $76,000 each." S. P. Lee Report, Mound City, July 27, 1865, ibid., 309.

107. WR Hackley to My Darling, Memphis May 28 1865, in "Hackley Letters," 104.

108. Thomas B. Van Horne, *History of the Army of the Cumberland Its Organization, Campaigns, and Battles, Written at the Request of Major-General George H. Thomas, Chiefly from His Private Military Journal and Official and Other Documents Furnished by Him* (Cincinnati: Robert Clarke, 1875), 1:xxv.

109. Ibid.

110. Ibid., xxvi.

Chapter 15: An Exasperating Peace (May 1865–December 1866)

1. "Recollections of Thomas," *Harpers New Monthly Magazine* 30, no. 180 (May 1865): 754–755 and 758.

2. William Bluffton Miller, *Fighting for Liberty and Right: The Civil War Diary of William Bluffton Miller, First Sergeant, Company K, Seventy-fifth Indiana Volunteer Infantry* (Knoxville: University of Tennessee Press, 2005), 339–340.

3. Francis F. McKinney, *Education in Violence: The Life of George H. Thomas and the History of the Army of the Cumberland* (Detroit: Wayne State University Press, 1961), 451.

4. Williams to My Dear Daughters, Near Washington, June 5th, 1865, in Alpheus S. Williams, *From the Cannon's Mouth: The Civil War Letters of General Alpheus S. Williams*, edited by Milo M. Quaife (Detroit: Wayne State University Press, 1959), 390–391.

5. Ibid., 391.

6. Lately Thomas, *The First President Johnson: The Three Lives of the Seventeenth President of the United States of America* (New York: William Morrow, 1968), 523–524. Johnson became angry because of the "despoiling" of his home and grounds, including their supposed use as a brothel, to which Thomas made inquiries and determined that as "abandoned property," the estate was under the jurisdiction of the Freedmen's Bureau, ibid.

7. Edwin M. Stanton to GHT, War Department, Washington City, June 7th, 1865, RG 94, General's Papers, Folder 11, NA. See also *OR*, vol. 49, pt. 2, 964.

8. Richard W. Johnson, *Memoir of Maj.-Gen. George H. Thomas* (Philadelphia: J. B. Lippincott, 1881), 232.

9. General Orders No. 41, Nashville, Tenn., June 19, 1865, *OR*, vol. 49, pt. 2, 1013–1014.

10. GHT to E. M. Stanton, Nashville, Tenn., June 22, 1865, ibid., 1022.

11. Stanton to GHT, Washington City, June 22, 1865, ibid.

12. General Orders No. 3, Nashville, Tenn., June 25, 1865, ibid., 1033–1034.

13. Stanton to GHT, Washington City, June 27, 1865, ibid., 1039.

14. General Orders No. 118, Washington, June 27, 1865, ibid., 1040–1041.

15. McKinney, *Education in Violence*, 452.

16. W. G. Brownlow to President Johnson, Nashville, June 8th, 1865, *The Papers of Andrew Johnson*, edited by Paul H. Bergeron (Knoxville: University of Tennessee Press, 1989), 8:200.

17. Lizzie to My dear Friend, Nashville, June 12th /65, ibid., 229. Lizzie also offered interesting political advice to Johnson following her comments about Thomas: "Do not give yourself into the hands of those ultra Northern men. Use them but remember that the south is your home," ibid.

18. GHT to Johnson, Nashville, July 20, 1865, ibid., 440.

19. Wilbur Thomas, *General George H. Thomas: The Indomitable Warrior* (New York: Exposition Press, 1964), 602.

20. Thomas B. Van Horne, *The Life of Major-General George H. Thomas* (New York: Charles Scribner's Sons, 1882), 457.

21. See Eric Foner, *Reconstruction: America's Unfinished Revolution 1863–1877* (New York: Harper & Row, 1988), 231–232 and 235–236.

22. Grant to GHT, Washington D.C., July 17th, 1865 [11:00 AM], in Ulysses S. Grant, *The Papers of Ulysses S. Grant*, edited by John Y. Simon (Carbondale: Southern Illinois University Press, 1988), 15:268–269.

23. U. S. Grant to Edwin Stanton, August 14, 1865, 6:30 PM, ibid., 308.

24. U. S. Grant to GHT, Galena, Ills., Aug. 21st 1865, ibid., 307–308. Editor John Y. Simon identifies *OR*, vol. 49, pt. 2, 1106, which is dated August 26, as "misdated," ibid., 308.

25. GHT to U. S. Grant, Aug. 23, 1865, ibid.

26. Jno. Overton to His Excellency, Andrew Johnson, Nashville, May 6th/65, *Johnson Papers*, 8:39–40.

27. Frank C. Dunnington to My dear Sir, Nashville, Nov. 2, 1865, *The Papers of Andrew Johnson*, edited by Paul H. Bergeron (Knoxville: University of Tennessee Press, 1991), 9:326–328.

28. Ibid., 328. Even with the action of the president, a resolution to the Overton question

did not occur until 1866. W. G. Brownlow to Sir, Nashville, Nov. 20th 1865 and notes, ibid., 405–406.

29. Benjamin H. Grierson, *A Just and Righteous Cause: Benjamin H. Grierson's Civil War Memoir,* edited by Bruce J. Dinges and Shirley A. Leckie (Carbondale: Southern Illinois University Press, 2008), 345.

30. GHT to Andrew Johnson, Nashville Sept 7th 1865, *Johnson Papers*, 9:41.

31. Stanton to Andrew Johnson, August 21st 1865, *Johnson Papers*, 8:637–638.

32. Johnson to GHT, Executive Office, Washington, D.C., July 20th, 1865, ibid., 440.

33. Andrew Johnson to GHT, Washington, D.C., Sept. 8th 1865, *Johnson Papers*, 9:48–49. See also *OR*, vol. 49, pt. 2, 1111.

34. GHT, Nashville Sept 9 1865, ibid., 57. See also *OR*, vol. 49, pt. 2, 1112.

35. GHT to U. S. Grant, Sept. 11, 1865, in *Grant Papers*, 15:309.

36. GHT to U. S. Grant, Sept. 13, 1865, ibid.

37 U. S. Grant to GHT, Springfield, Ill., Sept. 13, 10:00 AM, ibid.

38. Walter L. Fleming, *Civil War and Reconstruction in Alabama* (New York: Peter Smith, 1949), 24. Charles Reagan Wilson discussed Wilmer as part of his examination of religion and the Lost Cause of the Confederacy, *Baptized in Blood: The Religion of the Lost Cause, 1865–1920* (Athens: University of Georgia Press, 1980), 42.

39. S. D. McConnell, *History of the American Episcopal Church* (New York: Thomas Whittaker, 1904), 371–373.

40. Van Horne, *Life of General Thomas*, 409–410.

41. Ibid.

42. Fleming, *Civil War and Reconstruction in Alabama*, 327–329. The full text of the Thomas order of December 29, 1865, appeared in "Bishop Wilmer's Case," *New York Times*, January 7, 1866.

43. William Stevens Perry, *The History of the American Episcopal Church, 1587–1883* (Boston: James R. Osgood, 1885), 587–588.

44, See Daniel W. Stowell, "'We Have Sinned and God Has Smitten Us!': John H. Caldwell and the Religious Meaning of Confederate Defeat," *Georgia Historical Quarterly* 78, no. 1 (Spring 1994): 1–38.

45. George W. Cullum, *Biographical Register of the Officers and Graduates of the U.S. Military Academy at West Point, N.Y., from its Establishment, in 1802 and 1890, with the Early History of the United States Military Academy,* 2 vols. (Boston: Houghton, Mifflin, 1891), 2:35.

46. GHT to Stanton, Nashville, Tenn., December 12, 1865, in Brooks D. Simpson, Leroy P. Graf, and John Muldowney, *Advice after Appomattox: Letters to Andrew Johnson, 1865–1866* (Knoxville: University of Tennessee Press, 1987), 239–240.

47. Jno. B. Wilgus to GHT, Lexington, Ky., Oct, 24th 1865, Thomas Papers, DUL.

48. GHT to Dear Buell, Nashville, Tenn., Decr 13, 1865, Buell Papers, Filson.

49. James E. Sefton, *The United States Army and Reconstruction 1865–1877* (Baton Rouge: Louisiana State University Press, 1967), 62.

50. Garfield set the date at "1866," James A. Garfield, *Oration on the Life and Character of Gen. George H. Thomas Delivered before the Society of the Army of the Cumberland* (Cincinnati: Robert Clarke, 1871), 37; Ephraim A. Otis did not provide a time frame for the occasion, "General George H. Thomas," in *Military Essays and Recollections Papers Read before the Commandery of the State of Illinois, Military Order of the Loyal Legion of the United States* (Chicago: A. C. McClurg, 1891), 418; Einholf put the time in December 1865, Christopher J. Einholf, *George Thomas: Virginian for the Union* (Norman: University of Oklahoma Press, 2007), 306.

51. GHT Report, Louisville, Ky., November 12th, 1866, AG, General's Papers, RG 94, Box 18, NA.

52. Theodore S. Bowers to Sherman, January 22, 1866—9:50 AM; Bowers to Meade and Bowers to Thomas, January 24, 1866, Ulysses S. Grant, *The Papers of Ulysses S. Grant,* edited by John Y. Simon (Carbondale: Southern Illinois University Press, 1988), 16:42.

53. Grant to Stanton, January 29, 1866, ibid., 38.

54. Grant to U.S. Senator Henry Wilson, February 1, 1866, ibid., 42–43.

55. Sherman, Meade, and GHT to John A. Rawlins, February 1, 1866, ibid., 42–45. Grant sent Wilson the suggested changes for the third bill on February 2, ibid., 44–45.

56. Grant to Stanton, Washington Feby 8th 1866, ibid., 49.

57. Grant to Johnson, Washington, D.C., Feby. 9th, 1866, ibid., 52–53.

58. Robert M. Patton to GHT, December 30, 1865, and GHT endorsement, January 1, 1866, ibid., 54.

59. Grant endorsement, January 9, 1866, ibid.

60. Alvan C. Gillem to Dear Sir, Chattanooga, Tenn., Feb. 13, 1866, *The Papers of Andrew Johnson*, edited by Paul H. Bergeron (Knoxville, University of Tennessee Press, 1992), 10:90–91.

61. Bland Ballard to Dear Sir, Louisville, Ky., Apr. 28th 1866, ibid., 458–460.

62. General Orders No. 5½, Nashville, Tenn., February 13th, 1866, *General Orders, Military Division of the Tennessee, 1866*, USMAL.

63. Timothy B. Smith, *The Golden Age of Battlefield Preservation: The Decade of the 1890s and the Establishment of America's First Five Military Parks* (Knoxville: University of Tennessee Press, 2008), 20.

64. General Orders No. 8, Nashville, Tenn., April 10th, 1866, *General Orders, Military Division of the Tennessee, 1866*, USMAL.

65. "From Nashville," *Cincinnati Daily Enquirer*, May 31, 1866. It may well have been that the organization did not prove successful or that any benefits were short-lived, and thus little is known beyond the existence of the group.

66. Foner, *Reconstruction*, 261–262; Sefton, *U.S. Army and Reconstruction*, 82–83; George C. Rable, *But There Was No Peace: The Role of Violence in the Politics of Reconstruction* (Athens: University of Georgia Press, 1984), 33–42.

67. Grant to GHT, Washington, D.C., July 6th, 1866, *Grant Papers*, 16:230–231.

68. GHT Report, Louisville, Ky., November 12th, 1866, AG, General's Papers, RG 94, Box 18, NA.

69. Rable set the number of troops available "to use against the rioters" at 150, *But There Was No Peace*, 40.

70. Alvan C. Gillem to Dear Sir, Nashville Tenn June 29, 1866, *Johnson Papers*, 10:637.

71. Foner, *Reconstruction*, 262–263; Sefton, *U.S. Army and Reconstruction*, 84–86; Rable, *But There Was No Peace*, 43–58.

72. General Orders No. 44, [July 6, 1866], *Grant Papers*, 16:228.

73. Grant to GHT, Washington, D.C., July 6th, 1866, ibid., 230.

74. GHT to Grant, July 14, 1866, ibid., 243.

75. July 17, Tuesday [1866], Gideon Welles, *Diary of Gideon Welles, Secretary of the Navy under Lincoln and Johnson,* 3 vols. (Boston: Houghton Mifflin, 1911), 2:554–555.

76. Stanton to Grant, July 17, 1866, *Grant Papers*, 16:243. Welles noted the discrepancy in time and recorded the president as observing, "Yet, it does seem to have been some time on the way for a telegram," July 19, Thursday [1866], Welles, *Diary*, 2:557.

77. Grant to GHT, Washington, D.C. July 18th 186[6] [1:50 PM], *Grant Papers*, 16:243.

78. Sefton, *U.S. Army and Reconstruction*, 101.

79. Brooks D. Simpson, *Let Us Have Peace: Ulysses S. Grant and the Politics of War and Reconstruction, 1861–1868* (Chapel Hill: University of North Carolina Press, 1991), 201.

80. Ibid., 290.

81. GHT endorsement, August 3, 1866, *Grant Papers*, 16:536.

82. GHT Report, Louisville, Ky., November 12th, 1866, AG, General's Papers, RG 94, Box 18, NA.

83. Richard W. Johnson, *Memoir of Maj.-Gen. Thomas*, 233; McKinney, *Education in Violence*, 464.

84. Simpson, *Let Us Have Peace*, 201.

85. Sefton, *U.S. Army and Reconstruction*, 91.

86. William F. G. Shanks, *Personal Recollections of Distinguished Generals* (New York: Harper & Brothers, 1866), 63.

87. General Orders No. 84, October 4, 1866, *OR*, vol. III, 5, 1007–1009.

88. John Cimprich, "A Critical Moment and Its Aftermath for George H. Thomas," in *The Moment of Decision: Biographical Essays on American Character and Regional Identity*, edited by Randall M. Miller and John R. McKivigan (Westport, Conn.: Greenwood Press, 1994), 178.

89. James Guthrie to Sir, Louisville, Nov. 8th 1866, *The Papers of Andrew Johnson*, edited by Paul H. Bergeron (Knoxville: University of Tennessee Press, 1994), 11:430–431.

90. Stanton to GHT, Nov. 15, 1866, quoted in ibid., 431.

91. S. B. Franks to Sir, Woodbury, Cannon Co., Tenn, September 10th, 1866, ibid., 202–203.

92. GHT Report, Louisville, Ky., November 12th, 1866, AG, General's Papers, RG 94, Box 18, NA.

93. GHT Report, Louisville, Ky., Sept. 30th 1867, ibid.

94. Elvero Persons, "General George H. Thomas," *Christian Advocate* (1866–1905), April 19, 1894, 249.

95. J. G. Parkhurst to Mr. President Detroit Aug 19, 1867, *The Papers of Andrew Johnson*, edited by Paul H. Bergeron (Knoxville: University of Tennessee Press, 1995), 12:497.

96. William Passmore Carlin, *The Memoirs of William Passmore Carlin, U.S.A.*, edited by Robert I. Girardi and Nathaniel Cheairs Hughes Jr. (Lincoln: University of Nebraska Press, 1999), 123.

97. John M. Schofield, *Forty-Six Years in the Army* (New York: Century, 1897), 292.

98. "The Thomas Medal," *New York Times*, December 6, 1866.

Chapter 16: Final Stages (1867–1868)

1. Brooks D. Simpson, *Let Us Have Peace: Ulysses S. Grant and the Politics of War and Reconstruction, 1861–1868* (Chapel Hill: University of North Carolina Press, 1991), 188.

2. GHT Report, Louisville, Ky., Sept. 30th 1867, AG, General's Papers, RG 94, Box 18, NA.

3. Richard W. Johnson, *Memoir of Maj.-Gen. George H. Thomas* (Philadelphia: J. B. Lippincott, 1881), 242–243.

4. Thomas B. Van Horne, *The Life of Major-General George H. Thomas* (New York: Charles Scribner's Sons, 1882), 424.

5. Ibid., 427.

6. Alexander McClure, *Lincoln and Men of War-Times: Some Personal Recollections of War and Politics during the Lincoln Administration* (Philadelphia: Times Publishing, 1892), 370.

7. GHT to D. W. C. Senter, Louisville, March 4, 1867, in "Gen. Thomas Declines to be a Candidate for the Presidency," *New York Times*, March 10, 1867.

8. GHT to Cist, Louisville, Ky., March 11, 1867, printed in William H. Lambert, *George Henry Thomas: Oration before the Society of the Army of the Cumberland, at Rochester, N.Y., September 17, 1884* (Cincinnati: Robert Clarke, 1885), 40–41.

9. GHT to Cist, Louisville, Ky., April 8, 1867, printed in ibid., 41.

10. John Watts De Peyster, *Sketch of George H. Thomas from Representative Men* (New York: Atlantic Publishing, 1875), 559; Coppée, *General Thomas*, 295.

11. Francis F. McKinney, *Education in Violence: The Life of George H. Thomas and the History of the Army of the Cumberland* (Detroit: Wayne State University Press, 1961), 7.

12. Richard W. Johnson, *Memoir of Maj.-Gen. Thomas*, 234.

13. Alfred to My Dearest Mary, Head-Quarters Department of the Cumberland, Office of Commissary Musters, Chattanooga Nov 18 1863, in Alfred Lacey Hough, *Soldier in the West: The Civil War Letters of Alfred Lacey Hough*, edited by Robert G. Athearn (Philadelphia: University of Pennsylvania Press, 1957), 170.

14. Allan Peskin, *Garfield: A Biography* (Kent, Ohio: Kent State University Press, 1978), 209. Of Chickamauga, Peskin noted, "Garfield's admiration for Thomas from that day on amounted to hero-worship. He thought him the strongest general of the war," ibid.

15. Alfred to My Dearest Mary, Head-Quarters Department of the Cumberland, Office of Commissary Musters, Nashville, Tenn. July 3rd, 1864, in Hough, *Soldier in the West*. 203.

16. U. S. Grant to GHT, Washington, Apl. 30th 1867, Cooke Family Papers, VHS; Ulysses S. Grant, *The Papers of Ulysses S. Grant,* edited by John Y. Simon (Carbondale: Southern Illinois University Press, 1991), 17:135.

17. U. S. Grant to Hon. E. M. Stanton, Long Branch, N.J. July 23d 1867, *Grant Papers*, 17:236.

18. U. S. Grant to GHT, July 23, 1867, ibid., 237.

19. GHT to U. S. Grant, July 24, 1867, ibid.

20. GHT Report, Louisville, Ky., Sept. 30th 1867, AG, General's Papers, RG 94, Box 18, NA.

21. GHT to U. S. Grant, August 6, 1867, in *Grant Papers,* 17:238–239.

22. GHT Report, Louisville, Ky., Sept. 30th 1867, AG, General's Papers, RG 94, Box 18, NA.

23. Roy Morris Jr., *Sheridan: The Life and Wars of General Phil Sheridan* (New York: Crown Publishers, 1992), 291.

24. William S. McFeely, *Grant: A Biography* (New York: W. W. Norton, 1981), 261.

25. U. S. Grant to His Excellency, A. Johnson, Washington, D.C., Aug. 17th 1867, *Grant Papers*, 17:276.

26. Grant to Sir, Washington, D.C., Aug. 17th 1867, *The Papers of Andrew Johnson*, edited by Paul H. Bergeron (Knoxville: University of Tennessee Press, 1995), 12:489.

27. Andrew Johnson to Grant, Aug. 19, *Grant Papers*, 17:280–281. See also Johnson to Grant, Washington, D.C., Aug. 19 1867, *Johnson Papers*, 12:494–496.

28. U. S. Grant to GHT, Aug. 17, 3:00 PM, *Grant Papers*, 17:281.

29. James E. Sefton, *The United States Army and Reconstruction 1865–1877* (Baton Rouge: Louisiana State University Press, 1967), 157.

30. R. King Cutler to Mr. President, No. 27 Indiana Ave., August 20, 1867, *Johnson Papers*, 12:497–499.

31. Bvt. Lt. Col. Alexander B. Hasson to GHT, Louisville, Aug. 21, 11:30 AM, *Grant Papers*, 17:282.

32. GHT to Grant, Lewisburg, West Va., Aug. 22, ibid.

33. "Aug. 24, 1867," in W. G. Moore, "Notes of Colonel W. G. Moore, Private Secretary to President Johnson, 1866–1868," edited by St. George L. Sioussat, *American Historical Review* 19, no. 1 (Oct. 1913): 111.

34. Andrew Johnson to Sir, Washington, D.C. Aug 26th 1867, *Johnson Papers*, 12:511.

35. Johnson to GHT, Aug 23, 1867, ibid., 511–-512. The President and his interim secretary of war traded shots a final time on the Thomas/Sheridan business. Both resolved to hold their ground, which for Johnson was rapidly eroding from under him. See U. S. Grant to Sir, Washington, Aug. 26th 1867, and Johnson to Grant, Aug. 27, 1867, ibid., 512–513.

36. Henry Coppée, *General Thomas* (New York: D. Appleton, 1893), 296–297.

37. GHT to My dear Colonel, Louisville, Ky., Nov. 8th, 1867, Thomas Papers, Filson.

38. GHT to Adjutant General, Louisville, Ky., Sept. 24th 1867, in GHT Report, Sept. 30th 1867, NA.

39. Ben H. Severance, "Reconstruction Power Play: The 1867 Mayoral Election in Nashville, Tennessee," in *Sister States, Enemy States: The Civil War in Kentucky and Tennessee,* edited by Kent T. Dollar, Larry H. Whiteaker, and W. Calvin Dickinson (Lexington: University Press of Kentucky, 2009), 326.

40. Thos. Duncan to GHT, Nashville, Tenn., Sepr. 21, 67, in GHT Report, Sept. 30th 1867.

41. A. L. Hough to Duncan, Sepr. 24th, 1867, in ibid.

42. Grant to GHT, Washington DC, Sepr. 24th 1867 3:30 PM, in ibid.

43. GHT to Grant, Louisville, Ky., Sept. 25th 1867, in ibid.

44. Ben H. Severance, *Tennessee's Radical Army: The State Guard and Its Role in Reconstruction, 1867–1869* (Knoxville: University of Tennessee Press, 2005), 163. Severance repeated the assertion in "Reconstruction Power Play," 327–328.

45. September 27, Friday [1867], Gideon Welles, *Diary of Gideon Welles, Secretary of the Navy under Lincoln and Johnson,* 3 vols. (Boston: Houghton Mifflin, 1911), 3:212.

46. GHT to Grant, Nashville, Tenn., Sept. 26th 1867, 3 PM, in GHT Report, Sept. 30th 1867, NA.

47. Grant to GHT, Washington, D.C., 26 4 PM, 1867, in ibid.

48. GHT Report, Sept. 30th 1867, NA.

49. Grant to GHT, Washington, D.C., 26th 1867, 9 PM, in ibid.

50. GHT Report, Sept. 30th 1867, NA.

51. Mayor Brown to GHT, Sepr. 27th 1867, in ibid.

52. September 27, Friday [1867], Welles, *Diary*, 3:211–212.

53. W. Matt Brown [to Johnson], Nashville Tenn Sept 27 1867, *The Papers of Andrew Johnson*, edited by Paul H. Bergeron (Knoxville: University of Tennessee Press, 1996), 13:115–116.

54. GHT to Grant, 11 AM, Nashville, Tenn., Sepr. 27, 67, in GHT Report, Sept. 30th 1867, NA.

55. GHT to Mayor Brown, Nashville, Sepr. 27, 1867, in ibid.

56. GHT Report, Sept. 30th 1867, NA.

57. Special Order No. 147, Sepr. 27, 1867, in ibid.

58. GHT to Grant, 12 M., Nashville, Sepr. 28, 1867, in ibid.; Severance, "Reconstruction Power Play," 328 and 336. Severance attributed the State Guard's actions to an "agreement" between Thomas and Cooper, *Tennessee's Radical Army*, 163.

59. GHT Report, Sept. 30th 1867, NA.

60. GHT to Mayor Brown, Sepr. 28th 1867, in ibid.

61. Mayor Brown to GHT, 12 O'clock, Nashville, Sepr. 28, 1867, in ibid.

62. GHT to Grant, 5 PM, Nashville, Sepr. 28, 1867, in ibid.

63. GHT Report, Sept. 30th 1867, NA.

64. Severance, "Reconstruction Power Play," 329. The withdrawn Matt Brown tallied three votes, ibid.

65. GHT to My dear Colonel, Louisville, Ky., Nov. 8th, 1867, Thomas Papers, Filson.

66. GHT to My Dear Mr. Gibbs, Louisville, Ky., Nov. 18, 1867, Yale.

67. John Tyler Jr., to Mr. President, Washington City Novr. 26 1867, *Johnson Papers*, 13:263.

68. De Peyster, *Sketch of George H. Thomas From Representative Men*, 571.

69. "Febry 21, 1868," in Moore, "Notes of Colonel W. G. Moore," 120.

70. GHT to Johnson, Louisville Ky February 22, 1868, *Johnson Papers*, 13:586–587.

71. GHT to B. F. Wade, Louisville, February 22, 1868, in Edward McPherson, *The Political History of the United States of America during the Period of Reconstruction, (From April 15, 1865, to July 15, 1870,) Including a Classified Summary of the Legislation of the Thirty-Ninth, Fortieth, and Forty-First Congresses with the Votes Thereon; Together with the Action, Congressional, and State, on the Fourteenth and Fifteenth Amendments to the Constitution of the United States, and the Other Important Executive, Legislative, Politico-Military, and Judicial Facts of that Period,* 2nd ed. (New York: Negro Universities Press, 1969), 346.

72. Richard W. Johnson, *Memoir of Maj.-Gen. Thomas*, 232–233.

73. F. L. Thomas to My dear Col., Troy NY, Aug 29th 1881, Hough Papers, UCBL.

74. GHT to My dear Ramsey, Louisville, Ky., Feby. 17, 1868, Thomas Papers, Filson.

75. GHT to Dear Colonel, Louisville, Ky., March 7, 1868, Author's Personal Collection.

76. R. A. Bennett and Wm. Wright to Sir, Gallatin, Tenn., July 31st 1868, *The Papers of Andrew Johnson*, edited by Paul H. Bergeron (Knoxville: University of Tennessee Press, 1997), 14:461.

77. Jno W Leftwich to My Dear Mr President, Memphis, Tenn., Aug 7th 1868, ibid., 487.

78. GHT to Dear Colonel, Louisville, Ky., Augt. 1, 1868, Thomas Papers, Filson.

79. GHT to Dear Colonel, Louisville, Ky., May 14, 1868, Thomas Papers, Filson.

80. Francis MacDonnell, "The Confederate Spin on Winfield Scott and George Thomas," *Civil War History* 45, no. 4 (Dec. 1998): 262.

81. GHT to S. A. Letcher, August 11, 1868, HL.

82. MacDonnell, *Confederate Spin*, 262–263. Einholf used similar language and logic to assess the exchange. Christopher J. Einholf, *George Thomas: Virginian for the Union* (Norman: University of Oklahoma Press, 2007), 345–346.

83. GHT to Wm. R. Plum, Louisville, Ky., August 11, 1868, HL. In the text of the letter Thomas struck out the word "especially" with a line.

84. Mary M. Furguson to Johnson, Mount Hope [Tenn.], Sept. 4/68, *The Papers of Andrew Johnson*, edited by Paul H. Bergeron (Knoxville: University of Tennessee Press, 1999), 15:15.

85. GHT to Dear Colonel, Louisville, Ky., Sept. 11, 1868, Thomas Papers, Filson.

86. Of the numerous references to staff members appearing in various reports from General Thomas found in the *Official Records*, see especially General Orders No. 20, Nashville, Tenn., April 10, 1865, which featured Robert H. Ramsey as assistant adjutant-general, S. C. Kellogg as aide-de-camp, A. J. Mackay as chief quartermaster, J. G. Parkhurst as provost-marshal general. Other prominent names included William D. Whipple and Henry M. Cist, both also listed as assistant adjutant-general, J. P. Willard, aide-de-camp, G. P. Thruston, acting judge-advocate, and A. L. Hough, chief commissary of musters, *OR*, vol. 49, pt. 2, 308–309, and General Orders No. 3, Nashville, Tenn., June 25, 1865, ibid., 1033–1034.

87. GHT to Dear Colonel, Louisville, Ky., October 5, 1868, Thomas Papers, Filson.

88. GHT to Dear Colonel, Louisville, Ky., December 21, 1868, Thomas Papers, Filson.

89. GHT to Dear Colonel, Decr 23, 1868, Thomas Papers, Filson.

90. GHT to Dear Colonel, Louisville, Ky., December 26th 1868, Thomas Papers, Filson.

Chapter 17: Thomas's Last Battles (1869–1870)

1. Thomas B. Van Horne, *The Life of Major-General George H. Thomas* (New York: Charles Scribner's Sons, 1882), preface.

2. Thomas B. Van Horne, *History of the Army of the Cumberland Its Organization, Campaigns, and Battles, Written at the Request of Major-General George H. Thomas, Chiefly from His Private Military Journal and Official and Other Documents Furnished by Him* (Cincinnati: Robert Clarke, 1875), 1:xxv.

3. John Watts De Peyster, *Sketch of George H. Thomas from Representative Men* (New York: Atlantic Publishing, 1875), 575.

4. Freeman Cleaves, *Rock of Chickamauga: The Life of George H. Thomas* (Norman: University of Oklahoma Press, 1948), 300.

5. William T. Sherman, *Memoirs of General William T. Sherman* (New York: Charles L. Webster, 1892), 2:439–440. Thomas biographer Francis McKinney expressed his "grave doubt that Sherman reported correctly the details of their conversations," *Education in Violence: The Life of George H. Thomas and the History of the Army of the Cumberland* (Detroit: Wayne State University Press, 1961), 467. McKinney's conjecture was strong circumstantially given that Sherman recorded only one aspect of the range of topics the men were supposed to have discussed.

6. GHT Testimony, Washington, D.C., January 30, 1869, Army Organization, 40th Congress, 3rd Session, 113.

7. Ibid., 114.

8. Ibid., 115.

9. Ibid., 116.

10. GHT to Dear Colonel, Washington D.C., February 1, 1869, Hough Papers, UCBL.

11. GHT to Dear Colonel, Washington, D.C., February 10, 1869, Hough Papers, UCBL.

12. Ibid.

13. Van Horne, *Life of General Thomas*, 433–434.

14. GHT to Dear Colonel, Washington, D.C., March 2nd 1869, Hough Papers, UCBL.

15. GHT to J. S. Hale, Washington D.C., March 8, 1869, in Donn Piatt, *Memories of the Men Who Saved the Union* (New York: Belford, Clarke, 1887), 297.

16. Sherman, *Memoirs*, 2:439–440.

17. Ibid., 440.

18. Ibid., 440–441.

19. Cleaves, *Rock of Chickamauga*, 302–303.

20. GHT to Dear Hough, Washington, DC, March 16, 1869, Hough Papers, UCBL.

21. Van Horne, *Life of General Thomas*, 434.

22. GHT to Dear Hough, Washington, DC, March 16, 1869, Hough Papers, UCBL.

23. Van Horne, *Life of General Thomas*, 434.

24. GHT to Dear Hough, Washington, DC, March 16, 1869, Hough Papers, UCBL.

25. Donald B. Connelly, *John M. Schofield and the Politics of Generalship* (Chapel Hill: University of North Carolina Press, 2006), 148.

26. James Lee McDonough, *Schofield: Union General in the Civil War and Reconstruction* (Tallahassee: Florida State University Press, 1972), 191.

27. John M. Schofield, *Forty-Six Years in the Army* (New York: Century, 1897), 277.

28. GHT to Col. R. H. Ramsey, Washington DC, March 22, 1869, HL.

29. GHT to Dear Colonel, Louisville, Ky., May 12, 1869, Thomas Papers, Filson.

30. GHT to Dear Colonel, Washington D.C., April 5, 1869, Hough Papers, UCBL.

31. GHT to Dear Colonel, Washington D.C., April 14, 1869, Hough Papers, UCBL.

32. Cleaves, *Rock of Chickamauga*, 303.

33. General Orders No. 21, Head Quarters Military Division of the Pacific, San Francisco, Cal., June 1, 1869, RG 393, pt. 1, Entry 3691, NA.

34. General Orders No. 22, Head Quarters Military Division of the Pacific, San Francisco, Cal., June 1, 1869, RG 393, pt. 1, Entry 3691, NA.

35. Donn Piatt and Henry V. Boynton, *General George H. Thomas: A Critical Biography* (Cincinnati: Robert Clarke, 1893), 649. McKinney described the event as "a dinner in his honor" and explained that the revelations came in the form of a "conversation" that occurred during the meal, in *Education in Violence*, 469. Several biographers used the term "banquet" to characterize the setting for the Thomas-Halleck discussion. See, for example, Frank A. Palumbo, *George Henry Thomas: The Dependable General* (Dayton, Ohio: Morningside House, 1983), 382 and 388; Wilbur Thomas, *General George H. Thomas: The Indomitable Warrior* (New York: Exposition Press, 1964), 615; John F. Marszalek, *Commander of All Lincoln's Armies: A Life of General Henry W. Halleck* (Cambridge, Mass.: Belknap Press of Harvard University Press, 2004), 238, 239, and 244.

36. "The Battle of Nashville Affairs," *Cincinnati Commercial*, February 8, 1870. Marszalek made a point that Halleck took it upon himself to assist in whatever corrective measures might be necessary in setting historical records straight regarding Thomas, Schofield, and the 1864 Nashville Campaign. Marszalek explained of Halleck, "When he tried to right a historical wrong, however, he ended up making trouble for himself." Ironically, many of Halleck's views regarding Reconstruction were similar to those of Thomas. Both thought white Southerners should show more remorse and less stubbornness in their attitudes, particularly in public displays of Confederate flags and ministers' insistence on omitting the prayer for the president of the United States. An important distinction was that Thomas's views on race were much more far-reaching than Halleck's. Marszalek, *Commander of All Lincoln's Armies*, 230–231 and 239.

37. Van Horne, *Life of General Thomas*, 440.

38. Erasmus D. Keyes, *Fifty Years' Observation of Men and Events Civil and Military* (New York: Charles Scribner's Sons, 1884), 167.

39. General Orders No. 23, Head Quarters Military Division of the Pacific, San Francisco, Cal., June 1, 1869, RG 393, pt. 1, Entry 3691, NA.

40. General Orders No. 26, Head Quarters Military Division of the Pacific, San Francisco, Cal., June 17, 1869, ibid.

41. General Orders No. 27, Head Quarters Military Division of the Pacific, San Francisco, Cal., June 29, 1869, ibid.

42. General Orders No. 28, Head Quarters Military Division of the Pacific, San Francisco, Cal., June 30, 1869, ibid.

43. Richard W. Johnson, *Memoir of Maj.-Gen. George H. Thomas* (Philadelphia: J. B. Lippincott, 1881), 238.

44. James Pickett Jones, *John A. Logan: Stalwart Republican from Illinois* (Tallahassee: University Presses of Florida, 1982), 40–41.

45. "Army Reduction," *Cincinnati Commercial*, March 29, 1870.

46. George Crook, *General George Crook: His Autobiography,* edited by Martin F. Schmitt (Norman: University of Oklahoma Press, 1946), 160.

47. Cleaves, *Rock of Chickamauga*, 303.

48. Special Orders No. 100, San Francisco, Cal., June 15, 1869, RG 393, pt. 1, Entry 3693, 1869 Volume, NA. Both John P. Willard and Sanford C. Kellogg joined the expedition along with Hough as aides and inspectors with various responsibilities.

49. Robert W. Frazer, *Forts of the West: Forts and Presidios and Posts Commonly Called Forts West of the Mississippi River to 1898* (Norman: University of Oklahoma Press, 1965), 42, 92, and 93.

50. *Alaska Times*, July 2, 1869.

51. Ibid., July 23, 1869.

52. GHT to Dear Colonel, Portland, Oregon, July 7th, 1869, Thomas Papers, Filson.

53. Field Notes, "written by Maj. Gen. Thomas," n.d., Hough Papers, UCBL.

54. Christopher J. Einholf, *George Thomas: Virginian for the Union* (Norman: University of Oklahoma Press, 2007), 71–72 and 334.

55. Richard W. Johnson, *Memoir of Maj.-Gen. Thomas*, 239.

56. Alfred A. Hough, "An Army Officer's Trip to Alaska in 1869," edited by Robert G. Athearn, *Pacific Northwest Quarterly* 40, no. 1 (Jan. 1949): 44–49.

57. Alfred to My Dearest Mary, Junalaska, Aug. 20, 1869, Hough Papers, UCBL.

58. Alfred to My Dearest Mary, Sitka, Alaska, July 23, 1869, Hough Papers, UCBL.

59. Hough, "An Army Officer's Trip to Alaska in 1869," 51–52.

60. Ibid., 63.

61. Ibid.

62. Ibid., 64.

63. GHT to Dear Porter, West Point, NY October 18, 1869, Thomas Papers, USMAL.

64. *Executive Documents, House of Representatives of the United States, Third Session, Forty-First Congress, "Annual Report of the Board of Regents of the Smithsonian Institution Showing the Operations, Expeditions, and Conditions of the Institution, for the Year 1869,"* 29 and 57.

65. Hough, "An Army Officer's Trip to Alaska in 1869," 52–53.

66. Ibid., 57.

67. Palumbo, *The Dependable General*, 385.

68. Van Horne, *Life of General Thomas*, 437.

69. Keyes, *Fifty Years' Observation*, 167.

70. Alexander McClure, *Lincoln and Men of War-Times: Some Personal Recollections of War and Politics during the Lincoln Administration* (Philadelphia: Times Publishing, 1892), 371.

71. B. F. Scribner, *How Soldiers Were Made: Or the War as I Saw It under Buell, Rose-crans, Thomas, Grant and Sherman* (New Albany, Ind.: Donohue & Henneberry, 1887), 299. Sadly, when Scribner subsequently sent the general a picture of the child, he received a reply in black-bordered paper from Frances Thomas informing him that her husband had died, ibid.

72. GHT to Dear Porter, West Point, NY October 18, 1869, Thomas Papers, USMAL.

73. General Orders No. 42, Head Quarters Military Division of the Pacific, San Francisco, Cal., December 21, 1869, RG 393, pt. 1, Entry 3691, NA.

74. G. P. Thruston to GHT, Nashville, December 25, 1869, Thomas Papers, UT.

75. Thruston to GHT, Nashville, December 31, 1865, Thomas Papers, UT.

76. Quoted in Wilbur Thomas, *Indomitable Warrior*, 603.

77. Ibid., 616.

78. GHT to Sherman, San Francisco, Cal., March 14th, 1870, William T. Sherman Papers, LOC.

79. Special Orders No. 53, Head Quarters Military Division of the Pacific, San Francisco, Cal., March 28, 1870, RG 393, pt. 1, Entry 3691, NA.

80. The text of this last response can be found in several Thomas biographies. See, for example, Wilbur Thomas, *Indomitable Warrior*, 623–627, and Palumbo, *The Dependable General*, 408–411.

81. Van Horne, *Life of General Thomas*, 442.

82. Richard W. Johnson, *Memoir of Maj.-Gen. Thomas*, 255.

83. Van Horne placed the time of death at 7:25, *Life of General Thomas*, 442–443; as did McKinney, *Education in Violence*, 471. Johnson put the time at 7:15, *Memoir of Maj.-Gen. Thomas*, 255.

84. John Russell Young, *Around the World with General Grant*, edited by Michael Fellman (Baltimore: Johns Hopkins University Press, 2002), 304.

85. Sherman to Alfred L. Hough, Washington March 29th, 1870, quoted in Special Orders No. 56, San Francisco, Cal., March 29, 1870, RG 393, pt. 1, Entry 3693, 1869 Volume, NA. A copy of the Western Union telegram with the notation "Received at San Francisco, March 29, 1870, 9:14" can be found in the Hough Papers, UCBL.

86. Special Orders No. 56, San Francisco, Cal., March 29, 1870, RG 393, pt. 1, Entry 3693, 1869 Volume, NA.

87. McKinney, *Education in Violence*, 472–473.

88. Ibid., 472; Wilbur Thomas, *Indomitable Warrior*, 621.

89. Van Horne, *Life of General Thomas*, 444–445.

90. McKinney, *Education in Violence*, 473. Cleaves was unique among Thomas biographers in omitting Schofield from the proceedings, *Rock of Chickamauga*, 306.

91. J.E.B., "The Late Gen. Thomas," *New York Times*, April 9, 1870.

92. Ibid. Cleaves erroneously places Sheridan at the funeral, *Rock of Chickamauga*, 306.

93. J.E.B., "The Late Gen. Thomas," *New York Times*, April 9, 1870.

94. Palumbo, *The Dependable General*, 395.

95. J.E.B., "The Late Gen. Thomas," *New York Times*, April 9, 1870.

Epilogue: What History Has Done

1. David M. Jordan, *Winfield Scott Hancock: A Soldier's Life* (Bloomington: Indiana University Press, 1988), 213–214.

2. "Major-Gen. Thomas," *New York Times*, March 30, 1870.

3. "Thomas," *Chicago Times*, March 30, 1870.

4. "Honor to Gen. Thomas," Louisville *Courier-Journal*, March 20, 1870, Thomas Papers, Filson.

5. A. L. Hough to E. D. Thompson, San Francisco, Cal., Apl 1st 1870, Hough Papers, UCBL.

6. U. S. Grant to Frances K. Thomas, Washington, D.C., March 29, 1870, in Ulysses S. Grant, *The Papers of Ulysses S. Grant,* edited by John Y. Simon (Carbondale: Southern Illinois University Press, 1994), 20:128.

7. U. S. Grant to John Coon, Washington, D.C., Nov. 17, 1870, in ibid., 21:15.

8. Frances L. Thomas to Dear General, 90 Fourth Street, Troy, New York, April 30th, 1870, Sherman Papers, LOC.

9. Frances L. Thomas to Dear Col., Troy New York, April 29th, 1870, Hough Papers, UCBL.

10. Frank A. Palumbo, *George Henry Thomas: The Dependable General* (Dayton, Ohio: Morningside House, 1983), 397.

11. Ibid., 407.

12. Thomas B. Van Horne, *History of the Army of the Cumberland Its Organization, Campaigns, and Battles, Written at the Request of Major-General George H. Thomas, Chiefly*

from His Private Military Journal and Official and Other Documents Furnished by Him (Cincinnati: Robert Clarke, 1875), 1:xxvi.

13. Peter Cozzens, introduction of the 1988 edition of Thomas B. Van Horne, *History of the Army of the Cumberland Its Organization, Campaigns, and Battles, Written at the Request of Major-General George H. Thomas, Chiefly from His Private Military Journal and Official and Other Documents Furnished by Him* (Wilmington, N.C.: Broadfoot Publishing, 1988), xvi.

14. Oscar to Dear Mother, May 8, 1870 Fort Sully D.T., in Oscar Ladley, *Hearth and Knapsack: The Ladley Letters, 1857–1880,* edited by Carl M. Becker and Ritchie Thomas (Athens: Ohio University Press, 1988), 303.

15. Fort Thomas changed to Fort Pembina on September 6, 1870, and Fort Apache took the name Camp Thomas on the twentieth of the same month; in February of the following year it became Camp Apache. Robert W. Frazer, *Forts of the West: Forts and Presidios and Posts Commonly Called Forts West of the Mississippi River to 1898* (Norman: University of Oklahoma Press, 1965), 3, 112.

16. Carl Schurz, *Speeches, Correspondence and Political Papers of Carl Schurz,* edited by Frederic Bancroft, 4 vols. (New York: G. P. Putnam's Sons, 1913), 3:410.

17. Quoted in John Russell Young, *Around the World with General Grant,* edited by Michael Fellman (Baltimore: Johns Hopkins University Press, 2002), 303–304.

18. Kniffin, "Major-General William Starke Rosecrans," in *War Papers Being Papers Read before the Commandery of the District of Columbia Military Order of the Loyal Legion of the United States,* vol. 4, *Papers 1–26. March 1887–April 1897* (Wilmington, N.C.: Broadfoot Publishing, 1993), 71–72.

19. Albert Castel, "Prevaricating through Georgia: Sherman's *Memoirs* as a Source on the Atlanta Campaign," *Civil War History* 40, no. 1 (March 1994): 48–71, provided one of the most popular essays taking Sherman's *Memoirs* to task. John F. Marszalek, "Sherman Called It the Way He Saw It," ibid., 72–78, offered a response in the same edition.

20. Christopher J. Einholf, *George Thomas: Virginian for the Union* (Norman: University of Oklahoma Press, 2007), 342–343.

21. F. L. Thomas to editor of the *Herald,* Troy, December 31, 1875, in Hough statement, "Genl Geo. H. Thomas & Fitzhugh Lee," Fort Mackinnac, Mich., Jan. 8, 1876, Hough Papers, UCBL.

22. F. L. Thomas to My dear Col Hough, Troy NY, Nov 18th 1879, Hough Papers, UCBL.

23. Stanley Matthews, *Unveiling of Ward's Equestrian Statue of Major-General George H. Thomas, Washington, November 19, 1879* (Cincinnati: Robert Clarke, 1879), 4.

24. Richard W. Johnson, *Memoir of Maj.-Gen. George H. Thomas* (Philadelphia: J. B. Lippincott, 1881), 286.

25. Ibid., 287–288.

26. Walter H. Herbert, *Fighting Joe Hooker* (Indianapolis: Bobbs-Merrill, 1944), 295–296.

27. F. L. Thomas to My dear Col Hough, Troy, NY., May 27th 1880, Hough Papers, UCBL.

28. F. L. Thomas to My dear Col Hough, Troy, NY., January 10th 1881, ibid.

29. Sanford C. Kellogg to My dear Hough, Fort Laramie, Wyoming, June 6, 1881, ibid.

30. F. L. Thomas to My dear Col., Troy, NY., Aug 29th 1881, ibid.

31. F. L. Thomas to My dear Col Hough, Troy NY., Jany 6th 1883, ibid.

32. Quoted in James Lee McDonough, *Schofield: Union General in the Civil War and Reconstruction* (Tallahassee: Florida State University Press, 1972), 134.

33. Ezra J. Warner, *Generals in Blue: Lives of the Union Commanders* (Baton Rouge: Louisiana State University Press, 1964), 98.

34. "Brave By Act of Congress," *New York Times*, January 12, 1883.

35. F. L. Thomas to My dear Col Hough, Troy NY., Jany 20th 1883, Hough Papers, UCBL.

36. Ephraim A. Otis, "General George H. Thomas," in *Military Essays and Recollections Papers Read before the Commandery of the State of Illinois, Military Order of the Loyal Legion of the United States* (Chicago: A. C. McClurg, 1891), 397.

37. Francis F. McKinney, *Education in Violence: The Life of George H. Thomas and the History of the Army of the Cumberland* (Detroit: Wayne State University Press, 1961), 504; Einholf, *George Thomas*, 338.

38. See Nina Silber, *The Romance of Reunion: Northerners and the South, 1865–1900* (Chapel Hill: University of North Carolina Press, 1993), and David W. Blight, *Race and Reunion: The Civil War in American Memory* (Cambridge, Mass.: Belknap Press, 2001), for excellent treatments on popular attitudes regarding the war.

39. Byron A. Dunn, *On General Thomas's Staff* (Chicago: A. C. McClung, 1899), 7–8.

40. See Bill Thomas, *Fort Thomas* (Charleston, S.C.: Arcadia Publishing, 2006), for an illustrated history of the post and community.

41. Gregory Dean Chapman, "Army Life at Camp Thomas, Georgia, during the Spanish-American War," *Georgia Historical Quarterly* 70 (Winter 1986): 636.

42. Ibid., 637.

43. Ibid., 642. Chapman noted that by summer the camp held some 58,000 men and 10,000–15,000 horses.

44. Ibid., 643.

45. Ibid., 655.

46. Kenneth Ray Young, *The General's General: The Life and Times of Arthur MacArthur* (Boulder, Colo.: Westview Press, 1994).

47. J. Willliam Jones, "Thomas and Lee—Historical Facts," *Confederate Veteran* 11, no. 12 (Dec. 1903): 559.

48. William E. Reppert, "About Gen. G. H. Thomas's Side in the War," *Confederate Veteran* 16, no. 3 (March 1908): 126–127.

49. B. F. Grady, "What Gen. Thomas Wrote Gov. Letcher," *Confederate Veteran* 16, no. 5 (May 1908): 222–223.

50. Blight, *Race and Reunion*, 381.

51. Information on SS *George H. Thomas*, from a first-day cover featuring "Liberty Ships Honoring Famous Generals built during World War II," in author's collection.

52. John Gorley Bunker, *Liberty Ships: The Ugly Ducklings of World War II* (Annapolis, Md: Naval Institute Press, 1972), 184 and 211. The full range of vessels appears in appendixes at the end of the volume. Some of these underwent as many as nine transactions before being scrapped.

53. *Johnny Shiloh*, with the precocious Kevin Corcoran in the title role, was meant to appeal to young audiences by offering the legend of the "drummer boy" without apology or historical attribution. Although the largest adult role fell to Brian Keith as the sergeant who grudgingly embraced the young soldier, Edward Platt played General Thomas in the adaptation and introduced him in that manner to a generation of Disney viewers. See Brian Steel Wills, *Gone with the Glory: The Civil War in Cinema* (Lanham, Md.: Rowman & Littlefield, 2007), 106 and 192; Bell Irvin Wiley, *The Life of Billy Yank: The Common Soldier of the Union* (Indianapolis: Bobbs-Merrill, 1952), 297–298.

54. Quotes from Einholf, *George Thomas*, 227. Wilbur Thomas discussed the Clem/Thomas association in broader, popular terms, in *General George H. Thomas: The Indomitable Warrior* (New York: Exposition Press, 1964), 335–336.

Experience More at Marriott®

From island resort getaways to globe-trotting business trips,
Marriott is here to make sure all your journeys are everything you imagined—and more.

Over 500 Marriott Hotels & Resorts in 60 countries. Visit Marriott.com to book your next stay.

SHARE THE EXPERIENCES
YOU'VE COME TO LOVE.

Indulge the palate.
Massage your cares away.
Or tear through a brilliant back nine.

The Marriott Hotels & Resorts GiftCard
of experiences.

GiftCard

528	SCHMIDT/WILLIAM/MR/		08/12/12	11:00	9336
Room	Name		Depart	Time	ACCT#
CDBL	CRAWFORD AND COMPANY	Rate	08/11/12	13:04	
Type			Arrive	Time	
70					

				Payment	RWD#: XXXXX7022R
Room	Address				
Clerk					
DATE	REFERENCE	CHARGES	CREDITS		BALANCE DUE

$ .00

TO BE SETTLED TO: AMERICAN EXPRESS

WE HOPE YOU HAD A MEMORABLE EXPERIENCE WITH US, CAN WE BOOK
YOUR NEXT RESERVATION FOR YOU? STOP BY THE FRONT DESK AND
WE WILL BE GLAD TO ASSIST YOU.

AS REQUESTED, A FINAL COPY OF YOUR BILL WILL BE EMAILED TO:
            BILL.SCHMIDT@US.CRAWCO.COM
    SEE "INTERNET PRIVACY STATEMENT" ON MARRIOTT.COM

55. Einholf, *George Thomas*, 228.

56. Colgate W. Darden Jr., "Address," *Southampton County Historical Society,* Bulletin no. 3 (July 1976): n.p.

57. "Southampton's Civil War Hero, Like or Not," *Virginian-Pilot*, November 7, 2004.

58. Question and answer comments made following various public programs.

59. See Edward L. Ayers, *"A House Divided . . .": A Century of Great Civil War Quotations* (New York: John Wiley & Sons, 1997).

60. John D. Wright, *The Oxford Dictionary of Civil War Quotations* (New York: Oxford University Press, 2006), 403.

61. Victor Brooks and Robert Hohwald, *How America Fought Its Wars: Military Strategy from the American Revolution to the Civil War* (Conshohocken, Pa.: Combined Publishing, 1999), 482.

62. Ibid., 475. The authors gave the other generals listed with Thomas here A as well. (See 482–484.) Meade received an A– (483). Of most prominent Confederates Thomas faced, Joseph Johnston took the highest assessment with C (476), and Braxton Bragg and John Bell Hood both received Fs (477).

63. Larry J. Daniel, *Days of Glory: The Army of the Cumberland, 1861–1865* (Baton Rouge: Louisiana State University Press, 2004), 426.

64. Daniel W. Crofts, *Old Southampton: Politics and Society in a Virginia County, 1834–1869* (Charlottesville: University Press of Virginia, 1992), 206.

65. Albert Castel, *Articles of War: Winners, Losers, and Some Who Were Both in the Civil War* (Mechanicsburg, Pa.: Stackpole Books, 2001), 236–237.

66. Herman Hattaway and Archer Jones, *How the North Won* (Urbana: University of Illinois Press, 1983), 653–654.

67. W. J. Wood, *Civil War Generalship: The Art of Command* (Westport, Conn.: Praeger, 1997), 232.

68. James F. Rusling, *Men and Things I Saw in Civil War Days* (New York: Eaton & Mains, 1899), 102.

69. Archer Jones, *Civil War Command and Strategy: The Process of Victory and Defeat* (New York: Free Press, 1992), 214.

70. Wood, *Art of Command*, 229–230.

71. Earl J. Hess, *Trench Warfare under Grant and Lee: Field Fortifications in the Overland Campaign* (Chapel Hill: University of North Carolina Press, 2007), 93.

72. Wood, *Art of Command*, 242–243.

73. Horace Porter, *Campaigning with Grant* (New York: Century, 1907), 351.

74. Ibid., 352.

75. Ibid., 353.

76. Thomas J. Morgan, *Reminiscences of Service with Colored Troops in the Army of the Cumberland, 1863–1865* (Providence: Soldiers and Sailors Historical Society of Rhode Island, 1885), 48.

77. Thomas B. Van Horne, *The Life of Major-General George H. Thomas* (New York: Charles Scribner's Sons, 1882), 347.

78. John Cimprich, "A Critical Moment and Its Aftermath for George H. Thomas," in *The Moment of Decision: Biographical Essays on American Character and Regional Identity*, edited by Randall M. Miller and John R. McKivigan (Westport, Conn.: Greenwood Press, 1994), 174–175.

79. Einholf, *George Thomas*, 5 and 9.

80. Wood, *Art of Command*, 242–243.

81. Einholf, *George Thomas*, 354.

82. Benson Bobrick, *Master of War: The Life of General George H. Thomas* (New York: Simon & Schuster: 2009), 343.

83. James I. Robertson Jr. and Brian Steel Wills, *Civil War Sites in Virginia: A Tour Guide*, rev. ed. (Charlottesville: University Press of Virginia, 2011), 86.

84. Young, *Around the World with General Grant*, 261.

85. According to the Academy website, usma.edu, the motto dated from 1898.

86. Wiley Sword, *Embrace an Angry Wind: The Confederacy's Last Hurrah: Spring Hill, Franklin, and Nashville* (New York: HarperCollins, 1992), 425. Sword reached a similar conclusion in *Courage Under Fire: Profiles in Bravery from the Battlefields of the Civil War* (New York: St. Martin's Press, 2007), 239.

Bibliography

Primary Sources

Manuscripts

Archives, University of Colorado at Boulder Libraries, Boulder, Colo.
    Hough, Alfred Lacey, Papers
Author's Personal Collection
    Thomas Letter to R. H. Ramsey, Louisville, Ky., March 7, 1868
Eleanor S. Brockenbrough Library, Museum of the Confederacy, Richmond, Va.
    Thomas, George H., Papers
Filson Historical Society, Louisville, Ky.
    Allen, Theodore, Diary
    Anderson, Larz, Papers
    Bramlette, Thomas Elliott, Papers
    Bristow, Benjamin Helm, Papers
    Buell, Don Carlos, Papers
    Dow Family Papers
    Hammond, John Henry, Papers
    Hanback, Lewis, Papers
    MacKay, Andrew J., Papers
    Pirtle, Alfred, Journal
    Pirtle, Alfred, Letters
    Speed, Thomas, Letterbook
    Thomas, George Henry, Papers
    Thruston, Gates Phillips, Papers
    Tilford, John H., Diary
    Wood, Thomas J., Papers
Georgia Historical Society, Savannah, Ga.
    Olmstead, Charles H., Papers
Huntingdon Library, Huntingdon, Calif.
    Thomas, George Henry, Papers
Library of Congress, Washington, D.C.
    Anderson, Robert Anderson, Papers
    Garfield, James A., Papers
    Hartz, E. L., Papers
    Porter, Fitz John, Papers
    Sherman, William T., Papers
    Wilson, James H., Papers
Library of Virginia, Richmond, Va.
    Thomas Family Genealogical Notes

Francis P. McKinney, "The General Used No Stilts," ts., n.d., Accession Number 24290

"Widow's Declaration for Additional Bounty Laws," Accession Number 25436

Mississippi State University, Starkville, Miss.

Grant, Ulysses S., Papers

National Archives, Washington, D.C.

M331, R196, Correspondence, Reports, Etc.

M567, Correspondence, Letters Received, Office of the Adjutant General, 1822–1860

M617, Returns from U.S. Military Posts, 1800–1916

M619, Correspondence, Letters Received, Office of the Adjutant General, 1861–1870

RG393, Correspondence, Reports, Etc., Letters Received, Department of the Pacific, 1854–1858

Personal Collection of Wiley Sword

George Thomas Letter

Preston Library, Virginia Military Institute Archives, Lexington, Va.

Francis H. Smith Letters

Robert W. Woodruff Library, Emory University, Atlanta, Ga.

Gourdin, Robert, Papers

United States Army Military History Institute, Carlisle Barracks, Carlisle, Pa.

Scott, W. H. "An Enlisted Man's Estimate of General George H. Thomas," 96–108. N.p., n.d.

United States Military Academy Archives, West Point, N.Y.

Circulation Records, 1836–1841

Official Register of the Officers and Cadets of the U.S. Military Academy, West Point, New York. (The individual Official Registers are available online at www.library.usma.edu.)

Register of Delinquencies, 1836–1840

Thomas, George H. (Va.)

United States Military Academy Special Collections, West Point, N.Y.

Duncan, James, Letter from Thomas, March 18, 1847, in Cullum File, Manuscript Collections

Stuart Files, #1643

Special Collections, University of Tennessee, Knoxville, Tenn.

General George Thomas Letters

Special Collections, University of Virginia, Charlottesville, Va.

Blackford Family Papers, 1847–1872, Accession No. 5927

Virginia Historical Society, Richmond

Caperton Family Papers

Cobb, Daniel William, Diaries

Cooke Family Papers

Lee, Robert Edward, Papers

Lee Letterbook

Stuart, James Ewell Brown, Letters

Thomas, George Henry, Papers

Thomas Family Papers

Tompkins Family Papers

Zabriskie, George Albert, Papers

Virginia State Library, Richmond

McKinney, Francis, Papers

William R. Perkins Library, Duke University, Durham, N.C.

Bragg, Braxton, Papers

Scully, James, Papers
Thomas, George H., Papers
Yale University Library, New Haven, Conn.
George H. Thomas Letters

Government

Executive Documents, Senate of the United States, Second Session, Thirty-Second Congress, 1852–'53.

Executive Documents, House of Representatives of the United States, Second Session, Thirty-Third Congress, "Reports of Explorations and Surveys to Ascertain the Most Practicable and Economical Route for a Railroad from the Mississippi River to the Pacific Ocean." IV, 1856.

Executive Documents, House of Representatives of the United States, Third Session, Thirty-Fourth Congress, "Annual Report of the Board of Regents of the Smithsonian Institution Showing the Operations, Expeditions, and Conditions of the Institution, for the Year 1856."

Executive Documents, House of Representatives of the United States, Third Session, Fortieth Congress, "Report of the Secretary of War, 1868."

Executive Documents, House of Representatives of the United States, Third Session, Fortieth Congress, "Army Organization," February 26, 1869.

Executive Documents, House of Representatives of the United States, Second Session, Forty-First Congress, "Report of the Secretary of War, 1869."

Executive Documents, House of Representatives of the United States, Third Session, Forty-First Congress, "Annual Report of the Board of Regents of the Smithsonian Institution Showing the Operations, Expeditions, and Conditions of the Institution, for the Year 1869."

The Official Records of the Union and Confederate Navies in the War of the Rebellion. Washington, D.C.: Government Printing Office.

The War of the Rebellion: The Official Records of the Union and Confederate Armies. 70 vols. In 127 serials and index. Washington, D.C.: Government Printing Office, 1880–1895.

Newspapers

Chicago Times
Cincinnati Daily Enquirer
Harpers New Monthly Magazine
Knoxville Whig and Rebel Ventilator
Louisville Daily Journal
New York Times
[Richmond] *Daily Dispatch*
[Richmond] *Sentinel*
Southern Illustrated News
Virginian Pilot, Hampton Roads, Va.

Books

Anderson, Thomas M. *General George H. Thomas: His Place in History, A Paper Read before Oregon Commandery of the Military Order of the Loyal Legion of the United States, March 7, 1894.* Portland, Ore.: A. Anderson, 1894.

Bates, David Homer. *Lincoln in the Telegraph Office.* New York: Century, 1907.

Battles and Leaders of the Civil War. Vols. 1–4. Edited by Robert Underwood Johnson and Clarence Clough Buel. New York: Century, 1887.

Battles and Leaders of the Civil War. Vol. 5. Edited by Peter Cozzens. Urbana: University of Illinois Press, 2002.

Beatty, John. *Memoirs of a Volunteer, 1861–1863.* Edited by Harvey S. Ford. New York: W. W. Norton, 1946.

Bennitt, John. *"I Hope to Do My Country Service": The Civil War Letters of John Bennitt, M.D., Surgeon, 19th Michigan Infantry.* Edited by Robert Beasecker. Detroit: Wayne State University Press, 2005.

Bertsch, Friedrich, and Wilhelm Stangel. *A German Hurrah! Civil War Letters of Frederich Bertsch and Wilhelm Stangel.* Translated and edited by Joseph R. Reinhart. Kent, Ohio: Kent State University Press, 2010.

Bisbee, William Henry. *Through Four American Wars: The Impressions and Experiences of Brigadier General William Henry Bisbee as Told to His Grandson William Haymond Brisbee.* Boston: Meador Publishing, 1931.

Bradford, Gamaliel. *Union Portraits.* Boston: Houghton Mifflin, 1915.

Bull, Rice C. *Soldiering: The Civil War Diary of Rice C. Bull, 123rd New York Volunteer Infantry.* Edited by K. Jack Bauer. New York: Berkley Books, 1988.

Cadwallader, Sylvanus. *Three Years with Grant.* Edited by Benjamin P. Thomas. New York: Alfred A. Knopf, 1956.

Calkins, William Wirt. *The History of the One Hundred and Fourth Regiment of Illinois Volunteer Infantry. War of the Great Rebellion. 1862–1865.* Chicago: Donohue & Henneberry, 1895.

Campaigns in Kentucky and Tennessee Including the Battle of Chickamauga 1862–1864. Papers of the Military Historical Society of Massachusetts. Vol. 7. Boston: Military Historical Society of Massachusetts, 1908.

Carleton, James Henry. *The Battle of Buena Vista, with the Operations of the "Army of Occupation" for One Month.* New York: Harper and Brothers, 1848.

Carlin, William Passmore. *The Memoirs of William Passmore Carlin, U.S.A.* Edited by Robert I. Girardi and Nathaniel Cheairs Hughes Jr. Lincoln: University of Nebraska Press, 1999.

Chase, Salmon P. *The Salmon P. Chase Papers.* Edited by John Niven. Kent, Ohio: Kent State University Press, 1993.

Chesnut, Mary. *Mary Chesnut's Civil War.* Edited by C. Vann Woodward. New Haven, Conn.: Yale University Press, 1981.

Cist, Henry M. *The Army of the Cumberland.* New York: Charles Scribner's Sons, 1882.

Cobb, Daniel William. *Cobb's Ordeal: The Diaries of a Virginia Farmer, 1842–1872.* Edited by Daniel W. Crofts. Athens: University of Georgia Press, 1997.

Connolly, James A. *Three Years in the Army of the Cumberland: The Letters and Diary of Major James A. Connolly.* Edited by Paul Angle. Bloomington: Indiana University Press, 1959.

Cox, Jacob Dobson. *Military Reminiscences of the Civil War.* New York: Charles Scribner's Sons, 1900.

Cram, George F. *Soldiering with Sherman: Civil War Letters of George F. Cram.* Edited by Jennifer Cain Bohrnstedt. DeKalb: Northern Illinois University Press, 2000.

Crook, George. *General George Crook: His Autobiography.* Edited by Martin F. Schmitt. Norman: University of Oklahoma Press, 1946.

Dana, Charles A. *Recollections of the Civil War: With the Leaders at Washington and in the Field in the Sixties*. New York: D. Appleton, 1902.

Davis, Jefferson. *The Papers of Jefferson Davis*. Edited by Lynda Lasswell Crist. 8 vols. Baton Rouge: Louisiana State University Press, 1971–.

Dennett, John Richard. *The South As It Is, 1865–1866*. Edited by Henry C. Christman. Athens: University of Georgia Press, 1986.

De Peyster, John Watts. *Major General George H. Thomas*. New York: Atlantic Publishing, 1875.

———. *Sketch of George H. Thomas from Representative Men*. New York: Atlantic Publishing, 1875.

Doubleday, Abner. *My Life in the Old Army: The Reminiscences of Abner Doubleday from the Collections of the New-York Historical Society*. Edited by Joseph E. Chance. Fort Worth: Texas Christian University Press, 1998.

Dunham, Alburtus A., and Charles Laforest Dunham. *Through the South with a Union Soldier*. Edited by Arthur H. DeRosier Jr. Johnson City: East Tennessee State University, 1969.

Dunn, Byron A. *On General Thomas's Staff*. Chicago: A. C. McClung, 1899.

Edmonston, Catherine Ann Devereaux. *"Journal of a Secesh Lady": The Diary of Catherine Ann Devereaux Edmonston, 1859–1866*. Edited by Beth G. Crabtree and James W. Patton. Raleigh: North Carolina Division of Archives and History, 1979.

Ewell, Richard S. *The Making of a Soldier: The Letters of General R. S. Ewell*. Edited by Percy Gatling Hamlin. Richmond, Va.: Whittet & Shepperson, 1935.

Fitch, Michael H. *Echoes of the Civil War as I Hear Them*. New York: R. F. Fenno, 1905.

French, Samuel G. *Two Wars: An Autobiography of Gen. Samuel G. French*. Nashville, Tenn.: Confederate Veteran, 1901.

Garfield, James A. *The Diary of James A. Garfield*. Edited by Harry James Brown and Frederick D. Williams. 4 vols. [East Lansing]: Michigan State University Press, 1973.

———. *Oration on the Life and Character of Gen. George H. Thomas Delivered before the Society of the Army of the Cumberland*. Cincinnati: Robert Clarke, 1871.

Grant, Ulysses S. *Personal Memoirs of U. S. Grant*. 2 vols. New York: Charles L. Webster, 1886.

———. *The Papers of Ulysses S. Grant*. 31 vols. Edited by John Y. Simon. Carbondale: Southern Illinois University Press, 1988.

Green, Wharton J. *Recollections and Reflections: An Auto[biography] of Half a Century and More*. Raleigh, N.C.: Edwards and Broughton Printing, 1906.

Grierson, Benjamin H. *A Just and Righteous Cause: Benjamin H. Grierson's Civil War Memoir*. Edited by Bruce J. Dinges and Shirley A. Leckie. Carbondale: Southern Illinois University Press, 2008.

Guerrant, Edward O. *Bluegrass Confederate: The Headquarters Diary of Edward O. Guerrant*. Edited by William C. Davis and Meredith L. Swentor. Baton Rouge: Louisiana State University Press, 1999.

Gurowski, Adam. *Diary: 1863–'64–'65*. Edited by Charles Richard Williams. New York: Burt Franklin, 1886. Reprint, 1968.

Hartzell, John Calvin. *Ohio Volunteer: The Childhood and Civil War Memoirs of Captain John Calvin Hartzell, OVI*. Edited by Charles I. Switzer. Athens: Ohio University Press, 2005.

Hay, John. *Inside Lincoln's White House: The Complete Civil War Diary of John Hay*. Edited by Michael Burlingame and John R. Turner Ettlinger. Carbondale: Southern Illinois University Press, 1997.

Haynie, J. Henry. *The Nineenth Illinois: A Memoir of a Regiment of Volunteer Infantry Famous in the Civil War Fifty Years Ago for Its Drill, Bravery, and Distinguished Service*. Chicago: M. A. Donohue, 1912.

Hill, Daniel Harvey. *A Fighter from Way Back: The Mexican War Diary of Lt. Daniel Harvey Hill, 4th Artillery, USA*. Edited by Nathaniel Cheairs Hughes Jr. and Timothy D. Johnson. Kent, Ohio: Kent State University Press, 2002.

Hood, John Bell. *Advance and Retreat: Personal Experiences in the United States and Confederate States Armies*. Bloomington: Indiana University Press, 1959.

Hough, Alfred Lacey. "An Army Officer's Trip to Alaska in 1869." Edited by Robert G. Athearn. *Pacific Northwest Quarterly* 40, no. 1 (Jan. 1949): 44–64.

———. *Soldier in the West: The Civil War Letters of Alfred Lacey Hough*. Edited by Robert G. Athearn. Philadelphia: University of Pennsylvania Press, 1957.

Howard, Oliver Otis. *Autobiography of Oliver Otis Howard, Major General United States Army*. 2 vols. New York: Baker & Taylor, 1908.

Johnson, Andrew. *The Papers of Andrew Johnson*. 15 vols. Edited by Roy P. Graf, Ralph W. Haskins, and Paul Bergeron. Knoxville: University of Tennessee Press, 1967–2000.

Johnson, Richard W. *Memoir of Maj.-Gen. George H. Thomas*. Philadelphia: J. B. Lippincott, 1881.

———. *A Soldier's Reminiscences in Peace and War*. Philadelphia: J. B. Lippincott, 1886.

Johnston, Joseph E. *Narrative of Military Operations, Directed, during the Late War between the States by Joseph E. Johnston*. New York: D. Appleton, 1874.

Jones, John B. *A Rebel War Clerk's Diary at the Confederate States Capital*. Philadelphia: J. B. Lippincott, 1866.

Kean, Robert Garlick Hill. *Inside the Confederate Government: The Diary of Robert Garlick Hill Kean*. Edited by Edward Younger. New York: Oxford University Press, 1957.

Kenly, John Reese. *Memoirs of a Maryland Volunteer War with Mexico, in the Years 1846–7–8*. Philadelphia: J. B. Lippincott, 1873.

Keyes, Erasmus D. *Fifty Years' Observation of Men and Events Civil and Military*. New York: Charles Scribner's Sons, 1884.

Kimberly, Robert L., and Ephraim S. Holloway. *The Forty-first Ohio Veteran Volunteer Infantry in the War of the Rebellion, 1861–1865*. Cleveland: R. H. Smellie, 1897.

King, John M. *Three Years with the 92d Illinois: The Civil War Diary of John M. King*. Edited by Claire E. Swedberg. Mechanicsburg, Pa.: Stackpole Books, 1999.

King, William Henry. *No Pardons to Ask, nor Apologies to Make: The Journal of William Henry King, Gray's 28th Louisiana Infantry Regiment*. Edited by Gary D. Joiner, Marilyn S. Joiner, and Clifton D. Cardin. Knoxville: University of Tennessee Press, 2006.

Ladley, Oscar. *Hearth and Knapsack: The Ladley Letters, 1857–1880*. Edited by Carl M. Becker and Ritchie Thomas. Athens: Ohio University Press, 1988.

Lambert, William H. *George Henry Thomas: Oration before the Society of the Army of the Cumberland, at Rochester, N.Y., September 17, 1884*. Cincinnati: Robert Clarke, 1885.

Lee, Robert E. *The Daily Correspondence of Brevet Colonel Robert E. Lee Superintendent, United States Military Academy September 1, 1852 to March 24, 1855*. Edited by Charles R. Bowery Jr. and Brian D. Hankinson. Occasional Papers 5. West Point, N.Y.: United States Military Academy Library, 2003.

Lincoln, Abraham. *Collected Works of Abraham Lincoln*. Edited by Roy P. Basler. 9 vols. New Brunswick, N.J.: Rutgers University Press, 1953.

Logan, David Jackson. *"A Rising Star of Promise:" The Civil War Odyssey of David Jackson Logan*. Edited by Samuel N. Thomas Jr. and Jason H. Silverman. Campbell, Calif.: Savas Publishing, 1998.

Logan, John A. *The Volunteer Soldier in America*. Chicago: R. S. Peale, Publishers, 1887.

Logan, Mrs. John A. *Reminiscences of a Soldier's Wife: An Autobiography*. New York: C. Scribner's Sons, 1913.

Lyman, Theodore. *Meade's Army: The Private Notebooks of Lt. Col. Theodore Lyman*. Edited by David W. Lowe. Kent, Ohio: Kent State University Press, 2007.

Mansfield, Joseph King Fenno. *Mansfield on the Condition of the Western Forts, 1853–54*. Edited by Robert W. Frazer. Norman: University of Oklahoma Press, 1963.

Matthews, Stanley. *Unveiling of Ward's Equestrian Statue of Major-General George H. Thomas, Washington, November 19, 1879*. Cincinnati: Robert Clarke, 1879.

Maury, Dabney Herndon. *Recollections of a Virginian in the Mexican, Indian, and Civil Wars*. New York: Charles Scribner's Sons, 1897.

McClure, Alexander. *Lincoln and Men of War-Times: Some Personal Recollections of War and Politics during the Lincoln Administration*. Philadelphia: Times Publishing, 1892.

———. *Old Time Notes of Pennsylvania: A Connected and Chronological Record of the Commercial, Industrial and Educational Advancement of Pennsylvania, and the Inner History of All Political Movements Since the Adoption of the Constitution of 1836*. 2 vols. Philadelphia: John C. Winston, 1905.

McPherson, Edward. *The Political History of the United States of America during the Period of Reconstruction (From April 15, 1865, to July 15, 1870,) Including a Classified Summary of the Legislation of the Thirty-Ninth, Fortieth, and Forty-First Congresses with the Votes Thereon; Together with the Action, Congressional, and State, on the Fourteenth and Fifteenth Amendments to the Constitution of the United States, and the Other Important Executive, Legislative, Politico-Military, and Judicial Facts of that Period*. 2nd ed. New York: Negro Universities Press, 1969.

Meade, George. *The Life and Letters of George Gordon Meade, Major-General United States Army*. Edited by George Gordon Meade. 2 vols. New York: Charles Scribner's Sons, 1913.

Miller, Charles Dana. *The Struggle for the Life of the Republic: A Civil War Narrative by Brevet Major Charles Dana Miller, 76th Ohio Volunteer Infantry*. Edited by Stewart Bennett and Barbara Tillery. Kent, Ohio: Kent State University Press, 2004.

Miller, William Bluffton. *Fighting for Liberty and Right: The Civil War Diary of William Bluffton Miller, First Sergeant, Company K, Seventy-fifth Indiana Volunteer Infantry*. Knoxville: University of Tennessee Press, 2005.

Morgan, Thomas J. *Reminiscences of Service with Colored Troops in the Army of the Cumberland, 1863–1865*. Providence: Soldiers and Sailors Historical Society of Rhode Island, 1885.

Mosman, Chesley A. *The Rough Side of War: The Civil War Journal of Chesley A. Mosman, 1st Lieutenant, Company D, 59th Illinois Volunteer Infantry Regiment*. Edited by Arnold Gates. Garden City, N.J.: Basin Publishing, 1987.

Opdycke, Emerson. *To Battle for God and the Right: The Civil War Letterbooks of Emerson Opdycke*. Edited by Glenn V. Longacre and John E. Haas. Urbana: University of Illinois Press, 2003.

Palmer, John M. *Personal Recollections of John M. Palmer: The Story of an Earnest Life*. Cincinnati: Robert Clarke, 1901.

Peter, Frances. *A Union Woman in Civil War Kentucky, The Diary of Frances Peter*. Edited by John David Smith and William Cooper Jr. Lexington: University Press of Kentucky, 2000.

Piatt, Donn. *Memories of the Men Who Saved the Union*. New York: Belford, Clarke, 1887.

Pope, John. *The Military Memoirs of General John Pope*. Edited by Peter Cozzens and Robert I. Girardi. Chapel Hill: University of North Carolina Press, 1998.

Porter, Horace. *Campaigning with Grant.* New York: Century, 1907.

Richardson, Albert D. *A Personal History of Ulysses S. Grant, Illustrated by Twenty-six Engravings; Eight Fac-similies of Letters from Grant, Lincoln, Sheridan, Buckner, Lee, etc.; and Six Maps.* Hartford, Conn.: American Publishing, 1868.

Rusling, James F. *Men and Things I Saw in Civil War Days.* New York: Eaton & Mains, 1899.

Schofield, John M. *Forty-Six Years in the Army.* New York: Century, 1897.

Schurz, Carl. *Speeches, Correspondence and Political Papers of Carl Schurz.* Edited by Frederic Bancroft. 4 vols. New York: G. P. Putnam's Sons, 1913.

Scribner, B. F. *How Soldiers Were Made: Or the War as I Saw It under Buell, Rosecrans, Thomas, Grant and Sherman.* New Albany, Ind., and Chicago: Donohue & Henneberry, 1887.

Shanks, William F. G. *Personal Recollections of Distinguished Generals.* New York: Harper & Brothers, 1866.

Sheridan, Philip H. *Personal Memoirs of P. H. Sheridan, General United States Army.* New York: Charles L. Webster, 1888.

Sherman, Francis T. *Quest for a Star: The Civil War Letters and Diaries of Colonel Francis T. Sherman of the 88th Illinois.* Edited by C. Knight Aldrich. Knoxville: University of Tennessee Press, 1999.

Sherman, John. *John Sherman's Recollections of Forty Years in the House, the Senate and Cabinet, An Autobiography.* Chicago: Werner, 1895.

Sherman, William T. *Home Letters of General Sherman.* Edited by M. A. DeWolfe Howe. New York: Charles Scribner's Sons, 1909.

———. *Memoirs of General William T. Sherman.* 2 vols. New York: Charles L. Webster, 1892.

———. *Sherman's Civil War: Selected Correspondence of William T. Sherman, 1860–1865.* Edited by Brooks D. Simpson and Jean V. Berlin. Chapel Hill: University of North Carolina Press, 1999.

Sherwood, Isaac R. *Memories of the War.* Toledo, Ohio: H. J. Chittenden, 1923.

Simpson, Brooks D., Leroy P. Graf, and John Muldowney, *Advice after Appomattox: Letters to Andrew Johnson, 1865–1866.* Knoxville: University of Tennessee Press, 1987.

Smith, William F. *Autobiography of Major General William F. Smith 1861–1864.* Edited by Herbert M. Schiller. Dayton, Ohio: Morningside House, 1990.

Sorrel, G. Moxley. *Recollections of a Confederate Staff Officer.* Edited by Bell Irvin Wiley. Jackson, Tenn.: McCowat-Mercer Press, 1958.

Speed, Thomas. *The Union Cause in Kentucky, 1861–1865.* New York: G. P. Putnam's Sons, 1907.

Stanley, David S. *Personal Memoirs of Major-General D. S. Stanley, U.S.A.* Cambridge, Mass.: Harvard University Press, 1917.

Stockwell, Elisha, Jr. *Private Elisha Stockwell, Jr. Sees the War.* Edited by Byron R. Abernathy. Norman: University of Oklahoma Press, 1958.

Taylor, Benjamin F. *Pictures of Life in Camp and Field.* Chicago: S. C. Griggs, 1875, 1888.

Tennessee Civil War Veterans Questionnaires. Compiled by Gustavus W. Dyer and John Trotwood Moore. 5 vols. Easley, S.C.: Southern Historical Press, 1985.

Villard, Henry. *Memoirs of Henry Villard Journalist and Financier 1835–1900.* 2 vols. Westminster, UK: Archibald Constable, 1904.

Wainwright, Charles S. *A Diary of Battle: The Personal Journals of Colonel Charles S. Wainwright, 1861–1865.* New York: Harcourt, Brace & World, 1962.

Wallace, Isabel. *Life and Letters of General W. H. L. Wallace.* Chicago: R. R. Donnelley, 1909.

Wallace, Lew. *Lew Wallace: An Autobiography.* New York: Harper & Brothers, 1906.

Watkins, Sam R. *"Co. Aytch": A Confederate Soldier's Memoirs*. New York: Collier Books, 1962.

Welles, Gideon. *Diary of Gideon Welles, Secretary of the Navy under Lincoln and Johnson*. 3 vols. Boston: Houghton Mifflin, 1911.

Wilcox, Cadmus M. *History of the Mexican War*. Washington, D.C.: Church News Publishing, 1892.

Williams, Alpheus S. *From the Cannon's Mouth: The Civil War Letters of General Alpheus S. Williams*. Edited by Milo M. Quaife. Detroit: Wayne State University Press, 1959.

Wilson, James H. *Under the Old Flag: Recollections of Military Operations in the War for the Union, the Spanish War, the Boxer Rebellion, etc*. 2 vols. New York: D. Appleton, 1912.

Woodcock, Marcus. *A Southern Boy in Blue: The Memoir of Marcus Woodcock 9th Kentucky Infantry (U.S.A.)*. Edited by Kenneth W. Noe. Knoxville: University of Tennessee, 1996.

Woods, J. T. *Steedman and His Men at Chickamauga*. Toledo: Blade Printing & Paper, 1876.

Wyeth, John Allan. *With Sabre and Scalpel: The Autobiography of a Soldier and Surgeon*. New York: Harper & Brothers, 1914.

Young, John Russell. *Around the World with General Grant*. Edited by Michael Fellman. Baltimore: Johns Hopkins University Press, 2002.

Articles

Alcaraz, Ramon. "Description of the Battle of Buena Vista." In Ernesto Chavez, *The U.S. War with Mexico: A Brief History with Documents*, 107–109. Boston: Bedford/St. Martin's, 2008.

Beckwith, Samuel H. "Samuel H. Beckwith 'Grant's Shadow.'" Edited by John Y. Simon and David L. Wilson. In *Ulysses S. Grant: Essays and Documents*, edited by David L. Wilson and John Y. Simon, 77–139. Carbondale: Southern Illinois University Press, 1981.

Brinton, Daniel Garrison. "Dr. Daniel Garrison Brinton in the Army of the Cumberland." Edited by D. G. Brinton Thompson. *Pennsylvania Magazine of History and Biography* 90, no. 4 (October 1966): 466–490.

Buell, Don Carlos. "East Tennessee and the Campaign of Perryville." In *Battles and Leaders of the Civil War*, edited by Robert Underwood Johnson and Clarence Clough Buel, 3:31–51. New York: Century, 1887.

Cist, Henry. "Comments on General Grant's 'Chattanooga.'" In *Battles and Leaders of the Civil War*, edited by Robert Underwood Johnson and Clarence Buel, 3:717–718. New York: Century, 1887.

Crenshaw, Edward. "Diary of Captain Edward Crenshaw, of the Confederate States Army." *Alabama Historical Quarterly* 1, no. 4 (Winter 1930): 438–452.

Darden, Colgate W., Jr. "Address." *Southampton County Historical Society*, Bulletin no. 3 (July 1976): n.p.

Fullerton, Joseph F. "The Army of the Cumberland at Chattanooga." In *Battles and Leaders of the Civil War*, edited by Robert Underwood Johnson and Clarence Clough Buel, 3:719–726. New York: Century, 1887.

Grady, B. F. "What Gen. Thomas Wrote Gov. Letcher." *Confederate Veteran* 16, no. 5 (May 1908): 222–223.

Hackley, William Beverley Randolph. "The Letters of William Beverley Randolph Hackley: Treasury Agent in West Tennessee, 1863–1866." Edited by Walter J. Fraser Jr. and Mrs. Pat C. Clark. *West Tennessee Historical Society Papers* 25 (1971): 90–107.

Hill, Daniel H. "Chickamauga—The Great Battle of the West." In *Battles and Leaders of the*

Civil War, edited by Robert Underwood Johnson and Clarence Clough Buel, 3:638–662. New York: Century, 1887.

Howard, Oliver Otis. "Grant at Chattanooga." In *Personal Recollections of the War of the Rebellion: Addresses Delivered before the New York Commandery of the Loyal Legion of the United States, 1883–1891*, edited by James Grant Wilson and Titus Munson Coan, 244–257. New York: Published by the Commandery, 1891.

———. "Sketch of the Life of George H. Thomas." In *Personal Recollections of the War of the Rebellion: Addresses Delivered before the New York Commandery of the Loyal Legion of the United States, 1883–1891*, edited by James Grant Wilson and Titus Munson Coan, 285–302. New York: Published by the Commandery, 1891.

Jones, J. William. "Thomas and Lee—Historical Facts." *Confederate Veteran* 11, no. 12 (Dec. 1903): 559–560.

Kelly, R. M. "Holding Kentucky for the Union." In *Battles and Leaders of the Civil War*, edited by Robert Underwood Johnson and Clarence Clough Buel, 1:373–392. New York: Century, 1887.

Kniffin, Gilbert C. "The Life and Services of Major General George H. Thomas." *War Papers Being Papers Read before the Commandery of the District of Columbia Military Order of the Loyal Legion of the United States*. Vol. 1, *Papers 1–26. March 1887–April 1897*. Wilmington, N.C.: Broadfoot Publishing, 1993.

———. "Major-General William Starke Rosecrans." *War Papers Being Papers Read before the Commandery of the District of Columbia Military Order of the Loyal Legion of the United States*. Vol. 4, *Papers 1–26. March 1887–April 1897*. Wilmington, N.C.: Broadfoot Publishing, 1993, 69–90.

Livermore, Thomas L. "General Thomas in the Record." In *Critical Sketches of Some of the Federal and Confederate Commanders*, 210–244. Boston: Houghton Mifflin, 1895.

Loring, F. H. "General George A. [*sic*] Thomas." In *War Papers Being Papers Read before the Commandery of the State of Iowa, Military Order of the Loyal Legion of the United States*, 279–295. Wilmington, N.C.: Broadfoot Publishing, 1994.

Lyon, Hylan B. "Memoirs of Hylan B. Lyon, Brigadier General, C.S.A." Edited by Edward M. Coffman. *Tennessee Historical Quarterly* 18 (March 1959): 35–53.

McClatchey, Minerva Leah Rowles. "A Georgia Woman's Civil War Diary: The Journal of Minerva Leah Rowles McClatchey, 1864–65." Edited by T. Conn Bryan. *Georgia Historical Quarterly* 51, no. 2 (July 1967): 197–216.

Meigs, Montgomery C. "First Impressions of Three Days' Fighting: Quartermaster General Meigs's 'Journal of the Battle of Chattanooga.'" Edited by John M. Hoffmann. In *Ulysses S. Grant: Essays and Documents,* edited by David L. Wilson and John Y. Simon, 59–76. Carbondale: Southern Illinois University Press, 1981.

Merrill, W. E. "Block-Houses for Railroad Defense in the Department of the Cumberland." In *Sketches of War History 1861–1865, Papers Presented for the Ohio Commandery of the Military Order of the Loyal Legion of the United States, 1880–1890*, edited by Robert Hunter, 389–421. Cincinnati: Robert Clarke, 1890.

Moore, W. G. "Notes of Colonel W. G. Moore, Private Secretary to President Johnson, 1866–1868." Edited by St. George L. Sioussat. *American Historical Review* 19, no. 1 (Oct. 1913): 98–132.

Newton, George A. "Battle of Peach Tree Creek." In *The Atlanta Papers*, no. 15, 391–408. Dayton, Ohio: Press of Morningside Bookshop, 1980.

Otis, Ephraim A. "General George H. Thomas." In *Military Essays and Recollections Papers Read before the Commandery of the State of Illinois, Military Order of the Loyal Legion of the United States*, 395–407. Chicago: A. C. McClurg, 1891.

Persons, Elvero. "General George H. Thomas." *Christian Advocate* (1866–1905), April 19, 1894, 249. http://www.proquest.com.

Pirtle, Alfred. "Stone[s] River Sketches." In *War Papers Being Papers Read before the Commandery of the State of Ohio, Military Order of the Loyal Legion of the United States,* 95–110. Wilmington, N.C.: Broadfoot Publishing, 1992.

Putnam, Douglas, Jr. "Reminiscences of the Battle of Shiloh." In *Sketches of War History 1861–1865, Papers Presented for the Ohio Commandery of the Military Order of the Loyal Legion of the United States, 1880–1890,* edited by Robert Hunter. 3:197–211. Cincinnati: Robert Clarke, 1890.

Reppert, William E. "About Gen. G. H. Thomas's Side in the War." *Confederate Veteran* 16, no. 3 (March 1908): 126–127.

Sheridan, Michael V. "Charging with Sheridan up Missionary Ridge." In *Battles and Leaders of the Civil War,* edited by Peter Cozzens, 5:450–466. Urbana: University of Illinois Press, 2002.

Smith, William Farrar. "Comments on General Grant's 'Chattanooga.'" In *Battles and Leaders of the Civil War,* edited by Robert Underwood Johnson and Clarence Clough Buel, 3:714–717. New York: Century, 1887.

Stone, Henry. "The Battle of Nashville, Tennessee December 15 and 16, 1864." In *Campaigns in Kentucky and Tennessee Including the Battle of Chickamauga 1862–1864. Papers of the Military Historical Society of Massachusetts,* 7:479–542. Boston: Military Historical Society of Massachusetts, 1908.

———. "Major-General George Henry Thomas." In *Critical Sketches of Some of the Federal and Confederate Commanders,* 163–208. Boston: Houghton Mifflin 1895.

———. "Repelling Hood's Invasion of Tennessee." In *Battles and Leaders of the Civil War,* edited by Robert Underwood Johnson and Clarence Clough Buel, 4:440–464. New York: Century, 1887.

———. "The Siege and Capture of Atlanta, July 9 to September 8, 1864." In *The Atlanta Papers,* no. 3, 99–132. Dayton, Ohio: Press of Morningside Bookshop, 1980, 99–132.

Stuart, J. E. B. "J. E. B. Stuart's Letters to His Hairston Kin 1850–1855." Edited by Peter W. Hairston. *North Carolina Historical Review* 51, no. 3 (July 1974): 261–333.

Tidball, Eugene C. "A Subaltern's First Experiences in the Old Army." *Civil War History* 45, no. 3 (Sept. 1999): 197–222.

Wood, Thomas J. "The Battle of Missionary Ridge." *War Papers Being Papers Read before the Commandery of the Ohio Military Order of the Loyal Legion of the United States,* 4:23–51. Wilmington, N.C.: Broadfoot Publishing, 1991.

Woolworth, James M. "George H. Thomas." In *Civil War Sketches and Incidents. Papers Read by Companions of the Commandery of the State of Nebraska, Military Order of the Loyal Legion of the United States,* 145–151. Omaha: Published by the Commandery, 1902.

Yaryan, John Lee. "Stone River." *War Papers Being Papers Read before the Commandery of the State of Indiana, Military Order of the Loyal Legion of the United States,* 157–177. Wilmington, N.C.: Broadfoot Publishing, 1992.

Secondary Sources

Books

Albion, Robert Greenleigh. *Makers of Naval Policy, 1798–1947.* Edited by Rowena Reed. Annapolis, Md.: Naval Institute Press, 1980.

Ambrose, Stephen E. *Duty, Honor, Country: A History of West Point.* Baltimore: Johns Hopkins University Press, 1966.

————. *Halleck: Lincoln's Chief of Staff.* Baton Rouge: Louisiana State University Press, 1962.

Ash, Stephen V. *Middle Tennessee Society Transformed, 1860–1870: War and Peace in the Upper South.* Baton Rouge: Louisiana State University Press, 1988.

Ayers, Edward L. *"A House Divided . . .": A Century of Great Civil War Quotations.* New York: John Wiley & Sons, 1997.

————. *In the Presence of Mine Enemies: War in the Heart of America 1859–1863.* New York: W. W. Norton, 2003.

Baggett, James Alex. *Homegrown Yankees: Tennessee's Union Cavalry in the Civil War.* Baton Rouge: Louisiana State University Press, 2009.

Bailey, Anne J. *The Chessboard of War: Sherman and Hood in the Autumn Campaigns of 1864.* Lincoln: University of Nebraska Press, 2000.

Ballard, Michael B. *U. S. Grant: The Making of a General, 1861–1863.* Lanham, Md.: Rowman & Littlefield, 2005.

————. *Vicksburg: The Campaign That Opened the Mississippi.* Chapel Hill: University of North Carolina Press, 2004.

Barton, Michael. *Goodmen: The Character of Civil War Soldiers.* University Park: Pennsylvania State University Press, 1981.

Bauer, K. Jack. *The Mexican War: 1846–1848.* New York: Macmillan, 1974.

Bearss, Edwin C. *The Campaign for Vicksburg.* 3 vols. Dayton, Ohio: Morningside Press, 1985–1986.

Berry, Stephen W., II. *All That Makes a Man: Love and Ambition in the Civil War South.* Oxford: Oxford University Press, 2003.

Blight, David W. *Race and Reunion: The Civil War in American Memory.* Cambridge, Mass.: Belknap Press, 2001.

Bobrick, Benson. *Master of War: The Life of General George H. Thomas.* New York: Simon & Schuster, 2009.

Boney, F. N. *John Letcher of Virginia: The Story of Virginia's Civil War Governor.* Tuscaloosa: University of Alabama Press, 1966.

Boynton, Henry V. *Was General Thomas Slow at Nashville?* New York: Frances P. Harper, 1896.

Bradley, George C., and Richard L. Dahlen. *From Conciliation to Conquest: The Sack of Athens and the Court-Martial of Colonel John B. Turchin.* Tuscaloosa: University of Alabama Press, 2006.

Broadwater, Robert P. *General George H. Thomas: A Biography of the Union's "Rock of Chickamauga."* Jefferson, N.C.: McFarland, 2009.

Brooks, Victor, and Robert Hohwald. *How America Fought Its Wars: Military Strategy from the American Revolution to the Civil War.* Conshohocken, Pa.: Combined Publishing, 1999.

Brown, Kent Masterson. *The Civil War in Kentucky: Battle for the Bluegrass State.* Mason City, Iowa: Savas Publishing, 2000.

Buell, Thomas B. *The Warrior Generals: Combat Leadership in the Civil War.* New York: Crown, 1997.

Bunker, John Gorley. *Liberty Ships: The Ugly Ducklings of World War II.* Annapolis, Md: Naval Institute Press, 1972.

Burkhardt, George S. *Confederate Rage, Yankee Wrath: No Quarter in the Civil War.* Carbondale: Southern Illinois University Press, 2007.

Burne, Alfred H. *Lee, Grant and Sherman: A Study in Leadership in the 1864–65 Campaign.* New York: Charles Scribner's Sons, 1939.

Carpenter, John A. *Sword and Olive Branch: Oliver Otis Howard.* Pittsburgh: University of Pittsburgh Press, 1964.

Carter, Arthur B. *The Tarnished Cavalier: Major-General Earl Van Dorn, C.S.A.* Knoxville: University of Tennessee Press, 1999.

Carter, Dan T. *When the War Was Over: The Failure of Self-Reconstruction in the South, 1865–1867.* Baton Rouge: Louisiana State University Press, 1985.

Casdorph, Paul D. *Confederate General R. S. Ewell: Robert E. Lee's Hesitant Commander.* Lexington: University Press of Kentucky, 2004.

Castel, Albert. *Articles of War: Winners, Losers, and Some Who Were Both in the Civil War.* Mechanicsburg, Pa.: Stackpole Books, 2001.

———. *Decision in the West: The Atlanta Campaign of 1864.* Lawrence: University Press of Kansas, 1992.

Catton, Bruce. *The Hallowed Ground: The Story of the Union Side of the Civil War.* Garden City, N.Y.: Doubleday, 1956.

———. *U. S. Grant and the American Military Tradition.* Boston: Little, Brown, 1954.

Cleaves, Freeman. *Rock of Chickamauga: The Life of George H. Thomas.* Norman: University of Oklahoma Press, 1948.

Coffman, Edward M. *The Old Army: A Portrait of the American Army in Peacetime, 1784–1898.* New York: Oxford University Press, 1986.

Connelly, Donald B. *John M. Schofield and the Politics of Generalship.* Chapel Hill: University of North Carolina Press, 2006.

Connelly, Thomas Lawrence. *Autumn of Glory: The Army of Tennessee, 1862–1865.* Baton Rouge: Louisiana State University Press, 1971.

Cooling, Benjamin Franklin. *Fort Donelson's Legacy: War and Society in Kentucky and Tennessee, 1862–1863.* Knoxville: University of Tennessee Press, 1997.

Coppée, Henry. *General Thomas.* New York: D. Appleton, 1893.

Cornish, Dudley Taylor, and Virginia Jeans Laas. *Lincoln's Lee: The Life of Samuel Phillips Lee, United States Navy, 1812–1897.* Lawrence: University Press of Kansas, 1986.

Cozzens, Peter. *No Better Place to Die: The Battle of Stones River.* Urbana: University of Illinois Press, 1990.

———. *The Shipwreck of Their Hopes.* Urbana: University of Illinois Press, 1994.

———. *This Terrible Sound.* Urbana: University of Illinois Press, 1992.

Craven, Avery. *Edmund Ruffin Southerner: A Study in Secession.* Baton Rouge: Louisiana State University Press, 1966.

Crofts, Daniel W. *Old Southampton: Politics and Society in a Virginia County, 1834–1869.* Charlottesville: University Press of Virginia, 1992.

Cullum, George W. *Biographical Register of the Officers and Graduates of the U.S. Military Academy at West Point, N.Y., from its Establishment, in 1802 and 1890, with the Early History of the United States Military Academy.* 2 vols. Boston: Houghton, Mifflin, 1891.

Curtiss, John Shelton. *The Russian Army under Nicholas I: 1825–1855.* Durham, N.C.: Duke University Press, 1965.

Dabney, R. L. *Life and Campaigns of Lieut.-Gen. Thomas J. Jackson.* New York: Blelock, 1866.

Daniel, Larry J. *Days of Glory: The Army of the Cumberland, 1861–1865.* Baton Rouge: Louisiana State University Press, 2004.

———. *Shiloh: The Battle That Changed the Civil War.* New York: Simon & Schuster, 1997.

Davis, Stephen. *Atlanta Will Fall: Sherman, Joe Johnston, and the Yankee Heavy Battalions.* Wilmington, Del.: Scholarly Resources, 2001.

Davis, William C. *Jefferson Davis: The Man and His Hour*. New York: HarperCollins, 1991.

Dougherty, Kevin. *Civil War Leadership and Mexican War Experience*. Jackson: University Press of Mississippi, 2007.

Dunn, J. P., Jr. *Massacres of the Mountains: A History of the Indian Wars of the Far West, 1815–1875*. New York: Archer House, 1958.

Durham, Walter D. *Reluctant Partners, Nashville and the Union, 1863–1865*. Knoxville: University of Tennessee Press, 2008.

Einholf, Christopher J. *George Thomas: Virginian for the Union*. Norman: University of Oklahoma Press, 2007.

Elliott, Sam Davis. *Soldier of Tennessee: General Alexander P. Stewart and the Civil War in the West*. Baton Rouge: Louisiana State University Press, 1999.

Engle, Stephen D. *Don Carlos Buell: Most Promising of All*. Chapel Hill: University of North Carolina Press, 1999.

———. *Struggle for the Heartland: The Campaigns from Fort Henry to Corinth*. Lincoln: University of Nebraska Press, 2001.

Evans, David. *Sherman's Horsemen: Union Cavalry Operations in the Atlanta Campaign*. Bloomington: Indiana University Press, 1996.

Feis, William B. *Grant's Secret Service: The Intelligence War from Belmont to Appomattox*. Lincoln: University of Nebraska Press, 2002.

Fellman, Michael. *Citizen Sherman: A Life of William Tecumseh Sherman*. New York: Random House, 1995.

Fisher, Noel C. *War at Every Door: Partisan Politics and Guerrilla Violence in East Tennessee: 1860–1869*. Chapel Hill: University of North Carolina Press, 2002.

Fiske, John. *The Mississippi Valley in the Civil War*. Boston: Houghton Mifflin, 1900.

Fleming, Thomas J. *West Point: The Men and Times of the United States Military Academy*. New York: William Morrow, 1969.

Fleming, Walter L. *Civil War and Reconstruction in Alabama*. New York: Peter Smith, 1949.

Foner, Eric. *Reconstruction: America's Unfinished Revolution 1863–1877*. New York: Harper & Row, 1988.

Frank, Joseph Allan. *With Ballot and Bayonet: The Political Socialization of American Civil War Soldiers*. Athens: University of Georgia Press, 1998.

Frazer, Robert W. *Forts of the West: Forts and Presidios and Posts Commonly Called Forts West of the Mississippi River to 1898*. Norman: University of Oklahoma Press, 1965.

Freeman, Douglas Southall. *R. E. Lee: A Biography*. 4 vols. New York: Charles Scribner's Sons, 1934–1935.

Fuller, J. F. C. *The Generalship of Ulysses S. Grant*. New York: Dodd, Mead, 1929.

Furgurson, Ernest D. *Chancellorsville, 1863: The Souls of the Brave*. New York: Alfred Knopf, 1992.

Gallagher, Gary W. *Lee: The Soldier*. Lincoln: University of Nebraska Press, 1996.

Glatthaar, Joseph T. *Partners in Command: The Relationships between Leaders in the Civil War*. New York: Free Press, 1994.

Goetzmann, William H. *Exploration and Empire: The Explorer and the Scientist in the Winning of the American West*. New York: Alfred A. Knopf, 1966.

Grimsley, Mark *The Hard Hand of War: Union Military Policy toward Southern Civilians 1861–1865*. New York: Cambridge University Press, 1995.

Hafendorfer, Kenneth A. *The Battle of Wild Cat Mountain*. Louisville, Ky.: KH Press, 2003.

———. *Mill Springs: Campaign and Battle of Mill Springs, Kentucky*. Louisville, Ky.: KH Press, 2001.

Hallock, Judith Lee. *Braxton Bragg and Confederate Defeat.* Vol. 2. Tuscaloosa: University of Alabama Press, 1991.

Harrison, Lowell H. *The Civil War in Kentucky.* Lexington: University Press of Kentucky, 1975.

Hart, B. H. Liddell. *Sherman: Soldier, Realist, American.* New York: Frederick A. Praeger, 1958.

Hart, Herbert M. *Old Forts of the Southwest.* Seattle: Superior Publishing, 1964.

Hartje, Robert G. *Van Dorn: The Life and Times of a Confederate General.* Nashville, Tenn.: Vanderbilt University Press, 1967.

Hattaway, Herman. *General Stephen D. Lee.* Jackson: University Press of Mississippi, 1976.

Hattaway, Herman, and Richard E. Beringer. *Jefferson Davis, Confederate President.* Lawrence: University Press of Kansas, 2002.

Hattaway, Herman, and Archer Jones. *How the North Won.* Urbana: University of Illinois Press, 1983.

Hay, Thomas Robson. *Hood's Tennessee Campaign.* New York: Walter Neale, 1929.

Henry, Robert Selph. *"First with the Most" Forrest.* Indianapolis: Bobbs-Merrill, 1944.

———. *The Story of the Mexican War.* Indianapolis: Bobbs-Merrill, 1950.

Herbert, Walter H. *Fighting Joe Hooker.* Indianapolis: Bobbs-Merrill, 1944.

Hess, Earl J. *Banners to the Breeze: The Kentucky Campaign, Corinth and Stones River.* Lincoln: University of Nebraska Press, 2000.

———. *Trench Warfare under Grant and Lee: Field Fortifications in the Overland Campaign.* Chapel Hill: University of North Carolina Press, 2007.

Hoppen, K. Theodore. *The Mid-Victorian Generation, 1846–1886.* New York: Oxford University Press, 2000.

Horn, Stanley F. *The Army of Tennessee.* Norman: Oklahoma University Press, 1952.

———. *The Decisive Battle of Nashville.* Nashville: University of Tennessee Press, 1956.

———. *Invisible Empire: The Story of the Ku Klux Klan, 1866–1871.* Boston: Houghton-Mifflin,, 1939.

Hughes, Nathaniel Cheairs, Jr., and Roy P. Stonsifer Jr. *The Life and Wars of Gideon J. Pillow.* Chapel Hill: University of North Carolina Press, 1993.

Hughes, Nathaniel Cheairs, Jr., and Gordon D. Whitney. *Jefferson Davis in Blue: The Life of Sherman's Relentless Warrior.* Baton Rouge: Louisiana State University Press, 2002.

Hutton, Paul Andrew. *Phil Sheridan and His Army.* Norman: University of Oklahoma Press, 1985.

Johannsen, Robert W. *Frontier Politics and the Sectional Conflict: The Pacific Northwest on the Eve of the Civil War.* Seattle: University of Washington Press, 1955.

Johnson, Mark W. *That Body of Brave Men: The U.S. Regular Infantry and the Civil War in the West.* Cambridge, Mass.: Da Capo Press, 2003.

Jones, Archer. *Civil War Command and Strategy: The Process of Victory and Defeat.* New York: Free Press, 1992.

Jones, James Pickett. *John A. Logan: Stalwart Republican from Illinois.* Tallahassee: University Presses of Florida, 1982.

———. *Yankee Blitzkrieg: Wilson's Raid through Alabama and Georgia.* Athens: University of Georgia Press, 1976.

Jones, Terry L. *The American Civil War.* New York: McGraw-Hill, 2010.

Jordan, David M. *Winfield Scott Hancock: A Soldier's Life.* Bloomington: Indiana University Press, 1988.

Kennedy, Frances H., ed. *The Civil War Battlefield Guide.* 2nd ed. Boston: Houghton Mifflin, 1998.

Lamers, William M. *The Edge of Glory: A Biography of General William S. Rosecrans, U.S.A.* New York: Harcourt, Brace & World, 1961.

Lavender, David. *Climax at Buena Vista: The American Campaigns in Northeastern Mexico 1846–47.* Philadelphia: J. P. Lippincott, 1966.

Leonard, Elizabeth D. *Yankee Women: Gender Battles in the Civil War.* New York: W. W. Norton, 1994.

Lewis, Lloyd. *Captain Sam Grant.* Boston: Little, Brown, 1950.

———. *Sherman: Fighting Prophet.* New York: Harcourt, Brace, 1958.

Long, E. B. *The Civil War: Day By Day: An Almanac 1861–1865.* Garden City, N.Y.: Doubleday, 1971.

Longacre, Edward G. *From Union Stars to Top Hat: A Biography of the Extraordinary General James Harrison Wilson.* Harrisburg, Pa.: Stackpole, 1972.

Lonn, Ella. *Desertion during the Civil War.* New York: Century, 1928.

Losson, Christopher. *Tennessee's Forgotten Warriors: Frank Cheatham and His Confederate Division.* Knoxville: University of Tennessee Press, 1989.

Macartney, Clarence Edward. *Grant and His Generals.* New York: McBride, 1953.

Mahon, John K. *History of the Second Seminole War, 1835–1842.* Gainesville: University Press of Florida, 1967.

Mansfield, Edward D. *The Mexican War: History of Its Origins, and a Detailed Account of the Victories Which Terminated in the Surrender of the Capital; With the Official Despatches of the Generals.* New York: A. S. Barnes, 1849.

Marszalek, John F. *Commander of All Lincoln's Armies: A Life of General Henry W. Halleck.* Cambridge, Mass.: Belknap Press of Harvard University Press, 2004.

———. *Sherman: A Soldier's Passion for Order.* New York: Free Press, 1993.

Matloff, Maurice. *American Military History.* Washington, D.C.: Office of the Chief of Military History, United States Army, 1969.

McConnell, S. D. *History of the American Episcopal Church.* New York: Thomas Whittaker, 1904.

McDonough, James Lee. *Chattanooga—A Death Grip on the Confederacy.* Knoxville: University of Tennessee Press, 1984.

———. *Nashville: The Western Confederacy's Final Gamble.* Knoxville: University of Tennessee Press, 2004.

———. *Schofield: Union General in the Civil War and Reconstruction.* Tallahassee: Florida State University Press, 1972.

———. *Shiloh—in Hell before Night.* Knoxville: University of Tennessee Press, 1977.

———. *Stones River: Bloody Winter in Tennessee.* Knoxville: University of Tennessee Press, 1980.

———. *War in Kentucky: From Shiloh to Perryville.* Knoxville: University of Tennessee Press, 1994.

McDonough, James Lee, and Thomas L. Connelly. *Five Tragic Hours: The Battle of Franklin.* Knoxville: University of Tennessee Press, 1983.

McDonough, James Lee, and James Pickett Jones. *War So Terrible: Sherman and Atlanta.* New York: W. W. Norton, 1987.

McFeely, William S. *Grant: A Biography.* New York: W. W. Norton, 1981.

———. *Yankee Stepfather: General O. O. Howard and the Freedmen.* New Haven, Conn.: Yale University Press, 1968.

McKinney, Francis F. *Education in Violence: The Life of George H. Thomas and the History of the Army of the Cumberland.* Detroit: Wayne State University Press, 1961.

McKnight, Brian D. *Confederate Outlaw: Champ Ferguson and the Civil War in Appalachia*. Baton Rouge: Louisiana State University Press, 2011.

———. *Contested Borderland: The Civil War in Appalachian Kentucky and Virginia*. Lexington: University Press of Kentucky, 2006.

McMurry, Richard M. *Atlanta 1864: Last Chance for the Confederacy*. Lincoln: University of Nebraska Press, 2000.

———. *John Bell Hood and the War for Southern Independence*. Lexington: University Press of Kentucky, 1982.

———. *Two Great Rebel Armies: An Essay in Confederate Military History*. Chapel Hill: University of North Carolina Press, 1989.

McPherson, James M. *Battle Cry of Freedom: The Civil War Era*. New York: Oxford University Press, 1988.

McReynolds, Edwin C. *The Seminoles*. Norman: University of Oklahoma Press, 1957.

McWhiney, Grady. *Braxton Bragg and Confederate Defeat*. Vol. 1: *Field Command*. New York: Columbia University Press, 1969.

McWhiney, Grady, and Perry D. Jamison. *Attack and Die: Civil War Military Tactics and the Southern Heritage*. Tuscaloosa: University of Alabama Press, 1982.

Miller, Randall M., Harry S. Stout, and Charles Reagan Wilson, eds. *Religion and the American Civil War*. New York: Oxford University Press, 1998.

Missall, John, and Mary Lou Missall. *The Seminole Wars: America's Longest Indian Conflict*. Gainesville: University Press of Florida, 2004.

Mitchell, Joseph B. *Military Leaders in the Civil War*. New York: G. P. Putnam's Sons, 1972.

Mitchell, Reid. *Civil War Soldiers*. New York: Viking Penguin, 1988.

Morris, Roy, Jr. *Sheridan: The Life and Wars of General Phil Sheridan*. New York: Crown Publishers, 1992.

Morrison, James L., Jr. *"The Best School in the World": West Point, the Pre–Civil War Years, 1833–1866*. Kent, Ohio: Kent State University Press, 1986.

Mountcastle, Clay. *Punitive War: Confederate Guerrillas and Union Reprisals*. Lawrence: University Press of Kansas, 2009.

Myers, Raymond E. *The Zollie Tree: General Felix K. Zollicoffer and the Battle of Mill Springs*. Louisville, Ky.: Filson Club, 1964. Reprint, 1998.

Nicolay, John G., and John Hay. *Abraham Lincoln: A History*. Chicago: University of Chicago Press, 1966.

Noe, Kenneth W. *Perryville: This Grand Havoc of Battle*. Lexington: University Press of Kentucky, 2001.

O'Connor, Richard. *Thomas: Rock of Chickamauga*. New York: Prentice-Hall, 1948.

Palumbo, Frank A. *George Henry Thomas: The Dependable General*. Dayton, Ohio: Morningside House, 1983.

Parks, Joseph H. *General Edmund Kirby Smith, C.S.A*. Baton Rouge: Louisiana State University Press, 1954.

———. *General Leonidas Polk, C.S.A*. Baton Rouge: Louisiana State University Press, 1962.

———. *Joseph E. Brown of Georgia*. Baton Rouge: Louisiana State University Press, 1977.

Perry, William Stevens. *The History of the American Episcopal Church, 1587–1883*. 2 vols. Boston: James R. Osgood, 1885.

Peskin, Allan. *Garfield: A Biography*. Kent, Ohio: Kent State University Press, 1978.

Peters, Virginia Bergman. *The Florida Wars*. Hamden, Conn.: Archon Books, 1979.

Peterson, Norma Lois. *The Presidencies of William Henry Harrison and John Tyler*. Lawrence: University Press of Kansas, 1989.

Pfanz, Donald C. *Richard S. Ewell: A Soldier's Life*. Chapel Hill: University of North Carolina Press, 1998.

Piatt, Donn, and Henry V. Boynton. *General George H. Thomas: A Critical Biography*. Cincinnati: Robert Clarke, 1893.

Piston, William Garrett. *Carter's Raid: An Episode of the Civil War in East Tennessee*. Johnson City, Tenn.: Overmountain Press, 1989.

Prokopowicz, Gerald J. *All for the Regiment: The Army of the Ohio, 1861–1862*. Chapel Hill: University of North Carolina Press, 2001.

Prucha, Francis Paul *A Guide to the Military Posts of the United States, 1789–1895*. Madison: State Historical Society of Wisconsin, 1964.

Rable, George C. *But There Was No Peace: The Role of Violence in the Politics of Reconstruction*. Athens: University of Georgia Press, 1984.

Ramage, James A. *Rebel Raider: The Life of General John Hunt Morgan*. Lexington: University Press of Kentucky, 1986.

Rister, Carl Coke. *Robert E. Lee in Texas*. Norman: University of Oklahoma Press, 1946.

Robertson, James I., Jr. *Stonewall Jackson: The Man, the Soldier, the Legend*. New York: Macmillan, 1997.

Robertson, James I., Jr., and Brian Steel Wills. *Civil War Sites in Virginia: A Tour Guide*. Rev. ed. Charlottesville: University Press of Virginia, 2011.

Robertson, William Glenn, Edward P. Shanahan, John I. Boxberger, and George E. Knapp. *Staff Ride Handbook for the Battle of Chickamauga, 18–20 September 1863*. Fort Leavenworth, Kans.: Combat Studies Institute, U.S. Army Command and General Staff College, 1992.

Rodenbough, Theophilus F., and William L. Haskins, eds. *The Army of the United States: Historical Sketches of Staff and Line*. New York: Merrill, 1896.

Roland, Charles P. *Albert Sidney Johnston: Soldier of Three Republics*. Austin: University of Texas Press, 1964.

———. *An American Iliad: The Story of the Civil War*. New York: McGraw-Hill, 1991.

Sandburg, Carl. *Abraham Lincoln: The War Years*. 4 vols. New York: Harcourt, Brace & World, 1939.

Sefton, James E. *The United States Army and Reconstruction 1865–1877*. Baton Rouge: Louisiana State University Press, 1967.

Severance, Ben H. *Tennessee's Radical Army: The State Guard and Its Role in Reconstruction, 1867–1869*. Knoxville: University of Tennessee Press, 2005.

Sheehan-Dean, Aaron. *Why Confederates Fought: Family and Nation in Civil War Virginia*. Chapel Hill: University of North Carolina Press, 2007.

Shenk, Joshua Wolfe. *Lincoln's Melancholy: How Depression Challenged a President and Fueled His Greatness*. Boston: Houghton Mifflin, 2005.

Silber, Nina. *The Romance of Reunion: Northerners and the South, 1865–1900*. Chapel Hill: University of North Carolina Press, 1993.

Simpson, Brooks D. *Let Us Have Peace: Ulysses S. Grant and the Politics of War and Reconstruction, 1861–1868*. Chapel Hill: University of North Carolina Press, 1991.

———. *Ulysses S. Grant: Triumph over Adversity, 1822–1865*. Boston: Houghton-Mifflin, 2000.

Skelton, William B. *An American Profession of Arms: The Army Officer Corps, 1784–1861*. Lawrence: University Press of Kansas, 1992.

Smith, Derek. *In the Lion's Mouth: Hood's Tragic Retreat from Nashville, 1864*. Mechanicsburg, Pa.: Stackpole Books, 2011.

Smith, Justin H. *The War with Mexico*. Gloucester, Mass.: Peter Smith, 1963.

Smith, Timothy B. *The Golden Age of Battlefield Preservation: The Decade of the 1890s and the Establishment of America's First Five Military Parks.* Knoxville: University of Tennessee Press, 2008.

Sprague, John T. *The Origin, Progress and Conclusion of the Florida War.* Facsimile reproduction. Gainesville: University Press of Florida, 1964.

Squires, W. H. T. *The Days of Yester-Year in Colony and Commonwealth: A Sketch Book of Virginia.* Portsmouth, Va.: Printcraft Press, 1928.

Steiner, Paul E. *Medical-Military Portraits of Union and Confederate Generals.* Philadelphia: Whitmore Publishing, 1948.

Sun Tzu. *The Art of War.* Translated by Samuel B. Griffith. London: Oxford University Press, 1963.

Sword, Wiley. *Courage under Fire: Profiles in Bravery from the Battlefields of the Civil War.* New York: St. Martin's Press, 2007.

———. *Embrace an Angry Wind: The Confederacy's Last Hurrah: Spring Hill, Franklin, and Nashville.* New York: HarperCollins, 1992.

———. *Shiloh: Bloody April.* Dayton, Ohio: Press of Morningside Bookshop, 1988.

Symonds, Craig L. *Joseph E. Johnston: A Civil War Biography.* New York: W. W. Norton, 1992.

———. *Stonewall of the West: Patrick Cleburne and the Civil War.* Lawrence: University Press of Kansas, 1997.

Tatum, Georgia Lee. *Disloyalty in the Confederacy.* Chapel Hill: University of North Carolina Press, 1934.

Thomas, Benjamin P., and Harold M. Hyman. *Stanton: The Life and Times of Lincoln's Secretary of War.* New York: Alfred A. Knopf, 1962.

Thomas, Bill. *Fort Thomas.* Charleston, S.C.: Arcadia Publishing, 2006.

Thomas, Emory M. *Bold Dragoon: The Life of J. E. B. Stuart.* New York: Harper and Row, 1986.

———. *The Confederacy as a Revolutionary Experience.* Englewood Cliffs, N.J.: Prentice-Hall, 1971.

———. *The Confederate Nation: 1861–1865.* New York: Harper and Row, 1979.

———. *Robert E. Lee: A Biography.* New York: W. W. Norton, 1995.

Thomas, Lately. *The First President Johnson: The Three Lives of the Seventeenth President of the United States of America.* New York: William Morrow, 1968.

Thomas, Wilbur. *General George H. Thomas: The Indomitable Warrior.* New York: Exposition Press, 1964.

Trelease, Allen W. *White Terror: The Ku Klux Klan Conspiracy and Southern Reconstruction.* New York: Harper & Row, 1971.

Trudeau, Noah Andre. *Like Men of War: Black Troops in the Civil War, 1862–1865.* New York: Little, Brown, 1998.

Tucker, Glenn. *Chickamauga: Bloody Battle in the West.* Indianapolis: Bobbs-Merrill, 1961.

Utley, Robert. *Frontiersmen in Blue: The United States Army and the Indian, 1848–1865.* New York: Macmillan, 1967.

Vandiver, Frank E. *Mighty Stonewall.* New York: McGraw-Hill, 1957.

Van Horne, Thomas B. *History of the Army of the Cumberland Its Organization, Campaigns, and Battles, Written at the Request of Major-General George H. Thomas, Chiefly from His Private Military Journal and Official and Other Documents Furnished by Him.* 2 vols. and atlas. Cincinnati: Robert Clarke, 1875.

———. *History of the Army of the Cumberland Its Organization, Campaigns, and Battles, Written at the Request of Major-General George H. Thomas, Chiefly from His Private*

Military Journal and Official and Other Documents Furnished by Him. 2 vols. and atlas. Introduction by Peter Cozzens. Wilmington, N.C.: Broadfoot Publishing, 1988.

———. *The Life of Major-General George H. Thomas.* New York: Charles Scribner's Sons, 1882.

Wade, Wyn Craig. *The Fiery Cross: The Ku Klux Klan in America.* New York: Simon & Schuster, 1987.

Walker, Scott. *Hell's Broke Loose in Georgia: Survival in a Civil War Regiment.* Athens: University of Georgia Press, 2005.

Walzer, Michael. *Just and Unjust Wars: A Moral Argument with Historical Illustrations.* New York: Basic Books, 1977.

Warner, Ezra J. *Generals in Blue: Lives of the Union Commanders.* Baton Rouge: Louisiana State University Press, 1964.

———. *Generals in Gray: Lives of the Confederate Commanders.* Baton Rouge: Louisiana State University Press, 1959.

Weigley, Russell F. *Quartermaster General of the Union Army: A Biography of M. C. Meigs.* New York: Columbia University Press, 1959.

Weitz, Mark A. *More Damning Than Slaughter: Desertion in the Confederate Army.* Lincoln: University of Nebraska Press, 2005.

Wert, Jeffry D. *General James Longstreet: The Confederacy's Most Controversial Soldier—A Biography.* New York: Simon & Schuster, 1993.

Wiley, Bell Irvin. *The Life of Billy Yank: The Common Soldier of the Union.* Indianapolis: Bobbs-Merrill, 1952.

———. *The Road to Appomattox.* Memphis, Tenn.: Memphis State College Press, 1956.

Williams, David. *A People's History of the Civil War: Struggles for the Meaning of Freedom.* New York: New Press, 2005.

Williams, T. Harry. *The History of American Wars: From 1745 to 1918.* New York: Alfred A. Knopf, 1981.

———. *Lincoln and His Generals.* New York: Alfred A. Knopf, 1952.

Wills, Brian Steel. *A Battle from the Start: Nathan Bedford Forrest.* New York: Harper Collins, 1992.

———. *Gone with the Glory: The Civil War in Cinema.* Lanham: Rowman & Littlefield, 2007.

———. *The War Hits Home: The Civil War in Southeastern Virginia.* Charlottesville: University Press of Virginia, 2001.

Wilson, Charles Reagan. *Baptized in Blood: The Religion of the Lost Cause, 1865–1920.* Athens: University of Georgia Press, 1980.

Wood, W. J. *Civil War Generalship: The Art of Command.* Westport, Conn.: Praeger, 1997.

Woodworth, Steven E. *Davis and Lee at War.* Lawrence: University Press of Kansas, 1995.

———. *A Deep Steady Thunder: The Battle of Chickamauga.* Fort Worth, Tex.: Ryan Place Publishers, 1996.

———. *Jefferson Davis and His Generals: The Failure of Confederate Command in the West.* Lawrence: University Press of Kansas, 1990.

———. *Nothing but Victory: The Army of the Tennessee, 1861–1865.* New York: Alfred A. Knopf, 2005.

———. *Six Armies in Tennessee: The Chickamauga and Chattanooga Campaigns.* Lincoln: University of Nebraska Press, 1998.

———. *This Grand Spectacle: The Battle of Chattanooga.* Abilene, Tex: McWhiney Foundation Press, 1999.

Wright, John D. *The Oxford Dictionary of Civil War Quotations.* New York: Oxford University Press, 2006.

Wyeth, John Allan. *Life of General Nathan Bedford Forrest*. New York: Harper & Bros., 1899.

Young, Kenneth Ray. *The General's General: The Life and Times of Arthur MacArthur.* Boulder, Colo.: Westview Press, 1994.

Articles and Unpublished Manuscripts

Bailey, Anne J. "The USCT in the Confederate Heartland, 1864." In *Black Soldiers in Blue: African American Troops in the Civil War Era*, edited by John Davis Smith, 227–248. Chapel Hill: University of North Carolina Press, 2002.

Castel, Albert. "Prevaricating through Georgia: Sherman's *Memoirs* as a Source on the Atlanta Campaign." *Civil War History* 40, no. 1 (March 1994): 48–71.

Chapman, Gregory Dean. "Army Life at Camp Thomas, Georgia, during the Spanish-American War." *Georgia Historical Quarterly* 70 (Winter 1986): 633–656.

Cimprich, John. "A Critical Moment and Its Aftermath for George H. Thomas." In *The Moment of Decision: Biographical Essays on American Character and Regional Identity*, edited by Randall M. Miller and John R. McKivigan, 173–187. Westport, Conn.: Greenwood Press, 1994.

Coffman, Edward M. "Memoirs of Hylan B. Lyon, Brigadier General, C.S.A." *Tennessee Historical Quarterly* 18 (March 1959): 35–53.

Crane, R. C. "Major George H. Thomas on the Trail of Indians in 1860." *West Texas Historical Association Year Book* 20 (Oct. 1944): 77–85.

Crimmins, M. L. "Major George H. Thomas in Texas." *West Texas Historical Association Year Book* 14 (Oct. 1938): 73–82.

———. "Robert E. Lee in Texas: Letters and Diary." *West Texas Historical Association Year Book* 8 (June 1932): 3–24.

Crum, Tom. "Camp Cooper, A Different Look." *West Texas Historical Association Year Book* 68 (1992): 62–75.

Hattaway, Herman, and Michael L. Gillespie. "Soldier of Conscience, George H. Thomas, A Virginian Fights for the Union." *Virginia Cavalcade* 34 (Autumn 1984): 64–75.

Heidler, Jeanne Twiggs. "The Military Career of David Emanuel Twiggs." Doctoral dissertation, Auburn University, 1988.

Hsieh, Wayne Wei-siang. "'I Owe Virginia Little, My Country Much': Robert E. Lee, the United States Regular Army, and Unconditional Unionism." In *Crucible of the Civil War: Virginia from Secession to Civil War,* edited by Edward L. Ayers, Gary W. Gallagher, and Andrew J. Torget, 35–57. Charlottesville: University Press of Virginia, 2006.

MacDonnell, Francis. "The Confederate Spin on Winfield Scott and George Thomas." *Civil War History* 45, no. 4 (Dec. 1998): 255–266.

Marszalek, John F. "Sherman Called It the Way He Saw It." *Civil War History* 40, no. 1 (March 1994): 72–78.

Neighbours, Kenneth F. "The Assassination of Robert S. Neighbors." *West Texas Historical Association Year Book* 34 (Oct. 1958): 38–49.

———. "Indian Exodus Out of Texas in 1859." *West Texas Historical Association Year Book* 36 (Oct. 1960): 80–97.

Richardson, Rupert N. "The Saga of Camp Cooper." *West Texas Historical Association Year Book* 56 (1980): 14–34.

Roberson, B. R. "The Courthouse Burnin'est General." *Tennessee Historical Quarterly* 23 (Dec. 1964): 372–378.

Severance, Ben H. "Reconstruction Power Play: The 1867 Mayoral Election in Nashville, Tennessee." In *Sister States, Enemy States: The Civil War in Kentucky and Tennessee,* edited by Kent T. Dollar, Larry H. Whiteaker, and W. Calvin Dickinson, 320–337. Lexington: University Press of Kentucky, 2009.

Stowell, Daniel W. "'We Have Sinned and God Has Smitten Us!': John H. Caldwell and the Religious Meaning of Confederate Defeat." *Georgia Historical Quarterly* 78, no. 1 (Spring 1994): 1–38.

Wills, Brian Steel. "Brig. Gen. Hylan Benton Lyon." In *Kentuckians in Gray: Confederate Generals and Field Officers of the Bluegrass State,* edited by Bruce S. Allardice and Lawrence Lee Hewitt, 180–186. Lexington: University Press of Kentucky, 2008.

Index